PUBLIC EXPENDITURES IN COMMUNIST
AND CAPITALIST NATIONS

PUBLIC EXPENDITURES IN COMMUNIST AND CAPITALIST NATIONS

FREDERIC L. PRYOR

Department of Economics, Swarthmore College
Pennsylvania

1968
RICHARD D. IRWIN. INC., HOMEWOOD, ILLINOIS
IRWIN-DORSEY LIMITED, NOBLETON, ONTARIO

PRINTED IN GREAT BRITAIN

A study for
The Yale Economic Growth Center
New Haven, Connecticut, and
The Center for Research on Conflict Resolution
Ann Arbor, Michigan

To Zora

ACKNOWLEDGMENTS

For its programme on the empirical delineation of properties of nations with different economic systems, the Center for Research on Conflict Resolution of The University of Michigan provided me with a grant with which to finance the initial work on this study. I would especially like to express my appreciation to Robert Angell and Kenneth E. Boulding, the Directors of the Center, for their interest and support.

The Economic Growth Center of Yale University, as part of its programme of international economic comparisons, supplied the bulk of financing for this study as well as the physical facilities for research. I would particularly like to thank the Director of this Center, Lloyd G. Reynolds, for his great help and encouragement.

While working on this manuscript I received invaluable assistance from a large number of my colleagues at Yale. Among those to whom I owe special obligation are: Richard Cooper, Karl Deutsch, Donald Hester, Shane Hunt, Kenneth Kehrer, James Land, Andrea Maneschi, John Michael Montias, Peter Mieszkowski, Marc Nerlove, Howard Pack, Hugh Patrick, Joseph Pechman, Merton Peck, Charlotte Phelps, Derek Price, Charles Rockwell, Bruce Russett, Ronald Soligo, Steven Stevens, and Jan Tumlir.

I also drew heavily upon the expertise and aid of many outside of Yale. For advice, data, and manuscripts on various specific points, I would especially like to thank Henry Aaron, Thad Alton, C. Arnold Anderson, Stanisław Braun, Mark Field, and Alec Nove. Many others, to whom I am most grateful, aided in the estimations of the public consumption expenditures. These include G. Barbaruto, Abraham Becker, Dimitrije Dimitrijević, H. Freund, Daniel Gallik, A. Kalogeris, Anton Kausel, Auguste Klamecker, Vojan Konvalinka, Allen Manvel, Lyndon Mannon, Martin O'Donoghue, George Pall, Michael Simai, V. Siesto, Alan Tait, D. Tosato, Jindřich Veverka, and Vuk Živadinović. Another group also read and made many perspicacious comments on preliminary drafts of this study. Here I would especially like to acknowledge the aid

A*

of: Robin Barlow, Walter Hettich, Simon Kuznets, Staffan Linder, Fritz Neumark, Mancur Olson, Mary Pryor, Millard Pryor, Sr., Millard Pryor, Jr., and Ronald Riddle.

My greatest debt of gratitude is to my wife, who not only carried out the homely duties that earn the usual authorial encomia but also aided in the calculation of many tables, conducted much of the research based on exotic language materials, and helped to hone to a sharper edge many of the ideas expressed in this study.

CONTENTS

TABLES AND DIAGRAMS

DIAGRAMS

APPENDIX TABLES ARE LISTED ON PAGE 316

Chapter I

INTRODUCTION

A. The Aims of this Study
1. *Comparing Market and Centrally Planned Economies*
2. *Extending the Positive Theory of Public Expenditures*
3. *Refocusing the Study of 'Comparative Economic Systems'*

B. Some Preliminaries and the Selection of the Sample

C. Plan of Attack

A. THE AIMS OF THIS STUDY

Political passions about public expenditures run high. But underneath the policy controversies vital questions about the actual behaviour of these expenditures await dispassionate analysis: What services are or should be actually financed through the public sector? What are and should be the factors associated with changes in the relative volume of such expenditures? What are the effects of financing certain expenditures through the public rather than the private sector? At what levels of government are and should certain public expenditures be made? How similar or different are public expenditures between nations with different economic systems? Many, many more questions can be added to this list. Since public expenditures comprise from one-fifth to one-third of the national incomes of most industrialized nations, the desirability for research on such questions is manifestly clear.

For this study of public expenditures I have three basic purposes, each of which is briefly discussed below.

1. COMPARING MARKET AND CENTRALLY PLANNED ECONOMIES

The first purpose of this study is to analyse public expenditures of a group of nations with different economic systems. Comparing and contrasting public expenditures of many nations can lead to discoveries of relationships which, for lack of perspective, can never be unearthed from study of such expenditures in a single country. If nations with different economic systems are used in such comparisons, additional generalizations with political and ideological significance can be derived which are unobtainable if we limit such comparisons to nations with the same economic system.

But up to the present time no one has systematically attempted such a promising project on any scale. For the most part, empirical analyses in both East and West have focused on the experiences of single nations. For lack of suitable data few Western economists have attempted comparisons of public expenditures on a disaggregated level among the more developed market economies[1] or among the centrally planned nations[2] or between nations with different economic systems.[3] East European economists have shown considerably more interest in such comparative studies; unfortunately, their explorations of public expenditures among centrally planned economies have been marked by the use of incomparable data and primitive analytic techniques,[4] and their comparisons between

[1] Comparable data on public expenditures are available in very few sources. The most detailed estimates are for the European Common Market nations [European Economic Community, *Die Einnahmen und Ausgaben der oeffentlichen Verwaltung in den Laendern der EWG*, Studien 2, Reihe Wirtschaft und Finanzen (Brussels, 1964)]. A research group working under the direction of Alan Peacock and Jack Wiseman is also preparing such data for a number of nations, but most of these studies have not yet appeared. Other quantitative comparative studies of public expenditures among Western nations are carried on at an extremely high level of aggregation or else focus on only a single type of expenditure (e.g. for defence, health, or education). I cite the major conclusions of these analyses at appropriate places in this study.

[2] For analysis of public expenditures among the East European nations, two Western Studies are available: Nicolas Spulber, *The Economics of Communist Eastern Europe* (Cambridge, Mass., 1957) and Theo Surányi-Unger, *Studien zum Wirtschaftswachstum Suedosteuropas* (Stuttgart, 1964). Unfortunately, neither study has any adjustments of the data from different national sources to make them more comparable.

[3] There are also two monographs on public expenditures in East and West: Henry Laufenburger, *Finances comparées: Etats-Unis, France, Angleterre, URSS* (Paris, 1957), and Richard A. Musgrave, *Fiscal Systems* (New Haven, 1968). But neither author pays much attention to adjusting the data for comparability; and, moreover, both of these studies focus primarily on questions outside the frame of reference of this monograph.

[4] East European economists have written a number of mongraphs on public expenditures among the centrally planned economies. These include: B. G. Boldyrow, *Die Finanzen der europaeischen Laender der Volksdemokratie* (East Berlin, 1953) (a German translation of a Soviet study); D. Butakov, V. Bochkova, and I. Shevel', *Finansi stran narodnoy demokratii* (Moscow, 1959);

public expenditures in East and West have usually been very short and superficial.[1] Although such intra-system comparisons reached grotesque levels during the Stalin era (see below), East European economists, like their Western counterparts, have become increasingly cautious in generalizing about such matters.

The core of the empirical analysis in this study is a set of comparable estimates for the most important expenditures. These calculations were made after a thorough search of the primary source materials of each country and can easily be used by other scholars for further studies, even by those who may disagree with the interpretations I have made of the data. In order to maintain the continuity of analysis and the interest of the reader, however, I have excluded all descriptions of the sources of data and the estimating techniques from the text and have placed them in an appendix.

2. EXTENSIONS OF THE POSITIVE THEORY OF PUBLIC EXPENDITURES

A positive theory deals with empirical questions about the behaviour of measurable variables. As I shall discuss at greater length in the next chapter, four major questions compose the corpus of a positive theory of public expenditures: (1) What goods and services are publicly financed? (2) What are the determinants of these expenditures? (3) What are the behavioural properties of these expenditures—such as the degree of centralization, substitution effects, stability, or incidence—and what are the economic factors underlying such properties? And (4) what difference does it make whether a particular good or service is financed by the public or the private sector?

Questions about what expenditures 'should' be made or

Władyaław Jaworski, *Systemy kredytowe europejskich krajów socialistycznych* (Warsaw, 1962); V. P. Komissarov and A. N. Popov, *Den'gi, kredit, i finansy evropeiskich stran narodnoy demokratii* (Moscow, 1960); and Léon Kurowski, *Les finances dans les états socialistes* (Paris, 1962). In none of these studies is there any attempt to adjust the official data for incomparabilities.

[1] As far as I know, there are no East European monographs devoted to comparisons of public expenditures in centrally planned and market economies. All such comparisons are made within the context of other studies, primarily on public finance, and are usually based on scattered data from the most convenient standard reference sources, with few serious attempts to adjust the data for comparability.

whether certain public expenditures are 'beneficial' belong to the sphere of normative economics and are banished from this study. Of course, focus on positive theory does not mean that all value judgments are eliminated; for by the very choice of analytical methods and hypotheses to be examined, certain implicit value or ideological judgments are made. Whenever possible, however, I have tried to make such judgments explicit.

Although the importance of normative economics in policy making for public expenditures is clear, a positive theory of public expenditures also has a very vital role in this process. In order to place the relationship between positive and normative economics in greater perspective, it is useful to glance briefly at three important applications of a positive theory of public expenditures in the public policy making process.[1]

First, such positive theories can be used to determine certain costs and benefits of public expenditures. For instance, knowledge about the degree of substitution between public and private expenditures for health is certainly useful in evaluating whether planned increases in government health expenditures would result in additional health care or whether they would merely induce a reduction in private health expenditures for the same purpose. Or study of economies of scale and the levels of government at which certain expenditures are made would be quite helpful in evaluating the pros and cons of decentralizing the expending of specified public funds. Similarly, understanding of the economic factors underlying the stability of different public expenditures over time would aid in setting up feasible counter-cyclical public expenditure programmes. Or positive economic analysis can aid in the calculation of cost functions for particular public expenditures. Numerous other important examples could be given.

In addition, through empirical study of the behaviour of public expenditures, norms can be developed that can serve as preliminary aids in investigating whether specific expenditures should be made or changed. Let us suppose, for instance, that a regression analysis of public expenditures reveals that govern-

[1] Some of these points are discussed at much greater length by Elliott R. Morss, 'Some Thoughts on the Determinants of State and Local Expenditures', *National Tax Journal*, XIX, March 1965, pp. 95–104.

mental units with certain economic, geographical, and social characteristics (e.g. *per capita* income, urbanization, and age structure of the population) average a specified amount of public expenditures for education. If actual expenditures are very much less or greater, then an excellent starting point is provided for examining whether such expenditures should be changed. It must be emphasized that such a diagnostic use of a positive theory of public expenditures should be the beginning, not the end, point in the decision-making process for determining future public expenditures.[1]

Finally, positive public expenditure theories, especially concerning the determinants of such expenditures, are vital in making projections or for use in economic planning models.

In spite of the potential usefulness of a positive theory of public expenditures, Anglo-American opinions about the possibilities of developing such a theory were quite pessimistic, especially in the early 1950s. A distinguished American economist summarized such views when he noted:

'The tremendous growth of government expenditures here and abroad has been one of the most striking economic developments of recent years. Economic analysis of these changes has dealt primarily with the probable effects on levels of employment and prices ... Economists specializing in public finance have generally concentrated on taxation. Perhaps there is not much more the economist can say about spending. The nature of the problems, especially the unavailability of bases for appraising results, makes study difficult. Description, plus the statement of rather obvious generalities, may about exhaust the possibilities.'[2]

Although continental economists were not so defeatist, they had not made major advances in this area for many years.

Recently, however, economists have begun to study public

---

[1] This diagnostic use of positive public expenditure theories is especially emphasized and analysed by Alison Martin and W. Arthur Lewis, 'Patterns of Public Revenue and Expenditure', *Manchester School*, XXVI, September 1956, pp. 203–44.

[2] C. Lowell Harriss, 'Public Finance', in Bernard F. Haley, ed., *A Survey of Contemporary Economics* (Homewood, Ill., 1952), pp. 261–2.

expenditures again in order to construct positive theories. This task has been immeasurably aided through the increasing availability of public expenditures data and the use of electronic computers to process such information. But such work is really still in the beginning stages; there remains much to be done.

The second purpose of this study, therefore, is to extend the positive theory of public expenditures. I focus particularly on the determinants of public expenditures, substitution relations between public and private expenditures, and the centralization of expenditures. In addition I also try to develop a number of statistical and analytical techniques which have not hitherto been used in studying public expenditures and which can be of value to future investigators in the field.

3. REFOCUSING THE STUDY OF 'COMPARATIVE ECONOMIC SYSTEMS'

In the West the study of 'comparative economic systems' is a subject that has received relatively little serious attention. Although there are a large number of textbooks on the subject, there are very few monographs or special studies. Most empirical work has focused on institutions, price systems, economic planning, or comparative growth rates of production. Although there is an enormous amount of discussion about what and how economic systems should be compared, there are very few economists who actually make such comparisons. Above all, there is little consensus on what the subject is or should be about.

Among Marxists, however, the situation is quite different. Marx's theory is primarily a comparative theory of economic systems and institutions, with special emphasis on dynamic factors. Particular theoretical attention is paid to the relations between units of production, productive forces (e.g. the state of technology or the quantity and quality of capital equipment) and productive relations (e.g. property relations and the distribution of income between labour and others). However, by focusing on the processes of production and the primary distribution of income, Marxists usually neglect—or explicitly exclude[1]—the consumption process from their analyses. Indeed, the serious empirical comparisons by Marxists of various

[1] E.g. Oskar Lange, *Political Economy*, Vol. I (Oxford, 1962), pp. 1, 7.

aspects of socialist and capitalist economies in recent years seem to focus primarily around differences in growth rates of various types of production.

Although all these production themes are useful to analyse, the field of 'comparative economic systems' should cover a broader range of economic phenomena. In particular, many aspects of consumption deserve attention in the comparative study of economic systems. The relationship of this study to the broader area of consumption and to the comparative analyses of production phenomena can be quite easily viewed.

As a mirror image of the Marxist notion of 'units of production', let us define 'units of consumption' as the institutions through which decisions are made about the quantity and type of goods that are directly consumed by private individuals.[1] For many goods and services this unit is the consumer himself or his family; for other goods and services, various levels of government. In previous eras additional institutions such as the church or the feudal manor were important units of consumption as well.

It should be clear that if the unit of consumption extends wider than the individual or the family, the unit can potentially affect the distribution of consumption among families, just as the unit of production affects the distribution of income among those engaged in the productive process. If we are interested in problems of distribution, we must look at both the production and consumption units, rather than focusing exclusive attention on the former.

In analysing the effects of the level of economic development on public expenditures, we are studying at the same time the relations between productive forces and the relative importance of one type of consumption unit. In generalizing about substitution relations between public and private expenditures or about the degree of centralization of public consumption expenditures between different levels of government, we are also theorizing about the relations between different types of con-

[1] This concept is not new and has been employed in a useful manner by a number of non-Marxist economic anthropologists. For application in the analysis of modern economies, a number of difficulties arise in distinguishing intermediate and final consumption. For the purpose of this brief discussion, however, it is not necessary to dwell upon such knotty problems.

sumption units. In trying to determine the effect of the economic system on public expenditures, we are simultaneously investigating whether the structure (relative importance) of units of consumption is part of the economic 'base' or 'superstructure'.

Thus this study of public expenditures is also a study in the field of 'comparative economic systems', in which the focus of attention is shifted from production to consumption. I must emphasize, however, that there are many aspects of consumption that are not explored in this study but which would be of considerable use for future examination. Aside from the analysis of consumption and production there is also a wide range of other topics (e.g. the role of money or of foreign trade) which should be included in the study of 'comparative economic systems'.

B. SOME PRELIMINARIES AND THE SELECTION OF THE SAMPLE

In any broad interpretive study such as this, the basic purposes can be obscured in several ways. First, the reader may object to certain facts or statistics. Whenever possible, primary sources of information are used and documented; and sufficient data and description of the estimating procedures are supplied, so that indignant readers may recalculate any of the important results. Second, mystification can arise from the terminology and analytical methods that are employed. Although I could not avoid the use of technical terms and, in some places, complex statistical methods, I place definitions for all such terms and descriptions of such methods in a glossary at the end of the book (Appendix F). All abbreviations and new concepts coined in the course of analysis are listed there as well.

To avoid confusion it is also useful to define at the outset several key terms used in this study. *Public consumption expenditures* cover the current expenditures for goods and services and the transfer payments by governments that are financed exclusively through taxation or public borrowing. Such expenditures can be made either by institutions included in the government budgets or by parafiscal institutions which are excluded from budgetary review. The individuals or groups that utilize such goods and services or which receive such transfer payments make no direct payment for them. Public investment expenditures, government subsidies, and sales by government organs to the population are excluded.[1] Thus a modified 'expenditure concept', rather than a 'value added' (or national product) concept is used in the analysis.

The distinction between public consumption expenditures and the public ownership of the means of production is central to this study. Although both modes of collectivization must be taken into account in examining the economic role of the state, the distinction makes it easier to analyse the basic issues in a more systematic fashion.[2] Certain implications of this distinction can be seen by examining the four possible combinations that arise from the two concepts.

TABLE 1–1

Combinations of Modes of Collectivization[3]

Financing of expenditures	Ownership of means of production	Examples
Public	Public	Public education in the USA and the USSR
Public	Private	Government purchases of paintings for public museums from private artists in USA and USSR
Private	Public	Electricity sold to private individuals by publicly owned electric companies in the USA and USSR
Private	Private	Private purchases of vegetables in farmers' markets in the USA and USSR

[1] Social insurance payments are included in public consumption expenditures; but interest payments are excluded. I adopt this particular definition primarily for statistical convenience, although there are a number of analytical advantages for such a definition as well. A more detailed exploration of the concept is presented in Appendix A–1.

[2] E.g. Lionel Robbins, [*The Theory of Economic Policy in English Classical Political Economy* (London, 1952), Chapter II] outlines in a most interesting way the long list of functions which the classical economists believed should be fulfilled by the government. Nevertheless, stating the fact that Adam Smith [*An Inquiry into the Nature and Causes of the Wealth of Nations* (New York, 1937) Book V] favoured public education without noting that he also believed that such services should be financed by user-fees misses the flavour of Smith's remarks.

[3] Public production can be subdivided into two types: public ownership of the

The term *public expenditures*, in contrast to public consumption expenditures, is broader and covers all expenditures that are included in government budgets. This concept is not as analytically useful as public consumption expenditures and is not, therefore, used in the empirical part of this study.

For the sake of comparability it is absolutely necessary to consider public consumption expenditures at all levels of government. Although this injunction seems self-evident, it has been often violated, particularly by Marxist economists.[1]

In selecting a sample for the empirical comparisons, many conceptual and methodological problems face the investigator. The most important such difficulties and their solutions are briefly outlined below.

First, what do we mean by 'economic system'? Most frequently the term is used to designate socialist or capitalist economies (economies with relatively more or less government ownership of the means of production) or to distinguish market and centrally planned economies (where capital and inter-

means by which such goods and services are produced; and government management of the production of goods and services. Combined with public financing such a threefold classification gives rise to eight different cases; this taxonomic exercise (replete with examples) is carried out in Appendix E–1.

[1] A typical example can be found in a classic Soviet text on public finance by N. N. Rovinskiy, *Gosudarstvennyy byudzhet SSSR* (Moscow, 1949) in which the author begins with an hypothesis about the exploitative nature of capitalism and then notes that in 1949–50, 'nearly' 75 per cent of US government expenditures were for military purposes, while less than 5·4 per cent were for social purposes and less than 1 per cent were for education. From these data he paints a pitiful word-picture of the 'millions of American children' who could not obtain education and shows how this illustrates the real nature of the system, in contrast to socialist economies where such social and education expenditures are very high and where there is no exploitation. Aside from some data juggling (see below), the author does not seem to realize that most social and education expenditures in the United States are not made through the federal budget but rather through public trust funds or through state and local governments. Therefore, his demonstration lacks a certain credibility.

To back his argument, Professor Rovinskiy apparently obtained his data from: US Bureau of the Budget, *The Budget of the United States Government for the Fiscal Year Ending June 30, 1950* (Washington, DC, 1949), pp. 1397 ff. To place his argument in perspective, it is useful to compare his figures with data from the budget and with government expenditures on all levels. (Such data come from Appendix A–12. Of course, my data are not completely comparable since they exclude capital expenditures and research costs; include trust fund expenditures; are realized, rather than planned data; and cover calendar year 1950, rather than fiscal year 1949–50.) Rovinskiy includes certain transportation expenditures as mediate products are allocated relatively more or less through a market mechanism or by a set of legally binding government directives). These dichotomies are not the same, for both capitalist and socialist economies can have either a market mechanism or a centralized method of resource allocation. For instance, wartime Nazi Germany was an example of a centrally planned capitalist economy; and Yugoslavia is a socialist market economy.[1] I choose the method of resource allocation, rather than ownership of productive means, as the main criterion for 'economic system'. The only effect of this decision in grouping the countries of this study for analysis is placing Yugoslavia with the United States and other market economies, rather than with the Soviet Union and other socialist nations.[2]

military, a statistical adjustment which may be more indicative of Soviet than American budgetary practices. Percentages are included, since Rovinskiy's calculations are extremely peculiar (see above):

Expenditures (all monetary data in million dollars)

Item	Rovinskiy	% of total	Federal budget	% of total	All govt. levels	% of total
			(my data)			
External Security						
Direct military	14,300		14,268		13,805	
Foreign affairs and aid	6,700		6,709		3,478	
Atomic energy	⎰ 3,500		725		partly incl. above	
Transportation	⎱		not mil.		not mil.	
(Sub-total)	(24,500)	(58·3)	(21,702)	(51·8)	(17,283)	(24·6)
Social						
Welfare & health	1,986		2,358		15,021	
Education ⎱	414		414		7,228	
Culture ⎰					not incl.	
Veterans' benefits	not incl.		5,496		incl. in welfare	
(Sub-total)	(2,400)	(5·7)	(8,268)	(19·8)	(22,249)	(31·7)
Total government expenditures	42,000	(100·0)	41,858	(100·0)	70,234	(100·0)

[1] Most Western commentators on the Yugoslav economy [e.g. George Macesich, *Yugoslavia: The Theory and Practice of Development Planning* (Charlottesville, Va., 1964) or George W. Hoffman and Fred W. Neal, *Yugoslavia and the New Communism* (New York, 1962)] emphasize the importance of the market in allocating resources. It must be noted, however, that there are also a number of important non-market elements in the allocation system as well; certainly the price controls exercised during most of this period significantly modified market action.

[2] There is some doubt that Yugoslavia can be considered a socialist nation, since about one half of its productive capital during the period under examination

In comparing 'economic systems' the usual approach is to choose the 'leading nation' of each system for study, a procedure that ignores the great variety of experience within each system. Further, since the USA and the Soviet Union are usually selected, phenomena associated with the different levels of economic development in the two countries are confused with systemic differences. The obvious way to avoid such difficulties is to increase the size of sample. For the centrally planned (or, for short, centralized) economies the seven industrialized or semi-industrialized nations in East Europe are selected; for the market economies, countries are chosen with roughly similar levels of economic development, i.e. gross national products *per capita*. I also include the United States among the sample nations because, as the wealthiest nation in the world, it has a certain intrinsic interest.

The sample thus embraces fourteen nations—seven market economies and seven centrally planned economies. For certain purposes, subsets of nations can be examined separately, e.g. West and East Germany, Austria and Czechoslovakia, Italy and Poland, or Greece and Bulgaria. In most cases, however, all nations in the sample are used at one time for the analyses. Although the range of variability of the nations is limited in so far as all are at least semi-industrialized and have *per capita* GNPs over $400 during most of the period, in other dimensions they have greater diversity. Some of the cross-section properties (properties at a single point in time) of the fourteen nations can be seen in Table 1–2.

A problem arises in the selection of a time period for which the comparisons are made. At the time the basic estimates

was privately owned [I. Vinski, 'The National Wealth of Yugoslavia at the End of 1962', International Association for Research in Income and Wealth, Raymond Goldsmith and Christopher Saunders, eds., *Income and Wealth*, Series VIII, *The Measurement of National Wealth* (London, 1959), p. 167]. It must also be added that there were some periods in which all other socialist countries rejected the notion that Yugoslavia was 'socialist' [for documentation on this point, see Zbigniew K. Brzezinski, *The Soviet Bloc: Unity and Conflict* (Cambridge, Mass., 1960)].

For certain cases, e.g. education, there are good empirical indications that analytic advantages can be gained by classifying Yugoslavia among the socialist nations. In such situations, I do not hesitate to use the alternative criterion for economic system.

TABLE 1–2

Cross-Section Properties of the Sample Nations in 1956[1]

Nations	GNP *per capita* (index)	Mid-year population (1000s)	Density (persons per square kilometre)	Urbaniza-tion (per cent)
Market Economies				
USA	100	168,225	21	53
West Germany	61	52,022	209	55
Austria	41	6,983	83	43
Ireland	36	2,898	41	34
Italy	36	48,490	161	57
Greece	21	8,031	60	38
Yugoslavia	18	17,685	69	18
Centralized Economies				
Czechoslovakia	50	13,250	104	31
East Germany	50	17,716	164	49
USSR	38	199,600	9	37
Hungary	35	9,911	106	46
Poland	32	27,726	89	33
Romania	22	17,583	74	25
Bulgaria	21	7,576	68	29

were made, data were available for most countries only for the years 1950 through 1962, and therefore this period is used. For detailed cross-section comparisons, 1956 (1955 for Hungary) and 1962 are chosen, the former year coinciding with the last year of readjustment from the Stalinist excesses in East Europe (i.e. the end of the 'new course'), the latter year being the last year for which abundant data were available. Some idea about the properties of the sample nations over the time period used for this study can be gained from Table 1–3.

[1] *Per capita* GNP data for Hungary are for 1955. USA excludes Alaska and Hawaii; West Germany includes West Berlin but excludes the Saar; East Germany includes East Berlin. GNPS are calculated from quantity data, weighted by US prices. Urbanization is the percentage of population living in urban 'places' over 10,000.

Details and sources of GNP data are given in Appendix B. Sources for population and urbanization data are given respectively in Appendices D–1 and D–2. Densities are calculated from population data and from data on areas [from UN, *Statistical Yearbook* 1959 (New York, 1959) and US Bureau of the Census, *Statistical Abstract of the United States, 1962* (Washington, DC, 1962)].

TABLE 1–3

Time-Series Properties of the Sample Nations, 1950 through 1962
(Average Annual Growth Rates)[1]

Nations	Population	Labour force	Gross national product (constant prices)	Material product (constant prices)
Market economies				
USA	1·7%	0·9%	2·9%	2·4%
West Germany	0·9	2·0	7·0	7·2
Austria	0·2	0·7	5·4	5·7
Ireland	−0·5	−1·5	1·6	n.a.
Italy	0·6	2·0	6·2	6·5
Greece	0·9	0·7	6·2	7·0
Yugoslavia	1·1	0·5	8·0	7·4
Centralized economies				
Czechoslovakia	1·0%	1·0%	5·0%	6·8%
East Germany	−0·7	0·2	5·8	8·6
USSR	1·7	1·7	7·1	9·3
Hungary	0·6	1·3	4·3	5·7
Poland	1·8	1·1	4·8	7·2
Romania	1·2	1·0	7·0	8·5
Bulgaria	0·9	0·6	5·8	7·9

Additional cross-section and time-series data for the sample nations are given in the text and appendices.

[1] Data for Yugoslavia cover 1952 through 1962. Boundaries for the national units are chosen so as to make the data comparable for the entire period for each nation. Material product covers production of 'material goods' and is roughly equivalent to the GNP after the removal of all services. All of the gross national product data for the centrally planned economies are from calculations made in the West; however, the material product data for these economies are from official statistics. All average annual growth rates are calculated by fitting exponential curves to the data, using the method of least squares.

Sources for population, labour force, and gross national product data are given respectively in Appendices D–1, D–2, and B. Data on material products for the centralized economies and Yugoslavia are net (exclude depreciation) and are taken from the respective national statistical yearbooks. Data on material products are gross (depreciation is included) for Austria, Greece, Italy, USA, and West Germany and are obtained from OECD, *Statistics of National Accounts*, 1950–61 (Paris, 1964) and OECD, *General Statistics* January 1965, by summing the gross domestic product originating from agriculture, forestry, and fishing; mining and quarrying; manufacturing; construction; electricity, gas, and water works; and transportation and communications.

C. PLAN OF ATTACK

A basic problem of research strategy immediately arises: how should empirical evidence on expenditures, institutions, political intentions, and other matters be balanced? It is possible to focus primary attention on institutional, political, and ideological matters surrounding public expenditures. But such an approach runs the danger of obscuring important differences between how the public expenditures 'should' and actually do behave; moreover, one can become so enmeshed in the multitude of institutional similarities and differences as to lose complete sight of the actual public expenditures that are made. Or, one can start from certain notions about the 'essence' of each economic system or nation and find data supporting these ideas. But such an approach leads to the suppression of empirical evidence which is contrary to the propositions to be 'proved', a procedure that may result in debating points but which hardly serves to advance our understanding of economic reality.[1] Or one can even reject the empirical data completely and argue along with the romantic Argentinian socialist Estéban Echeverria who proclaimed: 'Theories are everything; facts alone matter little. What is a defective political fact? It is the result of an erroneous idea. What is its opposite, an act rich in good results? It is the product of mature, precise ideas.'[2]

The approach in this study is different from all of these and, I believe, more straightforward. For each expenditure that is analysed, a number of theoretical remarks and *a priori* predictions of the behaviour of public expenditures are deduced. If possible, such predictions are tested with the comparable expenditures data from the fourteen sample countries and the hypotheses are accepted or rejected according to what the data reveal. If the proper data are not available for the sample nations, then expenditures data from other governmental units are selected for testing purposes. A tangled skein of conceptual,

[1] Although the above discussed approaches may seem naïve, they are often used. For examples from two recent books on capitalism, see my 'Comparing Economic Systems: A Review Article', *Soviet Studies*, XVIII, January 1967, pp. 356–61.

[2] Cited by Laura Randall, 'The State of Economics Today', *Ararat*, Winter 1967, p. 52.

B

statistical, and analytical problems forces us to touch only briefly upon many important issues. But pointillism has its place in the social sciences, as in art; and although some of the details may be fuzzy, the theoretical and empirical outlines are, it is hoped, sufficiently clear.

Such an empirical approach does not preclude the inclusion of institutional or political information, and indeed such data are extremely useful for interpretive purposes. The key of the inquiry, however, lies in the testing of hypotheses on the data from the fourteen nations. Those who feel that such quantitative methods are inappropriate for dealing with problems of the political process where ideology plays such an important role, may use this book for meditating on the implications of Edmund Burke's famous lament: '. . . the age of chivalry is gone. That of sophisters, economists, and calculators has succeeded; and . . . glory . . . is extinguished forever.'[1]

The next chapter is addressed to specific problems of comparing public consumption expenditures, the major types of questions which can be asked, and the available information for answering them.

The subsequent four chapters are empirical analyses of the behaviour of individual public consumption expenditures. More lengthy studies are made of military, health, welfare, and education expenditures, which are quantitatively the most important. Shorter investigations of administration, internal security, diplomacy and foreign aid, and research and development expenditures are also carried out.

In the last chapter I summarize the previous results, extend the analysis to a number of topics not previously considered, and indicate certain promising areas for future research.

1 Edmund Burke, 'Reflections on the Revolution in France', in Philip Magnus, ed., *Edmund Burke, Selected Prose* (London, 1948), p 69.

Chapter II

ANALYSING PUBLIC CONSUMPTION EXPENDITURES

A. Introduction

B. Types of Goods and Services Publicly Financed

C. Determinants of Public Consumption Expenditures
1. *Three Approaches*
2. *Major Hypotheses to be Tested*
3. *Statistical Problems*

D. Behavioural Properties of Public Consumption Expenditures
1. *Substitution Effects*
2. *Centralization*
3. *Stability*
4. *Incidence*

E. Differential Effects of Public and Private Financing

F. Concluding Remarks

A. INTRODUCTION

On its most general level a positive theory of public expenditures is concerned with four basic questions: (1) What types of goods and services are publicly financed? (2) What are the determinants of the volume of public expenditures? (3) What are the factors underlying other behavioural properties of public expenditures such as substitution relations, centralization, or stability? (4) And what difference does it make whether a good or service is financed in the public or private sector? The analysis in this study of public consumption expenditures of market and centrally planned economies centres on these general questions.

Before plunging into the empirical study, however, we must pay some attention to the specific analytic techniques that can be employed with the available information. Otherwise we run the dangers either of misinterpreting the data or of incompleteness. In this chapter I examine the types of hypotheses to be tested, the kind of data that are necessary for the verification of these hypotheses, the statistical methods that are appropriate for such verification, and the types of approximations that are employed when the desired data are not at hand. Thus this chapter sets the guidelines for the empirical analyses in the remaining chapters. Those readers who are impatient with discussions of methodology and who are willing to accept my statistical and analytical methods on faith can skim designated parts of this chapter without serious loss of continuity.

Underlying the discussion in this chapter is an assumption that should be made explicit at once: for purposes of analysis it is permissible to isolate public consumption expenditures from taxes and to focus exclusive attention on the former. Of course, considerable controversy surrounds this assumption (even though it is implicit in a large majority of studies on public expenditures) and its importance depends on the level of aggregation and the time period chosen for exploration.[1] For the type of analysis carried out in this study, however, a number of statistical experiments suggest that it is a very reasonable hypothesis. The results of these experiments and further discussion of such issues are included in the appendices.[2]

B. TYPES OF GOODS AND SERVICES PUBLICLY FINANCED

First of all a positive theory of public consumption expenditures deals with a set of questions about what goods and services are publicly financed. Exploration of such questions raises one important ambiguity.

In many cases it is very difficult to define exactly what particular service is being publicly financed. For instance, military

[1] A number of economists have advanced arguments on a theoretical level to support the hypothesis that taxation phenomena must be taken into account in the discussion of public consumption expenditures. Such studies include: James M. Buchanan, *Public Finance in Democratic Process* (Chapel Hill, 1967); Alan Peacock and Jack Wiseman, *The Growth of Public Expenditures in the United Kingdom* (Princeton, 1961); Harley H. Hindrichs, *A General Theory of Tax Structure Change during Economic Development* (Cambridge, Mass., 1966); and James L. Barr and Otto A. Davis, 'An Elemental Political and Economic Theory of the Expenditures of Local Governments', *Southern Economic Journal*, XXXIII, October 1966, pp. 149–66. The last three studies also contain supporting empirical evidence.

[2] These experiments are described in Appendix E–2: The Propriety of Isolating Public Consumption Expenditures. The Peacock and Wiseman hypothesis is examined in detail in Appendix E–3: An Analysis of the Displacement Effect.

expenditures can be regarded as consisting of three basic services: land, sea, and air armed forces. Or we can view these military expenditures in the manner of the US Defence Department as consisting of the services of: strategic retaliation forces, continental air and missile defence, airlifts and sealifts, civil defence and home guard, etc.[1] The definition of 'service' depends upon the state of technology, policy decisions concerning the underlying purposes of expenditures, and administrative advantages of grouping certain highly specific activities together. Basically, this is an aggregation problem and raises some major problems for empirical research. First, reports that a specific activity or piece of equipment has been publicly financed often fail to mention what service is actually being produced. Second, reported expenditures may include items that the analyst may not consider pertinent; for instance, 'education' expenditures may include the cost of school athletics, free lunches to children, or bus transportation for children working on a nearby state farm. Finally, knowledge of the legislative intent behind the appropriation of funds must be supplemented by information about the administrative rules by which such funds are actually spent before decisions can be made concerning the 'services' publicly financed.

In the Marxist economic literature, I have been unable to locate any sustained analysis of what types of goods and services are or should be publicly financed, either from a theoretical or empirical viewpoint. In the Western economic literature there are three major theories about these matters;[2] such theories have focused respectively on 'public-goods properties', the 'exclusion principle', and the 'insurance principle'.[3] From considerations of such properties or principles it

---

[1] Such issues are discussed in a number of specific contexts in David Novick (ed.) *Program Budgeting: Program Analysis and the Federal Budget* (Cambridge, Mass., 1965).

[2] Aside from general theories, there are a number of different types of *ad hoc* explanations for special goods or services, e.g. public financing of ammunition for rifle clubs in the US is a 'frontier holdover'; public financing of churches in a number of European nations is a 'feudal holdover'; public financing of education occurs because education is a 'merit good'. [On the latter concept see Richard A. Musgrave, *The Theory of Public Finance* (New York, 1959)].

[3] The literature on public goods and exclusion properties is summarized by J. G. Head, 'Public Goods and Public Policy', *Public Finance/Finances publiques*,

is usually argued that because particular goods and services should be financed publicly, in most cases this public financing actually occurs. In other words, there is an Hegelian leap from the 'should' to the 'is'.

In some branches of economics, this argumentative leap from normative to positive analysis has proved a stimulating procedure,[1] but in the field of public finance and expenditures, the results have been decidedly unfortunate. For by assuming that the normatively derived properties listed above actually bring about the public financing of a good or service, meaningful empirical questions about the actual goods and services publicly financed cease to be asked.[2] Although discussions about the properties that justify public financing of a good or service have abounded in the economic literature for the last century, very few empirical studies of the actual publicly financed services have been made.[3]

In principle, it is quite easy to test hypotheses about which goods and services are publicly financed. One need merely draw up a long list of different goods and services, pick out the services with those properties which lead to their being financed through the public sector, and then examine the expenditure data of a number of governmental units in order to see whether such predictions are successful.

In practice, however, a number of difficulties arise. It is very difficult to obtain detailed public expenditure data for a large

XVIII, 3/1962, pp. 197–219. The insurance doctrine is presented in its most extreme form by Guiseppe Ugo Papi, 'Eine Theorie des oekonomischen Verhaltens des Staates', *Zeitschrift fuer die gesamte Staatswissenschaft*, CXVI, 1/1960, pp. 1–17.

[1] Ricardo's theory of foreign trade was essentially normative, but it has proved useful in the empirical analysis of trade flows as well, e.g. in the study by Donald MacDougall, 'British and American Exports: A Study Suggested by the Theory of Comparative Costs', *Economic Journal*, December 1951 and September, 1952.

[2] This point is emphasized in a much stronger way by Gunnar Myrdal, *The Political Element in the Development of Economic Theory* (Cambridge, Mass., 1955).

[3] The most extensive such study is by Henry J. Schmandt and G. Ross Stephens, 'Measuring Municipal Output', *National Tax Journal*, XII, 4/1960, pp. 369–75. For an international comparison between cities in the USA and UK, see William H. Form and Delbert C. Miller, *Industry, Labor and Community* (New York, 1960).

enough number of governmental units; and the more aggregative the data, the less useful such an analysis would be. Moreover, a simple 'yes' or 'no' on whether such services are publicly financed may not be sufficient since such services may be performed for part of the population in the unit under analysis but not for others. (For instance, in the United States, free school books for children in public elementary schools are provided in some but not all areas; or in the USSR, public health insurance used to be available to workers on state farms, but not on collective farms.) Further, generalizing on the basis of 'common knowledge' or of legal provisions can be misleading. For instance, in the realm of education we might expect similar socialist countries to behave in the same way; yet we find many important differences: in Czechoslovakia, free books are provided to all schoolchildren, while in East Germany (where such a public service is constitutionally guaranteed) only 25 per cent of all schoolchildren receive them.[1] Finally, the degree to which a certain service is financed respectively by the public and private sectors seems quite relevant to such analyses as well.

Of the four major questions composing a positive theory of public expenditures, this problem of which goods and services are publicly financed is the only one for which insufficient information is available for an adequate empirical analysis. Although a great many theoretical remarks about the nature of publicly financed goods and services can be made, it will be more worthwhile to turn to those matters which can be empirically investigated.

C. DETERMINANTS OF PUBLIC CONSUMPTION EXPENDITURES

Since the early 1950s the theoretical and empirical literature on determinants of the volume or changes in the volume of public consumption expenditures has experienced a rapid growth. Such studies are useful, not only for making projections or deriving

[1] 'Answers to Readers' Questions', *G D R Review*, Special Number, 1965, p. 6. Since this source is an East German governmental information magazine addressing itself to foreigners, it is hardly likely that this datum is understated. As provision of free education and free schoolbooks is written into the 1949 constitution, this statement is a surprising admission of unconstitutionality.

'norms' of public expenditures, but also for gaining insights into the causal mechanisms that underlie the collectivization of consumption. As a great deal of this study deals with determinants of public consumption expenditures, it is useful to explore the methods by which such determinants can be isolated and analysed.

1. THREE APPROACHES

The most rigorous approach toward exploring determinants of the volume of public consumption expenditures is through formal model building; and the most successful attempts have been in the field of military expenditures—an area in which one might expect economists to have little to say. By means of a simple indifference curve analysis, the assumption that governments are unitary entities with stable preferences, and the concept of a 'public good', Western economists can derive a series of testable hypotheses about the behaviour of military expenditures which turn out to be quite accurate (see Chapter III). Marxist economists, starting from Lenin's theory of imperialism,[1] also advance a set of different predictions that can be easily tested. Such causal models can be based on narrow economic considerations, such as the Western approach to military expenditures mentioned above, or on broad socioeconomic grounds such as the Marxist theory of these military expenditures or Adolph Wagner's proposition about the rising share of public consumption expenditures in the GNP (discussed in the next subsection).

Most such causal theories of public expenditures are based on assumptions that are gross simplifications and, therefore, descriptively false. Nevertheless, 'methodological nominalists'[2]

[1] V. I. Lenin, *Imperialism, The Highest Stage of Capitalism* (New York, 1939). Such hypotheses are also tested in Chapter III and, although it is not my intention to spoil the readers' suspense, they do not serve as accurate predictors.

[2] The term has been coined by Karl R. Popper [*The Open Society and Its Enemies* (Princeton, 1950), p. 34] and is contrasted with 'methodological essentialists', who hold that it is the task of science to discover the 'essence' of things and that once such an 'essence' is discovered, contradictory phenomena are considered of 'secondary' importance or a 'distortion' of the true essence. The 'methodological nominalists' (a more modern label would be 'methodological existentialists') argue that in examining entities or theories, 'by their fruits ye shall know them'.

assert that 'the relevant question is whether [the assumptions] are sufficiently good for the purpose in hand. And this question can only be answered by seeing whether the theory works, which means whether it yields sufficiently accurate predictions.'[1] Thus the hypothesis that governments are unitary entities with stable preferences, which is implictly or explicitly assumed in most empirical studies of public consumption expenditures is permissible only in so far as it allows us to make accurate predictions about the determinants of public expenditures. For this study I have also taken this nominalist position on methodology.

Two major objections can be raised against such an approach. In order to avoid misunderstanding, these must be answered.[2] First, some argue that the realism of the assumptions is an important aspect in judging the reasonableness of a theory, since a large number of positive theories can potentially explain the same phenomenon. Aside from some difficulties about the criteria of 'realism',[3] methodological nominalists can retort with justification that in evaluating theories for scientific use, the one with the greatest predictive power is chosen, no matter how unpalatable the assumptions behind the theory may be. Of course, dissatisfaction about such assumptions may act as an important spur to find 'better' theories, but the criterion for 'better' is always predictive power.

The position of methodological nominalism can also be attacked because such an approach does not really illuminate the problem of 'causation', since it neglects the entire problem of the mechanism by which the dependent variable is related to the independent variables. That is, although it is recognized that useful predictive models based on highly unrealistic

[1] Milton Friedman, 'The Methodology of Positive Economics', *Essays in Positive Economics* (Chicago, 1953), p. 15.

[2] There is a vast literature on these matters, and I cannot here discuss the various issues exhaustively. The above remarks are meant to indicate in a rough manner my position and to meet the most obvious objections.

[3] Friedman, *op. cit.*, argues that the assumption behind the statement 'the distance travelled by a falling body is equal to one half the gravitational constant multiplied by the square of the time the body falls' is extremely 'unrealistic', namely that the object is falling in a complete vacuum. Nevertheless, this did not prevent the theory from being generally accepted for several generations. Moreover, even though we can make corrections for air pressure and friction, porosity and density of the object, etc., the theory is extremely useful in a great many cases even today.

B*

assumptions do play an important role in the development of science, the end goal is the inclusion of all relevant aspects of reality into the theory.[1] Certainly there is justice to this objection, especially when the link between individual and group behaviour is not very clear. However, the discovery of the causal mechanism usually occurs after the quantitative relationships have been discovered; and, moreover, such mechanisms can only be demonstrated through empirical analysis of the quantitative relationship of the relevant variables.[2] Since fourteen nations are involved in this study, investigation of the causal mechanism in each country is obviously out of the question, and the relationships between macro- and microeconomic phenomena concerning public expenditures must be left to future investigators.

A second approach to the determinants of public consumption expenditures is the derivation of hypotheses from propositions that deal only with one or several important facets of the phenomena under examination. Such an approach is much less complete than the construction of causal models, and the deductive chains are usually considerably shorter. Such propositions may be based on institutional factors (e.g. the alleged expansionism of governmental bureaucracies) or on more standard economic considerations (e.g. nations with higher *per capita* incomes require a higher portion of their labour force with advanced technical training).

Such hypotheses are empirically tested in exactly the same way as the hypotheses derived from the more formal causal models. But interpretation of the results must be made more cautiously and a statistically significant relationship between two

[1] Tjallings C. Koopmans [('The Construction of Economic Knowledge', *Three Essays on the State of Economic Science* (New York, 1957)] places special emphasis on this point.

[2] This position is especially argued by R. M. MacIver [*Social Causation* (New York, 1964)], who has asserted that isolation of the quantitative factors associated with a certain phenomenon is the scientific sense in which we use the concept of causation. For example, a physical chemist investigating the relationship between temperature and the volume of gases (a rise in temperature 'causes' an increase in the volume of gases) worries considerably more about the quantitative relationships than about the mechanism by which the heat is transformed into molecular energy, which in turn affects the volume of gas. The difficulty with this methodological position lies in the fact that the methods by which such quantitative relationships are properly *isolated* are left completely undiscussed.

variables should be viewed as an 'association' or 'correlation' rather than as a causal relationship. The primary usefulness of such exercises is to direct future empirical and theoretical research toward further examination of such associations.

The third and final major approach toward the study of determinants of public consumption expenditures is strict induction. That is, on more or less intuitive reasons a number of factors are chosen to be statistically tested for significant associations with the volume or with changes in the volumes of specific expenditures. Thus, in many parts of this study I test whether the economic systems of nations are related to their differences in public consumption expenditures without any preconceived notions about what the results will be. But there are a great number of well-known dangers in using such a method and in interpreting the results, which render such an approach inadvisable except in special situations where possible correlations between particular variables are of special interest.

2. MAJOR HYPOTHESES TO BE TESTED

In this section I discuss three major groups of hypotheses: those relating to (1) economic system, (2) the level of economic development, and (3) 'other factors'.

Economic System

The influence of economic system on public consumption expenditures is, of course, a vital question in a world where the competition between such economic systems is so important.

Before turning to hypotheses about the differences between the systems, it will be worth while to review briefly the major differences in the institutions that are responsible for public consumption expenditures. Unfortunately, a great deal of nonsense has been written about the topic.[1] However, a number of important differences do seem clear.[2]

---

[1] E.g. D. Butakov, *et al.*, *Finansi stran narodnoy demokratii* (Moscow, 1959), pp. 81–2, assert that the organs of state in socialist nations are socially indispensable and serve *only* a positive economic function, while similar institutions in capitalist countries represent *only* a dead weight on the economy and are characterized only by red tape and bureaucracy. Many other examples in the writings of both Marxist and non-Marxist economists can be found.

[2] The best discussion of these differences is by the Hungarian economist

First, in the centrally planned nations the many organizations and institutions responsible for public consumption expenditures are much more hierarchically organized than in the market economies. Thus in the centralized economies there is a definite administrative arrangement of budgetary units, each being a part of a pyramid of responsibility and power and each using standard administrative tools. No such uniformity exists among the market economies. Although higher governmental instances in these nations may have the right to direct or to interfere in the operations of lower units, the administrative links between units are less well defined and the various budgetary units less standardized, not only in regard to function but also in regard to the use of administrative tools. It must be added that the greater hierarchical arrangement of budgetary units in the centrally planned economies, often referred to as 'unity of budgetary organs', does not necessarily imply that the economic interests of these units are more uniform. Indeed, such an inference represents an elementary confusion between form and content. The only valid way of arriving at such a conclusion is by defining certain measures for unity or conflict of interests and investigating the matter empirically, a formidable but useful task which seems to be beyond the capability of the ideologically oriented economists who pontificate about such matters.

Second, in the centralized economies the budget plan presents a set of binding instructions on the respective organs of government, while in the market economies the approved budget often represents a series of upper limits on government spending which may be reduced on certain occasions on the initiative of the executive branch of the government. This difference, which is related to the point discussed above, springs from the fact that in the centralized economies the state budget is part of a larger, economy-wide financial plan, which in turn is more or less related to the production plans for the entire economy.[1] On the other hand, the market economies do not

Stefan Varga, 'Die Eigenarten des Budgets der sozialistischen Staaten', *Finanzarchiv*, XXII, April 1963, pp. 185–203. This article should be read in conjunction with his worthwhile though long-winded twin study, 'Ueber den eigenartigen Charakter der sozialistischen Finanzwissenschaft', *Zeitschrift fuer die gesamte Staatswissenschaft*, CXIX, January 1963, pp. 83–117.

[1] I qualify with 'more or less' because in most of these countries the integration

have such yearly production plans, and although the central budget is sometimes presented in the context of the future growth of the economy, the many interrelations between the budget and the rest of the economy are usually not made as explicit as in the case of the centralized economies. The actual importance of this difference between binding instructions and upper limits is difficult to evaluate, especially because the differences between the actual and proposed expenditures are usually minor in the market economies; furthermore, the importance of the role of the stage budget in the national economy is receiving increasing attention in most market economies as certain types of national planning measures are being introduced.[1] If the socialist economies move closer to the 'Yugoslav model' and if the capitalist economies continue their trends toward increasing economic planning, the differences between the two systems in regard to the binding nature of budgetary laws and the integration of budgetary and national planning will become increasingly less.

One consequence of the greater integration of the state budget in the national plan of the centralized economies is that budget surpluses or deficits appear much less important in these countries than in the market economies, where the imbalances of governmental expenditures and receipts have important macro-economic consequences. This is because any surplus or deficit of state expenditures in the centralized economies can be more easily offset through government action in the banking sector. As a result, the budget deficit or surplus is an important tool of economic policy in many market economies while it seems virtually ignored in some of the centralized economies.[2]

of financial and physical planning has been an extremely difficult administrative problem.

[1] One alleged distinction between government expenditures and receipts in countries with different economic systems is that they are supposed to be more 'predictable' in the centralized economies. A glimpse at the difference between planned and actual budgetary amounts in these centralized economies casts some doubt on the proposition. A relatively simple statistical analysis can easily establish the validity of this proposition, but such an effort did not seem important enough to carry out for this study.

[2] John M. Montias ('Comments on Brzeski's Paper' in a forthcoming series of essays edited by Gregory Grossman) suggests that the Polish government

Third, budgetary accounting practices are quite different between the economic systems. In addition, the degree of uniformity of such practices is much greater in the centralized economies. In all the centrally planned economies except East Germany, the accounting methods and the statistical presentation of the data roughly follow Soviet procedures: a distinction is made between 'budget' and 'nonbudgetary' institutions; all expenditures of the former units are aggregated and reported net of receipts from the public; and roughly similar categories are used in reporting expenditures. Although there are differences as to whether capital expenditures are included with current or as to the exact definitions of the functional categories, many other differences are relatively minor. This means that intra-bloc comparisons are facilitated and, if it is desired, greater uniformity of expenditures among the nations can be achieved. In the market economies, on the other hand, there is considerable variation in accounting and reporting methods. Some nations still use certain types of 'fund' accounting systems; others distinguish between 'ordinary' and 'extraordinary' expenditures and revenues; and some expenditures are reported net of receipts from the public while others are recorded gross. In short, in the market economies the diversity is overwhelming and any desire for making comparisons in order to bring expenditures in different countries closer together is rapidly discouraged for lack of comparable data.

Fourth, in the market economies detailed data on the budget are quite easy to obtain, while in the centralized economies, with the exception of Poland, most of such data are withheld from the public. In regard to both budget plans and actual expenditures and receipts of governmental organs, a flood of information is available in the market economies—the most notable being the United States, where federal expenditures and receipts are presented in a document of over one thousand pages, covering in detail every governmental organ (including the Defence Department) except for the most highly secret institutions such as the Central Intelligence Agency. The real

consciously used budgetary surpluses and deficits in anti-inflationary policies. However, most of the brunt of these policies lay in changes in investment financed through the budget.

problem in dealing with the market economies is not obtaining information and data but in putting the data from different governmental units into some standardized form. (Fortunately, individual governments publish a number of statistical surveys to aid such a process.) In the centralized economies, again with the exception of Poland, the planned budgets are pitiful documents consisting of several pages which contain a few scattered data surrounded by a great amount of verbiage. Reporting of actual public expenditures is even more cursory in some of these nations, the nadir being Czechoslovakia and Hungary which do not report realized state expenditures in any accessible publication. There is a peculiar element of unpredictability here; for example, upon request the Finance Ministries of these two nations do supply considerable unpublished data on welfare, health, and education expenditures.

Reflecting this situation is the process by which the proposed governmental budgets, at least on the central level, are ratified by the respective legislatures. In the market economies, the budgets are debated by the political parties with great vigour, changes are made, and ambiguities are clarified. The degree to which the legislatures succeed in changing the budget proposals is a relatively unexplored question,[1] but at least government officials are forced to defend and sometimes modify the policy decisions underlying the proposed budget. In the centralized economies, the budgets are usually explained, rather than debated, and are unanimously and quickly approved intact. This ritualistic rubber-stamping of government budgetary requests by the legislatures has recently received criticism in the public press of some of these countries, but a strengthening of the actual use of legislative power in the budget-making process does not seem imminent.

A final major difference in public budgetary expenditures between centralized and market economies is the scope of the budget. The centralized economies, as shown in Chapter VI, finance a greater portion of total national investment through the state budget; in addition, they channel relatively more

[1] The only sophisticated study of this matter I could find is by Otto. A. Davis, *et al.*, 'A Theory of the Budgetary Process', *American Political Science Review*, LX, September 1966, pp. 529–47.

subsidies for production, short-term capital loans, and grants to productive units through the budget as well. This allows a greater redistribution of investment funds from one sector to another, a process which has certain disadvantages as well as advantages. Analysis of these expenditures, however, is more appropriately in the province of monographs on government economic administration, rather than public consumption expenditures.

What are the implications of these institutional differences on the volume of public consumption expenditures? Using a considerable amount of imagination, both Marxist and non-Marxist economists have made a number of deductions which, stripped of their polemical justifications, appear too weak to justify their recording here. Although such institutional information is useful as a background for studying the actual expenditures, it is extremely difficult to derive many very convincing hypotheses linking the institutions to the actual expenditures. Indeed, most of the current notions about the empirical differences in public consumption expenditures of centrally planned and market economies stem from very much different considerations.

Certain economists designate different types of public consumption expenditures as 'good' or 'bad' and, with knowledge about the orientation of economic systems, use this stipulated dichotomy to predict the relative volume of such expenditures in different nations. For example, the Marxists Paul Baran and Paul Sweezy, after identifying public consumption expenditures as 'good', note:

'In a rationally ordered socialist society with productive potential comparable to that of the United States, the amount and proportion of surplus absorbed by the state for the satisfaction of collective wants and needs of the people would certainly be larger, not smaller, than the amount and proportion absorbed by the government in this country today.'[1]

[1] Paul A. Baran and Paul Sweezy, *Monopoly Capitalism* (New York, 1966), p. 147. Oskar Lange [Lange and Fred M. Taylor, *On the Economic Theory of Socialism* (Minneapolis, 1952), pp. 103 ff.)] reaches a similar conclusion by reasoning that socialist nations can take greater cognizance of production and consumption externalities in their decision making about public expenditures.

Other economists approach the relationship between economic system and public expenditures in an even more categorical way. For instance, Richard Musgrave partly defines capitalist and socialist economies in terms of the relative amounts of public consumption expenditures.[1] That is, an economy is designated socialist if it interferes more with consumer (private) preferences for goods and services by public financing of 'merit goods', an approach which (in regard to education, health, and welfare) puts Austria as the most 'socialistic' country in the fourteen nation sample of this study. Underlying such a definitional approach is the common political observation in the West that advocates of greater economic planning and public ownership are almost always in favour of greater public consumption expenditures as well.

Relying on political or ideological evidence in regard to the relationship between economic system (defined in any way) and public consumption expenditures is dangerous, especially when political and ideological conflicts between nations are so intense. Although opinions of the relationships between economic system and public consumption expenditures appear quite fixed in the economic literature, the logical or empirical bases for such certainty seem quite inadequate. Many observers of such polemics must share the feelings of Lord Melbourne, who, after listening to the historian Thomas Macaulay, wished he were as sure on any subject as Macaulay was about everything.

Prior to the present study there has been no extensive empirical investigation of this relationship between economic system and public consumption expenditure, and, as a result, there is no extensive body of evidence to refute or to strengthen. Since I have seen no institutional or theoretical evidence on this systems-expenditure relationship that is convincing, it does not seem worthwhile to report any specific hypotheses for testing. Moreover, the relevant theoretical literature does not yield any model or set of *a priori* hypotheses on this relationship that would add much to an empirical analysis. Since it is extremely important to investigate this relation between economic system and public consumption expenditures in an empirical

[1] Richard A. Musgrave, *Fiscal Systems* (New Haven, 1968), Chapter I.

fashion, a purely inductive approach seems most advantageous; and this is the method which is followed throughout this study to explore such matters.

Level of Economic Development

The level of economic development is a second determinant of public consumption expenditures which is of great interest. Fortunately, this variable has received a great deal of attention in both theoretical and empirical studies of public consumption expenditures. The most famous early theorist in these matters was Adolph Wagner, who formulated a long run 'law' that in growing economies, public consumption expenditures become an increasingly larger share of the national income.[1] This represents on a governmental level the same type of generalization that Ernst Engel enunciated some years before for private consumption (that, in part, as family income increases, the portion of income expended on food declines). Wagner's 'law' has been the subject of comment and controversy in the public finance literature ever since.[2]

Economists have tried to justify Wagner's 'law' on a variety of theoretical grounds. On the demand side, some have asserted that the share of public consumption expenditures in the GNP rises with economic development because of tastes (income elasticities) or technological requirements. Others have emphasized the importance of correlates of *per capita* income such as urbanization, while still others have pointed out that public attitudes toward public expenditures change as nations grow wealthier. On the supply side, considerable emphasis is placed on the larger tax base accompanying economic development or

[1] For Wagner's major statements, see his *Finanzwissenschaft*, 1st Part, 3rd ed. (Leipzig, 1883), or *Grundlegung der politischen Oekonomie*, 1st Part, 3rd ed. (Leipzig, 1893). Wagner's style is so murky that my interpretation is open to some doubt. The best survey of his ideas is by Herbert Timm, 'Das Gesetz der wachsenden Staatsausgaben', *Finanzarchiv*, N. F., Band 21, September 1961, pp. 201–47.

It should be noted that Wagner was not the first economist to speculate on the growth of public expenditures. Wagner's predecessors include, among others, Adam Smith; but no one attempted to buttress his arguments with so much actual data or with such an elaborate theoretical structure.

[2] For a fairly detailed survey of the many views on these matters which have been advanced, see Appendix E–5: A Brief History of Doctrine on the Relationships of Income and Public Consumption Expenditures.

tax rate ratchet effects following wars and other periods of national emergency. Still other economists have pointed toward the behaviour of particular public consumption expenditures as critical in the operation of Wagner's 'law'.

Although certain associations between *per capita* income and public consumption expenditures seem clear, the quantitative relationships implied by Wagner's 'law' are not at all certain on theoretical grounds. For instance, it is highly likely that productivity grows faster in those sectors which are not financed by public consumption expenditures so that the opportunity costs of goods and services that are publicly financed increases. If the relative costs of certain goods and services increase, there is a strong tendency for other goods and services to be chosen for consumption instead. Or, on a less theoretical plane, there are no really convincing economic reasons why the share in the national income of a number of specific public consumption expenditures (e.g. for police) should increase. If the data presented in the following chapters have no other use, they should convince most readers that many commonly held notions about the quantitative relations between income and public consumption expenditures are quite misleading.

If the theoretical evidence for Wagner's 'law' is less than convincing, the empirical evidence is even weaker. Two important types of nations do not fit Wagner's generalization—the highly underdeveloped and the highly developed economies—and both deserve brief comment.

In certain highly underdeveloped economies noneconomic factors play a more important role as a determinant of public consumption expenditures than does income *per capita*. For instance, among primitive forest dwellers the functional equivalents of public expenditures show wide variation: they are almost nil among the Siriono in Bolivia, but are quite high among the Semang in South-East Asia.[1] Or, in cases of somewhat more

---

[1] Since the concept of 'public expenditures' is difficult to apply to primitive non-monetized economies, its closest functional equivalent, the sharing of food between producers and consumers, is used in the above example. The information comes from the Human Relation Area Files of Yale University. A short but useful sketch of more formal aspects of public finance among primitive tribes is given by Wilhelm Gerloff, 'Die oeffentliche Finanzwirtschaft der Naturvolker', *Die oeffentliche Finanzwirtschaft* (Frankfurt a. M., 1948), pp. 42–58.

developed economies, public consumption expenditures were relatively low in England in the seventeenth and eighteenth centuries, but seemed to reach incredible heights in Siam in the same period where, by law, everyone annually owed six months' work to the state (unfortunately information about the expenditures made from such revenues is not available).[1] Turning to cross-section data for the 1950s, we find that the best available statistics do not reveal any statistically significant relationship between the share of aggregate public consumption expenditures (defined in national income concepts) in the GNP and the level of economic development as measured by the GNP *per capita* for the most underdeveloped nations.[2]

Among the wealthiest nations there similarly appears to be no strong relationship between income *per capita* and the ratio of public consumption expenditures to the GNP.[3] And, for the postwar years, the data for the sample nations on both a time-series and cross-section basis do not provide positive evidence for Wagner's assertion either (these data are presented and discussed below).

It is extremely important to note, however, that the average ratio of public consumption expenditures to the GNP is very much higher in the highly developed than in the highly underdeveloped economies. Wagner's 'law' also seems applicable on both a time-series and a cross-section basis for nations that are in the process of transforming their economies from rural-agricultural to urban-industrial; and it was primarily from such nations that Wagner drew his empirical evidence. It

[1] Data on England can be found in B. R. Mitchell and Phyllis Deane, *Abstract of British Historical Statistics* (Cambridge, 1962), pp. 389–91; and Jindrich Veverka, 'The Growth of Government Expenditure in the United Kingdom since 1790', *Scottish Journal of Political Economy*, X, 1/1963, pp. 111–27. The case of ancient Siam is one of many examples of state parasitism discussed by Stanislav Andreski, *Elements of Comparative Sociology* (London 1964), pp. 227 ff.

[2] See esp. Hindrichs, *op. cit.*; Musgrave, *op. cit.*, Shibshankar Prasad Gupta, *The Size and Growth of Government Expenditures: A Time-Series and Cross-Section Analysis*, Ph.D. dissertation, University of York, 1966; Harry T. Oshima, 'Share of Government in Gross National Product for Various Countries', *American Economic Review*, XLVII, June 1957, pp. 381–90; and Simon Kuznets, 'Quantitative Aspects of the Economic Growth of Nations: Part VII, The Share and Structure of Consumption', *Economic Development and Cultural Change*, X, Part 2, January, 1962.

[3] See esp. Gupta, *op. cit.*, Kuznets, *op. cit.*, and Oshima, *op. cit.*

must be emphasized, however, that there are certain notable exceptions to his 'law'. For example, during the entire nineteenth century in the UK the ratio of public expenditures to the GNP did not have any upward trend.[1,2]

Since most of the nations in this study have levels of development toward the higher end of the scale, the influence of income *per capita* on the ratio of public consumption expenditures to the GNP is somewhat problematic. If there is such a relationship, it seems worthwhile to explore it not only on a highly aggregated level where all sorts of expenditures are combined, but also on the most highly disaggregated level as possible.

Other Factors

In the above discussion of determinants I speak primarily in the context of aggregative public consumption expenditures for national units. For examination of local expenditures, economists have carried out considerably more detailed studies, particularly of an econometric type, and have uncovered a covey of determinants.[3] The following list includes the most important of these discoveries:

Variables affecting both demand and supply of public consumption expenditures:

   (i) Income *per capita* (affects not only demand but reflects 'taxable capacity' and the cost of government services as well).
   (ii) Wealth *per capita* (operates similarly to income *per capita*).
   (iii) Population density (affects demand for certain services, such as roads, as well as the cost for supplying certain services such as transportation of children to school).

[1] Veverka, *op. cit.*
[2] A bibliography of long time-series data for seventeen countries is given in Appendix E–4.
[3] A bibliography of over 50 such studies is given in Appendix E–4.

(iv) Population growth (affects demand for government capital formation and also affects supply by creating certain lags in the apperception of citizens' needs).[1]

Variables affecting primarily demand for public consumption expenditures:

(i) Urbanization.

(ii) Industrialization.

(iii) Distribution of income (e.g. the more unequal the distribution of income, the more police services may be desired).[2]

(iv) Ethnic or religious homogeneity of the population (may act similarly to distribution of income).[3]

(v) Climate (e.g. snow removal is not necessary in warm climates).

(vi) Literacy level of the population.

(vii) The age composition of the population (e.g. affects demand for schools, old age homes).

(viii) Regional traditions.[4]

(ix) The amount of alternative private services supplied.[5]

(x) The absolute size of the population of a particular governmental unit (affects the actual number of government services provided).[6]

(xi) The type of housing (e.g. demand for fire protection is greater with wooden rather than brick houses, etc.).[7]

[1] See esp. Harvey E. Brazer, *City Expenditures in the United States*, (New York, 1959).

[2] See esp. Robert Frank Adams, *Determinants of Local Government Expenditures*, Ph.D. dissertation, U. of Michigan, 1963.

[3] *Ibid.*

[4] See esp. Sherman Shapiro, 'Some Socio-economic Determinants of Expenditures for Education', *Comparative Education Review*, VI, 2/1962, pp. 160–6.

[5] See esp. Jerry Miner, *Social and Economic Factors in Spending for Public Education* (Syracuse, 1963).

[6] See esp. Henry J. Schmandt and C. Ross Stevens, *op. cit.*,; and Harvey Shapiro, 'Measuring Local Government Output: A Comment', *National Tax Journal*, XIV, 4/1961, pp. 394–7.

[7] See esp. Adams, *op. cit.*

Variables affecting primarily the supply of public consumption expenditures:

   (i) Scale of production of government services.[1]

  (ii) Quality of production (e.g. a higher teacher/student ratio means higher education expenditures per student).

 (iii) The number of governmental units in a given area (affects costs by increasing difficulties of co-ordination, decreasing scale of production).[2]

 (iv) Intergovernmental grants (affects not only the amount of services that a particular governmental unit performs, but moreover, may affect the total amount of services provided in the entire area).[3]

  (v) Independence of unit for funds (e.g. education expenditures are higher in those units in which the main decision unit is also responsible for taxation, than in units where the decision unit receives tax funds from other governmental units).[4]

 (vi) Salary level of government employees.

It should be clear that many of these determinants overlap, that many play a relatively minor role, and that many important ones have been omitted, especially of a political[5] or socio-psychological[6] nature. In this study I test a number of hypotheses drawn from the above list as well as a number of additional propositions (e.g. for welfare expenditures, I use several different types of political variables). In any case, where variables other than the level of economic development or the type of economic system are selected for testing, I try to give

[1] See esp. Werner Z. Hirsch, 'Expenditure Implications of Metropolitan Growth and Consolidation', *Review of Economics and Statistics*, XLI, August 1959, pp. 232–41.

[2] See esp. Adams, *op. cit.*

[3] See esp. Robert L. Harlow, *Factors Affecting American State Expenditures*, Ph.D. dissertation, Yale University, 1966.

[4] See esp. Miner, *op. cit.*

[5] For an unsuccessful large-scale attempt to include political variables, see Thomas R. Dye, *Politics, Economics, and the Public: Policy Outcomes in the American States* (Chicago, 1966). There are also a number of unsuccessful smaller studies as well. In the research for this book, I also tried to include a number of political variables, but found that they had no predictive power.

[6] For a short summary of some such studies, especially in the area of 'fiscal psychology', see Appendix E–6: The Socio-Political Approach to Public Expenditures.

considerable theoretical justification for the choice, since a purely inductive approach would be endless.

3. STATISTICAL PROBLEMS

Although it is relatively easy to set up hypotheses, it is very much more difficult to actually carry out the proper statistical analysis to test them. Since the core of this study is such a statistical analysis, it is necessary to examine briefly seven particularly difficult problems dealing with the nature of the data, the prices which can be used in the analysis, the level of aggregation on which to carry out the examination, other types of comparisons which can be used for perspective, the regression models which are employed throughout the study, and the manner in which statistical inferences are made. Some of these are highly technical problems and the nonspecialist reader can skim this section without serious loss.

The Data of the Study

The first major problem is comparability of public consumption expenditures data, a problem which prevented extensive comparisons between centrally planned and market economies up until the present. There is a large literature on incomparabilities of public expenditures data[1] and, of course, it is necessary to adjust the data of each of the countries in the fourteen-nation sample to fit a common definitional framework. To this end I prepared a set of standard definitions (primarily based on the practices of the East European nations) for eight important functions of public consumption expenditures and then used as disaggregated data as possible to calculate the corresponding aggregates for all countries. In those cases where such disaggregated data were not available, adjustments were made by

[1] See e.g. Josef Berolsheimer, 'Probleme internationaler Finanzvergleich', in Wilhelm Gerloff and Fritz Neumark, *Handbuch der Finanzwissenschaft*, IV (Tuebingen, 1965), pp. 1–88; C. Lowell Harriss, 'Government Expenditure: Significant Issues of Definition', *Journal of Finance*, IX, December 1954, pp. 351–65; Institut international de finances publiques, *L'importance et la structure des recettes des dépenses publiques* (Brussels, 1960); United Nations, Department of Economic and Social Affairs, *A Manual for Economic and Functional Classification of Government Transactions* (New York, 1958); or N. T. Wang, 'Some Problems of International Comparisons of Public Social Expenditures', *Indian Economic Review*, II, February 1965, pp. 23–52.

other methods. The eight expenditures combined form the 'adjusted budget,' which is used for studying the behaviour of public consumption expenditures on the most aggregated level. I also investigate briefly some of the public expenditures excluded from the 'adjusted budget' in Chapter VI. The exact procedures employed in preparing the estimates and the definitions underlying the 'adjusted budget' are described in Appendix A.

In addition to the estimates for public consumption expenditures, GNP estimates had to be prepared as well. For the market economies, this was no problem since such data using standardized definitions are readily available. For the centralized economies, estimates of their gross national products according to Western definitions are available and are used whenever possible. Full details of the GNP estimates are given in Appendix B.

Prices

In computing ratios of public consumption expenditures to the GNP, two difficult problems arise. First, since the centrally planned nations do not have a functioning market for productive factors other than labour, the returns to land and capital are undervalued. In trying to adjust for such omissions it was discovered for the Soviet Union that the GNP varies considerably when different assumptions about the returns to these factors of production are made.[1] Additional difficulties are introduced because the ratios of net indirect taxes (indirect taxes minus subsidies) to the GNP are quite different in market and centralized economies.

To minimize such difficulties, all cross-section comparisons are made with factor price GNPs in the denominators (net indirect taxes are removed). However, for the centralized economies no estimates are made for the returns on land and capital. This means that within each economic system comparability is achieved, although comparisons cannot be made between the two systems until the direction of the statistical bias is determined. If all factor returns are included, the ratio of most government expenditures (especially for highly labour-intensive

[1] See Raymond P. Powell and Richard Moorstein, *The Soviet Capital Stock, 1928–61* (Homewood, Ill., 1965).

services such as education, health, or administration) to the GNP would be *lower* than they are in this study (i.e. the ratios for the centralized economies have an upward bias). This is because inclusion of such factor returns would increase the denominator of the ratio more than the numerator. Although the effect of this 'factor-income-effect' cannot be quantitatively determined, such a statistical bias can be taken qualitatively into account when evaluating the public consumption expenditures/GNP ratios. For this reason the direction of bias is explicitly stated whenever such comparisons are made.

The difficulties created by this 'factor-income-effect' seem considerable, but two heartening phenomena must be noted. First of all, this 'factor-income-effect' is partly offset because workers in services financed by public consumption expenditures receive somewhat lower wages *vis-à-vis* workers in manufacturing in the centrally planned than in market economies (which lowers the numerator of the expenditures/GNP ratio). Furthermore, when various kinds of physical indicators are analysed in the place of the expenditures data (e.g. data on soldiers for military expenditures; data on teachers and students for education expenditures; health personnel and mortality rates for health expenditures), the conclusions concerning the effect of economic system do not often conflict with the conclusions derived from the expenditures data.

A second aspect of prices that raises difficulties is the computation of constant price indices. In most kinds of analyses of public consumption expenditures, constant-price estimates are preferable to current-price series since there is a systematic upward bias when current-price data are used. More specifically, as *per capita* GNP increases, the ratio of current-price expenditures data to the current GNP can rise, even though a similar ratio computed in constant-prices remains the same. This comes about because productivity in sectors producing goods usually rises faster than in those sectors producing services; and, since wages in services parallel those in other sectors, services become relatively more expensive *vis-à-vis* goods. Because public consumption expenditures are used primarily to finance services, rather than goods, there is an upward bias in the change in the current-price public expenditures/GNP ratio. It must be noted that this bias occurs when using either cross-section or time-series data.

In other studies of public expenditures, current-price estimates are converted into constant-price series by deflating with various wage and price series which happen to be at hand (since the proper data for such purposes are generally unobtainable). This input-deflation procedure, of course, neglects any improvement in productivity for those services financed by public funds and, moreover, is particularly sensitive to the types of price and wage series that are chosen for the task. This sensitivity, in turn, raises obvious difficulties for international comparisons when price indices are not standardized.[1]

At one stage of investigation, constant price time-series public expenditures indices were calculated for all countries.[2] For the centralized economies, however, the results were completely unreasonable because of some serious inconsistencies between the various price and wage indices used for the individual countries. Further, for some of the market economies the results appeared dubious. Therefore, the following alternative procedure is used for analysing the data.

The relationships between income and public consumption expenditures in both the cross-section and time-series analyses are presented in terms of a 'ratio-elasticity', which is defined as the percentage change in the ratio of public consumption expenditures to the GNP that occurs when *per capita* income increases by one per cent. Thus, if the ratio-income-elasticity is positive, it means that the share of public consumption expenditures in the GNP increases as *per capita* GNP rises; similarly, if it is negative, this ratio decreases as *per capita* GNP rises.[3]

[1] There are also some extremely tricky index-number problems which arise with such a procedure. Most analysis of long-term public expenditures series use a constant base GNP series (Laspeyres index) and a current base expenditures series (Paasche index) because they deflate the current price government expenditures by a Laspeyres price index. (This might explain the peculiar calculation of Alan T. Peacock and Jack Wiseman, *op. cit.*, pp. 155–6) where the implicit price deflators of GNP and government expenditures rise at about the same rate from 1890 to 1955.

[2] I discuss in detail these estimates and a great many other problems in calculating constant price indices in Appendix C.

[3] This measure is chosen because it makes the cross-section and time-series results comparable, a feature which other elasticity measurements do not share.

In both the time-series and cross-section analyses the *per capita* income variable is expressed in constant prices. For the time-series studies a constant price base in the mid 1950s is used whenever possible; for the cross-section studies *per capita* incomes are expressed in dollar estimates (production weighted by US prices).

However, the ratio of public consumption expenditures to the GNP is calculated for both the time-series and cross-section studies in current prices. Thus the ratio-income-elasticities are calculated using mixed current-constant price data, and in interpreting the results certain statistical aids are necessary.

For perspective in the time-series studies, differences in ratio-income-elasticities for the market economies using constant price data for both the income *per capita* and the expenditures/ GNP ratio are presented so that some idea of the magnitude of statistical bias in the 'mixed-price' ratio-income-elasticities can be gained. Thus, if the 'mixed-price' ratio-income-elasticity for country X of expenditure A is $+0 \cdot 25$ (i.e. the ratio of A to the GNP increases a quarter of a per cent as the *per capita* GNP increases one per cent) and if the average constant-price ratio-income-elasticity for the market economies is $0 \cdot 50$ lower than the average mixed ratio-elasticity, then it would be most likely that the ratio-income-elasticity for country X would be negative if constant-price data for all parts of the calculation could be obtained.

For the cross-section studies no such calculations can be made of the extent of the statistical bias. From theoretical consideration of the factors involved, however, it seems likely that the statistical bias in the cross-section results is somewhat less than in the time-series studies;[1] therefore, the time-series calculations of bias can be utilized as a limit.

It is important to note that ratio-income-elasticities and regular income elasticities are monotonically related and that a zero ratio-income-elasticity can be interpreted as a unitary income elasticity. The formula for the ratio-income-elasticity is:

$$\frac{d(X/Y)}{(X/Y)} \bigg/ \frac{d(Y/P)}{(Y/P)}$$

where X = expenditure; Y = factor price GNP; and P = population. It is a pure number and has no units.

[1] By calculating the *per capita* GNPs with dollar price weights, the spread between countries is less than if the price weights of a poorer country had been

Of course, uncertainties are introduced into the statistical analysis because of the use of current-price data and it is also necessary to cross-check the conclusions with results obtained from physical indicators (discussed above). Again, the conclusions derived from the two sets of data are quite similar.

Aggregation Problems

At what levels of aggregation should the analysis be carried out? In almost all international comparison the greatest attention is focused on the behaviour of total public expenditures, and it is useful to examine briefly the type of results that are obtained from such an approach. In the table below (as in most tables in

TABLE 2–1

Ratios of 'Adjusted Budgetary Expenditures' to Factor Price
Gross National Products of the Sample Nations[1]

Country	1956		1962	
	Adj. budg. expend./GNP	Adj. budg. expend. excl. military/GNP	Adj. budg. expend./GNP	Adj. budg. expend. excl. military/GNP
Market economies				
USA	20%	11%	23%	15%
West Germany	26	22	30	25
Austria	25	24	28	27
Ireland	20	18	18	17
Italy	26	22	28	24
Greece	19	13	20	16
Yugoslavia	27	17	27	20
Centralized economies				
Czechoslovakia	31%	25%	30%	26%
East Germany	33	27	33	30
USSR	30	17	27	18
Hungary	23	17	17	15
Poland	21	16	20	16
Romania	20	14	18	16
Bulgaria	28	19	22	16

used (the relative *per capita* income of the USA in comparison to another country is lower if US price weights, rather than the other country's price weights are used). Thus there is a downward bias which partially offsets the upward bias discussed above.

[1] Data for Hungary are for 1955 and 1962. The 'adjusted budget' concept is

this study) countries are arranged by economic system with declining income *per capita* (1956) as one reads down the list for each system.

The data in the table have several curious features. Although there is an upward bias to the ratios of the centralized economies because of the 'factor-income-effect', there is no statistically significant (0·05 level) difference in the unweighted average ratios between the two economic systems in either year, either including or excluding military expenditures. Even in regression experiments with the economic system included as one of the explanatory variables, there appear to be no significant differences between the systems.

Second, no single variable (including income *per capita*) explains to a statistically significant extent the behaviour of these ratios for the entire sample in either year.[1] (However, *per capita* income is positive associated with these ratios for the centralized economies alone.)[2] Experiments using combinations of different explanatory variables also proved unsuccessful. One possible interpretation of such lack of success is that we are trying to explain the relative volumes of too many different types of expenditures at the same time. Certainly there are enormous differences that are brought about by the removal of military expenditures, and this suggests that there are certain disadvantages of lumping all sorts of diverse expenditures for many different purposes together. If a different causal factor

explained above in the text and in Appendix A–1. Sources and methods of estimation are given in Appendices A and B.

[1] Regressions of the following type were calculated: $\ln R = a + b \ln V$; where R = ratios in the above table; v = independent variables which were tested; and a, b = calculated regression coefficients. For the independent variables I used data in Tables 1–2 and 1–3. For more elaborate statistical experiments, dummy variables representing economic system were also added, but results were quite inconclusive. By lack of explanatory power I mean that no calculated regression coefficient was significantly larger than zero.

[2] Using only the centralized economies alone, income is significantly (0·05 level) correlated with both ratios in Table 2–1 for 1962 and almost significantly correlated with the 'adjusted budget minus military expenditures' ratios in 1956 as well. In addition the case of 'adjusted budget minus military expenditures' in 1962 is one of the few instances in this study where the elasticity coefficients coming from the two different samples are different enough (0·05 level of significance) to be considered as coming from different populations. Co-variance analyses to test for this phenomenon were made for all major statistical experiments in this study.

underlies each type of expenditure, then such an aggregative approach obscures more than it illuminates.

Examining the adjusted budgetary expenditures using time-series data also reveals several curious phenomena.

TABLE 2–2

Time-Series Behaviour of 'Adjusted Budgetary Expenditures',
1950 *through* 1962[1]

Country	Ratio-income-elasticity		Country	Ratio-income-elasticity	
	Total	Total excl. military		Total	Total excl. military
USA	+1·07*	+1·75*	Czechoslovakia	−0·02	+0·12*
West Germany	+0·06	+0·21*	East Germany	−0·37*	−0·19*
Austria	+0·38*	+0·35*	USSR	−0·45*	−0·03
Ireland	−0·30*	−0·28*	Hungary	−0·20	+0·52*
Italy	+0·35*	+0·51*	Poland	+0·08	+0·15
Greece	−0·03	+0·25*	Romania	−0·24*	+0·31*
Yugoslavia	−0·27	+0·33*	Bulgaria	−0·32*	+0·01

In the table most of the ratio-income-elasticities for the total adjusted budget are negative, and the unweighted average is −0·02, which is not significantly larger than zero. This means that the ratio of public consumption expenditures to the GNP (both calculated in current prices) does not effectively change as *per capita* income (constant prices) increase. When the expenditures/GNP ratios are calculated in constant prices for the market economies, the average ratio-income-elasticities are 0·22 below the mixed-price ratio elasticities presented in the table. Thus the share of public consumption expenditures in the GNP appears to be declining, a phenomenon that (as noted above) runs counter to Wagner's 'law'.

The unweighted average ratio-income-elasticity for civilian public consumption expenditures is somewhat higher (+0·29). Since the average constant-price ratio-income-elasticity for market economies is 0·24 below the mixed-price ratio-income-elasticity, this suggests that the average share of civilian public

[1] Ratio-income-elasticity is defined in the text above and in Appendix F. Data for Yugoslavia cover 1952 through 1962. Stastically significant coefficients (0·05 level) are designated by asterisks. Expenditure data come from Appendix A; GNP data, Appendix B.

consumption expenditures in the GNP would remain about the same if everything were calculated in constant prices.

The differences between the results when military expenditures are included or excluded in the calculations show again that analysis on a high level of aggregation can conceal a great deal of useful information and that disaggregation is desirable. Because of the availability of data certain limits are placed on the degree of disaggregation on which to conduct the statistical investigation. It is also possible that disaggregation can be carried too far. To explore this latter question, a number of experiments were carried out (especially for health and welfare) to determine whether useful results could be obtained by combining different types of expenditures. In all cases, however, the results of such experiments suggest that as much disaggregation as possible permits a wider range of determinants to be uncovered and introduces greater richness into the analysis.

Alternative Comparisons

In almost all studies of public consumption expenditures, exclusive attention is focused on one type of analysis (either cross-section or time-series) at one level of government (countries, states, counties, or cities). The consequence of such a narrow focus is incompleteness. For instance, in studying the public consumption expenditures of nations it is extremely important to note that in most cases, the time-series elasticities are considerably higher than the cross-section elasticities. This comes about, of course, because there are different causal factors or determinants of these expenditures operating over space and time.[1] By analysing both time-series and cross-section data, one can isolate and study such different determinants, and the subject matter is, as a consequence, much more deeply explored.

Another method of investigating the determinants of public consumption expenditures more deeply is to compare the determinants of expenditures on different levels of government. It is well known that it is impermissible to generalize from the

[1] A number of possible causal differences between time-series and cross-section results are explored in Appendix E-7.

results of one level of aggregation to another (e.g. from survey data about the actions of individuals to the behaviour of macro-economic aggregates) and this is true of public expenditures as well.[1] Nevertheless, by comparing results from nations and local governments, considerable perspective is gained into the different forces that are acting at each level. In certain cases in this study, therefore, the results of the analysis of determinants for the fourteen nations are compared with results of a similar analysis with US state and local government expenditures.

The Statistical Models and Procedures

Various statistical methods can be used to analyse the data on public consumption expenditures. One can, for instance, examine such data in matched pairs of nations and, at one point in this study, this proves a useful procedure. But in order to utilize all the data to the fullest extent, multivariate regression analysis serves as the primary statistical tool. In both the cross-section and time-series analyses, the following equational form is used for most hypothesis testing:[2]

$$E/Y = a(Y/P)^w(A)^x(B)^z;$$

where $E/Y =$ the ratio of the expenditure under examination to the GNP (current domestic prices),

$Y/P =$ income *per capita* (fixed domestic prices for time-series; dollar prices for cross-sections),

$A, B =$ other variables tested, and

$a, w, x,$ and $z =$ the calculated regression coefficients.

[1] For an analysis of these problems with examples from sociology and political science, see Erwin K. Scheuch, 'Cross-National Comparisons Using Aggregative Data: Some Substantive and Methodological Problems', in Richard L. Merritt and Stein Rokkan, eds., *Comparing Nations: The Use of Quantitative Data in Cross-National Research* (New Haven, 1966), pp. 131–67.

[2] This particular form was chosen for four reasons. First, for both international and intranational studies of public expenditures, such a form seemed to yield higher coefficients of multiple correlation than a linear form of the regression. Second, time-series and cross-section results are comparable. Third, interpretation of the coefficients as elasticities introduces a welcome simplicity into the analysis. Fourth, use of a logarithmic transformation reduces the importance in the regressions of very large or rich nations (esp. the USA and the USSR) and increases the possibility that the variables are normally distributed.

C

For the actual calculations the logarithmic form is taken and least-square regression of the following type are presented:[1]

$$\ln (E/Y) = a + w \ln (Y/P) + x \ln (A) + z \ln (B).$$

The coefficients w, x, and z express the relationships between the respective independent variables and the dependent variable (E/Y) in terms of elasticities. That is, w can be interpreted as the ratio-income-elasticity and x and z are the respective elasticities for the other variables.

In the cross-section analysis a special variable (a 'dummy variable') is introduced which designates economic system ($S = 0$ for market economies; $S = 1$ for centralized economies).[2] The (natural) anti-log of the calculated coefficient for S designates the effect of belonging to a certain economic system on the expenditures/GNP ratio. If the calculated coefficient for S is equal to $+0 \cdot 1823$, this means that the E/Y ratio is $1 \cdot 20$ times higher in centralized than market economies.[3] Thus we have a method of introducing the qualitative factor of economic system into the quantitative analysis.

The equational forms described above are utilized because of the small size of the sample; more sophisticated statistical models require considerably more data and a much larger sample, a task which is beyond the scope of this study. Such single equation reduced-form-models do not permit a separation of supply and demand factors; nevertheless an attempt is made to discuss beforehand the separate supply and demand factors that seem most important.[4,5]

---

[1] Natural logarithms, rather than common logarithms, are used for all regressions.

[2] In those cases in which the economic systems variable is chosen to be capitalist-socialist, the values of 0 and 1 are respectively assigned to these categories.   [3] $1 \cdot 20$ is the (natural) antilog of $0 \cdot 1823$.

[4] There are a number of statistical techniques, especially co-variance analysis, which permit time-series and cross-section data to be used together. Since GNP data in national currency units are used in the time-series analyses and GNP data in dollars for the cross-section studies, certain peculiar index-number problems arise. It was felt that more simple analytic techniques would sufficiently serve the purposes for which the data are meant and, at the same time, would be less confusing to the reader.

[5] Two caveats must be noted for such a procedure:

A. I am implicitly assuming that causation is only in one direction. For instance, in using income *per capita* to explain the ratio of expenditures for health to the

In making inferences from the data for a single year about associations between variables in the cross-section analyses, problems arise concerning the generality of results. In order to avoid drawing conclusions from any 'peculiar year', comparisons are made for two different years, one in the mid 1950s, one in the early 1960s. Although it would have been preferable to use data for the early 1950s as well, certain aspects of that period raise doubts as to the meaningfulness of such comparisons, e.g. the political repercussions of the Korean War, the Stalinization of the economies of the centralized economies, and the inadequate economic data reporting systems in some of the sample nations at that time. By comparing the coefficients in the regression equations for the two selected years, a certain impression about the stability of the relationships between variables can be gained.[1]

Significance Tests

For all of the comparisons I carry out tests for statistical signi-

GNP, I am assuming that the ratio of health to the GNP is not an important factor in determining the GNP *per capita*. Although this assumption seems reasonable as a first approximation, certain difficulties in market economies arise where Keynesian-type unemployment exists and when public expenditures directly affect the GNP through a multiplier action. Fortunately, such unemployment did not play a very important role in the economies of any of the sample nations, with the possible exception of the United States. (Other problems of causality between the determinants of public expenditures and such expenditures are briefly discussed by Elliott R. Morss, 'Some Thoughts on the Determinants of State and Local Expenditures', *National Tax Journal*, XIX, March 1965, pp. 95–101.)

B. Because of the lack of variables which adequately reflect cost factors, the primary emphasis in the study of the determinants of public expenditures is on the demand side. Certain economists e.g. Barry N. Siegel, 'On the Positive Theory of State and Local Expenditures', in Paul L. Kleinsorge, ed., *Public Finance and Welfare* (Eugene, Ore., 1966) emphasize the importance of separating demand factors from changes in the production function of 'public services' and changes in the unit costs of inputs. Although I am well aware of the statistical problems arising from the use of a one-equation model to capture all of these forces, I see no other method possible to analyse the data for the small sample that is used in this study.

[1] A number of tests were performed at an early state of investigation to see if it were statistically legitimate to pool the data for those two years. Although in most cases such a procedure is legitimate, results are reported for each year separately in order to show more concretely the range and direction of variation.

Similarly, other tests were conducted to test the legitimacy of pooling the data for countries with different economic systems for a single year. In almost all of the experiments performed, such pooling was permissible.

ficance and use the results for accepting or rejecting hypotheses. Underlying this procedure are several assumptions that should be made explicit.

In regard to the variable for economic systems I assume that there is a stochastic element in the public consumption expenditures for each of the nations of the sample and that each represents only one out of a very large number of possible cases of that particular economic system. For instance, even though the average expenditures for some purpose are higher in one type of economic system than another, this can be a chance occurrence and the difference is not accepted as positive evidence for some hypothesis unless it is statistically significant. For other types of variables the meaning of the significance tests should be clear.

Many of the methods of statistical inference that I use, especially the regression techniques, are based on a number of assumptions including the normal distribution of the variables. Indeed, one of the important reasons why a logarithmic transformation is used is to increase the possibility of such a distribution. However, these assumptions are not necessary to make, in which case the 'test of significance' may be interpreted just as the use of an *a priori* rule for excluding from consideration certain calculated statistics with low powers of differentiation.

Summary

The difficulties of analysis discussed above can be divided into two classes: some are the result of lack of sufficient data (the comparability problems and the difficulties arising from price considerations); the remainder are methodological (problems arising from choosing the proper level of aggregation, in selecting an adequate statistical model, and in determining the statistical significance of the results). These difficulties are not insurmountable; but most introduce uncertainties in interpreting the results. Such considerations should not deter us from trying to compare public consumption expenditures among the nations in the sample, but they suggest that we should not be too dogmatic in our conclusions.

D. BEHAVIOURAL PROPERTIES OF PUBLIC CONSUMPTION EXPENDITURES

In this study I focus on four types of behaviour properties of public consumption expenditures: substitution relations, centralization, stability, and incidence. Each is briefly discussed in turn below.

1. SUBSTITUTION RELATIONS

Substitution relations between public and private expenditures for the same service are essential to take into account when comparing public consumption expenditures among nations. The fact that a nation has relatively low public consumption expenditures for a particular service does not necessarily mean that the public does not enjoy such services, but may merely mean that the consumption of the service is privately financed. Such private expenditures do not play an important role in any country for internal or external security, but they may be extremely important for education, health, welfare, and research and development. Although data on such private expenditures leave much to be desired, I attempt whenever possible to take such substitution relations into consideration.

There are also substitution relations between different types of public expenditures. One variant of the guns-vs.-butter dilemma occurs when civilian public consumption expenditures decrease as military expenditures increase; similarly, other types of substitution relations, e.g. between health and welfare expenditures, can be imagined. This type of substitution relation is also investigated in this study, especially in regard to military expenditures.

Finally there can be a substitution between central and local public consumption expenditures for the same service. For instance, if the central government increases its contribution to primary and secondary education, do local governments cut down on their expenditures for the same purpose? In recent years there has been a growing body of literature on this matter, but primarily for the United States.[1] On a national level detailed data on intra-governmental transfers are necessary but

---

[1] Empirical studies in this area include: Robert F. Adams, 'The Fiscal Response to Intergovernmental Transfers in Less Developed Areas of the United States',

unfortunately not available. Therefore, this type of substitution relationship must be neglected. Nevertheless, certain aspects of the analysis of centralization of government expenditures are relevant in this regard.

It is surprising that the first two types of substitution relations have been completely neglected in the public finance literature. The theoretical framework for analysing such relationships can be borrowed from the generally accepted theory of consumer choice; the statistical results have extreme relevance to policy makers who must predict what effects changes in existing public consumption expenditures will bring. The empirical analyses of such substitution relationships is one of the major extensions of the positive theory of public expenditures in this study.

2. CENTRALIZATION OF EXPENDITURES

The 'centralization ratio' of public consumption expenditures is defined for total national public consumption expenditures as the share which is directly made at the central governmental level.[1] When only US state and local governmental expenditures are under examination, the centralization ratio is defined to be the share of these expenditures that are directly made by the state governments. Although centralization ratios of public consumption expenditures have been little studied, they have important implications not only for generalizations about the activity of different consumption units but also for the study of the determinants of public expenditures (see below).

The most extensive discussion of the factors underlying the change in the centralization ratio of public expenditures is by Peacock and Wiseman, who argue that centralization accompanies a rising *per capita* national income for the following reasons:[2]

(*a*) With improved transport and communications, pressure

Review of Economics and Statistics, forthcoming; George A. Bishop, 'Stimulative versus Substitutive Effects of State School Aid in New England', National Tax Journal, XVIII, June 1964; or E. F. Renshaw, 'A Note on Expenditure Effects of State Aid to Education', Journal of Political Economy, LXVIII, April 1960, pp. 170–4.

[1] Central governmental transfers to local governments that are spent by the latter for some particular good or service are included as local expenditures.

[2] Peacock and Wiseman, *op. cit.*

grows during the process of economic development for improved and uniform standards of public services, which can be met satisfactorily only by greater centralization of control over the size and character of public spending.

(b) With improved transport and communications, larger areas of control become economically efficient. That is, there are scale economies in public activities that are generated in the process of economic growth.

(c) Wars usually bring about a rapid increase in government spending and taxation, and after the war such expenditures usually do not return to the pre-war levels. Such a 'displacement effect' is particularly noticeable in central rather than local governmental spending.

(d) With economic development there is a change in the nature of the economic environment so that previously local problems such as education, pollution control, or unemployment begin to affect other governmental units to a much greater degree. The increasing importance of externalities, especially associated with increasing urbanization, demands a greater degree of central control over governmental expenditures at a local level.

(e) As government expenditures become an increasingly larger share of GNP, direct taxation at the central governmental level becomes a more efficient way of raising the required revenues than a patchwork-quilt system of local taxes. And, without strong pressures for the return of such revenues to the local governments through a grant-in-aid system, the superior taxing power of the central government results in increasing centralization of government expenditures.

(f) Accompanying economic development is a change in social ideas, so that people are more willing to accept central governmental interference and expenditures, particularly for functions previously considered to be in the local government domain.

There are some important counter-arguments, however. Martin and Lewis[1] point out that one characteristic of underdevelopment is the relative unimportance of local government;

1 Alison Martin and W. Arthur Lewis, 'Patterns of Public Revenue and Expenditure', *Manchester School*, XXVI, September 1958, pp. 203–44.

and although they do not develop a formal theoretical argument, it can be reasonably inferred from their remarks that this reflects the scarcity of qualified government personnel at lower

TABLE 2–3

Long Term Trends in the Centralization of Public Expenditures[1]

Country	Period	Trend
United Kingdom	1790–1910	Falling
	1910–61	Rising
United States: total	1902–13	Falling
	1913–62	Rising
United States: State and Local	1902–13	Relatively level
	1913–62	Rising
Canada	1913–60	Rising
Australia	1913–55	Rising
France	1871–1913	Falling
	1913–58	Rising
Germany	1881–1913	Rising
(Post-War West Germany)	1913–58	Rising
Norway	1913–57	Relatively level
Sweden	1913–58	Relatively level
Japan	1881–1910	Rising
	1910–60	Falling

stages of economic development and the necessity of conserving such scarce skilled manpower by centralizing expenditures as much as possible. Theodore Mesmer[2] argues, on the other hand, that the lower the *per capita* income, the greater the variability of centralization; and that as nations develop, their centralization ratios converge.

In analysing such matters three questions must be distinguished: What are the determinants of the aggregative centralization ratios? What are the determinants of the differential degree of centralization for different expenditures within a single nation? And what are the determinants of the differential degree of centralization of the same specific type of expenditure among many countries?

[1] Sources are given in the Appendix D–5.
[2] Theodore Charles Mesmer, *Government Expenditures and Economic Growth: An International Comparative Study*, Ph.D. dissertation Univ. of Wisconsin, 1962.

TABLE 2–4

Trends in Centralization Ratios of the Sample Nations,
1950 *through* 1962[1]

Country	Average annual growth rate of the centralization ratios	
	Total adjusted budget	Total adjusted budget excl. military expts.
Market economies		
USA	−0·8%*	−0·3%
West Germany	+0·6	+1·3*
Austria	−0·1	−0·2*
Ireland	−1·3	−1·4
Italy	+0·2*	+0·5*
Greece	−0·3*	−0·3*
Yugoslavia	−5·5*	+0·1
Centrally planned economies		
Czechoslovakia	−2·5%*	−2·5%*
East Germany	−0·2	+0·3*
USSR	−3·1*	−5·0*
Hungary	n.a.	n.a.
Poland	−2·1*	−2·7*
Romania	−1·7*	−0·9*
Bulgaria	−1·1*	−0·8*

(*An asterisk denotes that the growth rate is significally different from zero; 'n.a.'
means not available.*)

In trying to test the hypotheses about the aggregative centralization ratios, which are the main focus of attention of the
economists cited above, different conclusions can be drawn if
one examines either time-series or cross-section data alone. For
developed economies the time-series data of centralization
ratios can be easily summarized.

In the nineteenth and early twentieth centuries (see Table 2–3),
no pattern emerges. From 1913 to the present, however, most
countries have had a rising centralization ratio which has
accompanied a rising *per capita* GNP and population. In the
period from 1950 to 1962, however, the trend in centralization
ratios was quite mixed and, in the main, behave differently than
the long run trend.

[1] The series for Czechoslovakia covers 1953 through 1962; for East Germany,
1951 through 1962; and for Yugoslavia, 1952 through 1962. All data come from
Appendix A.
C*

Among the sample nations (see Table 2–4), with the exception of the Germanies and Italy, none of the countries shows a statistically significant rising trend in centralization, either including or excluding military expenditures. And in the case of the Germanies, the reverse behaviour of the centralization ratios can be easily explained from political and legal factors.[1] Although the pronounced tendency toward decentralization of public consumption expenditures in the centrally planned economies reflects a reaction from the Stalinist centralization in the late 1940s, the experience of most of the market economies suggests that destalinization is not the only factor at work. Similar to the analysis of determinants, the results differ considerably when military expenditures are removed from the total and suggest certain disadvantages of such an aggregate approach.

Turning to cross-section comparisons, we obtain some curious results. From data for the mid 1950s for fifty nations and for 1962 for state and local governments in the USA, the following regressions can be calculated:[2]

$$\ln C_1 = 0 \cdot 560 - 0 \cdot 068^* \ln Y/P - 0 \cdot 039 \ln P \qquad R^2 = 0 \cdot 17^*$$
$$\qquad\qquad (0 \cdot 029) \qquad\qquad (0 \cdot 020)$$
$$\ln C_2 = 4 \cdot 11 - 0 \cdot 18^* \ln Y/P - 0 \cdot 48^* \ln P \qquad R^2 = 0 \cdot 59^*$$
$$\qquad\qquad (0 \cdot 02) \qquad\qquad (0 \cdot 13)$$

where C_1 = centralization ratio for public expenditures for nations

C_2 = centralization ratio for US state and local public expenditures

[1] The East German result is partly due to a legal redefinition of the social insurance agency for East Berlin from the local to the central governmental level. The West German result may be partially attributed to a relaxation of the strictures against centralization which were initially placed on the country by the occupying military powers.

[2] The standard errors of the calculated coefficients are placed in parenthesis; the asterisks denote statistical significance (0·05 level). National centralization ratios come from Mesmer, *op. cit.*; population data, from UN, *Demographic Yearbook* (New York: annual); GNP data in dollar prices, from Paul N. Rosenstein-Rodan, 'International Aid for Under-developed Countries', *The Review of Economics and Statistics*, XLII, May 1961, pp. 126 ff. and from my own estimates. US state and local data from US Bureau of the Census, 'Historical Statistics on Government Finances and Employment', *Census of Government*, 1962 (Washington, DC, 1964).

$Y = $ GNP (nations) or personal income (states), both
in dollars

$P = $ population

These regressions show that on a cross-section basis, the
centralization ratio moves inversely to income *per capita* and
population—results that are completely opposite from those
obtained from the long time-series data in Table 2–3. For the
fourteen-nation sample, however, the centralization ratios seem
to behave differently from those of the world as a whole or of
the US state and local governments.

TABLE 2–5

Centralization Ratios of the Sample Nations in 1956 and 1962[1]

Country	Total adjusted budget		Total adjusted budget excl. military expt.	
	1956	1962	1956	1962
Market economies				
USA	81%	68%	50%	51%
West Germany	70	74	65	70
Austria	85	86	84	85
Ireland	71	70	69	68
Italy	84	86	82	84
Greece	91	90	87	87
Yugoslavia	43	32	10	10
Centralized economies				
Czechoslovakia	70%	62%	63%	54%
East Germany	74	74	69	71
USSR	71	54	51	29
Hungary	n.a.	n.a.	n.a.	n.a.
Poland	78	67	71	59
Romania	74	68	64	62
Bulgaria	73	71	60	60

The centralization ratios for the sample nations reveal an
enormous variation, ranging for total adjusted budgetary
expenditures from 32 to 91 per cent and for civilian public
consumption expenditures, from 10 to 87 per cent. Of the five
federal nations, four have the lowest centralization ratios in their

[1] The data come from Appendix A; 'n.a.' means not available.

respective economic systems.[1] Unfortunately, economic variables, either singly or together, or other political variables cannot explain to a statistically significant extent the behaviour of these ratios.[2,3] Again we are forced to look behind the data to discover why our predictive powers are so poor.

Underlying the different time-series and cross-section results is the influence of the composition of public consumption expenditures on the aggregate centralization ratio. This turns our attention to the centralization ratios of particular types of public consumption expenditures.

It is well known that military, diplomacy, and social insurance expenditures are made primarily at the central governmental level in most countries. When relative centralization ratios of other types of government expenditures are compared, some interesting results are obtained.

For the six European Common Market nations in 1958, the rank order of the centralization ratios for twelve major public expenditures of each of these nations is significantly correlated with the rank order of such expenditures in every one of the other nations.[4] And for the fifty US states in 1962 there is a significant coefficient of concordance[5] of the rank order of the centralization ratios for seven major expenditures in each state. (These are discussed in much greater detail in Appendix E–8).

These results mean that a change in the proportion of total expenditures which is spent for various services changes the aggregate centralization ratio. The importance of this change in

[1] The five federal nations are: the United States, West Germany, Austria, Yugoslavia, and the Soviet Union.

[2] If Yugoslavia is classified as a socialist country, then the centralization ratios of the socialist nations are significantly (0.05 level) lower in the socialist than capitalist nations in 1962, but not in 1956. For the economic systems as defined above, there is no statistically significant difference.

[3] A large number of experiments were attempted, using a number of economic and political variables both singly and in combination. Such variables are listed in Table 1–2 and in Appendix D–4.

[4] The data come from European Economic Community, *Die Einnahmen und Ausgaben der oeffentlichen Verwaltung in den Laendern der EWG*, Studien 2, Reihe Wirtschaft und Finanzen (Brussels, 1964), p. 114.

[5] The 'coefficient of concordance' [see Maurice G. Kendall, *Rank Correlation Methods*, 2nd ed. (New York, 1955)] would be equal to 1.00 if the rank order of the centralization ratios in all states were the same and would be equal to 0.00 if they were in a random pattern. The above calculated coefficient is equal to 0.59, which is statistically significant (0.05 level).

composition can be seen in the time-series data for the United States, where the aggregative centralization ratio appeared to rise from 32 per cent to 62 per cent between 1913 and 1962. However, if we hold the relative importance of the twenty major expenditures constant and recalculate the change in centralization ratios, we find that the rise was only from 32 per cent to 38 per cent (1913 structure) and from 46 per cent to 62 per cent (1962 structure).

In the time-series data the major force behind the centralization ratios of total public expenditures over time seems to be the increasing relative importance of social security expenditures and, in some countries, military expenditures as well, both of which are primarily made at the central governmental level.[1] The changing relative importance of different expenditures over time in relation to GNP *per capita* is greatly different from over space at one point in time. In other words, there are different time-series and cross-section determinants for public expenditures which bring about different compositions of expenditures and which greatly influence the aggregative centralization ratio as well.

Taking into account the effect of the composition of expenditures on the aggregate centralization ratio, an extremely important policy issue arises because two conflicting interpretations can be made of the different cross-section and time-series results reported above.

First, it can be argued that the variation of the centralization ratio of each specific public consumption expenditure is severely limited by economic factors (such as externalities, economies of scale, etc.), a hypothesis that is supported but not proven by the rank order relationships for the centralization ratios of specific expenditures that are noted above. Therefore, most of the differences in the aggregative centralization ratios of public expenditures can be attributed *solely* to a different mix of specific expenditures. This hypothesis also places considerable importance on isolating the different cross-section and time-series determinants for public consumption expenditures which

[1] Since this rise in the relative importance of military and social security expenditures did not occur in the nineteenth century, this might account for the mixed trends observed in this period in Table 2–3.

bring about such differential changes in structure in the two cases. Such an explanation also suggests that those cases of centralization or decentralization which lie far from the norm (e.g. Greece and Yugoslavia) are subject to certain inefficiencies that could be quite costly and that introduction of extensive intra-governmental transfer systems to decentralize expenditures may have few economic benefits in some of the other countries.

Second, the differential behaviour of centralization ratios in time-series and cross-section studies might also reflect the way in which public expenditure innovations have been introduced and have percolated through the economy. Some economists, such as Solomon Fabricant, have argued that a major force in the growth of government expenditures has been the extension of such expenditures to new services.[1] Further, such innovations seem to be made more often at higher levels of government; only slowly are such expenditure programmes transferred to lower levels of government. The rise over time in the centralization ratios can, therefore, be traced to the increase in overall public expenditures and the slowness of the new spending programmes to be transferred to lower governmental levels. The inverse relationship of income *per capita* and centralization at a single point in time might reflect the fact that such innovative public programmes are more easily decentralized in governmental units with higher *per capita* incomes. (Such an explanation seems more suitable for local, rather than national, units.) The similarity of rank order of centralization ratios would, according to this interpretation, reflect the time distribution of major expenditure innovations in nations or in local governmental units, rather than any intrinsic economic properties except in special cases (such as diplomacy and military), where public good properties seem to predominate. The great variation in centralization ratios between nations would reflect the levels at which public expenditure innovations are made and the efforts that nations have made to diffuse such innovations to other levels of governments. Intra-governmental grant programmes, therefore, do not necessarily have the adverse effects that one might deduce from the previous interpretation.

[1] Solomon Fabricant and Robert E. Lipsey, *The Trend of Government Activity in the United States* (New York, 1952).

In order to avoid the 'composition-effect' and to provide evidence in regard to these two conflicting interpretations of the centralization data, it is absolutely necessary to examine such ratios for each individual public consumption expenditure and, moreover, on both a cross-section and time-series basis. Certainly the advantages of an analysis on a disaggregated basis are as strong in the case of centralization as for the determinants of public consumption expenditures.

3. STABILITY

Although the stability of public consumption expenditures has been little studied on a comparative basis, it is a phenomenon having a number of important implications. If we define the stability of an expenditure over time as the relative degree of fluctuation around its trend, then several important questions arise. Are the fluctuations of public consumption expenditures greater or less than economic fluctuations in the economy as a whole? Are the fluctuations of these expenditures and the GNP in the same or the opposite directions? And in what way are fluctuations in public consumption expenditures and the GNP causally related?

On a cross-section basis the stability of a particular expenditure can be measured by the degree of variation of *per capita* expenditures or variation of the ratio of expenditures to income in different governmental units when key economic variables are held constant. This aspect of stability gives perspective on the range of options which policy makers face.[1] If, for instance, the coefficients of variation of two expenditures are 10 and 50 per cent, this suggests that the restraints on policy making in regard to the volume of expenditures are less severe in the latter case. In examining coefficients of variation of public consumption expenditures in different sub-units of a single nation, an interesting aspect of the geographic incidence of an expenditure is illuminated (a topic which is discussed below).

In the public finance literature there are relatively few hypo-

---

[1] This particular aspect of stability has been examined for US state and local governmental expenditures by Fabricant, *op. cit.*,; Harvey Brazer, *op. cit.* and Glenn W. Fischer, 'Interstate Variation in State and Local Government Expenditures', *National Tax Journal*, XVII, March 1964, pp. 57–74.

theses about the stability of public consumption expenditures on either a cross-section or a time-series basis. Nevertheless, empirical analysis of this phenomenon is quite straightforward and the results can be succinctly stated. Discussion of this matter is therefore deferred to the final chapter, where stabilities of aggregative public consumption expenditures can be examined together with each individual type of expenditure.

4. INCIDENCE

The incidence of public consumption expenditures is the impact of such expenditures on the distribution of income, and the first major analytical problem is to determine a base-point from which such effects can be measured. Starting in the classical way from some concept of 'neutral taxation' or a 'neutral government budget' presents a number of insurmountable difficulties, and, indeed, these concepts are becoming discredited.[1] Postulating an income distribution existing if there were no government budget at all also has a number of serious problems.

A more manageable approach should be based on three important considerations: First, the redistribution of income through the government budget is only one of the ways in which the government can affect the income distribution. In any nation where wages and prices are influenced by public policy or where the government actively attempts to carry out full employment or economic growth policies, redistribution of income through the budget is only one facet—perhaps of minor importance—of the total impact of the government on the income distribution.[2] Second, with our present information and economic tools, we can only hope to measure the most direct impact of the government budget on income distribution, so that secondary effects (such as the effect of the expenditures of the recipients of governmental transfer payments) or long-range effects must be omitted from discussion. Third, the redistributional effects of government expenditures must not be examined in isolation, but rather in conjunction with the

[1] See esp. Alan T. Peacock, 'Introduction', in Peacock, ed., *Income Redistribution and Social Policy* (London, 1954), pp. 7–15.

[2] This issue in regard to the centrally planned economies is discussed by Franklyn Holzman, *Soviet Taxation* (Cambridge, Mass., 1955), pp. 284 ff.

effects of taxation, so that the net effect of the government budget can be ascertained.[1] These three important considerations have been implicitly or explicitly assumed in most of the recent studies of the effect of government expenditures on the distribution of income.[2]

In an analysis of incidence, an important distinction between long-run and short-run incidence must also be observed. A long-run redistribution of income occurs when income is redistributed between income classes. A short-run redistribution of income comes about when those with higher incomes at a particular time are taxed and those with lower incomes at that time receive benefits such that a person's income is redistributed over his own lifetime. (For instance, a person can receive free education in his youth, pay taxes to cover this and a state pension during his working life, and receive the pension in his old age.) A special type of long-run redistribution through public consumption expenditures comes about if there is a redistribution of income between rich and poor geographical units in a particular country, an incidence phenomenon that can be measured considerably more easily than other types.

Many aspects of the questions that can be asked about the comparative incidence patterns of public consumption expenditures in different nations lie beyond the scope of this study. However, certain considerations of the above discussion are useful to take into account in interpreting the results of the analysis for specific expenditures. And the question of the spatial incidence of public consumption expenditures, which is

[1] Among Marxist economists the argument has been advanced that most budgetary receipts of the East European nations are not taxes, but rather deductions from the societal surplus value. Such a notion, particularly in regard to the turnover tax, is not affirmed by all. For the purposes of this discussion such governmental receipts are considered as taxes, even though they contain a number of non-tax elements. The issues surrounding whether or not turnover taxes in the Soviet Union are 'taxes' are discussed by Gertraud Menz, *Die Entwicklung der sowjetischen Besteurung* (West Berlin, 1960), 170–71.

[2] The most recent empirical studies on the national impact of government expenditures and taxes are contained in Peacock (ed.), *op. cit.*; Colin Clark and Geer Struvel, eds., *Income and Wealth, Series X: Income Redistribution and the Statistical Foundation of Economic Policy* (New Haven, 1964); and W. Irwin Gillespie, 'Effects of Public Expenditures on the Distribution of Income', in Richard A. Musgrave, ed., *Essays in Fiscal Federalism* (Washington, DC 1965).

also related to the cross-section stability of such expenditures, is one relevant aspect which does not require detailed micro-economic data and which can be explored with the data collected for this study. Because the spatial incidence of different expenditures can be easily handled at one time, discussion of such matters is deferred until the final chapter.

E. DIFFERENTIAL EFFECTS OF PUBLIC AND PRIVATE FINANCING

What difference does it make when a service is financed in the private, rather than the public sector? This is a question which involves consideration not only of substitution relations between public and private expenditures but also of the incidence of public consumption expenditures. The only expenditures that can be used for such an empirical study are those with a sufficient variation in the public/private mix among nations, so that a differential effect can be observed, a condition that effectively limits analysis to health, education, and welfare expenditures.

Several types of differential effects can be readily imagined. First, if a service is financed in the public sector, it seems likely that its consumption would be more evenly spread over the population than if the financing were left to the private sector. From such an assumption it can be argued that infant mortality should be lower and that the proportion of students in universities from lower socio-economic income classes should be higher if health and education are publicly, rather than privately, financed. These two propositions are empirically investigated in this study; sufficient data for similar propositions in other areas are unfortunately unavailable.

A second aspect of the effects of public and private financing concerns the relative efficiency of production and the relative quality of services produced that are associated with the two different methods of financing. These are difficult phenomena to investigate because in most cases highly detailed data are required and because the differential effects of public and private ownership must also be eliminated. For education, however, it did prove possible to investigate certain such quality effects.

For specific types of expenditures other hypotheses about the differential effects of public and private financing can also be set forth and, whenever possible, these propositions are empirically tested with the data from the sample nations.

F. CONCLUDING REMARKS

Sufficient information on the public consumption expenditures of the fourteen nations in the sample is available to explore empirically a large number of questions concerning their determinants, their behaviour properties, and the differential effects of financing such services in the public, rather than private, sector. To utilize such data in the most useful and thorough manner, the investigation is carried out on the most disaggregated level as possible. Special attention is focused on the effects of the economic systems and the level of economic development, although many other factors are taken into account as well.

Each of the following four chapters contains the analysis of one or several types of public consumption expenditures. Each chapter starts with a theoretical examination of the properties of the expenditures; in turn, this forms the framework from which specific hypotheses are derived and tested. Whenever possible, both monetary and physical data are used for such tests. The availability and accuracy of the data permit quite different types of questions to be investigated for each expenditure. Nevertheless, the guidelines set forth in this chapter shape all such explorations.

Chapter III

PUBLIC CONSUMPTION EXPENDITURES FOR DEFENCE

A. Introduction
B. Economic Properties of Defence Expenditures
C. Cross-Section Determinants
  1. *The Pact Theory*
  2. *Analysis of Components*
  3. *A Brief Summary*
D. Time-Series Determinants
E. Substitution between Defence and Civilian Expenditures
F. Summary and Conclusions

A. INTRODUCTION

Machiavelli's dictum that: 'The principal study and care and the special profession of a prince should be warfare and its attendant rules and discipline',[1] points up a curious phenomenon in scholarship about warfare and defence. Although enormous intellectual resources have been invested into studying methods by which men can kill each other more effectively, relatively little effort has been devoted to studying the macro-economic aspects of defence and war expenditures. Although military expenditures in the world in the early 1960s amounted anually to somewhere between $120 and $180 billion[2]—about equal to the income of the poorer half of mankind—few economists have attempted to analyse as a whole the defence expenditures of a nation or a set of nations; indeed, of the famous economists of

[1] Niccolo Machiavelli, *The Prince*, trans. T. G. Bergin (New York, 1947), Chapter XIV.
[2] The former datum is estimated by the UN, Department of Economic and Social Affairs, *Economic and Social Consequences of Disarmament* (New York, 1962), p. 3; the latter datum is estimated in a much more careful study by Emile Benoit and Harold Lubell, 'The World's Burden of National Defense', in Emile Benoit, ed., *Disarmament and World Economic Interdependence* (Oslo, 1966). In the comparison with world income I assume that the poorer 1 and 1/3 billion people in the world had a *per capita* income of less than $100 per year.

the past, only Adam Smith seemed interested in establishing generalizations about aggregative military expenditures.[1]

Although it is generally believed that the primary determinants of military expenditures are political, economic analysis of these expenditures reveals a considerable number of important phenomena which have not yet been rigorously explored. Indeed, formal economic model building is more successful for defence expenditures than for any other type of public consumption expenditure examined in this study.

In the cross-section analysis below, consideration of the public-good properties of defence results in the prediction that the ratio of defence expenditures to the GNP is positively related to the total national product of a nation, an hypothesis which is also substantiated by empirical evidence. For the time-series data, deductions from an hypothesis about the interaction of defence expenditures between enemy and allied nations also lead to a number of successful predictions.

Other types of questions dealing with these expenditures are also explored. The most important of these issues deals with trade-offs between defence and civilian public consumption expenditures, where I find that such substitution relations are quantitatively unimportant or nonexistent.

B. ECONOMIC PROPERTIES OF DEFENCE EXPENDITURES

Defence expenditures are defined to include all expenditures for the recruiting, training, and maintenance of an army, navy, air and rocket forces, and national security troops.[2] Because military expenditures are defined narrowly in the statistics of the centrally planned economies, a similar definition is adopted for the market economies so that expenditures on civil defence, veterans, military research and development, interest payments on war debts, reparations, military assistance abroad, and military construction are excluded and are placed in other

[1] Adam Smith, *An Inquiry into the Nature and the Causes of the Wealth of Nations* (New York: 1937), Book V, Chapter I, Part I.

[2] National security troops are defined to exclude those units which serve a domestic police function, a distinction that raises a number of difficulties for East Germany, Greece, and Italy. Full details are given in Appendix A.

budgetary categories.[1] The exact methods of estimation and sources of data for each country are outlined in detail in Appendix A.

Before the general economic properties of defence expenditures can be discussed, it is useful to consider exactly what is 'produced' by such expenditures. Although military preparations have little meaning except in their relation to the foreign policy goals of the nation, such goals and the relationships between these goals and the military means are often difficult to unravel.[2] However, for the sake of economic analysis, several underlying principles can be set forth.

The 'defensive aim' of military expenditures relates to the direct security of the home territory. One aspect of this is pure protection—the ability to protect an area against attack and to minimize the damage which another nation can impose. In military jargon this aspect of protection is called 'damage limitation capability'. Another facet of protection is deterrence of enemies against attacking which requires a force capable of inflicting sizeable losses on any other country and the willingness to use this force whenever attacked. These two aspects of defence are very different and imply greatly different conduct in foreign affairs.[3]

The 'offensive aim' of military expenditures is concerned with the security of a nation in relation to other territories. Although

[1] Such exclusions make little difference for the estimation of military expenditures of most market economies, but become large for the United States, especially in the later years when research and development expenditures assumed considerable importance. My 1962 estimate of us military expenditures is 72 per cent of the OECD estimate, the difference being due (expressed as percentages of the OECD estimate) to exclusion of: military R. and D., 13 per cent; construction, 3 per cent; military assistance, 3 per cent; defence related activities, welfare-type measures of the Defence Department and Veteran's Administration, economic development type expenditures of the Defence Department, expenditures of the national police agencies, etc., 9 per cent. Full details are given in Appendix A–13. Such a narrowing of the OECD definition is necessary, however, in order to achieve comparability with the data from the centralized economies.

[2] The interrelations between defence expenditures and foreign policy goals are analysed in an extremely stimulating case study by Warner R. Schilling, 'The Politics of National Defense: Fiscal 1950', in Warner R. Schilling, *et al.*, *Strategy, Politics, and Defense Budgets* (New York, 1962), pp. 1–267.

[3] The differences, interrelations, and advantages and disadvantages of these two basic protective postures are discussed in detail by Glenn H. Snyder, *Deterrence and Defense* (Princeton, NJ, 1961).

this covers the preparation and carrying out of wars of aggression to obtain economic or political advantages, it also includes the prevention of gains by enemy nations in other parts of the world, which would in some way affect the security of the home territory.

Both the defensive and offensive aims of military expenditures take place in an environment of uncertainty in which it is difficult to predict when or how or where the home nation will be challenged and in which it is also difficult to know the effect of a domestic defence measure on a similar measure taken by other nations. To complicate the problem even more, there are an enormous number of alternative means to achieve given political ends so that the allocation of defence expenditures among these means raises further knotty problems.

The deterrence aspect of protection has the properties of a pure 'public-good'. That is, no one in a nation with a deterrent force can be excluded from the benefits of such expenditures and, in addition, the cost of protecting an additional person in the country is zero. The situation is somewhat more difficult to analyse for other aspects of defence in which the public-good aspects depend on the military technology employed.

Certain types of protection expenditures, such as the building of a wall around a city in the Middle Ages or the ringing of a modern nation with antiaircraft guns can be considered as public-goods, at least until capacity constraints are met. Other types of protective measures, however, have high marginal costs and do not cover all citizens of a country.[1] For instance, the US Secretary of Defence, Robert McNamara, noted that in 1970 when the USA would have a population of about 210 million, zero investment in 1965 in air shelters and other similar defence measures would probably mean that about 149 million Americans would be killed in an unexpected enemy atomic attack, while investments of 5, 15, and 25 billion dollars in such shelters would mean that the level of deaths would fall respectively to 120, 96, and 78 million people. In other words, certain defence

---

[1] These ideas as well as the example below are taken from an excellent discussion of such issues by Jacques M. van Ypersele de Strihow, *Sharing the Defense Burden among Western Allies*, unpublished Ph.D. dissertation, Yale University, 1966.

measures are like a shield that protects only part of the body politic, rather than armouring all parts equally, a fact that brings about many interdependencies between various types of costs and benefits of specific protection measures.[1] Finally, certain protection measures can be considered completely as 'private-goods', e.g. a home bomb shelter for one family's use.

The public-good aspects of defence exepnditures have certain important implications. First, in *all* modern nations almost all defence expenditures are made by the central government. Defence expenditures of the various subnational territorial governmental units are limited to certain civil defence measures and possibly the maintenance of a small defence force; indeed, in many nations even these civil defence expenditures are made centrally. Since such civil defence measures are excluded from the statistical definition of defence expenditures used in this study, this means that in every one of the sample nations, 100 per cent of the defence expenditures are made on the central governmental level.

Second, at the present time there are no sizeable private armies or any sizeable private defence expenditures in any modern nation. This has not always been true, e.g. during the Italian renaissance private armies of mercenaries played an important role; and in the 1920s and 30s in Germany, private armies had an important political influence.[2] At the present time, however, such private armies are banned and nonexistent in most nations. Furthermore, private defence expenditures are usually small. Family air raid shelters, for instance, have not been a very fast selling item anywhere.

Finally, because a deterrent force has public-good qualities, a nation that enters into a mutual protection pact with another nation having such a force can receive at a very low cost, all of

[1] This phenomenon is also discussed by Fred S. Hoffman, 'The Economic Analysis of Defense: Choice without Markets', *American Economic Review*, XLIX, May 1959, pp. 368–76.

[2] Some of the condottieri must be considered as bandits since they were financed exclusively by plunder. The German groups, on the other hand, had many army characteristics. Their officers were paid from outside sources, had the traditional army hierarchy, and served both offensive and defensive functions. Classification of certain groups such as the ultra-right Minutemen in the United States raises some difficult problems of definition.

its benefits.[1] In other words, a deterrent force can be an international public-good among nations of a military alliance, a phenomenon which is discussed in much greater detail in the following pages.

Aside from the implications of the public-good aspects of defence expenditures, other types of economic relations should be briefly mentioned. In regard to the level of economic development, non-Marxists have offered no convincing reasons why, as the *per capita* GNP increases, the share of defence expenditures to the GNP either increases or decreases. On the other hand, Marxists who base their analysis on Lenin's theory of imperialism,[2] argue that as the *per capita* GNP increases, capitalist nations must resort to ever-increasing relative levels of defence expenditures in order to stave off the general crisis of capitalism. This is an hypothesis that can be easily tested.

A different type of relationship between defence expenditures and the GNP can also be argued.[3] If two nations have the same *per capita* GNP but if one nation has a much larger population (and absolute value of national product) then the government of the larger nation can obtain a higher absolute amount of 'security' for lower *per capita* defence expenditures. Holding *per capita* income constant, we would therefore predict that the ratio of defence expenditures to the GNP is inversely related to the absolute value of the GNP,[4] an hypothesis which turns out to be the exact reverse of one which I derive in the following pages for members in military alliances.

Another property of defence expenditures that is important in the empirical analysis is that the 'product' of such expenditures of one nation depends very much on the level and type of

---

[1] A number of aspects of this phenomenon are discussed by Ypersele, *op. cit.*; Malcolm W. Hoag, 'Economic Problems of Alliances', *Journal of Political Economy*, LXC, 6/1951, pp. 522–35; and Mancur Olson, Jr. and Richard Zeckhouser, *An Economic Theory of Alliances*, RAND Corporation Memorandum RM-4297-ISA (Santa Monica, Calif., November 1965).

[2] V. I. Lenin, *Imperialism, the Highest Stage of Capitalism* (New York, 1939). It should be noted that in recent years such views have been muted since they conflict with the Soviet Union's campaign for total world disarmament. Nevertheless, Lenin's basic views have never been repudiated.

[3] I would like to thank Mancur Olson for pointing out this relation to me.

[4] Underlying this hypothesis is, of course, the assumption that tastes in the nations in regard to military expenditures are similar.

similar expenditures in enemy countries. Such a well known interdependency suggests that certain time patterns of defence expenditures emerge when a number of nations are compared. On an abstract level, certain interaction models of defence expenditures of opposing nations have been constructed with special reference to arms races.[1] Although empirical work in this area is just beginning,[2] the analysis of interacting defence expenditures has been hampered in the past by the lack of comparable data, a difficulty which may be partly overcome by the public expenditures data developed for this study.

A final aspect of defence expenditures that must be briefly mentioned is the recent accelerated growth of military technology.[3] Production costs of old weapons have rapidly decreased, new weapons have been introduced, the speed at which warfare is conducted has accelerated, the range of warfare is drastically wider, and larger numbers of people can be killed with greater ease. Although military power of most nations has rapidly increased national security of all nations has declined. Since the greatest technological changes have occurred in offensive, rather than defensive, weapon systems, deterrent costs may have declined but defence costs have risen and the 'damage limitation ability' per dollar expenditure seems to be rapidly declining.[4] Thus a rising portion of the national product devoted to defence does not necessarily indicate that a nation is becoming more 'secure'; and the measurement of changes in the 'product' of defence expenditures is impossible to make

[1] Pioneering work in this area was done by Lewis F. Richardson, *Arms and Insecurity* (Pittsburgh, 1960) and has been carried forward in a number of more recent studies, such as Kenneth E. Boulding, *Conflict and Defense: A General Theory* (New York, 1962) and Paul Smoker, 'A Mathematical Study of the Present Arms Race', *General Systems*, VIII, pp. 51–60.

[2] E.g. Paul Smoker, 'Trade, Defense and the Richardson Theory of Arms Race: A Seven Nation Study', *Journal of Peace Research*, 2/1965, pp. 161–77.

[3] The changing technology of warfare and defence is carefully analysed by Quincy Wright in his monumental *A Study of War*, 2nd edition (Chicago, 1965). A shorter analysis with especial reference to military expenditures is made by M. Slade Kendrick, 'Technological Advances in the Weapons and Equipment of the Armed Forces', *A Century and a Half of Federal Expenditures*, National Bureau of Economic Research Occasional Paper 48 (New York, 1955), Appendix A. An interesting Soviet view may be found in G. I. Pokrovsky, *Science and Technology in Contemporary War* (New York, 1959), Chapter I.

[4] On this point, see especially J. B. Wiesner and H. F. York, 'National Security and the Nuclear Test Ban', *Scientific American*, Vol. 211, October/1964, pp. 27–35.

without a careful analysis of the purposes for which such expenditures are made, a difficult task which far transcends the purpose of this study.

C. CROSS-SECTION DETERMINANTS OF DEFENCE EXPENDITURES

The analysis of the cross-section determinants of defence expenditures is predicated on the assumption that there are no significant differences in the temporal response of nations to changes in the international environment. The correctness of this assumption is examined and confirmed in the following section.

The first step in the cross-section empirical analysis is the examination of the ratios of defence expenditures to the national products.

TABLE 3–1

Ratios of Defence Expenditures to Factor Price GNPs in the Sample Nations, 1956 and 1962[1]

Country	1956	1962	Country	1956	1962
USA	8·6%	7·8%	Czechoslovakia	5·6%	4·7%
West Germany	3·9	4·7	East Germany	6·0	3·9
Austria	0·7	1·2	USSR	12·3	9·4
Ireland	1·4	1·3	Hungary	6·6	2·5
Italy	3·7	3·2	Poland	4·7	3·9
Greece	6·2 (5·4)	4·3 (4·0)	Romania	5·5	2·9
Yugoslavia	10·0	6·7	Bulgaria	9·0	5·8

No apparent pattern emerges from the data. There is no relation between the ratios of defence expenditures to the GNP and *per capita* income. Further, in neither year is there any statistically significant difference in the average unweighted ratios in the two economic systems. In regression experiments where the influence of a number of economic variables can be held constant, there is still no significant difference in the ratios of the two systems.

[1] Data are from Appendix A. Data for Greece in parentheses are defence expenditures which are not financed by outside aid; data for Hungary are for 1955 and 1962.

Comparisons of these ratios of the nations in the sample might be misleading since all of the centrally planned nations are members of the Warsaw Treaty Organization (WTO), while three of the sample market economies are neutral nations. A more meaningful picture of the relative levels of defence expenditure might be gained from looking at such ratios for the entire NATO group of countries. In order to achieve comparability between the NATO countries, the broad OECD definition of defence expenditure is used for the NATO countries although certain incomparabilities with the Warsaw Pact countries are introduced. In the table below, the countries are arranged according to declining *per capita* income.

TABLE 3–2

Ratios of Defence Expenditures to Factor Price GNPs of the NATO Countries in 1956 and 1962, OECD Definitions[1]

Country	1956	1962	Country	1956	1962
USA	10·7%	10·9%	Belgium	3·7%	3·5%
Canada	7·0	5·1	Netherlands	6·4	5·0
Luxembourg	2·3	1·7	Iceland	0·0	0·0
West Germany	3·2	4·9	Italy	4·0	3·4
Norway	3·7	3·7	Greece	6·7	5·2
United Kingdom	7·4	6·3	Portugal	3·9	7·6
Denmark	3·3	3·4	Turkey	5·2	5·9
France	7·4	6·3			

From certain ideological notions about the nature of the nations in the two defence alliances, we might suspect that one group of nations would be significantly more highly 'militarized', i.e. have a higher defence expenditures/GNP ratio. However, the unweighted average ratios of the two groups are relatively similar and in neither year was the difference statistically significant.[2] Even if such expenditures were calculated with the

[1] Data on factor cost GNPS and defence expenditure come from OECD, *General Statistics*, January, 1965, supplemented by OECD, *Statistics on National Accounts, 1950–1961* (Paris, 1964) and, in several cases, from national statistical sources. Estimates of GNP *per capita* are described in Appendix B.

[2] A standard 't test' for determining the significance between means is used. Since the use of the OECD definition made little difference for most of the NATO countries (except the USA, Italy, and Greece), it is doubtful that the broader definition would lower the NATO mean to the point where it would be significantly lower than the average ratio of the Warsaw Pact nations.

same definition and if the factor-income-effect were taken into consideration, it is doubtful that such differences would be statistically significant.[1] This is due, of course, to the high degree of variability of the ratio among nations of both military groups.

For both the NATO and the WTO nations, the ratios of defence expenditures to the GNP are statistically unrelated to the GNP *per capita*,[2] a result that casts serious doubt on the hypothesis for the capitalist nations derived from Lenin's theory of imperialism. In a larger sample of fifty-five nations, a similar conclusion is reached.[3]

Although the ratio of defence expenditures to the GNP is unrelated to *per capita* income, other statistical relations can be found. In the discussion below implications of the public-good properties of defence alliances are discussed under 'the pact theory' while causal factors underlying individual components of defence expenditures are explored in the following subsection.

Even other statistical relations between the ratio of defence expenditures to the GNP and different socio-economic variables have been found, but these are not explored in the present study.[4]

[1] Estimation of the direction of bias of the factor-income-effect (defined in Chapter II and the Glossary, Appendix F) is difficult since there are offsetting factors. For the equipment part of military expenditures there is a downward bias in the actual defence/GNP ratios. However, because a considerable amount of defence expenditures go for salaries, there is an upward bias to the ratios in Table 3–1. The net effect of the two biases is probably quite small.

[2] Regressions of the following form were calculated: $\ln D/Y = a + b \ln Y/P$, where D = defence, Y = the GNP, P = population, and a and b are the calculated regression coefficients.

[3] Bruce M. Russett, 'Measures of Military Effort', *The American Behavioral Scientist*, February 1964, pp. 26–29.

[4] Bruce M. Russett, et al., *World Handbook of Political and Social Indicators*, (New Haven, 1964), p. 270, regresses the ratio of defence expenditures to the GNP against a series of different individual social, economic, and political variables. He finds statistically significant relationships (0·05 level) of defence expenditures as a ratio of GNP to the following variables: total population, general government, and social security expenditures as a percentage of GNP, military personnel as a percentage of the population between 15 and 65, percentage votes for Communist Party in total vote, percentage votes of non-communist secular parties, proportion of speakers of dominant language in the population, absolute value of GNP, foreign trade as a ratio of GNP (inverse relation), consumption as a percentage of GNP (inverse relation), students enrolled

1. THE PACT THEORY

Proponents of the pact theory[1] start with the notion that those people enjoying the benefits of public goods tend to understate publicly their desire for such goods if assessment of costs is based on the stated desire. Since none can be excluded from enjoying the benefits of public goods, there is a natural tendency to let others pay for it. In a military pact where one nation is defended not only by its own army but by the deterrent forces and armies of all signatory nations and where each nation bears only the cost of its own army (roughly the situation in both the WTO and the NATO)[2] there is thus the tendency to enjoy the defence benefits provided by other nations and to cut down on one's own defence expenditures.

Certain implications of this may be more clearly seen in the diagram opposite.

Curve $A''A'$ is the production possibility curve between 'military security' and civilian goods. Empirical evidence presented above on the effect of investment in air raid shelters suggests that there are diminishing returns to military expenditures and, for this reason, the production possibility curve is drawn concave to the origin.[3] If the nation enters into a mutual defence arrangement of the NATO or Warsaw Pact type, it receives $A''M$ ($=OM'$) worth of security from the other

in institutions of higher education per 100,000 population, marriage rate, equality of income before taxes, and non-Catholics as percentage of population. They offer no explanations to the causes of such relationships and many of the correlations seem spurious.

[1] This pact theory had its genesis in Mancur Olson, Jr., *The Logic of Collective Choice* (Cambridge, Mass., 1965) and is further developed in Olson and Zeckhouser, *op. cit.*, Olson and Zeckhouser, 'An Economic Theory of Alliances', *The Review of Economics and Statistics*, XLVIII, August 1966, pp. 268–79, and Ypersele, *op. cit.* The following paragraphs draw heavily from these analyses, and I would like to thank all three authors for allowing me to read their studies before publication.

[2] A crucial fact in the analysis is the method by which the military forces in the NATO and WTO are financed. If some sort of important enforceable pact-tax were levied on each nation, the situation would be quite different. However, such a situation exists neither in NATO nor, to the best of our knowledge, in the WTO.

[3] Of course, it can be argued that there are certain increasing returns, since there is probably a critical minimum size for a deterrent force, but this phenomenon can be taken care of by slightly changing the diagram, without substantially altering the conclusions of the argument.

countries.[1] This would shift the nation's production possibility to $A''MP'$ curve. I_1 and I_2 are the nation's indifference curves between military security and civilian goods. As noted above, the elasticities of these curves are not known. Before entering into the military pact it is optimal for the nation to produce OB'' units of civilian goods and OB' units of military security. After entering into a defence pact, it is optimal for the nation to produce ON'' units of civilian goods and $M'N'$ units of military security while reviewing free OM' units of military security from the other nations. In any kind of usual case, a nation would cut down on its own defence expenditures after entering

Diagram 3–1

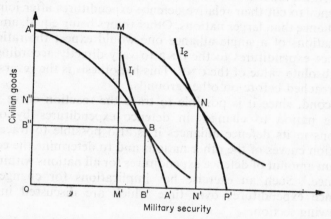

Effect on a pact member of fixed defence expenditures by other pact members[2]

[1] There is some difficulty in measuring the extent of $A''M$. For instance, Hoag, *op. cit.*, notes: 'It would be ridiculous, for example, to claim that Luxembourg's annual gain from NATO in money terms is several times as large as the total annual product because that is what comparable protection would cost if she were isolated.' This partly misses the point, however. $A''M$ represents the amount of 'defence' which the nation feels it is receiving from another nation with which it enters a defence alliance. It certainly does not represent all of the military expenditures of the other nation but only those which are applicable to the nation under analysis. Thus a certain subjective element enters into the evaluation of how ready the other nation is in honouring its agreement and supplying the agreed-upon support at any crucial moment.

[2] This diagram was conceived by Ypersele, *op. cit.*

into a defence treaty, although the extent depends upon the relative sizes of the nations involved. If the USA enters into a defence treaty with Canada, $A''M$ for America would be very small, so that the effect on total military expenditures would also be very small; on the other hand, for Canada, the $A''M$ received from the USA would be very large, relative to its own defence effort. By changing the size of $A''M$ so that the $A''MNP'$ curve shifts location, one can easily trace the reaction of a nation to different sizes of military expenditures by other pact nations.

Two important implications may be drawn from the use of this diagram:

First, the smaller nations of a defence alliance have a greater tendency to cut their relative defence expenditures after joining an alliance than larger nations. Other things being equal, among the nations of a single alliance one would expect the ratio of defence expenditures to the GNP to vary directly according to the absolute value of the GNP. This hypothesis is the reverse of one reached before on other grounds.

Second, since it is possible to trace the reaction curve of a single nation to changes in defence expenditures by other nations in its defence alliances it is also possible to trace the reaction curves of the other nations and to determine the equilibrium amount of defence expenditures for all nations within the alliance.[1] Such an exercise has implications for changes in defence expenditures over time which are discussed in the following section.

There is certain qualitative evidence to support the generalization about the relation of economic size to the ratio of defence expenditures to the GNP. Iceland, the smallest member of NATO (1956 population: 161,000) has no military expenditures, and political figures in Luxembourg, another small NATO country (1956 population: 307,000) are considering disbanding its army.[2] Furthermore, in some NATO countries (e.g. Belgium) there has been serious debate about reducing

[1] This type of analysis is carried out in depth by Olson and Zeckhouser, *op. cit.*, and is discussed in greater detail below.

[2] 'Luxembourg's Aid to NATO Debated', *New York Times*, February 6, 1966, p. 14.

defence expenditures on the grounds that other members of NATO supply most of the needed military security.[1]

A more formal quantitative analysis can be easily made by calculating regressions where the variable to be explained is the ratio of defence to the GNP (D/Y) and the absolute value of the GNP is one of the explanatory variables. The analysis can be broadened by considering a number of other independent variables and by including a number of non-pact nations as well. Because of comparability problems, separate regressions were calculated for Western Europe[2] (using the OECD definition of defence) and for Eastern Europe (using a narrow definition of defence expenditures).

The first set of regressions contains two explanatory variables: the absolute value of the GNP (Y) and income *per capita* (Y/P), both expressed in a common currency. The logarithm form of the regression was selected in order to minimize the effect of the very large GNPs of the United States and the Soviet Union.

TABLE 3–3

Statistical Relationships between the Ratio of Defence Expenditures to the Factor Price GNP and Other Economic Variables[3]

Western Europe   *Coefficients of Determination* (R^2)
1956: $\ln D/Y = -0\cdot62 + 0\cdot83^* \ln Y - 0\cdot71 \ln (Y/P)$ $0\cdot50^*$
                  $(0\cdot21)$ $(0\cdot68)$
1962: $\ln D/Y = -0\cdot88 + 0\cdot82^* \ln Y - 0\cdot63 \ln (Y/P)$ $0\cdot49^*$
                  $(0\cdot21)$ $(0\cdot67)$

Eastern Europe
1956: $\ln D/Y = -0\cdot59 + 0\cdot18 \ln Y - 0\cdot41 \ln (Y/P)$ $0\cdot33$
                  $(0\cdot13)$ $(0\cdot46)$
1962: $\ln D/Y = -1\cdot35 + 0\cdot26 \ln Y - 0\cdot22 \ln (Y/P)$ $0\cdot43$
                  $(0\cdot15)$ $(0\cdot61)$

[1] Evidence for this is given by Ypersele, *op. cit.*

[2] 'Western Europe' includes all NATO countries as well as Sweden, Switzerland, Austria, and Ireland. Spain and Finland had to be excluded for lack of comparable data. 'Eastern Europe' includes the seven centralized economies included in Table 3–2. Yugoslavia was excluded from both sets of regressions. The usefulness of including non-pact nations is discussed below.

[3] The standard errors of the calculated coefficients are placed below in parentheses. The asterisk denotes that the calculated number is significant at the 0·05 level. These regressions were also run in a straight arithmetical form with similar results. In addition, all regressions for Western Europe were run,

D

In Western Europe for both years the ratio of defence expenditures to the factor price GNP is statistically related (0·05 level of significance) to the absolute value of the GNP.[1] Furthermore, about half of the variance among these nations of the defence/GNP ratio is explained by the independent variable.[2] In Eastern Europe there are no significant statistical relations, although the signs of the calculated coefficients of the absolute GNP follows expectations.[3] The empirical evidence for the pact theory appears promising.

Two aspects of the regression results require comment. First, in none of the four regressions is the calculated coefficient for the *per capita* income variable statistically significant. This result reinforces our agnosticism about whether military expenditures are an inferior or superior good.

Second, disturbing thoughts arise because the analysis explains too much, since it covers both nations within and outside of military pacts. If, for Western Europe, a dummy variable denoting whether or not the nation belongs to NATO is added as an independent variable to the regressions, the resulting calculated regression coefficient is not statistically significant. Proponents of the pact theory might argue that this can be easily explained, since the non-NATO European countries act 'as if' they belonged to NATO. That is, the neutral West Europ-

excluding Greece and Turkey (whose military expenditures are partly financed by the USA) and the USA. These latter regressions were quite similar to the above results.

1 This hypothesis has also been empirically tested for noncommunist nations by Ypersele, *op. cit.* Olson and Zeckhouser, *op. cit.*, and Russett, *et al.*, *op. cit.*, all of whom also found a statistically significant relation between the two variables. Ypersele refined the data by adjusting the wages of conscripts to reflect the market wage rate and by including foreign aid. Russett's sample covers eighty-one nations.

2 A number of hypotheses can be offered to explain the rest of the variance. One aspect of the data that is particularly striking is the relatively high amount of defence expenditures among the Balkan nations, a feature that can be understood on historical grounds. Further exploration of such hypotheses must be left to other investigators. Certain countries in defence alliances might have high military expenditures to protect themselves against their allies!

3 When the regressions for Eastern Europe are recalculated with Y/P excluded, the calculated regression coefficients for Y are just a shade below statistical significance at the 0·05 level. It is interesting to note that in both years, those nations with Soviet troops stationed in them had ratios of defence expenditures to the GNP which are lower than that predicted by the regression equation.

ean countries such as Austria and Sweden somehow 'know' that the United States will defend them if they are attacked. This might well be true, but more institutional evidence is needed before such an explanation can be accepted.

The pact theory has considerable plausibility but the evidence is not completely convincing. Since other hypotheses discussed in Section B of this chapter are refuted by the data, confidence in the pact theory can be increased. However, the results are just enough unsettling to encourage us to search for other explanations and to examine additional evidence.

2. ANALYSIS OF COMPONENTS

The most promising supplementary approach to explore military expenditures lies in a disaggregation of defence expenditures and an examination of each component. Such a method also allows the separation of political and economic factors from certain institutional aspects which are glossed over in the analysis of expenditure aggregates. The three major components for examination are: the number of personnel involved in military activities; their remuneration; and the expenditures on equipment for them.

The Number of Military Personnel[1]

The concept of military personnel is somewhat ambiguous. In all modern military establishments there is a separation between producers and users of weapons, so that civilians engaged in weapons manufacturing are not considered as military personnel.[2] Nevertheless, there are also civilians attached to the armed forces of all nations, who are mostly engaged in financial, logistical, maintenance, and research functions, and who are difficult to classify. Since the carrying out of these tasks is performed by different mixes of civilian and military personnel

---

[1] A fascinating comparative sociological analysis of this problem covering many nations and centuries is made by Stanisław Andrzejewski, *Military Organization and Society* (London, 1954). Unfortunately, Andrzejewski's qualitative approach is not suited to this study, and a different type of analysis is developed below.

[2] In some defence establishments, military personnel are used to assemble weapons, but these account for only a very small proportion of the total personnel.

in various nations, it is necessary for the sake of comparability to include all such persons in the definition of military personnel.[1] Since such 'civilian-type jobs' are becoming relatively much more important in the armed forces, problems in obtaining comparable data on 'military personnel' increase with each year.[2]

There are a number of hypotheses about the relation between the number of military personnel and various socio-economic and political variables. For instance, it has been propounded that the key variable in determining the size of 'defensive armies' is the length of the frontier, while other variables play an important role in determining the size of 'offensive armies' including the absolute size of the population and the GNP *per capita*.[3] Since armed forces in the nineteenth century between the Napoleonic wars and the turn of the century were supposedly 'defensive' while armed forces in the twentieth century are supposedly 'offensive', such hypotheses can easily be tested.

For the statistical analysis, two years, a century apart, were chosen; both were relatively quiet years politically, and the data, it is hoped, reflect underlying forces rather than particular crises. The data exclude paramilitary personnel and reserves.[4]

---

[1] Problems in statistically determining the number of relevant civilians are very difficult to solve. Generally, a much higher proportion of civilian personnel are attached to defence establishments in market than in centrally planned economies. I was told by a former Hungarian officer that even the person in the Hungarian Central Bank responsible for disbursing funds to the military was an army officer.

[2] The quantitative increase in importance of 'civilian-type jobs' in the military establishment between 1860 and 1950 is shown by Morris Janowitz, *The Professional Soldier* (Glencoe, Ill., 1960), p. 65.

[3] These hypotheses are discussed by E. A. G. Robinson, 'The Size of the Nation and the Cost of Administration', in E. A. G. Robinson, ed., *Economic Consequences of the Size of Nations* (New York, 1960), pp. 223–39.

[4] Paramilitary forces are numerically important only in the centrally planned economies. Such forces are the military and sport organizations (DOSAAF in the USSR, DOSO in Bulgaria, SVAZARM in Czechoslovakia, GST in East Germany, MHS in Hungary, LPZ in Poland, and AVSAP in Romania) and, in a number of these countries, the factory fighting groups. None of these countries has an institution similar to the Red Guards in China. Comparable estimates of reserve forces are almost impossible to make, since the state of readiness of such reserves may differ greatly. Even though many of the centralized economies such as the Soviet Union have 'cadre-type' armies with skeletal divisions consisting primarily of officers, this does not necessarily mean that reserve forces are in a great state of readiness.

TABLE 3–4

Military Personnel as a Percentage of the Population, 1858 and 1958[1]

1858		1958			
European Countries		NATO Countries		Warsaw Pact Countries	
Austria	1·08%	Belgium	1·49%	Albania	3·12%
Bavaria	1·86	Canada	1·03	Bulgaria	2·77
Belgium	1·61	Denmark	1·22	Czechoslovakia	1·56
Denmark	0·81	France	2·47	East Germany	0·92
France	0·98	West Germany	0·41	Hungary	0·79
Great Britain	0·48	Greece	2·76	Poland	1·62
Greece	0·82	Iceland	0·00	Romania	1·68
Hanover	1·38	Italy	0·96	USSR	2·19
Lesser German		Luxembourg	0·64		
States	0·56	Netherlands	1·36	Non-Pact European	
Lesser Italian		Norway	1·44	countries	
States	0·34	Portugal	1·25		
Naples	1·29	Turkey	2·04	Austria	0·67%
Netherlands	1·72	United Kingdom	1·82	Finland	1·13
Portugal	0·72	USA	2·14	Ireland	0·32
Prussia	1·14			Spain	1·72
Russia	0·81?			Sweden	1·24
Sardinia	1·07			Switzerland	n.a.
Saxony	1·12			Yugoslavia	3·49
Spain	0·69				
Sweden and					
Norway	0·82				
Switzerland	2·84?				
Turkey	0·40?				

Before turning to the regression analysis it is worth noting that using an unweighted sample, there is a significantly higher ratio of military personnel to the population in 1958 (1·5 per

[1] For 1858, data on military personnel and population come respectively from: F. W. Hirst, *The Political Economy of War* (London, 1915), p. 81; and Frederick Martin, ed., *The Statesman's Yearbook 1864* (London, 1864). The data include only armed forces personnel; information on civilian personnel attached to the military establishment are not available but such personnel are believed to be numerically very small. Data for Russia, Switzerland, and Turkey are followed by question marks because information from other sources differ considerably for these countries. The source of difficulty is the handling of reserves, mercenaries, and non-national conscripts. In the regressions these three countries are omitted.

For 1958, data include civilian personnel attached to the defence establishment and internal security troops other than police personnel. Sources of data and methods of estimation are described in Statistical Note D–6.

cent) than in 1858 (1·0 per cent). Even if civilians attached to the armed forces could have been included in the data for the latter year, it is highly unlikely that such a conclusion would have been changed. This reflects an increasing militarization of Europe which a number of authors have noted.[1] It is also relevant that in 1958 the unweighted average ratio of military personnel to population is significantly greater in the Warsaw Pact nations than among the NATO countries. However, if *per capita* income is held constant or if security troops are removed, this statistically significant difference between the two groups of nations disappears.

Additional insights can be gained through using other statistical techniques. For each year regressions were calculated with total military personnel as the dependent variable and total population and area as the explanatory variables.

TABLE 3–5

Statistical Relationships of Military Personnel to Area and Population: 1858 and 1958[2]

	Size of sample	Coefficient of determination
1858		
$\ln M = 5 \cdot 07 + 0 \cdot 99^* \ln P - 0 \cdot 16 \ln A$ $\quad\quad\quad\quad (0 \cdot 15) \quad\quad\quad (0 \cdot 14)$	18	$0 \cdot 83^*$
1958		
$\ln M = -3 \cdot 80 + 1 \cdot 85^* \ln P - 0 \cdot 35 \ln A$ $\quad\quad\quad\quad (0 \cdot 17) \quad\quad (0 \cdot 18)$	29	$0 \cdot 81^*$

where M = total military personnel
P = population
A = area.

[1] The problems of changing intensities of war or militarization of economies over long periods are more adequately discussed by Richardson, *op. cit.*, Andrzejewski, *op. cit.*, and Pitirim Sorokin, *Social and Cultural Dynamics*, Vol. III (New York, 1937).

[2] An asterisk means that the coefficient is statistically significant; standard errors are placed in parentheses below each coefficient. Population is recorded in 1000s, area in 1000 km^2, and military personnel in absolute number. Regressions without transformation into natural logarithms were also carried out; the results were not different enough to warrant separate reporting. In addition, a series of regressions were calculated for Western Europe excluding Greece, Turkey, and the United States. Again, the results were not greatly different.

Not surprisingly, in both years the number of military personnel is significantly and positively related to population; however, in neither year is there a statistically significant relation with area and, indeed, even the signs of the calculated coefficient are different than expected. Since the area of a country and the length of its frontier are roughly related, the 'defence army' hypothesis can be rejected.[1]

The calculated coefficients relating military personnel and population reveal the following important information: if a country was 1 per cent larger in population than another, its armed forces in 1858 and 1958 were respectively about 1 per cent and 1·8 per cent larger. Changing the definition of the dependent variable to exclude security forces makes very little difference in the size of these calculated regression coefficients.[2]

To what may such differences in the two centuries be attributed? A 'pact theorist' might argue (*post hoc*) that in 1858, military technology excluded the effective use of deterrent forces, so that most defence expenditures were for services which did not have strong public-goods characteristics and that the basic argument behind Diagram 1 would not hold. More institutionally minded economists might argue that the nature of military alliances and, indeed, the whole concept of the balance of power were different in the two years. Unfortunately, a further exploration of this matter would take us too far from the main theme of this study.

A number of experiments were carried out with the 1858 data in order to determine other relationships with variables such as population density and various geographic factors. But no statistically significant correlations were found. Another series of experiments were attempted using the ratio of military personnel to the population as the dependent variable, but, as might be expected, none of these resulted in statistically significant

[1] It could, of course, be argued that the total frontier is not the relevant variable, but rather the frontier facing the enemy, or the land frontier. Proponents wishing to resuscitate the defence hypothesis must, therefore, be quite specific in defining which border they mean. Proving that nineteenth century wars were 'defensive' might also be difficult.

[2] If the regressions are recalculated so that the dependent variable is the ratio of military personnel to the population, then no statistically significant relations could be found for 1858. For 1958, this ratio is significantly related to the total population and to absolute size of the GNP.

relationships either. In 1858 it appears that the population of the country was the major explanatory variable for determining the size of the army. Introduction of certain political and social variables might prove to be statistically significant, but this lies more properly in the area of history and political science; unfortunately, up to now most historians and political scientists have been surprisingly unwilling to attempt analysing the vast amounts of historical data on the sizes of military establishments.[1]

More experiments were carried out on the 1958 data. First, a series of additional independent variables was introduced into the regression presented in Table 3–5. These included *per capita* income, density, and dummy variables designating whether the nation was a member of a military pact and whether the nation had a centrally planned economy. However, not one of the calculated coefficients of these variables either alone or in combination with others, was statistically significant. Such results were not changed when smaller groups of countries were examined separately.

Because these results appeared so surprising, over 80 different regression equations were calculated, using various combinations and forms of the above-mentioned variables. Yet in all of them, only population and occasionally (but with a negative sign) area proved to explain in a statistically significant fashion the amount of military personnel in a country; other economic and political variables played a statistically insignificant role.

The lack of statistical significance in the regression of dummy variables designating whether the nation belonged to the NATO or the WTO or was neutral seems the most interesting negative result.[2] A similar result is obtained when security forces are removed from the armed forces.

In order to make the analysis of the 1958 data comparable with the calculations presented in Table 3–3 with the expenditures data, the ratios of military personnel to the population were regressed against total population and also the total

[1] Some idea of the richness of quantitative information available can be gained from E. M. Rosenbaum, 'War Economics: A Bibliographic Approach', *Economica*, N.S., IX; February, 1942, pp. 64–94.

[2] This does not conflict with the results with the unweighted averages noted above because in this experiment, income *per capita* is held constant.

value of the GNP. Positive and statistically significant relationships are found in both cases. Indeed, such results can be predicted from a slight modification of the pact theory model.

The Remuneration of Military Personnel

Although there appears a simple empirical relationship explaining the number of military personnel, the payment of such personnel depends on three political-economic factors.

First, the system of recruiting plays a crucial role, and four types of recruiting systems must be noted: volunteer, conscript, mixed, and citizens' armies.[1] Armed forces relying completely on volunteers, such as in Canada and Australia, must pay high wages to attract sufficient manpower and, indeed, the wages of privates in the aforementioned two countries are the highest in the world.[2] Conscript armies, e.g. in France, USSR, or Turkey need pay their soldiers very little since, by force of law, the members of the army must serve. Thus, in some conscript armies, aside from living supplements (free food, clothing, lodging, etc.) soldiers receive wages little more in value than a few packs of cigarettes a week. Mixed volunteer-conscript armies, such as in Belgium, West Germany, and the United States, pay wages to their soldiers somewhere between those of completely conscript or completely volunteer recruitment systems. Finally, payment of members of citizens' armies, such as in Switzerland or Israel, depend on special political circumstances. For example, soldiers on yearly manoeuvres in Switzerland receive remuneration equal to their wages in civilian life.

Second, within the conscript, volunteer, or mixed conscript-volunteer systems, soldiers' wages seem to vary according to the general level of wages in the economy. Thus conscripts in France receive very much higher wages than conscripts in Greece or Turkey, and volunteers in Canada receive more than volunteers in East Germany.

---

[1] Recruitment systems are discussed in detail by M. R. D. Foot, *Men in Uniform* (New York, 1961). In the NATO alliance all countries have had conscript systems except Belgium (mixed), Canada (volunteer), the United Kingdom (mixed), and the United States (mixed). All of the WTO nations have had conscript armed forces except East Germany, which had a volunteer system until 1961.

[2] *Ibid.*, pp. 162–3, has a table of wages for privates for some thirty-one nations, as well as scattered observations on the subject throughout his study.

D*

Finally, the average wage of military personnel depends on the mix between civilians, officers, and enlisted men. Civilians attached to the military establishment generally receive salaries commensurate with salaries throughout the economy for their particular skills. Officers receive much higher wages than average industrial workers.[1] A more exact determination of relative officers' remuneration requires finding the proper civilian analogues for such officers and obtaining adequate data for both groups.

Thus three factors, the system of recruiting, the level of wages in the economy, and the relative proportion of different types of military personnel, combine to determine the average level of remuneration. Lack of detailed data on such matters hinders further analysis.

The Capital Flow/Labour Ratio

Owing to the complexity in the determination of the average remuneration for military personnel, the ratio of wage payments to non-wage military expenditures (a favourite ratio of some analysts) is generally not a very significant statistic. However, if wage and allowance payments can be isolated and if non-personnel expenditures can be estimated in some common currency, then an estimate of the capital flow/labour ratio of defence establishments can be calculated, a statistic on which a number of predictions can be made. In order to simplify estimation problems the ratio of non-personnel defence expenditures to military personnel is used, rather than the capital flow/soldier ratio directly.

First of all, it seems very likely that the ratio of non-personnel defence expenditures to military personnel is positively related to the GNP *per capita* because of a substitution effect. That is, as GNP *per capita* rises, military wages rise; in addition, as industrial productivity increases, the cost of military equipment

---

[1] Average officers salaries for the Soviet Union are estimated by Nancy Nimitz, *Soviet National Income and Product, 1956–1958*, RAND Corp., Memorandum RM-3112-PR (Santa Monica, 1962), p. 33; for Hungary by Thad P. Alton, *et al.*, *Hungarian National Income and Product in 1955* (New York, 1963), p. 148; and for the USA in *Statistical Abstract*, any issue. In all three cases, officers receive on the average about twice the average industrial salary. Since data for other nations could not be located, a more precise generalization cannot be made.

becomes relatively less expensive in terms of labour. Thus there is a change in the relative prices of labour and equipment which would encourage a change in the relative capital intensity of the army. Furthermore, there may also be a reinforcing income effect. Other things being equal, the higher the *per capita* income, the more a nation can afford highly expensive modern weapon systems such as rockets and hydrogen bombs.

A nation's role in international affairs and in military alliances is also important in determining the ratio of non-personnel defence expenditures to military personnel. If a nation aspires to be the continual leader of a defence alliance, then it must make heavy investments in military research and in the expensive deterrent systems whose benefits are enjoyed by the other pact members.

Testing these hypotheses is difficult because of problems in deriving an adequate exchange rate with which to value the non-personnel defence expenditures in a common currency. Therefore, the estimates below must be viewed indicative only of the relative magnitudes. The non-personnel defence expenditures per military person are calculated separately for East and West Europe and are indexed with the ratio of the largest country equal to 100. Countries are arranged in descending order of national product *per capita*. (See Table 3–6 on the next page.)

The United States, as the military leader of NATO, and the Soviet Union, as the military leader of the Warsaw Pact, have the highest ratios of non-personnel expenditures per military person. In the other countries in each military group there are statistically significant relationships between the GNP *per capita* and the index values.[1] Thus our general notions about the ratio seem confirmed by the available evidence. Complete certainty is not possible, however, because of the crudeness of the data.

3. A BRIEF SUMMARY

In explaining aggregative defence expenditures the pact theory has a theoretical elegance as well as a certain degree of empirical confirmation. The predicted positive relation between the

---

[1] Regressions were calculated for each set of separate nations, after the USA and the USSR had been excluded.

TABLE 3–6

Index Values of Non-personnel Expenditures per Military Person in 1962

Western Europe and America[1]		Eastern Europe[2]	
USA	100	Czechoslovakia	74
Sweden	59	East Germany	73
Canada	70	USSR	100
West Germany	61	Hungary	56
Norway	16	Poland	64
France	25	Romania	26
United Kingdom	46	Bulgaria	31
Belgium	15		
Netherlands	26		
Austria	4		
Greece	3		

ratio of defence to the GNP and the size of the total GNP occurs among the NATO nations and shows certain tendencies among the WTO nations as well. Theories that relate defence expenditures to the level of economic development, the economic system, or other factors are rejected when tested with the data of this study.

Additional insights can be gained by examining the separate components of defence expenditures. In regard to the number

[1] These estimates were made in three steps: First, data on military expenditures excluding wages and allowances of the armed forces were obtained from national accounts statistics. Second, an estimate of the wage bill of civilian workers was obtained by assuming that such workers received the average industrial wage. Third, the national data were converted into dollars by the exchange rate, a procedure based on the assumption that the international military equipment market had operated to equalize the dollar price of such equipment in the major countries and that other non-personnel expenditures are relatively unimportant. (Closer approximations of the Gilbert-Kravis type were unfortunately not available for all countries.) National accounts data come from OECD, *General Statistics*, January 1965, supplemented in several cases by national data. Sources for military personnel are given in Appendix D–6. For France, national data on military personnel, rather than OECD data, are utilized.

[2] These estimates were made in two steps. First, personnel expenditures of the armed forces were removed from total military expenditures. Second, the national data were converted into dollars by use of purchasing power parity exchange rates in industry which were derived from data presented by Frederic L. Pryor and George J. Staller, 'The Dollar Values of the Gross National Products in Eastern Europe', *Economics of Planning*, VI, 1/1966, pp. 1–27. No account was taken of wage expenditures for civilian employees because of the uncertainties in the number of such personnel. Wage bill data come from Appendix A; sources on military personnel are given in Appendix D–6.

of military personnel, the regression analysis shows that the population elasticity of such personnel is considerably greater than unity in the post World War II period. In terms of ratios this means that the ratio of military personnel to the population is related to the total population (and, as other regressions show, to the total GNP as well). The remuneration of military personnel depends on the system of recruiting, the average wage rates in the country, and the mix between officers, soldiers, and civilians. Finally, the ratio of new equipment per military person depends on the level of economic development and whether or not the nation is a pact leader.

The aggregative and disaggregative approaches are complementary in several ways. First, the determinants of the number of military personnel in 1958 can be predicted from the pact theory. Second, the higher non-personnel expenditure per military person of pact leaders is quite in accord with the fact that nations having the largest absolute gross national products also have the highest share of defence expenditures, since the leaders of the two pacts under consideration are also the largest nations in their respective military groupings. Third, the other results obtained in the two types of analyses are not inconsistent.

D. TIME-SERIES DETERMINANTS OF DEFENCE EXPENDITURES

In the cross-section analysis a given international environment is assumed; and, in addition, no considerations are taken of responses of one nation to the military expenditures of another. In a time-series analysis, on the other hand, such phenomena can be explored.

The analysis of most time-series data in this study begins with the calculation of ratio-income-elasticities. For military expenditures, such elasticity coefficients are negative for almost all nations and, in a surprising number of cases, statistically significant.[1] In constant prices such a downward trend might not

---

[1] Ratio-income-elasticities are the percentage change in the ratio of public consumption expenditures to the GNP which accompany a one per cent change in the GNP *per capita*. This statistic is described extensively in Chapter II, pp. 59 ff. The results of the calculation are presented in Appendix D–7.

be so pronounced.[1] The interpretation of such results is political, rather than economic: military expenditures were at a very high level during the Korean War in the early 1950s but, as international tensions subsided during the period, declined in relative importance. The economic meaning of such elasticity calculations does not seem very important. Considerations of the differential responses of a nation to changes in the military expenditures of its enemies and friends provide a much better starting point for the analysis of the time-series data for military expenditures.

Between enemies it seems likely that military expenditures of the nations would be related to each other in a direct manner. This could come about because both countries are reacting to some common phenomena such as changes in the state of tension between the two nations or changes in the state of military technology. Or such an apparent interaction could be due to the response of one nation to changes in the military budget of the enemy. Although such types of interactions may seem obvious, at least one distinguished political scientist, Samuel P. Huntington, claims that US military expenditures are less of a response than a residual item in the budget after funds have been allocated for other purposes.[2]

The most sensitive test for such interrelations should not be made directly on the defence expenditure series but rather on variations of such expenditures from their trends.[3] If there are such interrelations, then the deviations from the trend of enemy

[1] Average constant-price elasticities are 0·21 below average current price elasticities if we assume no productivity changes. However, there has been a rapid increase in military technology which, unfortunately, has not been quantitatively measured, so that it is impossible to assess its impact on the ratio elasticity measurements.

[2] In an extensive survey of the decision-making process for military expenditures Samuel P. Huntington [*The Common Defense: Strategic Problems in National Politics* (New York, Columbia University Press, 1961), p. 22] concludes that: 'In both the Truman administration before the Korean War and in the Eisenhower administration after the war, the tendency was: (1) to estimate the revenues of the government or total expenditures possible within the existing debt limit; (2) to deduct from this figure the estimated cost of domestic programs and foreign aid; and (3) to allocate the remainder to the military.'

[3] Examining the residuals around the trend minimizes the problems arising from different definitions of military expenditures as well as the difficulties arising from the fact that if two time series have trends in the same direction, they are usually highly correlated.

nations should be positively correlated. This procedure assumes that a given state of international relations exist (an exogenous factor) and tries to examine the implications, a task which is the exact opposite for political scientists who are interested in the causal factors underlying the international relations.[1]

There are two possible mechanisms of interaction that can be explored, and the exact definition of military expenditures used in the analysis depends on which mechanism is chosen. If we assume that nations respond to some common phenomenon such as the state of international tension, then we should examine such expenditures using fixed prices and a common definition. If we suppose that the interdependency is due to direct observations of military budgets, then current price budgetary data should be used instead. Although the first supposition seems more reasonable, it cannot be automatically accepted.

This problem can be easily cleared up by testing the various concepts of military expenditures and seeing which yield the highest correlation coefficient. This procedure was carried out in three steps. First, five different series of defence expenditures for the United States (OECD definition, current prices; OECD definition, constant prices; definition of this study, current prices; definition of this study, constant prices; US budget definition, current prices) and three different series of defence expenditures for the Soviet Union (definition of this study, current prices; definition of this study, constant prices; Soviet budget definition, current prices) were prepared. Second, the trend for each series was calculated and the deviations from this trend as a percentage of trend value were derived. Finally, the deviations from the trend of the various series were regressed against each other. Most of the calculated correlation coefficients are roughly the same; but the correlation co-

---

[1] An exception to this generalization are those political scientists who are studying arms race models. For two of the most recent and imaginative studies that have been made with defence expenditures data for the USSR and USA, see: Lloyd Jensen, 'Military Capabilities and Bargaining Behavior', *Journal of Conflict Resolution*, IX, June 1965, pp. 155–64; and Richard H. Brody and John F. Vesecky, 'Soviet Openness to Changing Situations: A Critical Evaluation of Certain Hypotheses about Soviet Foreign Policy Behavior', unpublished paper, Stanford University.

efficient derived from the two series in fixed prices using the definition employed in this study is somewhat higher, a result that not only adds evidence to the nature of interaction, but also, in a different context, offers some confirmation to my estimating techniques (see Appendix A).

Using the common definition, the average annual increase of military expenditures in constant prices from 1950 through 1962 was $1 \cdot 6$ per cent for the USA and $1 \cdot 4$ per cent for the USSR, a similarity that is not unexpected. The coefficient of determination (R^2) of the residuals from the trend is $0 \cdot 48$, which is statistically significant ($0 \cdot 05$ level). Thus it appears that there is an important interaction of military expenditures between the two nations and that this interaction is due to a response to some common phenomenon such as the state of tension between them or changes in military technology.[1] Since only about one-half of the variance between the two sets of deviations is explained by the interaction hypothesis, a number of other factors must also be brought into the analysis if a more exact explanation is to be offered. Unfortunately, consideration and testing of such variables would lead us too far afield.[2] Graphical comparisons of the deviations from the trend of the two countries yields additional useful information.

First, there do not seem to be any consistent lag relationships between the military expenditures of the two nations; both seem to be responding directly to common circumstances.[3] That is, neither nation appears to be responding to a change in military expenditures of the other nation after a discrete interval of time. Since the time period of analysis is a year, lag relationships of less than this period would not be properly reflected in the graph.[4] Second, after 1954 the military expenditures of both

[1] The results are partly due to the time period selected for analysis. From 1945 to 1950 there did not seem to be the type of interaction of military expenditures that characterized the later period. These early postwar year can be considered as a learning period in which the defence decision makers reoriented themselves to a different international situation.

[2] More detailed analysis of the state of military technology, especially the introduction of new weapon systems, seems a fruitful approach toward the explanation of part of the residual variance.

[3] Statistical tests also failed to reveal consistent lag relationships.

[4] A number of authors have argued that the United States military and foreign policy is characterized by a response to Soviet initiatives, rather than the reverse

nations seem all to lie quite close to their respective trends. The relatively greater deviation from the trend of the USA during the Korean crisis in the early 1950s was due to several well-known factors. Demobilization after World War II had proceeded much more rapidly in the United States than in the Soviet Union, so that there was a greater gap between potential and

Diagram 3–2

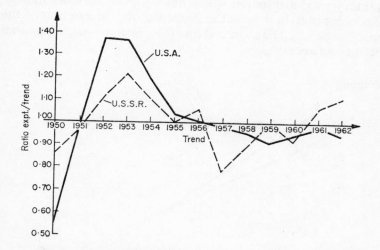

Ratio of deviations from the trend of military expenditures in the United States and the Soviet Union, 1950 through 1962

actual military power in the former country by 1950. Furthermore, the United States was a direct participant in the war, while the Soviet Union acted more as a supplier of equipment and advice.

The data presented in the diagram and the regression calculations thus give considerable positive evidence for the interaction hypothesis. Although the 'residual theory' of military expendi-

e.g. Arnold L. Horelick and Myron Rush, *Strategic Power and Soviet Foreign Policy* (Chicago, 1966). If this is true and if American response, as measured by changes in expenditures, was quick, then no lag relationship could be seen in the above diagram.

tures is not completely disproven by such results,[1] the empirical evidence presented above casts grave doubts on its validity.

In regard to the interrelations of military expenditures between allies, the pact theory has some interesting implications. As noted above, it is possible to derive from Diagram 1 the reaction curves of every nation to the military expenditures of other countries in its mutual defence alliance. If there is a stable equilibrium of defence expenditures among nations in a military pact, a situation which has considerable plausibility,[2] this point may be schematically seen as the intersection of the reaction curves. Diagram 2 shows this for a two-nation mutual defence alliance.

Diagram 3–3

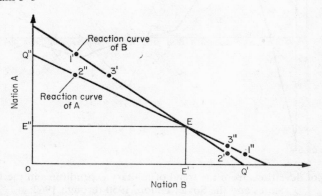

Military expenditure reaction curves of nations in a defence alliance[3]

In time period O, as the pact is signed, Nations A and B are expending for defence the amounts designated respectively Q'' and Q'. If the two nations can shift their resources instantaneously between civilian and defence purposes, both nations will

---

[1] It is possible that US military expenditures are a residual and that the Soviet Union has responded instantaneously to US decisions; such a situation does not seem very likely, however.

[2] See esp. Olson and Zeckhouser, *op. cit.*

[3] The diagram is taken from Olson and Zeckhouser, *op. cit.*; the analysis of dynamic behaviour is my own, and neither of them is responsible for the dynamic implications which I have drawn from their theory.

cut their defence expenditures in the next time period, so as to be spending respectively the amounts corresponding to $1''$ and $1'$. In time period 2, each will increase expenditures to the amounts corresponding respectively to $2''$ and $2'$. Defence expenditures of Nation A will converge toward E'' of Nation B, E'.

Since nations cannot shift resources instantaneously between civilian and defence production, it is doubtful that the cyclical fluctuations of defence expenditures toward the equilibrium point would occur, although both countries could slowly cut their defence expenditures so that equilibrium could be reached. From considerations discussed in the previous section and from the diagram, it should be apparent that the nation with the smaller defence expenditures in the beginning (Nation A) would cut its military expenditures relatively more than the nation with the larger initial expenditures (Nation B). Even if there are long-run shifts in the equilibrium point due to changes in the international environment, such a proposition should hold. By examining the time trends of military expenditures in constant prices, evidence on this matter can be obtained.

It should also be readily apparent from the diagram that the larger nation is closer to its equilibrium point than the smaller nation. If international conditions continually change so that the equilibrium point experiences a series of short-run shifts, there is a differential response of the two nations. The country farther from its equilibrium point can adjust to such shifts by changing the direction of its adaption path to equilibrium; the country nearer to its equilibrium point experiences more fluctuations from its long-run trend. The situation is complicated by certain asymmetries between increasing and decreasing defence expenditures, as well as by the possibility that changes in equilibrium defence expenditures may be long-run as well as short-run changes. All we can say, therefore, is that it is likely (but not certain) that fluctuations of defence expenditures around the trend are relatively more important in larger than in smaller nations belonging to a defence alliance, a proposition that can also be tested.

One corollary can also be drawn from the above two propositions: the larger a nation, the more the fluctuations in its military expenditures should approximate such fluctuations of the pact leader. In order to test this proposition, however, certain interrelations of military expenditures must be further explored and several institutional facts must be briefly noted.

The North Atlantic Treaty Organization was founded in April 1949 in the period of rising international tensions preceding the Korean War in 1950. Consisting originally of Belgium, Canada, Denmark, France, Iceland, Italy, Luxembourg, the Netherlands, Norway, Portugal, the UK, and the USA, it was later joined by Germany, Greece, Italy, and Turkey. The founding date corresponded roughly with the end of the reconstruction period of Western Europe and the beginning of a long-run period of sustained economic growth for most of the nations.

The Warsaw Treaty Organization was established in May 1955, in a period where international tensions were still high but receding from the peak reached during the Korean War. The signatory members were Albania, Bulgaria, Czechoslovakia, East Germany, Hungary, Poland, Romania, and the USSR, nations all of which had been militarily bound to each other for many years through an interlocking series of bilateral mutual assistance alliances.[1] Since then no new members have joined.

The military, economic, and political circumstances that led to the founding of both pact systems contribute a number of complications to the analysis of changes of defence expenditures over time, and these interfere with the relatively simple considerations discussed above. Therefore, considerable caution must be exercised in interpreting the empirical results.

In both military blocs the average trends of military expenditures in constant prices are lower for the smaller countries than for the larger countries; only in the Warsaw Pact nations is the difference statistically significant, however.[2] For fluctuations

---

[1] The Warsaw Pact Organization and the circumstances leading to its founding are discussed in detail by Kazimierz Grzybowski, *The Socialist Commonwealth of Nations: Organizations and Institutions* (New Haven, 1964), Chap. 5, and Zbigniew K. Brzezinski, *The Soviet Bloc: Unity and Conflict* (Cambridge, Mass., 1966).

[2] For the comparisons, West Germany, East Germany, and Austria are excluded because their military expenditures in the early 1950s were influenced by the decisions of their occupying powers. For the Warsaw Pact the larger

around the trend there are no statistically significant differences between larger and smaller countries for either bloc. Thus the empirical evidence for the two hypotheses derived above is mixed, and no definite conclusions can be drawn.[1] Comparison of trend values between blocs is ruled out because such values are highly sensitive to the definition of military expenditures which is employed.[2]

The fruitfulness of the hypothesis concerning the interaction of military expenditures between enemy nations and the uncertain results of the hypotheses about the interaction between allies suggests a different approach to the problem. This revolves around the degree to which other pact members respond to the tensions that affect the leaders of their respective pacts. If we assume that similarity of changes in military expenditures of pact members to changes in the military expenditures of the pact leaders demonstrates the cohesiveness and discipline of a pact and if we assume that the lines of influence extend from the pact leaders to the other members, then intra-pact relationships can be easily measured. To this end regressions between the deviations from trend of military expenditures of pact leaders (independent variable) and other pact members (dependent variables) were calculated with constant price series.[3] Three interesting results were obtained.

countries are USSR, Poland, and Czechoslovakia; and the smaller nations are Romania, Hungary, and Bulgaria. In NATO the larger countries are the USA, the UK, France, Italy, Canada, and the Netherlands; and the smaller countries are Belgium, Denmark, Norway, Greece, Portugal, and Luxembourg. Unweighted averages were calculated for each group and compared, using the standard 't test' of significance.

[1] Furthermore, some statistical problems also arise which make statistical inference difficult. In particular, variation around the trend was so wide for a number of countries that the calculated trends are not statistically significant. Thus, in the comparison of average trend values, a note of uncertainty is introduced.

[2] Unfortunately, it did not prove possible to calculate the military expenditures of all the NATO nations using the definition employed in the estimations for the WTO nations.

[3] Rather than directly regressing residuals, I used an equivalent procedure, and the following type of regressions were calculated (proof of the equivalence is given by Ragnar Frisch and Frederick V. Waugh, 'Partial Time Regressions as Compared with Individual Trends', *Econometrica*, I, Vol I, pp 387–402): $\ln M_1 = a + bT + c \ln M_2$, where M_1 are military expenditures of nations which are not pact leaders, T is time, M_2 are military expenditures of the pact leader, and

First, the correlation of residuals between the Soviet Union and its pact members are statistically significant in all cases; while between the United States and NATO countries, only five out of twelve are significant. This tells us something that most people already know; during the 1950–62 period there was more cohesiveness and unity of action among the WTO nations than among the NATO countries. This feature is partly due to the fact that certain NATO countries had military interests outside the scope of the alliance (e.g. France in Algeria) which found no parallel among the WTO members; and partly to the fact that the ability and interest of the Soviet Union and the United States in exercising influence among their respective allies were somewhat different. An analysis of the WTO since the Sino-Soviet difficulties reached the stage of open polemics might reveal a different degree of cohesion.

Second, the degree of response of pact members to changes in military expenditures of pact leaders is higher among the larger nations of each pact, than among smaller nations.[1] Although these differences are not statistically significant in either pact, the results are suggestive, especially in light of the above discussed corollary to the pact theory which can be used to predict such a phenomenon. Finally, the degree of response of pact members to changes in military expenditures of pact leaders is higher in the WTO than in the NATO, although, unfortunately, this difference is also not statistically significant.

Aside from the interaction between enemy nations, several different types of dynamic interactions for nations within defence alliances are suggested by the data. In short, WTO pact members are more disciplined than NATO pact members and it

a, b, and c are the calculated coefficients The key coefficient is c; its statistical significance denotes the 'similarity' of response, and its size designates the degree of response If it were equal to 0.5 between the USA and the UK, this would mean that for every 1 per cent increase of US military expenditures from its trends, UK expenditures would increase by 0.5 per cent. The regressions assume a particular type of causality which must be further examined.

[1] For the WTO the large nations are Poland and Czechoslovakia, while the small nations are Romania, Hungary, and Bulgaria. For the NATO, large nations are the UK, France, Italy, Canada, the Netherlands, and Belgium, while the small nations are Denmark, Norway, Greece, Portugal, and Luxembourg

appears that larger nations in defence alliances have relatively higher trends of military expenditures and seem to follow the military expenditures of the pact leaders more closely than smaller nations. The last two results can be predicted from dynamic considerations of the pact theory although, it must be added, other such predictions do not receive such confirmation. Because such calculations put a severe strain on the comparability of the data, caution must be exercised in interpreting such results.

In the economic literature there are also a number of other dynamic aspects of defence expenditures which are discussed.[1] Many of these do not seem promising and, unfortunately sufficient comparable data are not available for testing others. The results of experiments in this section, however, are sufficiently clear to demonstrate the fruitfulness of the underlying theoretical structure used to derive the hypotheses which could be empirically examined.

[1] Two problems discussed in the military literature deserve mention:

First, a number of authors have suggested that critical bottlenecks such as personnel or foreign exchange greatly affect the time pattern of defence expenditures. For instance, a decrease in size of the military age cohort or an adverse balance of trade might, in turn, act as a brake on higher military expenditures. Such hypotheses, especially in regard to military manpower, were very briefly examined for this study and were found to be unpromising. Although such bottleneck theories need further examination, I doubt whether any significant effect will be found.

Second, changes in the structure of military expenditures provide an interesting area for comparisons. The shift of military expenditures from surface weapons and manned aircraft to missile and space systems, the change of relative emphasis in procurement from airframes and other metal products to electronics, chemical propulsion, and other complex subsystems, and the increasing importance of military R and D affect not only the structure of military expenditures but the absolute amount as well. Unfortunately, comparative data are not sufficiently available for an analysis to be made at this time, although interesting aspects of this problem are discussed by Murray L. Weidenbaum, 'Problems of Adjustment for Defense Industries', in Emile Benoit and Kenneth E. Boulding, eds., *Disarmament and the Economy* (New York, 1963), pp. 66–89; and 'The Impact of Military Procurement on American Industry', in Jacob A. Stockfisch, ed., *Planning and Forecasting in the Defense Industries* (Belmont, Calif., 1962), pp. 135–75. From a much different viewpoint many insights can also be gained from Merton J. Peck and Frederic M. Scherer, *The Weapons Acquisition Process: An Economic Analysis* (Boston, 1962), esp. pp. 107–10.

E. SUBSTITUTION BETWEEN DEFENCE AND CIVILIAN EXPENDITURES

In economies with full employment, changes in the amounts of resources devoted to defence expenditures must be reflected by reverse changes in the amount of resources devoted to other sectors. Exploration of the substitution relations between defence and civilian expenditures yields, of course, useful information about the resolution of classical guns-vs.-butter dilemma. Furthermore, in the context of defence vs. civilian public consumption expenditures, such an analysis also gives important clues about the degree to which public consumption expenditures are limited by taxation restraints.

It has been pointed out that among economically developed nations in the early 1960s, the ratio of defence expenditures to the GNP (D/Y) and the ratio of investment to the GNP are inversely related to each other and that this suggests that defence and investment expenditures are substitutes for each other.[1] In trying to replicate this result for the OECD nations in 1956 and 1962, regressions of the following type were calculated: $\ln X/Y = a+b \ln (D/Y)$, where X/Y is the ratio of the investigated 'other sector' to the gross national product, and a and b are the calculated regression coefficients. If there is substitution between defence expenditures and the expenditures of the sector under examination, then coefficient b should be negative.[2]

In West Europe in 1962 statistically significant (0·05 level) substitution relations with defence exist only for investment (gross fixed investment plus inventories), a result that confirms the above mentioned effects. In 1956, however, such substitution relations with defence do not occur for investment or, for that matter, private consumption, but rather for current government civilian expenditures, including transfers. In order to explore this matter further and to use the data for the fourteen

---

[1] I would like to thank Richard Zeckhouser for showing me his unpublished paper 'Defense Spending, Capital Formation, and Economic Growth', which greatly helped me to clarify my ideas on this problem of substitution.

[2] This assumes that there was no Keynesian type unemployment, an assumption which underlies most of the other statistical exercises carried out in this section as well. With the exception of the United States, such unemployment was extremely low or nonexistent in all the countries under examination.

sample nations of this study, cross-section regressions of the following form were calculated: $\ln N/Y = a+b \ln D/Y$, where $N =$ non-military budgetary expenditure and where a and b are the calculated coefficients. Again substitution is demonstrated by a negative 'b'. Unfortunately, no statistically significant substitution relations could be found for either 1956 or 1962. More sophisticated experiments also lead to the same conclusions.

These results can be interpreted in two different ways. Either they suggest that the nature of the substitution relations changed between the two years or else they mean that the mechanisms of substitution are different among countries, so that cross-section analyses are not a useful method of exploring such relations. There are cogent reasons for accepting the latter explanation and it seems more useful to investigate such substitution relation for each individual country on a time-series basis.

For the time-series analysis we must distinguish between long- and short-run substitution relations. Short-run substitution relations are those which occur annually. Thus changes in defence expenditures may affect consumption in one year and investment in the next. Long-run substitution relations refer to trends in the relative shares over time; thus the share of defence expenditures in the GNP may decrease over time, while the share of education expenditures may rise. It must be emphasized that the short- and long-run substitution relations can be between different sectors. Because of the unavailability of adequate constant price data of different end-use sectors for the WTO nations, attention can be paid only to short-run substitution relations.

Investigating substitution relations with the formula used in the cross-section analysis described above raises a number of technical statistical problems, which make it worthwhile to search for an alternative formulation. One sensitive technique is to remove the time trend of the variables under examination and to regress the residuals, a procedure employed in the analysis of the interrelations of Soviet and US defence expenditures.[1]

[1] For the actual statistical work an equivalent formulation (used also in the determination of the interrelations of military expenditures among pact members) was employed.

This type of specification has a number of advantages, other than ease in calculation. Although it is desirable to make such calculations using fixed price data, substitution relations can also be determined using current price data if price changes in the two aggregates are linearly related to each other, an assumption that seems reasonable in most cases. Since certain types of fixed prices data are not available, this is an important consideration. Furthermore, although it is desirable to use the same type of series for the calculation of incidence in all countries, this is not completely necessary if the available series and the desired series are linearly related. Thus, while series for investment expenditures using a common definition are not available for all countries, we can nevertheless safely assume that the pattern of incidence of defence expenditures is the same for gross investment as it is for investment excluding depreciation. The specific definitions used in the calculations are noted below.

Two types of substitution analyses are carried out on the time-series data. First, the substitution of defence expenditures on non-military public consumption expenditures of the sample nations is examined. The data are taken from the current price estimates. Then, the substitution relations between defence expenditures on GNP end-use aggregates are explored. In this case constant price data are used for market economies and current price data are used for the centralized economies, since constant price data for all nations are not available on an end-use basis.[1]

For the various sample nations, defence expenditures do not have a statistically significant substitution relationship with non-military budgetary expenditures in any country, a result that appears paradoxical in the light of the well-known fall of civilian governmental expenditures during wartime as military

[1] For the market economies, data from OECD, *Statistics of National Accounts, 1950–1961, op. cit.*, and *General Statistics*, January 1965, and, for special cases, other issues of *General Statistics* were used. For the centralized countries, national statistics on net material product and accumulation were used in conjunction with my own estimates for defence and, for several years in several countries, my own estimates of net material product and accumulation. This meant that governmental civil expenditure was combined with private material consumption data.

expenditures rise, and the reverse of this movement at the end of the war. Several explanations of the empirical results seem most likely. Although the period under examination (1950–62) was politically tense, only minor wars occurred; certainly the mobilization accompanying the Korean crisis was quite mild in comparison to mobilization during World War II. Furthermore, many government expenditures programmes are contractual (e.g. social insurance payments), based on need for which the military situation has no relevance (e.g. primary education), or difficult to change in the short run so that incidence pattern would appear. Finally, although changes in defence expenditures might have had significant substitution relationships on non-defence public consumption during certain periods (e.g. the early 1950s) the situation might have changed during the latter 1950s and early 1960s, when defence expenditures were relatively much less important and changes in these expenditures were of much smaller magnitude, so that the results in the earlier period would be swamped.[1]

These results have certain implications for questions concerning the degree to which government revenues act as a restraint on public consumption expenditures. If tax rates remain the same, if defence expenditures increase, and if government revenues restrain government expenditures, then a substitution of defence for civilian public consumption expenditures would appear. Although the empirical analysis does not reveal any such substitution pattern for the sample nations, we cannot immediately conclude that state revenues no longer acted as a restraint on public consumption expenditures, since changes in government revenues in certain patterns could also lead to such empirical results.[2] But these revenue patterns also do not occur. Thus, although tax revenues may have once acted to restrain government expenditures in previous eras, for the time period under examination this revenue restraint did

---

[1] In the mid-1960s there might have been a certain substitution of civilian for military expenditures in the United States, owing to the rapid increase of military expenditures related to the Vietnam hostilities.

[2] For instance, tax revenues could rise and fall such that any change in the level of military expenditures is completely covered. A preliminary investigation of tax revenues did not, however, reveal such patterns and the matter did not seem worthwhile to pursue empirically any further.

not seem operative to an extent detectable through aggregative analysis.[1]

Investigation of substitution relations between defence expenditures and GNP aggregates such as private consumption, domestic investment, domestic plus foreign investment, and current civilian governmental expenditures leads to extremely interesting results. Among market economies in countries such as Austria, Denmark, Ireland, the Netherlands, or Norway, where defence expenditures are a relatively small proportion of the GNP, there are no statistically significant substitution relations between defence and any of the GNP end-use aggregates. Here changes in defence expenditures are of relatively small magnitude and are absorbed in different sectors in different periods, so that no consistent substitution pattern can be found. In countries where defence expenditures are relatively more important, such as Canada, Greece, West Germany, the UK, and the USA,[2] defence expenditures have a statistically significant substitution relationship with current governmental civilian expenditures (*excluding* transfers) although in almost every case the elasticity of substitution (the percentage change in governmental civilian expenditures accompanying a 1 per cent change in defence expenditures) is less than 0·1 per cent. This means that once transfer payments are removed, defence expenditures do have a significant substitution relationship with other types of government expenditures, although the magnitude of this substitution is very small. It is impossible to generalize about the results of the substitution experiments on other GNP end-use aggregates. In some countries, such as Greece or Canada, there is no statistically significant substitution relationship with any other sector. In some countries, such as the United States, there is a statistically significant substitution only with domestic investment, while in other countries such as France and West Germany this substitution relationship appears between defence and foreign investment. Finally, in a third group of countries, such as West Germany

---

[1] Of course, an increase in defence expenditures might bring about an attempt to reduce civilian public consumption expenditures, so that a subjective restraint might occur. The data do not reveal that such subjective restraints were very important in determining actual expenditures, however.

[2] France is an exception to this generalization.

and the United Kingdom, there is a statistically significant substitution relation between defence and personal consumption.

These mixed results have several important implications. First, market economies do not respond in any standard way to changes in defence expenditures, and, in order to predict what the response might be, attention must be paid to the individual features of each economy. In addition, the substitution patterns appear to remain relatively constant in some countries while changing considerably over time in other countries, so that any predictions about substitution must take into account the time period as well.

For the centralized economies, somewhat different results are obtained. With the exception of Czechoslovakia and the Soviet Union, no statistically significant pattern of substitution between defence expenditures and other major GNP end-use aggregates could be found.[1] In several of these countries the changes in magnitude of defence expenditures are quite small and are absorbed by different sectors at different times. For other countries the pattern of substitution has changed: in the early 1950s there were substitution relations between defence and consumption, while after destalinization, very mixed policies of substitution were introduced.[2] In Czechoslovakia there is a statistically significant substitution relationship between defence and total consumption (private consumption plus current civilian governmental expenditures). In the Soviet Union, for which data on all GNP aggregates are readily available,[3] defence expenditures are found to have statistically significant substitution relationships only with private consumption. This latter result is not unexpected because of the constantly reiterated Soviet statement of their desire to keep the ratio of investment to the net material product relatively constant.

This brief examination of substitution between defence and

[1] Romania is omitted from the analysis because of uncertainties surrounding the estimation of such GNP aggregates.

[2] This can be seen from a year-by-year comparison of substitution relations.

[3] Nimitz, *op. cit.*, and Abraham S. Becker, *Soviet National Income and Product, 1958–1962*, RAND Corporation memorandum RM-4294-PR (Santa Monica, June 1965).

other expenditures shows that few consistent patterns can be found for all nations with the same economic system. With regard to civilian public consumption expenditures, a certain substitution between defence appears if transfer expenditures are omitted; if such transfers are included, no substitution relations can be found for the sample nations. The substitution patterns between defence and other GNP aggregates are quite varied.

These few remarks and experiments do not, of course, exhaust the topic of substitution relations. The exact mechanism of such substitution, the existence of substitution with less-aggregative end-use sectors (e.g. investment for civilian production rather than total investment) and possible substitution relations between military expenditures and sector-of-origin GNP aggregates (e.g. industrial or agricultural production) await future investigation.

F. SUMMARY AND CONCLUSIONS

Although many more questions are raised in this chapter than are answered, a number of tentative conclusions can nevertheless be made.

In both the NATO and the WTO at a single point in time, the ratios of military expenditures to the GNP are related to the absolute values of the gross national product. In addition, the ratio of military personnel to the population is related to the total population. These two conclusions can be predicted from a theoretical model of military pacts. The major determinants of the non-personnel expenditures per military person are GNP *per capita* and the role of the country in its military bloc. In all of these cross-section analyses, the economic system does not appear to play a significant role.

Of the dynamic behaviour of defence expenditures in the Soviet Union and the United States, the discovered inter-relations between the two series and the hypothesized response to a common set of political circumstances is most striking. Within each pact the expenditures of the pact leader seem an important determinant for military expenditures of the other nations, although this phenomenon is more important in

Eastern Europe. From the pact theory certain differential behaviour of large and small nations can be predicted and also partially confirmed in the empirical investigation.

Substitution relationships between defence and total civilian public consumption expenditures are not statistically significant. If transfer expenditures are excluded, a significant but small substitution relationship can be seen. These results are important, not only in their own right, but because they suggest that in the post-war period public revenues no longer act as an important restraint on public expenditures to an extent sufficient to be revealed through aggregative analysis.

Although this investigation has been conducted primarily with the tools of economics, this has not meant that emphasis was placed solely on economic factors. Indeed, the entire examination of the interrelations between military expenditures of opposing nations is predicated on the hypothesis that the primary causes are political; and, in other parts of the study, political factors are explicitly brought into the discussion. Although the influence of institutional elements in the defence decision-making process are relatively neglected in the discussion for the sake of greater generality, the importance of such factors is recognized, especially in the mechanisms that are discovered through the quantitative analysis. It must be noted that through use of such quantitative techniques, particularly in a comparative framework, we can avoid some of the errors that have been made by examining the decision-making process for military expenditures of a single nation alone (e.g. the 'residual theory' of military expenditures mentioned above). Resolution of a great many issues concerning military expenditures is impossible without better data and more information; nevertheless, a number of important insights can be gained with even the limited information at hand.

Chapter IV

PUBLIC CONSUMPTION EXPENDITURES FOR WELFARE AND HEALTH

A. Introduction
B. Public Consumption Expenditures for Welfare
   1. *Demand Factors*
   2. *Supply Factors*
   3. *Empirical Relationships Between Public and Private Welfare Expenditures*
   4. *Determinants of Public Consumption Expenditures for Welfare*
   5. *A Brief Summary*
C. Public Consumption Expenditures for Health
   1. *Demand Factors*
   2. *Supply Factors*
   3. *Empirical Relationships Between Public and Private Health Expenditures*
   4. *Determinants of Public Consumption Expenditures for Health*
   5. *A Brief Summary*
D. Other Aspects of Welfare and Health Expenditures
   1. *Determinants of the Establishment of Social Insurance Systems*
   2. *Substitutions and Complementarities Between Welfare and Health Expenditures*
   3. *Centralization*
E. Summary and Conclusions

A. INTRODUCTION

Public consumption expenditures on health and welfare constitute the core of the 'welfare state', a subject on which political progressives in the nineteenth and twentieth centuries part company. Almost every economically developed country in the world has extensive public pension, welfare, and health programmes and reflecting this state of affairs the United Nations in its Universal Declaration of Human Rights (1948) proclaimed:

'Everyone has the right . . . to security in the case of unemployment, sickness, disability, widowhood, old age, or other lack of livelihood in circumstances beyond his control . . .'[1]

On the other hand, extreme disapproval of such sentiments by liberals (in the European sense of the word) can be easily found in the contemporary political-economic literature, e.g.:

'In democracies, the welfare state is the beginning and the police state is the end. The two merge sooner or later in all experience, and for obvious reasons . . . all modern dictators—communist, fascist, or disguised—have at least one thing in common. They all believe in social security.'[2]

The scholarly literature on such welfare state expenditures seems characterized by three major features. First, evaluation of the relative importance among nations of the magnitudes of such expenditures is still in the beginning stages. Although considerable progress has been made in collecting and presenting comparable information for a number of countries,[3] few extensive analyses of such data have been undertaken.

Second, substitution relations between public and private health and welfare expenditures constitute a virtually unexplored area and provide numerous points of disagreement in interpreting the available data on public expenditures. Two alternatives are open: On the one hand, it can be argued that it is impossible to discuss jointly public and private expenditures for health or welfare because the causal factors are so different. And, since data on private expenditures are so difficult to obtain, primary attention should be exclusively paid to public expenditures.[4] On the other hand, one can attempt, in a more or less primitive fashion, to look at public and private expenditures together, at

[1] Royal Institute of International Affairs, *Documents on International Affairs, 1947–1948* (London, 1952), pp. 855 ff.

[2] Melchior Palyi, *Compulsory Medical Care and the Welfare State* (Chicago, 1949), pp. 13, 18.

[3] E.g. such publications of the International Labour Office as: *The Cost of Social Security* (Geneva, various years), or *The Cost of Medical Care* (Geneva, 1959).

[4] Essentially this is the position of John Vaizey, 'The Theory of Social Expenditure', *Administration* (Dublin), V, 4/1957–58, pp. 77–88.

E

the cost of analysing in greater depth the public expenditures. In this chapter I lean toward the latter alternative.

Finally, a number of judgments have been made about the relative effectiveness of public programmes in different countries (especially between socialist and capitalist nations) on very inadequate factual and theoretical bases. For arriving at more reasoned judgments we need not only to have highly detailed data, but also to solve a number of difficult conceptual and theoretical problems concerning the criteria for evaluation.[1,2] Since the primary focus of this study is on other aspects of public consumption expenditures, such problems must be left for others.

From the empirical results in this chapter I draw several useful conclusions. First, substitution relations between public and private expenditures are important and must be taken into account. Second, the cross-section and time-series determinants are very different. At a single point in time the key variable affecting public consumption expenditures on health and welfare is the length of operation of the social insurance institutions; over time, other factors appear more influential. In neither case, however, does the economic systems variable appear to play an explanatory role. Finally, political and institutional factors seem most relevant in understanding the centralization of these public consumption expenditures for welfare

[1] Such difficulties may be seen in trying to compare the relative 'adequacy' of old-age pensions in the USA and USSR. One basic piece of information is that for given personal income levels, the pension rates as a percentage of total income received when working are slightly higher in the USA than the USSR. (Such data are presented by Robert J. Myers, 'Economic Security in the Soviet Union', *Transactions of the Society of Actuaries*, XI, Meeting 31, November 1963, pp. 723–45). But as such rates decrease with rising income levels in both countries and since the average income in the USSR is considerably lower than in the USA, the aggregative ratio of pensions to earnings is higher in the former country. Moreover, in the USSR urban coverage seems more complete than in the USA; but, on the other hand, overall coverage is considerably greater in the USA, at least during the period under examination.

[2] One example of such methodological difficulties may be seen in a report of the United Nations Research Institute for Social Development [*Aspects of Social and Economic Growth* (Geneva, October 1965)] in which the authors assert that a relatively high degree of social expenditures somehow brings about a higher rate of growth because in a cross-country analysis, the two factors are correlated. Although this assertion may well be true, the failure to present any explanation of the mechanism involved vitiates the analysis.

and health. I discuss the two expenditures separately, since certain causal factors influencing their behaviour are different. As public consumption expenditures for welfare are about three times greater in magnitude than public consumption for health in most countries, they are analysed first.

B. PUBLIC CONSUMPTION EXPENDITURES FOR WELFARE

Public consumption expenditures on welfare are defined to include all assistance payments, public pensions, public income-support programmes, and social insurance payments, excluding those for medical care. Payments by insurance schemes required by law but carried by private insurance companies are included as public consumption whenever possible. For the sake of comparability, pensions and assistance payments given by public-owned enterprises but financed by sales revenues are excluded. Price supports, rent subsidies,[1] payments for occupational safety measures, tax favours, and non-monetary welfare measures[2] are also excluded. Finally, expenditures for spiritual welfare are excluded, although it is possible that these may be quite similar among nations. For instance, in relation to the population, the number of clergymen in the United States is practically the same as the number of full-time Communist Party officials in the Soviet Union.[3]

The welfare expenditures discussed in this section are used to cover two basic human needs. First, there is the need for con-

[1] Both price supports and rent subsidies are excluded for two reasons. First the incidence of these expenditures is very uncertain. Second, comparable data are not available and could be estimated only with enormous effort. The magnitudes of rent subsidies in the centralized economies are discussed in Appendix D–14.

[2] Such privileges include special rights to housing or education. The East Germans have made an important innovation in this area by granting the elderly permission to travel or migrate freely to West Germany, an opportunity that is denied other population groups.

[3] In the United States about 0·1 per cent of the population were clergymen in 1960 [us Bureau of the Census, *Statistical Abstract of the US, 1966* (Washington, DC, 1966), p. 232]; in the Soviet Union the average number of full-time Communist Party officials between 1956 and 1961 was roughly similar (data from George Fischer, 'The Number of Soviet Party Executives: A Research Note', *Soviet Studies*, XVI, January 1965, pp. 330–33).

tinuity of family expenditures, which can be affected by such long-range factors as old age, disability or death of the bread-winner; or by such short run factors as temporary unemployment or illness. Second, there is the need for adequate family expenditures which can be influenced by such factors as the size of the family and its geographical location.

These two welfare needs can be met through a variety of public and private arrangements. Through the private sector one can finance such wants from personal savings, private insurance arrangements, or philanthropic efforts. Or the government can pass laws to make employers liable to certain welfare claims by employees, or to force the employers to take out certain types of group insurance or to compel them to set up certain types of providence funds, etc. Although statistical materials concerning such 'nonstatutory social insurance measures' are scanty, scattered evidence suggests that such measures have some quantitative importance in a number of countries.[1]

Before turning to the separate supply and demand factors underlying public consumption expenditures for welfare, two important aspects of these expenditures must be emphasized.

First, the major motivating factors behind the public financing of welfare expenditures do not seem related to consumption externalities or public-good properties, an observation which seems intuitively clear when examining old-age pensions, which constitute the bulk of all welfare expenditures.[2] In contrast to the examination of military expenditures in the previous chapter, such public-good properties cannot be used with profit in the analysis.

Second, as old-age pensions are quantitatively so important, it is imperative to discuss one possible determinant of such

[1] E.g. see 'The Costs of Non-Statutory Social Security Schemes', *International Labour Review*, LXXVIII, October 1958, pp. 388–403. One type of 'non-statutory' system that is particularly difficult to analyse quantitatively is a children's allowance scheme which is administered by enterprises following state guide-lines. Although data on government grants to such enterprises are available, adequate information on gross amounts dispersed are almost impossible to locate.

[2] This is quantitatively discussed in Appendix E-9.

expenditures which would affect both the demand and supply side together—the length of time in which the social insurance programmes for old-age pensions have been in operation. On the demand side, this time factor reflects two phenomena: the basic climate of opinion in nations for governmental intervention in the welfare field; and the desire to extend such programmes to increasingly broad groups of the population. The importance of this latter factor lies in the fact that most social insurance welfare programmes started on relatively small scales with relatively low benefits. However, over the years such programmes have been incrementally broadened in coverage, and the benefits have been extended.[1] On the supply side this time-period factor can be interpreted as reflecting the institutional momentum which appears to build up in certain public programmes or, in the terminology of American conservatives, 'creeping socialism'. Although the mechanism by which such momentum is generated is far from clear, certain aspects of the situation have been discussed in the general analysis of Parkinson's First Law.[2]

One implication of this time-period factor is that the ratios of public consumption expenditures for welfare to the GNP would not be related to the *per capita* GNP on a cross-section basis, but very strongly (and positively) in the time-series. And from such considerations, it also seems likely (but not conclusive) that the ratio of private to total welfare expenditures would decrease in the years following the introduction of a social insurance system.

Of course, use of this time-period factor (which is really a political variable) pushes one empirical question back into time: what factors underlie the establishment of social insurance programmes in the first place. This interesting problem is discussed briefly in Section D below.

---

[1] A number of economists (e.g. Süphan Andic and Jindřich Veverka, 'The Growth of Government Expenditures in Germany since the Unification', *Finanzarchiv*, *NF*, XXIII, January 1964, pp. 169–278) have suggested that such changes are used as tools to obtain votes and that the time pattern of such expenditures is tied to elections. Although exploration of the exact mechanism would take us too far afield, it is worth noting that this hypothesis can be empirically tested.

[2] C. Northcote Parkinson, *Parkinson's Law* (Boston, 1957).

1. DEMAND FACTORS

The effect of *per capita* income on welfare expenditures is mixed, and there are a number of arguments suggesting both an increasing and decreasing of welfare expenditures to the GNP as the level of economic development rises.

One reason for expecting that welfare expenditures increase in relative importance with a rising level of income is succinctly stated by John Kenneth Galbraith:

'As the real wage of the worker increases and also as employment becomes more certain, unemployment and the absence of income acquires its contrasting horror. With increasing income it also becomes possible to think of old age; the individual expects to survive, and old age without income is differentiated as it was not before, by the prospect of discomfort . . . Thus the notion, so sanctified by the conventional wisdom that the modern concern for security is the reaction to the peculiar hazards of modern economic life could scarcely be more in error. Rather, it is the result of improving fortune—of moving from a world where people had little, to one where they had much more to protect. In the first world, misfortune and suffering were endemic and unavoidable. In the second they have become episodic and avoidable. And as they became episodic and avoidable, reasonable men saw the merit of measures to avoid them and the possibilities for so doing.[1]

It must be noted that nothing in this paragraph specifically suggests that public (in contrast to total) welfare expenditures rise in relative importance.

The relationship between income *per capita* and welfare expenditures is viewed in a different way by Detlev Zöllner, who argues that the key factor in welfare expenditures in a nation is the portion of the population that is not engaged in agriculture.[2] He notes that although the agricultural workers

---

[1] John Kenneth Galbraith, *The Affluent Society* (Boston, 1958), pp. 108–09.

[2] Detlev Zöllner, *Oeffentliche Sozialleistungen und wirtschaftliche Entwicklung: Ein zeitlicher und internationaler Vergleich* (West Berlin, 1963). Zöllner actually has two theories: one for the developed West European and North American countries; one for the underdeveloped economies of Latin America, Africa, and Asia. Only the former theory is discussed above. Further, I have extended his

have considerable welfare needs, they can make certain provisions for such purposes that are non-monetary in nature and that are unavailable to those who have left the land. Further, with a rise in non-agricultural labour to total labour, public welfare expenditures should increase as a share of GNP, an hypothesis which Zöllner demonstrates with both time-series and cross-section data. Since this labour force ratio is related to the level of development, one can infer that the relative importance of welfare expenditures in the GNP probably rises with income *per capita*.

Another argument for an increasing relative importance of welfare expenditures with economic development is based on the well-documented observation that the proportion of the population over 65 increases as *per capita* income rises. This, in turn, means that the relative needs and demands for pensions and old age annuity arrangements rise with GNP *per capita* as well. Unfortunately, certain factors other than *per capita* income affect the age structure, and there are some analytic advantages of treating the age structure as an independent variable.

On the other hand, several arguments can be advanced for expecting welfare expenditures, particularly those financed publicly, to decline in relative importance.[1] First, as the level of economic development rises, the portion of population living in poverty declines, and there is therefore less relative need for transfer payments to the destitute. Unless the concept of destitution rises *pari passu* with the level of economic development (which some have argued is doubtful)[2] or unless public policy is designed to decrease continually the degree of income inequality,[3] the ratio of such welfare expenditures to the GNP should fall over time. Further, with economic development the

argument to cover all types of welfare expenditures, rather than the public welfare expenditures on which he primarily focussed. A number of objections can be raised concerning his statistical methods; in particular, his data are quite unrefined. Nevertheless, his study is provocative and has been undeservedly neglected.

[1] These arguments are made with particular emphasis by Henry Richardson, *Economic and Financial Aspects of Social Security* (Toronto, 1960), Chapter III; and Richard A. Musgrave, *Fiscal Systems* (New Haven, 1968).

[2] See esp. Vaizey, *op. cit.*

[3] As income *per capita* rises in a nation, the degree of income inequality usually decreases. For redistributional welfare expenditures to remain a constant share of GNP, a policy would have to be set to accelerate this natural equalization.

private financial sector increases in complexity and is more able to handle insurance and annuity needs of the population, so that the public welfare sector should decline in relative importance with a rising *per capita* GNP.

Underlying the argument about poverty levels is the assumption that such types of anti-poverty programmes constitute the bulk of public consumption expenditures for welfare, which, as noted above, is not the case. Further, such an argument may confuse the redistribution of individual income through time or the sharing of risk, which are obvious motives for social insurance measures, with the redistribution of income between income classes. But since most social insurance programmes are financed by payroll taxes or the equivalent, the redistribution of income between classes is not at all obvious and it seems much more reasonable to assume that the primary motive of welfare expenditures is risk-sharing.

The argument about the increasing ability of the private sector to handle private welfare needs is based on the assumption that private insurance firms avoid risk-skimming. This is a situation where competing insurance companies offer very low rates to 'low-risk' individuals and try to avoid high-risk situations. Of course, such 'experience rating' results in the most needy segment of the population being forced to pay extremely high rates, a feature which defeats the basic notion of wide-scale risk sharing. To avoid such a situation, either private insurance companies must be forced by law to insure all segments of the population or the public sector must take over a large share of the insurance function.

If I am correct that the primary purpose of public consumption on expenditures for welfare in most countries is the redistribution over time of income and the sharing of risk, rather than the redistribution of income between different income classes, then the type of economic system should make relatively little difference in the amount of such expenditures, since nations in either system face exactly the same problem. If, on the other hand, we believe that the primary (rather than secondary) aim of public consumption expenditures for welfare is to redistribute income between income classes, then it is likely that the centrally planned economies would have relatively lower public welfare expenditures, since they have considerably more policy tools with which to redistribute income (e.g. national wage and employment policies) than market economies.[1]

In regard to the relation between the level of economic development and public consumption expenditures for welfare, the arguments for a positive association of the welfare/GNP ratio and income *per capita* seem considerably stronger. It must be emphasized, however, that they are not conclusive by any means and that any prediction on this matter must be partly based on intuition.

A number of other demand factors have been adduced for explaining differences in welfare expenditures among nations. The predominance of Roman Catholics in the population is positively correlated to the importance of family allowances.[2] Participation in past wars, past currency reforms, pressures arising from changes in the class composition of the population, and other political-economic phenomena have also been suggested as factors increasing the aggregate demand for welfare expenditures.[3] Still others have advanced the hypothesis that the existence of large private savings acts to retard the growth of public welfare expenditures.[4] (It should be noted, however, that relatively small social insurance expenditures should act as a stimulus to private savings; a simultaneous equations model is therefore needed to separate the two different causal relationships.)

2. SUPPLY FACTORS

One extremely important but often neglected supply factor in welfare expenditures is that administration costs are generally much higher for private insurance companies than for public social insurance agencies. In 1962 in the United States, for instance, the ratio of administration costs to net benefits was about 20·6 per cent for the former and about 3·4 per cent for

[1] This argument is implied by Richard A. Musgrave, *op. cit.*

[2] Aaron, *op. cit.*

[3] See esp. Vaizey, *op. cit.*, and Henry Aaron, 'International Comparison of Income Maintenance Expenditures', in Otto Eckstein, ed., *Economics of Income Maintenance* (Washington, DC, 1966) for a review of this literature.

[4] See esp. Aaron, *op. cit.*

E*

the latter.[1] Such higher costs apparently exist for the Soviet individual insurance company (Gostrakh) as well.[2] In both countries these costs seem to be due primarily to selling costs and the additional expenses required to set up policies tailored to individual needs. Such a cost factor suggests that there are some cogent reasons for national decision makers to favour public over private insurance arrangements and to guide the development of insurance growth so that the public sector does not decline in relative importance.

Another supply factor that is important, at least for social insurance expenditures, is the method by which such expenditures are financed. According to a cross-section study by Henry Aaron, social insurance programmes financed from earmarked taxes are higher than those financed from general budget receipts, other things remaining equal. Unfortunately, lack of adequate data prevents testing of this factor for the sample countries.[3]

It might be argued that the method by which public consumption expenditures for welfare are distributed would also influence the volume of such expenditures. This argument, in turn, requires a brief glance at the three basic ways of administrating welfare programmes. *Social assistance* expenditures are payments (either in cash or kind) to 'needy recipients'. Such assistance is usually given only after investigation and determination of specific need and entails relatively high administration costs. Such a method of administrating might be chosen if welfare payments were to be conserved and allocated only to those with greatest need. *Social insurance* expenditures, on the other hand, are payments made to individuals who have

---

[1] The datum on private insurance companies comes from Institute of Life Insurance, *Life Insurance Fact Book 1965* (New York, 1965), p. 60, recalculating the base equal to total benefits, rather than total income. Taxes are excluded as a cost item. The datum for the Social Security Administration comes from sources cited in Appendix A–13. An interesting quantitative analysis of administration costs of a number of us public and private institutions for welfare expenditures has been made by Alfred F. Conard, *et al.*, *Automobile Accident Costs and Payments* (Ann Arbor, 1964).

[2] Robert J. Myers, 'Economic Security in the Soviet Union', *op. cit.*, p. 726.

[3] Aaron, *op. cit.* Some theoretical reasons for expecting such a result are given by James M. Buchanan, *Public Finance in Democratic Process* (Chapel Hill, 1967).

a legal right to such payments upon belonging to the insurance scheme and meeting certain relatively unambiguous qualifications (e.g. achieving a certain age or being unemployed). The benefits of such social insurance schemes are usually based on past contributions or earnings. (One exception among the sample nations is Ireland, which has followed the UK in giving quite similar payments to all recipients). *Social* or *public service* expenditures are payments for services to every member of the community falling within defined categories; such programmes are not limited to those who have joined some special insurance scheme or to those fulfilling a means test. Examples of such social service expenditures include automatic maternity grants or universal pension schemes (e.g. in Czechoslovakia). Such a method of administration might be selection if such welfare programmes were to be as extensive as possible.

On intuitive grounds one might suspect that the above three types of expenditures would be substitutes for each other, but this does not appear to be the case. Margaret Gordon has found that most of the nations with high relative (to the GNP) social insurance expenditures also tend to have high relative social assistance expenditures as well.[1] Although the distribution of welfare expenditures between the three categories may be somewhat different among nations, each type seems more suited to certain particular welfare needs, and thus they act in a complementary manner. Further, in most countries the bulk of such expenditures is channeled through social insurance institutions, so that isolating the effects of different proportions of the three types of expenditures would be quite difficult, especially with the data of the sample nations.

Much more can be said, of course, about the institutions for public consumption expenditures for welfare, but relatively few hypotheses that are testable can be derived from such information.[2] Therefore it seems more profitable to turn to other matters.

[1] Margaret S. Gordon, *The Economics of Welfare Policies* (New York, 1963), p. 20; other aspects of this are discussed by Aaron, *op. cit.* For the United States the problem is empirically analysed by Lora Collins, 'Determinants of Public Assistance Expenditures', in Eckstein, *op. cit.*

[2] A brief survey of the five major social insurance programmes in the sample countries is given in Appendix E–10.

In order to avoid interpreting data on public consumption expenditures for welfare as indicative of the 'welfare orientation' of the government, three specific phenomena must be mentioned. First, although welfare expenditures may be made to accomplish humanitarian aims, such expenditures can also be to achieve certain manipulated non-welfare ends as well. For instance, the Soviet Union has used differential benefits to workers in certain industries and to workers who have remained at one factory for specified periods of time to encourage employment in specific industries and to lower labour turnover;[1] or Poland has had a system of pensions for writers in which each writer had to make a special petition to the state for a pension, the amount of which is individually determined.[2] Second, unless welfare payments are made through a social arrangement, a certain potential discrimination exists against some groups, a feature which is the focus of considerable polemics concerning such expenditures. Proving that actual discrimination exists, however, involves determining whether there exists in the excluded group an unfairly frustrated demand for such services. Of course, this is a situation which is extremely difficult to prove, except in cases where benefits to a certain group are suddenly withdrawn without public demand for such action on the part of the group in question. Although such cases can be found for the sample nations,[3] they are quite rare; therefore, lack of coverage of certain groups for welfare expenditures cannot be interpreted as *prima facie* evidence of discrimination. Finally, welfare expenditures in a nation cannot be interpreted to reflect the relative degree of welfare among nations, because certain such expenditures may not be needed. This was pointed out almost a millenium ago by Maimonides, who noted that 'the most meritorious of all, is to anticipate charity by prevent-

[1] For the Soviet Union such measures are analysed in detail by Jack Minkoff, *The Soviet Social Insurance System since 1921*, Ph.D. dissertation, Columbia University, 1960 (Ann Arbor, University Microfilms, n.d.).

[2] Jerzy Putrament, *Trybuna Ludu*, November 21, 1965.

[3] According to the *New York Times*, August 2, 1963, the Soviet magazine *Science and Religion* announced that workers employed by churches and religious agencies, except for cleaners and watchmen, were withdrawn from the state pension system. Other cases of such removal from the state pension system occurred in several East European nations after the change-over to socialism, when pensions to certain groups were repudiated or withdrawn.

ing poverty . . . this is the highest step and the summit of charity's golden ladder'.[1] Consideration of the relative degree of welfare among the population of the sample nations would unfortunately lead us too far astray from the central theme of this study. It must be noted, however, that welfare expenditures designed to alleviate specific 'anti-welfare' features of certain economic systems (such as the need for unemployment compensation in capitalist economies) account for only a very small portion of total welfare expenditures in the sample nations;[2] as noted above, the bulk of welfare expenditures in most nations are for old age pensions.

3. EMPIRICAL RELATIONSHIPS BETWEEN PUBLIC AND PRIVATE WELFARE EXPENDITURES

Data on private expenditures are extremely difficult to obtain. Nevertheless, some idea about relative magnitudes can be gained from an examination of such data for the country with probably the relatively largest share of private financing of such welfare services. (See Table 4–1 on the next page.)

Although private welfare expenditures are supposed to be relatively important in the United States, they only made up 30 per cent of the total, or 2·4 per cent of GNP. The share of private to public welfare expenditures has very slowly declined in the USA since 1930,[3] but it seems extremely likely that such private expenditures were always a very small proportion of the GNP. Furthermore, in the other sample nations it is highly probable that private welfare expenditures are considerably less than 2 per cent of the GNP.

To what extent are the publicly financed expenditures for

---

[1] Cited by Solomon Fabricant, 'An Economist's View of Philanthropy', in Frank R. Dickenson, ed., *Philanthropy and Public Policy* (New York, 1962).

[2] Unemployment is not just a problem of capitalism. Several socialist nations including Poland and Yugoslavia have had considerable problems in this area and both nations alleviated such difficulties by exporting surplus workers to capitalist nations such as West Germany. At one time in the mid-1950s Bulgaria also exported workers, but only to other socialist nations. East Germany and Hungary feel the need for systems of unemployment compensation. Certain problems about comparing unemployment in different nations are discussed briefly in my 'Comparing Economic Systems: A Review Article', *Soviet Studies*, January 1967.

[3] J. Frederic Dewhurst, *et al.*, *America's Needs and Resources: A New Survey* (New York, 1955), p. 432.

TABLE 4–1

Total Current Public and Private Welfare Expenditures in the USA in 1957–58[1]

	Percentage of factor price GNP	Percentage of total
Public consumption	5·73	70
Private		
Insurance and enterprise payments for short-term income losses	0·48	6
Insurance and private enterprise payments for pensions	1·68	21
Philanthropy	0·24	3
Total	8·14	100

welfare encroaching upon the privately financed expenditures? In the following section I present evidence for the USA that the ratio of public consumption expenditures for welfare to the GNP is quite low, but that this ratio is increasing at a very fast rate over time. Since the ratio of total welfare expenditures to the GNP is rising and the share of privately financed welfare expenditures in the total is very slowly declining, this suggests that a large part of the growth of public expenditures can be traced to the filling of unmet welfare needs, rather than en-croachment on the private sector. This problem of encroach-ment can be explored in a different way by looking at the sub-stitution relations between public and private welfare expendi-tures with which to answer the following question: if public consumption expenditures were cut, how many welfare needs financed by these funds would be unmet?

On an international level this substitution relation can be quantitatively examined by analysing the relative amounts of private life insurance *vis-à-vis* old age pensions from the social insurance system. As social insurance arrangements are infrequently changed, it seems likely that private insurance buyers adjust to the social insurance payments, rather than the reverse. It is therefore possible to analyse such substitution effects with a simple single equation model. The following cross-

[1] Statistical sources and methods are given in Appendix D–8.

section regression calculation is for sixteen West European and North American nations for 1960.[1]

$$\ln (I/Y) = -10\cdot19 + 1\cdot01^* \ln (Y/P) - 0\cdot98^* \ln (S/Y)$$
$$(0\cdot32) \qquad\qquad (0\cdot30)$$

$$R^2 = 0\cdot63^*$$

where I = private life insurance in force,
   Y = GNP
   P = population
   S = public social insurance expenditures for old age, invalidism, and death.

Two important conclusions can be drawn from this regression calculation. First, the share of private insurance in the GNP is significantly and positively related with *per capita* GNP a phenomenon which gives empirical support to Galbraith's analysis of needs for security which are cited above. Second, the relative amount of private life insurance is significantly and inversely related to the relative amount of social insurance expenditures for the same purpose.[2] In other words, there appears to be a substitution effect of private for public welfare expenditures. Furthermore, the elasticity of substitution is about $1\cdot0$ (i.e. for every $1\cdot0$ per cent change in social insurance expenditures, private insurance expenditures change in the opposite direction by $1\cdot0$ per cent). Because of the nature of the data for private life insurance, however, this calculated elasticity of substitution must be regarded only as a first approximation. More refined investigation of such substitution relationships using US data for different income groups and areas raises a

[1] Total life insurance in force, rather than annual life insurance benefits, are used because data on the latter could not be located. In the regression standard errors are placed below the coefficients in parentheses, and asterisks denote coefficients that are significantly ($0\cdot05$ level) greater than zero. The data on private life insurance come from the Institute of Life Insurance, *op. cit.*; social insurance expenditures come from the International Labour Office, *The Cost of Social Security*, 1958–60 (Geneva, 1964); and sources for GNP data are given in Appendix B.

[2] With a smaller sample Aaron, *op. cit.*, also finds an inverse relation between statutory and non-statutory social insurance arrangements.

number of technical problems which prevent comparisons from being made.[1]

Even though there is seldom substitution of private for public welfare expenditures, various income groups are quite differently affected if the financing of these expenditures is primarily in either the public or the private sectors. For instance, under a completely private old-age insurance system, certain poorer groups of the population might not have any insurance at all, especially because of the higher risk associated with these groups and the higher administration costs of reaching them. Under a completely public system such risk-skimming might not exist.

While the discussion on social and private insurance has been in the context of market economies, it should not be thought that such considerations are inapplicable for the centralized economies. Each of these nations has a state insurance company from which it is possible to buy individual insurance to supplement the state social security programmes. Although little information is available about such organizations,[2] we know that sizeable portions of the population of these countries— ranging up to 50 per cent in East Germany—have such policies.[3] The lack of detailed information about such insurance

[1] A number of experiments were performed on us states using data from public and private insurance in order to test such substitution relations in a more refined way. Difficulties arose in predicting total social insurance payments by state, owing to the fact that people receiving benefits often move to different states after retirement and because there are certain upper limits on benefits from social security that are difficult to catch in the regression equations. Similar difficulties hindered the analysis of private insurance benefits. Although there appeared to be a complementarity, rather than a substitution, between public and private insurance benefits, the results seemed very unsatisfactory. Micro-economic data on insurance expenditures per family [Survey Research Center, Institute for Social Research, University of Michigan, *Life Insurance 1954* (Ann Arbor: n.d.)] show some puzzling nonlinear relations which provide further grounds for distrusting the results obtained from linear statistical models

[2] A few scattered articles on the subject are available, e.g. Robert J. Myers, 'Voluntary Insurance in the ussr', *Eastern Underwriter*, May 22, 1959.

[3] Data from Staatliche Zentralverwaltung fuer Statistik, *Statistisches Jahrbuch der deutschen demokratischen Republik 1965* (East Berlin, 1965), p. 416. The statistical yearbooks of most of the centralized economies have a brief section on statistics about individual life insurance policies. Since the data are usually presented on a highly aggregated level—without any separation between individual and group life insurance policies, etc.—interpretation is quite difficult.

systems precludes further analysis of such organizations at this time.

4. DETERMINANTS OF PUBLIC CONSUMPTION EXPENDITURES FOR WELFARE

The cross-section data for the sample countries show an extremely varied picture.

TABLE 4–2

Ratios of Public Consumption Expenditures for Welfare to the Factor Price GNPs in 1956 and 1962

Country	1956	1962	Country	1956	1962
USA	4·8%	6·7%	Czechoslovakia	11·9%	13·7%
West Germany	13·5	15·0	East Germany	10·7	13·1
Austria	15·6	17·8	USSR	6·4	8·1
Ireland	9·5	7·6	Hungary	5·6	5·4
Italy	10·7	11·7	Poland	6·5	6·6
Greece	5·9	8·1	Romania	3·8	5·6
Yugoslavia	7·4	7·7	Bulgaria	5·5	6·2

The unweighed average ratios are higher in the market than centralized nations in both years, but the differences between the two systems are not statistically significant. Although interpretation of such results is complicated by the 'factor-income-effect', the standard deviations of the ratios in both groups of nations are so high that, even if more comparable GNP data were available, the same conclusion would probably be reached.[2]

In the regression analysis the calculated coefficient of the

---

[1] Public consumption data come from Appendix A; factor price GNP data from Appendix B. Data for Hungary are for 1955 and 1962.

[2] Evaluating the factor income effect is difficult since the goods and services for which such welfare expenditures are made are unknown. Two important statistical biases must be considered. On the one hand, sales taxes on consumer goods are much higher in the centrally planned than market economies so that the actual resources commanded by welfare expenditures in relation to the GNP is smaller than the fraction in Table 4–2. On the other hand, a large portion of such welfare expenditures is used for food. As agricultural products may be relatively under-priced because of the exclusion of land rents in price calculations, there may be a downward bias to the ratios in Table 4–2. Since the two biases work in opposite directions and their relative strengths are not known, no conclusions can be drawn except that the net effect is probably quite small.

variable representing economic system is also not statistically significant. Thus the hypothesis presented in previous pages of the unimportance of economic system as a determinant of public consumption expenditures for welfare seems confirmed.[1]

The level of economic development plays a peculiar role as a determinant of the welfare expenditures. For the sample nations, all of which have semi- or fully-developed economies, *per capita* GNP is not significantly related to the ratio of public consumption expenditures for welfare to the GNP.[2] For cross-section samples embracing economies over the entire range of economic development, however, it is clear that there is an important positive relation between *per capita* GNP and the relative importance of state welfare expenditures.[3] For long-period time-series analysis the same phenomenon can be observed. All of this suggests that the level of economic development is an underlying but not an immediate causal determinant of such expenditures.

Turning to the hypothesis linking public consumption welfare expenditures to the length of operation of the social insurance system, we obtain more encouraging results:[4]

For 1956 $\ln W = -2\cdot62 + 0\cdot66^* \ln T$ $R^2 = 0\cdot41^*$
$$(0\cdot23)$$

For 1962 $\ln W = -2\cdot85 + 0\cdot73^* \ln T$ $R^2 = 0\cdot42^*$
$$(0\cdot24)$$

[1] Phillips Cutright, 'Political Structure, Economic Development, and National Social Security Programs', *American Journal of Sociology*, LXX, March 1965, pp. 537–51, also reaches a similar conclusion in regard to political structure using a much different type of analysis.

[2] As noted in the time-series analysis, constant price income elasticities are quite similar to current price elasticities so that the above results would probably hold if all expenditures were calculated in a common currency. See also ftn. 2, p. 145.

[3] This relation can be seen especially in the studies by Zöllner, *op. cit.* and Cutright, *op. cit.* It must be noted that both of these studies cover only social insurance programmes. Since such expenditures constitute the bulk of total public consumption expenditures for welfare, it seems safe to generalize.

[4] Standard errors are placed in parentheses below the coefficients; an asterisk denotes statistical significance at the $0\cdot05$ level. Information on founding dates of social insurance systems for old age pensions comes from US Department of Health, Education, and Welfare, Social Security Administration, *Social Security Programs Throughout the World*, 1964 (Washington, DC, 1964).

where W = ratio of public consumption expenditures for welfare to the factor price GNP.

T = number of years of operation of the social insurance system for old age pensions.

For both years relative public consumption expenditures for welfare are significantly and directly related to the length of operation of the social insurance expenditures for old age pensions.[1] As noted in the theoretical discussion, this variable has implications for both the demand and the supply side.

However, this time-period variable is not the only factor that can be used to explain the data in Table 4–2. Variables representing the age structure of the population (population over 65 as a share of total population; and population over 65 as a ratio of the employed labour force)[2] are also significantly and directly associated with the ratios of public consumption expenditures for welfare to the GNP.

Since we have two different explanations for the data, both of which have theoretical justification, additional information is necessary to make the proper choice of determinants, and two additional factors seem particularly relevant. First, if a multiple regression is calculated using both the time-factor and the pupulation structure variables, only the coefficient for the former variable is statistically significant. Second, as noted in Section D of this chapter, the age structure of the population is not associated with the establishment of social insurance systems for old age pensions.

Thus it seems most probable that the primary determinant of the ratios of public consumption expenditures for welfare to the GNP at a single point in time is the length of time that the social insurance system for old age pensions has been in operation. Although the age structure of the population is undoubtedly an important factor underlying the demand for welfare expenditures, its role as a determinant of welfare expenditures seems secondary. This conclusion is also reached by Aaron, who uses

---

[1] From much different samples Aaron, *op. cit.*, and Gordon, *op. cit.*, also obtain similar results.

[2] Labour force and population data come from sources cited in Appendices D–1 and D–2.

a much different sample and somewhat different method of analysis as well.[1]

There are, of course, a number of variables of tertiary importance which can be used to explain certain special aspects of public consumption expenditures for welfare. Because of the relatively small size of the sample, I do not feel that much could be gained by presenting the results of further empirical exploration of such potential determinants.[2]

Other facets of the determinants of public consumption expenditures for welfare can be viewed from time-series analyses. The results of ratio-income-elasticity calculations are given in Table 4–3 below.

TABLE 4–3

Time-Series Behaviour of Public Consumption Expenditures for Welfare, 1950 through 1962[3]

Country	Ratio-income-elasticity	Country	Ratio-income-elasticity
USA	+2·61*	Czechoslovakia	+0·22
West Germany	+0·14	East Germany	+0·10
Austria	+0·33*	USSR	+0·50*
Ireland	−1·29*	Hungary	+0·96*
Italy	+0·77*	Poland	+0·45*
Greece	+0·24	Romania	+1·28*
Yugoslavia	−0·24	Bulgaria	+0·48*

The unweighted average ratio-income-elasticity is equal to +0·46, which means that the ratio of public consumption expenditures for welfare to the GNP increases quite rapidly as GNP *per capita* increases. But the variations among the sample nations of these elasticities are quite great.[4] Since the current

[1] Aaron, *op. cit.*

[2] I carried out a number of experiments with the data from the sample nations to satisfy myself that the most important potential determinants were tested. Exploration of other variables are carried out by Aaron, *op. cit.*, Cutright, *op. cit.*, Gordon, *op. cit.*, and Zöllner, *op. cit.*

[3] Yugoslav expenditures cover only the period from 1952–62. Statistically significant (0·05 level) coefficients are designated with an asterisk. Data come from Appendices A and B. 'Ratio-income-elasticities' are defined in Chapter II, pp. 59ff., and in the Glossary (Appendix F.)

[4] The average ratio-income-elasticity is not significantly greater than zero, even though such elasticities are positive in twelve out of fourteen cases. Even

and constant-price ratio-income-elasticities for the market economies are about the same, conversion into constant-prices for the entire sample would not greatly change the results from the current-price data.

In the table, differences in the unweighed average ratio-income-elasticities between the nations of the two economic systems are not statistically significant. Further, no single independent variable explains the differences in such elasticities between nations.

However, if the ratio of public consumption expenditures for welfare to the GNP (in 1956) and the *per capita* income are used together as explanatory variables in the regression, both show statistically significant relation (the former, inverse; the latter, direct) with the calculated ratio-income-elasticities.[1] The former relationship means that, other things remaining the same, the higher the public welfare expenditures/GNP ratio, the lower the calculated ratio income elasticity. In other words, there appears to be a convergence of the public welfare expenditures/GNP ratio of the sample nations toward a common point. Such a convergence appears most striking in the fact that in three out of four countries where welfare expenditures are relatively highest (West Germany, East Germany, and Czechoslovakia), the time-series ratio-income-elasticities are not significantly greater than zero. The direct and significant relation between income *per capita* and the ratio-income-elasticity defies a simple interpretation. It does suggest, however, that public consumption expenditures for welfare as a ratio of GNP continues to rise as GNP *per capita* increases, a conclusion for which theoretical evidence (presented above) exists as well.

---

if Ireland (which has an apparent substitution relation between health and welfare expenditures) is omitted, this is still the case.

[1] The calculated regression is:

$$E = 0 \cdot 216 - 11 \cdot 039 * W + 0 \cdot 0011 * Y/P \qquad R^2 = 0 \cdot 59*$$
$$(3 \cdot 819) \qquad (0 \cdot 0003)$$

where E = time series ratio-income-elasticity,
W = ratio of public consumption expenditures for welfare to the GNP in 1956,
Y/P = income *per capita*.

The regression is not calculated in logarithms because some of the time-series ratio-income-elasticities are negative.

It must also be noted that the size of the coefficient linking these two economic magnitudes is very small, so that this relationship appears to be of secondary quantitative importance.

If a rising level of economic development creates an increasing demand for public consumption expenditures for welfare and if, for political reasons, the relative magnitude of such expenditures do not correspond to the *per capita* income of the nation, then there is a differential unmet need for such welfare expenditures in the various nations. Thus the major factor underlying the differences in the time-series ratio-income-elasticities appears to be the elimination of these differential unmet public welfare needs through more rapid increases where such unmet needs are greatest. Further, for countries with a given *per capita* income there also appears to be an upper limit on public consumption expenditures for welfare.

5. A BRIEF SUMMARY

First, two empirical results of this study support the hypothesis about the positive relation between the level of economic development and the ratio of total welfare expenditures to the GNP. In the examination of private life insurance expenditures on a cross-section basis, the ratio of such expenditures to the GNP increases with a rising GNP *per capita*. Further, in the time series analysis, the ratio-income-elasticities of public consumption expenditures for welfare are positive for most nations.

Second, a certain substitution relation of private for public welfare expenditures appears, and privately financed welfare expenditures are higher in those countries where social insurance expenditures are low. Nevertheless, this substitution relation is not complete, and private financing appears to cover only part of the potential demand for welfare expenditures.

Third, in the cross-section analysis, the most important explanatory variable of the data in the sample nations is the length of time in which the social insurance system for old-age pensions has been in operation. On the demand side, this factor could reflect the relative desire on the part of the population for government intervention in this area; on the supply side, 'creeping socialism', i.e. the bureaucratic extension of social insurance systems.

Fourth, the economic system does not seem to play an important role as a determinant for public consumption expenditures for welfare. This result is also predicted on theoretical grounds.

Finally, the time-series ratio-income-elasticities are positive and are greatest in those countries which have the lowest ratio of public consumption expenditures for welfare to the GNP. Thus there appears a convergence of these expenditure/GNP ratios.

C. PUBLIC CONSUMPTION EXPENDITURES FOR HEALTH

Public consumption expenditures on health are defined to include expenditures for hospital or nursing care; payments for physicians, dentists, and other personnel; and payments for drugs, X-rays, and prosthetic devices; whether given directly to the recipient through a national health service or indirectly through the reimbursement of medical expenses or through third party expenditures for medical services. For the sake of comparability, medical payments by health insurance schemes required by law but carried by private insurance companies (such as the US Workmen's Compensation in some states) are included as public consumption. All payments for income support during sickness are excluded from health expenditures and are placed in welfare.

The economic analysis of health expenditures and of education expenditures have many similarities.[1] Both are part consumption, part investment services; and both have certain externalities. On the other hand, there are important differences. Health expenditures affect not only the quality of the population, such as education, but the number as well. Furthermore, while education acts to *improve* the quality of an individual,

---

[1] However, there is still considerable controversy about the proper use of economic analysis in the field of health. A limited role of such techniques is seen by Eli Ginzberg ['Medical Economics—More than Curves and Computers', Bureau of Public Health Economics and the Department of Economics, University of Michigan, *The Economics of Health and Medical Care* (Ann Arbor, 1964)]; a more extensive role is argued by Herbert E. Klarman, *The Economics of Health* (New York, 1965), esp. pp. 10–11.

health expenditures act to *maintain* the quality, i.e. to counter a hostile environment from maiming or killing. Thus, in judging the effect of health expenditures on a person, it is not only necessary to have data on that person today, but also his past history in order to judge what his situation today would have been if certain health expenditures had not been made. Although the economic effects of education expenditures can be judged by income and productivity differentials among individuals, the economic effect of health expenditures must be judged from the reduced incidence of disease and death and the benefits resulting from such a development.[1]

Before turning to the separate demand and supply factors underlying health expenditures, two important aspects of these expenditures must be noted.

First, a number of different types of medical expenditures have public-good properties. These include the draining of malaria-breeding swamps, inoculation of children against diphtheria, quarantining individuals with infectious diseases, or city-wide rat control. In these cases no one can be excluded from enjoying the benefits of these measures and the increased costs of these services for an additional person are very low. These services that have public-good properties are usually financed publicly. Through a sad history of plagues and epidemics, mankind has learned that these matters cannot be adequately handled on an individual basis but must be attacked collectively, the costs of which are covered through taxes. On the other hand, it must be noted that the benefits of many medical expenditures are individual and entirely 'exclusive', e.g. the setting of a broken arm, prenatal care, or appendectomies. Although sufficient data are not available for a precise judgment to be made, it seems highly likely that most health expenditures are for services without public good properties.[2]

Second, since expenditures financed by national health insurance plans or by governmental public services constitute

[1] The various economic similarities and differences between health and education expenditures are analysed in much greater depth by Selma Mushkin, 'Health as an Investment', *Journal of Political Economy*, LXX, October 1962, Part 2, pp. 129–37.

[2] The relatively small magnitude of health services with public-good properties is emphasized by D. S. Lees, *Health through Choice* (London, 1961).

the bulk of public consumption expenditures for health in most of the sample nations, we might expect some relation between such public expenditures and the length of time such public health insurance programmes have been in operation.[1] The reasons for such a relation on both the demand and the supply side are similar to those presented for public consumption expenditures for welfare in the previous pages.

1. DEMAND FACTORS

There are a number of demand factors for health care that might influence public and private expenditures for such purposes.

First, the effect of income on medical services demanded is quite uncertain. On the one hand, it can be argued that medical need is generally greater at lower income levels; e.g. studies have shown an inverse relationship between income and sick-days *per capita*.[2] This is due partly to the lack of preventive medical care in low-income areas and partly to the well-known disease-creating conditions accompanying such low incomes. (Both factors are neatly summarized by Henry Sigerist, who noted, 'Nicotinic acid cures pellagra but a beefsteak can prevent it'.)[3] Thus we might expect that medical expenditures as a share of income would decline as income *per capita* rises (although the relationship is complicated by the unfortunate fact that low-income individuals or nations might not be able to afford the necessary expenditures).[4] On the other hand, increasing urbanization and longer life expectancies accompany a rising level of

[1] It must be noted that a number of the sample countries finance health expenditures as a public service; nevertheless, in all of these countries such programmes started out on an insurance basis. The variable used in the regressions below is the number of years that have elapsed since the introduction of a public national health insurance scheme (or, for the United States, which had no such national system until 1966, the years since the introduction of such a public insurance scheme on a state level).

[2] This is documented in many places, e.g. Seymour E. Harris, *The Economics of American Medicine* (New York, 1964), p. 242.

[3] Cited by Herman Miles Somers and Ann Ramsey Somers, *Doctors, Patients, and Health Insurance* (Washington, DC, 1962), p. 20.

[4] Hippocrates, in his essay 'On Diet' noted that the mass of people 'by necessity must lead a haphazard life and . . . neglecting all, cannot take care of their health'. [Cited by George Rosen, 'The Evolution of Social Medicine', in Howard E. Freeman, *et al.*, eds., *Handbook of Medical Sociology* (Englewood Cliffs, NJ, 1963).] Of course, consideration of this factor is more complicated if health expenditures are publicly financed.

economic development. Since urbanization increases the need for medical expenditures (due to greater dangers of contagion, etc.) and since medical needs rise with age,[1] we might expect medical expenditures to rise as a share of income with an increasing level of *per capita* income. With two offsetting factors it is likely that the ratio-income-elasticities will not be statistically significant unless one of these factors is very much stronger than the other.

Second, there are several important uncertainties that the buyer of medical services must take into account.[2] The incidence of illness for specific individuals is quite unpredictable and, for a particular person, there is an uncertainty surrounding the need for future medical expenditures. Since the incidence of illness is fairly predictable for large masses of people, risk-sharing devices can be set up, e.g. medical insurance. If these devices are inadequate, however, it is likely that at specific times many people will be unable to afford the medical expenditures which they want. This, in turn, suggests that aggregate medical expenditures are higher in nations where such risk-sharing mechanisms function in an adequate manner. Another uncertainty surrounds the effects of medical care and the possibilities of recovery. Of course, things were much worse in the past, e.g. 1910–12 has been identified as the 'great divide' in US medical care when 'for the first time in human history, a random patient with a random disease consulting a doctor chosen at random stood better than a 50–50 chance of benefiting from the encounter'.[3] The less this uncertainty, the greater the probability that patients needing medical care will actually attempt to obtain such services. The rising level of medical technology over the years suggests that the time-series ratio-income-elasticities for medical expenditures should be higher than the cross-section ratio-income-elasticities.

[1] Grover Wirick and Robin Barlow, 'The Economic and Social Determinants of the Demand for Health Services', Bureau of Public Health Economics, *op. cit.* Health economists have noted that many health expenditures are made by individuals who in previous eras would have died at a much earlier age.

[2] These uncertainties are analysed in detail by Kenneth J. Arrow, 'Uncertainty and the Welfare Economics of Medical Care', *American Economic Review*, LIII, December 1963, pp. 941–73.

[3] Lawrence Henderson, cited by Somers and Somers, *op. cit.*, p. 136.

Third, a number of commentators have asserted that a relationship exists between the demand for health care and economic system. Marxists and other critics of capitalism have argued that capitalism leads to an excessive rate of work injuries and occupational diseases, since employers neglect protection measures in their relentless search for profits.[1] On the other hand, many non-Marxists have suggested that the extreme pressure for plan fulfilment in socialist nations leads to a neglect of adequate occupational protection measures.[2] At least in regard to work injuries, substantial differences between nations in the two systems do not seem to emerge; since only a few socialist countries publish such data, however, the statistical picture is still quite murky.[3] Although other examples of supposed differences that are due to economic system can be given, it does not seem worthwhile to pursue such matters on a theoretical level.

Fourth, the relation of price and expenditures for health is also difficult to analyse. For certain types of medical services, the price elasticity seems very low. For example, there is evidence that after the introduction of the national health service in the United Kingdom, general health check-ups increased very little.[4] On the other hand, for drugs the price elasticity seems very high and a number of national health services, such as the Czechoslovak or Soviet, have had to introduce nominal fees for drugs in order to cut down on their use.[5] Furthermore, we know that in some centralized economies, the demand for very high quality medical care is unfulfilled and that special

[1] See, for instance, K. William Kapp, *The Social Costs of Private Enterprise* (Cambridge, Mass., 1948).

[2] Some of these views are briefly discussed by Mark G. Field, *Doctor and Patient in Soviet Russia* (Cambridge, Mass., 1957).

[3] Some data are given in ILO, *Yearbook of Labour Statistics* (Geneva, annual).

[4] D. S. Lees and R. C. Rice, 'Uncertainty and the Welfare Economics of Medical Care: Comment', *American Economic Review*, LX, March 1965, pp. 140–54.

[5] Complaints of 'drug-chiselling' or wastage seem endemic with most national health services, even among the centrally planned economies [e.g. Miroslav Tuček, *et al.*, *Socialistické finance* (Prague, 1965), pp. 364–65]. On the system of fees for drugs in Czechoslovakia and the Soviet Union, see *Rude pravo*, June 6, 1964; and Alberta Edwards, 'Some Observations on the Distribution of Pharmaceuticals in the Soviet Union', *Report of the American Marketing Delegation to the Soviet Union, 1960* (Cambridge, Mass., n.d.)

'closed clinics' have had to be established to provide for such care for selected segments of the population.[1,2] Such factors suggest that, *ceteris paribus*, the ratio of total health expenditures (public and private) should be higher in those nations in which such expenditures are financed primarily through insurance (public or private) arrangement or through taxation, rather than privately. Another complicating factor in the relation between price and demand for medical services is introduced because relative prices of medical services are apparently rising over time and this change can affect elasticity calculations at any one point in time.[3]

Finally, two demand factors must be mentioned, the effects of which cannot be evaluated empirically because of lack of suitable comparable data. One of these factors is the considerable lack of knowledge on the part of the consumer of medical services about what he is obtaining. Part of this is due to the obvious fact that most of the public does not understand the technical aspects of medical science. Another part is due to difficulties in evaluating the medical services received.[4] And a final part is due to certain false attitudes toward disease, physicians, and symptoms of ill-health by many segments of the population. A second factor relates to the fact that health

1 For the Soviet Union, such 'closed clinics' are discussed by Mark G. Field, *op. cit.*, pp. 185–8. On the other hand, such a system does not seem to exist in East Germany, although certain special hospitals, which have many important patients receive much higher quality drugs and equipment than other hospitals [according to the memoirs of an East German doctor, Herbert L. Schrader, *No Other Way* (New York, 1964)].

2 In a system where medical care is entirely financed by the state, the rationing of high quality medical care is a very difficult matter. Ffrangcon Roberts [*The Cost of Health* (London, 1952)] divides medical expenditures into three categories: wealth restoring (e.g. aiding productive workers to regain their health), wealth consuming (e.g. keeping retired persons alive for a few extra years), and neutral. He then proposed that wealth restoring expenditures on health receive priority. Such a proposal, while unacceptable to many people, is one of the few serious attempts to solve the question of priorities in the allocation of free health care.

3 Klarman, *op. cit.*, pp. 28–9, discussed this phenomenon and tries to attack the elasticity problem using such data. However, he neglects the important fact that the productivity of medical care is rising over time so that changes in relative current prices do not reflect changes in relative real prices.

4 In studies in North Carolina and in England, investigators have found no positive correlation between the popularity of a doctor or his patient-load and the quality of his practice. (These studies are discussed by Somers and Somers, *op. cit.*, p. 32.)

expenditures have certain investment features. The quantitative assessment of the returns of such investment or the determinants of such investment has only just begun and requires highly detailed micro-economic data.[1]

2. SUPPLY FACTORS

Certain aspects of the supply of medical services also have considerable effect on the behaviour of aggregate expenditures.

First, since health is a labour intensive service, this would affect the cost of medical care *vis-à-vis* other goods and services in the economy and, other things remaining the same, a substitution from medical to other goods and services might occur as wages of health personnel rise over time. This substitution effect, in turn, suggests that the cross-section income elasticities would be higher than the time-series income elasticity. But other things do not often remain the same over time and the rising costs of medical service are partly or, perhaps, wholly offset by the rising productivity of medical workers.[2] It seems likely the reasons on the demand side given in the section above for expecting a higher time-series income elasticity than cross-section elasticity would prevail over the reasons on the supply side for expecting the reverse.

Second, although the inputs of medical care can be easily designated (physicians, nurses, laboratory technicians, drugs, hospital beds, etc.) the substitution relationships between these inputs must be taken into account when making comparisons between nations. For instance, in the United States over

[1] Such evaluations of the economic effect of health expenditures on income or productivity have been carried out by Mushkin, *op. cit.*; Walter Galenson and Graham Pyatt, *The Quality of Labour and Economic Development in Certain Countries* (Geneva, 1964); Rashi Fein, *Economics of Mental Illness* (New York, 1958); Burton A. Weisbrod, *Economics of Public Health* (Philadelphia, 1961); or, in a more qualitative way, Hector Correa, *The Economics of Human Resources* (Amsterdam, 1963), Chapter IV. Klarman, *op. cit.*, Chapter VII, has a summary of other such studies.

[2] Productivity seems to have increased for four distinct reasons: First, the level of medical technology is rising, owing to the discovery of new techniques, drugs, etc. Second, physicians have much more equipment, and medicine is becoming increasingly capital intensive. Third, patients are now coming to physicians or to hospitals, so that health personnel can examine more patients per hour. Fourth, there seem to be certain economies of scale (analysed by Arrow, *op. cit.*). Measurement of such productivity changes is discussed by Klarman, *op. cit.*, Chapters IV to VII.

the past sixty years there was a substitution between untrained hospital attendants for trained nurses in the first part of the century, a substitution of paramedical personnel (such as laboratory technicians) for physicians, dentists, and nurses in the latter part of the period, and an apparent substitution of hospital beds for physicians for almost the entire period.[1]

If we look at direct health personnel (physicians, dentists, registered or certified nurses and midwives, and *feldschers*)[2] and hospital beds in the sample nations a different facet of these substitution relations can be viewed. For the market economies, income *per capita* is directly and significantly related to *per capita* health personnel but not to hospital beds *per capita*; in the centrally planned economies the reverse is true[3] (see Table 4–4). Holding *per capita* income constant and testing for a trade-off between the above two medical inputs does not reveal a statistically significant relationship. It is likely, none the less, that statistically significant substitution effects could be found if much more detailed data on health inputs were available.[4]

Since the personnel covered in the table account for only about half of total health personnel, and since certain crucial health inputs such as hospital equipment or drugs do not enter, the data give a very inadequate reflection of the total health inputs. The substitutability of health inputs, the incompatibility of data on inputs other than those given in the table, and the variation in relative wages of physicians[5] suggest that a de-

---

[1] Data are given in Appendix D–9.

[2] A *feldscher* is a physician's assistant or highly trained male nurse who fulfils a number of physician's duties in Eastern Europe.

[3] The datum on hospital beds for Ireland (which has been checked in original sources and found to be correct) is so much out of line with the data from other nations because a large share of hospital expenditures in Ireland is financed from the betting receipts of the Irish Sweepstakes, a horse race that draws revenues from most parts of the world.

[4] Regressions of the following form were calculated:

$$\ln I_1/P = a + b \ln Y/P + c \ln I_2/P + d \ln V$$

where I_1 and I_2 are health inputs, Y = income, P = population, and V = other variables (e.g. economic system).

The only calculated regression coefficient that is statistically significant is 'b'. A number of experiments were tried with both the 1956 and 1962 data but without success.

[5] For a brief discussion of the wages of medical personnel, see Appendix D–13.

composition of expenditures into components, similar to the analysis for military expenditures, would be both infeasible and of little use.

TABLE 4–4

Health Inputs and Outputs for the Early 1960s[1]

Country	Health inputs per 100 population		Health outputs		
	Health personnel	Hospital beds	Infant mortality rate	Life expectancy (Years) Men	Women
Market Economies					
USA	0·60	0·90	25·3	66·8	73·4
West Germany	0·48	1·04	29·2	66·9	72·4
Austria	0·48	1·06	32·8	65·0	71·0
Ireland	n.a.	2·13	29·1	64·5	67·1
Italy	0·32	0·92	41·8	65·8	70·0
Greece	0·22	0·58	40·4	67·5	70·7
Yugoslavia	n.a.	0·50	84·2	62·2	65·3
Centralized Economies					
Czechoslovakia	0·59	1·25	22·8	67·2	72·8
East Germany	0·37	1·21	31·6	67·3	72·2
USSR	0·70	0·85	32	65	73
Hungary	0·50	0·70	47·9	65·2	69·6
Poland	0·39	0·72	54·8	64·8	70·5
Romania	0·37	0·74	60·3	64·2	67·7
Bulgaria	0·43	0·77	37·3	64·2	67·6

A third aspect of health expenditures on the supply side is the difficulty in determining the results of such expenditures. Key morbidity indicators are not yet internationally standardized,

[1] Infant mortality is defined as infant deaths per 1,000 live births; life expectancy is measured at birth. The data cover primarily 1962; life expectancy rates for Ireland, Italy, and Bulgaria are for 1956, however. More detailed data for 1962, as well as 1956, and sources and notes on the information in the table are given in Appendix D–10.

Although these represent the most standardized health data compiled on an international basis, many problems of comparability still exist. For health personnel, standards of qualification differ in the various countries. And for hospital beds the statistical handling of beds in nursing homes, or of bassinets differs among nations (e.g. both are excluded in the US data; both are apparently included in the East German data). Therefore, I have not attempted to draw conclusions from minor differences.

and thus present comparison difficulties.[1] Although mortality and life expectancy are more standardized, other problems arise. Examination of infant mortality rates at one point in time can be misleading because of the very rapid decline in such rates during the period under examination.[2] Furthermore, although life expectancies and infant mortality rates are significantly related to *per capita* income, they are affected by a variety of other factors, such as the degree of urbanization, which have not been very well explored on a macro-level.

Finally, the linkage between health inputs and health outputs is quite uncertain.[3] Part of this is due to problems in measuring inputs and outputs. Another part is due to the extreme importance of the organization of medical care. For instance, certain types of health measures are extremely important and effective and are very inexpensive. Home quarantining of people with contagious diseases need cost very little; most aspects of pre-natal care can be carried out at low marginal costs; only inexpensive eyedrops are needed to cure glaucoma or to prevent ophthalmia neonatoram; and Papanicolaou smear tests for the detection of uterine cancer or inoculations against polio can be made at very low average costs. One particular aspect of the organization of medical care is the spatial distribution of health personnel and facilities. Using the ratio of physicians to the population as an indicator it can be shown that the coefficient of variation of this ratio is about twice as high in the Soviet Union as in the United States, i.e. the spatial distribution of

---

[1] For instance, it is known that in the mid-1950s, American workers lost a *per capita* average of 6·3 work days a year on account of sickness, while in the Soviet Union, the figure was 14·6 days. However, maternity leaves in the two statistics seem to be handled differently, which makes comparability difficult; and, furthermore, even the concept of 'days of sickness' is ambiguous, e.g. it may cover only actual sick days or it may also cover the days after illness in which the employee is not sick, but when for various reasons he does not report to work.

USA datum from: United States Public Health Service, *Health Statistics from the US National Health Survey* (Washington, DC, March 1961); USSR datum, cited by Murray S. Weitzman, *Comparison of the US and USSR Employment in Industry: 1939–1958* (Washington, DC, January 1963).

[2] Data are given in Appendix D–10.

[3] Experiments were carried out to determine whether infant mortality and life expectancy could be better predicted (higher correlation coefficient) from information on economic system and income *per capita* or from data on health personnel and hospital beds *per capita*. In no case did the second group of variables prove superior.

physicians to the population is very much more uneven in the former than in the latter country.[1] This probably accounts for an important part of the considerable difference in infant mortality in the two nations.

3. Empirical Relationships between Public and Private Health Expenditures

Empirical evidence on the portion of total (public+private) health expenditures in the GNP does not reveal any relation with the level of economic development, a result which is predicted from the theoretical evidence provided above. Scattered data on nations show that these health expenditures/GNP ratios fall within a band between 3·5 and 5·0 per cent and have no apparent link with the GNP *per capita*.[2] For US states, for which data are much more comparable and abundant, statistical tests did not reveal any significant relationship either.[3]

There is, however, evidence for a high degree of substitution between public and private health expenditures. From the data

[1] The derivation of this result is described in Appendix D–12. Although the Soviet Union has a much higher percentage of the population living in rural areas than the United States, the above statistic was calculated by taking large areas together, and the maldistribution of health personnel caused by the urban-rural distribution of the population does not influence the results.

The great differences in spatial distribution of medical personnel seem due to three factors, none of which are related to economic system. First, the lower the *per capita* income of a nation, the more uneven the spatial distribution of physicians tends to be (because of the relatively much greater attractiveness of living in the cities). And this certainly seems operative between the Soviet Union and the United States. Second, about 3/4 of all Soviet physicians are women; since women tend to marry men of similar or higher educational standards, and since the occupation of such men keep them in a few major cities, it is very difficult to induce such women to leave their husbands to practice medicine in small towns. Third, although physicians in the United States in rural areas or in small towns tend to have higher earnings than physicians in large cities (Somers and Somers, *op. cit.*, p. 206), there is no indication that such economic incentives for physicians are used on a large scale in the Soviet Union.

[2] Data are available in the International Labour Office, *The Cost of Medical Care* (Geneva, 1959). However, these figures have been severely criticized for lack of comparability by Brian Abel-Smith, *Paying for Health Services: A Study of Costs and Sources of Finance in Six Countries* (Geneva, 1963).

[3] Data on public and private expenditures on health in the different US states come from Appendix D–11. I tried a number of different regression experiments including polynomial forms, but no statistically significant relation between the total health expenditures/personal income ratio and *per capita* personal income could be found.

F

for nations, the ratio of total health expenditures to the GNP appears unrelated to the way in which these expenditures are financed, which indicates an inverse relation between the two different health expenditures. For the sample nations, reliable data on private health expenditures are available for only a few countries; comparison of two polar cases is enlightening, however.

TABLE 4–5

Total Current Public and Private Health Expenditures in the USA and Czechoslovakia[1]

	USA 1957–58		Czechoslovakia 1958	
	Percentage of GNP	Percentage of Total		Percentage of GNP	Percentage of Total
Public consumption	0·96%	19%	Public consumption	3·95%	96%
Private			Private		
Direct	2·55	51	Direct, enterprise		
Paid by health			etc.	0·17	4
insurance	0·90	18			
Paid by private	0·48	12			
enterprises, phil-					
anthropy, or through					
tort liability, etc.					
Total	4·89	100		4·12	100

Public consumption expenditures on health as a ratio of GNP are vastly different in the two countries. However, total health expenditures are relatively similar, which suggests that a considerable substitution between private and public health expenditures occurs. Neither the mechanism of substitution nor the extent of substitution can be adequately judged from such individual cases, however, and a more sensitive approach is needed. Since a deeper examination of this problem of sub-stitution of public and private health expenditures can only

[1] Factor price GNPs are used. For Czechoslovakia, public consumption data come from Appendix A–4 and private expenditures on health were calculated from data from Abel-Smith, *op. cit.*, pp. 72, 74. My definition of public consump-tion expenditures is somewhat different from Abel-Smith's. Sources and methods used for estimating US data are given in Appendix D–8.

be made by obtaining comparable data for public, private, and insurance expenditures on health for a large number of political units, and since such data do not exist on the national level, the individual states within the United States are chosen as a sample.[1] One of the difficulties which arises is the estimation of private health expenditures, a task of sufficient magnitude to prevent analysis of the problem for more than one year (1962).

In a preliminary investigation using simple least squares regressions, governmental health expenditures *per capita* were found to be significantly related to *per caputa* income and urbanization. Other economic variables such as the percentage of poor families or portion of labour force in manufacturing, or political variables such as the degree of interparty competition, the degree to which the state voted Republican or Democratic, and the degree to which the state could be considered a one-party state, had little explanatory power and were dropped from further investigation.[2] *Per capita* private health expenditures were found to be primarily related to *per capita* income, and other independent variables did not offer much explanatory power.

If there is substitution between public and private health expenditures, then they should be inversely related to each other after the influence of other explanatory variables is removed. But after numerous experiments, I could find no such substitution relation.[3] Thus health expenditures on an intra-national level seem to act very differently than on an inter-national level.

To resolve this apparent paradox I performed a number of

[1] Public consumption expenditures for health exclude those for military personnel but include all other major types by all levels of government (see Appendix D–11), Washington, D C and Alaska are omitted from the sample because of special federal programmes designed especially for these two areas.

[2] Others have also tried to test for the influence of political variables on health expenditures, but without success. E.g., see Thomas R. Dye, *Politics, Economics, and the Public: Policy Outcomes in the American States* (Chicago, 1966).

[3] According to some of the results of experiments on this matter, public and private health expenditures are complements, rather than substitutes. I tried a variety of statistical models to investigate possible substitution relations including those with simultaneous equations where the regression coefficients are calculated using a three-stage-least-squares method. But no substitution relation could be found. For aid in these calculations I would like to thank Andrea Maneschi.

additional statistical experiments on the two components of private health expenditures: those financed by health insurance payments[1] and those which are out-of-pocket. Using simple least squares regressions the former expenditures were found to be directly related to income *per capita*, urbanization, and the labour force in manufacturing (since a very considerable portion of health insurance is sold on a group basis through factories in the United States). Other explanatory variables were tried and rejected. Out-of-pocket health expenditures seemed related only to *per capita* income.

A statistically significant inverse relation between out-of-pocket and insurance-financed health expenditures can be calculated after removing the influence of *per capita* income. Thus, between these two aggregates there is a substitution relation. If we further make the reasonable assumption that people adjust their out-of-pocket health expenditures to their health insurance benefits, rather than the reverse (in most group health insurance plans there is little room for choice on the amount of insurance that is purchased), then we can calculate elasticity of substitution of out-of-pocket insurance expenditures of about $0 \cdot 36$ (for every $1 \cdot 00$ per cent change in health insurance payments, out-of-pocket expenditures change $0 \cdot 36$ per cent in the opposite direction).[2]

In combining these quantitative results with certain qualita-

---

[1] I used payments of insurance companies, rather than receipts of these enterprises, as the variable under examination. Underlying this decision is the assumption that administrative expenditures of these companies (which constitute the major difference between their receipts and their payments for health benefits) are more a payment for the socialization of risk than for health.

[2] This elasticity coefficient is derived from a regression calculation of the following type: $\ln(H/P) = a + b \ln(Y/P) + c \ln(I/P)$, where H = out-of-pocket health expenditures; P = population; Y = personal income; and I = insurance benefits for health; and a, b, c = calculated regression coefficients. The sample includes Alaska and Washington, DC. The data are from Appendix D–11 and other sources cited there. If the assumption about the adjustment mechanism is rejected, then the elasticity of substitution must be calculated from a simultaneous equations model, and its numerical value would vary from that given above.

It must be added that this substitution relation between out-of-pocket and insurance-financed expenditures conflicts with the results of survey data presented by Odin W. Anderson and Jacob J. Feldman, *Family Medical Costs and Voluntary Health Insurance: A Nationwide Survey* (New York, 1956). As noted in Chapter II one cannot generalize from survey data to aggregates, since different causal factors may operate at different levels of aggregation.

tive evidence, we find that three important factors appear to play a role in the existence of a substitution effect on an international level and the lack of such an effect on an intra-national level within the United States.

First, after examination of the different US public programmes for health it appears that most were deliberately designed to minimize substitution except those for war veterans. That is, from institutional evidence it seems as if a relatively large portion of US governmental health programmes are devoted to health care for the 'medically indigent' (those who, by definition, would have very much less health care if government aid were not given) or for measures with considerable public-goods aspects such as epidemic control, which private citizens would probably not finance alone.

Second, a considerable portion of the public expenditures on health in other economically developed nations are really expenditures of the nationalized health insurance companies. Thus much of the substitution relation noted on an international level could be between out-of-pocket and health insurance expenditures, a phenomenon which is demonstrated for the United States.

Third, the degree of substitution need not be invariant to the relative expenditures for health by the public and private sectors. That is, it seems possible that the degree of substitution might increase as the public share of total health expenditures increases. Thus public consumption expenditures might have to rise to considerable levels before any substantial substitution of public for private expenditures would take place. Since US public consumption expenditures amount to only about 1/5th of total health expenditures (see Table 4–5) the USA might not have reached the point where substitution of public for private expenditures would begin. It is also possible that after a certain point the degree of substitution between public and private health expenditures would decline.[1]

---

[1] Private health insurance can in many cases take the place of public health insurance and has the advantage of being tailored more to the individual demands of the buyer. In the United Kingdom after the introduction of the national health insurance, private health insurance sales continued to rise.

Another factor concerns the buying of higher quality medical aid. A Polish economist suggested to me that the share of publicly financed medical expenditures

Therefore, the different results obtained from the international and intra-national cross-section analyses are not necessarily contradictory. Indeed, their confrontation yields additional insights into the substitution process.

From this brief discussion of the substitution of public and private expenditures for health, we can turn to several relevant problems that arise in this general policy area.

If there is a relatively low degree of substitution between public and private health expenditures in the United States, then any major increase in public expenditures should lead to a considerable strain on medical facilities. Thus there were certain ominous prospects (including the overcrowding of hospitals and nursing homes) which the United States faced with the introduction of Medicare in 1966.[1]

A second implication of public rather than private financing of medical expenditures lies in the distribution of medical services among the population. A number of advocates of increased public consumption expenditures for health have argued that such expenditures would reduce the high rate of infant mortality among the poor to such an extent that total

will fall because, as people become wealthier, they will increasingly buy private health care in order to obtain higher quality medical aid. But as income *per capita* of a nation increases, public medical care might also increase in quality so that there will be increasingly less need for such extra-high quality privately financed medical care. Unfortunately, little empirical evidence on these matters is available.

1 Although the Medicare programme brought an approximate 20 per cent increase in public consumption expenditures on health in its first year of operation, such overcrowding of hospitals did not occur. Three offsetting factors might have been in operation: the data used in making the estimations of substitution between public and private expenditures did not include the free care given to medical indigents by physicians and hospitals. Therefore, the introduction of Medicare might merely have resulted in payments for services previously rendered gratis. A clear demonstration of this phenomenon could be seen if hospital revenues and physicians' incomes take a sudden jump in the first few post-Medicare years. Another offsetting factor might be a substitution of Medicare for other public funds. That is, once Medicare funds were available, expenditures from other public programmes covering health care for the elderly would be diverted to other uses. Or, the Medicare programme might still be too new for many of the elderly to know how to utilize fully its potential, so that the strain on hospital facilities would not appear for several years. Finally, the elderly might not have been in such need of medical care as previously believed. Until more facts are available, further elaboration of these explanations does not seem fruitful, especially since the predicted strain on medical facilities might have actually occurred.

infant deaths would be considerably lower. In other words, the marginal benefits gained by giving a certain amount of additional medical care to the poor offsets the marginal losses of taking away such benefits from the rich. And, indeed, one dramatic piece of evidence for this assertion is readily available: from the 1920s to the early 1940s, the United States had a lower infant mortality rate than the UK, but after the introduction of the national health service in the UK in 1948, its infant mortality rate dipped below that of the United States and has remained below ever since.[1] One would therefore expect that infant mortality might be related to the relative degree to which health expenditures are financed in the public sector where the degree of substitution between public and private health expenditures is low.

Using the data for the United States I attempted to test statistically this hypothesis;[2] unfortunately, the results were negative. Although a number of explanations can be given for this failure, I believe the key factor in the picture which cannot be adequately measured is the organization of medical care— a variable which, I noted above, seems to explain differences in Soviet and US infant mortality rates.[3]

This question of the effects of different methods of financing medical expenditures can be approached on a more microeconomic level, and a considerable body of literature exists on the relative merits of fee-for-services, insurance financing, and

[1] The data come from League of Nations, *Statistical Yearbook* (Geneva, various years) and the United Nations, *Demographic Yearbook* (New York, various years).

[2] Using the data from Appendix D–11 plus data on infant mortality by race and twenty-six different characteristics of the population which various medical authorities have considered to play a causative role in infant mortality, a number of different single and simultaneous equation models were tested. Although over 400 separate statistical experiments were tried, I could not find a statistically significant relationship between the ratio of public to private health expenditures and infant mortality.

[3] There are also other interpretations of the failure. First, the data might be too aggregative, and an important effect on infant mortality might be discovered if just expenditures on maternal and child care by the public and private sectors were examined instead. Unfortunately, such detailed data do not exist at the present time. Second, the effects of financing might be washed out by other much stronger causal factors. For most of the regressions, factors such as ratio of illegitimate births, race, and median family income explained most of the variations of the infant mortality rates. Finally, the hypothesis might be wrong.

public service financing of medical care. These questions are far from resolved, for even in the Soviet Union important spokesmen are calling for a retreat from the public service financing of medical care and a return to fee-for-service in certain areas.[1] Further exploration of this explosive issue would, unfortunately, lead us too far astray from the main theme of this study.[2]

4. DETERMINANTS OF PUBLIC CONSUMPTION EXPENDITURES FOR HEALTH

Similar to the welfare expenditures the cross-section data for health expenditures look extremely varied.

TABLE 4–6

Ratios of Public Consumption Expenditures for Health to the Factor Price GNPs in 1956 and 1962[2]

Country	1956	1962	Country	1956	1962
USA	0·9%	1·2	Czechoslovakia	4·2%	3·6%
West Germany	2·7	3·2	East Germany	n.a.	n.a.
Austria	2·8	3·2	USSR	3·0	2·5
Ireland	3·6	3·4	Hungary	2·6	2·6
Italy	3·3	3·9	Poland	2·6	3·4
Greece	1·1	1·2	Romania	2·7	2·9
Yugoslavia	3·1	4·1	Bulgaria	3·4	2·4

The unweighted average ratios of the centralized economies are larger than those of the market economies, but not to a significant extent. Since health expenditures are relatively labour intensive, the factor-income-effect discussed in Chapter II gives the data from the centralized economies an upward bias, and the differences between the two systems would be less than

[1] See Aleksandr M. Luk and Vladimir Tardov, 'Bol'noy i rodstvenniki: zametki vracha', *Literaturnaya gazeta*, December 8, 1966, p. 2; this article is translated and reprinted under a different title in *Current Digest of the Soviet Press*, XVIII, January 4, 1967, pp. 8–9.

[2] For the United States this debate is summarized by Klarman, *op. cit.* For the sample nations, see Appendix E–11: The Effects of Financing Medical Care Expenditure Different Ways.

[2] Data come from Appendix A. Although estimates were made for East Germany, they are not considered reliable enough for inclusion in the above table or for hypothesis testing. For Hungary, data are for 1955 instead of for 1956.

indicated in the table. The redefinition of economic systems to place Yugoslavia among the socialist economies does not substantially change the picture. The systems variable is also not statistically significant in the various regression experiments.

The calculated ratio-income-elasticities for each of the two years are also not significantly larger than zero. Inclusion of the economic systems variable does not change the situation.

The key explanatory variable appears to be the number of years in which the national health insurance system has been in operation, the theoretical importance of which is discussed in the previous pages. In regression calculations, the following results are obtained:[1]

For 1956, $\quad \ln H = -4 \cdot 10 + 0 \cdot 73^* \ln T \qquad R^2 = 0 \cdot 61^*$
$$(0 \cdot 18)$$

For 1962, $\quad \ln H = -4 \cdot 10 + 0 \cdot 72^* \ln T \qquad R^2 = 0 \cdot 52^*$
$$(0 \cdot 21)$$

where H = public consumption expenditures on health as a percentage of GNP.

T = years since start of social insurance programme for health.

In both years the length of operation of the social insurance programme for health is positively and significantly related to the ratio of public expenditures for health to the GNP, i.e. the longer the operation of the social insurance programme for health, the higher the relative public expenditures for health purposes. A number of other possible explanatory variables were added to the above regressions; in no cases, however, were the calculated regression coefficients for these other variables statistically significant while the length of operations variable maintained its explanatory power.

Calculating time-series ratio-income-elasticities yields an entirely different picture.

[1] For the United States, which did not have such a national system, the year in which the first public state health insurance programme was introduced (1942) is used instead. All information on founding dates of health insurance programmes comes from US Department of Health, Education, and Welfare, Social Security Administration, *op. cit.* An asterisk denotes statistical significance (0·05 level).

F*

First of all, the average unweighted ratio-income-elasticity is +0·86, which is among the two highest such elasticities for the different public consumption expenditures. Since the average current price elasticities for the market economies is +0·48 higher than the constant price income elasticities, the data indicate that even in constant prices, public consumption expenditures for health as a ratio of GNP rise at a respectable rate. The greater time-series than cross-section ratio-income-elasticities confirms a prediction that was made on the basis of theoretical considerations discussed above.

TABLE 4–7

Time-Series Behaviour of Public Consumption Expenditures for Health, 1950 *to* 1962[1]

Country	Ratio-income-elasticity	Country	Ratio-income-elasticity
USA	+1·73*	Czechoslovakia	−0·05
West Germany	+0·19*	East Germany	n.a.
Austria	+0·34*	USSR	+0·18
Ireland	+1·96*	Hungary	+1·09*
Italy	+0·67*	Poland	+1·50*
Greece	+0·99*	Romania	+0·96*
Yugoslavia	+1·09*	Bulgaria	+0·02

Attempts to explain statistically the differences between time-series ratio-income-elasticities prove somewhat disappointing. Although a negative relationship between the ratio of health expenditures to the factor price GNP and the ratio-income-elasticities appears, the calculated regression coefficient is slightly below statistical significance at the 0·05 level. That is, a tendency toward equalization of the expenditure/GNP ratio among countries appeared, but the statistical significance of this result falls short of the previously set criterion for acceptance of hypotheses. A number of other variables (e.g. *per capita* income, economic system) can be also tried as independent variables, both singly and in combinations, but none of the

---

[1] The data come from Appendices A and B. For Yugoslavia the time period covered is 1952 through 1962. An asterisk designates statistical significance at the 0·05 level.

calculated regression coefficients gives statistically significant results.[1] It is also possible that part of the time-series increase might be due to the encroachment of public on private health expenditures. For the few countries where data on this matter are available (e.g. the US), this factor does not appear of any importance. Indeed, since the portion of publicly financed health expenditures seemed so high a share of the total in most of the sample countries in 1950, this encroachment explanation does not appear to have importance in those cases for which data are not available either.

Although cross-section determinants for health and welfare expenditures are similar, the time-series data for health do not show in such a striking way the 'unmet need effect' which is observable in the welfare data.

5. A BRIEF SUMMARY

From the general theoretical considerations and the empirical analysis, certain important generalizations about public consumption expenditures for health can be drawn.

First, the data for nations reveal a considerable substitution between public and private health expenditures. Substitution between out-of-pocket and insurance financed health expenditures can also be found in an intra-national study of the United States.

Second, the economic system seems to play no significant role in the determination of public consumption expenditures for health. The system variable is also not significantly related to the measurable health inputs or outputs.

Third, expenditures data on health cannot measure well the amount of health services being produced, especially because of the uncertain relationships between health inputs and outputs. The latter phenomenon is due not only to the fact that measurable and unmeasurable health inputs are substitutable for each other but also because of the importance of the organization of medical care and the spatial distribution of health inputs. Such

[1] The time pattern of public consumption expenditures on health is quite peculiar in a number of countries, such as the United States, where the ratio-income-elasticities in different periods are greatly different. These time patterns are a promising area for future exploration.

factors might account for the much higher infant mortality in the USSR than in the United States.

Fourth, in the cross-section analysis the most important explanatory factor for the ratio of public consumption expenditures for health to the GNP is the number of years in which the national health insurance programmes have been in operation. No other statistically significant explanatory variables can be found.

Finally, the ratio-income-elasticities over time are very high, especially in relation to other public consumption expenditures. Part of this seems to stem from the fact that as the technological level of medical services rises, the demand for such services increases.

D. OTHER ASPECTS OF WELFARE AND HEALTH EXPENDITURES

Up to now I have focused primarily on the determinants of public consumption expenditures for welfare and health and on the substitution relations between public and private expenditures for these services. But underlying the determinants for these expenditures is the problem of identifying the causes for the establishment of the social insurance programmes for these purposes. In addition there are questions about the centralization of these expenditures and substitution and complementarity relations between them that have not yet been explored. These problem areas form the core of this section.

1. DETERMINANTS OF THE ESTABLISHMENT OF SOCIAL INSURANCE SYSTEMS

In the previous pages I show that the length of operation of the social insurance system plays a crucial role in explaining the relative amount of public consumption expenditures for welfare and health. But the use of this political factor as an explanatory variable raises an obvious question: what are the determinants of the establishment of social insurance systems?

If we look at the world in 1913, we find that only nations with relatively high levels of economic development had social insurance programmes for old-age pensions.[1] Therefore it appears that the level of economic development and its correlates—industrialization, urbanization, and a high GNP *per capita*—underlay the establishment of such programmes. But among a sample of nations including all of the European countries and the relatively developed nations in North America and the British Commonwealth, the existence of such social insurance programmes is not significantly related to the *per capita* GNP or its correlates.[2] In other words, the level of economic development appears an underlying, but not an immediate, cause for the establishment of such programmes.

After a considerable amount of experimentation I found that the existence of such social insurance programmes in 1913 could be predicted quite accurately by reference to only one factor—the relative importance of unionization.[3] This association does not necessarily imply that social insurance programmes were brought about by unionization, for both could have been the result of the mobilization of the political power of the working classes. Although exploration of the exact relationships of these two variables must be left to the historian, their correlation is highly plausible.

Thus two factors seem at work in the establishment of social insurance systems—the level of economic development, which is the deeper and more basic cause and the relative importance of unionization, which is related to more immediate and political influences. The importance of the political factor seems to be increasing—witness the establishment of social insurance programmes in economically highly underdeveloped nations after World War II where political mobilization of the masses was strong.[4]

2. SUBSTITUTIONS AND COMPLEMENTARITIES BETWEEN WELFARE AND HEALTH EXPENDITURES

The definitions of health and welfare expenditures that are adopted in this study deviate considerably from standard

[1] Data on the establishment of social insurance programmes can be obtained from US Department of Health, Education and Welfare, *op. cit.*
[2] These experiments are described in Appendix E–12.
[3] For a description of sources and methods for this result, see Appendix E–12.
[4] Zöllner, *op. cit.*, has an interesting theoretical discussion about this situation.

statistical practices, especially in the placing of income supports during short-term illness into welfare expenditures. Nevertheless, this particular division of expenditures does have the advantage of placing the most substitutable types of expenditures together (e.g. public assistance and income supports during illness), so that there is less interaction between major separate categories of expenditures.

This matter of interaction between welfare and health expenditures raises a number of difficulties. It can be argued that public expenditures for health and welfare are substitutes for each other, since certain public health expenditures nullify the need for certain public welfare expenditures, and vice versa. On a personal level this is reflected by the fact that part of the transfer payments to individuals (recorded under 'welfare') are really spent for health purposes by the recipient. On the other hand, good reasons can be given that health and welfare expenditures are complementary, since the same set of political attitudes that result in higher expenditures for one would also result in higher expenditures for the other.

Up to now it has been implicitly assumed that there are neither substitution nor complementary effects between welfare and health. If there were, it might be advantageous to analyse the combined total of such expenditures instead of such expenditures separately. It is to this problem that we now briefly turn.

If we hold economic system and income *per capita* constant, a significant cross-section complementarity appears between health and welfare expenditures.[1] That is, other things remaining equal, higher relative public consumption expenditures on health are associated with higher relative public consumption

[1] For the results in this paragraph, I calculated regressions of the following type:

$$\ln E_1/Y = a + b \ln (E_2/Y) + c \ln (Y/P) + d(S) + e \ln V$$

where E_1 = one type of public consumption expenditure,
E_2 = another type of public consumption expenditure,
Y = GNP,
P = population
S = economic system
V = other variables (length of time in which social insurance system had been in operation).

The expenditures are designated as substitutes if the calculated coefficient 'b' is negative; and complements, if 'b' is positive.

expenditures on welfare. Since both types of public expenditures are related to the length of time in which the social insurance system has been in operation (which, in turn, reflects to a certain extent public attitudes toward government intervention in this field), this complementarity is to be expected. If, however, we hold constant the length of time in which the social insurance system has been in operation as well,[1] the complementarity disappears, and the crucial calculated coefficient is not significantly larger than zero.

TABLE 4–8

Behaviour of Combined Public Consumption Expenditures for Health and Welfare[2]

Country	Ratio of expenditures to factor price GNP		Ratio-income-elasticities 1956 through 1962
	1956	1962	
Market economies			
USA	5·7%	7·9%	+ 2·47*
West Germany	16·2	18·2	+ 0·14*
Austria	18·4	21·0	+ 0·33*
Ireland	13·0	11·0	− 0·53*
Italy	14·0	15·5	+ 0·74*
Greece	7·0	9·3	+ 0·32*
Yugoslavia	10·6	11·8	+ 0·14
Centralized economies			
Czechoslovakia	16·1	17·3	+ 0·16
East Germany	n.a.	n.a.	n.a.
USSR	9·4	10·6	+ 0·41*
Hungary	8·2	8·0	+ 1·00*
Poland	9·0	10·0	+ 0·75*
Romania	6·6	8·4	+ 1·16*
Bulgaria	8·9	8·6	+ 0·33

Looking at the problem in a different way, we may ask: Can we predict the cross-section difference between nations better by looking at public consumption expenditures for welfare and

[1] Since social insurance systems for health and old-age pensions were usually set up at different times, the earliest date is chosen.

[2] Data come from Appendix A; ratio-income-elasticity for Yugoslavia covers the period from 1952 through 1962. The cross-section data for Hungary are for 1955 and 1962.

health separately or by combining them? A number of tests were carried out and it appears that combining the two expenditures does not aid cross-section prediction to any appreciable extent.[1]

Testing for complementarities and substitution relations with the time-series data leads to mixed results.[2] Statistically significant complementarities appear for five countries: the United States, West Germany, Austria, Hungary, and Romania. That is, holding income *per capita* constant, an increase in relative public consumption expenditures for health is directly associated with an increase in relative public consumption expenditures for welfare. In one country, Ireland, a substitution relation appears, although it is a shade below statistical significance. For the other countries, the coefficients representing substitution or complementarity are not statistically significant. In explaining the differences in time-series ratio-income-elasticities among nations, combining health and welfare expenditures leads only to slightly better predictions.[3]

From such experiments the conclusion can be drawn that although certain ostensible complementarities between public consumption expenditures on health and welfare appear, such effects do not greatly affect the separate analyses of each expenditure. And, indeed, in combining public welfare and health expenditures, we lose certain useful information about the behaviour of each type of expenditure.

3. CENTRALIZATION

Examination of the centralization of public consumption expenditures on health and welfare leads to several

[1] Tests were made by computing regressions with similar independent variables but different dependent variables (i.e. public health expenditures/GNP, public welfare expenditures/GNP, public welfare and health expenditures/GNP) and looking at the resulting coefficients of multiple correlation. Since the separate cross-section correlation coefficients are quite high, combining expenditures does not result in very much higher coefficients.

[2] I calculated regressions of the following type:
$$\ln E_1/Y = a + b \ln E_2/Y + c \ln Y/P$$
where the symbols have the same significance as in the footnote above, and where substitution and complementarity relations are determined by the sign of the coefficient 'b'.

[3] Tests similar to those performed on the cross-section data were carried out. It must be emphasized that the improved predictive power was quite small.

important insights about the nature of the centralization process.

First of all, there is considerably more cross-section variation in centralization ratios than between the two points in time. This seems to indicate the importance in historical continuity of centralization ratios.

TABLE 4–9

Centralization Rates of Public Consumption Expenditures for Health and Welfare[1]

Country	1956		1962	
	Health	Welfare	Health	Welfare
Market economies				
USA	29%	64%	35%	68
West Germany	87	85	91	89
Austria	91	88	89	90
Ireland	2	85	2	85
Italy	75	91	79	93
Greece	100	100	100	100
Yugoslavia	———6———		———6———	
Centralized economies				
Czechoslovakia	6	86	4	70
East Germany	n.a.	79	n.a.	87
USSR	22	61	18	40
Hungary	n.a.	n.a.	n.a.	n.a.
Poland	35	89	22	86
Romania	n.a.	n.a.	n.a.	n.a.
Bulgaria	21	92	12	93

In most cases public consumption expenditures for health are much more decentralized than such expenditures for welfare. This seems to reflect the institutional fact that the bulk of welfare expenditures come from the central social insurance

[1] Centralization ratios give the share of public consumption expenditures which are directly financed at the central governmental level.

For Greece, 1961 is used instead of 1962; for the Soviet Union, 1960 instead of 1962; for East Germany, 1958 instead of 1956.

The increase in the centralization ratio for welfare of East Germany is due to the inclusion of the social institutions serving East Berlin into those serving the rest of the country. It is not known to what extent other changes in the table are due to such legal or institutional changes.

The data come from Appendix A and are, in several cases, rough estimates.

fund, while many health expenditures are made by local government agencies, even though they are financed originally by transfers from a central fund.

There is, of course, no great necessity for making old-age pension expenditures at the central government level.[1] For instance, Yugoslavia has completly decentralized its social insurance system, and the Soviet Union is moving slowly in this direction. Indeed, in certain cases, the classification of social insurance agencies as belonging to the central government rests on an arbitrary legal distinction. (For example, the 2,000 or so West German social insurance agencies, each of which primarily serves a local area or industry, seem often to function as strictly local agencies.) The reason why most social insurance organizations have remained agencies of the central government appears to lie less in such economic matters as economies of scale[2] than in the historical fact that in most of the sample nations the initiative for social insurance originally came from the central government, and that decentralization has not been a policy goal of sufficient importance to warrant changing the original status of the social insurance agencies. This is not to deny that there are considerable administrative problems in decentralizing a social insurance system, especially in devising transfer mechanisms to take into account the geographical mobility of the population. Rather such considerations suggest that institutional inertia is an important factor in the determinants of centralization.

Exploring correlates to these centralization ratios must be done quite inductively since, as noted in Chapter II, we have few hypotheses to test. For public expenditures for welfare the centralization ratio is related in both years to a variable indicating whether the nation is federal or unitary and to the *per*

[1] It can be argued that because there are economies of scale in risk taking [see Don Patinkin, *Money, Interest, and Prices* (Evanston, Ill., 1956), appendix to Chpt. V by Aryeh Dvoretzky] there are economies of scale in social insurance agencies. However, risk-sharing devices between social insurance agencies can be devised to as to reduce in importance or perhaps eliminate this type of scale effect.

[2] Such arguments are seldom raised in the literature about social insurance systems. I do not know whether this neglect is due to the fact that such economies in this case are unimportant or whether the literature about such matters is incomplete.

capita income. Other things being equal, centralization is less in federal nations and seems to rise with increasing *per capita* income.[1] The former result is quite expected; the latter conclusion is met in several other public consumption expenditures but seems difficult to explain. For health, none of the variables related to the phenomenon of centralization seems to explain the ratios in the table.[2] This is not surprising, for a neglected accounting factor appears to play the crucial role. In some nations health insurance payments are given to individuals who then reimburse the different health-care institutions. (Sometimes this reimbursement is merely an accounting transaction between the institution and the social insurance agency.) Thus expenditures are recorded for the level of government to which the social insurance agency belongs. In other countries, however, social insurance funds given to health-care institutions are recorded as expended by that level of government to which the health institution belongs. As far as I could ascertain, this latter accounting arrangement seemed more prevalent in the centralized economies. In those countries financing health care as a public service, e.g. Ireland, health expenditures are also recorded on the level of government to which the different health care institutions belong.

E. SUMMARY AND CONCLUSIONS

A number of factors important to a positive theory of public expenditures have emerged from this analysis of public consumption expenditures on health and welfare.

The portion of health and welfare expenditures made for services with public-good properties is small indeed, and

[1] The variable designating the type of government (federal or unitary) is statistically significant in both years in several forms of equations that were tried. The statistical significance of the income *per capita* variable depended on the form of the regression. Although the economic system variable appears to play a role, its exact effect cannot be determined from the sample since data were not available for two centralized economies, which are known to have highly centralized fiscal systems. I tested a number of other variables, but with negative results.

[2] The economic systems variable appears significant, but, for reasons given in the footnote above, its importance is in doubt because of the omission of data for Hungary and Romania.

therefore, the justification of public expenditures in these general areas must be made on other grounds. The crucial consideration appears to be the sharing of risk over as broad an area as possible, a function that is not carried out by the private sector because of such phenomena as risk-skimming and the relatively high administration costs of private insurance companies *vis-à-vis* social insurance agencies.

The public financing of health and welfare expenditures does not mean that some expenditures would not be otherwise made, for substitution effects are found for both types of expenditures. Nevertheless, this substitution does not always occur, as health expenditures data for the Unites Stated show, and the public financing of such expenditures has an effect on the distribution of recipients.

In analysing the determinants of public consumption expenditures, we can make useful predictions from propositions that have intuitive appeal but which cannot be considered a model in the same sense that applies for military expenditures in the previous chapter. Although the deductive chain is considerably shorter, predictions are made that do receive empirical confirmation.

The most important factor explaining the variation of public consumption expenditures for health and welfare among nations is the number of years in which the social insurance systems have been in operation. On the demand side this factor denotes the degree to which the population favours state intervention in these expenditure areas; on the supply side, this variable represents the expansion of the social insurance system to include wider coverage and higher benefits. The origins of the social insurance systems are related to a political variable— the relative importance of unionization. It appears likely that both factors are related to a more basic political phenomenon— the political mobilization of workers.

On theoretical grounds we do not expect much effect of the economic system on public consumption expenditures for welfare and health, and the empirical results confirm such expectations.

The effect of the level of economic development is more complicated. In the cross-section analysis the *per capita* GNP is not related to the ratio of public consumption expenditures for health or welfare to the GNP. However, in the time-series data the ratio-income-elasticities for both types of expenditures are quite high. An upper limit of relative welfare expenditures can be detected, however, since those nations with the highest expenditure/GNP ratios have the lowest time-series ratio-income-elasticities. For health expenditures there is less certain evidence that a similar upper limit may also exist.

In the exploration of the degree of centralization of these two public consumption expenditures, political and legal factors seem to play a much more important role than do economic variables.

Finally, health and welfare expenditures appear more as complements than substitutes in most cases. However, many more analytical insights can be gained by studying these expenditures separately rather than combined.

Chapter V

PUBLIC CONSUMPTION
EXPENDITURES FOR EDUCATION

A. INTRODUCTION

Within the past century a radical shift in attitudes toward public consumption expenditures on education has taken place in most countries. In 1832 a respected member of the British Parliament could declare:

'It is not proposed that the children of the poor be educated in an expensive manner or even taught to write and cypher. Utopian schemes for the universal diffusion of general knowledge would soon . . . confound that distinction of ranks and classes of society, on which the general welfare hinges, and the happiness of the lower orders, no less than that of the higher, depends.'[1]

---

[1] Cited by Frederick Harbison and Charles A. Myers, *Education, Manpower and Economic Growth* (New York, 1964), p. 140. In the same vein a Russian decree of June 18, 1887 proscribed that: '*Gymnasiums* and *pro-gymnasiums* should prevent the entrance of children of coachmen, manservants, cooks, laundrywomen, small shopkeepers, and the like; the children of whom, with the exception perhaps of unusually gifted ones, ought not to be allowed to escape from the environment

In 1948 the United Nations General Assembly unanimously proclaimed in the Universal Declaration of Human Rights [Article 26 (1)]:

'Everyone has the right to education. Education shall be free at least in the elementary and fundamental stages. Elementary education shall be compulsory. Technical and professional education shall be made generally available and higher education shall be equally accessible to all on the basis of merit.'[1]

Only relatively recently, however, have economists begun to apply their analytic skills to problems of education. Although pioneers in the empirical economic study of education such as Dublin, Lotka, and Strumilin had shown in the 1920s and 1930s how such analyses could be carried out, significant interest in such work came only in the 1950s. Since then the economic literature devoted to such problems has been growing at an overwhelming pace.[2] Moreover, international organizations have begun to collect a considerable amount of comparable information on various aspects of the education systems of most countries in the world. In spite of all this recent theoretical and empirical work, however, we are far from understanding the causal factors underlying the behaviour of education expenditures.

In this chapter I focus not only on problems surrounding the determinants of education expenditures but also on a number of other issues, such as the substitution between public and private expenditures in education and the centralization of education expenditures, which have not yet received their proper attention from economists.

to which they belong; because the experience of many years has proven that it leads them to scorn their parents and to be dissatisfied with their way of life, and that it instills hatred against the existing inequality of property status, which is inescapable by the nature of things . . .' [Adapted from a citation by Arcadius Kahan, 'The Development of Education and the Economy in Czarist Russia', in C. Arnold Anderson and Mary Jean Bowman, eds., *Education and Economic Development* (Chicago, 1965), p. 370.]

[1] Cited by UNESCO, *World Survey of Education*, III (New York, 1961), p. 11.

[2] Theodore W. Schultz, *The Economic Value of Education* (New York, 1963), has a selected bibliography of over 200 items on the economics of education, most of which were written between 1958 and 1963.

B. ECONOMIC PROPERTIES OF EDUCATION EXPENDITURES

Education expenditures discussed in this chapter cover expenditures connected with primary, secondary, and higher level education; formal vocational schooling; and adult education. Expenditures on nurseries or kindergartens, out-of-school activities of youth, factory training programmes, or political work labelled as education are excluded whenever possible. Although empirical evidence can be brought forward that the costs of formal education considered in this chapter constitute less than half of the cost of knowledge-producing activities in at least one of the sample nations,[1] inclusion of more informal types of education makes the analysis considerably less tractable.

Education is both a consumption and an investment service for which there are different private and social costs and benefits. By focusing on these different costs and benefits, insight can be gained into the supply and demand factors that influence expenditures on education.

On the supply side, the current monetary costs of schooling include the cost of personnel engaged in the education process, the teaching and learning materials (books, blackboards, etc.), and the upkeep of school buildings. The current non-monetary costs of schooling include certain privileges accorded educational institutions (e.g. tax rebates) and the production foregone by pupils and students by not participating in the labour force.[2] All of these current costs occur regardless of the economic system or the state of development. Depending on the system of transfer payments, however, the share of these costs that is privately borne may vary. In one country, for instance, students may bear the brunt of educational costs, not only paying for their schooling but also in bearing their income loss in not working while attending school. Or the system can be entirely socialized so that schooling is free and further, the

[1] Fritz Machlup, *The Production and Distribution of Knowledge in the United States* (Princeton, 1962), pp. 354 ff.

[2] The different private and public costs of education are outlined in much greater detail in a number of excellent recent studies, e.g. Theodore W. Schultz, *op. cit.*; Rudolph Blitz, 'The Nations' Educational Outlay', in Selma J. Mushkin, ed., *Economics of Higher Education* (Washington, DC, 1962); and Gary S. Becker, *Human Capital: A Theoretical and Empirical Analysis with Special Reference to Education* (New York, 1964).

student receives a salary from the government to compensate for his income loss during the time spent at school.

Although considerable attention has recently been paid to such costs, relatively little effort has been made by economists to derive cost functions for schooling, i.e. to relate education inputs (teachers, buildings, materials, etc.) to education outputs (scores on achievement tests, etc.).[1] Indeed, our knowledge of the cost function seems limited to a few prominent features: as the level of education increases (primary, secondary, vocational, college and university), the average cost of supplying a pupil or student with one year of schooling increases. Moreover, there are considerable returns to scale in schooling. It is of course obvious that twenty children in a class with one teacher can receive the same amount of education at much less cost per pupil than if these children were individually educated at home by tutors. But it has also been shown that costs per pupil are lower in schools that have 200, rather than 100, pupils and, indeed, economies of scale extend for a considerable range.[2] Finally, the productivity of teachers seems not to have kept pace with the rise in productivity of other sectors of the economy, and, until such mechanical aids as teaching machines are introduced on a large scale, such a situation is expected to continue.

Such factors should make it evident that the average costs of educating a child should rise over the years for two major reasons: First, the average duration of schooling is rising, which increases not only the total amount but the average cost per school year (because the average grade level of the pupil is rising). Second, if teachers' wages keep pace with wages in other sectors of the economy, then the monetary costs of a pupil year of schooling rises because of the differential produc-

[1] Psychologists and educationists have, of course, spent considerable effort on such problems but the economic implications of such studies have been neglected. However, for a promising start in this direction, see H. Thomas James, *et al.*, *Wealth, Expenditure, and Decision Making for Education* (Stanford, 1963).

[2] Most economists studying such matters have defined economies of scale in terms of the number of children served by one school system. Critical analyses of such attempts and a much more refined empirical treatment of these problems are made by Walter Hettich (*Equalization Grants, Minimum Standards and Unit Cost Difference in Education*, Ph.D. dissertation, Yale University, 1966) and John Riew 'Economies of Scale in High School Operation', *Review of Economics and Statistics*, XLVIII, August 1966, pp. 280–8). Both properly measure costs as a function of school size and both find economies of scale for a considerable range.

tivity effect mentioned above. The relationship between the rising average costs of educating a child and the increasing income *per capita* in a nation has an effect on the substitution of private for public education and is discussed in section C.

The demand for education is considerably more difficult to outline briefly. There are, of course, such well-known elements as the increasing technological complexity of society, which in turn means that individuals must be exposed to more years of formal schooling in order to be able to function effectively in the economy. Further examination of such issues can be carried out more systematically if we separate the benefits of schooling to the individuals receiving it and the benefit of such expenditures to other members of society.[1]

To the private individual, the *production* benefits of his own schooling include his higher productivity due to the knowledge and skills acquired through education, the opportunity of obtaining even more education and higher income,[2] and the opportunity for hedging against the vicissitudes of technological change by being more flexible and by being more able to carry out a wider variety of tasks. On the *consumption* side, the benefits of education to an individual include his enjoyment in participating in the schooling process, the enrichment of his life through the new tastes and sensibilities acquired at school, the added consumption gained from saving on certain expenditures that would be necessary if education had not been obtained (e.g. in many countries an illiterate must hire someone to write his letters), and, finally, the increased consumption from the income obtained through the added productivity due to his schooling. Although the production benefits to the individual occur only after education has been completed, the consumption benefits may occur either during the education process itself or afterwards, depending upon the particular situation.

---

[1] The most extensive economic discussion of the benefits of education is by Burton A. Weisbrod, *External Benefits of Public Education* (Princeton, 1964), from which many of the ideas presented below are drawn. In regard to externalities, Maurice Peston ('The Theory of Spillover and its Connection with Education', *Public Finance/Finances publique*, XXII, 1–2/1966, pp. 184–99) also has a useful discussion.

[2] Weisbrod, *op. cit.*, notes that this opportunity (which he calls the 'financial option') is formally similar to a manufacturer buying certain capital equipment with the option of purchase at a discount of a replacement machine in the future.

The benefits of schooling accrue not only to those individuals receiving it but to others as well. One type of such externality operates in a direct manner, e.g. the costless transmission of education and skills by students and pupils to others.[4] Although such simple cases seem rare, there are several kinds of important but less obvious externalities.[2]

One type concerns the quality of society and government which is made possible by schooling. It is a commonplace idea that a stable and democratic society is impossible without a minimum degree of literacy, knowledge, and acceptance of a common set of values and that for all these purposes formal schooling plays a major role. Furthermore, empirical studies have shown that in the United States the more highly educated persons have a considerably greater degree of political awareness and participation than those with less education, which it is hoped contributes to the quality of government and society.[3] Moreover, education provides a means for social mobility by able individuals and thus serves as a stabilizing force in society. Other types of externalities can also be designated.[4] Although all these externalties can be discussed in much greater detail, I argue later that they lay a relatively unimportant role in financial decisions concerning education.

The type and quantity of government expenditures is also

[1] One manifestation of this externality is revealed in a number of successful mass campaigns against illiteracy (e.g. in Cuba in the early 1960s) which have utilized 'each one teach one' techniques. There are, however, certain opportunity costs of such a technique. A better example is the large number of immigrant parents in the United States who have learned to read and write English from their children in school. In other cases parents have obtained quite an extensive informal education in helping their children with schoolwork.

[2] The technical distinction which must be drawn is between 'technological' and 'pecuniary' externalities. The discussion below embodies this distinction imprecisely, since there are many mixed cases, but allows classification of empirical examples to be made more simply.

[3] Documentation on these points is provided by Burton Weisbrod, 'Preventing High School Dropouts', in Robert Dorfman, ed., *Measuring Benefits in Government Investments* (Washington, DC, 1965).

[4] Viewing workers with more and less education as two different production factors it should be clear that in a market economy where everyone is paid his marginal productivity, an increase in the number of more educated workers can in many circumstances lead to an increase in wages of the less educated worker. Another type of pecuniary externality occurs when goods appear on the market at lower prices when production costs have fallen (because of a more educated and skilled labour force).

affected. For example, there is a saving of government unemployment benefits and transfer payments to the destitute since schooling contributes to the ability of people to obtain work in a rapidly changing urban economy. In addition, education expenditures may save police expenditures in both the present and the future by providing for the constructive occupation of children's time and by inculcating them with the values of society. Furthermore, a higher level of literacy allows certain government services to be performed at a lower cost, e.g. an income tax, which cannot be extensively used in a non-literate society, is said to be less expensive to administer than a sales tax.[1]

It must be noted that economists have taken only the first steps to measure quantitatively such benefits. For instance, the determination of increased income due to additional education is difficult to separate from the income due to higher intelligence, although promising econometric studies have been made on this problem.[2] And assessing other benefits of education requires the surmounting of additional hurdles.[3]

In addition to the supply and demand properties of education

[1] Weisbrod, *op. cit.*, presents evidence on this as well as other cases. It must be noted, however, that in his quantitative analysis he pays no attention to the opportunity cost of the man-hours spent in filling out income tax forms and searching for tax loopholes.

[2] Shane J. Hunt, 'Income Determinants for College Graduates and the Returns to Educational Investment', *Yale Economic Essays*, III, 2/1963, pp. 305–57), has devised an ingenious but controversial method of separating the effects of intelligence and education. Unfortunately, the standard deviations of his derived returns to education are too great to permit firm policy conclusions to be drawn. A more sensitive separation of education and intelligence effects but with a more limited sample, is made by Daniel Rogers (*The Effect of Education on Earnings: A Case Study*, unpublished Ph.D. dissertation, Yale University, 1967), who does find significant returns to education when intelligence is held constant.

[3] An excellent survey of the statistical and methodological problems involved in isolating the economic effects of education is: William G. Bowen, 'Assessing the Economic Contribution of Education: An Appraisal of Alternative Approaches', in OECD, *Economic Aspects of Higher Education* (Paris, 1964), pp. 177–201. Special problems in determining the benefits of education expenditures to the economic growth of nations are discussed in detail in OECD, *The Residual Factor and Economic Growth* (Paris, 1964). In one recent empirical study it is suggested that the beneficial effects of schooling on the labour force have been considerably over-exaggerated in recent years, especially when other factors such as the health of the labour force are properly taken into account [Walter Galenson and Graham Pyatt, *The Quality of Labour and Economic Development in Certain Countries* (Geneva 1964)].

expenditures, the two most important ways public consumption expenditures for education directly act to redistribute income between income classes must be briefly mentioned. First, it is well known that a large share of labour income can be considered as an investment return to human capital accumulated through publicly financed education. And it is highly likely that the distribution of income is considerably more equal than it would be if personal income consisted only of the returns from tangible capital and illiterate labour (a situation that exists in underdeveloped economies with highly unequal income distributions). Thus public consumption expenditures for education act to change the income distribution in a progressive manner. Second, lower income groups have on the average more children. With compulsory primary and secondary education financed by the public sector, these poorer families receive a larger per family share of such education than upper income groups.

What are the implications of the supply and demand factors on the behaviour of expenditures for education? If a higher portion of a nation's children are receiving education, if the education lasts a longer period, and if the monetary costs of education are rising because of the differential productivity effect noted above, then education expenditures increase rapidly as *per capita* GNP rises. Nevertheless, from theoretical grounds it is not at all clear that education expenditures increase as a share of the GNP, especially when constant-price series are used. In other words, the operation of Wagner's 'law' for education expenditures cannot be predicted from abstract reasons.

Because of the increasing technological complexity of the world economy, education expenditures respond differently to *per capita* income over time and over space at a single point in time. More specifically, one can predict that education expenditures have a higher ratio-income-elasticity in the time-series than in the cross-section data.

The theoretical considerations give a few further clues on other determinants of total education expenditures. From the demand side, one would expect that education expenditures and the relative number of children in the population would be positively related. Taking into account the investment aspects of education expenditures one might also predict that there would be an empirical link between such expenditures and the prevailing interest rates, the relative rates of return to education *vis-à-vis* other investments, and the degree of substitution between private and public expenditures for this service. Unfortunately, comparable data to test these hypotheses from investment considerations are not available.

C. PUBLIC AND PRIVATE EDUCATION EXPENDITURES

Three problem areas receive attention in this section. First, I examine empirically the properties of total education expenditures and various key components of such expenditures. Then the relative shares of publicly and privately financed expenditures for this service, with particular attention to substitution effects, are explored. Finally, I investigate a number of implications of financing different shares of these education expenditures through the private or the public sectors.

1. BEHAVIOUR OF TOTAL EXPENDITURES FOR EDUCATION[1]

A number of cross-section empirical studies have shown a significant and positive relation between the share of total education expenditures in the GNP and the *per capita* GNP, at least for nations that are not economically highly underdeveloped.[2] For the most part, however, such investigators have calculated only simple regressions, and it is quite possible that other determinants might influence the numerical value of the estimated elasticity. In order to avoid this difficulty I calculated a number of multiple regressions to explore the behaviour of the total education expenditures/GNP ratios for a sample of OECD and other economically developed nations. The most important results are that (*ceteris paribus*) the

[1] In addition to the studies cited below, the following recent major empirical investigations of factors relating to education expenditures have also been made: Donald Perry Sanders, *Patterns of Educational Change During Economic Growth*, Ph.D. dissertation, Stanford University, 1962; Galenson and Pyatt, *op. cit.*; and Hector Correa, *The Economics of Human Resources* (Amsterdam, 1963).

[2] Such investigations include: Daniel Blot and Michel Debeauvais, 'Educational Expenditure in Developing Areas: Some Statistical Aspects', in Lucille Reifman, ed., *Financing of Education for Economic Growth* (Paris, 1964), and Harbison and Myers, *op. cit.*, pp. 36 ff.

ratio-income-elasticity is positive (about $+0\cdot45$) and that this education ratio is also significantly and directly related to the proportion of school-age children (5 to $14\cdot9$) in the population as well.[1] If the expenditures/GNP ratios could be reliably calculated in terms of a single currency, the ratio-income-elasticity would be much closer to zero, but would probably still be positive.

Long period time-series data also show a positive ratio-income-elasticity[2] and the size of the calculated coefficient increases if opportunity costs of education (e.g. income forgone by pupils and students engaged in the educational process) are included.[3] Because of the different statistical methods that are employed by the various investigators, it is unfortunately not possible to compare the time-series and cross-section elasticities.

Once the question of economic system is injected into the analysis, what can we expect? On the basis of classical doctrines, Marxists would predict that total education expenditures in socialist nations would be higher than in capitalist nations at a similar stage of development.[4] Non-Marxists have had little to say on the subject.

Unfortunately sufficient data on total education expenditures in the sample nations do not exist for studies to be made of the

[1] Current education expenditures data come from Ingvar Svennilson, *et al.*, 'Targets for Education in Europe in 1970', *Policy Conference on Economic Growth and Investment in Education* (Paris: OECD, 1962); GNP data in dollars, from my Appendix B; and other data, from standard statistical sources.

[2] Such studies include: Friedrich Edding, *Internationale Tendenzen in der Entwicklung der Ausgaben fuer Schulen und Hochschulen*, Kieler Studien 47 (Kiel, 1958); and Michael Kaser, 'Educational and Economic Progress: Experience in Industrialized Market Economies', in E. A. G. Robinson and J. E. Vaizey, *The Economics of Education* (New York, 1966), pp. 89–174.

[3] See especially Theodore W. Schultz, 'Education and Economic Growth', in Nelson B. Henry, ed., *Social Forces Influencing American Education* (Chicago, 1961).

[4] According to Friedrich Engels, 'In capitalist society the bourgeoisie gives the worker only as much education as it is in its own interests. And that indeed is not much.' [Cited by US Department of Health, Education, and Welfare, Education in the *USSR*, Publ. 14/1957 (Washington, DC, 1957).] Although Marx saw a much greater potential need for education of workers in capitalism, he was convinced that only in socialism or communism would workers receive the proper amount of education for their moral and intellectual well-being [see especially, Karl Marx, *Capital*, Vol. I (Moscow Foreign Languages Publishing House, 1961), Chapter XV, Sections 3 and 9].

ratio-income-elasticities or of the differences resulting from the type of economic system. We can, however, study certain key components of such education expenditures by the use of physical indicators in order to make inferences about the total. For education on the primary (1°) and secondary (2°) levels the following data are relevant to the analysis.

The percentage of the population in school ages, defined for

TABLE 5–1

Primary and Secondary Education Indicators for 1956[1]

Country	School age population as % of total population	Enrolment rate (full time 1° and 2° school pupils as a % of school age population)	Full time pupils per 1° and 2° school teacher
Market economies			
USA	19	109	28
West Germany	14	88	26
Austria	15	79	21
Ireland	20	74	29
Italy	16	74	21
Greece	17	82	40
Yugoslavia	18	69	31
Centralized economies			
Czechoslovakia	18	82	26
East Germany	13	78	22
USSR	16	87	20
Poland	16	84	24
Hungary	19	74	31
Romania	17	62	21
Bulgaria	18	83	24

[1] School-age population covers age groups from 5 to 14·9; teachers include both full- and part-time teachers in regular and primary and secondary schools; pupils include only full-time pupils attending regular primary and secondary schools and exclude kindergarten pupils.

Sources of data and methods of estimation of students and teachers are given in Statistical Note D–15. In general the definitions of UNESCO [*Manual of Educational Statistics* (Paris, 1961)] are followed.

Data similar to those in the above table for 1962 are given in Statistical Note D–17.

convenience as the children from 5 to 14·9 years, is an important demographic factor in the demand for education. For both 1956 and 1962 this ratio is unrelated both to the economic system and the *per capita* GNP.

The enrolment rate is a measure of the relative effort of a nation toward educating its youth. (The United States had a rate over 100 per cent because the school age population is defined above to include children from 5 to 14·9, while a large number of children who are from 15 to 18 also attend school.)[1] There is no statistically significant difference in the average enrolment rates between the two systems, even when *per capita* income and other variables are taken into account. This result tends to discredit the prediction made from Marxist considerations discussed above, although it can be argued that primary and secondary education are 'necessary' for the working class, so that this is not a fair test of the proposition that capitalist economies do not provide the 'proper' amount of education.

In both 1956 and 1962 there is a statistically significant relationship between the enrolment rate and the level of economic development, with the enrolment rate increasing about 0·2 per cent for every 1 per cent increase in the *per capita* GNP. (Such a relationship is obscured somewhat in the centrally planned economies primarily because of the extraordinarily high enrolment rate in Bulgaria, which has heavily emphasized such education ever since its liberation from Turkey in the nineteenth century.) Other quantitative studies using different samples have also shown similar relations between the two variables under consideration. Once *per capita* income is taken into account, the enrolment rate does not seem significantly related to any other variables (including the ratio of school-age children to the total population).

The number of pupils per teacher is a very rough measure of the quality of education, as students are supposed to learn better

[1] The US data are not completely comparable for two reasons. First they contain high school pupils concentrating on vocational subjects, a situation that does not exist in Europe. Second, they exclude the students in the first year of US colleges which are on the educational level about equal to the last year of European secondary schools. Although the net effect of these two factors is probably very small, no adjustment could be made for lack of data.

G

in smaller classes.[1] It seems reasonable to believe that the pupil/teacher ratio is inversely related with *per capita* income, especially since the pupil/teacher ratio has declined in most nations as economic development has occurred. However, the situation is complicated when considerations of teaching efficiency are taken into account. That is, if teachers are better trained or if teaching machines are used, then lower pupil/teacher ratios might not be necessary for the pupil to acquire the same amount of education. Although regression calculations yield an inverse relation between the pupil/teacher ratio and *per capita* income, the coefficients are not statistically significant and no definite conclusions can be drawn. There are also no significant correlations between this ratio and the economic systems.

In experimenting with other variables associated with the pupil/teacher ratio, a positive relationship (statistically significant at about the $0 \cdot 10$ level) was found with the share of school-age children in the population, i.e. the correlation suggests that the number of teachers is a key bottleneck in the educational systems of the sample nations, a proposition that seems intuitively plausible. As no other important associations could be inductively uncovered, the age composition must be considered as the most important determinant of the pupil/teacher ratio at any single point in time. The lack of a significant relationship between the level of economic development and the pupil/teacher ratio on a cross-section basis, in contrast to the time-series data (see below) seems to reflect partly this demographic constraint.

The available data on teachers' wages are not very comparable.[2] As a first approximation, however, wages of industrial workers and teachers move parallel with each other so that remuneration of teachers is generally higher in nations with higher levels of economic development.

Other types of education are more difficult to explore. Comparable physical indicators are not available for vocational

---

[1] Many dispute this proposition. Riew, *op. cit.*, cites a number of quantitative studies which purport to show that within a given range the teacher/student ratio is unrelated to student learning, other things remaining the same.

[2] Such wages are discussed below and in Appendix D–16.

education since the type and intensity of training are so very different in the various sample nations. Data are, however, available for institutions of higher learning, and although such education accounts for only a small part of total education expenditures, comparisons are enlightening. Because of the varying proportion of part-time students and teachers, it seems useful only to compare the number of students receiving degrees.

TABLE 5–2

Students Receiving Degrees from Institutions of Higher Learning per thousand in the Student Age Group[1]

Country	1956	1962	Country	1956	1962
USA	35·9	43·5	Czechoslovakia	10·6	15·4
West Germany	10·0	12·3	East Germany	8·3	12·6
Austria	7·2	7·4	USSR	14·8	15·9
Ireland	10·0	15·1	Poland	10·6	10·2
Italy	5·3	5·7	Hungary	9·1	9·7
Greece	6·1	8·3	Romania	7·4	7·5
Yugoslavia	4·7	14·8	Bulgaria	9·2	12·0

Any statistical tests performed on the data are likely to be misleading because of the very great difference between the United States and all other nations. If the United States is removed from the sample, no statistically significant relations between the data and a variety of variables such as income *per capita* and economic system emerge that are consistent for

[1] The UNESCO definition of 'institution of higher learning' is followed whenever possible. The data include both undergraduate and graduate degrees for natives and foreigners as well as college degrees received from evening and correspondence courses. The student age group is defined from 20 to 24·9. For Austria and West Germany the data are for 1957 and 1962.

The data come from the national statistical yearbooks, supplemented for Austria and West Germany by data from UNESCO *Statistical Yearbook*, various issues; and, for West Germany, by my own estimate of graduates in fine arts. Population data come from Appendix D–1.

It should be noted that the data from the national statistical yearbooks and the UNESCO *Statistical Yearbook* are quite different for the two Germanies and Austria. For West Germany and Austria this is due to the much broader definition of 'institutions of higher learning' employed by UNESCO; for East Germany, because the UNESCO inexplicably excludes degrees obtained through night and correspondence courses.

Data on degrees received as a ratio of the total population are given in Appendix D–17.

the two years. However, if matched pairs of countries from the two economic systems are selected (Austria and Czechoslovakia, West and East Germany, Ireland and Hungary, Italy and Poland, and Greece and Bulgaria), four out of the five pairs show a higher ratio in the table for the centralized economies. The only exception is the Ireland–Hungary pair, which contains some difficulties in comparison, especially since Ireland has such a high portion of foreign students. Thus the centrally planned economies appear to be making a somewhat greater relative effort in giving higher education to its youth if the United States is excluded from the sample.

The analysis of components of education expenditures can also be carried out with the time-series data as well. (See Table 5–3.)

The growth rate of the population and the ratio of school-age population to the total population determine the increase in the absolute number of school-age children, which is the basic demographic constraint to the increase in expenditures on education. It is noteworthy that only in the United States, Czechoslovakia, and Poland did the average increase in the number of school-aged children exceed 2·5 per cent.

For enrolment rates in primary and secondary schools, only one country has a statistically significant decrease, and this can be satisfactorily explained by reference to a number of special domestic considerations in that country.[1] The other nations have either a statistically significant increase or do not significantly change. The unweighted average rate of increase for the entire sample is 0·6 per cent, which gives further evidence that enrolment rates rise over time. There are no significant relationships between the growth rate of the enrolment rate and such variables as *per capita* income, the economic system, or any demographic variable.

[1] The negative coefficient for the Soviet Union seems surprising and has been double checked for accuracy. It can be explained as due to four factors: changes in education policy concerning length of school; changes in the mix between academic (regular primary and secondary schools) and vocational schools; changes in policy concerning full- and part-time schooling; and the time period chosen for comparison (between 1960 and 1965 the enrolment rate rose considerably). Nicholas DeWitt, *Education and Professional Employment in the USSR*, National Science Foundation 61–40 (Washington, DC, 1961), pp 130 ff., has a much more detailed analysis of these themes.

In regard to the teacher/pupil ratio, no country has a statistically significant decrease; and excepting the two countries with the most rapid rise in enrolment rates (Yugoslavia and Romania) these ratios increase significantly in all the sample countries. The growth rates of this teacher/pupil ratio are not significantly related to either the level of *per capita* income, the

TABLE 5–3

Average Annual Growth Rates of Important Components in the Expenditures for Primary and Secondary Education from 1950 through 1962[1]

Country	Population	School age population as a % of total pop.	Enrolment rates in primary and secondary schools	Teachers per pupil	Rough est. average teachers' wages (current prices)
Market economies					
USA	+ 1·7%*	+ 2·0%*	+ 0·1%	+ 0·3%*	+ 5·5%*
West Germany	+ 1·0*	− 1·6*	− 0·2	+ 2·3*	+ 6·4*
Austria	+ 0·2*	− 1·1*	− 0·4	+ 0·9*	+ 8·4*
Ireland	− 0·5*	+ 1·1*	+ 0·7*	+ 0·7*	+ 5·1*
Italy	+ 0·6*	− 0·4*	+ 0·9*	+ 2·0*	+ 4·9*
Greece	+ 0·9*	− 0·3*	+ 0·0	+ 2·9*	+ 6·6*
Yugoslavia	+ 1·1*	+ 1·3*	+ 2·9*	+ 0·6	+ 12·5*
Centralized economies					
Czechoslovakia	+ 1·0%*	+ 1·7%*	− 0·2%	+ 1·9*%	+ 3·5%*
East Germany	− 0·7*	− 1·7*	+ 0·9*	+ 3·7*	+ 3·6*
USSR	+ 1·7*	+ 0·6	− 1·4*	+ 2·3*	+ 2·5*
Hungary	+ 0·6*	+ 0·8*	+ 0·7*	+ 2·8*	+ 6·9*
Poland	+ 1·8*	+ 2·4*	+ 0·5	+ 1·0*	+ 10·3*
Romania	+ 1·2*	+ 0·4	+ 2·9*	− 0·6	+ 8·4*
Bulgaria	+ 0·9*	+ 0·7*	+ 0·8*	+ 1·1*	+ 4·4*

[1] The asterisks denote that the derived growth rate is statistically significant at the 0·05 level.

Data for Greece are from 1954–62; data for Yugoslavia are from 1952–62. Data on all (public and private) full-time primary and secondary pupils and on all teachers in these schools are given. No adjustments have been made for private schools in the calculation of the ratio of total educational expenditures to total teachers' wages; such an adjustment would not greatly change the growth rate of this ratio.

Sources of data and methods of estimation are given in Appendices D–15 and D–16.

change of income, or the economic system. It is important to note, however, that there is an inverse and significant relation with the average annual change of the proportion of school age children in the population, a result that provides confirmation of the conclusion from the cross-section analysis that demographic considerations are important determinants of the teacher/pupil ratio.

Although the time-series data on teachers' wages leave much to be desired for several countries, it appears that the increase of such wages is the most important factor in the increase of expenditures on primary and secondary education. Indeed, for most countries this wage factor is as important as the previously discussed factors combined.

The results of a similar analysis for degrees received by students in institutions of higher learning are unenlightening and are therefore not presented. Unfortunately, comparable data for vocational schools are not available.

The results of the discussion above can be easily summarized. From a number of cross-section and time-series studies it appears that the ratio-income-elasticity of education expenditures is positive. From the time-series analysis of the sample countries, the major factors behind the increases in total education expenditures are the rising enrolment rates, the rising teacher/pupil ratios and the rising salaries of teachers. In the cross-section analysis the factors that influence international comparisons the most are the positive relationships of *per capita* income with the enrolment rate and teachers' salaries.

For primary and secondary education no statistically significant differences in regard to enrolment rates, pupils, or teachers can be found between nations with different economic systems. For institutions of higher learning, however, the centralized economies appear to have a somewhat higher number of degrees granted in relation to the population in the student-age group.

2. RELATIVE SHARES OF PUBLIC AND PRIVATE FINANCING

In this section I present both quantitative and qualitative information concerning the financing of education by the public and private sectors in the sample nations. Before beginning, however, it is useful to examine briefly the various types of costs of education that enter the analysis.

'Resource-use costs' cover the expenditures on teachers, maintenance of school buildings, transportation of students, teaching materials and supplies, and books and school supplies of the students. 'Resource-loss costs' of education cover the opportunity costs of the resources in the education system—the income forgone by students and pupils while attending school and the interest and profits foregone by investing the capital into school buildings and equipment rather than for some other purpose.[1] Finally there are 'resource-transfer costs,' which are transfer payments to pupils and students to enable them to attend school by supplying them with some of the income they have forgone by not participating in the labour force. These resource-transfer costs do not represent a cost to society in terms of production (other than the cost of their administration) but are rather monetary payments or monetary expenditures on goods and supplies in the budget of the donor and a corresponding source of monetary income or income-in-kind by the recipient. (See Table 5-4 on the next page.)

The resource-use costs of education in relation to the GNP are somewhat higher (about 15 per cent) in the Soviet Union than in the United States. One would expect the reverse on the basis of evidence from the positive ratio-income-elasticities from the cross-section studies discussed in the previous section or the fact that the United States has a considerably larger portion of its children in primary and secondary schools and of its college-age youth in institutions of higher learning. To what may these surprising results be attributed? Both statistical and 'real' phenomena must be taken into account.

On the statistical side the 'factor-income-effect' gives an

---

[1] In the calculation of such resource-loss costs, there are not only a number of extremely knotty theoretical problems (e.g. see discussion of these matters by Schultz, *op. cit.*, Chapter II) but a great number of estimating difficulties as well. Consequently, a number of arbitrary decisions must be made. For instance, not all returns to child labour are included but only the income forgone by the older children; opportunity costs of teachers not working in other sectors are also excluded. Even rough estimations such as those in Table 5-4 given us some ideas about the magnitudes of these opportunity costs, however.

upward bias to the Soviet data, since education expenditures consist primarily of payment for services.

In addition, differences in the cost structure of education seem to reinforce this upward bias. Although salaries of primary and secondary school teachers, which are the largest single item of expenditures, are roughly equal to industrial workers' wages in both countries,[1] other factors complicate the situation. If the cost of educating a pupil for a year in a primary school is indexed at 100, the cost of educating a student in a university for a year is about 480 in the USA and about 1,400 in the USSR in the mid 1950s.[2] If comparable salaries could be used in calculating expenditures in both countries, the Soviet data would probably be somewhat lower *vis-à-vis* the United States' expenditures.

TABLE 5–4

Current Education Costs and Sources of Financing in the USA and the USSR[3]

	USA 1957–58		USSR 1957	
	Percentage of factor price GNP	Percentage of total	Percentage of factor price GNP	Percentage of total
Costs				
Resource-use costs	3·24%	47%	3·74%	68%
Resource-loss costs	3·67	53	1·77	32
Total	6·91	100	5·51	100
Financing				
Direct government	2·45	35	3·58	65
Monetary transfers	0·23	3	0·60	11
Other				
Gifts and endowment	0·18	3	0·00	0
Private	4·05	59	1·33	24
Total	6·91	100	5·51	100

[1] Sources for data on teachers' wages are given in Appendix D–16.

[2] Nicholas DeWitt, 'Soviet and American Higher Education: Magnitude, Resources, and Costs', in OECD, *Economic Aspects of Higher Education* (Paris, 1964), p. 149. For a more complete discussion of these matters, see his monumental *Costs and Returns in Education in the USSR*, unpublished Ph.D. dissertation, Harvard University, 1962.

[3] Details may not add to totals because of rounding. Sources and methods for the calculations are given in Appendix D–18.

From reading the relevant literature, one receives the impression that in one area of education—vocational training—the Soviet Union outdistances the United States and that this might be a 'real' factor influencing the resource-use comparisons. Unfortunately, it is extremely difficult to estimate such expenditures, especially for the United States, where a considerable amount of such schooling is financed with out-of-pocket expenditures or by private enterprises and labour unions. Without reliable estimates of such expenditures for either country, this difference in vocational training expenditures must remain a conjecture.

The differences in the relative resource-loss costs in the two countries are due to a number of factors, including differences in the distribution of students and pupils at various levels of education and in the relative resource-loss costs at various levels of education. In comparison to a number of other countries, the proportion of total costs represented by the resource-loss costs are very low in the Soviet Union.[1]

Although certain difficulties arise in interpreting the data on the cost side, the data on financing are quite unambiguous. In the Soviet Union the public sector finances a much larger share of education expenditures than in the United States. Four important aspects of this difference must be emphasized.

First, in the USA, contrary to the Soviet Union, an important share of the direct resource-costs of education are borne by the pupils or students, since direct government expenditures and other sources of income do not cover all resource-use costs. Second, transfer payments to students and pupils are relatively much more important in the Soviet Union than in the United States. Third, there are a number of sources of finance for education in the USA (gifts and endowments) that are absent in the USSR; finally, a much greater relative burden of resource loss costs are borne by the student or his family in the United States. For the other sample countries a qualitative assessment of these four factors can also be made in order to arrive at some conclusions concerning the relative shares of the public and private sectors in financing education in the two systems.

[1] Schultz, *op. cit.*, pp. 29 ff. has data on other nations.

G*

For all the nations under consideration except Greece, fees for primary and secondary schools play little or no role in the financing of these institutions. Furthermore, tuition fees for most institutions of higher learning are relatively low in all countries except the United States.[1] (Unfortunately, data about fees for vocational schools and semi-professional training in various nations are not available.) Thus it seems safe to generalize that in all the sample countries with the exception of the United States (and possibly Greece), almost all of the current resource-use costs of education are borne by the state.

On the other hand, transfer payments to pupils and students seem much more important in the centralized than the market economies. There is evidence that the proportion of college and university students receiving monetary grants is much higher in the centrally planned economies[2] and that pupils in vocational schools receive much more financial aid as well.[3] Non-monetary

[1] The United States is the only nation in the sample with an extensive network of private colleges and universities The importance of students' fees in the financing of us universities is discussed by Dolfe Vogelnik, 'A Comparison Between the Financing of Higher Education in the United States and Yugoslavia', in oecd, *Economic Aspects of Higher Education* (Paris, 1964), pp 120 ff.

[2] For instance, in the latter part of the 1950s about 25 per cent, 29 per cent, and 7 per cent of all students in institutions of higher learning in, respectively, the United States, West Germany, and Austria, received such aid; while in East Germany, the Soviet Union, and Czechoslovakia, the recipients were respectively about 90 per cent, 80 per cent, and 23 per cent of the student body.

These data come from the following sources: John B Lansing *et al.*, *How People Pay for College* (Ann Arbor, 1960), p. 20; Stifterverband fuer die deutsche Wissenschaft, *Wissenschaft in Daten* (Essen, 1962), p. 56; Austria, Oesterreichisches Statistiches Zentralamt, 'Oesterreichische Hochschulstatistik, Wintersemester 1959/60', Heft 60, *Beitraege zur oesterreichischen Statistik* (Vienna, 1961); East Germany, Staatliche Zentralverwaltung fuer Statistik, *Statistisches Jahrbuch der Deutschen Demokratischen Republik*, 1965 (East Berlin, 1965), p. 459; Nicholas DeWitt, *Education and Professional Employment in the USSR*, *op. cit.*, p. 67; and Czechoslovakia, Ústřední úřad státní kontroly a statistiky, *Statistická ročenka ČSSR 1962* (Prague, 1962), Tables 16–19, 16–20, and 16–28.

[3] Scattered data on scholarships to vocational students can be found in the national statistical yearbooks of most centralized economies. [The Czechoslovak data (*Statistická ročenka ČSSR 1962, op. cit.*, Tables 16–28) show this most clearly and indicate that scholarships to vocational students are of much greater magnitude than to college and university students.] Reliable data for the market economies could not be located, but interviews with students and teachers in the above-mentioned nations suggested to me that transfer payments to vocational students are very low.

transfers (e.g. through free or subsidized textbooks and low-cost student housing) may have also been higher in these centralized economies as well.

Other sources of finance for education seem to have had little importance in all the sample nations except the United States. In these sample nations there has not been a tradition of alumni donations to institutions of higher education or large grants to education by charitable foundations. Although the notion of such foundations seems to be gaining in popularity in West Germany and Sweden, schemes of voluntary giving to education are still in their infancy in most European nations.

Finally, from independent and much less authoritative information, it appears that in the centralized economies a lower percentage of monetary expenditures of full-time students is financed by their parents or from part-time jobs[1] than in the market economies. In the United States about 61 per cent of the average monetary expenditures of unmarried full-time college students are borne by the students' parents and about 23 per cent of these expenditures are financed by the students' earnings from work; in West Germany, these percentages for all students are respectively 58 and 13.[2] The portion of a student's education financed from work is partly a sociological feature and depends on society's attitudes toward such work and the availability of such opportunities.[3]

All of these factors point toward the conclusion that the public sector bears a higher portion of the costs of education in

---

[1] Information about student finances was obtained from a small number of interviews with students from different East European nations.

[2] Data from Lansing, *et al.*, *op. cit.*, p. 22; and Stifterverband der deutschen Wissenschaft, *op. cit.*, p. 58.

[3] Soviet visitors to US universities usually vehemently denounce the system by which certain students help support themselves by work in dormitories or cafeterias. Such criticism is particularly manifest in an article by a Soviet editor about his visit to Oberlin College (Boris Pankin, 'Young Communist Paper Views the American Campus', *Current Digest of the Soviet Press*, XIII, 23/ 1961, pp. 14–17, rept. from *Komsomolskaya pravda*, May 28, 1961, p. 3) in which he notes how some students are forced to be 'servants' of others through kitchen work because of financial need. As an ex-dishwasher of this college I was not aware that my fellow kitchen workers considered the work to be servile; rather, such work was considered merely as means toward a desirable end—a college education. Pankin's statement seems more indicative of Soviet attitudes toward work, a curious view for a nation ideologically committed to the labour theory of value.

the centrally planned nations than in the market economies (with the exception of Yugoslavia, for which some contrary evidence is provided in section D). This conclusion is, of course, congruent with the generally accepted belief about such matters. The relative mix of public and private financing is related to several interesting economic phenomena which are analysed below.

3. IMPLICATIONS OF DIFFERENT METHODS OF FINANCING EDUCATION

Financing education in different ways has many possible important implications. First, if the elasticity of substitution of private for public expenditures is low, then a larger share of public financing should result in the production of a greater relative amount of education services. Second, a greater public share should also result in a higher proportion of pupils and students from poorer income groups. Third, there should be certain predictable relations between the financing of education and the ownership of facilities where education is produced. Fourth, differences in curricula should be related to different ways in which education is financed. And finally, the way in which education is financed should be related to the theoretical motives for placing such a service in the public sector. Each of these implications is briefly discussed in turn.

If the elasticity of substituting private for public education is unity, then the way in which education is financed should make no difference in the relative amount of education that is produced; on the other hand, if this elasticity is below unity, then public financing of education should result in a higher ratio of total education expenditures to the G N P, other things remaining equal. Considerable evidence on the total amount of education has already been presented. As noted above there are no significant differences in enrolment rates or pupil/teacher ratios for primary and secondary education in the two systems. The centrally planned economies appear to have a higher proportion of their youth in institutions of higher learning, but only if the USA is omitted from the sample.[1] The only bit of evidence suggesting that the relative amount of education expenditures in the two systems is not similar comes from the comparison of

[1] Other evidence is presented in Appendix D–17.

resource-use costs of education in the USSR and the USA. Since these expenditure data contain some quirks and are therefore ambiguous, the physical indicators seem the more reliable basis on which to reach a judgement.

Thus it appears that the differences in total education expenditures in the two systems are relatively small. Since the method of financing does not greatly affect the total amount of educational services that are produced,[1] we can conclude that the elasticity of substitution of private for public education expenditures is close to unity.

The effect of the method of financing education expenditures on the social class composition of those being educated can also be empirically studied. Since the system of transfer payments to students appears to operate most extensively on the higher levels of education we can explore these matters most sensitively by looking at the available evidence for colleges and universities. Although data on the social-class composition are not completely comparable, several broad generalizations can nevertheless be made.[2] In both systems, the proportion of students from worker and peasant backgrounds show considerable differences, ranging in the late 1950s in the centralized economies from about 35 per cent in the USSR to about 63 per cent in Bulgaria and in the market economies from about 8 per cent in Austria to 48 per cent in Greece. On the average the proportion of students of working-class backgrounds is greater in the centralized economies, although this ratio seems to be increasing in the market economies and decreasing in the centralized economies. For comparisons of the Soviet Union and the United States or of East and West Germany where the class composition of the student body can be calculated as a ratio of the class composition of the labour force, the similarities between nations with different economic systems are more

---

[1] Certain interrelations between public and private expenditures on education for local government units in the United States are also statistically analysed by Jerry Miner [*Social and Economic Factors in Spending for Public Education* (Syracuse, 1963)]. Although the manner in which he presents his empirical results do not allow the elasticity of substitution to be easily calculated, it also appears that the substitution between public and private expenditures is high.

[2] For a discussion of the data on which these generalizations are based, see Appendix E-14: Discrimination in Higher Education.

striking than the differences; indeed, the Soviet Union and the United States appear almost the same!

Although the data for such comparisons leave much to be desired, it appears that the financing of education does make a difference in the class composition of students, but that the family background and culture of students is a much more important determinant in all countries. Furthermore, in a number of nations there is evidence that other factors such as the location of institutions of higher learning greatly influence the social class composition of students as well.[1]

What is the relationship between the method by which education expenditures are financed and the ownership of educational facilities? Non-economic factors of course play an extremely important role in this relationship. However, on the basis of purely economic criteria alone, a number of economists of different political stripe have argued that a system of public education grants to pupils and students which would permit them to study at any private school of their choice would result in an economically more efficient educational system.[2] And, indeed, in several countries (notably Belgium, Ireland and the Netherlands) such a system of state grants to schools permits a considerable portion of education to be carried out in non-state facilities. However, in other countries (notably the United States and Greece) it is a matter of policy that private schools on the primary and secondary level receive no major direct governmental financial support.[3] We can see a more exact picture of

[1] Some striking evidence for this is shown in a sociological exploration of junior colleges in California by Burton R. Clark [*The Open Door College: A Case Study* (New York, 1960)]. For the Netherlands, econometric evidence on the importance of this geographical factor is cited by J. B. D. Derkson, 'Some Comments on the Report of Professor Orłowski and Dr Pirozynski, '*Public Finance/Finances publiques*, XXII, 1–2/1966, pp. 184–99.

[2] In the nations where grants of this type are extensively used, such arguments are, of course, common. In the Anglo-American economic literature, Milton Friedman, *op. cit.*, in the United States, and Alan Peacock and Jack Wiseman [*Education for Democrats: A Study of the Financing of Education in a Free Society*, (London, 1964)] in the United Kingdom, have most eloquently argued this point in recent years.

[3] In the United States there are a number of indirect governmental supports for private primary and secondary education. For instance, such institutions are exempt from paying many types of taxes; moreover, gifts to these schools have certain tax advantages to individuals in high income-tax brackets. In addition, considerable public funds are channelled to private institutions of higher learning.

the extent of the private production of education among the sample nations by examining the ratio of pupils in private primary and secondary schools to the total number of pupils at these levels.

TABLE 5–5

Relative Importance of Private Primary and Secondary Schools in 1957–58[1]

Country	Ratio of pupils in private schools to total pupils	Country	Ratio of pupils in private schools to total pupils
USA	13·2%	Czechoslovakia	0·0%
West Germany	2·7	East Germany	0·0
Austria	4·4	USSR	0·0
Ireland	92·7	Hungary	0·2
Italy	9·5	Poland	0·1
Greece	7·4	Romania	0·0
Yugoslavia	n.a.	Bulgaria	0·0

For the socialist nations, of course, the importance of private schools is very small or non-existent. But among the market economies less than one-seventh of primary and secondary school pupils are enrolled in private schools except in Ireland, which has a well-functioning grant system allowing for such private education to be provided without cost to all pupils. This in turn implies that a very large part of the monetary costs of primary and secondary schools are publicly financed in the sample nations, since fees to public schools in these countries

[1] Only full-time pupils in regular primary and secondary schools are included; pupils in special, vocational, night, and other types of schools are excluded. For Hungary, denominational secondary schools are considered private; although the number of pupils attending denominational primary schools is not known; it is considered to be negligible. For Italy, data are for 1956–57. For Ireland, only the national schools vested in the Minister of Education are considered public. Since data on pupils in different types of vested national schools are not available, the datum in the table was estimated by assuming that the average number of pupils in all types of vested schools were the same. It must also be added that data on pupils in non-recognized private primary schools are not available, which means that the datum in the table is slightly understated. For Yugoslavia, although data on pupils in private primary and secondary schools are not available, it is believed that the number is very small. Sources for all data are given in Appendix D–15.

are non-existent or minimal, at least in the latter part of the period.[1] It should be added that of all the industrialized or semi-industrialized nations in the world, private schools educate an important share of pupils only in those three nations listed above which have extensive grant systems.[2]

The demonstrated link between the financing of education and the ownership of facilities where such services are produced allows predictions about the respective roles of the public and private financing to be tested empirically, since physical data on ownership can be substituted for expenditures data.

One type of prediction concerns special determinants for private education. For instance, since private education is quite expensive, the more skewed the income distribution, the higher the relative amount of such private production should be, other factors remaining the same.

Other predictions concern the relative amount of privately supplied education at different levels. For instance, after a fairly low level of education has been achieved, the measurable rate of return to investment in schooling seems to fall, paralleling the falling rate of return of other types of investment when the amount invested is increased.[3] This suggests that, *ceteris paribus*, pupils or their parents would be more willing to pay for private education at lower educational levels where the return is highest. On the other hand, education at higher levels is usually more specifically related to knowledge and skills needed for particular types of work and, in so far as such education can be tied to a particular job in the future, the benefits of higher level education may seem more real than the benefits of primary

[1] For the market economies, information is available for all countries except Ireland from: International Bureau of Education, *Financing of Education*, Publ. No. 163 (Geneva, 1955). For the other countries, information on fees is available from a number of scattered sources. It must also be noted that although every centralized economy had fees for secondary schools and universities in the early 1950s, most of these fees were relatively minor and were gradually eliminated before 1962.

[2] UNESCO, *World Survey of Education, III* (New York, 1961). A significant percentage of secondary students attend private schools in a number of countries; for primary and secondary schools combined, however, the generalization in the text still holds true.

[3] For the US, calculations are made by W. Lee Hanson in 'Total and Private Rates of Return to Investment in Schooling', *Journal of Political Economy*, LXXI, April 1963, pp. 128–40.

education. Furthermore, as private schools may be able to adjust more quickly to changing demands for skills and knowledge by specific employers than public schools, this specific benefit factor is reinforced.[1] Such considerations suggest that private schooling would be more prevalent at higher levels, *ceteris paribus*. Since good *a priori* reasons can be given for either a rising or a falling relative importance of private schooling with a rising level of education, we can expect a mixed picture when we turn to the relevant data for the sample nations.

Should the importance of private education increase with a rising *per capita* income? One well-known economist asserts that as a community becomes wealthier, the individual citizens are more able to afford private education and, in addition, will more strongly desire private education which can be individually tailored to the specific needs of the pupils.[2] On the other hand, it is pointed out above that the average unit costs of education rise over time *vis-à-vis* other goods and services as *per capita* income rises, and moreover, the schooling process for the average pupil becomes longer. Thus we have income and substitution effects working in opposite directions, and we should expect a mixed picture from the available data as well.

Comparable data for nations on the degree of inequality and the extent of private schooling are not readily available.[3] On the other two questions, mixed results are predicted, and, upon examination of the empirical evidence, mixed results are obtained.[4] Although it is heartening to obtain predicted results, the nature of the evidence does not allow a judgment on whether non-economic factors also influenced the situation.

[1] The line between regular secondary and vocational schools is often difficult to draw. It must also be noted that this 'specific benefit' factor may be more apparent than real.

[2] George Stigler, 'The Economic Role of the State', in Helmut Schoeck and James W. Wiggins, *The New Argument in Economics: The Public Versus the Private Sector* (Princeton, 1963), p. 14.

[3] The hypothesis can be tested, however, with cross-section regressions for the United States. A number of experiments were tried, using the gini coefficient as the measure of the inequality of income, but the results were negative and the proposition must be rejected for the USA.

[4] Such evidence is presented in Appendix E–13: The Production of Private Education.

However, the arguments that I use demonstrate the possibilities of exploring the interrelations between public financing and public ownership in a rigorous manner.

Does the share of public financing of education expenditures affect the school curricula? For primary and secondary schools, which are primarily financed through the public sector in all nations, there appear few important differences among most of the sample nations.[1] However, in institutions of higher learning, where the shares of public and private financing differ much more, the curricula between market and centralized economies vary considerably. Market economies grant a higher percentage of degrees in humanities, law, and the social and natural sciences, while centrally planned economies grant a greater portion of degrees in engineering and agriculture, fields that are most directly related to material production. From qualitative evidence it appears that in the market economies student demand plays a much more important role in what subjects are taught than in the centralized economies, where the government attempts to link the production of specialists to anticipated (rightly or wrongly) future needs. In other words, in the sample nations, the larger governmental role in financing education has also been accompanied by greater governmental control of the curricula. This link, however, seems due more to political than economic factors.[2]

The evidence presented in this entire section on public and private education expenditures has considerable bearing on the motives behind financing education through the public sector and these deserve brief attention.

A number of political conservatives have advocated that while

[1] Data for the generalizations in the paragraph are given in Appendix E–15: School Curricula Differences Among the Sample Nations. Mr Kenneth Kehrer, who is preparing a dissertation on the subject, informs me that upon detailed examination of curricula, certain systematic differences can be found.

[2] In regard to the share of education expenditures financed through the public sector, Yugoslavia appears more similar to the socialist nations. However, in regard to the distribution of degrees of students in institutions of higher learning, Yugoslavia appears more similar to the market economies. The policies in Eastern Europe in regard to the share of students receiving degrees in various fields seems due to the fact that these nations have been heavily influenced by the Soviet example, a situation that belies the fact that several of these countries (Czechoslovakia, East Germany, and Poland) have much longer traditions of higher education than does the Soviet Union.

primary and secondary education should be publicly financed because of the externalities associated with such expenditures,[1] higher education or specific vocational training, should be privately financed because of the identifiable monetary gains which accrue to the recipient of such schooling after its completion. Any argument for public financing of education based on externalities is nebulous, however, especially since there have been few noteworthy attempts to value such externalities in monetary terms. Indeed, one august institution recently published a book opposing public financing of almost all education on the grounds that such externalities are completely unimportant![2] Perhaps externalities 'should' be a reason why certain education expenditures should be publicly financed; but its actual importance in the decisions to finance such expenditures publicly is doubtful.

Several other arguments for public financing of education revolve around questions of risk and rationality. The capital market that might enable hard working and talented poor children to borrow funds to finance their own education is highly imperfect in every country because of the very high risks that are involved in such a borrowing process. Part of this risk springs from the fact that many of the talents of a person are not revealed until he has participated in the education process itself. Another aspect stems from the difficulties in obtaining repayment of education loans, especially when education increases a person's geographical mobility. The problem of rationality also arises, because in many cases a child and his parents are not able to make a rational decision about the relative costs and benefits of education to the child and how much education he should receive. By placing part of the financing of education in the public sector, part of the risks inherent in this cost-benefit decision are borne by society.

Public education is also one of the most socially acceptable methods of redistributing income. The previous citation from the Universal Declaration of Human Rights is an instance of

[1] E.g. Milton Friedman, *Capitalism and Freedom* (Chicago, 1962), pp. 86 ff. Implicit in such arguments is the assumption that much less education would be forthcoming if the system were privately financed.

[2] E. G. West, *Education and the State: A Study in Political Economy* (London, Institute of Economic Affairs, 1965).

this belief. Moreover, as noted above, it seems likely that such a net redistribution occurs not only over a person's lifetime but also between income classes as well. In the terminology introduced in the second chapter, this is a long-run as well as a short-run redistribution. The extent of the educational process that is publicly financed depends on the importance the national decision makers place on the desirability of such a redistribution.

Finally, in a society controlled by a certain group (class, racial, or other types of groups) the ruling elite may feel it worth while to finance education publicly in order to inculcate its values into the children and to try to maintain its own power position in this way. Unfortunately, it is difficult to find empirical evidence to support such an hypothesis.

These last two arguments rest on political, social, and value judgments that are not directly economic. Education is one of the many examples of an expenditure where traditional considerations of public-good properties and externalities appear to play a very minor role in justifying its financing through the public sector.

4. A BRIEF SUMMARY

Both cross-section and time-series studies show a positive ratio-income-elasticity of total education expenditures, although the underlying factors are somewhat different. In both cases, however, increases in the enrolment rate with rising *per capita* incomes play a major role. In examining the physical indicators for education production, I could find no significant differences between the two economic systems except perhaps in higher education.

The systems do appear to differ, however, in the share of public expenditures that is financed through the public sector. From quantitative evidence in regard to the Soviet Union and the United States and from qualitative evidence for the other countries it appears that a much larger portion of education expenditures are publicly financed in the centralized economies.

Five implications of the methods for financing education are explored and a number of useful conclusions can be drawn. First, it appears that the elasticity of substitution of private for public consumption expenditures for education is close to unity, at least on a cross-section basis. Second, the degree to which education expenditures are financed in the public sector has made a certain difference in the social-class composition of students, but at least one other factor seems overwhelmingly more important—the status of the parents. Quantitative evidence about this matter for the Soviet Union and the United States shows that these two nations are similar. Third, in almost all nations, publicly financed education is also produced primarily in public facilities, at least on the primary and secondary school levels. Fourth, the share of public financing of education, particularly on the higher levels, affects the distribution of students studying various subjects. Finally, the most cogent reasons for financing education in the public sector seem to be political or social (freedom of opportunity for children, redistribution of income, and social stability), rather than directly economic in the traditional sense (externalities or public good properties). Indeed, the most important economic justification for publicly financing education lies in the insurance function of a government—the sharing of risk over the largest possible number of people.

D. DETERMINANTS OF PUBLIC CONSUMPTION EXPENDITURES FOR EDUCATION

1. CROSS-SECTION ANALYSIS

Public consumption expenditures for education behave differently than total expenditures. The starting point for the empirical analysis is the information presented in Table 5–6 below.

TABLE 5–6

Ratios of Public Consumption Expenditures for Education to the Factor Price GNPs of the Sample Nations in 1956 and 1962[1]

Country	1956	1962	Country	1956	1962
USA	2·4%	3·0%	Czechoslovakia	3·8%	4·0%
West Germany	2·2	2·4	East Germany	3·8	4·3
Austria	2·5	2·6	USSR	4·4	3·8
Ireland	2·5	2·7	Hungary	2·7	2·6
Italy	3·0	4·0	Poland	2·9	3·1
Greece	1·5	1·6	Romania	3·4	3·7
Yugoslavia	2·1	4·0	Bulgaria	5·1	3·6

[1] Data for Hungary are for 1955 and 1962. The public consumption expenditures data come from Appendix A; the GNP data from Appendix B.

The unweighted average ratios of public consumption expenditures for education to the GNP are significantly higher in the centralized than market economies (and in the socialist than capitalist nations as well). Moreover, taking other factors such as *per capita* income into account, this significant difference still remains. Because education expenditures are highly labour intensive, the 'factor income effect' gives an upward bias to the ratios from the centralized economies, but the observed differences between the two systems are too great to be accounted for by this statistical effect. Thus these results support the conclusion previously reached concerning the relative share of the public education expenditures in the two systems.[1] It is worth noting, however, that the observed differences between the two systems are considerably smaller in 1962 than in 1956.

For both years the ratio-income-elasticities are positive, but the calculated elasticity coefficients are not significantly greater than zero.[2] There is, of course, no necessary theoretical reason for such an elasticity to be positive; indeed, in cross-section experiments for the local governments in the United States, the calculated elasticities are usually negative.[3]

I tried a variety of other statistical experiments to test relationships between the ratio of public consumption expenditures to the GNP and other variables (such as the ratio of school-age children to the population or the growth rate of the GNP). But no positive results were obtained which would illuminate the analysis.

Education thus appears to be the only major public consumption expenditure in which the economic system is related to the expenditures/GNP ratio. To demonstrate conclusively that this

[1] For reasons given below, it seems more useful to classify Yugoslavia with the centralized economies so that the systems variable is capitalist-socialist.

[2] The calculated elasticity coefficients for 1956 and 1962 are respectively $+0\cdot22$ and $+0\cdot16$.

[3] Jerry Miner, *op. cit.*, summarizes the results of a great many econometric cross-section analyses of education expenditures of US state and local governments. My own experiments on these matters are reported in Appendix E–16. One reason for lower cross-section ratio-income-elasticities for US local government expenditures than for nations is that within a nation, there is a greater tendency for decision makers in one governmental unit to take into consideration expenditure decisions made in other governmental units. In other words, for local governments there is a greater 'demonstration effect' than for nations. This brings the ratio-income-elasticity closer to zero in intra-national studies.

systems variable is a causal factor, it is necessary to have comparable data of these countries during a period when they were still market economies. Nevertheless, qualitative evidence on these matters is so strong that we can accept the conclusion without the necessity of such a demonstration with the pre-war data.

In order to explore further implications of the data in Table 5-6 it is necessary to disaggregate the data and to separate expenditures for primary and secondary school teachers' salaries (the largest single educational expenditure) from other types of public consumption expenditures for education.[1] Of course, the portion accounted for by 'other expenditures' is much greater in the centralized than in the market economies since relatively more funds in the former group of nations go for vocational training, institutions of higher learning, and transfer payments to students and pupils. Unfortunately, detailed quantitative data on these matters are not available for a more probing analysis, but, as discussed above, there is considerable qualitative information that is relevant.[2]

In regard to the share of public consumption expenditures accounted for by primary and secondary school teachers' salaries, Yugoslavia behaves much more similarly to the East European nations than to the other market economies. From such a consideration it appears more useful to employ a systems variable designating capitalist and socialist nations for further explorations of education expenditures.

Three factors should be taken into account in this decomposition of education expenditures. First, it appears that teachers are relatively better paid *vis-à-vis* industrial blue-collar workers in the capitalist than in the socialist nations. We cannot be completely sure of this fact, because of the nature of the available salary data. But if this is correct, then the differences

[1] Sources for estimating teachers' salaries are given in Appendix D–16. As noted in this appendix, difficulties arise in obtaining comparable data on non-wage payments in the form of bonuses, living supplements, and so forth as well as deriving average salary estimates from scattered data on salaries of teachers with particular qualifications.

[2] For instance, in East Germany most factor vocational training programmes seem to be financed through the state budget. Comparable expenditures data on vocational training could not be located; and physical data on students and teachers are also not comparable.

between the two economic systems in regard to the ratio of public consumption expenditures to the GNP would be even greater if calculations were made in standard prices for all nations.

Second, it seems reasonable to suspect that the ratio of primary and secondary school teachers' wages to total expenditures for education would be inversely related to *per capita* income.[1] But in regard to public consumption expenditures such a relation cannot be observed because of relative differences in teachers' wages and in the shares of education expenditures that are publicly financed.

Finally, the cost structure of schooling by level of education is quite different and this introduces an additional distorting element. Although considerable data on this matter are available, comparability is doubtful.[1] Nevertheless, it appears that relative costs of educating students in institutions of higher learning are very much greater in the socialist than in the capitalist nations, just as the comparison between the USSR and the USA above also demonstrates.

In brief, the cross-section comparisons of ratios of public consumption expenditures for education to the GNP show that the systems variable is the only significant determinant of the differences among the sample nations. This is due, of course, to the fact that a higher share of total education expenditures is financed publicly in the socialist nations. Further, in these socialist nations salaries of primary and secondary school teachers *vis-à-vis* industrial workers' wages appear to be lower and the relative costs of educating students in institutions of higher learning seem to be higher than in the capitalist nations.

[1] This would come about because as *per capita* income rises, a greater share of education expenditures would be devoted to institutions of higher learning or to non-teaching auxiliary expenditures in primary and secondary schools, such as counselling services, health services, or pupil transportation. For the US these factors are quantitatively analysed by Werner Z. Hirsch, *Analysis of the Rising Costs of Public Education*, Study Paper No. 4, Joint Economic Committee, Congress of the United States (Washington, DC, 1959), pp. 25 ff.

[2] In different UNESCO publications (e.g. *Statistical Yearbook*, various issues; and *World Survey of Education*, various issues) such data are presented. Although certain economists have made use of these data (e.g. C. d'Hoogh, 'Systèmes de financement et optimalisation des dépense d'enseignement', *Public Finance/Finances publiques*, XXI, 1–2/1966, pp. 236 ff.), they seem much too rough to elicit much confidence in their comparability.

2. TIME-SERIES ANALYSIS

Quite different factors enter into the examination of the time-series data of public consumption expenditures, for which data are presented in Table 5–7 below.

TABLE 5–7

Time-Series Behaviour of Public Consumption Expenditures for Education,
1950 *through* 1962[1]

| | Elasticities | | | Elasticities | |
	A	B		A	B
USA	+ 1·07	− 1·51*	Czechoslovakia	+ 0·42*	− 0·20
West Germany	+ 0·16*	+ 0·29*	East Germany	+ 0·18*	+ 0·56*
Austria	+ 0·47*	+ 0·65*	USSR	− 0·50*	− 0·91*
Ireland	+ 0·44*	+ 0·18	Hungary	+ 0·40	+ 0·04
Italy	+ 0·58*	+ 0·54*	Poland	+ 0·37*	− 1·01*
Greece	+ 0·64*	+ 0·62*	Romania	− 0·02	− 0·28*
Yugoslavia	+ 1·34*	+ 1·00*	Bulgaria	− 0·02	− 0·30

Elasticity A is the ratio-income-elasticity. The unweighted average of these elasticities for the fourteen countries is about +0·40 which, as predicted is higher than the cross-section ratio-income-elasticities. In econometric studies of public expenditures for education in the United States, ratio-income-elasticities are also greater than unity and higher than the cross-section elasticities.[2]

In regressions to determine factors associated with these elasticity coefficients, I found that these elasticity coefficients are significantly and inversely related to the 1956 ratios of public consumption expenditures to the GNP (Table 5–6); that is, the lower the expenditure/GNP ratios, the higher the ratio-income-elasticity. Similar to the case of public consumption expenditures for welfare, there seems to be a convergence of the

[1] Elasticity *A* is the ratio-income-elasticity and is defined in Chapter II and in Appendix F; Elasticity *B* is a modified ratio-income-elasticity and is explained below and in Appendix F. The data for Yugoslavia cover 1952 through 1962. An asterisk denotes that the calculated regression coefficient is significantly (0·05 level) greater than zero. The data come from Appendices A, B, and D–1.

[2] Results from studies on US state and local government expenditures for education are also similar and are summarized by Jerry Miner, *op. cit.* My own experiments on these matters are presented in Appendix E–16.

education expenditures/GNP ratios of the sample nations toward a single value.

I also tested the relationships of the above elasticities with other variables such as economic system, growth rate of GNP, growth rate of school-age population, and GNP *per capita.* However, no useful results were found.[1]

For the market economies the average constant-price ratio-income-elasticities are $0 \cdot 43$ below the current price elasticities, which means that most of the constant-price ratio-income-elasticities of the sample nations are negative or close to zero. In view of the great emphasis on education during the post-war years this seems very peculiar until one considers the relationship between income and population growth rates. The gross national products of most of the sample nations grow at an average annual rate of 4 per cent or above (Table 1–3). On the other hand, the increase in the number of school-age children in most cases is considerably below this, so that this population factor acts as a restraining factor on the growth of education expenditures. In previous eras when the GNP did not grow at such a rapid rate this demographic restraint was probably much less important.

In order to eliminate the effect of the growth rate of the school-age population on education expenditures, it is necessary to focus attention on education expenditures per school-age child and to calculate the relationship between the ratio of such expenditures to the GNP and the *per capita* income to derive a modified ratio-income-elasticity without any demographic distortions.[2] This is elasticity B in Table 5-7 and is designated in the discussion below as the 'modified ratio-income-elasticity'.

In all countries but three (in which the number of school-age children is decreasing) the modified ratio-income-elasticity is smaller than the regular ratio-income-elasticity, a result that is quite expected. There is no statistically significant difference in

---

[1] From data on the portion of private school children it seems doubtful that these elasticities are greatly affected by changes in the ratio of public to total education expenditures during the period.

[2] The formula for this elasticity is: $\dfrac{d(E/C/Y)}{(E/C/Y)} \div \dfrac{d(Y/P)}{(Y/P)}$

where E = public consumption expenditures for education; C = school-aged children; Y = GNP; and P = population.

the average modified ratio-income-elasticity between capitalist and socialist nations. The modified ratio-income-elasticities are, however, significantly and inversely related to the 1956 education/GNP ratio, the rate of increase in the school-age population, and the 1956 GNP *per capita*.[1] The first of these relationships shows another aspect of the convergence effect noted above. The second relationship shows that, *ceteris paribus*, the modified ratio income elasticity is greater, the lower the growth rate of the school age population; that is, that the education expenditures per school-age child increase more if the school-age population grows less. This indicates that in the sample nations there are certain demographic constraints placed on the growth of education expenditures per child, an effect which confirms some of the theoretical considerations about relative growth rates discussed in the above paragraphs. The casual factors of the inverse relationship between GNP *per capita* and the modified ratio-income-elasticity are unfortunately obscure.

In brief, the time-series analysis shows three important phenomena. First, the elasticities from the cross-section calculations are smaller than those from the time-series, which demonstrates that the rising level of technology (which accompanies a rising income *per capita* in time-series but not in cross-section data) is an important determinant of education expenditures. Second, there is an important demographic constraint on the growth of education expenditures—the number of school-age children. And in time-series comparisons this factor must be taken into account. Finally, there seems to be a convergence of the ratio of public consumption expenditures for education to the GNP, a phenomenon that is found for other types of public consumption expenditures as well.

E. CENTRALIZATION OF EDUCATION EXPENDITURES

In analysing public consumption expenditures on education, the level of government at which such expenditures are made is an important feature and deserves attention. Examination of this phenomenon is complicated by the fact that centralized

[1] These variables are statistically significant only when taken together.

expenditures and control do not necessarily parallel each other. Before turning to the data on centralization of expenditures, it is useful to survey briefly some important interrelations between control and expenditures.

Perhaps the most important type of control exercised by a central government over education at the local level is the determination of school curricula, a topic on which considerable information is available.[1] Curricula established by central authorities may be absolutely binding, as in the case of primary schools in Czechoslovakia and Hungary, or may be binding only in general outline, as in the case of primary schools in Greece, East Germany, Poland, Romania, and Bulgaria. On the other hand, centrally established curricula may merely designate minimum standards, as in the case of primary-schools in Austria, Ireland, Italy and Yugoslavia, or may not have any formal *legal* force as in the case of primary schools in the United States, West Germany, and the Soviet Union. For the last group of countries, the Laender in West Germany and the states in the United States set minimum standards; while in the Soviet Union the republics set a compulsory curriculum. Nevertheless, in the Soviet Union the federal government seems to play an extremely strong informal role especially through selection and the approval of textbooks.[2]

Since control over the curricula can be enforced without financial incentives, such control can be completely divorced from the level of government at which education expenditures

[1] Information for all the sample nations except East Germany may be obtained from: International Bureau of Education; *Preparation and Issuing of the Primary School Curricula*, Publ. Number 194 (Geneva, 1958); and *Preparation of General Secondary School Curricula*, Publ. Number 216 (Geneva, 1960). For East Germany, information is available from a number of sources, the most accessible of which is: Paul S. Bodenman, *Education in the Soviet Zone of Germany*, US Department of Health, Education, and Welfare, Bulletin 26/1959 (Washington, DC, 1959). The information below comes from these various sources.

[2] According to Alexander G. Korol [*Soviet Education for Science and Technology*, (Cambridge, Mass., 1957), p. 1]. 'For the present we need to note only one of the most distinguishing characteristics of the Soviet ten-year school: the uniformity of its curricula, textbooks, and methods of instruction, grade for grade, with only minor regional variations throughout the Soviet Union. In Moscow or Irkutsk, Russians or Buryats, boys or girls in corresponding grades follow the same curriculum prescribed by the Ministry of Education and study identical subjects following uniform syllabi and, except for the language in which they are written, identical "approved" textbooks.'

are made. This is particularly clear in those cases where a nation decentralizes expenditures but maintains the same type of curricula control.

Other types of governmental control that seem independent of the centralization of expenditures include: determination of qualifications of teachers,[1] designation of specific people or groups that are or are not allowed to teach, and the setting of salary schedules. Non-governmental influences in the decision-making process for education that seem independent of the centralization or decentralization of expenditures are also important to consider, especially if this influence includes that of a centralized religious group or political party.[2] Unfortunately, comparable information on such matters is difficult to obtain.

A final important relation between the degree of control and the centralization of expenditures is the degree to which a central government can specify the extent to which education expenditures are made at the various local levels of government. If, for instance, the local schools are greatly dependent on grants from the central government, then they may effectively have little power to determine the amount of their education expenditures if the central government allocates such grants on the basis of some type of central education plan. On the other

---

[1] The employment status of teachers is described for many nations by the International Bureau of Education: *Primary Teachers' Salaries*, Publ. No. 147 (Geneva: 1952); and *Secondary Teachers' Salaries*, Publ. No. 157 (Geneva, 1954).

[2] Western commentators have emphasized that the degree of political party control of education in various Eastern European nations acts as a centralizing force and cite a considerable body of qualitative information about this. E.g. in East Germany the Secretary of the Central Committee of the Socialist Unity Party declared: 'When some non-Party scholars raise the question whether the Party has the right to interfere in the affairs of the universities, we must answer that the Party not only has the right, but the duty . . .' (cited by Bodenman, *op. cit.*, p. 96); or in the Soviet Union, Party control seems extensive, not only on the level of policy making but also daily operations (Nicholas DeWitt, *Education and Professional Employment in the USSR, op. cit.*, pp. 42–5). On the other hand, party control in the day-to-day operations appeared less extensive in several other socialist countries, notably Poland. Quantitative evidence on this matter, which would permit reliable comparisons to be made, is not available. Furthermore, in some countries where a non-governmental organization has considerable control over education (e.g. Ireland), such a control can act as a decentralizing force if the organization in question has not centralized its policy on the matter.

hand, if the central and local governments share certain taxes at previously specified ratios and if the local governments have the legal power to use such funds in the best manner they see fit, then the central government may have almost no control over the amount of local expenditures on education, even though all of the local funds for education appear as a grant from the central to the local governments.

All of these considerations lead to the conclusion that for education, there need be little relation between the centralization of control and the centralization of expenditures. Such a divorce between economic and political factors makes the analysis of centralization of expenditures considerably easier, for we can focus exclusive attention on economic factors. A number of hypotheses to explain the differential degree of centralization of education expenditures in various governmental units can be offered.

First, there is a possible influence of geographical mobility of the population. Other things remaining the same, the greater the net emigration from certain subnational territorial units to others, the larger the share of public education expenditures which are financed at the central level (either directly or indirectly through a grant system). This would come about because citizens in one subnational territorial unit usually object strongly to being taxed for the education of children who later move out of the area. Furthermore, if there is considerable geographical mobility of families, it is generally desirable to have a fairly uniform system of education in every area, and this too requires central financing. Certain empirical evidence in favour of this proposition is available for the United States.[1]

Second, there is the influence of scale. Other things remaining equal, the smaller the size of the largest subnational units, the larger the share of education expenditures which may be financed at the central government level. This should come about because certain types of education, especially at the college and university level, appear to have lowest average unit costs when the number of students is quite large. Indeed, for a

[1] Weisbrod, *External Benefits* . . ., *op. cit.*, pp. 105 ff. presents some positive results of a regression analysis on this matter.

particular kind of advanced training, one institution may well serve an entire nation.

Third, the form of government of a country, whether it is federal or unitary, may also play a role. In a federal system, the proportion of education expenditures financed directly at the federal level should be lower, since local governments supposedly have more political autonomy and, therefore, more control over their own expenditures.

A final factor concerns the effects of income inequalities among the different subnational territorial units. *Ceteris paribus*, the greater the inequality of income in different parts of the country, the greater may be the degree of central governmental financing of education. If there is a desire for uniformity of education of children throughout a nation and if there is not an effective mechanism for the transfer of funds between different levels of government, then central government financing may be the only way in which such uniformity is brought about. I have carried out a number of experiments using data for state and local governments in the United States to see if this hypothesis is useful in analysing US centralization data, but the results were negative. Unfortunately, adequate information for testing this hypothesis on an international level is not available. Data on the centralization ratios of expenditures for testing the other hypotheses are given in Table 5–8 below.

TABLE 5–8

Centralization Ratios of Public Consumption Expenditures for Education[1]

Country	1956	1962	Country	1956	1962
USA	10%	4%	Czechoslovakia	16%	10
West Germany	0	2	East Germany	42	37
Austria	82	79	USSR	31	4
Ireland	92	93	Hungary	n.a.	n.a.
Italy	85	86	Poland	48	20
Greece	84	83	Romania	n.a.	n.a.
Yugoslavia	1	0	Bulgaria	40	24

[1] The centralization ratio is the percentage of public consumption expenditures made directly at the central governmental level. For Greece, the data are for 1956 and 1961; for East Germany, 1958 and 1962; and for the USSR, 1956 and 1960. All data come from Appendix A.

The most striking feature of the data in Table 5–8 is the enormous variation between countries and, for the centralized economies, between the two years. However, the variation at one point in time is considerably greater than between the two years.

In using the data to test the different hypotheses discussed above, several technical difficulties arise[1] which encourage caution in interpreting the data.

It appears that the form of government (federal or unitary) plays an important role. Four out of the five federal nations (USA, West Germany, Yugoslavia, and the USSR) have among the lowest centralization ratios in the two years.

One variable that reflects both the mobility and scale factors discussed above is the average size of the largest subnational territorial unit. That is, the larger this unit, the less important the mobility and scale factors would become and, therefore, the lower the degree of centralization would be. Such an inverse relation is found in 1956, but not in 1962. Moreover, in conjunction with the variable representing the form of government, its statistical significance disappears.

Per capita income would be another variable which should be related to the mobility factors discussed above. That is, the higher the *per capita* income of the nation, the greater the intra-country mobility and the higher the degree of centralization would be. Unfortunately, no such relation can be found, even when *per capita* income is tested in conjunction with form of government, average size of largest subnational territorial unit, and other such variables.[2]

Although the average centralization ratio is considerably higher in the capitalist than socialist nations, this seems to be due partly to the exclusion of Hungary and Romania, both of which are known to have highly centralized fiscal systems.

[1] Three major problems arise. First, the form of equation used in the regression calculations makes a considerable difference for the statistical significance of the independent variables. Second, a number of the independent variables are related to each other, so that multicollinearity difficulties are encountered. Finally, there are considerable differences in the calculated regression coefficients in the two years.

[2] In addition a series of regressions with *per capita* income and population were calculated, but the expected inverse relations of these variables and the centralization ratio did not appear.

In regard to the trends of the centralization ratios between 1956 and 1962, a fairly uniform pattern emerges. In most countries a decline occurs, and for the other countries no great changes occur. In the light of the four hypotheses discussed above, this trend is unexpected and the explanation seems to lie more in the realm of politics, rather than economics. In the socialist countries except for Yugoslavia, there was a general decentralization of public expenditures paralleling a retreat from earlier centralization excesses in many fields. In the United States direct central governmental participation in education expenditures declined with the fall in war veterans' benefits for education.

It must be added that for multi-level governments the indicator for centralization in the table masks changes in centralization occurring at other levels of government. For instance, in the United States the degree of centralization of education expenditures between state and local government increased at the same time that the degree of centralization between the federal and other governmental units declined.[1]

F. SUMMARY AND CONCLUSIONS

From this analysis of expenditures for education a number of major conclusions emerge.

To start with, the elasticity of substitution between private and public expenditures for education is such that the public/ private mix in financing education makes very little difference in the total amount of education which is produced. However, the method of financing does influence the social class structure of university students, the curricula of institutions of higher learning, and the ownership of facilities in which education is produced.

The most important motives for financing education in the public sector seem to be social and political; the most relevant economic motive appears to be the sharing of risks in education over the entire population. Externalities and public good properties seem to play little role.

---

[1] Such matters are discussed in much greater detail in Appendix E–8: Centralization of Public Expenditures in US State and Local Governments.

H

For total education production and expenditures the most important determinants appear to be the level of economic development and the proportion of school-age children in the population. Because of the relationship between the technological level of the world economy and *per capita* income over time, it can be predicted and evidence confirms the fact that the time-series ratio-income-elasticities of education expenditures are greater than those calculated with cross-section data. Other variables such as the type of economic system do not seem to play any significant role in explaining total education expenditures.

On the other hand, in the cross-section analysis of the share of public consumption expenditures for education in the GNP, the economic system (defined in terms of capitalist-socialist) is the most important explanatory variable, since the socialist nations finance publicly a much greater portion of education expenditures. However, the time-series analysis shows that there is a convergence of these expenditure/GNP ratios toward a common value, which means that the influence of economic system is diminishing.

The ratios of public consumption expenditures for education to the GNP are related to the *per capita* income in the time series data. Nevertheless, the number of school-age children acts as a constraint on the increase of total expenditures. If the ratio-income-elasticities of public consumption expenditures for education are made in constant prices, the calculated coefficients are close to zero, which reflects this demographic constraint.

In exploring the centralization of public consumption expenditures for education, we find that there can be a complete divorce between centralization of control and of the expenditures. The most important explanatory variable in the degree of centralization is whether the nation is unitary or federal.

Chapter VI

OTHER PUBLIC BUDGETARY EXPENDITURES

A. Introduction
B. Public Consumption Expenditures for Administration
C. Public Consumption Expenditures for Internal Security
D. Public Consumption Expenditures for Non-military External Security
E. Public Consumption Expenditures for Research and Development
F. Other Public Expenditures
G. Summary and Conclusions

A. INTRODUCTION

The most important public consumption expenditures are for defence, welfare, health, and education; together these comprise over 70 per cent of the adjusted budgets of all the sample nations. Various aspects of these four expenditures have received attention by economists and both my empirical and theoretical analyses of these expenditures utilize with considerable profit such previous studies.

For reasons that are obscure, however, social scientists have virtually ignored public consumption expenditures for administration, internal security, non-military external security, and research and development, that are examined below. This chapter focuses on the most fundamental aspects of these expenditures and the analysis is primarily empirical rather than theoretical. However, many of the results run contrary to commonly held notions about these expenditures and thus have significant theoretical implications.

Other types of public expenditures such as interest payments, subsidies, capital grants, and investment lie outside the range of expenditures that are explored in detail in this study. While the lack of comparable data precludes any tenable quantitative analysis of these expenditures at the present time, they are of interest, nevertheless, and are here examined in a qualitative manner so that greater perspective can be gained on the state budget as a whole.

B. PUBLIC CONSUMPTION EXPENDITURES FOR ADMINISTRATION

Expenditures for administration include those for the highest governmental organs, for financial administration of all levels of government, and for general control purposes, including civil defence. All interest charges, administrative expenditures of the nationalized enterprises, expenditures for low-level administration in the functional areas (e.g. education, defence, and so forth), or expenditures for justice and police are excluded whenever possible.

Government administration expenditures have several relevant theoretical properties which are worth while to consider. For one thing, they are an exclusive function of the public domain and, moreover, such administrative services are almost inevitably produced in public-owned facilities.[1] Thus the distinction between government financing and ownership cannot be used for differentiating the handling of such administrative services in different countries.

Such government administration also exhibits certain public-good properties. That is, some of the benefits of these expenditures cannot be excluded from anyone, and, furthermore, an additional person can enjoy these benefits for no extra costs. In trying to outline some of the benefits of administration expenditures such as a stable political order, co-ordination between other governmental services with public-good properties, or the pride of nationhood (or of locality), one encounters an important theoretical dilemma.

---

[1] Historically, such functions as defence and, as noted in the following section, even police and judicial expenditures have been financed, at one time or another, by the private sector. The ideology of technocracy, however, has not spread to such an extent that any group of people have yet chosen to let themselves be governed by a private-enterprise 'government administration company'.

It should be noted that in the United States, various government agencies are increasingly leasing private buildings for use. Such 'production' of public administration in private facilities is still quite unimportant, however.

It is extremely difficult to determine just what specifically is being produced by such administration expenditures. While looking at a number of the sample nations, one is reminded of George Trevelyan's assessment of the state of public administration in England under George III:

'The most serious minded and keensighted foreign critics . . . could not understand how it came about that a nation, which apparently possessed an unlimited supply of sagacious and successful men, numbered so very few of them among its rulers . . .'[1]

In trying to relate the benefits with the costs of governmental administration expenditures, the chances seem more likely that the relation is inverse, rather than direct.

While analysing empirically the data on government administration expenditures, it is also important to realize that the reporting of such expenditures is not standardized between nations or, for several sample countries, over time as well. Three basic reasons for this difficulty are apparent:

1. The decision as to whether to include or exclude the costs of high-level policy-making groups for the nationalized industries (e.g. Ministry of Heavy Industry) under 'government administration' varies among the sample countries. For instance, in West Germany all costs of administering the state industries are excluded from general governmental administration costs; in East Germany, on the other hand, some such costs (e.g. at one time the top administration of the Reichsbahn) are reported to be included under general government administration. Since detailed information on administration expenditures were unavailable for all centralized economies except Poland, and for some of the market economies as well, no major adjustments could be made to the published data.

2. The decision as to whether high level administration expenditures in the different functional fields (e.g. the expenditures for the operation of the Ministry of Education) are assigned to that function or to the general administration fund is also

[1] George Otto Trevelyan, *George the Third and Charles Fox*, Vol. II (New York, 1914), pp. 174–5.

handled differently in a number of the sample nations. It is also possible that government budgetary accounting systems in the more developed economies tend to be more complex and to allocate more costs to specific programmes or functions, rather than broader administrative or overhead categories. The quantitative significance of this is not known, however, and few adjustments could be made to take this phenomenon adequately into account.

3. Several nations among the centralized economies, have changed the statistical definition of administration expenditures over time. This has come about either because of some major administrative change (e.g. in the USSR, the introduction of the Sovnarkhozy and the abolition of the production ministries in 1957; or the selling of MTSs to the collective farms in 1958); or because of certain incentives to make administration expenditures appear to be growing more slowly than they actually are.[1] Since detailed information on how these definitions have changed over time is not available for most countries, no major adjustment could be made and several anomalies appear in the data.

Such statistical problems preclude meaningful cross-country comparisons of the ratios of administration expenditure to the GNP and of the degree of centralization of such expenditures, and force us to exercise caution in interpreting the time-series data for nations. It is quite useful, however, to examine administration expenditures of US state and local governments, which are much more comparable.

Taking into account the above discussed theoretical and empirical difficulties, several possible approaches are available to analyse the data on public consumption expenditures for administration. We could start with various types of theoretical models, derive some simple hypotheses, and test them. But few

---

[1] In order to fulfill plan goals for the reduction of administration expenditures, budgetary authorities have a considerable incentive to redefine such expenditures and transfer certain 'administration costs' to the functional areas. The much higher degree of year-to-year variation of administration expenditures in the centralized than in the market economies (see Chapter VII) is one indication that some type of accounting skulduggery may be afoot. Although such incentives may also exist in market economies, the existence of a multi-party political system creates certain hazards for anyone attempting such statistical manipulations.

such models in the scholarly literature seem very useful.[1] Or we can turn further afield to certain empirical studies that may be relevant. In particular, it seems reasonable to believe that administration problems in manufacturing and in government bear great similarity to each other. Therefore, we might be able to derive a number of hypotheses about the behaviour of governmental administration expenditures from studies of such costs in industry.[2] In weighing the benefits and costs of constructing a theoretical model or of turning to industry to obtain hypotheses about the behaviour of public consumption expenditures for administration, the latter alternative seems considerably more worth while.

Over time, the ratio of administrative to production expenditures (and the ratio of personnel in these two branches) in manufacturing has steadily risen. This rise cannot be attributed to any change in the relative importance of different industries

[1] One interesting type of model of administration costs, based on co-ordination problems arising from the 'combinatorial effect', is presented by William Baumol, 'Interaction of Public and Private Decisions', in Howard Schaller, ed., *Public Expenditure Decisions in the Urban Community* (Baltimore, 1962). Unfortunately, none of the important empirical implications of his model is borne out by the empirical results of this study.

One well-known lengthy theoretical treatment of governmental administrative expenditures is by C. Northcote Parkinson, *Parkinson's Law* (Boston, 1957). For all his wit and superb examples, his conclusions seem to be wrong on several important points which are discussed below.

[2] The most extensive empirical studies are by Seymour Melman: 'The Rise of Administrative Overhead in the Manufacturing Industries in the United States, 1899–1947', *Oxford Economic Papers*, III, February 1951, pp. 62–112; 'Production and Administration Cost in Relation to Size of Firm', *Applied Statistics*, III, March 1954, pp. 1–11; and *Dynamic Factors in Industrial Production* (New York, 1956). Briefer empirical examinations of this topic have been made by Michael Gort, *Diversification and Integration in American Industry* (Princeton, 1962), esp. pp. 87–91; and David Granick, *The European Executive* (Garden City, NY, 1962), Chapter 22. One empirical micro-study whose results seem to conflict with the Melman, Gort, and Granick conclusions is by Mason Haire, 'Biological Models and Empirical Histories of the Growth of Organizations', in Haire, ed., *Modern Organization Theory* (New York, 1959). A very relevant but early theoretical analysis of such problems is by Kenneth Boulding, *The Organizational Revolution* (New York, Harper, 1953).

In most of these empirical studies administrative employees are defined so as to include white-collar workers. It must be noted that the line between white and blue-collar workers is becoming increasingly more indistinct, especially between white-collar supervisors and blue-collar working foremen or between white-collar engineers and blue-collar highly skilled workers of automated equipment.

or of different size firms or to any change in industrial concentration or in the form of organization of the firm (partnership, corporation, etc.).

Seymour Melman tries to explain the rising time trend in relative administration expenditures (and the rising ratio of administration to production personnel) in terms of the development of new managerial functions and the efforts by administrators to rationalize their decision-making process by increasingly placing more resources in such functions as cost accounting and budgeting, market research and analysis, personnel and public relations, and operations research.[1] In Western Europe, on the other hand, David Granick suggests that the rise in relative administrative expenditures is primarily due to the rise of technical personnel such as engineers and scientists.[2]

Another explanation lies in the fact that technical change probably occurred faster in the production side than in the administration side of manufacturing, so that the unit labour costs of administration rose *vis-à-vis* production. Of course this does not mean that productivity should always increase faster in production; certainly the large-scale introduction of electronic data processing machines suggests that recently, administration productivity has increased at a considerable rate.

From these results as well as from ordinary 'common sense' it seems obvious that in time-series government administration expenditures would rise as a percentage of total government expenditures and, since the percentage of total government expenditures to the GNP has risen over the long run, government administration expenditures should also rise as a share of the national product. Unfortunately, neither of these hypotheses seems to be borne out by the data.

Studies of governmental expenditures over very long periods of time for all countries show dramatic falls in the ratios of administration of expenditures to the total budgetary expenditures. Indeed, these declines were precipitous enough to offset the rising overall share of government expenditures in the GNP, so that the share of governmental administration expendi-

---

[1] Melman, *Dynamic Factors in Industrial Productivity, op. cit.*, Chapter XVII.
[2] Granick, *op. cit.*

tures in the GNP remained the same or fell. For instance, in the United Kingdom, the ratio of administration expenditures to the GNP fell slightly between 1890 and 1955,[1] and in the United States from 1927 to 1963, the ratio-income-elasticity of government expenditures was substantially less than zero.[2]

For the analysis of the time-series data from the sample nations, two statistics are calculated: the ratio-income-elasticity and the ratio-budget-elasticity, i.e. the percentage change of the public administration expenditures/adjusted budget ratio as income *per capita* increases by 1 per cent. The results are presented in Table 6–1 below.

The calculated ratio-income and ratio-budget-elasticities are negative or are not significantly positive with the exception of

TABLE 6–1

Time-Series Behaviour of Public Consumption Expenditures for Administration, 1950 through 1962[3]

Country	Ratio-income elasticity	Ratio-budget-elasticity	Country	Ratio-income-elasticity	Ratio-budget-elasticity
USA	+ 0·93	− 0·14	Czechoslovakia	− 1·08*	− 1·06*
West Germany	− 0·21*	− 0·28*	East Germany	− 1·32*	− 0·95*
Austria	+ 0·54*	+ 0·16*	USSR	− 1·75*	− 1·30*
Ireland	+ 0·37*	+ 0·67*	Hungary	+ 1·22*	+ 1·43*
Italy	− 0·05	− 0·40*	Poland	− 2·80*	− 2·88*
Greece	− 0·21	− 0·18*	Romania	− 1·10*	− 0·86*
Yugoslavia	− 0·62	− 0·34	Bulgaria	− 1·30*	− 0·98*

[1] Alan T. Peacock and Jack Wiseman, *The Growth of Public Expenditures in the United Kingdom* (Princeton, 1961), pp. 191–2. The ratio of government administration to the GNP in current prices remained the same in the period; since the price index for services rose faster than for the GNP as a whole, this means in fixed prices that administration as a percentage of GNP fell.

[2] Elasticities were computed from data in the following sources: US Bureau of the Census, 'Historical Statistics on Governmental Finances and Employment', Vol. VI., No. 4, *Census of Governments, 1962* (Washington, DC, 1964); *Statistical Abstract of the United States, 1965* (Washington, DC, 1965); *Historical Statistics of the United States* (Washington, DC, 1960); and *Survey of Current Business*, XLV, 8/1965. A price index for administration expenditures was estimated from a government wage index and the wholesale price index. A number of different definitions of administration were used; all gave about the same results.

[3] The ratio-budget-elasticity is defined in the text. Expenditures data come from Appendix A. Yugoslav elasticities cover 1952 through 1962. Asterisks denote statistics significance at the 0·05 level.

H*

three nations. In the market economies, the constant-price ratio-income-elasticities are on the average about 0·45 lower than such elasticities calculated in current prices, which means that the negative tendencies of the ratio-income-elasticities are even greater than shown in the table.[1]

As indicated above, some of the countries—especially the centralized economies—changed their definition of administration expenditures over time so that the above calculated elasticities appear too low. From the budget literature, this appears especially to be the case in East Germany,[2] Czechoslovakia, and the USSR, although the exact changes made are not known. While such data problems suggest why experiments in explaining the differences between ratio-income-elasticities or between ratio-budget-elasticities are not promising,[3] we cannot pass off the fact that such elasticities are quite low or negative in the market economies where the data are more consistent. Before concluding that causes in the change of administration expenditures are different in government and the manufacturing sector, however, it seems worth while to consider whether we are measuring the same phenomenon in the two sectors.

In the manufacturing sector a line between administration and production workers or expenditures is drawn such that all

[1] The constant-price ratio-budget-elasticities are somewhat below the current-price budget elasticities for the market economies but, because so many assumptions are involved in calculating both the numerator and the denominator, the exact results are not reported.

[2] It is possible that certain reparation costs were included in East German administration expenditures for the early years; in any case, such administration expenditures on a *per capita* basis were much higher in East Germany than in West Germany for most of the period. East and West German administration costs are analysed in more detail in my 'East and West German Governmental Expenditures', *Public Finance/Finances publiques*, XX, 3–4/1965, esp. pp. 317–20, 356.

[3] Nevertheless, a number of experiments were attempted, trying to relate the ratio elasticities in Table 6–1 to the following explanatory variables (both singly and in different combinations): economic system, growth rate of GNP, the GNP *per capita*, the ratio-income-elasticity of the adjusted budget, the ratio of public administration expenditures to the GNP, and the ratio of public administration expenditures to the adjusted budget. With the exception of the economic systems variable, which seems to reflect data problems rather than any economically important phenomenon, no statistically significant relations were discovered.

'white-collar' personnel are included in 'administration'. Although it is noted above that this distinction in manufacturing is becoming increasingly more hazy, such a procedure certainly has important justifications. In the public sector where 'white-collar services' are produced, the distinction between administration and production is even less clear-cut. Since it is easier to define 'administration' to cover institutions, rather than a certain function, a statistical illusion may arise. That is, when governments expand their activities in the various functional areas (e.g. defence or education), it is quite possible that actual administration expenditures greatly expand while the measured expenditures, which cover just the top administrative bodies outside the functional area, remain the same. This phenomenon would give the data in Table 6–1 a strong downward bias. Until much more detailed data are available about the administration expenditures within each function, we cannot know whether the discovered differences between the governmental and manufacturing sectors are statistical or real.

In the cross-section analysis of industry, the ratio of administration to production expenditures (the ratio can also be defined in terms of personnel) is inversely related to the size of the firm or industry. Other factors such as industrial concentration, profit rates, the corporate form, pricing practices, age of firm, or degree of mechanization do not seem to affect significantly this ratio of administration to production expenditures. Furthermore, in comparing the manufacturing sector in different nations, the ratio of administrative to productive workers seems quite similar, although the overall labour productivity varies greatly among such countries.[1]

The inverse relation of the size and relative administrative expenditures seems primarily due to economies of scale within the administrative structure. This empirical result seems contrary to the contention of many who maintain that beyond a certain size, co-ordination of a firm becomes increasingly difficult so that, in the long run, average costs rise.[2] In addition,

[1] Melman, op. cit.
[2] The question cannot be settled from data on the ratios of administrative to production expenditures alone since profits are completely omitted from consideration and there is empirical evidence that the largest firms have lower

such an inverse relation offers a certain contrary evidence to the 'inexorable' action of Parkinson's law.[1]

Such data for industry suggest three behavioural relationships of the ratio of public consumption expenditures for administration to total public consumption expenditures (the 'administration/budget ratio'): (1) it is unrelated to *per capita* income; (2) it is unrelated to *per capita* budgetary expenditures; (3) it is inversely related to the absolute value of administration expenditures (the scale effect). If cross-section and time-series determinants for governmental administrative expenditures are the same,[2] then we would expect that: (4) the administrative/budget ratio is inversely related to *per capita* income [a prediction different from (1) which is made from industry results]; and (5) the ratio-income-elasticity is negative when the ratio of budgetary expenditures to the GNP is held constant.

Since data for the sample nations cannot be utilized for cross-sectional analysis, we must use public expenditures data for US state and local governments. To test the above hypotheses the following regressions can be calculated:[3]

average profit rates than firms in a smaller size category. Considerably more empirical analysis must be carried out before definite conclusions can be drawn.

[1] Of course, Parkinson, *op. cit.*, was primarily concerned with time paths of administration expenditures. *Contra* Parkinson, Melman found that the relative size of company administrative staffs is unrelated to the age of the company.

[2] Since US state and local government expenditures are used for the statistical analysis, it is necessary to derive the cross-section predictions from the corresponding data for the same type of governmental units. The following regressions can be calculated for such state and local expenditures for the period 1950 to 1962:

$$\ln (A/B) = -\ 6 \cdot 65 - 1 \cdot 02^* \quad \ln (Y_c/P) \qquad\qquad R^2 = 0 \cdot 75^*$$
$$(0 \cdot 18)$$

$$\ln (A/Y) = -\ 3 \cdot 16 + 1 \cdot 09^* \quad \ln (Y_c/P) \qquad\qquad R^2 = 0 \cdot 43^*$$
$$(0 \cdot 38)$$

$$\ln (A/Y) = -\ 3 \cdot 71 - 0 \cdot 39^* \quad \ln (Y_c/P) + 0 \cdot 70^* \ln (B/Y) \qquad R^2 = 0 \cdot 98^*$$
$$(0 \cdot 12) \qquad\qquad (0 \cdot 04)$$

where A = administration expenditures; B = current budgetary expenditures; Y_c = GNP in constant prices; Y = GNP in current prices; and P = population.

Time-series results are sensitive to the time period chosen for analysis. For instance, between 1902 and 1950 the ratio of public expenditures for administration to the GNP fell, while between 1950 and 1960 it rose.

[3] Administration includes both current and capital expenditures for financial administration and general control. They were calculated by averaging such expenditures for the fiscal years 1962 and 1963 in order to eliminate the variation in state expenditures because legislatures meet only once every two years. A number of experiments were made with different definitions of administration

$$\ln (A/B) = -12\cdot85 + 0\cdot53^* \ln (Y/P) - 0\cdot17 \ln (B/P) - 0\cdot03 \ln A$$
$$(0\cdot16) \qquad\qquad (0\cdot15) \qquad\qquad (0\cdot02)$$
$$R^2 = 0\cdot24^*$$

$$\ln (A/Y) = -12\cdot63 + 0\cdot34^* \ln (Y/P) + 0\cdot91^* \ln (B/Y$$
$$(0\cdot11) \qquad\qquad (0\cdot14)$$
$$R^2 = 0\cdot46^*$$

where A = administration expenditures of state and local governments,

B = current budgetary expenditures of state and local governments,

Y = personal income,

P = population

R^2 = coefficient of determination

Of the three predictions made from the results from industry, only one appears successful: that there is no relation between the administration/budget ratio and *per capita* budgetary expenditures. And this is a quite unexceptional forecast. Of the two predictions made from the assumption that the cross-section and time-series determinants are similar, both are spectacularly wrong since the calculated coefficients of the ratio-income-elasticity and the budget-elasticity are statistically significant, but with positive rather than negative signs.[1]

It is not too surprising that there is no 'scale effect' (i.e. the administration/budget ratio is inversely related to the absolute

expenditures and of total budgetary expenditures, but the results are roughly the same and are, therefore, not reported.

Data come from US Bureau of the Census: *US Census of Governments 1962*, *op. cit.; Governmental Finances in 1963* (Washington, DC, 1964) and *Survey of Current Business*, XLV, April 1965. Asterisks denote statistical significance at the $0\cdot05$ level.

[1] If the ratio-income-elasticity is calculated without holding the ratio of budget expenditures to income constant, the following results are obtained: $\ln (A/Y) = -13\cdot00 + 0\cdot12 \ln (Y/P); R^2 = 0\cdot02$. The symbols are the same as $(0\cdot14)$ those used above.

value of administration expenditures) because, as noted in a footnote above, the existence of such an effect in industry is not entirely clear.

The positive ratio-income-elasticity and budget-elasticity are quite unexpected, and an adequate interpretation is not possible until more detailed data are available. But we can infer that the cross-section and time-series determinants of public consumption expenditures for administration are quite different.

Certain factors influencing administration expenditures should be clear from this brief investigation. First, for international comparisons, data on public consumption expenditures for administration are not very comparable. Second, in using comparable data there are still a number of statistical biases, especially since administration is defined primarily in institutional rather than functional terms. Third, the data for administration expenditures of governments and industry, at least in the United States, behave very differently both in time-series and cross-section analyses. Finally, the cross-section and time-series determinants of public consumption expenditures for administration appear to be different, although the underlying factors cannot be isolated. Although negative results are seldom as exciting as positive results, they often have the advantage of destroying old prejudices which, in the case of administration expenditures, do not seem related to reality.

Before turning to analysis of another government expenditure, several additional remarks must be made about administration expenditures. In this era of bourgeoning bureaucracies, it seems extraordinary that so little empirical work has been carried out on the costs of administration. As to the Marxist literature it is unpardonable that those who believe in the 'withering away of the state' (a tenet in Marxist theology that is functionally equivalent to the apocalyptic-eschatological vision of Christian theology foreseeing the lion and the lamb lying together in peace) have not attempted to draw the necessary conclusions concerning governmental administration expenditures. Indeed, the 'economics of administration' awaits its founder in both the East and the West.

C. PUBLIC CONSUMPTION EXPENDITURES FOR INTERNAL SECURITY

Internal security covers expenditures on police, courts, prisons, and other institutions connected with the internal law and order of the nation. Fire protection is excluded; expenditures for civil defence from external aggression are included in administration.

In a democracy, internal security services have certain public good properties, especially in regard to the 'production' of protection and justice for all. Nevertheless, the extent of such public good properties is integrally related to the type of political order; and in dictatorships, for example, such properties are very much more limited. It should also be evident that the private sector can, as demonstrated in the past, play an important role in providing and financing such a service. For instance, in feudal times the state role in justice and protection was shared with a number of non-governmental groups such as the church and the aristocracy. In later periods, such private-sector internal security activities continued in different forms; devotees of American wild-west movies appreciate the important role of private posses and kangaroo courts in the nineteenth century.

In the period under examination such private internal security activities still exist. Among the market economies, in the field of justice many legal disputes in business are adjudicated by private arbitrators in the United States, rather than by court officials of the state, and are privately financed. Furthermore, a number of small, unincorporated American communities have hired private groups for police patrolling, rather than setting up a formal government and establishing their own police force.[1] In certain backward regions of that country, private vigilante groups have also sometimes played a role in producing justice

[1] The state of Florida also engaged such private police service in a widely publicized but not greatly efficacious drive against racketeering and corruption. The work of private police and detective forces in the countries with legal systems based on English common law is facilitated by the legality of 'citizen's arrests', by which any citizen may arrest any person in the act of committing a felony. The basic problem in citizens' arrests is, of course, enforcing the arrest long enough to bring the apprehended person to a police station.

(or injustice, as the case may be), a phenomenon which is also not unknown in some parts of other sample nations such as southern Italy. Nevertheless, in all market economies such para-police activities are of small importance and, indeed, many such activities are quite illegal.

Among some East European nations, however, relatively more security work is performed by those outside the formal law-and-order units. For instance, in the Soviet Union there are such para-police units as the Voluntary People's Militia (Dobro-volnaya narodnaya druzhina), which in 1960 included 2·5 million members, and the home-and-family-life detachments (Bytovyye otryady) of the Komsomol, which visit Soviet citizens in their homes to check on family matters and to inculcate the principles of the new society.[1] In a similar spirit, East German children who report on people listening to West German radio and television stations are encouraged and rewarded with gifts. However, in the other socialist nations, such para-police work seems much less important.

In addition to private participation in the internal security function, a certain role is also played by governmental agencies other than the police, the courts of the prisons. Supplementing the courts in the judicial field in most countries are a series of governmental administrative organs which regulate certain aspects of the industrial sector and which adjudicate certain legal disputes. Moreover, for police work, the army has often served an important role. For instance, in the US the Army and National Guards have been used to quell disorders arising from school desegregation, and in Hungary in 1956, certain groups did not hesitate to call in a foreign army to re-establish order after the domestic police and army failed in the task.

[1] These organizations are analysed in an interesting way by George L. Kline, ' "Socialist Legality" and Communist Ethics', *Natural Law Forum*, VIII (1963), pp. 21–34. Officially, the Komsomol home-and-family-life detachments do not serve a police function. It does not seem accidental, however, that two First Secretaries of Komsomol, A. Shelepin and V. Ye. Semichastny, later assumed top positions in the state security apparatus. In addition, V. S. Tikunov, who was a high official in Komsomol for ten years, was appointed Deputy Chairman of the KGB in 1961 and Minister of Public Order in the Russian Republic from 1961 to 1966. As long as Pavlik Morozov (a small boy who betrayed his parents to the police during the collectivization drive in the 1930s) is honoured in Soviet textbooks, such para-police work will undoubtedly continue.

Other examples of police work by military or para-military forces in Nazi Germany and Fascist Italy also come to mind.

Assessing the relative importance of participation in the internal security function by groups other than the formal public internal security organs is extremely difficult because of the lack of adequate statistics. Therefore, we are forced to focus our attention only upon the specified public expenditures for this purpose.

In the economic literature there are several contradictory hypotheses concerning the behaviour of public internal security expenditures. Starting from a basically pessimistic view of the nature of man, Adolph Wagner believed that the ratio-income-elasticity for internal security expenditures is greater than zero because of the increasing social strains arising from urbanization and the increasing need for judicial settlement of disputes stemming from the ever-growing complexity of life.[1] On the other hand, Henry Carter Adams, starting from Kantian notions about the perfectability of man, foresaw a ratio-income-elasticity for internal security expenditures of much less than zero.[2] Since analyses of such issues from the viewpoint of the 'nature of man' tend to degenerate into debates about the existence of original sin, such an approach is avoided in this section. It must be emphasized, however, that the empirical results presented below do have important implications for the science of theometrics (sometimes called hierometrics).[3]

[1] Adolph Wagner: *Finanzwissenschaft*, 1st Part, 3rd ed. (Leipzig, 1883); and *Grundlegung der politischen Oekonomie*, 1st Part, 3rd ed. (Leipzig, 1893).

[2] Henry Carter Adams, *The Science of Finance* (New York, 1899).

[3] Theometrics, the application of statistical methods to problems of theology, was founded in the nineteenth century by Francis Galton, who endeavoured to measure the power of prayers for the long life of the clergy and the royal family by determining the added life expectancy of these groups. Unfortunately, their life expectancy was somewhat shorter than average, and the science of theometrics seemed to stagnate for a long period thereafter. [Galton's experiment is discussed by Karl Pearson, *The Life, Letters and Labours of Francis Galton* (Cambridge: Cambridge U. Press, 1911–30), esp. Vol. II.] In the twentieth century, theometrics has been carried on by such scholars as A. T. Court, who attempted to relate the distribution of different kinds of crime with the religious beliefs and background of the criminals and by holding such factors as social class and age constant to see the behaviouristic implications of various types of theological systems. For a number of reasons, most theometric work has not been published; the science has been advanced through the work of solitary scholars, and the ideas of theometrics have been spread through the furtive exchange of manuscripts.

On the supply side, relations between the volume of expenditures for police or the number of police personnel and their ostensible effects are quite complex. Certain intricacies can be seen by looking at two dimensions of such effects: the suppression of political opposition to the government ('police terror') and the prevention of crime.

Police terror, which most people regard as the result of large police expenditures, can actually be carried out quite inexpensively, at least in monetary terms. For instance, in the late 1930s in Nazi Germany, the Gestapo numbered only about 32,000 and the Sicherheitsdienst (the internal intelligence army of the party, at one time connected with the ss) was about the same size.[1] (For perspective, it must be noted that these two units together numbered only slightly more than the border police and amounted to only about $0 \cdot 10$ per cent of the German population.)[2] In the Soviet Union under Stalin in the 1930s some evidence is available that the secret-police personnel were numerically very small.[3] This suggests that internal security expenditures in totalitarian dictatorships need not be particularly high, an economic factor which suggests that the degree of dictatorship may not be as important a causal element in determining different relative expenditures for internal security among nations as other functions such as traffic control, that take considerable manpower.

The influence of police expenditures on the suppression of crime is a difficult topic for analysis. It seems intuitively clear

[1] Jacques Delarue, The Gestapo: A History of Horror (New York, 1964), pp. 127, 183 ff. At its peak in 1944, the Gestapo numbered between 35,000 and 50,000.

[2] In 1962 in the United States, the Federal Bureau of Investigation had a staff of about 14,200 [US Bureau of the Budget, The Budget of the US Government. Fiscal 1964 (Washington, DC,) 1963], which amounted to $0 \cdot 008$ per cent of the population. In 1955 in Hungary, the permanent staff of the central political police numbered about 13,000 [Thad P. Alton, et al., Hungarian National Income and Product in 1955, (New York, 1963), p. 146] or about $0 \cdot 13$ per cent of the population. In East Germany, according to West German information (see Appendix A–5) the regular members of the Central State Security Service (excluding the Guard Regiment) numbered about 15,000 in 1962, or $0 \cdot 09$ per cent of the population.

[3] In an interview with General Orlov, the highest ranking member of the Soviet secret police to escape to the United States, I was told that the full-time members of this organization during the 1930s numbered about 40,000. Although such evidence must be taken with considerable caution, it does add supporting evidence to the conclusion about police expenditures for terror discussed in the text.

that for certain types of crime, the existence of a large police force discourages such attempts. But it is also evident that there are a great many social and psychological factors that may play an even more important role. For the United States, a number of experiments were made to test the relationship between police personnel and rates for different crimes in the various states, but no statistically significant results were obtained.[1] Although this does not prove that there is no such relationship, considerably more statistical research must be carried out on the problems before any statistical connections between police personnel and the crime rate can be firmly established.

A second factor that must be taken into account in the analysis of internal security expenditures is that the demand for these expenditures by the citizenry appears to be related to the amount of internal disorder, even though such expenditures may do little to relieve such situations (especially in the area of crime). If this is true, then we can generalize about the demand for such expenditures by considering the relationships between internal disorders and other social and economic factors.

During or after severe social crises such as wars or depressions, it seems likely that there is a greater demand for expenditures on internal security than in quiet periods. Thus it does not seem surprising that a much larger share of the GNP was devoted to such purposes in Europe in the years immediately following World War I than in the pre-war years.[2] Similarly, we would expect to see relatively low time-series ratio-income-

[1] There is a statistical identification problem since the crime rate may not only be determined by the relative police personnel but the relative personnel may be the result of a response to the crime rate. Experiments were made not only with single equation models but with simultaneous equation models as well, but the results were not greatly different. Data on seven different kinds of crime come from US Federal Bureau of Investigation, *Crime in the United States: Uniform Crime Reports* (Washington, DC, annual); data on police personnel come from US Bureau of the Census, *Census of the Government 1962, op. cit.* In order to reduce the variations induced by fluctuations in the crime rate of states in different years, the average crime rates for 1961 to 1963 were used in regressions. A considerable number of explanatory variables of the aggregative crime rates were also tested. Some of these results are reported below.

[2] For the United Kingdom, data are available in Peacock and Wiseman, *op. cit.*; for Germany, in Suphan Andic and Jindřich Veverka, 'The Growth of Government Expenditures in Germany since the Unification', *Finanzarchiv*, NF XXIII, January 1964.

elasticities of internal security expenditures in most of the sample nations in the post-World War II years because of the gradual subsiding of the social strains brought about by the war. Thus the particular years chosen for the time-series analysis make a crucial difference to the results of such a calculation.

The demand for internal security expenditures among a number of governmental units at a single point in time can also be similarly analysed. For instance, in the United States, crime rates are highly correlated not only with *per capita* income but also such variables as percentage of poor families (family incomes under $3,000), urbanization, racial composition, and other such characteristics.[1] Indeed, in some cases the causal connection between crime and social variables is quite direct, as in the relation between youth unemployment and juvenile delinquency.[2] Thus we could use such social and economic variables in the demand function for internal security expenditures.

Unfortunately, crime rates in different nations do not lend themselves so easily to analysis. The most comparable crime statistics are for murders, and for the sample nations the data are quite varied (see Table 6–2).

The murder rates in the table below are correlated neither with *per capita* income, economic system, urbanization, or other likely explanatory economic variables. If such rates are to be explained, we must explore more social, historical, and political causes: certain traditions of violence seem important factors underlying the high murder rates in the United States and the Balkans and political peculiarities seem to bring about the low East German rate.[3] Of course, such crime rate statistics

[1] Data on seven different kinds of crime come from Federal Bureau of Investigation, *op. cit.* A number of regression equations were computed to determine the broad economic correlates of the different crime rates. Correlation coefficients greater than 0·70 (or R^2 greater than 0·50) were obtained for all the cross-section state regressions for the different crime rates except for rapes. Murder rates, for which the data are the most comparable, were the most predictable.

[2] This problem is empirically analysed by Belton M. Fleisher, 'The Effects of Unemployment on Juvenile Delinquency', *Journal of Political Economy*, LXXI, December 1963, pp. 543–55.

[3] East Germany forced a large portion of its criminal elements to emigrate to West Germany. Although the East German government has officially denied such a policy, a visit to the camps for 'non-recognized refugees' in West Berlin gave me convincing evidence that such a systematic policy was carried out during the late 1950s and early 1960s.

reflect only part of the demand for internal security expenditures.

Another aspect of the demand for internal security expenditures relates to the increasing need of police personnel for traffic

TABLE 6–2

Murder Rates in the Sample Nations in 1962[1]

Country	Murders per 100,000 population	Country	Murders per 100,000 population
USA	4·9	Czechoslovakia	1·1
West Germany	1·3	East Germany	0·3
Austria	1·0	USSR	n.a.
Ireland	0·4	Hungary	1·9
Italy	1·1	Poland	1·2
Greece	1·5	Romania	n.a.
Yugoslavia	3·5	Bulgaria	2·1

control as the density of motor vehicles increases. In cross-section studies of nations the number of automobiles *per capita* rises considerably faster than income *per capita*.[2] Moreover, economic system plays an extremely important role, since for countries with similar *per capita* incomes the number of auto-

[1] Data from World Health Organization, *Epidemiological and Vital Statistics Report*, Vol. 18, 11/1965; Staatliche Zentralverwaltung fuer Statistik, *Statistisches Jahrbuch der Deutschen Demokratischen Republik* (East Berlin, annual); and Savezni zavod za statistiku, *Statistički godišnjak SFRJ* (Belgrad, annual). The East German datum includes East Berlin and is for 1960, the last year for which such information is given; the West German datum includes West Berlin.

In all countries, suicide rates were much higher than murder rates, with East Germany (30·1 suicides per 100,000) and Hungary (24·9 suicides per 100,000) as the leaders. It is interesting that there appears to be an inverse correlation between murder and suicide rates, although the rank order correlation coefficient is not quite statistically significant for the sample nations. The underlying psychological reasons for this inverse relation are explained in a number of textbooks on psychiatry [e.g. Otto Fenichel, *The Psychoanalytic Theory of Neurosis* (New York, 1945), pp. 400 ff.]. One full length study of this phenomenon is by A. F. Henry and J. F. Short, *Suicide and Homicide* (Glencoe, Ill., 1954).

[2] Data on the stock of automobiles in most countries can be obtained from the United Nations, *Statistical Yearbook* (New York, annual).

mobiles *per capita* in 1962 ranged from two to ten times greater in market than in centrally planned economies.[1]

For other aspects in the demand for internal security expenditures little quantitative information is available. The empirical bases of our knowledge of the demand factors for these expenditures on an international level seem too narrow for predictions about the behaviour of these expenditures to be made with any confidence.

A third major factor to consider in the analysis is that not all internal security personnel are used for internal security purposes. Indeed, in some of the centrally planned economies, the internal security system has played an important role in the industrialization of the country.[2] On the other hand, it is in these countries that there seem to be significant para-police units. The biases which these two factors introduce into the data are in opposite directions and partially cancel each other out.

A final important economic factor to be considered concerns the centralization of internal security expenditures. Among the market economies such expenditures are exclusively financed at the central governmental level in only Ireland and Greece, while in the centralized economies, internal security expenditures are not made at the local level in any of the sample countries except for the Soviet Union (after 1959). Although the small population size appears to be the most important determining factor in such centralization of expenditures in Ireland, certain obvious political considerations dominate the centralization decision for internal security expenditures in the other countries. A deeper analysis into the economic factors

[1] In 1962 the number of passenger automobiles *per capita* in Yugoslavia was twice that in Bulgaria; was five times greater in West Germany than in East Germany; and was ten times greater in Ireland and Italy than in Hungary and Poland. Data for the market economies and Poland come from the United Nations, *op. cit.* The Bulgarian datum comes from *Statesmen's Yearbook, 1963/64*, (London, 1963). The East German datum can be estimated from data given in the *Statistisches Jahrbuch der DDR, 1965, op. cit.*, p. 430.

[2] See, e.g. S. N. Swianiewicz, *Forced Labour and Economic Development: An Enquiry into the Experience of Soviet Industrialization* (London, 1965). The most thorough description of the internal structure and activities of the Soviet internal security apparatus is: Simon Wolin and Robert M. Slusser, eds., *The Soviet Secret Police* (New York, 1957).

behind the degree of centralization of internal security expenditures seems profitless.

Turning to the actual behaviour of internal security expenditures, it is more convenient to begin the analysis with the time-series data since they are less ambiguous than the cross-section information.

From the 1920s to the present the share of public consumption expenditures for internal security in the GNP appears to have declined in the United States, the United Kingdom, and Germany.[1] Therefore, we might expect the ratio-income-elasticities of the sample nations to be negative. However, a somewhat mixed picture appears instead.

TABLE 6–3

Time-Series Behaviour of Public Consumption Expenditures for Internal Security, 1950 through 1962[2]

Country	Ratio-income-elasticity	Country	Ratio-income-elasticity
USA	+ 1·92*	Czechoslovakia	—
West Germany	− 0·20*	East Germany	− 0·62
Austria	+ 0·19*	USSR	—
Ireland	− 0·06	Hungary	− 1·72*
Italy	− 0·14*	Poland	− 0·35*
Greece	+ 0·44*	Romania	—
Yugoslavia	+ 1·02*	Bulgaria	—

The average ratio-income-elasticity is slightly greater than zero but there is a very high variation among nations. Since the ratio-income-elasticities calculated in constant prices for the

[1] For Germany, see Suphan Andic and Jinřdich Veverka, 'The Growth of Government Expenditures in Germany since the Unification', *Finanzarchiv*, NF 23, January 1964; for the UK, Alan T. Peacock and Jack Wiseman, *The Growth of Public Expenditure in the United Kingdom* (Princeton, 1961). For the United States an income-elasticity was computed from 1927–62 data on police expenditures [Bureau of Census, 'Historical Statistics on Governmental Finances and Employment', Vol. VI, No. 4, *Census of Governments 1962*, Washington, DC, 1964], deflated by a price index derived from a government wage index and a wholesale price series.

[2] Expenditures data from Appendix A, Data for Yugoslavia cover 1952 through 1962. An asterisk designates statistical significance (0·05 level) and a dash indicates that estimates are given in Appendix A but are considered too rough to be included in the table.

market economies is about 0.42 lower than the current-price elasticities, such constant-price elasticities are probably zero or negative for all countries excepting the United States and Yugoslavia (the two nations that incidentally have the highest murder rates).

From the unweighted data the economic systems variable appears important in explaining differences between nations in the table. However, in analyses where *per capita* income and other factors can be held constant, the systems variable is no longer significantly related to the elasticities data.

Using a regression calculation it appears that these ratio-income-elasticities for internal security purposes are significantly and inversely related to the ratio of public consumption expenditures for these purposes to the GNP.[1] That is, the higher the expenditures/GNP ratio in 1956, the lower the ratio-income-elasticity. Thus internal security expenditures act similarly to public consumption expenditures for welfare and education in that there appears to be a convergence of the expenditure/GNP ratios toward a common point when other factors are held constant.

Furthermore, the ratio-income-elasticities for internal security expenditures are significantly and directly related to the murder rates. If such expenditures are viewed as a response to domestic disorders, such a result makes intuitive sense. Unfortunately, there is a problem of double causation which lends a certain element of uncertainty to such an interpretation.[2]

For the cross-section data conflicting predictions can be made on the basis of political factors.[3] From economic considerations

---

[1] The regression calculation in which the discussion in the next two paragraphs is based is:

$$E = 2.27 - 0.00067\,(Y/P) - 144.1^*\,(S/Y) + 0.442^*\,M \qquad R^2 = 0.88^*$$
$$ (0.00033) \qquad\quad (32.7) \qquad\quad (0.107)$$

where E = ratio-income-elasticity of public consumption expenditures for internal security (Table 6–3); Y/P = GNP *per capita;* S/Y = ratio of public consumption expenditures for internal security to the GNP in 1956 (Table 6–4); and M = murder rates (Table 6–2).

In a simple regression the ratio-income-elasticities are also significantly and directly related to the expenditures/GNP ratio.

[2] This identification problem is discussed in footnote 1, p. 243.

[3] Non-Marxist commentators generally believe that police expenditures are relatively higher in the socialist nations because of the necessity to repress the population in order to maintain political control. On the other hand. Marxist

two predictions can be made. First, if the cross-section and time-series determinants are similar, then the ratio-income-elasticity should be negative. Second, because of the traffic-control problem, internal-security expenditures in the centralized economies should be lower. The basic data for testing these propositions are given in Table 6–4 below.

TABLE 6–4

Ratios of Public Consumption Expenditures for Internal Security to Factor Price GNPs in 1956 and 1962[1]

Country	1956	1962	Country	1956	1962
USA	0·7	0·8	Czechoslovakia	—	—
West Germany	1·2	1·1	East Germany	1·9	1·5
Austria	1·3	1·3	USSR	0·7	—
Ireland	1·3	1·2	Hungary	2·6	1·4
Italy	1·8	1·7	Poland	1·9	1·6
Greece	1·3	1·3	Romania	—	—
Yugoslavia	2·0	2·0	Bulgaria	—	—

Analysis of the systems variable is complicated. Although the internal security expenditures/GNP ratios are significantly higher in the centralized economies for both years, two other factors must be considered. First, the factor income effect give the data for the centralized economies an upward bias, although probably not sufficient to account for the difference. Second, once *per capita* income is taken into account, the systems variable loses its statistical significance and the situation appears more complex, as the following calculations show:[2]

commentators such as K. Butakov, *et al.* [*Finansi stran narodnoy demokratii* (Moscow, 1959), pp. 81–2] believe relative police expenditures in capitalist nations to be higher because of the necessity of repressing workers discontented with being exploited. Their evidence—rising police expenditures—lacks credibility, however, since the absolute amount of police expenditures have risen in almost all countries, regardless of system.

[1] The data for Hungary are for 1955 and 1962. All expenditures data come from Appendix A. A dash designates that estimates are given in the Appendices but are considered too rough to be included in the table. The estimate for the Soviet Union represents an inference based on several scattered bits of budget information. Data from Poland and Hungary are based on official sources. The data for East Germany were estimated from information on personnel in various police units.

[2] The E/Y data come from Table 6–4; the *per capita* GNP data from Appendix B. Calculations with the systems variable as capitalist-socialist yielded about the same results.

1956: including USSR

$$\ln E/Y = -1\cdot11+0\cdot20S-0\cdot47\ln(Y/P); \qquad R^2 = 0\cdot34$$
$$(0\cdot25)\quad(0\cdot26)$$

1956: excluding USSR

$$\ln E/Y = -1\cdot15+0\cdot48^*S-0\cdot47^*\ln(Y/P); \qquad R^2 = 0\cdot77^*$$
$$(0\cdot14)\quad\;(0\cdot14)$$

1962: excluding USSR

$$\ln E/Y = -1\cdot51+0\cdot16S-0\cdot40^*\ln(Y/P); \qquad R^2 = 0\cdot55^*$$
$$(0\cdot14)\quad(0\cdot15)$$

where E = public consumption expenditures on internal security

Y = GNP

P = population

S = economic system (=0, market economies; =1, centralized economies).

In 1956 the centrally planned economies had a significantly higher relative public consumption expenditures for internal security only when the Soviet Union is omitted; and in 1962, even in this case the difference is not significantly different. In interpreting such results in the light of the *a priori* considerations discussed above, it seems likely that the centrally planned economies do devote a significantly higher relative amount of expenditures to internal security services other than traffic control and that this difference can be explained only on political grounds.

As expected the ratio-income-elasticity is negative, although in one out of the three regression calculations the calculated coefficient falls slightly short of statistical significance. Although the reasons underlying the lower ratio-income-elasticities with the cross-section than time-series data are obscure, it does appear that the basic determinants of both types of data in regard to income are similar.

In a cross-section analysis of internal security expenditures in the United States, there appears to be a ratio-income-elasticity slightly greater than zero in 1962. When the number of motor vehicles is held constant (so that only those expenditures not used for traffic control are considered), the ratio-income-elasticity is even higher. One possible explanation for such a difference with the data for nations is a 'demonstration effect'; that is, decision makers of internal security expenditures pay considerable attention to *per capita* norms derived from the experience of other local governments within the nation. It should certainly not be surprising that there is greater *per capita* standardization of public expenditures within a nation than between nations and this would bring the ratio-income-elasticity closer to zero.

In order to explore the data in Table 6-4 more deeply, a number of other experiments were attempted using such independent variables as urbanization, murder rates, and so on. But no additional insights were gained. Corroborating evidence about the determinants that can be made from study of the number of internal security personnel is unfortunately not available.[1]

From this brief empirical analysis several conclusions may be drawn. First, over long periods of time the ratio-income-elasticities of public consumption expenditures for internal security are negative. For the period under examination, most but not all such elasticities are also negative. The most important discoveries in regard to these elasticities is that such internal security expenditures appear to be converging toward a common ratio with the GNP, other things remain the same. The degree of internal disorder, as represented by the murder rate, also seems to influence these elasticities.

In the cross-section analysis the internal security expenditures also have a negative ratio-income-elasticity. The differences in relative public consumption expenditures for internal security between the two systems are not statistically significant. If expenditures for traffic control are removed, however, it appears

---

[1] Data on police personnel are available in the statistical yearbooks or other such official publications for most Western nations. These data are not very comparable because of different practices in classifying internal security employees into 'police' and civilians' and the omission of the latter. Estimates of internal security personnel in the centrally planned economies are scattered and are usually very difficult to evaluate.

likely that such relative expenditures are higher in the centrally planned economies, a difference that can be explained only from political grounds.

D. PUBLIC CONSUMPTION EXPENDITURES FOR NON-MILITARY EXTERNAL SECURITY

Non-military external security includes expenditures for diplomacy and for long-term foreign military and economic aid (both loans and grants). External intelligence expenditures, where they could be isolated, are within. Although forced reparation payments are excluded, voluntary governmental reparation payments, such as the West German Wiedergutmachung (restitution to the Jews),[1] are also included.

The most extensive theoretical treatment of these non-military external security expenditures was made by Adolph Wagner at the end of the nineteenth century.[2] According to his 'second law of state expenditures', in the course of economic development, expenditures for purposes of repression decline *vis-à-vis* expenditures for the prevention of the necessity for the use of force. Over the long run, therefore, he expected a relative decline in military expenditures and a relative increase in other external security expenditures. Although he did not foresee the institution of governmental foreign aid, such a development appears to fit neatly into his general theoretical views.

Since Wagner, however, such theoretical exercises have generally been avoided by economists, primarily because of the supposed importance of transitory political factors which cannot be adequately handled in an economic analysis. Before abandoning the analysis of such non-military external security expenditures to the political scientists, certain important economic factors should be briefly considered.

At first sight, a large portion of non-military external security appears to have the characteristics of a public good. Many

---

[1] The only apparent concession of East Germany to the Jews who were persecuted by the Germans in previous years was the calling off of a show trial to be patterned after the anti-Semitic trial of R. Slánský in Czechoslovakia. [This East German trial is discussed by William Griffith, *The New Course and Thaw* (New Haven, Yale University Press, forthcoming).]

[2] See esp. Adolph Wagner, *Finanzwissenschaft, op. cit.*

aspects of diplomacy benefit an entire nation and have a very low marginal cost. Furthermore, many political gains of foreign-aid expenditures also accrue to a nation as a whole. One result of these public-good characteristics is that in all the sample countries but West Germany, such non-military external security expenditures are made entirely at the central governmental level. (In West Germany, part of the restitution payment to Jews are made at the Laender levels; but all of the remaining expenditures are made solely at the federal level.)

It must be noted, however, that there are a number of services carried out by the diplomatic corps that are not public goods, such as the gathering of general political information or the performing of certain commercial and legal functions. Furthermore, because foreign economic assistance serves not only diplomatic functions but also charity and investment functions, many portions of such governmental assistance do not have public good properties. This problem causes particular difficulties in deriving an adequate definition of non-military external security expenditures and is discussed below.

Thus it does not seem unusual that over time and space the functions of the diplomatic services of nations have differed and that there have been considerably different mixes of 'foreign tasks' performed by the public and private sectors in this regard. Furthermore, the private sector has played an important role in the function of giving of grants and loans to foreign countires. For instance, in the United States from 1950 through 1962, the private sector accounted for 10 per cent of the total net grants given abroad and about 70 per cent of the long-term loans (or 32 per cent of total net grants and long-term loans).[1] In the centrally planned economies, however, all foreign grants and loans are accounted for directly by the government, except for occasional foreign trade loans.

In addition to the difficulties surrounding the economic nature of inter-governmental foreign aid programmes, there are also considerable ambiguities about the political results of such expenditures. In both the Soviet Union and the United States

[1] Data from Department of Commerce, Office of Business Economics, *Balance of Payments: Statistical Supplement* (Revised edition, Washington, DC, 1963) and various issues of *Survey of Current Business*.

strong groups of conservatives are opposed to such foreign aid programmes on the ground that such aid reaps very few political advantages, can create many enemies (e.g. aid to India alienates Pakistan), sets up expectations on the part of the receivers for continual aid in the indefinite future, and diverts needed resources from vital domestic programmes.[1] Furthermore, in both countries many citizens seem in favour of a reduction of such programs, if we are to believe public opinion polls in the USA[2] and certain political signs of such sentiments in the Soviet Union.[3]

The importance of the private sector in foreign economic grants and loans and the ambiguities surrounding the political effect of such programmes cast some doubt on whether such programmes would, in actuality, fit so nicely into Wagner's classification of 'preventive' expenditures. Further problems arise in trying to arrive at an appropriate concept by which to measure such expenditures as well as to obtain the appropriate data.

In determining an adequate statistical concept for measuring the extent of foreign loans and grants, it seems reasonable to try to distinguish the motives for the various types of international payments. Obviously, short-term trade credits should be excluded since these are usually given at commercial interest rates and serve primarily to encourage trade. The problem is more difficult for development loans with the purpose of creating production of goods and raw materials that are then exported to the donor country. Many loans of the centralized economies are directly tied to future trade in such specific commodities and could be considered primarily as 'domestic' investment

[1] The conservative opposition to Soviet foreign aid is discussed by Milton Kovner, 'Soviet Aid Strategy in Developing Countries', *Orbis*, VIII, 3/1964, pp. 624–41. In the USA, conservatives have banded together in the Citizens' Foreign Aid Committee to oppose foreign aid legislation.

[2] E.g. Eva Mueller, 'Public Attitudes Toward Fiscal Programs', *Quarterly Journal of Economics*, LXXVII, May 1963, pp. 210–35.

[3] According to Marshall I. Goldman, 'A Balance Sheet of Soviet Foreign Aid', *Foreign Affairs*, XLIII, October 1964, pp. 87–99, dock workers in Odessa refused to load butter destined for Cuba when their own stores were empty. Soviet presentation of foreign aid programmes to their citizens [N. Derkach, *The Differences in Soviet Portrayal of Their Aid to Underdeveloped Countries in English and Russian*, RAND Paper P-2853, Santa Monica, January 1964], suggests that there is considerable mass opposition to such expenditures.

carried out in a foreign country. Finally, the distinction between economic and military aid raises another group of thorny problems concerning motive. For it is well known that much 'military' aid has gone into the building of social overhead capital which only indirectly increases military potential, while, on the other hand, some 'economic' aid has been used directly for defence purposes.

Many have also felt it useful to distinguish the geographical direction of foreign aid. The fact that considerable US loans and grants went to Western Europe during the early 1950s or that considerable Soviet loans went to Eastern Europe (and that the Soviet Union has received foreign aid from other centralized economies)[1] suggests again that much so-called foreign aid is less a security than an economic expenditure and should be so classified.

A last important conceptual difficulty concerns the cost of such aid. A number of economists have argued that there is no real cost to governmental loans which are made to other governments at the prevailing market interest rate and that the 'aid element' can only be measured from the difference between the rate of the foreign loan and the market rate.[2] By isolating the 'aid element so that grants and loans can be put on some common basis, more meaningful comparisons of foreign aid can be made.[3] Difficulties arise, however, in separating the loan and grant elements of loans made in soft currencies or in evaluating aid given in kind.[4]

[1] According to the Polish Vice-Premier Piotr Jaroszewicz (cited by Arthur J. Olson, 'East Bloc Sends Capital to Soviet', *New York Times*, Nov. 11, 1962, p. 21) Czechoslovakia and several centralized economies are lending the USSR funds for mineral development.

[2] This point is argued by John A. Pincus, 'The Cost of Foreign Aid', *Review of Economics and Statistics*, XLV, November 1963, pp. 360–7; Alastair McAuley and Dubravko Matko, *The Real Cost of Soviet Foreign Aid* (Glasgow, 1966); and I. M. D. Little and J. M. Clifford, *International Aid: A Discussion of the Flow of Public Resources from Rich to Poor Countries* (Chicago, 1966).

[3] Milton Kovner ('Soviet Trade and Aid', *Current History*, XLIX, October 1965, pp. 227–34) does this by calculating a weighted average of interest rates on US grants and loans (2 per cent); Pincus, *op. cit.*, and McAuley and Matko, *op. cit.*, do this by calculating the difference between the face value of the loan and the discounted stream of repayments; Little and Clifford, *op. cit.*, use a variation of this latter method.

[4] These problems are discussed in detail by Pincus, *op. cit.*

In order to keep the statistical problems to manageable proportions, certain drastic simplifying procedures must be adopted. Acting on the premise that all long-term intergovernmental assistance has political repercussions for all the citizens in the involved nations, three simplifications are made: First, all (economic and military) intergovernmental grants and loans, except for short-term trade credits, are included. Second, no distinctions are made about the geographical direction of such aid.

Finally, the political impact of loans and grants is judged to be proportional to the gross value of such aid so that both types of aid are lumped together with no account taken of the different terms of such aid.

The type of analysis that can be performed on the data depends on the quality of the estimates, and several brief remarks must also be made on this matter. No centralized economy publishes data on actual aid expenditures and, with the exception of Poland, none publishes data on diplomatic expenditures either. Although estimates are possible to make, they are rough and preclude any detailed statistical analysis. We must, therefore, be content with a more qualitative approach.

In regard to public consumption expenditures for non-military purposes as a whole, it seems clear that there is no substitution relation with public expenditures for defence. In general, higher non-military external security expenditures seem to accompany higher military expenditures when the situation is viewed at a single point in time. Over time such a substitution relation is similarly not evident.[1] Thus in regard to non-military external security expenditures acting in place of military expenditures, Wagner's prediction is incorrect.

In regard to the components of non-military external security expenditures, the area of foreign aid seems the most promising for comparative analysis, and several generalizations can be made about the relationships of foreign aid with income *per*

[1] Using time-series data of market economies I carried out experiments similar to those in Chapter III for determining substitution relations of military expenditures. With the exception of West Germany (whose military expenditures were partly determined by the occupying powers during the early 1950s), no statistically significant substitution of military for non-military external security expenditures was found.

capita and economic system. To arrive at such an assessment, average ratios of foreign loans and grants to the factor price GNP were calculated for the period of 1957 through 1962.[1] Of the market economies, the United States and West Germany had respective ratios of 0·7 per cent and 0·2 per cent; the remaining nations had less than 0·1 per cent. Among the centralized economies, Czechoslovakia's ratio of 0·6 per cent was the highest, followed by the USSR with a ratio between 0·4 and 0·5 per cent. East Germany and Hungary had ratios of about 0·2 per cent; Romania and Poland, about 0·1 per cent; and only Bulgaria provided less than 0·1 per cent of its factor price GNP for such purposes. Two rough conclusions can be drawn. First, within the sample the relative non-military external security expenditures of the centralized economies are higher than those of the market economies; second, such relative expenditures are positively related to income *per capita*, i.e. the ratio-income-elasticity is positive. Thus in regard to the relation of 'preventive expenditures' with income Wagner's prognosis seems correct.

Because many of the sample nations did not begin to give foreign aid until the mid-1950s, calculation of ratio-income-elasticities for the period would not be very useful to analyse. In addition, the time patterns of these expenditures are extremely irregular in most countries. For the United States the ratio of such expenditures to the GNP reached a peak in 1953 with the termination of Marshall Plan aid to Western Europe; and for the Soviet Union the peak occurred in 1957 when loans to other centrally planned economies were at their highest.

Several contrasts exist in regard to the terms of the foreign aid. The United States and West Germany tend to give a larger portion of grants than the centralized economies and, on the loans, to charge somewhat higher interest rates.[2] Second, the

[1] The data on foreign loans and grants are a component of the data on non-military external security expenditures described in Appendix A. Because of an irregular pattern of foreign aid payments of the Soviet Union, data both including and excluding 1956 are given below for that country.

[2] Although most credits of the centralized economics carry an interest rate of about 2·5 per cent, Klaus Billerbeck [*Soviet Bloc Foreign Aid to the Under-developed Countries* (Hamburg, 1960), p. 44] notes that certain Czechoslovak loans have carried interest rates up to 6 per cent. It must be noted that a number of Marxist economists [e.g. Karl Herscher, *Der Zahlungsverkehr der DDR mit*

I

centrally planned economies channel a lower portion of their foreign aid through international aid-giving organizations such as the United Nations.

A final marked contrast between foreign aid of the two groups of nations is the relatively greater geographical dispersal of foreign aid by the market economies.[1] This situation seems to be slowly changing, however.

A number of other differences between foreign aid of market and centralized economies are also alleged to exist. For instance, most Marxist economists[2] claim that foreign aid from socialist nations, in contrast to aid from capitalist nations, has no political strings and, furthermore, is much more 'productive'. The statements about political conditions are factually incorrect[3] and the claims about 'productivity' are open to considerable dispute.[4] On the other hand, many non-Marxists have made exaggerated claims about the evils of foreign aid from the centralized economies which appear quite incorrect.[5] For a balanced judgment to be made on these matters, more information than a few spectacular anecdotes is required.

dem Ausland, East Berlin, 1958)] have asserted that US grants to the developing countries are 'really' loans for which repayment conditions have not been agreed upon. This is utterly false and indicative of the kind of cold-war propaganda that has characterized Marxist writings on the subject.

[1] This point is especially analysed by Joseph S. Berliner, *Soviet Economic Aid* (New York, 1958), Chapter III.

[2] E.g. Karl Heinz Domdey, *Neokolonialismus oder Unabhaegigkeit und sozialistische Wirtschaftshilfe* (East Berlin, 1962); Victor V. Rymalov, *Economic Cooperation Between the USSR and Underdeveloped Countries* (Moscow, 1962); S. M. Smirnov, *Mezhdunarodnye valutnye i kreditnye otnoshenia SSSR* (Moscow, 1960).

[3] Soviet political conditions on foreign loans to a number of countries are documented by Marshall I. Goldman, *Soviet Foreign Aid* (New York, 1967). Such strings are most apparent when aid projects are suddenly withdrawn and numerous examples in the aid programmes of most nations can be given (e.g. US aid commitments to Egypt in 1956; Soviet aid to China in 1961; Chinese aid to Burma in June 1967; and so forth). I would like to thank Mr Goldman for sending me an advance copy of his book.

[4] Soviet loans for stadiums in Guinea, Mali, and Indonesia, and for luxury hotels in Burma and the Congo (Brazzaville); East German construction of sugar beet factories in Indonesia where only sugar cane is grown; and many other such examples are discussed by Goldman, *op. cit.* Wastefulness of a number of foreign aid projects by market economies, such as the US financed Helmand valley project in Afghanistan is also widely known.

[5] E.g. Melvin Lasky, *The Ugly Russian* (New York, 1965). Many of Lasky's assertions are challenged by Goldman, *op. cit.*

In summary, the expenditures data show that a single point in time, non-military external security expenditures have a positive ratio-income-elasticity and, furthermore, are greater in the centrally planned than market economies. The time-series data show extremely irregular patterns and lend themselves more to a political rather than economic interpretation.

E. PUBLIC CONSUMPTION EXPENDITURES FOR RESEARCH AND DEVELOPMENT

The concept of R and D used in this section is broad: research is defined to include the 'systematic, intensive study directed toward fuller scientific knowledge of the subject studies'; while 'development' covers the 'systematic use of scientific knowledge directed toward the production of useful materials, devices, systems, and methods, including design and development of prototypes and processes, but excluding quality control, routine production testing, and production'.[1]

In the analysis of R and D expenditures it is important to note a number of theoretical properties of such services.

First of all, once new knowledge is discovered through research or development activities, it can often be supplied to others at very low costs. Furthermore, many types of knowledge are not patentable, and selling such knowledge is difficult since, if it can be written down or graphically portrayed, a monopoly of knowledge can be broken by anyone with printing facilities. Even if a patent is possible, the mere knowledge that certain discoveries have been made may be of commercial use to others. Such non-exclusive benefits and low marginal costs of reproduction mean that certain R and D expenditures are for services with public-good properties.[2] For this reason, it should be expected that some R and D expenditures are financed

[1] These are the definitions used by the US National Science Foundation in its statistical reports; they are taken from: *Federal Funds for Research, Development, and Other Scientific Activities*, Vol. XIV (Washington, DC, 1965), pp. 56–7.

[2] This public-goods aspect of R and D expenditures is analysed in much greater detail by Richard R. Nelson, 'The Simple Economics of Basic Scientific Research', *Journal of Political Economy*, LCVII, June 1959, pp. 297–306; and Kenneth J. Arrow, 'Economic Welfare and the Allocation of Resources for Invention', in Richard R. Nelson, ed., *The Rate and Direction of Inventive Activity: Economic and Social Factors* (Princeton, 1962), pp. 609–25.

through the public sector. Since such public-good properties apply more to 'basic' than 'applied' research (where patents can be more easily obtained and where research is directed toward highly specific ends), it should also not be surprising that relatively more basic than applied research is publicly financed.[1]

On the basis of such considerations it can be argued that it would be profitable for a nation to devote all its efforts to applied research and to import costlessly the results of basic research from other countries.[2] A more extreme form of this argument is that a nation need not use its scarce brain power for research at all but just import licences and buy new production techniques from abroad as with any other good or service. This overlooks not only the importance of basic research in the teaching of new generations of scientists but the increase in productivity of both basic and applied research workers when they are in close proximity.[3] Furthermore, a country that tried to rely exclusively on importation of technical knowledge would be, according to one specialist, a decade or more behind its competitors in every industry.[4] Additional evidence on this point is supplied by the Federation of British Industries, which argues that licensing arrangements for new technological processes are almost always supplementary, rather than a substitute, to a firm's internal research efforts.[5] This, of course, makes good sense since those who are grappling with certain research problems are usually best able to appreciate the significance of discoveries made elsewhere.

---

[1] For the United States this may be seen quite clearly in the data on the financing of R and D which are presented in various editions of: Bureau of Census, *Statistical Abstract of the United States* (Washington, DC, annual).

[2] See, for instance, Harry G. Johnson, 'Federal Support of Basic Research: Some Economic Issues', *Minerva*, III, Summer, 1966, pp. 500–14.

[3] This point is argued in detail by A. Marechal, *et al.*, *Fundamental Research and the Policies of Governments* (Paris, 1966).

[4] Christopher Freeman, *Science, Economic, and Government Policy* (Paris, 1963), p. 34.

[5] *Ibid.*, p. 35. The effect of importing technologies and scientific results depends on a number of institutional factors as well. For instance, enterprises in Ireland, many of which are owned by British interests, may be able to rely more on foreign R and D than enterprises in countries where enterprises are owned by nationals. Further, the way in which governments encourage such imports is also important. For instance, among the nations of the Council of Mutual Economic Assistance, there used to be a costless sharing of certain technological

Such arguments suggest a second important economic characteristic of R and D activities—namely, the important complementarities between different types of scientific work. In a very rough way, this may be seen in the high degree of correlation between scientific papers published in the sample nations in the fields of chemistry and physics, but also within the specialized areas within these disciplines.[1] Although it may be premature to speak of a 'law of balanced science development' within nations, such complementarities must nevertheless be recognized.[2]

A third important economic property of R and D expenditures concerns the elements of risk that must be taken into account by any financer of such activities. There is not only the possibility that R and D efforts may result in failure but also the chance that the results will not be useful to the particular purchaser although they may be extremely profitable to someone else. Unless there is some type of mechanism for insurance against such risks, a non-optimal allocation of R and D resources will result within a perfect market system. In actual economies such insurance devices do not extensively exist, and indeed, there are a number of compelling reasons why such a system cannot be created.[3] These risk elements are also relevant for decision making in centralized economies since the relationship between

advances (this is described in my article 'Forms of Economic Cooperation in the European Communist Bloc—A Survey', *Soviet Studies*, XI, 2/1959, pp. 173–94). Some features of this programme led to commercial frictions, however, and recently it has been proposed to put such a programme on a paying basis (Harry Schwartz, 'Soviet Asks East Bloc Members to Pay for Use of Technology', *New York Times*, November 27, 1966, p. 20).

[1] Derek J. deSolla Price, 'The Distribution of Scientific Papers by Country and Subject—A Science Policy Analysis', forthcoming essay.

[2] One way of approaching this problem quantitatively is to look at the relative amounts of basic research conducted by each country. For instance, from data on the distribution of scientific personnel in the Soviet Union [Alexander Korol, *Soviet Research and Development: Its Organization, Personnel, and Funds* (Cambridge, Mass., 1965)] and from NSF data for the USA, it appears that both countries devote about 10 per cent of total research funds to basic research. On the other hand this ratio varies considerably in other countries (data are given by W. R. Williams, 'Research and Economic Growth—What Should We Expect?' *Minerva*, III, Autumn 1964, pp. 57–71; and Christopher Freeman, *op. cit.*), although caution should be exercised in interpreting such results because of the possible lack of comparability of the data.

[3] See esp. Arrow, *op. cit.* on this point.

rewards for successful innovating and the risks of different R and D efforts may determine what kind and extent of research an enterprise or production ministry may carry out, especially in regard to basic research.[1]

Fourth, on the demand side of R and D services there seems to be an increasing appreciation of the possibilities of such expenditures on a micro-economic level for aiding the reduction of production costs, the creation of new products, and the gaining of competititive advantages in international markets or, for capitalist enterprises, domestic markets as well. Although R and D expenditures may have contributed relatively little to national growth in the past (e.g. Edward Denison estimates that only 20 per cent of US growth between 1929 and 1957 can be attributed to such a source)[2] such expenditures seem to be increasingly viewed as a very important source for future economic growth. Moreover, the climate of opinion toward such R and D expenditures seems to be more favourable among those who are highly educated.

Another demand factor of considerable importance is the relationship between R and D expenditures and the industrial structure of a nation. Certain industries (especially 'growth industries' such as aircraft, electronics, chemicals, or instruments) seem to be much more 'research intensive' than other industries such as lumber and forestry, transportation, or textiles.[3] Furthermore, research expenditures seem also related to the size distribution of firms and the absolute sizes of enter-

[1] The whole problem of the handling of risk by centrally planned economies is very unexplored territory. The fact that governmental agencies are allocating R and D funds does not mean that an optimal allocation of such funds can be reached. Charles J. Hitch [*The Character of Research and Development in a Competitive Economy*, RAND Corp. Paper P-1297, (Santa Monica, Calif., 1958)] has argued that within the US government, for instance, certain biases arising from the decision-making process make the allocation of these funds definitely non-optimal.

[2] Edward F. Denison, *The Sources of Economic Growth in the United States and the Alternative Before Us* (Washington, DC, 1962), p. 230.

[3] This point is analysed in detail by: Christopher Freeman, 'Research and Development: A Comparison between British and American Industry', *National Institute Economic Review*, May 1962, pp. 21–39; James S. Worley, 'The Changing Direction of Research and Development Employment Among Firms', in Nelson, ed., *op. cit.*; and Richard R. Nelson, Merton Peck, and Edward Kalachek, *Technology, Economic Growth, and Public Policy* (Washington, DC, 1967), Chap. III.

prises.[1] From such factors it has been argued that nations such as Australia, Finland, Canada, Iceland, and Norway show lower amounts of R and D expenditures than one would expect from their *per capita* income because of the relatively greater importance of industries in these countries which are not research intensive or which are characterized by small production units.[2] Unfortunately, adequate data on these matters are not available for the sample nations.

Finally, unit costs of R and D services seem to be rising. J. K. Galbraith speaks for many when he notes:

'There is no more pleasant fiction than that technical change is the product of the matchless ingenuity of the small man forced by competition to employ his wits to better his neighbour. Unhappily, it is a fiction. Technical development has long since been the preserve of the scientist and the engineer. Most of the cheap and simple inventions have, to put it bluntly, been made.[3]

All these various supply and demand properties of R and D expenditures suggest a number of *a priori* predictions about the behaviour of the expenditures data. Certainly from the demand and supply characteristics it seems likely that the ratio-income-elasticities are positive and, moreover, that the time-series elasticities are greater than those from the cross-section data. (This latter prediction assumes that a single point in time, the

[1] These features are examined by: Nelson, Peck, and Kalachek, *op. cit.* Chap. IV; Edwin Mansfield, 'Industrial Research and Development Expenditures: Determinants, Prospects and Relation of Size of Firm and Inventive Output', *Journal of Political Economy*, LXXII, August 1964, pp. 319–40; US National Science Foundation, *Industrial R and D Funds in Relation to Other Economic Variables* (Washington, DC, 1964); and Yale Brozen, 'R and D Differences Among Industries', in Richard A. Tybout, ed. *Economics of Research and Development* (Columbus, Ohio, 1965), pp. 93–100.

[2] Christopher Freeman, *Science, Economic Growth, and Government Policy*, *op. cit.*

[3] John Kenneth Galbraith, *American Capitalism* (Boston, 1952), p. 91. Certain contrary evidence on this point exists, e.g. on a *per capita* basis a number of countries outrank the United States on inventions and patents, although research is conducted on a larger scale in the US than in these other countries. Further, the continued existence of small research units or individual inventors also suggests that Galbraith overstates his case.

level of scientific and technological knowledge are roughly the same in different nations.) From the public good properties it seems likely that the largest share of the public consumption expenditures are financed at the level of the central government.

Hypothesis about the complex interaction of the public good properties, risk elements, complementarities, and substitution relations are difficult to make.[1] Although it is clear that part of the R and D expenditures are publicly financed, the share of the public sector is impossible to predict on theoretical grounds. Decision makers in the various nations must make subjective evaluations of these various elements, and since informed judgment on these matters is far from unanimous, one might predict that no discernible pattern of public and private financing can be found.

It also seems likely that there would be substitution between public and private financing of these R and D expenditures. This would come about not only because of the highly inelastic short-run supply curve of R and D personnel but also because the industrial demand for such services should be relatively independent of the methods of their financing.

In the empirical analysis to test these hypotheses, three difficulties arise which must be briefly discussed. First, of course, are the well-known problems of definition.[2] In some countries 'scientific' activity covers work only in the physical and biological sciences; in the United States, the social sciences are included; while in a number of European nations 'science' (*Wissenschaft, nauka,* etc.) covers all fields of scholarship including the humanities, law, and theology. Since the available data on R and D reflect conceptual differences and only a few adjustments could be made, small differences in the data that are presented should not be considered as significant.

[1] For market economies, one other matter also enters. Since R and D efforts of a production unit and its future economic growth are related, the amount of current R and D expenditures affects the future size distribution of the enterprises. A nation wishing to forestall certain antitrust activities in the future might do so by financing research in certain enterprises at the present time.

[2] Such definitional problems are surveyed by Lawrence A. Seymour, 'Problems of International Comparisons of R and D Statistics', mimeo, paper delivered at the OECD conference on 'Measurement of Scientific and Technical Activities', Frascata, Italy, June 1963. See also Kramish, *op. cit.*, and Freeman and Young, *op. cit.*

A second problem arises in the handling of military R and D. The distinction between military and civilian R and D does not necessarily correspond to the institutions financing such research. For instance, the United States Department of Defence finances a considerable amount of pure research quite unrelated to military problems, while, on the other hand, some private civilian R and D is exclusively military.[1] Since highly detailed information is necessary to adequately define and remove military R and D and since such information is not available for most countries, it seemed best to combine all types of R and D to circumvent this problem, even though some statistical biases might be introduced.[2]

A final problem occurs in isolating public consumption expenditures for R and D in the centrally planned economies. In these nations such expenditures are financed in three ways: directly through the state budget (and recorded as 'science expenditures'); indirectly by means of subsidies from the Ministries and similar governmental organs (which are recorded as grants under the budget rubric 'financing the national economy'); and by the enterprises (which do not appear in the budget at all). Clearly those expenditures explicitly designated as science are public consumption expenditures. I have classified the remaining R and D expenditures as 'privately' financed, since in large part such services are paid for by receipts of goods sold to other enterprises or individuals. This distinction also corresponds to the institutional fact that the 'science' section of the state budget enters quite directly into the budget decision-making process while the other R and D expenditures are only indirectly affected by this process.

In regard to the relative shares of public and private financing

[1] An interesting attempt to separate military and civilian R and D in the United States is by J. Herbert Hollomon. 'Technical Policies in the Context of Economic Needs', mimeo. paper prepared for the Federal Council of Science and Technology, July 18, 1963. I would like to thank Robert A. Fish for bringing this paper to my attention and for discussing with me methodological problems of separating civilian and military defence expenditures.

[2] A major bias is that certain military R and D is not completely included. Korol, *op. cit.*, has argued that Soviet rocket research expenditures are contained in the military, rather than in the science budget, so that my procedure would understate total R and D expenditures. Unfortunately, we have no concrete information about such matters.

I*

considerable scattered evidence on this matter is available. In the market economies of Western Europe the percentage distribution of the financing of R and D between government, business, and non-profit institutions (e.g. universities and foundations) varies greatly between nations.[1] Furthermore, the distribution of expenditures that are directly used by these sectors for R and D is also considerably different in the various countries. Finally, the relationships between these two distribution patterns is obscure. In the centrally planned economies, Czechoslovakia finances only about a quarter of its total R and D through public consumption expenditures; the Soviet Union finances roughly two thirds of its R and D expenditures in this way; while the other nations seem to finance almost all their R and D expenditures in this manner.[2] Thus the prediction about the unpredictability of the relative public and private shares in financing R and D seems confirmed.

An important substitution relationship appears to exist between the public and private financing of R and D expenditures. For Western Europe the ratios of total R and D expenditures to the GNP are roughly the same in nations with similar *per capita* incomes, although the financing of such expenditures varies considerably.[3] In the United States, a similar substitution relationship is found for firms working with and without government research contracts.[4] For the sample countries (see Table 6-5) some sort of substitution mechanism between public and private R and D expenditures also seems to be in operation. This may be seen from the fact that in relation to income, total R and D expenditures and total published scientific papers (a

[1] Data for this and the following statements come from Freeman, *op. cit.*, p. 78; and Christopher Freeman, A. Young, *et al.*, *The Research and Development Effort in Western Europe, North America, and the Soviet Union* (Paris, 1965), p. 72.

[2] Data for Czechoslovakia and the Soviet Union are given in Table 6–5. For East Germany institutional evidence on this matter is available in Vladimir Slamecka, *Science in East Germany* (New York, 1963). For the other countries I rely on a qualitative impression gained from a number of scattered statements in the economic literature on the state budget.

[3] These relationships can be seen from data presented by Freeman, Young, *et al.*, *op. cit.* and by Arnold Kramish, *Research and Development in the Common Market vis-à-vis the UK, US, and USSR*, RAND Corp. Paper P-2742 (Santa Monica, Calif., 1963).

[4] David M. Blank and George J. Stigler, *The Demand and Supply of Scientific Personnel* (New York, 1957), pp. 57–62.

physical indicator of R and D output) are much more related to income than public consumption expenditures for R and D. In other words, relatively more R and D is privately financed in those countries where public consumption expenditures for this service are relatively low.

Other types of properties of public consumption expenditures for R and D can be analysed in a more quantitative fashion. Cross-section and then time-series data are explored below.

TABLE 6–5

Cross-Section Indicators of Research and Development[1]

| | Ratios to the factor price GNP | | Numbers of published scientific papers per million population | |
| | Public consumption expenditures on R and D | | Total current expenditures on R and D | | |
Country	1956	1962	1962	Physics 1961	Chemistry 1965
Market economies					
USA	0·98%	2·13%	3·05%	34·4	288
West Germany	0·22	0·55	1·30	n.a.	208
Austria	0·04	0·04	n.a.	5·4	n.a.
Ireland	0·04	0·03	n.a.	3·2	n.a.
Italy	0·08	0·15	0·59	13·4	103
Greece	0·04	0·10	0·12	0·4	n.a.
Yugoslavia	0·46	0·90	n.a.	0·9	50
Centralized economies					
Czechoslovakia	0·69%	0·71%	2·80%	13·6%	220%
East Germany	1·43	1·89	n.a.	n.a.	252
USSR	0·90	1·58	2·46	14·3	174
Hungary	0·46	0·60	n.a.	10·0	192
Poland	0·38	0·48	n.a.	10·3	179
Romania	0·49	0·63	n.a.	6·7	92
Bulgaria	0·56	0·54	n.a.	3·8	119

[1] Hungarian data are for 1955 and 1962. For Greece, a broader definition of total R and D expenditures yields a ratio of 0·19 per cent of the factor price GNP. The data on scientific papers designate the papers appearing in the scholarly journals of these nations and do not necessarily represent the nationality of the authors. Total physics papers per million in East and West Germany together was 16·9 in 1961.

Public consumption expenditures data come from Appendix A. Sources for data on total R and D expenditures are given in Appendix D–19. For scientific papers the sources are: Dale B. Baker, 'Chemical Literature Expands,' *Chemical*

The data suggest that Yugoslavia belongs more with the socialist nations than with the market economies and, therefore, the system variable that is employed is socialist-capitalist. For the unweighted samples the average ratios of public consumption expenditures for R and D to the GNP are higher in the socialist than in the capitalist nations for both years, although the difference is statistically significant only in 1956. The factor-income-effect gives the data for the centralized economies a slight upward bias, but the differences between the systems are too great to be accounted for by this factor. If income *per capita* is held constant, the socialist nations have significantly higher public consumption expenditures/GNP ratios for both years (see below). In these socialist nations total R and D expenditures also seem significantly greater. This is an important conclusion that can not be predicted from economic considerations. Its cause may be traced, perhaps, to the greater commitment of decision makers in these socialist nations to economic growth and their belief in the positive relation between R and D efforts and rising productivity.

The importance of income *per capita* can be tested not only for public consumption expenditures but also for total expenditures on R and D as well.[1] The results of the regression calculations are:[2]

$$\text{For 1956: } \ln (E/Y) = -12 \cdot 71 + 2 \cdot 28^* S + 1 \cdot 50^* \ln (Y/P)$$
$$(0 \cdot 34) \quad (0 \cdot 37)$$
$$R^2 = 0 \cdot 81^*$$

$$\text{For 1962: } \ln (E/Y) = -14 \cdot 59 + 1 \cdot 98^* S + 1 \cdot 78^* \ln (Y/P)$$
$$(0 \cdot 50) \quad (0 \cdot 63)$$
$$R^2 = 0 \cdot 62^*$$

and Engineering News, XLIV, June 6, 1966, pp. 84–87; and Stella Keenan and Pauline Atherton, *The Journal Literature of Physics* (New York, 1964).

[1] For the socialist nations for which data were not available I assumed that public consumption expenditures represented 90 per cent of total R and D expenditures; for the capitalist nations, 50 per cent of the total.

[2] When the systems variable is defined in terms of centralized and market economies, somewhat different numerical results are obtained. Nevertheless, the same general conclusions can be drawn. Because of the relatively low ratios of several countries which may distort the results, the regressions were also calculated in several alternative forms; again there are no changes in the general conclusions.

For 1962: $\ln (T/Y) = -16 \cdot 33 + 1 \cdot 63^*S + 2 \cdot 13^* \ln (Y/P)$
$$(0 \cdot 44) \quad (0 \cdot 55)$$
$$R^2 = 0 \cdot 67^*$$

where E = public consumption expenditures on research and development,

Y = GNP,

S = economic system (capitalist nations = 0; socialist nations = 1), and

T = total current expenditures on research and development.

For all three cases there are very high positive ratio-income-elasticities. Although such a result for total public and private R and D expenditures is quite expected, nothing in the theoretical considerations presented above would have suggested such a high elasticity coefficient for the public consumption expenditures.

The high cross-section ratio-income-elasticities for total R and D expenditures has, of course, been noted by others. It has one extremely important political implication that must be mentioned:[1] Since the relative amount of R and D depends directly on the level of *per capita* income, the gap between rich and poor countries may continue to widen unless effective mechanisms for the transfer of science and technology between such nations are established.

If the number of scientific papers published is a good index of scientific output, then we should also be able to predict such output on the basis of the information about resources devoted to science. In order to provide some basis of comparison, tests were also made to predict the papers published in chemistry and physics with the GNP *per capita* as the explanatory variable. In all cases unfortunately, GNP *per capita* served as a better pre-

[1] This point has been greatly emphasized by Steven Dedijer in a number of articles, e.g. 'Underdeveloped Science in Underdeveloped Countries', *Minerva*, II, Autumn 1963, pp. 61–82; or 'International Comparisons of Science', *New Scientist*, XII, February 20, 1964.

dictor of such 'output' than any indicator of monetary inputs into R and D.[1]

If, as I argue above, science requires a certain 'balanced growth', this result is disturbing. Although this failure can be blamed solely on the crudeness of the input and output data, three other factors also seem to be important here. First, diminishing returns to science manpower might be in operation; certainly as a higher portion of the labour force is drawn into R and D work, the average quality of such personnel probably declines. Second, the composition of science activity (not only between pure and applied science but also between different types of applied work) could also affect the published output if the complementarity relationships between each type of scientific work are not rigid. Finally, although the United States 'should', according to the regression, publish a great many more physics papers, a portion of US physicists are working on projects of military importance, the results of which are classified. In other words, the relative importance of military research might affect the quantity of published materials. Until more detailed data on the quantity and quality of R and D inputs and outputs are available, these factors can not be more adequately explored.

It is well known and documented that over the years R and D expenditures have grown considerably faster than the GNP.[2]

[1] Since the income *per capita* variable explained over 70 per cent of the variation between nations (the cross-section correlation coefficients were all over 0.85) the test which was set up was severe. For the experiments, regressions of the following sort were calculated:

$\ln (Q/P) = a + b \ln V$, where (Q/P) is published papers per million population (physics, chemistry, and physics + chemistry); and V is the explanatory variable (either GNP *per capita* or monetary science inputs *per capita*). Monetary science inputs were calculated by multiplying the GNP *per capita* times the ratio of R and D expenditures to the GNP. Since the GNP data were in dollars and the ratio data were in national currency units, such a procedure neglected the possible relative price differences between R and D.

It is interesting that introduction of the economic systems variable into the regression as an explanatory variable with GNP *per capita* resulted in the calculated regression coefficients of both having statistical significance. This provides further evidence that total R and D expenditures were relatively higher in the socialist economies.

[2] See esp. Derek J. deSolla Price, *Science Since Babylon* (New Haven, 1961) and *Little Science, Big Science* (New York, 1963). In a very different context Fritz Machlup [*The Production and Distribution of Knowledge in the United States*

One implication of the rapid growth of science is the estimation that 80 to 90 per cent of all scientists in history are alive and working today.[1] Unfortunately, data on total R and D expenditures over time are available for only a few of the sample nations.[2] Nevertheless, the data on public consumption expenditures for this purpose are revealing.

TABLE 6–6

Time-Series Behaviour of Public Consumption Expenditures for R and D, 1950 through 1962[3]

Country	Ratio-income-elasticity	Country	Ratio-income-elasticity
USA	+ 5·53*	Czechoslovakia	+ 3·02*
West Germany	+ 1·62*	East Germany	+ 1·43*
Austria	+ 0·44*	USSR	+ 1·68*
Ireland	− 0·36	Hungary	+ 2·36*
Italy	+ 1·44*	Poland	+ 1·30*
Greece	+ 3·47*	Romania	+ 0·81*
Yugoslavia	+ 1·68*	Bulgaria	+ 1·37*

The unweighted average time-series ratio-income-elasticity is +1·84. With one exception the time-series ratio-income-elasticities are positive and statistically significant. Even though the average constant-price ratio-income-elasticities of the market economies are 0·43 below the current-price elasticities, calculation of constant-price elasticities would result in high positive coefficients for most countries.

(Princeton, 1962)] supplies additional evidence. Several Soviet economists, in discussing the 'law' that the production goods industry must grow faster than the consumer goods industry, have broadened their analysis and have tried to demonstrate that the 'knowledge industry' must grow even faster than the production goods industry.

[1] Price, *Little Science, Big Science, op. cit.*

[2] At the present time very little is published about the R and D expenditures of any of the socialist nations except the Soviet Union. Most Western research work on the subject has focused on institutional aspects [e.g. Slamecka, *op. cit.* or Slamecka, *Science in Czechoslovakia*, (New York, 1963).] The research work on this topic done in Eastern Europe is extremely sketchy and incomplete, and international comparisons of expenditures seem to be primarily impressionistic [e.g. Artur Bodnar, *Gospodarka europejskich krajów socjalistycznych* (Warsaw, 1962), pp. 200–04.]

[3] Expenditures data come from Appendix A; GNP data, from Appendix B. Yugoslav data cover 1952 through 1962.

The degree to which the time-series-elasticities reflect the growth of R and D expenditures in general or a change in the publicly financed share of such expenditures as well is not known for most nations. However, for the United States the very high elasticity coefficient does reflect the growing public share of R and D expenditures,[1] while the datum for Ireland suggests the reverse phenomenon.

Contrary to expectations, the average time-series ratio-income-elasticity is not greater than the cross-section elasticity. In trying to explore some of the determinants of these elasticities, a number of useful results are obtained. First, economic system seems to play no role in explaining the differences between nations. Further, the ratios of public consumption R and D expenditures to the gross national products of different nations do not appear to converge in the period under examination, unlike expenditures for welfare or education. Indeed, GNP *per capita* is the only variable that seems to be associated in a significant way with differences in these R and D ratio-income-elasticities among nations. Moreover, the higher the level of development, the higher the ratio-income-elasticity.[2] Although this factor would serve to increase the 'R and D gap' discussed above, it must be noted that diminishing returns in R and D output might occur if expenditures increase too fast.

One last aspect of public consumption expenditures for R and D—the centralization—can be quickly examined. In all the sample nations, with the possible exception of Yugoslavia,[3] the preponderant share of such expenditures is directly financed by the central government. This accords with expectations derived above that a large part of the R and D expenditures financed by the government have public good properties.

In short, the empirical investigation of public consumption

---

[1] Data on the publicly financed share of R and D in the USA since 1920 are reported by Nelson, Peck, and Kalachek, *op. cit.*, p. 46.

[2] This variable is statistically significant both alone and in combination with other independent variables in the regressions.

[3] As noted in Appendix A–15 an estimate of such centralization had to be made for Yugoslavia. My impression in reading Yugoslav budget materials is that a considerable share of these expenditures are made by the Republics through the Republic Academies of Science and other local research bodies.

expenditures for R and D has shown that the ratio-income-elasticities calculated from both cross-section and time-series data are very high. Furthermore, such expenditures are relatively greater in socialist than capitalist nations, a phenomenon that reflects not only the fact that a higher share of R and D expenditures are publicly financed in socialist nations but also that these nations have relatively higher total expenditures for this purpose. Substitution relationships between public and private financing of these services also seem to occur. Finally, for almost all nations the public consumption expenditures for R and D are financed primarily at the central governmental level.

F. OTHER PUBLIC EXPENDITURES

In addition to the eight public consumption expenditures examined in this study there are a number of other budgetary expenditures that would be useful to explore if adequate data were available. Within the government budgets of the centrally planned economies, such expenditures fall primarily within the budgetary rubrics 'culture' and 'financing the national economy'; in the market economies, these expenditures are either scattered within the budget or, in a number of cases, excluded from the budget and financed through para-fiscal institutions.

Some idea of the magnitudes of these expenditures omitted from discussion can be gained by examining the relationship between total 'adjusted budgetary expenditures' (the sum of the eight public consumption expenditures analysed above) and total gross budgetary expenditures. Since gross expenditures are defined differently in each country, the data in the table must be interpreted as reflecting both real factors and budgetary accounting differences. (See Table 6–7 on the next page.)

The average ratios are significantly lower in the centralized than in the market economies. This means that the expenditures omitted from detailed examination in this study are considerably more important in these nations than in the West. In order to gain perspective on these matters it is useful to consider briefly what expenditures are excluded from the analysis up to this point.

TABLE 6–7

Ratios of 'Adjusted Budgetary Expenditures' to Gross Budgetary Expenditure[1]

Country	1956	1962	Country	1956	1962
USA	66%	67%	Czechoslovakia	39%	42%
West Germany	66	64	East Germany	55	52
Austria	71	70	USSR	56	56
Ireland	69	64	Hungary	47	41
Italy	70	72	Poland	40	37
Greece	74	61	Romania	34	34
Yugoslavia	n.a.	n.a.	Bulgaria	41	36

First of all, four types of public consumption expenditures are omitted from the empirical analysis in this study: expenditures for culture and recreation, for fire protection, for the administration of natural resources, and for the administration of the economic interests of the state (e.g. current expenditures for roads, harbours, agriculture, industry, or trade). For some of these functions (e.g. culture) the budgetary accounting practices of the different nations are extremely obscure, and in the centralized economies the line between units operating on the 'budget principle' and the 'principle of economic accounting' is so tenuous (e.g. the handling of newspapers and theatres) that meaningful comparisons with the available data are impossible. In other cases (e.g. fire protection or administration of natural resources), data are unavailable or so widely scattered that estimates could not be made. In a final set of cases (e.g. administration of economic interests), conceptual difficulties coupled with lack of data prevent further analysis at the present time. In all the sample nations, the combined volume of these four expenditures is without doubt quite small in relation to the total adjusted budgetary expenditures. There is also no *a priori* reason to believe that these expenditures are relatively higher in the centrally planned economies.

Three other types of current budgetary expenditures are also

[1] The data come from Appendix A. Using a very rough estimate of gross budgetary expenditures for Yugoslavia, I found that the portion accounted for by the adjusted expenditures was roughly the same as in the other market economies.

omitted from discussion: interest payments, subsidies, and expenditures financed by sales to the public. By definition, the last type of expenditure is not public consumption and, moreover, is excluded from the gross expenditures data used above for all the sample nations except East Germany. The former two types of expenditures may or may not be considered public consumption and, therefore, deserve brief comment.

Originally, interest expenditures were included as a public consumption expenditure, but this decision was abandoned for both statistical and conceptual reasons. With the exception of Hungary, estimates would have had to be made for all the other centralized economies on the basis of highly dubious scattered information.[1] Furthermore, there is considerable doubt that data on interest payments are economically meaningful for this study since many of the sample countries carried out currency reforms during the 1940s (and, in the case of a number of the centralized economies, in the 1950s as well), at which time portions of the public debt were cancelled or written off.[2] This means that interest payments reflect the various currency reforms in the past more than any general 'need' for state borrowing. From such considerations it should be clear that relative interest payments from the state budgets are much higher in the market economies.

Subsidy payments are excluded from consideration because of insurmountable problems in obtaining comparable data.[3] In defining subsidies in an economically meaningful way, it is necessary to include not only indirect and direct payments in cash or kind by the government to different private citizens or

[1] Poland gives data on interest payments, but since these are also combined with repayments of the principle, such information is not very helpful.

[2] Brief monetary histories of many of the centralized economies are given by John M. Montias, 'Inflation and Growth: The Experience of Eastern Europe', in Werner Baer and Isaac Kerstenetzky, eds., *Inflation and Growth in Latin America* (Homewood, Ill., 1964), pp. 216–50.

[3] Even for the United States there are considerable difficulties in calculating the 'real' value of subsidies. This is explored by Robert L. Hubbell, 'Concealed Subsidies in the Federal Budget', *National Tax Journal*, September 1957; and Julius W. Allen, *Subsidy and Subsidy-like Programs of the US Government*, Materials prepared for the Joint Economic Committee, Congress of the United States (Washington, DC, 1960). The national income definition of subsidies, for which data are readily available in most countries, is quite arbitrary and, in many cases, not completely comparable with similar data for other countries.

groups but also the cash value of the provision of goods, services, fees, and loans which do not reflect the full competititve market value. In addition, we should also include the cash value of all tax exemptions[1] and the value of all cross subsidies which are netted out in most presentations of subsidy data.[2] For the centralized economies these tasks are particularly insurmountable because the market value of commodities, services, and loans are in many cases quite artificial. Scattered evidence suggests that such subsidy expenditures are considerably higher in the centrally planned economies, especially in the 1950s when many enterprises were quite highly subsidized. Nevertheless, the difference in the relative amount of subsidies probably accounts for only a small portion of the differences between market and centralized economies recorded in Table 6-7.

The major share of the differences between gross budgetary expenditures in market and centralized economies appears to stem from short and long-term capital grants and loans which are financed through the budget in the latter group of nations.

In the centrally planned nations during the period under examination the state enterprises had relatively small discretionary cash reserves. Instead they received at periodic intervals short term grants and loans from the state budget to cover certain expenditures. Such short-term capital grants were an important form of financial control of such enterprises and constituted a policy tool unique to these countries.[3]

In addition, these firms received long term capital grants for the purpose of financing certain capital investments. Countless Marxist economists have implicitly or explicitly justified this procedure by arguing that a large share of investment financed

[1] This task is, of course, extremely difficult to carry out. As far as I know, West Germany [Ministerium der Finanzen, *Finanzbericht* (Bonn, annual)] is the only nation that published official estimates of such hidden subsidies.

[2] Cross subsidies occur in nations with large nationalized industrial sectors when government enterprises in one industry are subsidized from the profits of other government enterprises in the same industry. Many times only the net subsidies (i.e. the subsidies which are not covered by profits but are financed by a grant from the Ministry of Finance) are recorded in the budget.

[3] Such grants are discussed by many Western economists, including: Joseph S. Berliner, *Factory and Manager in the USSR* (Cambridge, Mass., 1957); and George R. Feiwel, *The Economics of a Socialist Enterprise: A Case Study of the Polish Firm* (New York, 1965).

directly through the budget is necessary in order to mobilize funds for use in achieving rapid economic growth. Indeed, among the centralized nations from the mid 1950s through the early 1960s, direct government investment financed by the budget seemed to account for $\frac{1}{4}$ to $\frac{1}{2}$ of total gross investment, in contrast to the $\frac{1}{10}$ to $\frac{1}{3}$ of total gross investment financed directly through the budget in market economies (including Yugoslavia).[1] On the other hand, the mobilization of investment funds, as measured by the ratio of investment to the GNP, has not been very different between the two groups of nations until recently. From the early 1950s to the early 1960s, the investment share in the GNP in Western Europe rose from 20 per cent or less to near 25 per cent, while those in Eastern Europe (excluding East Germany) went from near 20 per cent to near 30 per cent.[2]

The portion of direct budgetary participation in investment, of course, only reveals part of the picture. If we add to direct investment, governmental grants to investment banks, investment subsidies and guarantees, interest subsidies, etc., governmental participation in the investment process rises considerably in both groups of countries. Although adequate data are

[1] Except for Yugoslavia, data for the market economies come from Appendix A and OECD, *General Statistics*, various issues. For Yugoslavia, data were taken from Savezni zavod za statistiku, Jugoslavija, *1945–64, Statistički pregled* (Belgrade, November 1965), p. 85.

For the centralized economies the official data on 'gross investment' are based on nonstandardized definitions, all of which differ from standard practices in the West. For comparability, therefore, such data must be recalculated using standard Western definitions. For the USSR I used the estimates of Abraham S. Becker, *Soviet National Income and Product, 1958–62*, Part I, RAND Corporation Memorandum RM-4394-PR (Santa Monica, Calif., June 1965); and Nancy Nimitz, *Soviet National Income and Product*, 1956–58, RAND Corporation Memorandum RM-3112-PR (Santa Monica, June 1962). For Eastern Europe I used the estimates of Thad P. Alton, *Czechoslovak National Income and Product*, 1947–48 and 1955–56 (New York, 1962); *Hungarian National Income and Product in 1955* (New York, 1965); and *Polish National Income and Product in 1954, 1955, and 1956* (New York, 1965). Estimates for the gross investment (Western definition) of the other centralized economies were not available.

[2] The measurement of the ratio of investment to the GNP for the centralized economies is greatly complicated by the fact that investment goods are priced relatively low *vis-à-vis* consumption goods in these countries and adjustments must be made. I have used the time series estimates of Maurice Ernst ['Postwar Economic Growth in Eastern Europe—A Comparison with Western Europe', in Joint Economic Committee, Congress of the United States, *New Directions in the Soviet Economy*, Part IV (Washington, DC, 1966), pp. 873–917] for the above generalizations.

not available, it appears that the financial participation of the government in investment in all the centralized economies has been well over 75 per cent, while in the market economies the percentage of such participation has been much less. (In West Germany during the 1950s, for instance, all types of government net saving amounted to over 40 per cent of total net savings while such governmental savings plus the subsidies granted through tax exemptions for investment raised this percentage to somewhat over 50.[1] West Germany appears to have a relatively high share of publicly financed investment among the market economies; further, a share of this investment is not included among the gross budgetary expenditures.)

Thus the major differences in the public expenditures among nations of the two economic systems seem to lie in the funds which are channelled for use by production enterprises, e.g. subsidies, and short- and long-term capital grants and loans. Although it might be argued that such expenditures are a direct outcome of the form of property ownership in the economy, the evolving experience of Yugoslavia (which has socialism but which is developing a decentralized system of enterprise financing) suggests that such a system is more historically linked to the specific experiences and economic problems of the Soviet Union. The future budgets of many socialist economies may have a ratio of adjusted budgetary expenditures to total gross budgetary expenditures which may be considerably nearer to Western ratios than now; everything depends, of course, on the limits to which economic decentralization will proceed.

G. SUMMARY AND CONCLUSIONS

Certain services financed by the public consumption expenditures for administration, internal security, non-military external security, and research and development have public-good properties. Except for administration, the relative shares financed through the public sector are different in the various sample nations and depend not only upon the public good properties but also upon a wide variety of other factors.

[1] Karl W. Roskamp, *Capital Formation in West Germany* (Detroit, 1965), p. 160.

Administration expenditures present analytic problems because it is difficult to measure what is being produced. In any case, such expenditures behave in a much different manner than similar expenditures for industry. Part of these differences may be due to the fact that these expenditures are recorded in different ways. From time-series data for the sample nations, it appeared that in most cases these expenditures as a share of GNP decline as *per capita* income increases. At a single point in time the reverse relation occurs, which suggests that time-series and cross-section determinants are quite different.

For internal security expenditures the effects are also difficult to measure. Both the cross-section and the time-series ratio-income-elasticities are negative. In addition, the ratios of these expenditures to the GNP appear to be converging. For the period under examination, however, the relative amount of these expenditures excluding those for traffic control appear to be greater in the centralized economies, a phenomenon that can be explained only from political considerations. Political factors also seem to underlie the most important differences in centralization of these expenditures.

For non-military external security expenditures two important generalizations can be made: these expenditures appear higher in the centrally planned economies; and at a single point in time their share in the GNP increases as the level of development rises. The pattern of these expeditures over time is irregular and cannot be explained from economic considerations.

Finally, public consumption expenditures for R and D show very high ratio-income-elasticities for both time-series and cross-section data. In addition, both public consumption expenditures and total expenditures for R and D are higher in the centralized economies. Because of public-good properties most of the public financing of these services is carried out at the central governmental level.

In regard to the public expenditures not discussed in detail in this study the major differences between the centrally planned and market economies lies in the relatively greater amount of subsidies and capital grants and loans in the former group of nations.

Chapter VII

AN OVERALL VIEW

A. Introduction
B. The Structure of Public Consumption Expenditures
C. Determinants of Public Consumption Expenditures Reassessed
   1. *The Influence of the Economic System*
   2. *The Role of the Level of Economic Development*
   3. *Other Factors: A Brief Summary*
D. Behavioural Properties in Perspective
   1. *Substitution Relations*
   2. *Centralization*
   3. *Stability*
   4. *Incidence*
E. Differential Effects of Public and Private Financing
F. Concluding Remarks

A. INTRODUCTION

The empirical analyses in the last four chapters have focused on a wide number of issues in the field of public consumption expenditures. It is now time to draw the major conclusions together and to supplement them with an exploration of several important issues that could not be readily analysed until the individual expenditures had received attention.

The chapter begins with a discussion of the 'structure' of public consumption expenditures. This topic is related to the problem of determinants and has been the theme of a considerable body of public finance literature. The next three sections focus on some major questions of the positive theory of public expenditures—the determinants, behavioural properties, and differential effects of public and private financing—which are outlined in the introductory chapters. In the last section I place the results of this study in a broader perspective by returning to the underlying purposes of the study and the differences between normative and positive economic analyses of public expenditures.

B. THE STRUCTURE OF PUBLIC CONSUMPTION EXPENDITURES

Questions about the 'structure' of government budgetary expenditures or receipts usually refer to the quantitative relations between various expenditure or tax magnitudes. Such an approach has been used in the past when GNP aggregates were not available and perspective could be gained only by comparing the amount of one type of budget aggregate with another. This approach is not often employed in the previous chapters because I believe that the factors underlying the behaviour of public consumption expenditures can be better explored in other ways. However, to link my study to those utilizing this older methodology, a brief glance at some structural properties seems useful.

One type of structural property has already been examined— the relationship between public consumption expenditures and other expenditures within the government budget (see especially Table 6–7). The relatively greater amounts of 'other expenditures' in the centrally planned economies can be traced to their relatively greater production subsidies and budgetary capital expenditures. Such a structural analysis is quite unexceptional; difficulties arise, however, when other structural magnitudes are explored.

Two magnitudes within the government budget that have received considerable propagandistic attention are public consumption expenditures for security (military, non-military external security, and internal security) and for social welfare (welfare, health, and education). These two expenditure aggregates reflect two very different motives for making public expenditures, and their confrontation may illuminate the relative strengths of such motives in the budget-making process. (See Table 7–1 on the next page.)

Understandably the USA and the Soviet Union, which have the relatively greatest military expenditures, also have the highest ratio of security to social welfare expenditures; while West and East Germany, which have relatively high social welfare expenditures, have relatively low ratios in the table.

Nevertheless, few positive generalizations can be drawn from the table. The ratios are not correlated with income *per capita* or economic system, either singly or together. There is also no

TABLE 7–1

Public Consumption Expenditures for Security as a Ratio of Public Consumption Expenditures for Social Welfare[1]

Country	1956	1962	Country	1956	1962
USA	126%	85%	Czechoslovakia	42%	34%
West Germany	32	35	East Germany	43	26
Austria	10	11	USSR	101	73
Ireland	18	19	Hungary	63	38
Italy	34	26	Poland	56	43
Greece	90	74	Romania	76	35
Yugoslavia	96	58	Bulgaria	79	62

statistically significant difference in these ratios among nations of the two military alliance systems or between members of military alliances and neutrals.[2] Indeed, the only useful bit of information extractable from the data is that the average ratio of security to social welfare expenditures decreased between 1956 and 1962. From results in the previous chapters we know that this is due both to a relative (to the GNP) decrease in military expenditures and to a relative increase in the various social welfare expenditures in most of the sample nations.

A second structural feature of interest is the distribution of social welfare expenditures between the three major functions. These are presented in Table 7–2 below.

If we exclude Yugoslavia from the analysis,[3] certain relationships seem clear. In both years the cnetrally planned economies have significantly higher ratios for education and health and significantly lower ratios for welfare. It therefore seems as if these centralized economies prefer those social welfare expenditures which have some positive effect on present or future production to those which do not act to increase the gross national product. But considerable caution must be exercised at this

[1] The data come from Appendix A.

[2] For the Warsaw Treaty Organization nations, all of the centralized economies are used; for the NATO countries, the USA, West Germany, Italy, and Greece are included; for the neutrals, Austria, Ireland, and Yugoslavia are used.

[3] Yugoslavia is in a peculiar position since it appears to be more like the market economies in 1956 and more like the socialist nations in 1962. Because most of the differences between the systems are on the borderline of statistical significance, considerable clarity is gained by omitting Yugoslavia from the analysis.

point. Taking into account other determinants of these public consumption expenditures, there are statistically significant differences between the two systems only for education; for welfare and health the economic system is definitely not a determinant. The data in the table thus reflect the combined influence of a number of factors such that attribution of differences in Table 7–2 to any single one is quite misleading. Additional relationships of these structural data for social welfare expenditures with such variables as *per capita* income, and so forth, are not apparent.

TABLE 7–2

Distribution of Public Consumption Expenditures for Social Welfare[1]

Country	1956			1962		
	Education	Health	Welfare	Education	Health	Welfare
Market economies						
USA	30%	11%	59%	27%	11%	62%
West Germany	12	15	73	11	15	73
Austria	12	13	75	11	13	75
Ireland	16	23	61	19	25	55
Italy	18	19	63	20	20	60
Greece	18	13	69	15	11	74
Yugoslavia	17	27	56	25	26	49
Centralized economies						
Czechoslovakia	19	21	60	19	17	64
East Germany	20	23	57	19	33	58
USSR	32	22	46	26	17	56
Hungary	25	24	51	24	25	51
Poland	24	21	54	23	26	51
Romania	34	27	39	31	23	46
Bulgaria	36	24	39	30	20	50

Other types of structural relationships can also be investigated: for example, the relative importance of transfers and direct expenditures or the distribution of different security expenditures. But the determinants of most of these expenditures have already been examined in the previous four chapters, and again statistical identification problems seem much greater for structural ratios. That is, in the structural analysis we must distinguish

[1] The data come from Appendix A.

the forces at work in both the numerator and denominator;[1] and in such a situation, forces affecting both sides of the fraction at the same time can be obscured, while other causal factors can be misinterpreted. Since too many economic forces operate on these ratios to be isolated in an adequate fashion, it seems better to examine each expenditure separately.

C. DETERMINANTS OF PUBLIC CONSUMPTION EXPENDITURES REASSESSED

Several methods are used in this study to isolate the determinants of the public consumption expenditures. For military expenditures, a rigorous model using implications of the public-good properties of such expenditures is constructed, and a number of hypotheses are generated which are statistically confirmed. Other types of hypotheses are derived from more intuitive notions and receive affirmation, at least in so far as the expected associations between variables are statistically significant. Such propositions stem from considerations of the nature of the relevant institutions which expend public funds (e.g. health and welfare expenditures) or 'commonsense' ideas about the supply and demand properties of these expenditures (e.g. interactions between military expenditures of enemy nations or differences between time-series and cross-section income elasticities for education). Finally, for some expenditures no adequate theory can be devised, and the empirical analysis is purely inductive (e.g. for administration and internal security expenditures).

1. THE INFLUENCE OF THE ECONOMIC SYSTEM

In the empirical analyses the economic system variable plays a statistically significant role in accounting for variations in the ratio of public consumption expenditures to the GNP for education, research and development, non-military external security, and possibly internal security excluding traffic control. In the case of education, the total amount of such services produced is

---

[1] In the analysis of expenditure/GNP ratios there is also, as noted in Chapter II, a statistical identification problem. Nevertheless, in this case it is easier to sort out the factors that seem to influence the numerator alone.

probably quite similar in the two cases; for the other expenditures the total amount of such services is greater in the centralized economies. The reasons underlying these systemic differences are primarily political or social, and such differences could not have been predicted from *a priori* economic considerations. It is noteworthy that for both education and internal security there is clear evidence that the difference between systems diminished between 1956 and 1962.

The economic systems variable is not a statistically significant determinant for public consumption expenditures for defence, welfare, and health; for all the time-series ratio-income-elasticities; and for the physical indicators examined in this study (except for R and D). In these cases two empirical factors related to this economic systems variable must be especially noted. First, in a great many cases the degree of variation among nations with the same economic system is much greater than the variation between the two economic systems, even after the influence of other determinants has been removed. This phenomenon overrides in importance any of the statistical difficulties in comparing public consumption expenditures between systems such as the factor-income-effect. Second, a number of general economic features (discussed below) underlie the differences in public consumption expenditures between nations that are related neither to the system of property ownership nor to the method of resource allocation.

Such results can be interpreted in several ways. They suggest to me that the policy dilemmas facing decision makers of public consumption expenditures are quite similar in all nations, regardless of system. Such policy problems include: the desirability of financing a service through the public rather than the private sector; the proper relationship of different public consumption expenditures to the tax revenues which must be raised; and balancing citizens' demand for particular services with the adjudged interests of the state. If the basic economic circumstances (in Marxist terminology 'productive forces') are similar and if the policy dilemmas are similar, it should not be surprising that the decisions taken are also roughly similar. Of course, such an argument relies on some notion of economic determinism, the validity of which has been denied in regard to comparisons between socialist and capitalist nations by a number of Marxists.

An alternative interpretation of these empirical results can be based on Musgrave's contention that it is only in those cases where goods and services do not have public-good properties (i.e. 'merit goods') that public consumption expenditures in capitalist and socialist nations would differ.[1] Now for some 'merit goods' such as education, this does appear to be the situation. But for 'merit goods' such as health and welfare services (for which I argue that public-good properties are relatively unimportant), there are no significant differences between the two economic systems. And in examining the other side of this proposition, significant differences between the two systems do appear for those services for which public-good properties are important (e.g. non-military external security and R and D expenditures).

In actuality the general problems in financing 'merit goods' appear quite similar in any economic system: If a service is publicly financed, some of it is bound to be wasted by the recipients because it has a zero price. If there are capacity restraints in producing the service, considerable administrative expense is involved in attempting to allocate it where the need is greatest. Further, collecting taxes to finance such public consumption expenditures presents difficulties in all nations. Thus, using the financing of 'merit goods' as a criterion for classifying nations may not necessarily yield the same results as when other criteria such as property ownership or method of allocating productive resources are employed.

The relative unimportance of economic system in many cases also has two extremely important methodological implications. First it should be manifestly clear that misleading results can be obtained in determining the differences between economic systems by comparing only two nations, each of which 're-presents' one particular system. Indeed, by carefully picking the pair of nations, almost any conclusion can be 'proved'. The real differences between economic systems can only be ascertained by comparing a number of nations in both systems, an obvious proposition which is necessary to emphasize only because of its

[1] Richard A. Musgrave, *Fiscal Systems* (New Haven, 1968).

constant violation by economists of both Marxist and non-Marxist persuasions.

Second, public finance institutions which appear different may actually act in very similar ways. In Chapter II a number of differences in these institutions of the two economic systems are outlined; these include the greater hierarchical arrangement of budgetary units, the closer integration of budgetary and production plans, and the greater scope of the budget in the centrally planned economies. But most of the differences are the consequence of ideology, custom, convenience, or political influences of other countries and do not reflect basic economic factors. For questions concerning the determinants of public consumption expenditures—in contrast to problems dealing with the politics surrounding their administration—Anglo-American economists seem considerably more justified in their neglect of the differences in budgetary institutions in the two systems than some continental economists and their fetishisms with institutional details.

It should not be surprising that with the decline of ideological dogmatism since the early cold-war years, the similarity of public consumption expenditures in nations with different economic systems has been increasingly recognized by economists in both East[1] and West.[2]

2. THE ROLE OF THE LEVEL OF ECONOMIC DEVELOPMENT

The level of economic, as measured by *per capita* income, plays a statistically significant role in the cross-section analyses to explain the public consumption expenditures/GNP ratios for only internal security, foreign aid, and research and development. For military, welfare, education and health expenditures, on the other hand, this *per capita* income variable has little explanatory power.

However, in almost all of the time-series analyses carried out in this study, the behaviour of the public consumption expenditures/GNP ratios is significantly related to *per capita* income (that is, the ratio-income-elasticity coefficients are statistically

[1] E.g. Miroslav Tuček, *et al.*, *Socialistické finance* (Prague, 1965), esp. pp. 283 ff.
[2] E.g. Jan Tinbergen, 'Do Communist and Free Economies Show a Converging Pattern?' *Soviet Studies*, XII, April 1961, pp. 333–41.

significant). Such time-series results do not necessarily contradict the cross-section conclusions for two reasons. First, there are different determinants for public consumption expenditures in time-series and cross-section bases. Second, a great many more factors are related to *per capita* income over time than over space, and there are manifold statistical problems in separating the various causal factors (or, in other words, problems of multicollinearity are greater with time-series than cross-section data).

To further evaluate the relationships between *per capita* income and public consumption expenditures, it is also useful to recall some major conclusions of other studies covering different countries or a longer span in time. On both cross-section and time-series bases it appears that during the course of economic development there is a secular shift in the ratios of total public consumption expenditures to the GNP. However, this shift seems to occur primarily during the economic transformation of societies from rural-agricultural to urban-manufacturing, when the average *per capita* income rises from around $200 to $600. After this shift, however, the pattern of public expenditures in regard to *per capita* income appears more random.

In considering the behaviour of both aggregative public consumption expenditures as well as individual expenditures, four factors appear most important to take into account.

First, for certain public consumption expenditures there are direct causal relationships with *per capita* income. These may spring from the subjective desires of individuals transmitted through the government or, more likely, be traced to specific socio-economico-political changes which accompany all nations with a rising *per capita* income, such as urbanization, increasing personal mobility, and greater stress on objective rather than traditional values. These causal relationships between income and expenditures occur on both cross-section and time-series bases and can be positive (e.g. public consumption expenditures for R and D) or negative (e.g. public consumption expenditures for internal security).

Second, the rise or fall of other public consumption expenditures approach asymptotes and, in many of these cases, a time element associated with *per capita* income is important for a certain period.[1] The relative rise of some expenditures is due to an increasing share of the expenditure which is publicly financed, a process which ceases after the public share reaches 100 per cent. For long-period analyses this shift in relative public-private share is important to take into account; for the thirteen-year period under analysis it played a negligible role in the time-series data in most sample nations. Other types of expenditures are limited by population constraints, e.g. for primary education where the enrolment rates are practically 100 per cent in all nations but the least economically developed. Other population constraints are quite obvious in the case of old-age pensions; indeed, the empirical analysis in Chapter IV shows a definite limit on the ratio of public consumption expenditures for welfare to the GNP.

Third, much of the growth of public consumption expenditures has been due to the extension of public financing into new areas. But as the population becomes wealthier and increasingly more expenditure options are open to all individuals, there will be fewer goods and services for which the price elasticities of demand are low because they are absolute necessities of life.[2] Public financing of goods and services with high price elasticities incurs not only the administrative difficulties noted above but social frictions as well. For instance, if free public housing is provided for the very poor, the allocation problem is of manageable proportions because absolute need can be recognized; however, if free housing is provided for all, everyone will naturally demand the most luxurious house in the most convenient locations, and obvious difficulties will arise. Although it is difficult to foresee the type of consumers who will inhabit future affluent societies, it is possible to predict that for the next few decades a price allocation of goods will still have many advantages.[3]

[1] This point is discussed and documented in Chapter II.

[2] This does not mean that people will have 'a lower demand' for goods in general but that they will have a sufficient amount of them such that the price elasticity of demand for any particular one is quite high.

[3] These problems are brilliantly analysed in much greater detail by Peter Wiles, the foremost Western economic eschatologist [see his *The Political Economy of Communism* (Cambridge, Mass., 1962), Chapters XVII to XX].

K

A final argument is based on more macro-economic considerations. If the ratio of public consumption expenditures to the GNP rises, the average ratio of taxes to income also rises. Now in market economies it has been observed empirically that as the *per capita* GNP rises, the inequality of income decreases slowly.[1] Therefore, as the tax/income ratio rises there is a relatively declining number of very rich on which the burden of new taxation can be shoved. In addition, there are certain limits of a person's income that can be taxed. Thus it is highly likely that rising tax rates affect an increasingly larger portion of the population. At some point the majority of the population is no longer able to receive benefits from public consumption expenditures without paying for them, a phenomenon that may act as a disincentive toward very rapid increases in the public consumption expenditures/GNP ratio thereafter.[2]

The relative importance of these four considerations depends upon the specific cases and the individual properties of the expenditures. Nevertheless, it should be clear that the relationship between various public consumption expenditures and *per capita* income is complex, and that the situation is complicated even more when determinants of these expenditures, that are not related to the level of economic development, are taken into account. In situations where numerous determinants can be easily separated—especially cross-section studies—*per capita* income often plays a relatively minor explanatory role.[3]

It should not be necessary to add that these considerations provide additional weaponry against simple-minded generalizations such as Wagner's 'law'. But unfortunately Wagner's 'law' is like Hydra and since public finance has not yet sired

---

[1] This phenomenon is empirically explored by many, including Simon Kuznets, 'Quantitative Aspects of Economic Growth of Nations: VIII. Distribution of Income by Size', *Economic Development and Cultural Change*, XI, January 1963, Part II. Between geographical areas in a single country such as the United States, income inequalities also decrease with rising level of economic development in the nation.

[2] This point is argued with special vigour by Shibshankar Prasad Gupta, *The Size and Growth of Government Expenditures: A Time-Series and Cross-Section Analysis*, Ph.D. dissertation, University of York, England, 1966.

[3] This conclusion is empirically demonstrated in several studies of US state and local public expenditures. See esp. Robert F. Adams, *Determinants of Local Government Expenditures*, Ph.D. dissertation, University of Michigan, 1963.

its Hercules, each adversary must join the attack whenever possible.

3. OTHER FACTORS: A BRIEF SUMMARY

For military expenditures, the absolute size of the national product plays an important role in explaining the cross-section differences between nations as well as certain differences in the time-series behaviour of these expenditures between small and large nations. The underlying cause of this relationship is the public-good nature of defence services among nations in military alliances. In addition, other properties of these expenditures over time can be explained by changes in the international political environment, which can be seen most dramatically by the close correlation between Soviet and American military expenditures.

For health and welfare expenditures, the date of the introduction of the social insurance system seems crucial in explaining cross-section differences. On the demand side, this indicates the desire of the population for public intervention in these areas; on the supply side, the incremental expansion of social insurance bureaucracies ('creeping socialism'). The actual date of the introduction of these social insurance systems is most immediately related to the political mobilization of workers, as reflected in the strength of unionization. For welfare expenditures and, to a lesser extent, health expenditures, there seems to be an upward limit to the public consumption expenditures/GNP ratio, such that those nations with the lowest relative expenditures have the fastest increase in public consumption expenditures.

Other factors also seem to play important roles in explaining the behaviour of the public consumption expenditures. For instance, the rising level of technology suggests that time-series ratio income-elasticities for both health and education are higher than cross-section elasticities, predictions that are confirmed by the data. The age structure of the population also appears important in explaining certain components of education expenditures.

The necessity of keeping this study within a reasonable size has permitted only a small number of such factors to be adequately explored. Nevertheless, several conclusions are immediately evident from the analysis. First, much more interesting and useful explorations of the determinants of public consumption expenditures can be made when such expenditures are disaggregated. This is especially true because disaggregation allows the isolation of special causal influences on one particular expenditure. Second, the determinants should be studied on both time-series and cross-section bases and, if possible, for different levels of government as well, so that the confrontation of results can lead to a deeper understanding of the causal forces at work in all situations.

D. BEHAVIOURAL PROPERTIES IN PERSPECTIVE

In each chapter I investigate a number of different types of behavioural properties of public consumption expenditures, particularly concerning centralization and substitution relations. The results of these analyses are summarized and further explored. For two additional behavioural properties, stability and incidence, discussion of both aggregates and individual expenditures are presented below at the same time to round out the analysis.

1. SUBSTITUTION RELATIONS

Substitution between public and private expenditures for the same service is shown to be important for the following four public consumption expenditures examined in this study: welfare, health, education, and R and D. Although difficulties arise in the exploration of this phenomenon, the empirical evidence is sufficient for considerable certainty about the general conclusions. On a state and local level the substitution relations between publicly financed, insurance financed, and out-of-pocket expenditures for health in the United States can be econometrically examined. The results show that there is no substitution between public and private expenditures, primarily because of some institutional features peculiar to this country; but that between out-of-pocket and insurance-financed expenditures, the substitution is considerable. Since most insurance financed health expenditures in the other sample countries are channelled through state social security systems, they are considered as public consumption expenditures; thus the general international and intra-national results about substitution relations are consistant.

The importance of these results for further empirical study of public consumption should be clear. In particular, it is impossible to evaluate the effects of such public consumption expenditures without taking into account the volume and effects of private expenditures for the same service. For policy making, knowledge of such substitution relations is also a strong necessity, espcially in the estimation of the costs and benefits of a particular programme. If the public expenditures are substituted for private expenditures, then some of the intended effects of public financing might be nullified; if there is no substitution, certain capacity limits in providing the service might be reached. In either case, more beneficial public programmes can be designed if these substitution relationships are reliably known.

One other type of substitution relation is also examined in this study—the substitution between different types of public consumption expenditures. However, between military and civilian public consumption expenditures such substitution is slight. Furthermore, a discovered lack of substitution between military and non-military external security expenditures is used to refute a theoretical contention to the contrary which was propounded by Adolph Wagner. Finally, for public consumption expenditures for health and welfare, complementary rather than substitution relations appear to predominate.

Such a lack of substitution between different types of public consumption expenditures has two important implications. First, in this post-Keynsian era revenue restraints on public expenditures are not as important as they supposedly were in the past especially for central governments. Second, major decisions about the magnitudes of various public consumption expenditures appear to be made in relative isolation from each other; other decision-making mechanisms for public consumption expenditures might lead to considerably more inter-expenditure substitution.

2. CENTRALIZATION

In the beginning of this study two major hypotheses about the centralization of public expenditures are offered. The first is that there is a high degree of determinancy of the degree of centralization for particular public consumption expenditures and that any deviation from certain limits results in adverse effects. The second is that many of the factors underlying the degree of centralization are institutional and that overcoming certain institutional constraints is the major difficulty in changing the degree of centralization of any public consumption expenditure. Certain empirical evidence in the last four chapters supports both hypotheses.

In regard to public consumption expenditures for external security (both defence and non-military external security expenditures) and for research and development, the provided services have considerable public-good properties for the nation as a whole. In these cases it seems likely that most such public consumption expenditures would be directly financed by the central government, a proposition that is also borne out in the empirical analysis. If the financing of these expenditures were decentralized, subnational governmental units could receive the benefits of these expenditures without paying for them, which would encourage 'freeloading' and other costly effects. Thus for certain expenditures there are severe limitations on variations of the degree of centralization without adverse consequences.

Further evidence for this proposition is also available. For the E.E.C. nations, the ratios of centralization for specific expenditures are quite similar.[1] And for state and local governments in the United States the ratios of centralization can be predicted for most expenditures with a considerable degree of accuracy by taking into account only such economic variables as *per capita* income and population.[2] It is noted in Chapter II, however, that certain institutional features might also be related to these economic variables (i.e. there is a possibility of multicollinearity) so that such evidence is not completely free of ambiguity.

On the other hand, for welfare, health, education, and

[1] Such evidence is documented in Chapter II.

[2] For us state and local expenditures there is a detailed empirical study of centralization ratios for various expenditures in Appendix E–8.

internal security public consumption expenditures in the sample nations, there is considerable variation in the centralization ratios, and each expenditure deserves brief comment. For welfare in countries such as the USSR there are only a small number of social insurance agencies, but some of these are designated as local organs; in other countries such as West Germany, there are several thousand social insurance agencies but these are defined as organs of the central government. The exact designations seem quite arbitrary, at least from an economic point of view. For health and education the legal nature of the government—whether it is federal or unitary—seems to be the most important factor underlying the degree of centralization. For internal security expenditures political factors rather than the economic system are vital in explaining differences between nations. Thus, for these expenditures the degree of centralization seems quite dependent on institutional factors.

Some additional supporting evidence can also be found. For the sample nations for the expenditures listed above, the degree of variation in the centralization ratios between nations at one point in time is considerably greater than for single nations over time. This suggests that institutional factors in individual nations are more powerful in regard to determining the centralization ratio than economic factors. The same differences between interspatial and intertemporal variation of the centralization ratios can be found for almost all expenditures of US state and local governments. In addition, for these US local governments the degree of centralization cannot be predicted from economic variables for expenditures for health and natural resources, at least in the experiments I tried.

Thus both of the offered hypotheses seem true—but in regard to different expenditures. Several other discoveries about the centralization of public consumption expenditures must also be emphasized.

Much of the change of the degree of centralization of aggregative public consumption expenditures is due to the changing composition of expenditures. Since there are different time-series and cross-section determinants for public expenditures, we would expect that the aggregative centralization ratios behave much differently in the two types of analyses, and indeed they do.

Again, disaggregation of total public consumption expenditures yields much more useful and interesting results than if the analysis is carried on only at highly aggregative levels.

It must finally be noted that no statistically significant relationships between the economic system and the degree of centralization for any individual public consumption expenditures except for internal security can be found.

3. STABILITY

Several vital economic questions concern the stability of public consumption expenditures over time: Are the fluctuations of such expenditures greater or less than fluctuations in the economy as a whole? Are the fluctuations of public consumption expenditures and the GNP in the same or opposite direction? And in what way are these fluctuations causally related?

The first two questions can be easily handled with the data from this study. Investigating the causal relations of these fluctuations requires an analysis of the fiscal policy-making process in each nation and does not lie in the scope of this study.

The exploration of economic fluctuations in centrally planned economies is still in its early stages.[1] Nevertheless, from the accumulated evidence it appears that aggregative economic variables in the centralized economies are not only subjected to important fluctuations, but that such fluctuations are equal to or greater than corresponding fluctuations in market economies.[2]

[1] The best quantitative comparative study is by George Staller, 'Fluctuations in Economic Activity in Planned and Free Market Economies', *American Economic Review*, LIV, June 1964, pp. 385–96. An interesting Marxist approach to the problem is by Joseph Goldman, 'Fluctuations and Trend in the Rate of Economic Growth in Some Socialist Countries', *Economics of Planning*, IV, 2/ 1964, pp. 88–98, (a condensation of his two articles in *Plánované hospodárstvi*, 9/1964, and 11/1964). Other important recent studies are: Eugene Zaleski, *Planification de la croissance et fluctuations économique en URSS*. (Paris, 1962); Julio G. H. Olivera, 'Cyclical Economic Growth under Collectivism', *Kyklos*, XIII 2/1960, pp. 229–55; and Holland Hunter, 'Priorities and Shortfalls in Prewar Soviet Planning', in Jane Degras, ed., *Soviet Planning: Essays in Honour of Naum Jasny* (Oxford, 1964), pp. 1–31.

[2] See esp. Staller, *op. cit.* Staller uses constant price data taken from official sources for all the centralized economies and compares the results with data from a large number of market economies. My results (see below) of fluctuations in the current price GNP show that fluctuations are higher in the centralized than market economies, although the differences are not statistically significant. The

It is useful, therefore, to see if such a generalization holds for public consumption expenditures.

Deciding on a useful empirical measurement of fluctuations raises a number of apparent difficulties. However, in previous comparative studies of economic fluctuations in various nations, most investigators have found that the type of measure for fluctuations which is finally chosen makes relatively little difference in the generalizations that are reached.[1] Moreover exploration of the fluctuations of public expenditures and of the GNP using both current and constant prices yield about the same results.[2] Therefore, it seems best to use the simplest type of measurements to ease problems of interpretation. In Table 7-3 below the coefficients of variation of current price data are presented. If public consumption expenditures grow at the same rate every year, the coefficient of variation is 0 per cent. If, on the other hand, the standard deviation of the yearly growth rates is twice as high as the average annual growth rate, the coefficient of variation is 200 per cent.

Several important generalizations can be drawn from the results. First, contrary to certain intuitive expectations, fluctuations in total public expenditures are about the same as fluctuations in the GNP. Fluctuations of public expenditures excluding the military are somewhat lower than fluctuations of the GNP or total public expenditures including the military, but these differences are not statistically significant.

Second, although the unweighted average fluctuations of public expenditures or the GNP are lower in the market than in the centralized economies, the differences are also not quite

fluctuations are, however, significantly and inversely related to *per capita* income. This reflects the fact that in less developed economies, agriculture (which is subject to considerable variation because of changing weather conditions) is relatively more important. The data in Table 7–3 for GNP fluctuations do not seem related to any other economic or political factor.

[1] E.g. Joseph D. Coppock, *International Economic Instability* (New York, 1962); or George Staller, *op. cit.*

[2] In my own experiments on these matters I used a number of measurements with both the current and constant-price data, including Coppock's log variance statistic. The rank orders of nations using standard deviation measures or log variance measures on the data were in all cases significantly related. The only countries to be significantly affected when current or constant-price series were chosen are noted below.

K*

TABLE 7–3

Fluctuations of Public Consumption Expenditures, 1950 through 1962[1]

	Coefficient of variation of the growth rates		
	Public consumption expenditures		Gross national product
Country	Total	Total excluding military expenditures	
Market economies			
USA	103%	40%	71%
West Germany	47	34	37
Austria	—	—	67
Ireland	74	68	60
Italy	35	34	32
Greece	49	38	66
Yugoslavia	56	30	42
Centrally planned economies			
Czechoslovakia	93%	88%	95%
East Germany	47	56	48
USSR	82	74	36
Hungary	108	80	—
Poland	72	67	77
Romania	74	58	101
Bulgaria	54	26	105

statistically significant. When Marxist economists deride the
'anarchical' fluctuations in economic activity in the West, they
may also be criticizing certain features of their own centrally
planned economies.

To what are the fluctuations in public consumption expenditures related? In simple regression experiments the degree of
these fluctuations in both expenditure series are significantly and
positively related only to the coefficients of variation of the

[1] The coefficient of variation is the standard deviation of the annual growth
rate divided by the average annual growth rate, with a slight modification to
make the two parts of the fraction more comparable. More precisely, I divided
the standard deviation of the ratios of E_{t+1}/E_t (where E_t = expenditures in
year t and E_{t+1} = expenditures in the following year) by the mean of these
ratios minus one. Public consumption expenditures for Austria and the GNP
for Poland are omitted because these were the only two instances where results
in current and constant-price data significantly differ. The current price data
for consumption expenditures come from Appendix A; the current price GNP
data, Appendix B.

gross national products.[1] No other simple associations could be found. More complex associations with two or more explanatory variables depend on the regression form and do not warrant reporting.

Can generalizations be made about the relative fluctuations of individual types of public consumption expenditures? *A priori* hypotheses can be made by considering the stability of supply and demand. Since it is always possible to spend more public funds quite rapidly (whether or not more results are obtained is a different question), the stability of demand seems the critical factor. On the basis of common observation one would suspect that short-term changes in demand are greatest for defence and non-military external security (including foreign aid) expenditures and least for health, education, and welfare expenditures. The results of the empirical investigation of fluctuations in public consumption expenditures follow in a gratifying manner such predictions.[2] The greatest fluctuations occur for military, diplomacy, and research and development expenditures. The inclusion of R and D expenditures in this list seems due to the fact that they are the most rapidly growing of any public expenditure in the period under examination and that rapid growth is often accompanied by considerable changes in year-to-year growth rates. The least fluctuations occur for internal security, health, and education. The inclusion of internal security in this list is not surprising when it is realized that for police needs, short-run changes in demand and supply are probably not great. The exclusion of welfare expenditures from the stable expenditures probably reflects the fact that there is a strong political element in transfer expenditures, particularly for old-age pensions.

For evaluating the effects of fluctuations in public expenditures, it is useful to know if such expenditures are used as a tool of countercyclical policy. A number of economists have

---

[1] Regressions of the following type were calculated: $\ln C = a + b \ln E$, where C = coefficient of variation and E = other explanatory variable. Among those variables used in these experiments were growth of public consumption expenditures, growth of GNP, fluctuations of GNP, *per capita* GNP, and economic system.

[2] In making these conclusions I omit from consideration administration and internal security expenditures in the centralized economies, as there are uncertainties about the accuracy to which the data reflect year to year changes.

suggested that such countercyclical use of public expenditures occurs primarily in capitalist economies since decision makers in socialist economies have a great many more policy tools with which to maintain economic stability.[1] It must also be noted that the desirability of such a countercyclical policy in capitalist economies, particularly with the use of current expenditures, is open to some doubt since rapid short-run changes in these expenditures can be quite disruptive. For example, cutting back on public consumption expenditures for education or R and D when the business cycle is in an upward phase has certain obvious disadvantages. Although a number of other pros and cons of such a counter-cyclical expenditures policy for nations with different economic systems can be given, it seems more promising to examine the actual situation for the sample nations.

There are a number of statistical difficulties in investigating this phenomenon, not the least of which is an identification problem and the lack of quarterly data to examine leads and lags. But because cyclical swings of the GNP in most of the countries lasted more than one year, the problems mentioned above were side-stepped and the following procedure was adopted. From series for public expenditures and the GNP, the trends were removed. If public expenditures had been counter-cyclically used, then the deviations from the trends of these public expenditures and the GNP should be negatively correlated.[2] Although we would not expect such an inverse relation among the centrally planned economies, the market economies might act differently.

In none of the countries examined this way, however, did there appear to be countercyclical fluctuations of public consumption expenditures. Indeed, in all countries the deviations of current public expenditures and the GNP from their respective

---

[1] See Richard A. Musgrave, *Fiscal Systems* (New Haven, 1968).

[2] If public consumption expenditures are used to offset countercyclical tendencies with perfect precision, then there would be no fluctuations from the trend for the GNP but considerable fluctuations for public consumption expenditures. Since there are policy lags, however, it is likely that public expenditures would not be used for countercyclical purposes until the GNP series had definitely turned downward. Therefore, the above procedure does have theoretical justification.

trends are positively correlated and, in most, to a statistically significant extent. If any of these countries use budgetary policy as a stabilization tool, it seems certain that primary emphasis is placed on the side of taxation or on types of budgetary expenditures, such as investment, that are not for public consumption purposes.

On a cross-section basis, the degree of variation in the expenditure/GNP ratios can be interpreted to indicate the range of choice facing policy makers in determining the particular volume of an expenditure. If, for instance, the coefficients of variation of these ratios for expenditures A and B are respectively 10 and 100 per cent, then such experience suggests that there are more open options for decision makers in regard to the second expenditure. For the sample nations in both 1956 and 1962, the coefficients of variation of the expenditure/GNP ratios are largest for public consumption expenditures for non-military external security, research and development, and defence; and are smallest for education, health, and internal security.[1] Surprisingly these results parallel exactly the findings from the time-series data! It is also noteworthy that the coefficients of variation are larger for civilian than for total public consumption expenditures.

If there are forces in the economies of these nations that 'determine' public consumption expenditures, then a better measure of the range of options open to decision makers can be obtained by measuring the variation of these expenditure/GNP ratios after the influences of these determinants have been removed. The basic statistical materials for such a project are already at hand form the analyses of the determinants of each individual public consumption expenditure discussed in the last four chapters.[2] Even taking these determinants into account,

[1] It is surprising that both internal security and administration expenditures, for which the data are perhaps the least comparable, show relatively small variation of the expenditures/GNP ratios.

[2] For each public consumption expenditure for which cross-section determinants were found, such determinants were used in the calculations. For the other expenditures I put into the regressions *per capita* income and economic system as the independent variables.

The best measure of the variation to be measured is the ratio of the standard error of estimate to the mean expenditures/GNP ratio. Since the regressions are calculated with a logarithmic transformation, this is a difficult statistic to calculate.

the largest variations again appear for R and D, defence, and non-military external security expenditures. At the other end of the scale, the results are slightly different, since the smallest variations appear for education, health, and welfare expenditures. All in all, removing the determinants of these public consumption expenditures does not greatly change the rank order of their variations. We can therefore conclude that the forces influencing the variation of public consumption expenditures over a period of time appear similar to those affecting the variation of such expenditures over many countries at a single point in time. That is, there is an association between rapid short-term changes in supply and demand for public consumption expenditures and the expenditure options that are open to policy makers.

From the lack of an inverse relation between fluctuations in public consumption expenditures and in the GNP we also conclude that these expenditures are not used in the sample nations as an important countercyclical policy tool. And from the explanation of the forces underlying the relative fluctuations of different expenditures over time, it should be clear that they should not be so utilized either.

4. INCIDENCE

Empirical estimations of the incidence of taxes and government expenditures are a frequent subject of discussion in the Western economic literature. However, Marxist economists seem extremely uninterested or unwilling to analyse empirically such politically inflammatory matters in regard to the East European nations.[1]

One way to determine empirically the impact of the govern-

However, the antilog of the deviation between predicted and observed variables in these logarithmic regressions is the ratio of the predicted and observed expenditures/GNP ratio. Therefore, the antilog of the standard error of estimate of the logarithmic regressions is used as the measure of variation after the influence of the determinants was removed.

[1] Much of the East European literature on these matters is summarized by Stefan Varga, 'Die Eigenarten des Budgets der sozialistischen Staaten', *Finanzarchiv*, XXII, April 1963, pp. 185–203. The only title of a Marxist monograph on the subject that I could locate is: Adám Schmidt, *Az adóztatás igazságossága: az alapvető problémát eltakaró részletkérdés* (Budapest, 1962). Unfortunately, it proved impossible to obtain this book for use for this study.

ment budget on the income distribution of the sample nations is to start from survey data of the governmental services that families with different incomes enjoy and their expenditure and income items on which taxes are placed.[1] But such survey data are not available for most nations included in my sample. One could also begin with information about the income distribution and then, on the basis of certain assumptions, allocate the various government expenditures and taxes.[2] But income distribution data and highly detailed data on government expenditures and taxes, from which assumptions could be made about their distribution among different income classes, are also not available for the centrally planned economies. The discussion in this section is, therefore, confined to some qualitative remarks about the incidence of the government budget in four sample nations plus the results of a brief experiment on one particular aspect of this problem which offers some quantitative insights into such matters.

In comparing the impact of certain public consumption expenditures among the sample nations, several factors become quite apparent. First of all, the redistributional aspects of some public consumption expenditures often depend less on their economic properties than on their exact administration. For instance, in Chapter IV it is noted that most of the US public consumption expenditures on health seem designed to aid the lower income groups and therefore can be said to act in a very progressive manner.[3] However, in a country such as the USSR where there is an extensive network of 'closed clinics' for high

[1] The only extensive use of such an approach is: J. L. Nicholson, 'Redistribution of Income in the United Kingdom in 1959, 1957, and 1953', in Colin Clark and Geer Struvel, eds., *Income and Wealth, Series X, Income Redistribution and the Statistical Foundation of Economic Policy* (New Haven, 1964).

[2] The usefulness of the following procedure for centralized economies has been challenged by Edward Ames, *Soviet Economic Processes* (Homewood, Ill., 1965).

[3] Taxes paid by individuals or families are 'progressive' if the ratio of taxes to income decreases as individual or family income decreases; a government expenditure is 'progressive' if the value of the service enjoyed by individual or families as a ratio of income increases as income decreases. The particular concept of income used as a base is a tricky analytical problem and is discussed in detail by W. Irwin Gillespie, 'Effect of Public Expenditures on the Distribution of Income', in Richard A. Musgrave, ed., *Essays in Fiscal Federalism* (Washington, DC, 1965).

officials and where rest cures and visits to sanitoria are often allocated to those workers who have most overfulfilled their production norms (and thus who are the most highly paid), public consumption expenditures may act in a less progressive manner.[1] (In this specific case, however, not enough information is available for any type of adequate evaluation; also the situation is complicated by the fact that Soviet public consumption expenditures for health are relatively so much greater than in the United States.) On the tax side, similar problems are evident. For instance, turnover taxes in the Soviet Union before and during World War II appear quite regressive because of the importance of the bread tax. After 1950, however, the bread tax diminished in importance, and the turnover tax became less regressive.[2] Properly structured, a turnover tax or a sales tax can even act in a very progressive manner.[3]

From previous studies about the impact of public expenditures and taxes on the income distribution in a number of countries one easy generalization is possible: public expenditures are considerably more progressive than taxes, at least in a short run sense (i.e. between people with different incomes at a single point in time; whether this represents a net lifetime redistribution between income classes is not known). The reasons for this phenomenon are quite apparent. Most government transfer payments (e.g. social insurance), which are quite extensive in the sample countries, are designed to increase the income of the groups with the lowest income at that particular

[1] This discussion does not take into account a topic that is discussed below, namely whether or not the consumption of health services is more evenly spread over the population when both public and private expenditures are considered together.

[2] Empirical evidence on this matter is presented by Franklyn D. Holzman, *Soviet Taxation* (Cambridge, Mass., 1955), pp. 146–58.

[3] In writing about taxes in capitalist economies, a number of Marxist economists have asserted that indirect taxes such as sales taxes are inherently regressive and exploitative. However, the ratios of such indirect taxes to the GNP are considerably higher in East Europe than in most West European nations. Furthermore, these ratios have risen from the prewar times in all the East European nations that were formally capitalist. [Considerable data on various indirect taxes in a number of centrally planned economies are presented by Theo Surányi-Unger *Studien zum Wirtschaftswachstum Suedosteuropas* (Stuttgart, 1964.)] Of course, any broad generalization about the effect of indirect taxes on the income distribution or on 'exploitation' without reliance on detailed micro-economic data is almost always superficial.

moment in time. Other types of government services, such as primary education, are available to all; and, since lower income groups usually have larger families, act in a progressive manner. Indeed, in this case a long-run distribution also seems apparent. That is, since earning power is directly related to education and since the value of human capital from education is a large percentage of the reproducible wealth,[1] the public consumption expenditures on education serve to modify considerably the income distribution from what it would be if tangible wealth were the only type of capital from which income could be derived.[2] On the other hand, the impact of taxes on the distribution of income (especially those taxes which are most easy to collect) is rarely progressive, as empirical studies of this phenomenon for various market economies have so frequently shown.

Comparisons of the net short-run effect of the government budget on the income distribution of different pairs of countries can be made with various degrees of exactness. For the USA and the Soviet Union, we can say only that the net effect on the government budget is quite progressive in the United States, and is probably progressive in the Soviet Union as well.[3] For East and West Germany we can make a more quantitative comparison of the progressiveness of a part of the budget in the following manner: The structure of consumption in similar income groups is roughly the same in the two areas, so that we can calculate in an unambiguous manner (i.e. with no serious index number problems) the purchasing power parities of the East and West German currencies for the consumption pattern of these different income groups. Since the cost structure in industry is also roughly similar, such parity ratios should reflect the respective incidence of indirect taxes and government subsidies. Although there were considerable differences in the

[1] For the United States see Theodore W. Schultz, *The Economic Value of Education* (New York, 1963), p. 51.

[2] These points are extensively discussed by James E. Meade, *Efficiency, Equality, and the Ownership of Property* (London, 1964).

[3] This very rough judgment of the Soviet budget is made on the basis of information on taxation supplied by Holzman, *op. cit.*, and a number of very crude qualitative assumptions about the incidence of expenditures. For the USA this generalization is derived from data presented by Gillespie, *op. cit.*

parity ratios for the various income groups in the early 1950s, the differences by the end of the decade were quite small and the incidence of indirect taxes and subsidies thus appeared roughly the same in the two nations.[1] It must be emphasized that such an approach does not include the effect of direct taxes (e.g. income taxes), transfer payments, or public consumption expenditures, although in these respects the two nations do not appear to differ greatly either.[2] For other pairs of sample nations, adequate information is not available for even the rough comparisons that are made above.

Another way to approach the problem of incidence of the government budget on different income groups is to explore the spatial distribution of public consumption expenditures and taxes between richer and poorer regions, and to measure the extent of any net redistribution. Although quantitative information on central governmental expenditures in various geographic areas is not available for most of the sample nations, I could conduct such experiments for regional and local government where suitable data are obtainable for the two Germanies, the USSR, and the USA. The data were assembled in three steps. First, the local governmental units were combined into ten regions so that the effects of a different number of units would be minimized. Second, only education, health, and welfare (excluding social insurance) expenditures were chosen since they are the most comparable. Finally, to estimate the net redistribution, a group of taxes was selected, the incidence of which lay primarily on the population in the respective regions.

The simplest analytic approach is to measure the differences in *per capita* government expenditures among regions. Here I calculated coefficients of variation of *per capita* expenditures

[1] Such calculations are made every few years by the Deutsches Institut fuer Wirtschaftforschung in West Berlin and are summarized for the 1950s in my book, *The Communist Foreign Trade System* (Cambridge, Mass., 1963), p. 241.

[2] In their ratios of public consumption expenditures to the GNP the two nations appear quite similar. The relative distribution of these expenditures among income classes is not known, although for one expenditure item-higher education—we have some clue through the social class distribution of students (see Appendix E–14). In regard to taxes, the income tax is relatively more important in West than in East Germany but the relative progressiveness in the two countries is not known.

where these expenditures for each region were weighted by the population, so that differences in size among these geographical units could be taken into account. The results are as follows: USA, 18 per cent; West Germany, 22 per cent; East Germany, 7 per cent; and the USSR, 6 per cent. These data indicate that *per capita* local government expenditures are much more evenly distributed in the centrally planned than market economies.[1] (It is interesting that *per capita* expenditures on education are the most evenly distributed in all countries, while *per capita* expenditures on welfare are, in most cases, the most unevenly spread.) Such results, while useful, do not tell us anything about budgetary redistribution *per se*, for which information about taxes and regional income differentials must be taken into consideration.

Testing the degree of the *net* spatial redistribution of government expenditures and taxes presents a number of additional problems since we have neither information on the average incomes in the different regions of all the sample nations nor the amount of redistributed budgetary funds among regions. We can evade most of these problems, however, by examining the relationship between taxes and expenditures in the different regions, arranging these areas from the lowest *per capita* public expenditures to the highest. If the ratio of expenditures to taxes remains the same as *per capita* expenditures rise then no apparent spatial redistribution occurs. If the ratio falls as *per capita* expenditures increase, then an apparent spatial progressive redistribution of income through the government budgets has taken place. In experiments conducted on these ratios, West Germany and possibly East Germany appear to be the only countries in which such a net spatial redistribution from richer to poorer regions occurs, a feature that might be traced to the extensive 'Finanzausgleich' systems inherited from prewar Germany. Results for the USA and the USSR are about the same and show no important net redistribution. Unfortunately, a number of difficulties arise concerning the way in which

[1] Sources and exact methods are noted in Appendix E–17. East Berlin is omitted from consideration in the East German datum; if it is included, the East German coefficient of variation of *per capita* expenditures is 17 per cent. For the Soviet Union it makes very little difference whether the Russian and Ukrainian republics are included in the calculation.

provinces are aggregated. An element of uncertainty must thus be taken into account when interpreting the outcomes of such experiments. Nevertheless, such results should make us wary about the facile generalizations concerning redistribution that are being made by ideologically oriented economists on the basis of 'intuitive' notions about the inherent 'goodness' of one or another economic system without the benefit of any type of quantitative analysis.

There are also a number of other types of interesting problems associated with the geographical distribution of government expenditures. For example, over time in both the USA and the USSR, the coefficient of variation of government expenditures seems to be decreasing. Furthermore, the pattern of such expenditures exhibits a number of peculiarities. For instance, under Stalin in the Soviet Union, the Georgian republic had the highest *per capita* social welfare expenditures for many years; under Khrushchev the Georgian republic losts its relative position, but it was not replaced by the Ukranian republic. In the United States, interesting relationships occur between the distribution of certain federal funds among the states and the control of certain committees in the Congress.

The incidence of public consumption expenditures thus appears the most difficult behavioural property to explore empirically. It seems likely that public consumption expenditures act in a much more progressive manner than the burden of taxes to finance them. In regard to the spatial distribution of local public expenditures, the degree of differences among regions appears less in the Soviet Union and East Germany than in the United States and West Germany. However, when both public revenues and expenditures of these local governments are taken into account, a net redistribution from richer to poorer regions seems to occur only in the Germanies.

E. DIFFERENTIAL EFFECTS OF PUBLIC AND PRIVATE FINANCING

One major hypothesis in this study about the differential effects of public and private financing is that public financing of services brings about a more even *per capita* consumption of such services over the entire population. Sufficient data are available for investigating various facets of this hypothesis in the areas of education and health. However, one important difficulty in any cross-section analyses of this phenomenon is that the inequality of income varies considerably in the different nations and this must somehow be taken into account.

From data presented on public consumption expenditures for health, considerable differences appear between the United States and some of the continental countries. If health services are more evenly consumed, then their infant mortality rate should be lower. I present evidence that between the UK and the USA, such a phenomenon is observable. Between the Soviet Union and the United States, however, the hypothesis breaks down because the Soviet rate is influenced by a highly uneven spatial distribution of physicians. For the United States I present the results of a number of unsuccessful experiments to link the infant mortality rate to the amount of public consumption expenditures on health. Here again the organization of medical care seems an important modifying factor.

I also show that in the centrally planned economies a much higher share of education expenditures is financed publicly, and it therefore seems likely that the portion of working-class children at institutions of higher learning should be much greater there. Although this is generally true, it does not occur in all cases, e.g. there are great similarities between the USA and the Soviet Union. Aside from the tentative nature of the data two factors complicate the analysis. First, in some centrally planned economies there has been an explicit policy of discrimination against children from other than working-class backgrounds. Second, the spatial distribution of colleges and universities also seems to play an important determining role in this matter of social-class composition.

F. CONCLUDING REMARKS

To place the many empirical results in a greater perspective I would like to return briefly to the three underlying reasons for making this study and then to re-examine briefly the relations between positive and normative analyses of public consumption expenditures.

As a study between market and centrally planned economies, one important conclusion stands out: in regard to public consumption expenditures there are few essential differences between nations of the two systems, at least on the macroeconomic level on which the analysis is carried out. Of course, on a micro-economic level there may be a great many important differences; unfortunately, comparable information in this regard is much more difficult to assemble and to analyse systematically.

This particular varient of the hypothesis about the convergence between economic systems—that the two systems are already the same—should not be interpreted to mean that this is also true in other areas. Indeed, in a great many more important respects the two economic systems are very different and, let me add without proof, are *not* becoming more similar.[1]

To broaden the scope of comparative economic studies, I proposed to examine the role of one particular type of consumption unit. Of course, this study does not present a complete theory of public consumption expenditures, especially since it proved impossible to investigate what specific services are publicly financed. And it should be clear that there are a number of other types of consumption units broader than the individual or the family that also deserve study. Nevertheless, showing certain impacts of the financing of a service on the distribution of consumed income and demonstrating that the importance of governments as units of consumption seems largely independent of property ownership certainly have important implications for any broader theory of consumption units. Furthermore, the evidence provided in this study that public consumption expenditures are not inextricably bound to the level of development in the manner enunciated by Wagner suggest that fruitful research on various units of consumption can be carried out which focus attention on other types of variables.

---

[1] On this matter see Peter Wiles, 'Will Capitalism and Communism Spontaneously Converge', *Encounter*, June, 1963, pp. 84–90; and, on a political level, Zbigniew Brzezinski and Samuel P. Huntington, *Political Power: USA/USSR* (New York, 1964).

Difficulties abound, of course in making comparisons between nations with different economic systems, and on a number of specific points we must be content with only first approximations. But it should be evident that sufficient information is available for systematic comparisons to be made, and, with the rising quantity and quality of data being published by all nations, such work is becoming easier to carry out with every passing year. Thus we are gradually receiving the proper information to separate propaganda from reality and to isolate the actual rather than the theoretical differences between economic systems. Of course, decision makers in each nation have certain vested interests in publicizing the merits of their own particular economic institutions. But scholars should be able to penetrate such rationalizations through comparative analysis of special aspects of these economies. I hope that this study will be followed by many large-scale empirical comparisons of nations with such different economic systems.

In advancing the positive theory of public expenditures, three particular aspects of this study deserve mention. First, I hope to have demonstrated conclusively the benefits of disaggregation in analysing public consumption expenditures. More aggregated analyses have masked a number of important facets of these expenditures which deserve attention. Second, the exploration of behavioural properties in public consumption expenditures, which has also been quite neglected up to now, yields a number of useful and interesting results. Although many issues in regard to substitution relations, centralization, stability, and incidence can not be adequately discussed with the data of this study, I hope to have shown the desirability and feasibility of further research in this area. Finally, a number of new aspects about the determinants of public consumption expenditures and the ways in which these determinants can be isolated and explored are herein presented. Even without rigorous model building, such as the pact theory presented in regard to military expenditures, new aspects of these determinants can be demonstrated, especially through the confrontation of time-series and cross-section analyses.

Bearing in mind the results of this study, we turn for a final glance toward the relationships between positive and normative economics in the field of public consumption expenditures. As noted in the first chapter, positive economic analyses can help the policy maker by setting up diagnostic norms, making projections, and specifying some of the costs and benefits of particular expenditures that must be taken into account.

Although positive theory can aid in the normative analysis of public consumption expenditures, it can not displace it. For in searching out of particular expenditures to make, in weighing of costs and benefits, and in deciding whether such expenditures are worthwhile to undertake, value judgments enter at all points. Whether this policy process is carried out in a highly formal fashion with the aid of sophisticated statistical analysis and economic theory, or hortatorily, or so casually that no intellectual process is apparent, normative evaluation of the available evidence both includes and transcends positive economics.

An apparent conflict may arise because it is the task of the positive-theory analysts to search out patterns of behaviour connected with public expenditures, while it is the duty of the normative-theory analysts to work toward changing these patterns. Any hope that we can more adequately solve our problems, however, lies in the possibility that both such groups can successfully accomplish their respective tasks.

TABLE OF CONTENTS OF APPENDICES

APPENDIX TABLES

Appendix A

ESTIMATES OF PUBLIC CONSUMPTION EXPENDITURES

APPENDIX A–1: INTRODUCTION

A. *Expenditure Concept*

Public consumption expenditures cover all current expenditures plus transfer payments (except for interest payments) that are financed by taxes. Capital expenditures, interest payments, subsidies, and government expenditures financed by sales to the public or by user-fees are excluded.

To arrive at comparable data for the fourteen countries, several arbitrary decisions have to be made. All social insurance expenditures are included as public consumption expenditures. Second, expenditures on military equipment are included as current expenditures for such items as buildings or bases are considered as capital expenditures and are excluded whenever possible. Third, rent allowances are considered as subsidies and are omitted whenever possible. Finally, social insurance expenditures carried by private insurance companies (e.g. Workmen's Compensation payments in the USA) are considered as public consumption expenditures.

Whenever possible a cash basis, rather than an accrual basis, of expenditures is used. This means that implicit interest on capital and depreciation expenses are not taken into account. All fiscal year data are converted into calendar year data by assuming that public consumption expenditures are spread evenly over the year.

For several countries it did not prove possible to follow the above definitions exactly. The basis of the estimates for Greece and Italy are GNP accounts which are based on an accrual method and which include implicit interest on capital and exclude depreciation. Yugoslav data are also on an accrual basis but do not take into account interest and depreciation. Finally, for East Germany it is not possible to eliminate all sales to the public. The statistical bias introduced in the data for these four countries is relatively small, however.

The separation of current and capital expenditures in the centralized and market economies is slightly different in that most of the latter countries follow the Soviet system of including capital repairs as current expenditures; while the official statistics of most market economies include such repairs under capital expenditures. No account is taken of this difference but the bias which is introduced is negligible.

B. *Functional Categories*

1. The data on 'gross expenditures' are not comparable but show the budgetary expenditures of the various countries as defined by the national statistical services of the specific nations.

2. Adjusted expenditures: these include the public consumption expenditures for administration, external and internal security, education, health, welfare, and research and development.

3. Administration: expenditures cover the costs of the highest organs of government for each level of government plus the cost of the financial system of the government. Whenever possible costs of administering the state enterprises producing goods sold on the market are removed.

4. Defence: expenditures cover costs of the armed forces and of the security units (e.g. border guards, and heavily armed internal protection forces). Certain internal security units serve both police and military purposes and, whenever possible, expenditures for such units are split into the two functions.

5. Other external security: expenditures cover costs of diplomacy, foreign grants and long term loans and, whenever it is possible to isolate such expenditures, costs of foreign espionage.

6. Internal security: expenditures cover costs of police, courts, and prisons. The expenditures of the internal political police are included whenever possible.

7. Education: expenditures cover costs of primary, secondary, and tertiary education. Expenditures for kindergardens, out-of-school activities of youth, sport, and 'culture' are excluded.

8. Health: expenditures cover direct costs of health institutions and payments for direct health care. Income supports during illness and sport expenditures are excluded.

9. Welfare: expenditures cover all welfare and social insurance payments not included in health or education. Expenditures for sports and culture are excluded.

10. Research and development: expenditures cover all current R and D expenditures including those for military purposes which could be located in the budget. For the centrally planned economies those expenditures included in 'financing the national economy' are excluded, however.

C. *Major Problems*

1. The estimates are based primarily on information from government documents from each individual country. For some of the centrally planned economies it proved necessary to collect and collate data from a very large number of sources, of which only the most important are cited.

2. Removing the expenditures which are financed by user fees raised several difficulties. In the centralized economies (with the exception of East Germany) most such expenditures are put in special 'extra-budgetary accounts' and are excluded from the budget; although for Poland, at least, some such expenditures are still included in the budget and had to be removed (e.g. nursery schools run by the various Ministries). Although the exact handling of such expenditures for the other centralized economies is not known, it is apparent from the economic literature of these countries that such expenditures that are possibly included in the budget are of relatively small magnitude. For the market economies removal of public expenditures financed by user fees required for several countries considerable patience to remove.

3. Removing capital expenditures and intragovernmental transfers raised few major difficulties. In most of the centralized economies current and capital budgetary expenditures are given separately and for the rest of the countries reasonable estimates for such capital expenditures can be made. Furthermore, in all these countries except East Germany intragovernmental transfers are netted out in the consolidated state budget. In the market economies there were few problems in separating current and capital expenditures or in removing intragovernmental transfers except for Yugoslavia.

4. Adding expenditures of para-fiscal institutions raised few major problems. (Para-fiscal expenditures are those expenditures financed by taxes but made through special funds which do not appear in the main governmental budgets. A classic analysis of these expenditures is by J. Merigot [P–80, XLI, 2/1949 and 3/1949].) In the centralized economies where the published budgets are 'consolidated', very few para-fiscal institutions exist and the public consumption expenditures of these organizations are very minor (e.g. certain sport and cultural expenditures are financed by state lotteries in Romania and East Germany). In the market economies data on such para-fiscal expenditures are available for all countries. One problem of definition arose—should the social expenditures financed from the profits of state enterprises be considered as para-

fiscal? Since such profits are not in the nature of a true tax, such expenditures are omitted.

5. The major difficulties arose in the separation of different types of functional expenditures since the budgetary data of most of the centralized economies are not very detailed. Although administration, military, and different types of social welfare expenditures are usually differentiated, almost all other types of public consumption expenditures are lumped together. Therefore, the analysis in this study is limited to the eight expenditures for which estimates could be made.

D. *Plan of Discussion of Sources and Methods*

1. Acknowledgements. Although I am responsible for all estimates, I received considerable help, without which these estimates could never have been made. I have tried to mention all those who supplied me with data or who helped me with the estimates for specific countries.

2. Main problems. In this section I discuss the general problems arising in adjusting the published data to fit the conceptual scheme used in this study. Such remarks cover the different sources of data, the most important estimating techniques, and the major assumptions underlying the estimates.

3. Subjective evaluation. An objective evaluation about the reliability of the estimates is impossible to make until more detailed data are published. To aid the user of these statistics I have tried to give my subjective impressions about the reliability of the estimates and to indicate with which estimates I am most displeased. Three overall ratings are given: '*A*' = very reliable; '*B*' = fairly reliable; '*C*' = reliability unknown or in doubt.

4. Sources of data. Whenever the estimates are based on information from a small number of sources, these are indicated.

5. Prices used. To avoid confusion about those countries with currency reforms, the currency units in which the estimates are made are specified (e.g. post 1961 roubles, etc.).

6. Notes on individual expenditure estimates. These are the footnotes to the table which is given for each country.

APPENDIX A–2: ESTIMATES FOR AUSTRIA

A. *Acknowledgments*

I owe a special debt of gratitude to Dr Anton Kausel of the Oester-reichisches Institut fuer Wirtschaftsforschung, who not only helped

L

me work out the method for making the estimates but also supplied considerable unpublished data and promptly answered a number of letters of inquiry about special points. Needless to say, he is not responsible for any mistakes which I may have made. Additionally I would like to thank Dr Auguste Klamecker of the Oesterreich-isches statistisches Zentralamt for her comments and Mrs Schlesinger and Mr Hirsch of the Finanzministerium for giving me certain unpublished data on federal expenditures. The Hauptverband der oesterreichischen Sozialversicherungstraeger also supplied unpublished data on transfer expenditures.

B. *Main Problems*

The primary difficulty lay in the lack of official calculations of total governmental expenditures on a functional basis so that estimates had to be made for all levels of government for many years. Nevertheless, sufficient data are available so that good estimates can be made, especially from the middle 1950s on.

Before turning to the two step estimation method which was employed, it must be noted that the delineation of the public sector was difficult in regard to the expenditures of the 'Chambers' (*Kammer*) and to the pensions of state enterprises. For the sake of comparability it was decided to include in the public sector the expenditures of the *Kammer* but to exclude the pensions of public enterprises except those financed by grants from the government budget.

The first step in the estimations was making calculations of public consumption for 1958, a year in which functional and economic breakdowns of public expenditures are available for the central government (including 'funds'), the Chambers, and the Laender [G47, pp. 19–21]. In addition, a breakdown of social insurance payments [G43] and of local expenditures on a functional basis are also available [G46, 1958]. The main problems in using these data are: the elimination of transfers between different levels of government; the removal of sales to the public ('*Kostenersaetze*'); the removal of capital expenditures; and adjusting the data to fit the standard functional categories.

1. Eliminating intra-governmental transfers from the expenditures of the central and Laender governments and the Chambers was easy since these are designated in the functional-economic breakdowns. The intra-governmental transfers within the social insurance expenditures present no difficulties and the intra-governmental transfers from the social insurance system and from the

adjusted local governments were assumed to be small enough to be completely neglected.

2. The sales to the public were estimated for each category for the federal level from data from [G41, 1958]. Such sales were assumed to be negligible for the Chambers and for the social insurance system. For the Laender and local governmental units, they were assumed to be equal to the total receipts of these units for the various specific categories except social-welfare (data from [G46, 1958]). Since such receipts were a small percentage of expenditures, such a procedure introduces little error.

3. Capital expenditures were isolated in the functional and economic estimates for the central and Laender governments, the Chambers and the social insurance system and provided no problems. For the local governmental units it was assumed that the ratio of capital to current expenditures was the same as in Vienna (data from [G42]), whose expenditures comprised about 40 per cent of all local governmental expenditures. Again, little error is introduced since local governmental capital expenditures were a very small portion of total expenditures in the different categories.

4. Adjusting the functional data to fit the standard functional definitions on the federal level was made with the help of budget data from [G41, 1958]. For the social insurance system detailed data are also available [G44] but for the other levels of government, only data on large functional aggregates could be located. Fortunately, these data are arranged in roughly the same way as the standard definitions so that few adjustments were necessary. Refined adjustments of these data could not be attempted.

The second step in the estimation procedure was using the 1958 calculations as a benchmark for estimating the other years. The procedures employed varied according to level of government.

1. For the federal level functional-economic breakdowns of governmental expenditures are available for 1957 on [G41, various issues] and, moreover, detailed data on realized budgetary expenditures are readily available for all years [G41]. For certain expenditures (e.g. science, military) data were taken directly from the realized budgetary expenditures data. In other cases, especially for the years in which functional-economic breakdowns are not available, it was assumed that certain functional expenditures remained a constant ratio of certain expenditures of the relevant ministries (i.e. that the annual rate of change of the functional expenditures was the same as the expenditures of the relevant ministries).

2. For the social insurance data, expenditures for different

programmes are available from [G43], [G44], and unpublished data from the social insurance agencies.

3. For the Chambers functional expenditures data are available only for 1958. Since unpublished economic breakdowns of Chambers expenditures are available, functional estimates were made by assuming that the functional division of expenditures remained about the same for all years. Since the expenditures of the Chambers are miniscule in relation to other governmental expenditures, little error should be introduced by such a method of estimation.

4. Functional breakdowns of Laender and local governmental expenditures are available [G46, various issues] from 1955 on and economic breakdowns of these expenditures [ûnpublished national accounts data] were located for all years. Therefore, the estimates from 1955 on presented no major difficulties. Before 1955, the transfer part of local and Laender governmental expenditures could be easily estimated from data on total transfers of these governmental units, but for the other types of expenditures, estimates could be made only by assuming that the functional division of expenditures between 1950 and 1955 remained the same. However, since Laender and local adjusted expenditures comprise only about 14 per cent of total adjusted expenditures, little error should be introduced by such methods.

C. *Subjective Evaluation*

Although a number of estimates had to be made, the range of error could be quite narrowed. I give the data in Table A-1 an overall rating of 'B'.

D. *Sources of Data*

Data used in these estimates were taken from [G42], [G47], [G48], and [G49] and various issues of [G41], [G43], [G44] and [G46]. These were supplemented by unpublished national accounts data and data from the Ministry of Finance.

E. *Notes on Individual Expenditure Estimates*

1. Data cover expenditures for goods and services, subsidies, interest payments, transfer payments and savings [G48, p. 48], [G49, p. 24].

2. The adjusted budget covers expenditures for administration, security, social purposes and science.

3. Central government includes the social insurance system, the federal 'funds', and the Chambers as well as the proper central

TABLE A-1

Public Consumption Expenditures of Austria (*Million Schillinge*)

		Adjusted Budget[2]					External Security		
						Adminis-		Occupation	
Year	Gross Budget[1]	Central[3]	Länder[3]	Local[3]	Total	tration[4]	Military[5]	Costs[6]	Other[7]
1950	15,020	8,005	345	847	9,197	599	0	383	52
1951	19,625	11,610	552	1,322	13,484	916	0	623	54
1952	25,470	14,685	683	1,548	16,916	1,094	0	476	64
1953	28,250	15,702	708	1,715	18,125	1,172	0	443	66
1954	30,200	16,609	759	2,003	19,371	1,324	0	0	80
1955	32,400	18,613	885	2,660	22,158	1,646	188	0	88
1956	36,490	21,914	992	2,931	25,837	1,902	717	0	97
1957	41,460	25,594	1,141	3,278	30,013	2,188	1,417	0	110
1958	43,180	27,604	1,191	3,406	32,201	2,386	1,651	0	125
1959	45,140	29,155	1,276	3,704	34,135	2,501	1,729	0	115
1960	50,680	31,011	1,359	4,032	36,402	2,635	1,681	0	150
1961	59,930	34,886	1,447	4,439	40,772	2,815	1,710	0	175
1962	65,600	39,276	1,634	4,881	45,791	3,075	1,881	0	190

		Social				Other	
Year	Internal Security[8]	Education[9]	Health[10]	Welfare[11]	Science[12]	Interest[13]	Direct Investment[14]
1950	503	874	1,060	5,713	13	177	1,786
1951	728	1,279	1,484	8,379	21	187	2,644
1952	895	1,557	1,884	10,921	25	216	2,727
1953	965	1,646	2,057	11,751	25	211	2,943
1954	1,124	1,828	2,239	12,739	37	287	3,322
1955	1,246	2,280	2,539	14,135	36	441	4,043
1956	1,391	2,613	2,884	16,192	41	536	4,267
1957	1,581	3,006	3,281	18,383	47	646	4,593
1958	1,597	3,163	3,489	19,740	50	783	5,401
1959	1,794	3,340	3,672	20,926	58	1,055	6,077
1960	1,895	3,647	4,072	22,249	73	1,329	6,918
1961	1,987	3,945	4,576	25,511	53	1,502	7,813
1962	2,150	4,320	5,143	28,968	64	1,596	8,354

government. Vienna is included in the local (rather than the Laender) government expenditures.

4. On the federal level administration expenditures cover expenditures of 'other governmental administration' excluding an estimate for reparations, foreign relations, and administration of state industry and similar 'economic' units (the latter from unpublished data supplied by the Ministry of Finance). For 1950–57 these expenditures were assumed to change at the same rate as the sum of expenditures of the presidential offices, the legislature, the comptroller, the Chancellor's offices, and the administration of state finances.

On Laender and local governmental levels these included expenditures for general administration and financial administration and excluded expenditures for pensions and for administration of economic units (estimated as zero on the Laender level and as the same percentage as in Vienna [G42] for the local governments). For 1950–55 these were assumed to change at the same rate of total expenditures for goods and services of the respective levels of government (unpublished national accounts data).

5. Military expenditures are the total expenditures of the Ministry of Defence. Although published national accounts data of military expenditures also include certain capital investments made by the Ministry of Commerce which have military purposes, these are excluded for the sake of comparability.

6. These data (from unpublished national accounts data) cover only those occupation costs which were paid by Austria. Toward the end of the occupation period, a large share of the occupation costs were borne by the occupying powers. These data do not include reparations.

7. These are expenditures of the Ministry of Foreign Affairs. Capital expenditures and sales to the public had to be estimated by extrapolation for the early years.

8. On the federal level these are the expenditures for 'state security and law'. From 1950 to 1957 they were assumed to change at the same rate as the combined expenditures for the High Court, the Ministry of Justice, and the Ministry of Interior.

On the Laender and local levels these covered expenditures for police. From 1950 to 1955 these were assumed to change at the same rate as total expenditures for goods and services of the respective levels of government.

9. On the federal level these cover expenditures for 'education and culture' with the removal of expenditures for art, scientific institutions, youth activities and sport (all from [G41]). Between 1950 and 1957 total expenditures for 'education and culture' were assumed to change at the same rate as expenditures of the Ministry of Education. Expenditures of the Chambers for education were assumed to be two-thirds of the expenditures for education and culture and to change at the same rate as total expenditures of the Chambers for goods and services.

On the Laender and local levels these cover expenditures for schools. For 1950 to 1955 it was assumed that the Laender and local expenditures for education changed at the same rate as total expenditures for goods and services of the respective levels of government.

10. On the federal level these include only the expenditures for health. They were assumed to change from 1950 to 1957 at the same rate as total expenditures of the Ministry of Social Welfare. The

health expenditures of the Chambers were estimated in the same way as for education (see footnote 9).

From the published data on health insurance payments, death payments and funds for income supports during illness were removed.

For Laender and local governments, data on expenditures for health and physical culture were used, with the removal of an estimate for physical culture (10 per cent of the total expenditures). For 1950 to 1955 it was assumed that expenditures for health changed at the same rate as total expenditures for goods and services of the respective levels of government.

11. On the federal level welfare expenditures include all current and transfer expenditures for social welfare (but excluding 'welfare price supports'), plus welfare grants to 'institutions of common purposes' plus pensions of state enterprises financed by grants from the federal government, plus expenditures for youth activities (see footnote 9). The series for transfer payments come from unpublished national accounts data; the expenditures for goods and services were assumed to change at the same rate as expenditures of the Ministry of Social Welfare.

Welfare expenditures of the Chambers consist of transfers and current expenditures. Data on transfer payments for all years come from unpublished national accounts data; current expenditures were assumed to be a constant ratio of total expenditures for goods and services of the Chambers.

Welfare expenditures of the social insurance system were derived as the residual from total social insurance payments after the removal of expenditures for health (see footnote 10).

On the Laender and local levels welfare include expenditures for welfare and aid to youth, pensions, and physical culture (see footnote 10). These expenditures were divided into transfer payments and expenditures for goods and services. Data for the former are available from unpublished national accounts data; for the latter estimates were made for 1950 to 1955 by assuming that the change in these expenditures was the same as the change in total expenditures for goods and services for the respective levels of government.

12. On the federal level science expenditures were taken from data on expenditures of the Ministry of Education for scientific institutions. On the Laender level, expenditures are for the 'science services' (*Wissenschaftspflege*). For 1950 to 1955 it was assumed that such expenditures changed at the same rate as Laender expenditures for goods and services. It is most likely that these esti-

mates on research and development are understated; the extent that such expenditures are financed through the expenditures for higher education is not known, although the fact that the Ministry of Education has a special science budget suggests that non-reported science expenditures may not be too large.

13. From unpublished national accounts data.

14. From unpublished national accounts data.

APPENDIX A-3: ESTIMATES FOR BULGARIA

A. *Main Problems*

In making estimates of the public consumption expenditures of Bulgaria there are five major problems:

1. Data on details within the main budgetary categories are not available except for scattered years. Although a great number of Bulgarian books and pamphlets have been written about the state budget, almost none of these contains more detailed data on the budget than one can find in various editions of the statistical year-book [G51]. This means that estimates for the subcategories of budgetary expenditures must be made from scattered plan data and other such information which are often of questionable reliability or consistency.

2. For the main expenditures within the social-cultural category, data for certain years are missing in the statistical yearbook and must be estimated by interpolations and extrapolations. However, in making such estimates data from other sources [B162, p. 55], [B196, pp. 366–69], [B211, p. 65], and [B194] were utilized with caution since they are not entirely consistent with each other or the yearbook data. (Another source [B100] presents certain social-cultural data which conflict with every other source; since no explanation is supplied, they were not used in the estimates.)

3. The available data on individual budgetary expenditures include both current and capital expenditures and the latter must be removed to make the Bulgarian figures consistent with the data for the other countries. Data on three major types of 'non-productive' investments are published [G51, various issues], section on investment. By assuming that the average ratio between 'above-limit' and 'limit' investment for the individual types of investment was the same between 1950–57 as in the following years, a complete series can be derived for these three types of 'non-productive' investments. Unfortunately, this derived series is higher than actual budgetary investment for total social-cultural activities for the two

years (1956 and 1957) for which such data are available [G51, 1959, p. 216], which means that such 'non-productive' investments were partially financed through non-budgetary means, as in the Soviet Union. Lacking any more information I assumed that the relation of budgetary to non-budgetary investment in these 'non-productive' sectors was the same for all years as in 1956 and 1957. Although such estimation methods are crude, the error introduced in the estimates of current expenditures should be relatively small.

4. The degree to which my estimates of public consumption expenditures are biased by the exclusion of expenditures not reported in the detailed part of the budget is unknown. However, the extra-budgetary expenditures (one datum on such expenditures is available but it is not very helpful) have a similar nature to those of the Soviet Union and, therefore, they can be neglected. The unspecified budgetary residual causes more problems. According to Bulgarian sources [B196, p. 359] this residual contains expenditures for fire prevention, unspecified subsidies, etc. Now some of these expenditures have a purely 'economic' character since one source [P28, 2/1963, p. 58] places part of these under the budgetary category 'financing the national economy'. However, it seems likely that the unspecified budgetary expenditures also contain certain kinds of security expenditures and, indeed, the sum of the preliminary estimations of expenditures for security troops and police were only slightly larger than the 'non-economic' part of the unspecified residual (i.e. the unspecified residual reported in [P28, 2/1963], rather than [G51]). Since there is other evidence that such security expenditures are not financed through the specified expenditures for defence (the equipment/soldier ratios computed in the text make good economic sense when the security troops are omitted), I have therefore assumed that both security troops and police were financed from the unspecified budgetary residual.

5. A final problem concerns the functional classification of expenditures. According to a detailed description of the contents of the various budgetary categories [B319, Chap. IX], the most major adjustment which needed to be made was the transfer of expenditures for kindergardens from 'education' to 'social'. All other needed adjustments were relatively minor and were neglected for lack of adequate data.

B. *Subjective Evaluation*

For most of the published Bulgarian budgetary data, the meaning is clear and the reliability seems good. Although a number of

L*

estimates had to be made for the security sector and a number of minor adjustments also had to be carried out, the errors and biases which are introduced should be small. I would give the data in Table A–2 a 'B' rating.

C. Sources of Data

The primary source of data was [G51], supplemented by the sources listed in the discussion.

D. Prices used

All data are stated in the new (1962) leva, which means that the data for the period from 1952 to 1962 had to be divided by 10 in accordance with the monetary reform at that time. Since the data for 1950

TABLE A–2

Public Consumption Expenditures in Bulgaria (Million New Leva)

| Year | Gross Budget[1] | Adjusted Budget[2] | | | | External Security | |
		Central[3]	Local[3]	Total	Administration[4]	Military[5]	Other[6]
1950	793·4	335·8	105·2	441·0	50·7	143·1	3·2
1951	1,141·2	415·4	115·0	530·4	53·4	199·8	4·3
1952	1,433·9	451·0	127·0	578·0	51·2	229·9	4·3
1953	1,579·8	490·6	146·3	636·9	59·2	257·9	4·3
1954	1,624·7	517·8	164·3	682·1	61·4	264·2	4·3
1955	1,710·2	543·0	169·1	712·1	58·8	271·2	4·4
1956	1,738·7	522·5	192·9	715·4	60·5	230·6	4·9
1957	1,890·2	565·6	215·7	781·3	61·3	241·4	4·9
1958	2,037·3	603·1	220·3	823·4	63·0	249·4	3·9
1959	2,634·2	603·2	261·4	864·6	62·0	228·6	3·9
1960	3,003·1	653·2	303·3	956·5	62·9	234·4	4·2
1961	3,285·7	733·5	328·8	1,062·3	61·3	275·6	5·0
1962	3,244·1	833·6	343·7	1,177·3	68·1	318·0	6·1

| Year | Internal Security[7] | Social | | | | Other Direct Investment |
		Education[8]	Health[9]	Welfare[10]	Science[11]	
1950	34·9	63·9	39·8	102·1	3·3	202·4
1951	41·8	79·0	44·3	103·0	4·8	269·2
1952	42·9	91·4	52·7	98·2	7·4	328·5
1953	43·9	97·3	62·2	103·7	8·4	366·3
1954	41·5	99·8	80·2	119·8	10·9	375·6
1955	44·6	106·5	78·5	135·6	12·5	359·3
1956	47·7	130·2	87·7	139·6	14·2	317·3
1957	51·6	142·5	89·0	174·8	15·8	218·5
1958	63·5	142·3	88·7	195·1	17·5	251·5
1959	74·2	145·2	94·4	237·1	19·2	467·6
1960	79·2	173·1	113·8	264·6	24·3	628·8
1961	84·3	190·7	121·2	297·8	26·4	577·5
1962	91·4	196·7	131·0	336·5	29·5	649·1

and 1951 were reported in terms of the leva used from 1952 to 1962, no further adjustments had to be made for this period.

E. *Notes on the Individual Expenditure Estimates*

1. These are published gross budgetary expenditures plus payments of the social insurance agencies in the early years (see footnote 9) and payments of the mutual insurance companies for the co-operatives (see footnote 9), which were formally incorporated into the budget in 1963.

2. Adjusted budgetary expenditures include current expenditures for security, social activities, administration, and research and development.

3. In allocating adjusted expenditures to central and local governmental units, it was assumed that the capital expenditures (which were removed) were divided between local and central governments according to their ratio in 1956 [G51, 1959, p. 216].

4. These data were derived from published data on administrative expenditures with the removal of expenditures on foreign affairs, justice, and capital expenditures. Details on the estimation of expenditures for foreign affairs are given in footnote 6. It must be noted that certain payments to international organizations are paid from the unspecified budget residual [B196, p. 359], rather than from diplomacy expenditures; but according to the available data on such international expenditures [G24], such expenditures are extremely small so that any error introduced in this way should be negligible. Expenditures for justice were estimated from data on employees in the 'administration of justice' [G51, various issues], data on the average industrial wage, and the assumption that other 'justice' expenditures amounted to 25 per cent of total wages. My estimates differ with [B8] but I believe that the official claims about the accounting of such expenditures [B319, Chap. 9] seem reasonable. Police expenditures could not be financed under administration, as they are too large. Capital expenditures were estimated by assuming that the ratio of current to capital expenditures in administration were the same for 12 years as for 1956 when data are available [G51, 1959, p. 216].

5. Military expenditures include both published expenditures for this purpose plus an estimate for security troops. According to [P92, various issues], security troops numbered 80,000 from 1950 through 1957 and 45,000 from 1960 through 1962. Since other scattered Western sources provide similar estimates, these data were accepted and were interpolated for the missing years. The wage fund

for security troops was calculated by assuming that the average wage was equal to the average industrial wage. It was further assumed that other costs for the security troops averaged 30 per cent of total wage payments.

6. Other external security expenditures include expenditures on diplomacy and foreign aid. Diplomacy expenditures were made by assuming that such expenditures as a percentage of material production were approximately the same as in Poland for each year. These were then adjusted slightly to smooth the series and to assure that such expenditures remained the same or increased every year. Foreign aid expenditures are discussed in Appendix D-20.

7. Internal security expenditures include expenditures for regular police, security police, courts, and prisons. Although an estimate can be made of expenditures for courts (see footnote 4), these constitute only a small proportion of total internal security and, since no other data are available, a fairly arbitrary estimation method must be employed. Assuming that the published data on internal security expenditures for Poland and Hungary are inclusive of all such expenditures for these countries, the ratio of these expenditures to the net material product can easily be calculated for each year. Since these ratios are quite similar in the two countries, it seems likely that such expenditures for Bulgaria have a similar ratio to the net material product. This preliminary estimate was added to the estimate of expenditures for security troops and was found to be only slightly larger than the 'non-economic' part of the unspecified budget residual (see above). Now it is unlikely that these two expenditure items entirely exhausted the 'non-economic' budgetary residual so that their sum was probably lower. On the other hand, since expenditures for courts have been financed from 'administration', the sum of expenditures for security troops and police could have been higher. Assuming that these two factors cancelled each other out, I estimated total internal security expenditures by subtracting the estimate for security troops from the 'non-economic' budgetary residual and made several minor adjustments in order to smooth the series. Data for the missing years were estimated by assuming that the 'non-economic' budgetary residual grew at the same rate as the sum of the originally estimated expenditures of security troops and police.

8. Education expenditures were derived by subtracting expenditures for capital expenditures and for kindergartens from the published data on education. Kindergarten expenditures are available for scattered years from the state budget plans [P28, 1/1960,

p. 9], [P28, 10/1961, p. 12], and [B195, p. 34]. Using these data (with certain minor adjustments as they were not entirely consistent) as benchmarks, such expenditures for other years were derived from a series on total wages of kindergarten teachers by assuming that total kindergarten expenditures moved at the same rate as these wage fund expenditures. The wage fund data were derived from data on the total number of kindergarten teachers and the average industrial wage [G51, various issues]. Capital expenditures for education were derived by assuming that the ratio of current to capital expenditures was the same in education as for expenditures in art and culture. The series on capital expenditures for education, art and culture were derived from published investment data [G51, various issues] and the above described adjustment for extra-budgetary investment expenditures.

9. Health expenditures were derived from published data after removing capital expenditures. Here it was assumed that 90 per cent of the budgetary investment expenditures for health and social purposes were placed in the health sector. The series on budgetary health and social welfare capital expenditures was derived from published investment data [G51, various issues] and the above-described adjustment for extra-budgetary investment expenditures.

10. Welfare expenditures were estimated from the published data by four adjustments. For the early years expenditures of the social insurance agencies [G51, various issues] were added in. Second, the expenditures (excluding increases in reserves) of the mutual insurance agencies for co-operatives were also included. Such data are available for the period 1953–62 [G51, various issues] and were estimated by extrapolation for the remaining years. Finally, kindergarten expenditures (see footnote 8) were added and capital expenditures (see footnote 9) were removed.

11. Scattered data on expenditures for science are available (Lazarov [P40, 2/1960, pp. 26 ff.], [B100, pp. 289 ff.], [B195, pp. 24, 34], and (Lazarov [P40, 2/1958, pp. 15 ff.]). Data from the first source seem inconsistent with each other and with the data from the other sources and, therefore, were neglected. Two methods are available for estimating the expenditures for science for the period. From [P40, 2/1958], data for 1948 and the mid-1950s are given and a geometric interpolation can be made and extended. Alternatively, from data on science expenditures in the mid and late 1950s ([P40, 2/1958] and [B195]), after capital expenditures are removed, and from data on the total number of scientists and their average wages [G51, various issues] a series can be constructed if the ratio of wages

for scientists to other science expenditures is assumed constant. Since the second method allowed a much more reasonable estimate of expenditures for art and culture (excluding science expenditures) to be made, it was chosen.

12. These data come from [G51, section on financing of investment] and have not been adjusted. They include grants from the budget for investment purposes. It is not known whether the small amount of investment financed through the individual budget categories (administration, social, or cultural) are also included.

APPENDIX A–4: ESTIMATES FOR CZECHOSLOVAKIA

A. *Acknowledgments*

I would like to thank the Czechoslovak Ministry of Finance for replying to a letter of inquiry and sending a number of unpublished series on different types of socio-cultural expenditures.

B. *Main Problems*

Four major difficulties arise in making estimates of Czechoslovak budgetary expenditures.

First, Czechoslovakia has published few official data on budgetary expenditures since 1955. A preliminary set of estimates was made from plan data (external and internal security and administration) and from isolated data from scattered sources (social expenditures) The major problem in this procedure is the discrepancy between sources, e.g. the most dramatic case is socio-cultural expenditures for 1955, for which four different figures are cited in different Czechoslovak sources ([G55], cited by [B9, p. 201], [G56], [B329] and [G51a]). Fortunately, the data supplied by the Czechoslovak Ministry of Finance seemed consistent with some of the data from the scattered sources and could be used for improving the original estimates.

Second, the concepts employed in Czechoslovak budgetary reporting cause difficulties. Although extra-budgetary expenditures are excluded from the budget [B329, p. 271], the exact contents of these expenditures are not known. I have assumed that the extra-budgetary expenditures are financed by fees and sales to the public and, therefore, have made no estimates of these except for the investment components which are described below. Finally, I have also assumed that the expenditures of the para-fiscal institutions were small enough to be neglected. Although the Revolutionary

Trade Union Movement did make certain small expenditures probably of a para-fiscal nature (e.g. for children's recreation) in the early 1950s, most of these seemed to be included in the budget in later years and to be of negligible size.

Third, the handling of capital expenditures changes over the period. From comparisons of the data from the Ministry of Finance, which excluded capital expenditures, and the scattered published data, it appears that capital expenditures were excluded from the reported socio-cultural expenditures up to 1955 and were included thereafter. On the other hand, for administration expenditures it appears as if a consistent methodology was employed for all years, as a change in reporting could be seen from a discontinuity in the series. Since Czechoslovak commentators usually mention that the budgetary data include capital expenditures, I have assumed that this was the case in administration; for social expenditures, I have followed the current expenditures data supplied by the Ministry of Finance.

Fourth, there were several other types of reorganization of budgetary reporting which raise additional difficulties. In 1950 local governmental expenditures were included in the state budget for the first time, which makes data for this year incomparable with those from previous years. In 1953, the scope of the budget category 'financing the national economy' was broadened to include certain gross expenditures previously reported net. Moreover, the social insurance system began to be included on a gross, rather than net basis, as well. On the basis of previous studies [B252, Chapter 4 and Appendices], adjustments can be made for these changes so that the data for 1950–53 are comparable with later years; the exact adjustment methods are described below. In 1958 a further change in the handling of 'financing the national economy' expenditures was made, but no comparability adjustments could be made. Finally, in 1955, the following evidence suggests that there was also a change in budgetary reporting of police and internal security expenditures:

1. The Czechoslovak budget has no unspecified residuals, so that security expenditures are either masked under some other category (e.g. 'financing the national economy') or are left out of the budget and financed by funds which are not reported. The former alternative seems much more likely.

2. Due to the emerging political détente the number of soldiers decreased each year from 1954 through 1956. However, reported military expenditures increased and a calculated ratio of equipment expenditures per soldier rose to a very high level.

3. There are curious discrepancies in various reported expenditures for 'financing the national economy' and defence in 1955. (Data in mil. Kr.)

Item	[B329, pp. 210, 332]	[G55, cited by B9, p. 201]	Differrence
FNE	43398	40757	2641
Defence and security	9620	12643	—2906

4. The differences between the two sources are very close to my estimation of internal security expenditures (2722 mil. Kr.).

TABLE A–3

Public Consumption Expenditures in Czechoslovakia (Million Koruny)

Year	Gross Budget[1]	Adjusted Budget[2]			Adminis- tration[4]	External Security	
		Central[3]	Local[3]	Total		Military[5]	Other[6]
1950	41,709	n.a.	n.a.	22,175	1,495	3,345	143
1951	60,042	n.a.	n.a.	28,042	1,495	4,120	143
1952	94,478	n.a.	n.a.	31,633	1,728	5,538	249
1953	86,182	25,613	9,781	35,394	2,012	8,368	250
1954	81,230	25,972	10,541	36,513	2,296	7,787	289
1955	83,943	26,767	11,231	37,998	2,204	7,774	356
1956	95,930	26,349	11,500	37,849	2,151	6,915	647
1957	100,854	26,739	13,868	40,607	2,239	6,609	767
1958	91,621	25,220	16,106	41,326	2,322	6,205	965
1959	99,194	25,474	17,104	42,578	2,015	6,041	859
1960	107,097	26,562	19,019	45,581	2,085	6,018	933
1961	111,612	28,728	19,385	48,113	1,637	6,629	1,037
1962	121,386	31,304	19,559	50,863	1,773	7,904	1,329

Year	Internal Security[7]	Social[8]			Science[12]	Other Direct Investment[13]
		Education[9]	Health[10]	Welfare[11]		
1950	2,367	2,248	2,798	9,652	127	10,785
1951	2,580	2,985	3,435	13,129	155	14,300
1952	2,616	3,318	3,785	14,142	257	13,806
1953	2,651	3,918	4,126	13,697	372	14,137
1954	2,687	4,223	4,940	13,888	403	16,595
1955	2,722	4,625	5,003	14,855	459	13,712
1956	2,758	4,709	5,181	14,643	845	13,913
1957	2,780	4,722	5,176	17,391	923	18,351
1958	2,802	4,728	5,300	18,022	982	20,600
1959	2,824	5,034	5,546	19,265	994	21,765
1960	2,846	5,750	5,626	21,287	1,036	27,028
1961	2,969	6,418	5,875	22,454	1,094	30,026
1962	3,038	6,689	6,001	22,937	1,192	30,730

5. If we assume that internal security expenditures were transferred from FNE to defence and security, then military expenditures decreased from 1954 to 1957 and, furthermore, the ratio of military equipment expenditures per soldier appears to behave much more reasonably.

Therefore, I have assumed that this hypothesized change in reporting actually occurred and have adjusted the published defence expenditures data accordingly.

C. *Subjective Evaluation*

For expenditures for social purposes and for R and D, I have considerable confidence; on the other hand, the estimates for the other categories leave something to be desired. I would give the data in Table A–3 a rating of 'B—'.

D. *Prices Used*

Data are presented in post-1953 koruny. All data from 1950 to 1953 were converted at the official conversion rates.

E. *Notes on the individual Expenditure Estimates*

1. The data for 1950–52 were adjusted for comparability in two ways. First, estimates for 1952 of the section 'financing the national economy' using both old and new budgetary definitions were located [B252, unpbl. Appendices]. It was assumed that the ratio of expenditures defined in both ways was the same in 1951 and 1950. Second, the net deficit (surplus) of the social insurance system was added. (Data from [B252, p. 28].) Gross budgetary expenditures data for 1950 through 1953 come from [B252, p. 28]. It must be noted that the final results are quite different from the data for these years which were supplied by the Czechoslovak Ministry of Finance (1950, 51166; 1951, 67046; 1952, 71236; 1953, 73899). Since I do not know in what way the Ministry of Finance adjusted its data for comparability, I have chosen to report my data instead of theirs. Data for 1954 through 1962 come from the Czechoslovak Ministry of Finance and are somewhat different from scattered data for such expenditures (e.g. [B329, p. 51], [sources cited by B9, p. 201], and [G22]).

2. Adjusted expenditures include those for administration, security, social purposes, and science.

3. It was assumed that the ratio of capital to current expenditures for the various individual budgetary items was the same for both central and local governments. Data on local budgetary expenditures

from 1954 through 1962 come from [G56, various issues]. Local budgetary expenditures for 1953 come from [G54, April 30, 1953].

4. Published administration data include current and capital expenditures of the highest organs of state, and of the courts and procuracy [B311, p. 370]. In addition, they are said to include penditures of the highest social-cultural organs as well [B22], although the cut-off point between social-cultural and administrative expenditures must be at a very high governmental level for such functions. The estimates were made in three steps. First, data for published administrative expenditures were collected. Since information on such expenditures was available for only 1954 and 1955 [B329, p. 315], plan data had to be used for the remaining years. Second, expenditures for diplomacy, courts and procuracy, and capital investment were removed. Expenditures on diplomacy were estimated by assuming that the ratio of such expenditures to the net material product each year was the same as in Poland. The resultant estimates were smoothed so that such expenditures would remain the same or increase every year. Expenditures on courts and the procuracy (the judicial system) were estimated by assuming that the ratio of such expenditures to the net material product was the same as in the Soviet Union in 1955. Expenditures for investment of administrative organs were obtained from [G56, various issues] (see above). Although such capital expenditures were a relatively high percentage of total administrative expenditures, it is unlikely that part of these investments were financed from extra-budgetary means so the entire amount of these investments were removed. Finally, the results for 1950 and 1953 were very much out of line with the results for other years. Since these were years in which major reorganizations of the budget occurred and for which plan data were used, it seems reasonable to believe that these were inaccurate estimates of actual expenditures. Therefore, the 1953 datum was replaced with the arithmetic mean of the 1952 and 1954 administration expenditures and the 1950 datum was replaced by the 1951 expenditures.

5. Plan data for defence and security ([G54, various issues] and [B178, p. 12]) were used as the basis of the estimates. For 1950 through 1953 these data appear to omit expenditures for border guards and military security troops and an estimate for these, based on the number of personnel in such units and the average industrial wage, was added. (See Statistical Note D–6 for sources of data.) Based on the change in budgetary reporting described above, internal security expenditures (see footnote 7) minus expenditures

for the judicial system (see footnote 4) were removed from defence and security from 1955 onward.

6. Other external security expenditures cover costs for diplomacy (see footnote 4) and foreign aid (see Appendix D-20).

7. Internal security expenditures were estimated in two steps. First, it was assumed that the ratio of internal security expenditures for each year was equal to the average ratio of such expenditures to the net material product in Poland and Hungary. Second, the series of preliminary estimates were smoothed and adjusted for the mid-1950s to take account of the different periods in which destalinization occurred in each country.

8. The composition and accounting of social-cultural expenditures is described in detail by [B311, pp. 369 ff.]. Data are available in a number of sources including the following: [G51a], [G52], [G53], [G55], (Pancak and Petrenka [P26, 5/1964, pp. 265 ff.]), and [B329, pp. 270–304]. Although my estimates were based primarily on the data supplied by the Ministry of Finance, these latter data were checked for consistency with the data from the above cited sources.

9. The Ministry of Finance supplied data only for education and culture combined. Data on separate expenditures for these items come from: 1952, [B328, p. 277]; 1953, 1954, and 1955, [B329, pp. 296–99]; 1960, 1961, and 1962, [P26, 5/1964, p. 265]. The remaining years were estimated through interpolations, using as a guidepost in the 1955–60 period, the series of selected education and cultural expenditures from [G56, various issues]. Capital expenditures had to be removed from the published data and were obtained from [G56, various issues], deflated (when constant price data were presented) with investment price indices from [B252, p. 44]. For 1957 about 50 per cent of total investment expenditures for education and culture were for education [G34, p. 406] and the same was assumed to hold for other years. By also assuming that all capital expenditures for education were made through the budget (rather than through extra-budgetary expenditures) current education expenditures could be calculated and current expenditures on culture could be derived as a residual. Expenditures on kindergartens (supplied by the Ministry of Finance) were removed from education and placed in welfare expenditures.

10. Current health expenditures data come from the data supplied by the Ministry of Finance and are very similar to data presented in other sources.

11. Social expenditures were estimated as the residual of total

current socio-cultural expenditures (from Ministry of Finance data) after the removal of expenditures for education, culture, health, and science (see footnote 12). One major ambiguity exists concerning these data. According to [B311, pp. 423 ff.], the losses of the housing authorities (presumably housing subsidies) are covered in the 'financing the national economy' portion of the budget, while certain housing construction is financed from the socio-cultural portion of the budget. On the other hand, most other Czechoslovak sources suggest the opposite. While the latter view seems much more reasonable, especially in the light of budgetary practices of other socialist nations, conclusive evidence is not available. For the purposes of these estimates, I have assumed this source to be wrong.

12. Science expenditure data vary considerably in the Czechoslovak economic literature; the estimates are based on the data supplied by the Ministry of Finance. Other sources, e.g. [B329, p. 298] and [B279, p. 24], present expenditures data considerably smaller than the Ministry of Finance series, but since none of the sources supply any explanation of the contents of such expenditures, the longest consistent series was chosen.

13. These data are from the materials supplied by the Ministry of Finance and are considerably higher than the estimates of [B252, p. 28]. Since the latter source has several extremely disturbing and unexplained discontinuities, the former series was chosen.

APPENDIX A–5: ESTIMATES FOR EAST GERMANY

A. *Acknowledgments*

I would like to thank Dr Leimbach at the Bundesministerium fuer gesamtdeutsche Fragen for his aid in using the files and materials at the ministerial archives.

B. *Main Problems*

The published data on the East German budgetary expenditures contain a number of extremely peculiar features which allow very favourable comparisons to be made with West Germany, especially in the handling of administration, military, police, and health expenditures. Indeed, of all the budgets examined in this study, the East German budget appeared to be the most deliberately misleading. There are four major problems of estimations:

1. Unlike the other centralized economies East Germany does

not follow the Soviet system of reporting all budgetary expenditures net of sale to the public (see esp. the comments by [B278, p. 94]). Since I was able to locate no data on the amount of such sales and since there are almost no references to such revenues in the vast East German literature on public finance, I have assumed that the volume of these sales to the public were relatively small and could be neglected.

2. Intra-governmental transfers are doubly accounted. Although this makes some difference in social expenditures, the major problem occurs in health where social insurance expenditures to health agencies are included under social insurance payments as well as under the expenditures of such agencies. Elimination of such double accounting proved extremely difficult and only the roughest estimates could be made. The details of the procedures employed are described in the notes on individual expenditure items.

3. Although data are available on most parts of the East German budget, they are scattered in a large number of isolated sources. In addition, there have been several major changes in budgetary accounting practices and it is often difficult to know the relationships of conflicting data presented in different sources. These estimates are a revised version of my preliminary published calculations [P74, 3 & 4/1965] and include several changes in definition and corrections of mistakes.

4. Military expenditures are greatly understated in East German sources, and, in addition, police expenditures are not published. Estimates for such security expenditures were made on the basis of personnel data and are described in the notes on individual expenditure items. Moreover, it is highly likely that certain security expenditures connected with the Soviet occupation are included under 'administration'. Unfortunately, these could not be removed (see below).

C. *Subjective Evaluation*

In spite of the considerable difficulties in obtaining or making estimates for different categories, I have considerable faith in the estimates for all sectors except administration and health. I give the estimates in Table A–4 a 'B–' rating.

D. *Notes on Individual Expenditure Items*

1. Total expenditures data for 1953 to 1962 come from [G61, 1962, p. 224], and [G61, 1963, p. 371]. For the overlap years (1958–62) these sources differ by about 2 per cent because of a change in

TABLE A–4

Public Consumption Expenditures in East Germany
(Million DM-East)

Year	Gross Expenditures		Adjusted Expenditures[3]			Administration[5]	External Security		
	With Double Accounting[1]	Excluding Double Accounting[2]	Central[4]	Local[4]	Total		Military[6]	Occupation[7]	Other
1950	21,814	21,584	n.a.	n.a.	11,592	2,594	512	1,600	18
1951	28,308	23,969	9,583	3,220	12,803	2,580	739	1,798	29
1952	33,353	27,615	10,884	3,812	14,696	2,511	1,188	1,884	48
1953	34,753	32,146	11,426	4,280	15,706	2,475	1,392	1,664	74
1954	36,143	33,458	12,057	4,486	16,543	2,494	1,421	1,600	92
1955	38.327	34,796	12,504	4,561	17,065	2,508	1,598	1,600	124
1956	35,856	32,906	13,568	4,627	18,195	2,491	1,725	1,600	124
1957	36,377	33,635	14,334	5,176	19,510	2,444	1,632	800	244
1958	42,248	38,738	14,419	5,755	20,174	2,381	1,870	600	232
1959	47,444	43,230	15,632	6,420	22,052	2,531	1,977	0	298
1960	50,555	44,522	16,660	6,894	23,554	2,751	2,018	0	204
1961	51,239	46,523	17,897	6,795	24,692	2,574	2,511	0	303
1962	55,802	49,071	19,051	6,549	25,600	2,560	2,980	0	276

Year	Internal Security[9]	Social[10]			Science[14]	Other Direct Investment[15]
		Education[11]	Health[12]	Welfare[13]		
1950	605	974	1,739	3,370	180	1,600
1951	698	1,113	1,790	3,850	206	2,800
1952	782	1,462	1,966	4,537	318	3,200
1953	860	1,819	2,129	4,907	386	4,300
1954	931	1,997	2,275	5,207	526	3,700
1955	986	2,005	2,370	5,266	608	2,900
1956	1,049	2,105	2,417	5,896	788	3,800
1957	912	2,561	2,576	7,472	869	4,400
1958	1,022	2,653	2,828	7,582	1,006	5,300
1959	1,062	2,934	3,176	8,940	1,134	6,200
1960	1,080	3,121	3,439	9,615	1,326	7,200
1961	1,135	3,234	3,690	9,813	1,432	8,100
1962	1,172	3,280	3,851	10,030	1,451	8,610

the treatment of the expenditures of the Deutsche Versicherungs-anstalten (DVA); these are discussed in the following footnote. There are conflicting data on total budgetary expenditures for 1950–52 [P94, October 10, 1955] data by E. Frenkel which are also printed in [G154, various issues], [B217], [P15, 19/1959, pp. 371–74] and [P15, 7/1956, pp. 270–73; 8/1956, pp. 328–31; 9/1956, pp. 380–82] (hereafter abbreviated as [P15, 7/1956, pp. 370–73) but most of these differences can be traced to different definitions of public expenditures. The 1950 datum was derived from a figure of government expenditures of East Germany excluding East Berlin [B217,

p. 91], plus an estimate of expenditures of East Berlin plus the expenditures of the social insurance system [P100, 42/1953] which were not included in the published consolidated budget until 1951. Nineteen fifty-two and 1953 data come from [P94, October 10, 1955] and are consistent with the data for later years.

2. In order to make the series consistent and to remove the double accounting, the following four types of adjustments must be made: First, the *'Finanzausgleich'* (intra-governmental transfers) between the central and Bezirke governments are doubly accounted and must be removed. (It is not clear if the intra-government transfers within the individual Bezirke are doubly accounted: I have assumed that this was not the case). Second, transfers from the central budget to the social insurance system are also doubly accounted and must be removed. Third, in 1956 and 1957 only government subsidies to the DVA were included in the consolidated budget, while in later years, gross expenditures of the DVA were included. Therefore, adjustments must also be made here. Finally, the health expenditures which are doubly accounted were removed.

For the *Finanzausgleich*, the 1951–55 data are from [P94, October 10, 1955] (the 1955 datum is a planned figure); the 1956–62 data are planned figures obtained from [G59, various issues]. No adjustment was necessary for the 1950 datum.

Budgetary grants to the social insurance system for 1950 were zero because receipts of the social insurance system were greater than expenditures. Data for such grants for 1951–55 come from [P94, October 10, 1955] (1955 is a planned figure). The 1956 datum is a planned figure from [G59 I, 19/1956]; the 1957–61 data are realized grants and were obtained from [B20, p. 197]. The 1962 datum comes from [P15, 24/1962, pp. 3–8]. It must be noted that these estimates differ from the usually cited data presented by [B200, p. 49], which exclude East Berlin and contain a number of other quirks as well.

Gross expenditures of the DVA for 1956 and 1957 were estimated by extrapolation. Since the budgetary subsidies to the DVA during these years appear to have been part of the total budgetary subsidies of the social insurance system and have already been removed, there is no need for their estimation.

The doubly accounted health expenditures were estimated according to a method described below (footnote 12) and were removed.

4. Local government units include the Laender (up to 1953), the Bezirke, and all lower units. According to [B278, pp. 57–58], local government units have financed only a limited number of activities;

all security expenditures and a large share of the socio-cultural expenditures have been financed at the republic level. Expenditures on administration for units below the Bezirke and Laender were obtained for 1951, 1955, 1958, and 1959 from [B323, p. 50] who claims to be citing an article [P15, 18/1959, pp. S–349–50] which, unfortunately does not contain the cited data. Nevertheless, these data were used and the expenditures for the missing years were estimated by interpolation or extrapolation. Administration expenditures of the Bezirke and Laender governments were estimated to amount to 20 per cent of local governmental administration expenditures. For socio-cultural expenditures conflicting data on local government expenditures are presented by [P15, 18/1959, pp. S–349–50] and [B323]; since the data of the former sources are similar to those for 1958 which are given in [G61, 1958, pp. 243–45] I constructed a series from these two sources and interpolated for the missing years. From this, local expenditures for culture were removed. Data for 1958, 1959, 1960, and 1962 were obtained from [G61, various issues]; an estimate for 1961 was made by interpolation; and estimates for 1951–57 were made by assuming that the ratio of local to total expenditures were the same in these years as in 1958. Any error introduced by such a procedure should be negligible because of the small size of cultural expenditures in relation to the expenditures for social purposes.

Although certain data are presented for expenditures of different levels of local government [G60, July 27/1959] [P15, 18/1959, S–349–50], [B20, p. 105], and [B323], the data are too conflicting for any estimates to be made.

5. Administration expenditures are a shadowy item in the East German budget. According to [B278] administration expenditures include expenditures for diplomacy and the judicial system and, therefore, these were removed. Although there is no indication whether any capital expenditures are included in administration expenditures, I have assumed that budgetary accounting procedures are the same for these as for socio-cultural expenditures where such capital items are excluded.

The 1950 datum is from [P15, 7/1956, pp. 270–73]; the 1951–55 data, from [P94, October 10/1955] (1955 datum is a planned figure); the 1956 datum, from [P15, 24/1957, p. 715]; the 1958 datum, from [G60, July 1/1959, pp. 6–8]; the 1960 and 1961 data (plan 1961), from [P15, 8/1962, pp. 3–8]. Data for 1957 and 1959 were estimated by interpolation; the 1962 expenditure was placed equal to the 1961 datum.

For derivation of data on costs of diplomacy and judicial system, see footnotes 8 and 9.

6. Published data for military expenditures for 1956–58 come from [P15, 19/1959, pp. 371–74); 1959 plan datum, from [P98, January 28, 1959, p. 5)]; 1960 plan datum, from [G60, May 6, 1960]; 1961 plan datum, from [P15, 7/1961, pp. 197–200]; 1962 plan datum from [P15, 8/1962, pp. 3–8]. However, comparison of these data with an estimated wage bill of military personnel (see below) suggest strongly that for every year except 1962, the published data covered primarily wages and allowances; furthermore [G142, June 19, 1958] has convincing evidence that military equipment was financed from the investment, rather than the military budget. Although there are a number of scattered estimates of hidden East German military expenditures in the Western literature ([P32, April 24, 1960], [P99, 6/1960, pp. 17–18], [P68, January 2, 1960], [G147, December 22, 1959], and [G27, p. 62]) these differ greatly from each other and do not seem very useful. Therefore, estimates were calculated in five steps.

First, the number of personnel in the various police and army units were determined. The data were obtained from the following accessible sources: [B42], [G143, various issues], [B81], [B103], [P87, 2 & 3/1962, pp. 6–10], [G148, various issues], [G149, various issues], and [P92, various issues]. These were supplemented by information for 1956–62 from the files of the Bundesministerium fuer gesamtdeutsche Fragen.

Second, the 'Barracked People's Police' and its successor, the National People's Army were designated as military units; the border guards (which were co-opted into the armed forces in 1961), the alert police (*Bereitschaftspolizei*), and the motorized alert police were designated as security troops and all other units (People's Police, Transportation Police, Secret Police, and Guard Regiments of the Secret Police) were considered as police units.

Third, a wage fund was estimated for the various military and security units. For the security units it was assumed that the average wage was equal to the average industrial wage. For the armed forces this was done by taking the 1955 wages for the various ranks (data from [G142, 6/1955, pp. 80–81]), weighing them by assuming that the distribution of men in various ranks was the same as in Hungary in 1955 (data from [B10, p. 148]), estimating officers' bonus payments as 20 per cent of their base pay, and assuming that for the other years the wages of officers and men moved at the same rate as the average industrial wages. To this was added an estimate of payments in kind, made for 1955 by estimating the assumed cost of clothing and food which military personnel received and estimated for other years by assuming that such payments in kind remained the same for all years and that the value of such payments varied according to changes in the retail price index.

Fourth, an estimate of non-personnel military expenditures was made in the following manner. In 1962 the relation between the calculated military wage fund and the published military expenditures figure seemed reasonable; for the other years, the published expenditures seemed only to cover personnel costs. Although the East Germans claimed that the increase in military expenditures in 1962 was due to an increase in military personnel, the real explanation seems to lie in a change in reporting. Therefore, the 1962 published military figure was accepted as representing total costs of the border guards and armed forces. After removing the total cost of the border guards (see below) a ratio of non-personnel expenditures per soldier was derived. It was assumed that such non-personnel per soldier expenditures increased at the same rates between 1955 and 1958 and between 1958 and 1962 as in the rest of Eastern Europe excluding the Soviet Union. From 1950–55 it was assumed that such non-personnel expenditures per soldier increased at an average annual rate of 11 per cent.

Fifth, an estimate of non-personnel expenditures of the security troops was made by assuming that such expenditures amounted to 30 per cent of the wage costs of these units. Since the Alert Police units are not financed through the Ministry of National Defence, it was assumed that they were not included in the published defence expenditures datum in 1962.

It must be noted that it is not known whether or not the expenditures of the 'Enterprise Fighting Groups' were included in the published military expenditures datum for 1962 or not. Therefore, no estimate of such expenditures has been made.

7. The data are from [B176] which contain the most thorough study of East German reparation payments available. After 1958 the East Germans did not need to make any direct payments for support of the Soviet army. However, according to one emigré newspaper, the Soviet Union did not relieve the East Germans from bearing the cost of certain auxiliary costs of the Soviet troops which amounted to 500 mil. DM–E in the late 1950s. I made no allowances for such costs, since I do not know if they really exist.

8. Other external security expenditures consist of costs of three different activities:

(*a*) Diplomatic expenditures were estimated by assuming that *per capita* expenditures were one-third those of West Germany, since East Germany has diplomatic relations with many fewer countries. My 1954 and 1955 estimates of 14 mil. DM–E and 18 mil. DM–E are partially confirmed by a refugee report (archive of the Bundesministerium fuer gesamtdeutsche Fragen, Bonn) which stated that the East German Foreign Ministry spent 10 mil. roubles for trade and diplomatic representatives in 1954 and asked for 14 mil. roubles in 1955. This represents about 11 mil. DM–E and 16 mil. DM–E.

(*b*) The estimating of foreign aid expenditures is discussed in Appendix D–20. These estimates are quite different from those of [B176].

(*c*) For intelligence expenditures I assumed that one-third of the full-time employees of the Ministry of State Security were involved in foreign intelligence work, that they received 25 per cent more than the average industrial worker, and that the other expenditures on foreign intelligence were equal to the payroll expenditures. This is a deliberately low estimate (75 mil. DM–E in 1960), especially in relation to the 10,000 spies which various Western commentators have asserted East Germany has placed in West Germany.

9. Internal security expenditures were estimated in three steps:

(*a*) Expenditures on wages of the various police units were estimated by assuming that all the personnel in these units, with the exception of the secret police, received the average industrial wage. For the secret police engaged in domestic activities (see footnote 8c) it was assumed that they receive 25 per cent more than the average industrial wage.

(*b*) Non-personnel expenditures of the various police units were estimated by assuming that they amounted to 30 per cent of the wage costs of all units except the secret police. For the secret police, it was estimated that such non-personnel expenditures amounted to the total of the estimated wages.

(*c*) Costs of the administration of justice were estimated by assuming that the East German *per capita* expenditures amounted to one-half of those (for '*Rechtspflege*') of West Germany. This fraction was chosen for two reasons: to take account of the fact that part of the costs of the administration of justice (prison guards) have already been estimated; and to reflect the fact that the court system in East Germany is much smaller, since justice is determined by much simpler criteria.

10. Data on current socio-cultural and science expenditures are

given in great detail for the years 1953–62 and are given in moderate detail for the years 1951–53 (but ostensibly exclude expenditures for East Berlin). The 1951–57 data come from [G61, 1958, pp. 240–45]; the 1958–62 data, from [G61, 1963, pp. 372–78]. The estimation of current socio-cultural and science expenditures including East Berlin for 1951 and 1952 present a problem. If socio-cultural and science expenditures for East Berlin alone for 1951 [B217, p. 97] are added to such expenditures excluding East Berlin, a figure is obtained which is very close to that presented by [P15, 7/1956, pp. 270–73]. However, there is some double accounting since the data excluding the East Berlin budget nevertheless includes transfers from the 'republic budget' to the East Berlin budget. On the other hand, [P94, October 10, 1955] and [P15, 19/1959, pp. 371–74] present data for all of East Germany for these years which are close to the data of [G61], excluding East Berlin. Since [G61, 1958] presents socio-cultural and science expenditures from the budgets of the Bezirke and since no other data by individual Bezirke are available, the following procedure was adopted: The expenditures of the East Berlin budget for various socio-cultural and science expenditures were calculated as percentages of the total expenditures for such purposes, and these percentages were used to adjust upwards the 1951 and 1952 data excluding Berlin. The amount of double accounting in the data from [P15, 7/1956, pp. 270–73] for 1951 was estimated by the difference between the former set of data and the calculated data and the double accounting contained in the 1950 data was assumed to be the same. Then the amounts of specific expenditures in the different branches were estimated by assuming that the percentage distribution of the socio-cultural and science expenditures was the same in 1950 as in 1951.

11. Education expenditures includes those for general and trade schools, special education schools, night schools, and adult education classes, colleges and universities, and payments to non-state educational facilities.

12. Health expenditures include those for hospitals and outpatient treatment, homes for women before and after child birth convalescence homes, payments from the DVA and social insurance for direct health care, public health measures, drug stores, and payments to non-state health facilities. Without adjustment health expenditures as a percentage of GNP were about twice as high as in any other nation; the cause seemed due to the double accounting of social insurance expenditures to health agencies (i.e. those expenditures which did not go directly to physicians or to the

patients). Since no data are available on the size of such double accounting, it was arbitrarily assumed that one half of the health insurance expenditures were doubly accounted and these were removed from the estimates. Although the resulting estimates as a ratio of GNP still seemed high, no further adjustments were made.

13. Welfare expenditures include those for pre-school training for children, children's homes, out-of-school activities for children, care of mothers and children, social welfare payments to the general population, administration costs of social welfare, 'labour expenditures' (certain housing expenditures plus bonuses for labour heroes, etc.), pensions, social insurance payments excluding those for health, and payments to non-state welfare institutions. The social insurance expenditures of the DVA (footnote 2) are also included. A certain problem arises about the elimination of housing subsidies. The housing expenditures contained in the budget are unexplained and the amount of rent subsidies administered by the local governments is not published. Nevertheless, since only 10 per cent of the apartments and homes in 1961 were built after 1945 (for more information see [B19] and [G61, 1962, pp. 374 ff.]) and since a majority of these were built by co-operatives or by private individuals, the amount of such rent subsidies was probably extremely small and little error could be introduced by neglecting them.

14. Science expenditures include those for academies, scientific institutes and research, scientific libraries, technical-scientific co-operation with foreign countries, and work on standards. Research expenditures are not given for 1961–62 and were estimated by separating expenditures for scientific institutes and research into three components (institutes concerned with physical sciences, institutes concerned with other disciplines, and research) and assuming that the ratio of expenditures of institutes of physical science (which are given for these last years) and research expenditures remained constant. Expenditures of institutes for other disciplines were small and were assumed to remain constant.

15. These data must be considered as only rough estimates since it is not known how inclusive they are, i.e. it is possible that certain investments in agriculture or communal economy are excluded.

The 1950 datum is a plan figure [G59, 1950, p. 114]. The 1951–58 data come from [P15, 19/1959, pp. 371–74]. Although these data are very close to those of [P94, October 10, 1955] and [G60, July 1, 1959, pp. 6–8] the 1957 datum is 800 mil. DM–E smaller than that reported by [P15, 4/1959, pp. 61–64] or the planned amount. The difference may lie in the fact that military equipment or housing are included in the latter sources. The figures for 1959–60 were calculated from data presented in [G60, July 26, 1961, Beilage]. The 1961 and 1962 figures are plan data [G59 I, 4/1961] and [G59 I, 3/1962] and include housing.

APPENDIX A–6: ESTIMATES FOR GREECE

A. *Acknowledgments*

I would like to thank Mr S. Geronimakis of the Ministry of Coordination of Greece for supplying unpublished data and explanations of the definitions used in the official statistics, Professor A. Kalogeris for his help in estimating expenditures for R and D, and Dr Jan Tumlir for his general aid in making these estimates.

B. *Main Problems*

Two major problems arose in making these estimates.

Although the Greek national accounts statistics [G64], [G65], and [G66] include a functional breakdown of public expenditures, these are based on definitions not quite the same as those used in this study. Although other Greek sources present data on public expenditures (e.g. [G67], [G68], [G69], it proved impossible to use these to build up alternative functional estimates. Fortunately, the national accounts data could be adjusted to correspond more to the definitions used here.

Another difficulty occurred because the national income data, at the time these estimates were prepared, were calculated only through 1961. Nineteen sixty-two data were estimated by assuming that the respective functional aggregates increased at the same rate as the expenditures of the Ministries whose functional responsibilities were roughly the same (data from [G68, pp. 71 ff.]).

C. *Subjective Evaluation*

Since the basic data are based on a GNP concept, rather than the expenditure concept used for most of the other countries in this study, and since the published and unpublished data are available only on a fairly high degree of aggregation, the congruence of these data with the concepts used here is not exactly known. Therefore, I give the estimates in Table A–5 as a rating of 'B–'.

D. *Sources of Data*

Unless otherwise specified, all data come from [G64, pp. 24–25, 34–37], [G65, pp. 26–27, 72–76], and [G66, pp. 18, 30–31] and unpublished GNP data.

TABLE A–5

Public Consumption Expenditures in Greece (Million Drachmae)

		Adjusted Budget[2]				External Security	
Year	Gross Budget[1]	Central[3]	Local[3]	Total	Administration[4]	Military[5]	Other[6]
1950	8,546	4,826	340	5,166	957	1,678	39
1951	8,630	5,977	361	6,338	1,027	2,523	46
1952	9,563	6,447	465	6,912	1,086	2,202	52
1953	10,338	7,126	635	7,761	1,152	2,421	82
1954	11,706	8,492	860	9,352	1,352	3,042	116
1955	14,345	10,044	982	11,026	1,707	3,360	128
1956	17,750	12,061	1,153	13,214	2,005	4,255	146
1957	19,457	12,478	1,155	13,633	2,110	3,938	160
1958	20,920	13,518	1,249	14,767	2,334	3,931	175
1959	22,469	14,303	1,423	15,726	2,365	4,086	206
1960	25,474	15,320	1,507	16,827	2,519	4,338	237
1961	29,434	16,742	1,844	18,586	2,722	4,497	210
1962	33,488	18,410	2,106	20,516	3,046	4,455	279

		Social				Other	
Year	Internal Security[7]	Education[8]	Health[9]	Welfare[10]	Science[11]	Interest[12]	Direct Investment[13]
1950	206	201	144	1,938	3	8	2,336
1951	342	439	285	1,672	4	25	1,673
1952	407	458	310	2,391	6	89	1,512
1953	539	569	317	2,670	11	9	1,910
1954	676	734	349	3,069	14	49	2,281
1955	766	871	633	3,541	20	76	2,590
1956	909	1,032	776	4,064	27	71	3,281
1957	1,048	1,055	818	4,470	34	51	3,417
1958	1,057	1,157	893	5,175	45	53	4,296
1959	1,106	1,273	982	5,646	62	171	5,153
1960	1,144	1,364	1,011	6,141	73	286	6,513
1961	1,197	1,525	1,177	7,169	89	365	7,572
1962	1,332	1,699	1,252	8,350	103	482	8,977

E. *Prices used*

Data are presented in post-1952 Drachmae.

F. *Notes on Individual Expenditure Estimates*

1. These include public expenditures for goods and services, subsidies, interest payments, transfer payments, gross fixed asset formation, and changes in government stocks. The above mentioned sources were supplemented by [G67, 1964, pp. 473–74].

2. Adjusted budget includes expenditures for administration, security, social purposes, and science.

3. Local expenditures include not only expenditures of local

governmental units but also those of special governmental funds excluding the social insurance system. Data for 1952–61 come from unpublished information supplied by the Ministry of Co-ordination. Data for 1950, 1951 and 1962 were estimated by extrapolation using as a guideline data on total 'local' governmental expenditures (from [G64] and [G65]).

4. These are the administrative expenditures presented in the national account statistics minus expenditures on goods and services for diplomatic purposes and expenditures of the Finance Ministry for the Central Chemical Laboratory. The expenditures on goods and services for diplomatic purposes were calculated from total expenditures for diplomacy (see footnote 6) minus an estimate for transfer payments, which were assumed to be one-half of the total governmental transfer payments abroad (subscriptions to international organization, international contributions and subscriptions, expenses for participating in international conferences and exhibitions, etc.). Although such an estimation method is crude, the amount of such transfers was small and little error should be introduced.

5. Published military data include expenditures of the Ministry of National Defence for military purposes, of NATO common interest works, and of the 'security forces' under the Ministry of Interior. Since the 'security forces' play an important police role as well, one half of such expenditures were assigned to internal security. Data on the expenditures for the 'security forces' for 1950 to 1955 are rough estimates based on data from various issues of [G69], [G62], and [G63]; data for 1955 through 1962 come from various issues of [G67] and [G68].

6. These are current expenditures of the Ministry of Foreign Affairs. Data for 1950–55 come from various issues of [G69], [G62], and [G63]; data for 1955 through 1962 come from various issues of [G67] and [G68].

7. Internal security covers expenditures for law and order, courts, prisons, and one half of the expenditures for the 'security forces' under the Ministry of Interior (see footnote 5).

8. Education includes expenditures for goods and services for educational purposes plus transfer payments to students. Since the handling of expenditures for pre-primary schools is not known, no adjustments in the published data were made to exclude them. However, since such expenditures in Greece are very small, little error should be introduced for this reason.

9. Health includes expenditures for goods and services for health

purposes plus transfers to hospitals and minus expenditures for sports. The latter were estimated as the expenditures of the General Secretariat of Athletics (data from [G68, 1963, p. 71]).

10. Welfare includes expenditures for goods and services for social services plus administration costs of the social security system plus all governmental transfer expenditures not included in education and health. Administration expenditures of the social security system (included in the published data under 'other government activities') were estimated as 4 per cent of total social insurance benefits.

11. Total governmental expenditures for R and D for 1961 are given in [B167] and [G16]. The bulk of such expenditures are accounted for by three organizations: the Demokritos Centre for Atomic Research, the Central Chemical Laboratory under the Ministry of Finance, and the agricultural experimentation stations. Expenditures data for all three organizations were obtained for most years from various issues of [G69], [G62], and [G63]; expenditures of the remaining budgetary R and D expenditures were assumed to move at the same rate as the combined R and D expenditures of the Central Chemical Laboratory and the agricultural experimentation stations. For the early 1950s, budgetary data are fragmentary and, since comparability is doubtful, only very rough estimates could be made.

12. These data are reported in the national income statistics; no adjustments have been made.

APPENDIX A-7: ESTIMATES FOR HUNGARY

A. *Acknowledgments*

I would like to thank Dr George Pall and Dr Michael Simai for their aid in locating materials for these estimates. I would also like to express my appreciation to the Hungarian Central Statistics Office for supplying certain data on the budgetary plan and to the Hungarian Ministry of Finance and the Ministry of Culture for supplying certain unpublished data on realized budgetary expenditures.

B. *Major Problems*

The primary difficulty in making the estimates stemmed from the fact that Hungary does not publish official data on realized state budgetary expenditures. Furthermore, in the entire Hungarian

M

economic literature, there are only two sources (Sugar [P93, October, 1962)] and [B321] which contain time series from which estimates can be based. Unfortunately these two sources present contradictory data and a decision had to be made on which source would be chosen.

Source [B321] was written by an economist who later became Minister of Finance and contains data in absolute terms which are consistent with certain scattered data found in other sources. Source [P93, October, 1962] presents data in index number form which seem inconsistent with data from all other sources which I was able to find. Therefore, the first source was chosen as the starting point for the estimates. These data were supplemented by unpublished detailed data on socio-cultural expenditures which were supplied by Ministry of Finance. Unfortunately, these unpublished data and the data from [B321] were slightly different, although the differences were not of an appreciable magnitude. The unpublished data on education expenditures supplied by the Ministry of Finance were slightly different than similar data supplied by the Ministry of Culture. However, since the latter only covered a few years, they were not used.

In addition to the above mentioned sources, scattered data from over 80 sources were gathered and collated. These were supplemented by data on planned expenditures (gathered primarily from [G72, various issues], [G73], [G74], [G75] and from data supplied by the Central Statistical Office). Most of the data from the scattered sources turned out to be planned, rather than realized expenditures. Moreover, some of these data were so out-of-line with other estimates that they could not be used. The remaining data proved useful as a source of alternative information although only rarely were they incorporated into the final estimates.

Two minor problems remained. The data from [B321] only covered the years through 1961 and, in several cases, it seemed as though the 1961 data were provisional. Therefore, for 1961 and 1962 certain simple extrapolations had to be made. Finally, the handling of sales to the public by budgetary organizations is not clear. Hungary, like the Soviet Union, has extra-budgetary accounts which finance non-reported expenditure of budgetary organizations. Although these are financed by sales to the public, George Pall has suggested to me that certain turnover tax receipts may also be transferred to these accounts. (This speculation is based on certain discrepancies between total turnover taxes and such taxes reported in the budget [B10, pp. 173 ff.]).

C. *Subjective Evaluation*

Because of the difficulties in obtaining comparable data and in determining the meaning of the available data, I give a rating of 'B–' to the estimates in Table A–6.

TABLE A–6

Public Consumption Expenditures in Hungary (Million Forint)

Year	Gross Budget[1]	Adjusted Budget[2]	Administration[3]	External Security Military[4]	External Security Other[5]
1950	25,277	8,675	827	2,042	84
1951	33,584	11,625	853	4,100	106
1952	41,468	16,821	1,195	5,924	107
1953	49,028	19,244	1,435	7,381	128
1954	43,980	19,610	2,320	5,429	128
1955	43,100	20,266	2,437	5,683	107
1956	42,171	19,831	2,631	4,090	128
1957	51,873	19,000	2,705	1,912	148
1958	46,500	20,823	2,920	2,078	153
1959	52,059	25,304	3,882	2,408	159
1960	67,400	28,741	4,478	3,100	153
1961	75,724	30,425	4,307	3,376	160
1962	82,000	33,891	4,340	4,913	193

Year	Internal Security[6]	Social Education[7]	Social Health[8]	Social Welfare[9]	Other Science[10]	Other Direct Investment[11]
1950	1,664	1,067	953	1,961	77	9,000
1951	1,774	1,369	1,017	2,287	119	11,700
1952	2,372	1,998	1,442	3,532	251	19,000
1953	2,110	2,435	1,719	3,711	325	15,700
1954	2,302	2,554	2,126	4,366	385	11,000
1955	2,211	2,365	2,234	4,829	400	9,800
1956	2,246	2,597	2,453	5,254	432	7,800
1957	1,937	2,916	2,826	6,069	487	5,000
1958	2,075	3,174	3,187	6,651	585	6,300
1959	2,370	3,873	3,796	8,104	712	14,700
1960	2,597	4,358	4,277	8,968	810	20,500
1961	2,692	4,570	4,632	9,789	899	21,486
1962	2,712	4,952	5,140	10,482	1,159	34,800

D. *Notes on Individual Expenditure Estimates*

1. The data for 1950 through 1954 came from (Timár [P51, May, 1955]); the 1955 datum, from [B179, p. 201], and the 1958 datum from ([P64, February 20, 1959], transl. by [P72, 41/1959]). The 1962 datum was derived from information from [P16, p. 175]. Data for the remaining years are plan data [G72, various years] and, while reflecting actual expenditures only within a percentage range

(especially the datum for 1956), should provide a useful indication of the trend of such expenditures.

2. Sum of expenditures for administration, security, social and scientific activities.

3. Published administration expenditures [B321, pp. 106–7] with the removal of an estimate of expenditures for diplomacy (see footnote 5). These administration expenditures are quite similar to the plan data for certain early years but deviate radically so that by 1960 they are almost double the planned administration expenditures. In dynamic terms the planned administration expenditures grew at an average annual rate of 7·1 per cent between 1950 and 1963, while the actual expenditures reported by [B321] grew at an average annual rate of 15·5 per cent between 1950 and 1962. Part of these differences lies in different coverage of the two series; there is much less difference between the planned data and the data presented by [B321] when administration expenditures are combined with expenditures for law and order. The data from [B321] probably also contain certain administrative expenditures which were transferred to 'financing the national economy' in the budget.

4. These are plan data for military expenditures, collected primarily from [G72, various years]. The 1950 datum comes from [G73] and is different from that reported by [G29, VII, 2/1955, p. 97]. Data on actual expenditures are available for only certain years: (all in mil. ft.) 1953, 6319 [G71]; 1955, 4900 [B58, p. 85]; 1961, 2900 [B238, p. 247]. (Data for 1956 and 1959 are also available [B186, p. 104] but are of questionable validity if these data are judged by the accuracy of other data presented in the same source). It is noteworthy that all three of these actual expenditure figures lie below the plan data, as does an estimate of actual defence expenditures for 1955 presented by [B10, p. 170]. Furthermore, the ratio of planned to actual expenditures is about the same in 1955 as in 1961. Two explanations for this phenomenon are possible: either the defence budget was underfulfilled in these three years or else the plan data contain some other types of expenditures as well. Now planned expenditures in both 1953 and 1955 were higher than such planned expenditures in the preceeding or following years and, moreover, occurred in a period where defence expenditures were falling. But this is not the case in 1961 and, therefore, the first explanation does not seem likely to cover all three cases. The second explanation could cover all three cases, especially if planned expenditures included internal security troops and if reported actual expenditures excluded such expenditures. Without additional

information, a firm judgement is impossible; nevertheless, the second explanation seems a much more likely explanation and, therefore, no additional estimates were made to cover the costs of the security troops.

5. Other external security expenditures include expenditures for diplomacy and foreign aid. Diplomacy costs were estimated by assuming that such expenditures were the same ratio of net material product as in Poland and by smoothing the derived series so that diplomacy expenditures either increased or remained the same each year. Estimation of foreign aid expenditures is discussed in Appendix D–20.

6. Internal security expenditures include costs of police, courts, and prisons, and were obtained from [B321, pp. 106–7]. The expenditures for 1955 are somewhat higher than the estimate by [B10, p. 170] of total expenditures for police, political police, and border guards. The data on expenditures for 'law and justice' reported by [B321] are quite similar to the plan data until 1957–59, when planned expenditures suddenly increased until they were about 35 per cent greater in 1961. This suggests that there was a change in definition in the budget plan. (See also footnote 3.)

7. Education expenditures were derived from the data supplied by the Ministry of Finance with the removal of expenditures for kindergartens and for science financed through the education budget. Kindergarten expenditures for 1955, 1957, and 1958 were obtained from [J.P.R.S., transl. 1203/1962, p. 68] and for 1960–62 from unpublished materials obtained from UNESCO. The kindergarten expenditures for the remaining years were estimated by interpolating or extrapolating the ratio of these expenditures to the total expenditures on education and culture. For estimation of science expenditures, see footnote 10.

8. Health expenditures include total health expenditures from data from Ministry of Finance (which are equal to those reported in [G70, 1959, p. 305; 1958, p. 308; and 1957 (English edition), p. 297] plus expenditures for medicine from the social insurance [G70, 1962, p. 323].

9. Welfare expenditures were obtained from the data on health and welfare expenditures [B321, pp. 106–7] plus kindergarten expenditures (see footnote 7) and minus expenditures for medicine and for subsidies for organized holidays at reduced rates.

10. Science expenditures include direct expenditures from the budget for scientific institutes as well as expenditures for research in universities which are financed from education funds. Data for the

former for 1953, 1957 through 1962 are available from [G70, 1962, p. 402]. Data for the missing years were estimated by interpolating and extrapolating the ratio of these science expenditures to total expenditures on education and culture taking into account planned expenditures for 1951 and 1952 [G74] and [G75]. Data on expenditures for science from educational institutions are available for 1957–59 from (Partos [P93, 5/1961] transl. J.P.R.S. 5576/1962). The ratio of these expenditures to total educational expenditures was assumed the same for other years. Such expenditures did not amount to over 5 per cent of total science expenditures in any year.

11. Data for 1950, 1951, 1953, 1954, 1955 and 1961 are realized expenditures from [G29, 2/1955, p. 97; 1/1956, p. 27] and [B238, p. 247]. Data for the remaining years are plan data from scattered sources. Since budgetary investment expenditures cover about 90 per cent of total stated gross investment for some years, it should be clear that such reported budgetary expenditures include grants to the investment banks.

APPENDIX A–8: ESTIMATES FOR IRELAND

A. *Acknowledgments*

I would like to thank Dr Alan Tait and Dr Martin O'Donoghue of Trinity College Dublin for allowing me the use of their unpublished estimates of Irish public expenditures and for patiently answering my many questions concerning their sources and methods. I would also like to express my appreciation to Mr J. B. Broderick of the Central Statistical Office of the Republic of Ireland for the use of unpublished government estimates of Irish public expenditures. However, Messrs Tait, O'Donoghue and Broderick are in no way responsible for the use I made of their estimates nor of any errors which I may have committed.

B. *Main Problems*

My estimates were based primarily on the calculations of Irish public expenditures for 1950–59 by Alan Tait and Martin O'Donoghue [P44 and P74, forthcoming] and [B49a, Chpt. 1] and for 1959–62 by the Irish Central Statistical Office. The major problems arose in reconciling two discrepancies of these to sets of estimates:

1. The studied expenditures are divided somewhat differently between administration and economic services. For the sake of comparability with other nations, I chose to follow the definitions of the cso.

2. Although the aggregate estimates for 'social services' are very similar in the two studies, the designation of the governmental level on which certain expenditures were made are somewhat different. This discrepancy arose in the handling of certain central

TABLE A–7

Public Consumption Expenditures in Ireland (Million Pounds)

Year	Gross Budget[1]	Adjusted Budget[2]			Adminis- tration[3]	External Security	
		Central	Local	Total		Military[4]	Other[5]
1950	90·7	49·5	13·5	63·0	4·8	4·2	0·3
1951	98·2	57·6	15·8	73·4	5·0	5·5	0·4
1952	111·8	62·7	16·5	79·2	5·8	6·9	0·4
1953	119·1	65·0	18·3	83·3	6·1	7·9	0·4
1954	122·8	63·0	22·7	85·7	6·5	6·4	0·4
1955	128·3	64·9	25·7	90·6	7·0	6·9	0·4
1956	136·6	67·2	27·5	94·7	7·3	6·9	0·5
1957	142·5	66·2	28·2	94·4	7·1	6·4	0·5
1958	146·0	65·8	29·2	95·0	7·6	6·4	0·5
1959	150·2	68·0	30·0	98·0	7·9	6·9	0·5
1960	159·3	71·6	32·3	103·9	8·6	7·4	0·6
1961	176·2	77·6	34·1	111·7	9·4	8·0	0·6
1962	186·6	84·3	36·0	120·3	10·6	8·6	0·7

Year	Internal Security[6]	Social			Science[10]	Other	
		Education[7]	Health[8]	Welfare[9]		Interest[11]	Direct Invest- ment[12]
1950	4·3	7·8	6·8	34·7	0·1	6·6	9·1
1951	4·9	8·8	8·2	40·5	0·1	7·2	10·1
1952	5·1	9·4	8·5	42·9	0·2	8·6	11·9
1953	5·4	10·1	9·0	44·2	0·2	10·2	12·8
1954	5·8	10·9	13·0	42·5	0·2	11·4	13·1
1955	5·9	11·1	15·3	43·8	0·2	13·0	14·3
1956	6·0	11·8	17·0	45·0	0·2	14·2	14·3
1957	6·1	12·3	17·8	44·0	0·2	15·4	11·6
1958	6·3	13·0	18·4	42·6	0·2	15·8	11·7
1959	6·8	14·0	18·8	42·9	0·2	16·7	12·6
1960	7·3	14·7	19·7	45·4	0·2	18·3	12·9
1961	7·9	15·7	21·0	48·9	0·2	20·3	16·1
1962	8·4	17·9	23·0	50·9	0·2	21·7	17·7

governmental expenditures administered by the local governments. The CSO definitions were also followed in this case

Minor problems arose because the functional aggregates of the two sets of estimates did not correspond to the standard schema. Due to the availability of highly disaggregated data for both local [G79, various issues] and central [G76, various issues] governments, adjustments could be easily made.

C. *Subjective Evaluation*

Since two somewhat different sources of data were used as the bases of my estimates, certain small errors are introduced in reconciling these sources with the conceptual scheme of this study. Nevertheless I give a rating of 'B +' to the estimates in Table A–7.

D. *Sources of Data*

Unpublished estimates of Dr Alan Tait and Dr Martin O'Donoghue for 1950 through 1959 and other unpublished estimates of the Central Statistical Office for 1959 through 1962 served as the basic sources for my estimates.

E. *Notes on Individual Expenditures Estimates*

1. Gross expenditures include current expenditures on goods and services, subsidies, interest payments, transfers and net savings. The data come from [G17, p. 124] and [G12, January, 1965, p. 75].

2. The adjusted budget covers expenditures for administration, security, social purposes, and science. As the estimates for each category were made separately for the two levels of government, there were no difficulties in calculating the total adjusted expenditures for each.

3. Administration covers expenditures for general administration and for finance and tax collection. For 1959 through 1962 cso estimates are used. For the central government in the other years it was assumed that administration expenditures changed at the same rate as the sum of total expenditures to 16 most important administrative offices [G76, various issues]. For local government administrative expenditures (where the differences between the Tait–O'Donoghue and the cso estimates were not so great), it was assumed that the administrative expenditures according to the cso definition changed at the same rate as such expenditures according to the Tait–O'Donoghue definition in the years 1950 to 1958.

4. The cso and Tait–O'Donoghue estimates are practically the same and no adjustments for incomparability were made. Army pensions [G76, various issues] were removed and transferred to welfare expenditures.

5. Other external security cover expenditures for diplomacy and for 'international co-operation'. Data on expenditures of the Department of External Affairs and for international co-operation come from [G76, various issues].

6. The cso and Tait–O'Donoghue estimates are practically the same and no adjustments for incomparability were made.

7. Tait and O'Donoghué do not disaggregate expenditures for different social services and the CSO calculations were based on definitions different from those employed in this study; therefore, new estimates for education and health had to be made.

Data on different types of education expenditures for all levels of government combined are readily available from [G78, various issues, education section]. My estimates include expenditures for administration of education, primary and secondary schools, vocational schools, universities and colleges (including Department of Agriculture schools), and reformatory and industrial schools. Costs of preprimary education were removed from the data on primary schools; these were estimated by assuming that costs per child were the same in primary and pre-primary classes. Estimates were made for public expenditures to universities and colleges for 1950 to 1955 by extrapolation. In the calculation of education expenditures by level of government, use was made of data supplied by Martin O'Donoghue from his unpublished OECD report on education expenditures in Ireland.

8. Central government expenditures on health were estimated from data presented in [G76, various issues] with the careful removal of capital expenditures, grants to local agencies, grants to the social insurance system, etc. Data for local governmental expenditures on health as well as data on payments by the public for services from local health agencies come from [G79, various issues]. In this source the definitions used in the presentation of health and welfare expenditures were changed in 1955 in order to reflect more faithfully the purpose for which the funds were being used. Therefore, health expenditures for 1950–55 were estimated by assuming that the percentage of health expenditures in total payments for health and welfare remained at the same level as in the following years.

9. Welfare expenditures (including social insurance payments) were derived as a residual from the sum of expenditures for 'social services' plus army pensions after the removal of expenditures for education, health, culture, and science (excluding the national laboratories, which are not considered a social service). As discussed above, the CSO definition of local expenditures was used and a rough adjustment was made to make the Tait–O'Donoghue data comparable.

10. These are the sum of expenditures of the State Laboratory, the Institute of Advance Studies, and one-half of the expenditures in the budgetary category 'science and art'. All data come from [G76, various issues].

M*

11. Data from [G17, p. 124] and [G12, January, 1965, p. 75].
12. Data from [G17, p. 124] and [G12, January, 1965, p. 75].

APPENDIX A-9: ESTIMATES FOR ITALY

A. *Acknowledgments*

These estimates could not have been made without the very great co-operation of the Istituto Centrale di Statistica (ISTAT) in Rome and I would like to express my very great appreciation especially to Mr G. Barbaruto and Mr V. Siesto for their help. I would also like to thank Mr D. Tosato of the Società per la Matematica e l'Economia Applicate (SOMEA) for his constant aid and Mr Frillici of the Ministero del Tesoro who also supplied useful information.

B. *Main Problems*

There were four major estimation problems; none of these provided very great difficulties, however.

1. Although a functional breakdown of government expenditures for 1951 to 1965 has been published by ISTAT [G85, Supplement, March, 1966], these data cover only salaries; expenditures on goods, services, and rents; and amortization. The published data on transfers and subsidies [G85, May, 1966] are only presented as an aggregate and, therefore, they must be functionally divided. For different levels of government, different methods were used:

(*a*) Central government: data on the main transfer payments are published in [G83, various issues] and [G80, various issues] and it is clear that almost all should be assigned to social expenditures. An estimate was made of the few transfer expenditures under administration and the remainder was assigned to social expenditures.

(*b*) Social insurance institutions: a breakdown of transfer payments by function was obtained from ISTAT worksheets.

(*c*) Local governments: very detailed functional-economic data for local governments are available in [G84, various issues]. Although the definitions employed are different from those used in the national accounts, a key to the relationship between the definitions for the years 1959 through 1962 was supplied by ISTAT. Before 1959 the local accounts were less detailed and transfer payments are impossible to isolate on a functional basis. Therefore, it was assumed that the functional composition of the transfer payments were the same proportions as in the later years.

(*d*) Other central and local government institutions: ISTAT economic accounts for each institution were used to build up the estimates; the expenditures of each institution were wholly assigned to one function.

For subsidies a very conservative approach in estimating was followed. Only those subsidies whose functional purpose was definitely known were included which means that only a small volume of subsidies were incorporated into the estimates. The remainder of the subsidies were considered to cover economic purposes and were therefore excluded.

2. In the official statistics the public sector is defined quite broadly so that certain institutions, such as the Casse Mutue Aziendali were included. Although the inclusion of some such

TABLE A-8

Public Consumption Expenditures in Italy (Billion Lire)

| Year | Gross Budget[1] | Adjusted Budget[2] | | | Adminis- tration[3] | External Security | |
		Central	Local	Total		Military[4]	Other[5]
1950	n.a.	1,300	280	1,580	220	318	31
1951	2,662	1,524	307	1,831	254	366	30
1952	3,184	1,849	344	2,193	277	402	28
1953	3,560	2,030	374	2,404	287	403	31
1954	3,921	2,314	419	2,733	332	452	35
1955	4,368	2,530	480	3,010	375	450	34
1956	4,826	2,855	525	3,380	412	488	30
1957	5,186	3,009	570	3,579	430	487	36
1958	5,606	3,441	612	4,053	456	521	38
1959	6,129	3,724	665	4,389	477	534	39
1960	6,691	4,019	701	4,720	507	582	42
1961	7,189	4,368	756	5,124	552	612	45
1962	8,332	5,152	871	6,023	637	694	50

| Year | Social | | | | | Other | |
	Internal Security[6]	Education[7]	Health[8]	Welfare[9]	Science[10]	Interest[11]	Direct Invest- ment[12]
1950	134	190	199	485	3	n.a.	n.a.
1951	154	222	218	582	5	176	247
1952	176	264	240	798	8	212	319
1953	188	281	273	933	8	223	400
1954	202	308	309	1,086	9	299	475
1955	218	341	357	1,226	9	328	505
1956	231	387	425	1,396	11	368	498
1957	242	430	487	1,454	13	370	540
1958	265	484	519	1,756	14	359	586
1959	278	551	601	1,893	16	448	605
1960	295	615	639	2,018	22	481	682
1961	344	675	723	2,148	25	503	710
1962	367	867	841	2,534	33	544	757

institutions is open to debate, the ISTAT definitions were followed since the importance of such questionable cases is very small.

3. The official functional breakdowns of government expenditures go back only to 1951. Nineteen-fifty expenditures for each function were estimated for the different levels of government by assuming that the expenditures changed at the same rate as parallel series. For the central government and other central government institutions such series came from budgetary data ([G88, various years]); for social insurance, from [G83]; for local governments and other local government institutions, data from [G84].

4. The definitions employed to define the various functions in the official statistics do not correspond exactly to the definitions employed in this study. Although a number of adjustments could be made, these covered only the most major differences, since detailed data for the less important adjustments were not easily available.

C. *Subjective Evaluation*

Since the basic data are based on a GNP concept, rather than the expenditures concept used for most of the other countries in this study, a slight bias is introduced in the comparison. On the other hand, good data on a very dis-aggregative basis were available. Therefore, I give the estimates in Table A–8 a rating of 'B +'.

D. *Sources of Data*

Unless otherwise stated the data come from [G85, March, 1966, supplement] or from the unpublished worksheets of ISTAT.

E. *Notes on Individual Expenditure Estimates*

1. The data come from [G85, May, 1966, p. 195].

2. The adjusted budget covers expenditures for administration, security, social purposes, and science. Local governments include regions, provinces, and towns as well as other local government organizations such as the universities.

3. The original data were adjusted by removing expenditures for goods, services, and salaries for international affairs (from ISTAT worksheets) and adding the estimated transfer payments.

4. The original data exclude expenditures for the Carbiniere, an organization which serves many domestic police functions but which is militarily armed and also acts as a defence force. Since detailed data of expenditures of the Carbiniere for military and police functions are not available, one half of such expenditures (from

ISTAT worksheets) were arbitrarily assigned to defence. Military R and D expenditures were removed from defence expenditures.

5. These data are budgetary expenditures for international purposes (from various issues of [G80] and [G88] and include expenditures for goods, services, salaries, and transfers. Government foreign aid expenditures carried on outside the budget are not included, which means that the non-military external security expenditures are slightly understated in the early 1960s.

6. From the original data were removed one half of the expenditures of the Carbiniere (see note 4) and an estimate for fire protection expenditures. For 1962, fire protection expenditures are available from the planned budget [G87, 1962] but for other years, such data were not presented in the budget. Therefore, it was assumed that such expenditures remained a constant ratio of total expenditures for public security during the entire period, a crude assumption which does not introduce any major error because of the small relative magnitude of fire protection expenditures.

7. To the basic data were added estimated transfer payments; from these were removed science expenditures (see note 10). These estimates contain two known biases; certain transfer payments of local governments to private schools could not be estimated and were thus excluded; and certain expenditures for the purpose of encouraging culture could not be estimated and were thus included. It is hoped that these two biases cancel each other out. The inclusion of expenditures for pre-primary education is uncertain, although it is most likely that such expenditures were excluded and, therefore, no adjustment was made. Any error introduced at this point should be less than 3 per cent.

8. To the basic series were added estimated transfers.

9. To the basic series were added estimated transfers. These estimates contain two biases: certain transfer payments of local governments to private schools were included here, rather than in education, and certain subsidies are excluded because their exact functional purpose could not be determined. Hopefully these two biases cancel each other out.

10. Estimates for current science expenditures were made in three steps. First, the expenditures of the special independent science institutions (CNR, CNEN, INSC, INEA, CNP, etc.) were obtained from ISTAT worksheets. Second, estimates of science expenditures of Ministries were made in the following way. For 1963 data are available from the only official survey of science expenditures [G86, June, 1966]; for the other years science expenditures of the five

major ministries were taken from the budget [G81] and, when unavailable, [G87] and were assumed to constitute a constant fraction of total science expenditures. A more direct estimating procedure is not available since the budgetary accounts do not indicate intra-governmental payments for R and D and such flows are important. Finally, university expenditures on science were estimated in a rough fashion taking the following considerations into account. The university financial accounts understate R and D expenditures (a brief discussion of this point is given by [B185, pp. 53 ff.]). The official estimate of university science expenditures [G86, June, 1966] or the estimate by Alexandro Quaranta ('*La spesa, il co-ordinamenti e la programmazione della ricerca*', [B258, p. 13] both account for over 40 per cent of total expenditures of universities (ISTAT worksheets), which means that such expenditures are defined very broadly. To narrow the definition I have taken an estimate of current expenditures for pure research in universities ([G86, June, 1966], adjusted to remove capital) and have assumed that they remained a constant ratio of total university expenditures over the period. Such a method leaves much to be desired; unfortunately no other method is available.

11. Data from [G85, May, 1966, p. 195].

12. Data from [G85, May, 1966, p. 195].

APPENDIX A–10: ESTIMATES FOR POLAND

A. *Main Problems*

Although considerable amounts of data on Polish public expenditures have been published, several difficulties are encountered.

1. There have been a number of reclassifications of different types of budgetary expenditures. Although these changes have been carefully noted in the Polish economic literature, making the proper adjustments so that the various series are consistent, means that in certain cases, rather rough estimation procedures must be employed as the proper data are not available.

2. Data for 1950 which are comparable with data for 1951 and succeeding years are not available and must be estimated. The estimates for local governments were made from data on realized expenditures of these units [B99, pp. 159–61], data on the payments of the social insurance system [B99, p. 244], and from planned expenditures of the central government [G92, 16/1950] which were reclassified on an item by item basis according to the system used

in the later years. All 1950 data were converted into post-reform Złoty at a 100:3 ratio.

3. Although most budgetary data are reported net of sales to the public, it is apparent from examination of the detailed central government budget that some such receipts are included. Some of these receipts are given in [691, various issues]; most had to be estimated on the basis of ratios of such receipts to total expenditures of the central government in the plan for 1958 [G92, 16/1958]. Such revenues of local governments had to be ignored, although it is believed that they were very small. In addition, the financing of certain special extra-budgetary institutions is tricky [P27, XIV, 5/1963, trans. by J.P.R.S., 15809/1963] and it could be argued that

TABLE A–9

Public Consumption Expenditures in Poland (Million Złoty)

Year	Gross Budget[1]	Adjusted Budget[2]			Adminis-tration[3]	External Security	
		Central	Local	Total		Military[4]	Other[5]
1950	33,356	14,627	1,802	16,429	1,742	2,571	170
1951	51,650	18,454	4,378	22,832	3,772	3,544	221
1952	61,314	22,252	5,464	27,716	3,848	6,063	238
1953	96,345	31,526	7,601	39,127	4,928	9,792	255
1954	116,485	34,172	9,007	43,179	5,840	10,403	238
1955	123,194	38,419	9,959	48,378	6,577	11,907	271
1956	133,877	41,196	11,695	52,891	4,842	11,950	339
1957	153,929	42,620	15,904	58,524	5,658	9,684	457
1958	168,356	46,171	18,346	64,517	5,351	10,660	644
1959	182,516	51,620	22,081	73,701	5,171	13,472	473
1960	200,115	53,861	23,773	77,634	5,016	14,156	495
1961	233,521	57,430	27,124	84,554	4,793	16,233	785
1962	249,970	61,483	30,235	91,718	4,946	17,531	962

Year	Internal Security[6]	Social			Science[10]	Other Direct Investment[11]
		Education[7]	Health[8]	Welfare[9]		
1950	1,377	2,248	1,648	6,474	199	12,407
1951	1,907	3,355	2,909	6,785	339	19,387
1952	2,745	3,602	2,901	7,828	491	21,147
1953	3,597	5,262	4,174	10,451	668	28,115
1954	3,585	5,865	4,717	11,751	780	29,066
1955	3,937	6,514	5,389	12,846	937	30,934
1956	4,702	7,348	6,464	16,276	970	34,576
1957	4,550	8,584	7,995	20,321	1,275	40,012
1958	5,129	9,397	9,085	22,986	1,265	38,166
1959	5,657	10,685	11,323	25,514	1,406	47,856
1960	6,276	11,526	12,351	26,134	1,680	47,945
1961	6,625	12,471	14,082	27,746	1,819	57,392
1962	7,137	13,806	15,316	29,859	2,161	58,436.

public consumption expenditures are spent here. Nevertheless, the magnitudes have been so small that neglect of such expenditures does not bias the results to any appreciable extent.

4. Capital expenditures are not given for individual items in the reported realized expenditures data and had to be estimated by assuming that the ratios of current to capital expenditures were the same as in the plan. In the cases where plan data were not available, an average current/capital ratio was derived and used.

5. For certain years between 1951 and 1954, data for individual types of expenditures are not available, and had to be estimated from interpolations, aided by data on various larger aggregates.

B. *Subjective Evaluation*

In spite of the number of estimates which had to be made, the margin for error is small. I give the estimates in Table A–9 a rating of 'A –'.

C. *Sources of Data*

The main source of data was the national statistical yearbook [G91, various issues] (exclusively in the section on finance). This was supplemented by [B99] and other sources mentioned below.

D. *Prices Used*

The data are reported in post-1950 Złoty.

E. *Notes on Individual Expenditure Estimates*

1. The 1950 datum is only a rough estimate. There were a number of insurmountable estimation problems due to double accounting and to overfulfillment of the central governmental planned budget. Fortunately, the biases introduced from these two factors are offsetting.

2. The sum of expenditures for administration, security, social (education, health, and welfare) and science are included.

Since detailed data on a functional basis are not available for different levels of government, the following assumptions were made in these estimates: actual capital expenditures were distributed in the same way as in the plan: and two-thirds of cultural expenditures (which are included in the official data on social expenditures) were made on the local level.

3. From official Polish data on administration expenditures, expenditures on internal security, foreign affairs, and capital investment were removed.

4. Except for the removal of capital expenditures, no adjustments were made.

5. These include expenditures on foreign affairs and on foreign economic aid. Data on expenditures for foreign affairs were taken from the plans for 1950 and 1957 through 1962. Estimates for the missing years were made by a parabolic interpolation where it was assumed that the low point was reached in 1952 and was 60 per cent of the average expenditures in 1950 and 1957. Details on the foreign aid estimates are given in Appendix D-20.

6. All data are planned expenditures of the Ministry of Interior, all courts, and procurators.

7. These data were derived from the aggregative data on expenditures for education, vocational schools, and science and higher education, with expenditures for the following activities removed: preschools and kindergartens, children's reading rooms, children's culture houses, homes and rest homes for children, assistance to children, camps, and playgrounds (all to welfare); science (to science); science libraries and archives. Capital expenditure and payment for certain educational services were also removed.

8. Health expenditures estimates were derived from budgetary data on health and physical education and from data on sanitoria expenditures of the social insurance system. From these were removed expenditures for urban and rural nurseries (to welfare), sports and tourism.

9. These estimates were derived from aggregate data on expenditures for 'other social benefits' plus social insurance expenditures (excluding those placed in health), expenditures covering a variety of children's activities (from education), and nurseries (from health).

10. Science expenditures have been handled differently in the official data in three different periods. The data in Table A-9 are based on the widest definition and include current expenditures of the Academy of Science and related research institutes, other research on non-economic problems, research on economic problems, and central laboratories. This means that in the 1956–60 period, total expenditures on economic research and on the central laboratories [B99, p. 212] had to be added and in the 1961–62 period, non-budgetary funds from the Central Technology Funds for research in the central laboratories had to be added.

11. Investment data exclude capital repairs.

A. *Main Problems*

Data on expenditures from the major budgetary categories are readily available from [G93, various issues]. Unfortunately, a search of the Romanian economic literature yielded very little additional data and very little information about the content of the various budgetary categories or the concepts used in the expenditures statistics. Indeed, even the best sources of information on the Romanian budget [B259] and [B13] are excessively vague on such matters.

The major difficulty in analyzing the Romanian data is accounting for the unspecified residuals. The most important such residual occurs in the consolidated state budget between the total expenditures and the expenditures of the four major categories. This generally has amounted to less than 5 per cent of total expenditures, although in 1955 and 1956 this residual was over 10 per cent of total expenditures. In addition, there has been an unspecified residual in the local government expenditures, which has been larger than the unspecified residual in the consolidated expenditures since the late 1950s. Finally, there has also been a small unspecified residual within the socio-cultural expenditures.

Two reasonable explanations may be given for the unexplained residual in the consolidated budget: either these expenditures included reparations and payments for Soviet troops which the Romanians wanted to hide; or these expenditures cover certain types of security expenditures. Although reparation payments [B101, p. 192] are the approximate size of this residual in 1950 and 1951, such payments stopped at the end of 1951, while the residual continued to increase. Furthermore, the residual was larger in the early 1960s after Soviet troops had been withdrawn. Therefore, the first explanation does not seem to fit the facts.

If one compares an estimate of internal security expenditures (see footnote 7) to the residual and to the administration expenditures, one is struck by two readily apparent facts. The internal security expenditures are too large to be contained within administration and are, for most years, the approximate magnitude of the residual. The two years in which the budget residual was very much larger than the estimate of internal security expenditures occurred in the two years following the sale of the Soviet share of the Soviet–Romanian mixed corporations to Romania. Therefore, the second explanation of the consolidated budget residual seems reasonable.

The unexplained residual in the local government expenditures is due to the fact that certain major categories of expenditures, such as administration and investment are not reported. The unexplained residual in the socio-cultural expenditures must remain a mystery.

One other major problem concerns the concepts which are used in the reported statistics. From a comparison of data presented by Craiu [P73, 1/1961] of budgetary expenditures specifically excluding capital expenditures and expenditures data from [G93], it is clear that the data in the latter source also exclude such capital expenditures. Furthermore, the published data also exclude the extra-budgetary expenditures which, according to [B259, Chpt. 7] are financed by entrance fees, sales to the public, fines, and penalties. Since the services financed by such extra-budgetary revenue are

TABLE A–10

Public Consumption Expenditures in Romania (Billion Lei)

Year	Gross Budget[1]	Adjusted Budget[2] Central	Adjusted Budget[2] Local	Adjusted Budget[2] Total	Administration[3]	External Security Military[4]	External Security Other[5]
1950	19·073	7·294	1·634	8·928	1·438	3·246	·069
1951	21·707	8·482	1·779	10·261	1·183	4·365	·070
1952	28·988	9·194	2·140	11·334	1·047	5·135	·070
1953	35·638	10·319	2·518	12·837	1·449	5·276	·070
1954	38·352	8·921	2·809	11·730	1·285	3·717	·074
1955	42·916	10·037	3·320	13·357	1·294	4·227	·123
1956	41·934	10·616	3·786	14·402	1·401	3·984	·124
1957	43·854	12·637	4·352	16·989	1·374	3·817	·166
1958	44·689	12·487	4·759	17·246	1·412	3·597	·197
1959	48·299	12·973	5·280	18·253	1·443	3·446	·180
1960	55·522	13·937	6·103	20·040	1·564	3·392	·130
1961	63·813	15·214	6·979	22·193	1·673	3·639	·122
1962	73·186	16·778	7·946	24·724	1·825	3·924	·136

Year	Internal Security[6]	Social Education[7]	Social Health[8]	Social Welfare[9]	Science[10]	Other Direct Investment[11]
1950	·800	1·332	·644	1·251	·148	n.a.
1951	·840	1·682	·720	1·225	·176	5·99
1952	·920	1·936	·769	1·271	·186	11·23
1953	1·000	2·296	·965	1·544	·237	14·38
1954	1·100	2·141	1·363	1·798	·252	10·18
1955	1·223	2·196	1·798	2·189	·307	9·27
1956	1·346	2·446	1·962	2·786	·353	9·71
1957	1·364	2·717	2·251	4·881	·419	9·11
1958	1·380	2·771	2·530	4·882	·477	9·23
1959	1·487	2·971	2·772	5·432	·522	10·86
1960	1·558	3·496	2·955	6·311	·634	13·49
1961	1·629	4·244	3·356	6·836	·694	n.a.
1962	1·700	4·995	3·824	7·474	·846	22·50

directly related to the source of such revenues, there was no need to estimate any extra-budgetary expenditures. However, there are also expenditures of certain para-fiscal institutions which are not reported. For instance, in 1959–62 certain expenditures for sport and physical culture were financed through such an institution. In this one case I have made estimates for these three years; other cases are not known but are presumably of very small importance.

B. *Subjective Evaluation*

Because of the paucity of information about the meaning of the published data, I give estimates in Table A–10 a 'C' rating.

C. *Sources of Data*

Unless otherwise stated all data come from [G93, 1963, pp. 408–9].

D. *Prices Used*

Data are presented in post-1952 lei.

E. *Notes on Individual Expenditure Estimates*

1. Romanian public data omit sport expenditures financed through the national lottery in the 1959–62 period. For consistency these were estimated and added in.

2. All security expenditures were assumed to be financed on the central government level. Data on local government expenditures for administration and for culture (to be removed from socio-cultural expenditures) are not available and had to be estimated. I assumed that the ratio of local to central government administrative expenditures were similar to those in Bulgaria and that two-thirds of the expenditures on culture were made by local governments.

3. Expenditures on diplomacy (see footnote 5) were removed from the published data.

4. The published data most likely contain expenditures of the militarized security troops for two reasons: the main budgetary residual is covered by internal security expenditures (see above); and the Romanian equipment/soldier ratios seem more consistent with the results of the other countries if this assumption is made. Two peculiar features about Romanian military expenditures must be noted. The non-personnel expenditures are quite high *vis-à-vis* total military expenditures for most of the 1950s and I strongly suspect that certain payments for Soviet troops are included in the military expenditures. Second, the published datum for 1955 is considerably out of line (too high) with the 1954 and 1956 data,

although the numerical size of the armed forces was similar. The purchase of certain militarily important stocks from the SovRom companies might have been included in this year and have caused this sudden increase.

5. Diplomatic expenditures were estimated by assuming that the ratio of such expenditures to the net material product was the same as in Poland. The derived series was then smoothed by use of moving averages. Estimates of foreign aid expenditures are discussed in Appendix D-20.

6. A preliminary estimate for law and justice expenditures was made by assuming that the ratio of such expenditures to the net material product was the same as the average for each year in Hungary and Poland. The resultant series was slightly larger than the major budgetary residual and was therefore adjusted downward so that the final results were slightly smaller than the budgetary residual.

7. Since the official data are lower than the estimates for education expenditures excluding kindergartens which are reported in the unpublished UNESCO questionnaire covering the years 1957–59, no adjustments were made.

8. The official data are taken without adjustments.

9. Social expenditures include the published data on expenditures for social welfare, children's allowances, and social insurance plus one-half of the expenditures on physical education and sport and all of the unspecified social-cultural residual.

10. Science expenditures were estimated in two steps. From the number of scientists and science workers [G93, 1962, pp. 114–15] and from the average wage of workers and employees (derived from such a datum for 1956 [G29, August, 1956, p. 38] and an index of money wages [G93, 1964, p. 138] a wage fund for scientists was estimated. Then it was assumed that this estimated wage fund was only 60 per cent of total expenditures on science, not only to take into account expenditures on supplies but also the fact that scientists earn more than the average wage workers. The exact place in the budget where all such expenditures are financed is not known, although some science expenditures are financed through expenditures for culture. Nevertheless, an estimate of science expenditures from this source in 1951 (derived by comparing data on 'culture' from [B88, p. 544] and data on 'culture with science' from [G93]) is considerably less than the science expenditures which I have presented.

11. Data from 1951 through 1959 come from [B88, p. 541]; 1959

is a plan figure. The 1960 datum comes from ([P29, 7/1964] transl. JPRS 20404/1964), which also presents a figure of 9·30 for 1956. The figure for 1962 is a plan datum from ([P29, 2/1962], transl. JPRS 15776/1962).

APPENDIX A–12: ESTIMATES FOR THE USSR

A. *Acknowledgments*

I would like to thank Mr Daniel Gallik for several enlightening conversations about Soviet budgetary accounting and Dr Abraham S. Becker for not only answering my numerous requests for information but also criticizing my initial attempt at estimating military expenditures. Professor Alec Nove also gave me several very useful suggestions.

B. *Main Problems*

Two major problems arise in making estimates of the Soviet public consumption expenditures:

1. There are three different unexplained residuals within the budget which probably contain hidden military expenditures. A number of Western economists have expended considerable amounts of effort in analysing these residuals and I have based my estimates of such hidden military expenditures upon these previous studies.

2. There are two different kinds of extra-budgetary accounts. One type of such expenditures is made by enterprises, kolkhozy, and labour unions for the 'educational, social, and cultural needs of workers and employees' [G99, 1962, p. 690] and is reported in official statistical publications. Another type of extra-budgetary expenditure (discussed by [B5, pp. 418–21], [B193, pp. 182–86], and [B256, pp. 379–80] are social expenditures of 'budgetary institutions' which are financed by user fees and non-tax income (except, apparently, for the 'self-tax' in rural areas for certain school costs) and which are earmarked for special purposes. It is not known whether all of this second type of extra-budgetary expenditure is included in the published data on extra-budgetary expenditures or whether some such expenditures are included in the published data on budgetary expenditures. (This second hypothesis was suggested to me by Daniel Gallik who pointed out that data on certain types of budgetary expenditures may be collected from the bank accounts of 'budgetary institutions', where budgetary and extra-budgetary expenditures are sometimes not separated). I have assumed that all

extra-budgetary expenditures have been excluded from the published budgetary data and that all extra-budgetary expenditures have been entirely financed by non-tax income. On the basis of these assumptions the estimates were based solely on the published budgetary data with no adjustments to take into account any reported extra-budgetary expenditures.

C. Subjective Evaluation

Considerable published data on Soviet public consumptions are available, and in addition, many Western economists have explored quite thoroughly many aspects of these data. Although a number of estimates had to be made, especially in the area of security, I give the estimates in Table A–11 a rating of 'B'.

TABLE A–11

Public Consumption Expenditures of the USSR (Million New Rubli)

Year	Gross Expenditures[1]	Adjusted Expenditures[2]				Administration[3]	External Security	
		Local[2]	Republic[2]	Union[2]	Total		Military[4]	Other[5]
'50	41 323·7	5.087	1,516	18,296	24,899	1,300	10,482	937
'51	44,304·1	5,241	1,554	20,016	26,811	1,312	12,067	935
'52	46,020·8	5,382	1,592	21,665	28,639	1,341	13,685	846
'53	51,469·6	5,545	1,725	23,339	30,609	1,340	15,558	698
'54	55,386·7	5,601	1,884	23,095	30,580	1,242	14,434	728
'55	53,953·8	5,834	2,151	21,341	29,326	1,167	12,770	768
'56	56,348·1	6,310	2,688	22,476	31,474	1,131	13,020	1,024
'57	60,731·5	6,879	4,533	20,442	31,854	1,113	10,018	1,013
'58	64,275·0	7,305	5,163	22,061	34,529	1,114	11,588	908
'59	70,399·1	7,909	6,530	22,867	37,306	1,034	13,126	862
'60	73,126·2	8,569	8,303	21,414	38,286	1,013	12,557	832
'61	76,300·0	9,439	9,761	23,886	43,086	1,020	14,782	1,042
'62	82,200·0	10,167	11,086	24,680	45,933	1,018	15,842	1,080

Year	Internal Security[6]	Social			Science[10]	Other	
		Education[7]	Health[8]	Welfare[9]		Interest[11]	Capital[12]
1950	1,053	3,671	1,929	5,037	490	194	n.a.
1951	1,053	3,805	1,972	5,162	505	262	n.a.
1952	1,009	3,954	2,033	5,254	517	331	n.a.
1953	742	4,132	2,185	5,376	578	445	n.a.
1954	743	4,446	2,637	5,723	627	494	n.a.
1955	696	4,580	2,796	5,784	765	543	n.a.
1956	711	4,695	3,161	6,778	954	619	11,840
1957	750	4,801	3,392	9,521	1,246	235	12,960
1958	769	4,844	3,604	10,184	1,518	185	14,270
1959	790	5,006	3,863	10,854	1,771	345	16,370
1960	809	5,310	4,174	11,515	2,076	350	18,060
1961	842	5,961	4,292	12,765	2,382	400	19,500
1962	871	6,462	4,254	13,734	2,672	400	19,700

D. *Source of Data*

The major sources of information are: [G94, p. 7], [G95, pp. 18–19], [G96], [G97], and [G99, various issues]. These are supplemented by the sources discussed below.

E. *Prices Used*

All data are given in post-1961 rubli.

F. *Notes on Individual Expenditure Estimates*

1. Data come from major sources of information listed above.

2. Local expenditures cover those of all government units below the republics (including the ASSRS). Two types of estimates had to be made for these calculations. The distribution of capital expenditures between various levels of government (which were removed) were made by taking data on capital expenditures on a disaggregative basis and assuming that the ratios of current to capital expenditures were the same for all levels of government for that specific function. Estimates were also made of the distribution of administrative and social expenditures between republic and local governments from 1958–60 and 1960–62 respectively by extrapolating the ratio of distribution of these expenditures between these two levels of government.

3. The basic data for administrative expenditures come from the sources cited above. From these were removed expenditures for 'the maintenance of the organs of justice' and capital investment. Data for expenditures for the organs of justice are given for 1950–55 in [G94] and range from 46 mil. R to 48 mil. R. For 1956–58 these expenditures were estimated as 48 mil. R; for 1959–62, 49 mil. R; and for 1962, 50 mil. R. Capital expenditures were estimated at 3 per cent of the total administrative expenditures on all levels.

4. The published data on defence expenditures are supposedly the expenditures of the Ministry of Defence and include, according to Soviet sources (e.g. [B6, p. 310]) monetary pay of Soviet armed forces, procurement of military supplies, military construction, maintenance of military institutions, and other military requirements (see also [B30, p. 4]). Several points are worth noting:

(a) There is no certainty that all of the expenditures of the Ministry of Defence are included. For instance, those portions of it which are related to the administrative costs of the Ministry could have been assigned to 'government administration', etc. (This point is discussed in some detail in [B114, pp. 68–9]). However, it is highly unlikely that such expenditures are very large.

(b) Military expenditures by other agencies have probably not been included in the data. For instance one economist [B30, p. 10] points out that Soviet discussions of the contents of military expenditures do not seem to mention military research and development, military stockpiling, civil defence, foreign military aid, space activities or atomic energy activities. Since many of such expenditures are excluded from the definition for military expenditure used throughout this study, this means we can avoid making certain highly speculative estimates which others (esp. Sosnovy, [P31, April, 1964]) have made.

(c) If we reject the hypotheses that defence expenditures have been put under other categories or have been kept out of the budget and covered by hidden revenues ([B30, pp. 2–4] gives convincing evidence against these hypotheses), then the only place for concealment of military expenditures are the unexplained budget residuals of which there are three. The analysis of these residuals has been pioneered by [B30] and (Godaire [G132]) and I am following very closely the method of the former.

The 'budgetary expenditures residual' (BER) is obtained by subtracting all the major categories of expenditures (administration, defence, socio-cultural, financing the national economy, and debt service) from the total. However, this residual contains three items which must further be removed, namely the BER of the republic and local budgets, grants to investment banks, and expenditures for the police and secret police. Data for the BERs of republic and local governments come from [G94] and [G95]; data for police and secret police are explained in footnote 6; data for grants to investment banks come from [B30, p. 8] for 1955–62 and were estimated to 1950 by extrapolation. The republic and local BERs were adjusted in 1960 and thereafter to take into account the police expenditures which were transferred to this portion of the budget at that time.

The 'national economy residual' (NER) is obtained by removing all published parts of the budget category 'financing the national economy' (namely expenditures for industry and construction, agriculture, machine tractor stations, transportation, communications, trade, and communal economy) from the total. In addition, certain known procurement subsidies must also be removed; these include subsidies for agricultural procurement and accounting subsidies for procurement from state enterprises. Data for calculating the unadjusted FNE residual come from [G94] and [G95], with expenditures on trade and communal economy for certain years estimated by interpolation. Data on agricultural procurement for 1950 to 1954 come from [B149, p. 213]; for 1955–60 from [B30, p. 14]. Data on subsidies to procurement from state enterprises for 1955–60 come from [B30, p. 14]; data for 1950–54 were estimated by extrapolation. Since data past 1960 are not available, the unidentified FNE residual had to be extrapolated for 1961 and 1962.

The 'industry and construction residual' (ICR) is contained within the industry and construction expenditures which are within the major budgetary category 'financing the national economy'. Information concerning the components of this item is very limited and somewhat different estimates of this residual have been made by different Western economists. I have used the estimates of [B30, p. 16] for 1955–60. Since data for estimates for 1950–55 are not available, this residual for these years was estimated by taking the average ratio of the residual to military expenditures and assuming that it was the same during the previous years. A similar procedure was followed in estimating the residual for 1961 and 1962.

The remaining residuals yields a sum ranging from about 50 per cent to 100 per cent of total published military expenditures. The next problem is determining what part of this combined residual represents hidden military expenditures for procurement and stockpiling. Arbitrarily I assumed one-half of the combined residual to be such hidden military expenditure, a procedure similar to that followed by [B30]. Evidence that this estimate is within the proper range of magnitude for certain hidden military expenditures is presented by [B30]. It must also be noted that the derived hidden expenditures item plus estimates of equipment expenditures within the published data are broadly consistent with estimates of military equipment production which have been calculated by much different methods (e.g. see the comments on this by [B30, sections 3 and 4]; and the data of Boretsky [G132, p. 104]).

There is some evidence that the results for 1961 and 1962 might be high since a certain amount of hidden military expenditures might have 'surfaced' during those years. Such evidence, however, is disputable [B30, pp. 50 ff.] and, in a completely different context, is partially refuted by Thornton [P86, September, 1964]). Without more information, it is impossible to resolve this debate; nevertheless, the evidence does not seem sufficient enough to require the adjustment of my data for those two years.

Three other adjustments were made to the derived military expenditures series (published data plus estimates of hidden expenditures). First, military pensions (data from [B149, p. 177], [B240, p. 119], and [B31, p. 170]) were removed and transferred to social expenditures. Second, 5 per cent of the remaining military expenditures were estimated to be capital expenditures and were removed. This was the approximate percentage of such expenditures in total military expenditures in the US. Finally, an estimate of border guards and internal security troops was added. These expenditures were made in the following way:

According to [P58, 1963–64] there were 300,000 security and border troops in 1963 and according to [P92, various years] security and border troops numbered 400,000 from 1955 to 1959 and 350,000 from 1960 to 1964. Alec Nove has pointed out to me that such estimates are also consistent with budget data and data from the Soviet 1959 census of occupations. For lack of other information I have assumed that such security personnel numbered 300,000 through the entire period, that their wages were the same as the average industrial wages, and that non-personnel expenditures amounted to thirty per cent of total expenditures.

5. Estimates for other external security expenditures were made in three parts:

(*a*) The estimates for expenditures for foreign aid payments are discussed in Appendix D–20.

(*b*) The expenditures for diplomacy were estimated as three-fourths of the US diplomacy costs, converted into roubles at the official exchange rate.

(*c*) Foreign intelligence expenditures not included in the military budget (i.e. other than military espionage carried out by the GRU, which is a branch of the armed forces) was estimated in the following way. In January 1960 the Ministry of Internal Affairs (MVD) was abolished at the Union level and was replaced by the republican Ministries for the Preservation of Public Order (MOOP). The unspecified BER of the republic and local governments increased in that year by 650 mil. R, compared to the increases in the residual of 64 mil. R in 1959. Assuming that MOOP expenditures represented 600 mil. R in this increase means that remaining secret police expenditures amounted to about 1100 mil. R (for total police and secret police estimate, see footnote 7). Since the other organ of police expenditures are contained in this amount, (the Committee for State Security (KGB) has had both internal and external functions which are described respectively by [B184, pp. 251 ff.] and [B124]) there is the problem of assigning expenditures to each function. Arbitrarily, I assumed that one-half of KGB expenditures went to external intelligence activities, which, in turn, amounted to about 30 per cent of the total assumed police and secret police expenditures. This percentage was used to derive a very rough estimate of KGB espionage expenditures in all other years.

6. The expenditures for 'maintenance of the organs of justice' (described in footnote 4) seem to cover only the costs of the courts and the procuracy, if the clues provided by [B184] are correctly interpreted. The expenditures for police and secret police were estimated in the following manner.

Data in the 1949 Soviet budget can be used to estimate outlays of the Ministry of Internal Affairs and the Ministry of State Security for that year. Moreover, from a number of isolated statements and pronouncements, a fair notion of the trend of these expenditures can be deduced until 1955. For these years, therefore, I have used the estimates of [B149, pp. 172–5]. For the succeeding years I assumed that the aggregate amount of expenditures rose at the same rate as average industrial wages ([G129, p. 66] and [G99, 1962, p. 485]), i.e. that the number of personnel in the police units remained about the same. From the total police and secret police expenditures, a certain amount for foreign espionage (see footnote 6) and security troops (see footnote 5) was deducted.

7. Education includes expenditures for general, trade, and vocational schools, adult education classes, colleges and universities, and other special schools. Official data on education were adjusted to exclude expenditures on R and D, cultural-enlightenment measures, theatres, museums, radio broadcasting, press and publishing, clinics attached to higher institutions of learning, pre-school education of children, children's homes, orphanages, child receiving centres, and institutions for supervision and work with children outside of schools.

Detailed data for most of the relevant categories are from [G97] and [G99, various years]. For the latter years data for several of the categories are not available and were estimated on an individual basis by extrapolation, using as guidelines series on similar expenditures.

Capital expenditures for the years 1950–57 are available in [G97] and, since the ratios of capital to current expenditures were relatively stable, such ratios were used to estimate capital expenditures for the remaining years on an individual expenditures basis whenever possible.

8. The Soviet budgetary data on health include expenditures for hospitals and dispensaries, medical centres and feldscher centres in

enterprises, emergency medical centres, blood centres, tuberculosis and other sanitaria, etc. To these were added expenditures for clinics attached to higher institutions of learning (from 'education') as well as social insurance payments directly related to health care (e.g. expenditures for health resorts, etc.). From budgetary health expenditures were removed expenditures on nursery schools and infant homes.

Capital expenditures were estimated in the same way as for education.

9. Welfare includes expenditures on kindergartens, children's homes, child receiving centres, supervision and work with children outside of schools, nursery schools, infant homes, support of single mothers, social insurance payments (except those for health care), social welfare, and military pensions (see footnote 5). Capital expenditures were estimated and removed in the same way as for education.

10. Data on budgetary R and D expenditures are readily available from the sources cited above. Some of the difficulties in interpreting these data as well as convincing evidence that not all military R and D are included here are presented by [B182, pp. 199–228]. Capital expenditures were estimated in the manner outlined for education.

11. The category 'debt service' in the Soviet budget includes interest payments on the state debt, repayment of this debt, and certain expenditures of the state lottery. The data on debt service vary somewhat among Soviet sources (e.g. data from the sources cited by [B151, p. 331] and [B149, p. 97] differ in certain years from the data in [G99, various years]) and probably such discrepancies are due to definitional differences among the various sources although the situation is not entirely clear.

My series was based primarily on the data from [G99, various issues], supplemented by interpolations and additional data from [B240]. The interest portion of the debt service was estimated from the rough rule of thumb devised by [B149, p. 84] for the period 1950–56. Following a partial cancelling of the debt and a suspension of most debt repayment, the 'debt service' expenditure fell drastically in 1957 and, lacking any more concrete information, I have arbitrarily assumed that the interest component amounted to 50 per cent of total 'debt service' expenditures from 1957–62.

12. Data were estimated from scattered sources.

APPENDIX A-13: ESTIMATES FOR THE UNITED STATES

A. *Acknowledgments*

I would like to thank Allen D. Manvel, Lynden Mannen, and Howard S. Ryan, all of the Bureau of the Census, for their assistance in using the data from the Census Bureau calculations of government expenditures and for the use of their unpublished worksheets. Also I would like to express my appreciation to Jacob Perlman, Kathryn Arnow, and Jane E. Pugh, all of the National Science Foundation, for use of unpublished data.

B. *Main Problems*

Although considerable data are available on public expenditures at various levels of government, there are several difficulties:

1. The various data on US government expenditures are quite different since they are compiled using different definitions by a number of agencies. My estimates are primarily based on the data of the US Bureau of the Census because the Census concepts are closer to those used in this study than any other estimates and because such data are available at a greater level of disaggregation for state and local governments than in any other source.

2. The basic data come in an aggregated form and adjustments were difficult to make in some cases. On the federal level where highly disaggregated data from other sources are available (e.g. [G101]), the Census data could be fairly accurately recast to fit the definitions used in this study, but for state and local government expenditures only the most important adjustments could be made. Little error should be introduced in this way, however.

3. Data on capital expenditures or sales to the public are not available for certain types of expenditures in several years. These were estimated by interpolating or extrapolating ratios of these to expenditures for other years.

4. Certain welfare and central bank expenditures, which are normally part of public consumption expenditures in other countries, are not included in the public sector in the USA. For comparability, payments of the Workmen's Compensation system of non-public carriers and administration expenditures of the Federal Reserve System were added to the estimates of public consumption expenditures.

5. The Census estimates are not geographically consistent since state and local government expenditures of Alaska are included in the second half of 1958 and succeeding years; and for Hawaii, in

BLE A–12

Public Consumption Expenditures of the USA (Million Dollars)

Year	Gross Budget[1]	Adjusted Budget				Adminis-tration[3]	External Security	
		Federal	State[2]	Local[2]	Total		Military[4]	Other[5]
0	70,234	30,153	6,598	8,292	45,043	1,899	13,805	3,478
1	84,823	42,998	6.321	8,894	58,213	2,082	26,947	3,884
2	101,759	56,410	6,400	9,683	72,493	2,252	38,298	4,872
3	107,294	57,604	7,026	10,533	75,163	2,318	38,554	5,164
4	107,340	53,272	7,834	11,579	72,685	2,278	34,502	4,356
5	109,281	52,335	7,993	12,427	72,755	2,359	32,104	3,883
6	116,383	55,354	8,420	13,653	77,427	2,552	33,392	3,691
7	125,586	58,884	9,904	15,193	83,981	2,750	34,704	3,472
8	135,493	62,571	11,498	16,701	90,770	2,856	35,490	3,708
9	143,522	65,468	12,013	18,100	95,581	3,100	35,452	3,512
0	152,774	68,272	12,926	19,862	101,060	3,431	35,200	3,122
1	165,070	73,589	14,008	21,690	109,287	3,986	37,300	3,060
2	175,456	79,382	14,631	23,194	117,207	4,631	39,394	3,280

Year	Internal Security[6]	Social				Other	
		Education[7]	Health[8]	Welfare[9]	Science[10]	Interest[11]	Direct Inv.[12]
0	1,560	7,228	2,241	12,780	2,052	4,794	9,889
1	1 731	6,962	2,506	11,717	2,384	4,770	12,012
2	1 881	6,806	2,701	12,407	3,276	5,146	12,798
3	2,027	7,065	2,823	13,784	3,428	5,496	13,180
4	2,184	7,666	2,964	15,637	3,098	5,600	14,152
5	2,364	8,626	3,180	16,954	3,285	5,990	14,190
6	2,566	9,468	3,494	18,454	3,810	6,450	14,724
7	2,803	10,360	3,730	21,628	4,534	6,982	16,188
8	3,082	11,246	4,066	25,102	5,220	7,160	17,420
9	3,341	12,065	4,452	27,113	6,546	8,146	17,857
0	3,603	13,193	4,861	29,459	8,191	9,320	18,494
1	3,842	14,140	5,350	32,139	9,470	9,241	19,553
2	4,069	15,134	5,885	34,016	10,798	9,754	20,338

the second half of 1959 and succeeding years. Since these two new states accounted for an extremely small part of total US public consumption expenditures, it was not felt that the benefits of estimating such expenditures back to 1950 would outweigh the costs, and, therefore, no adjustments have been made.

C. *Subjective Evaluation*

Although a number of estimates had to be made, I give the data in Table A–12 a rating of 'A'.

D. *Sources of Data*

The primary source of data was 'Historical Statistics on Governmental Finances' [G105]. This was supplemented for almost all categories by various issues of [G101], [G107], [G108], [G113], and [G117]. In addition, unpublished data from the worksheets of the Governments Division of the US Census Bureau were used, although the Census Bureau takes no responsibility for their accuracy or use in my estimates. Finally, for several categories additional sources, which are noted below, were employed.

E. *Notes of Individual Expenditure Estimates*

1. Gross expenditures include general and insurance trust expenditures, and exclude expenditures of government corporations, utilities, and liquor stores.

2. Expenditure of Washington, DC, are considered as local expenditures.

3. Administration includes expenditures from the following categories: financial administration, general control, and 'other and unallocable'. To these were added current expenditures of the Federal Reserve System (from [G135, various issues]). From these were removed expenditures for the following functions and services: selective service (to external security); prisons, administration, unemployment and employment compensation for federal employees, Indian Tribal funds, and veterans expenditures not elsewhere classified (to social expenditures); research and development libraries, (to science); and cultural facilities and miscellaneous commercial activities (fully removed).

4. Military includes expenditures for military functions, atomic energy, and defence related activities (stockpiling and expansion of defence production, including defence activities of the RFC). To these were added expenditures for selective service; from these were removed all expenditures for military pensions (to welfare) and for research and development. It should be noted that defence related activities of state and local governments (national guard, civil defence, and armoury activities) are classified under administration.

5. Other external security includes expenditures for foreign aid (military, economic, and financial assistance) and for foreign affairs. From these were removed expenditures for research and development.

6. Internal security include expenditures for local and state police, prisons, pardon, probation and parole activities, administration of justice, and protective inspections and enforcement of administrative regulations on all levels. (On the federal level these include most of the expenditures classified by the Budget Bureau as 'regulation of commerce and finance').

7. Education includes expenditures for the provision and support of schools, colleges, and other educational facilities and services except agricultural experimental stations and agricultural extension services. All expenditures for research and development, state expenditures for non-school libraries (which are included in the Census category for education from 1950 to 1959) and expenditures for kindergartens were removed. Kindergartens expenditures were estimated from the number of kindergarten teachers, the average wages of teachers, and the assumption that total kindergarten expenditures were 130 per cent of the total wages of kindergarten teachers. Data for all of these came from [G122, various issues] and [G116, various issues]. The number of kindergarten teachers was estimated by assuming that the pupil/teacher ratio was the same for kindergartens as for all primary school grades.

8. Health includes expenditures for hospitals, clinics, nursing, immunization, and other categorical, environmental, and general public health activities, From these, research and development expenditures were removed.

9. Welfare includes expenditures for: public welfare (both cash assistance payments and vendor payments, as well as expenditures of all welfare institutions and programmes), government insurance trusts (including social security payments), and veteran payments not elsewhere classified. Expenditures from the President's Disaster Relief Funds and the Indian Tribal Funds (administered by the Department of Interior) and expenditures for military pensions, unemployment and employment compensation for federal employees (administered by the Department of Labour), kindergartens (see footnote 7) and social security administration were added. (The latter were estimated for the period 1950–56 from administration costs/trust expenditure ratios derived from the later period.) Finally, workmen's compensation payments of private carriers were added. Expenditures for research and development in all these categories were removed.

10. Total federal expenditures for research and development come from [G136, Vol. XII]. An adjustment for D T and E support from military procurement appropriations before fiscal 1954 and another adjustment for pay and allowance of military personnel in R and D before fiscal year 1953 were made to make the data comparable for all years. (These adjustments were carried out partly on the basis of ratios of these expenditures to other components of military R and D and partly on the basis of unpublished information supplied by the NSF). Estimates of the R and D activities financed

N

by different federal government agencies but carried out by educational institutions (and thus classified as education by the Bureau of the Census) were made on the basis of data on federal obligations presented in [G136, various issues] and [G137, various issues]. State government expenditures for R and D are not available for any year and were estimated in the following way: In [G136] data on R and D expenditures are presented for fiscal year 1954 for California, Connecticut, New Mexico, New York, North Carolina, and Washington. These are classified under four major headings and from [G108, 1954] the total expenditures of the six states for these categories were obtained. Ratios of R and D expenditures in total expenditures in each category were calculated and it was assumed that these ratios were the same for all states for the period 1950 through 1962. City government R and D expenditures were assumed to be zero. Sales of R and D services by state universities were assumed to be one half of R and D expenditures financed by industry in *all* universities [G116, 1965, p. 545].

11. Interest expenditures include all interest except that paid on debts of local utilities.

12. These are total capital outlay expenditures [G105, VI, No. 4, p. 50] excluding military equipment and purchase of land and existing structures (est. from [G117, various issues]).

APPENDIX A–14: ESTIMATES FOR WEST GERMANY

A. *Acknowledgments*

I would like to thank Mr Weyershaeuser and Dr Freund of the Statistisches Bundesamt, the Bundesministerium fuer Arbeit und Sozialordnung, and the Bundesministerium der Finanzen for supplying information used in the making of these estimates. In an interview, Dr Freund also provided a number of very useful suggestions for these calculations.

B. *Main Problems*

West Germany has, without doubt, the most extensive published statistics on public expenditures in the world. Therefore, the main problems arose in the manipulation of the data, rather than the estimation of different series. Four major sets of difficulties were encountered:

1. Since public expenditures for the Saar are not available for most of the 1950s, local expenditures from this area are excluded

from the estimates for all years. However, expenditures for West Berlin are included for all years.

2. The expenditures of the 'Zweckverbaende' raised some conceptual problems. For comparability I included only budgetary transfers to these organizations as public consumption expenditures.

3. Integrating the social insurance expenditures into the budgetary accounts required elimination of double accounting of expenditures financed by transfers from various levels of government to the social insurance agencies. In addition, social insurance expenditures for West Berlin had to be estimated for the period 1950 through 1953. With the available data such matters did not prove difficult to overcome.

BLE A–13

lic Consumption Expenditures in West Germany (*Million DM-West*)

| ar | Gross Budget[1] | Adjusted Budget[2] | | | | External Security | | | |
		Central	Land	Local	Total	Administration[3]	Foreign Troops[4]	Military[5]	Other[6]
0	34,543	14,696	5,662	3,873	24,231	1,643	4,580	0	209
1	42,610	22,414	3,900	3,981	30,295	1,907	7,132	30	201
2	49,129	25,932	4,283	4,457	34,672	2,203	7,900	55	349
3	54,355	26,504	4,793	5,099	36,396	2,478	6,117	72	540
4	59,259	27,553	5,080	5,661	38,294	2,669	5,775	104	717
5	63,170	29,888	5,744	6,181	41,813	2,810	5,938	211	1,016
6	71,403	33,002	6,794	7,251	47,047	3,130	4,418	2,500	1,639
7	82,910	39,403	7,808	7,994	55,205	3,442	2,556	4,495	2,308
8	92,527	45,488	8,477	8,394	62,359	3,661	1,150	6,624	2,540
9	100,242	48,333	8,954	8,398	65,685	3,711	591	7,530	2,878
0	109,915	52,038	10,071	8,854	70,963	3,994	523	8,519	3,367
1	124,546	58,566	11,358	9,716	79,640	4,533	319	10,353	5,595
2	141,054	67,035	12,296	10,845	90,176	4,898	327	13,718	4,383

| ar | Internal Security[7] | Social | | | | | Other | |
		Education[8]	Health[9]	Welfare[10]	Science[11]		Interest[12]	Investment[13]
0	1,098	1,815	2,424	12,288	174		552	2,288
1	1,315	2,174	2,864	14,475	197		694	2,813
2	1,509	2,555	3,301	16,579	221		767	3,321
3	1,685	2,969	3,606	18,676	253		947	3,794
4	1,807	3,287	3,829	19,828	278		1,189	4,186
5	1,912	3,573	4,245	21,797	311		1,320	5,093
6	2,117	4,010	4,808	24,024	401		1,434	6,087
7	2,340	4,457	5,508	29,573	526		1,512	6,414
8	2,543	4,984	6,229	33,924	704		1,692	7,573
9	2,568	5,208	6,823	35,552	824		1,857	9,171
0	2,755	5,650	7,552	37,543	1,060		2,143	11,202
1	3,069	6,440	8,412	39,101	1,818		1,985	13,306
2	3,318	7,087	9,544	45,236	1,665		2,246	16,452

4. Public expenditures of West Berlin for 1950 had to be integrated into the main government accounts. Although this required a number of small estimations, no difficult problems arose.

C. *Subjective Evaluation*

Although a number of small problems arose in the estimations, especially for non-military external security and R and D expenditures, the errors introduced should be very small. For the data in Table A–13 I give a rating of 'A'.

D. *Sources of Data*

The primary sources of data were publications of the Statistisches Bundesamt on public expenditures at different levels of government [G155, issue numbers 54, 56, 57, 58, 59, 88, 99, 117, 118, 138, 139, 163, 164, 192, 197, 216, 217, 227, 236, 237, 256, 257, and 259] and [G152, various issues].

These were supplemented for social insurance data by [G141, 1957, pp. 342–5; 1962, pp. 42–3; and 1964, pp. 199–204]. For special expenditures categories, additional sources noted below were utilized.

E. *Notes on Individual Expenditure Estimates*

1. These are 'immediate expenditures' of the budget and social insurance expenditures, with budgetary subsidies to the latter netted out.

2. The '*Stadtstaaten*' (Bremen, Hamburg, and West Berlin) are considered here as cities, rather than as Laender.

3. Administration includes expenditures for 'highest state organs', 'general internal administration' and 'financial administration'. Expenditures for diplomacy, Dienststelle Blank, and Bundesamt fuer Verfassungschutz, are removed (see footnotes 4, 6, and 7).

4. In the period before 1955, military expenditures include those for the border police and for Dienststelle Blank (the precursor of the Ministry of Defence). Beginning 1955 military expenditures include those for border police and for defence, with occupation costs, auxiliary occupation costs, and research and development expenditures removed. Data on expenditures for Dienststelle Blank come from [G150, 1961, p. 293]; for military R and D, from [B185, p. 42] and [G145, p. 149], with the missing years interpolated.

5. Occupation costs include both direct and auxiliary costs of occupation troops.

6. Other external expenditures include those for foreign affairs, current restitution to the Jews ('*Wiedergutmachung*'), loans and grants to foreign countries, and payments to international organizations. Data on payments to European international organizations, as well as data on expenditures of the Office of Foreign Affairs (for early years) come from unpublished materials supplied by the Statistisches Bundesamt and the Bundesministerium der Finanzen. Foreign aid expenditures up to 1959 come from [G144] and consist of grants and new (bilateral) public credits to the developing nations. (Multilateral foreign aid is included elsewhere.)

7. Internal security expenditures cover 'preservation of justice' (which includes courts and prisons) and 'the public maintenance of order (which includes costs of inspections and of tasks handled by the former 'Administration Police') and police. Police expenditures include those for the Alert Police and the Bundesamt fuer Verfassungsschutz, but exclude those for the Border Police. Data on expenditures for the Bundesamt fuer Verfassungsschutz come from unpublished data supplied by the Bundesministerium der Finanzen.

8. Education includes expenditures for schools, colleges and universities, and communal expenditures for colleges, all with expenditures for research and development removed. Communal expenditures for colleges are contained in communal expenditures for 'other science' and were arbitrarily assumed to constitute 50 per cent of these expenditures. R and D expenditures of the colleges and universities were assumed to amount to 25 per cent of total expenditures of these institutions (see footnote 11).

9. Health includes expenditures designated for this purpose (excluding physical education), health and accident insurance payments from the social insurance agencies for direct health care payments and expenditures of university clinics excluding an estimate of R and D expenditures. The R and D expenditures were estimated as a constant ratio of these expenditures; the base year for the ratio is 1962 for which data are available [G145, p. 143].

10. Welfare includes expenditures for 'social purposes' and for physical education as well as all payments of the social insurance agencies except those included under health.

11. Data on expenditures for research and development are not isolated in the West German data and were estimated in the following way: The expenditure category 'other science' includes not only expenditures on research and development, but also on libraries and archives, conservatories, communal payments to colleges, and

several other cultural items. Expenditures for archives and libraries and estimated communal payments to colleges (see footnote 8) and for cultural purposes were removed; and R and D expenditures from the military sector (see footnote 5) and from colleges and universities (see footnote 10) were added. Cultural expenditures contained within 'other science' were estimated to be 3 per cent of total expenditures of this category.

There are two independent estimates for government science expenditures with which my estimates can be compared. The most commonly cited science expenditures data [B313] were very crudely estimated and contain expenditures of colleges and universities as well. If these latter expenditures are removed, the data from [B313] are somewhat lower than my estimates, especially for the early years. The most thorough estimates are [G145, pp. 142–43] which, for 1962, are 19 per cent higher than mine after their data are adjusted to my definitions. Nevertheless, their estimates for R and D expenditures from colleges and universities constitute about 67 per cent of all expenditures of these institutions, which seems manifestly too high. If my estimate of R and D expenditures (25 per cent of total expenditures of these institutions) is substituted, then their estimates are 7 per cent lower than mine. Due to ambiguities in defining expenditures for science, I made no further adjustments to make my estimates more comparable with those of these other sources.

12. This includes not only interest within the formal budgetary classification for this purpose but also interest payments removed from all other expenditures in the budgetary accounts.

13. These data cover all budgetary categories.

APPENDIX A–15: ESTIMATES FOR YUGOSLAVIA

A. *Acknowledgments*

For supplying unpublished data on social expenditures and for a number of useful conversations concerning the Yugoslav public accounts, I would like to thank Dimitrije Dimitrijević of the Narodna banka, Vojan Konvalinka of the Zlužba drustvenog knjigovodstva, and Vuk Živadinović of the Savezni zavod za statistiku. I am deeply indebted to Jindřich Veverka of Leicester University for his generous aid in helping to devise the estimation procedures employed below. I also wish to thank Charles Rockwell for his assistance in understanding Yugoslav national accounts.

B. *Main Problems*
The Yugoslav public accounts are a statistical nightmare, and, for lack of sufficient information, a number of important uncertainties exist in interpretation of the data. Three major problems arise.

1. There are four different and conflicting primary sources of data on public expenditures. The most detailed data for the period are published by the Federal Institute of Statistics ([G163, various issues], [G164, No. 119], and [G165]). These estimates are not consolidated accounts, however, and, as far as I could determine, are calculated on an accrual rather than a cash basis. Data for the period published by the National Bank [G158, various issues] are quite close to the FIS data (the differences can be attributed mostly to the cash basis and the slightly different sectoring principle) but are so highly aggregated as to be unusable for the present study. A third set of estimates published by the Social Accounting Service (Vojan Konvalinka, 'Rashodi neprivrednih delatnosti', [G160, 11–12/1965, pp. 680–707]) cover the 1956–64 period and differ from the first two estimates in the following ways: they are in constant prices; only net wages and salaries are included (i.e. social insurance payments, income taxes, and other such items are removed); they are consolidated; and a different sectoring principle is employed. However, adjustments can be made so that they are quite similar to the FIS data. Finally, sets of consolidated accounts for all 'non-productive' organizations have been published [G164] and [G158, various issues] but only as far back as 1962. These two sources differ not only from each other but also include organizations which are not financed by tax revenues. The data for the period under examination which are published by the FIS were chosen as the basis of the estimates because they were sufficiently detailed to permit enough adjustments to be made to make the data comparable with those from other nations.

2. Consolidating the FIS data to estimate public consumption expenditures raised a number of difficulties since there are three sets of accounts to take into consideration, each of which is presented on a different basis. The accounts of the budgetary institutions, which include expenditures for social assistance ('*socijalna zastita*'), exclude investments, grants to other public organizations, and expenditures financed by sales to the public. There are no difficulties in using such data. The accounts of the 'social funds' (which included in the period under examination the social insurance funds, the school funds, and several minor health and social funds) include investments and payments to the 'independent institutions' (dis-

cussed below) and exclude sales to the public. Since investment expenditures of the funds can be easily removed (investments in welfare expenditures can be considered negligible; and a series of current education expenditures financed from the social funds are quite accessible), these data can be made comparable with the expenditures from the budgetary institutions. Finally, the published accounts of the independent institutions ('*samostalne ustanove*') include expenditure financed by sales to the public but exclude investments. On the revenue side of the accounts of these independent institutions, grants from the state budget are separated from the combined receipts from the 'social funds' and the sales to the public. The difficulty in using such data lies in the estimating (and excluding) the sales to the public.

Several methods of consolidating these three accounts are possible. The method chosen is by far the most simple. The current expenditures of the budgetary institutions and the estimated current ex-

TABLE A–14

Public Expenditures of Yugoslavia (Billion Dinari)

| | Adjusted Expenditures[1] | | | | External Security | |
Year	Central[2]	Local[2]	Total	Administration[3]	Military[4]	Other[5]
1952	200·1	147·0	347·1	20·7	183·4	1·5
1953	185·2	167·6	352·8	28·1	167·4	1·9
1954	185·2	197·2	382·4	37·1	162·7	2·2
1955	184·1	210·3	394·4	23·3	159·3	2·8
1956	184·9	240·6	425·5	24·1	158·5	3·4
1957	187·0	281·5	468·5	23·0	158·3	4·0
1958	214·6	325·6	540·2	29·7	178·5	4·6
1959	237·9	392·4	630·3	34·5	195·6	5·2
1960	262·0	477·9	739·9	45·4	207·7	5·9
1961	314·7	604·9	919·6	58·5	247·7	9·7
1962	356·9	739·0	1,095·9	61·0	270·1	14·2

| | | Social | | | | Other |
Year	Internal Security[6]	Education[7]	Health[8]	Welfare[9]	Science[10]	Direct Investment[11]
1952	10·4	13·2	21·2	94·2	2·5	20·
1953	13·1	14·8	25·9	98·2	3·4	14·
1954	18·7	23·8	34·5	99·2	4·2	93·
1955	23·8	28·4	41·8	109·3	5·7	28·
1956	31·5	33·4	49·6	117·7	7·3	23·
1957	40·6	39·7	62·6	132·1	8·2	19·
1958	46·4	50·1	73·2	146·5	11·2	29·
1959	56·0	60·9	92·0	173·3	12·8	41·
1960	60·2	72·1	125·2	204·7	18·7	61·
1961	71·6	103·8	155·2	247·4	25·7	63·
1962	82·6	158·9	163·5	309·4	36·2	54·

penditures of the social funds were combined with the grants to the independent institutions. To the extent that the independent institutions are financed by funds which do not come from the budget of the social funds (e.g. from the enterprises), the expenditures of the independent institutions are undervalued. However, as far as I could determine such additional financing was extremely small or non-existent.

3. Adjusting the FIS data to the concepts used in this study involved a number of difficult estimations. Although certain unpublished data could be obtained in the social field, the other estimates had to be made by rather rough statistical methods. No adjustments could be made to take into account that the basic data are on an accrual, rather than a cash basis.

4. Although some public consumption data are available for 1950 and 1951, they are not completely comparable with the data for the later years. In addition, it can be argued that Yugoslavia did not really become a market economy until 1952. Finally, inflation was extremely severe from 1949 through 1951 and the meaning of the expenditures data is not entirely clear. For these reasons it was decided to make estimates only from 1952 through 1962.

C. *Subjective Evaluation*

Due to a number of uncertainties about the basic data I give the overall estimates in Table A–14 a rating of 'B —'.

D. *Sources of Data*

The main sources of data were [G164, No. 19, August, 1963] and [G165]. These were supplemented by the sources noted below.

E. *Notes on Individual Expenditure Estimates*

1. The adjusted budget includes expenditures for administration, security, social purposes, and science. The Yugoslavs have not published any consolidated government accounts for the entire period, so that no gross expenditures data are available.

2. The estimation of expenditures at various levels of government raised a number of difficulties and, as a result, republic and local government expenditures could not be separated. The expenditures of the social funds and the independent organizations (*samostalne ustanove*) were assumed to be made entirely on the republic and local levels since a very small fraction of such expenditures were made by organizations covering the entire country. Budgetary

N*

expenditures on education were assumed to be divided between the two levels of government in the same ratio as budgetary expenditures for education and culture. Finally, 67 per cent of the science expenditures were assumed to be financed at the Federal level. Since the magnitudes involved in each assumption are quite small, none of these assumptions introduces a very large error into the calculations.

3. The original data were adjusted by removing expenditures for internal security (see Note 6) and those portions of diplomatic expenditures included in administration (see Note 5).

4. No adjustments were made to the original data, which represent the expenditures of the Ministry of Defence. It must be noted, however, that Yugoslav soldiers are used for certain civilian construction projects such as road-building, so that these data might overstate defence expenditures unless such civilian work were financed through a special account which did not appear in the defence budget. Since information on such matters is not available, no adjustments were made.

5. Expenditures for the Ministry of Foreign Affairs were taken from the budgetary accounts [G159], [G166], and [G167]; (whenever possible, the final accounts were used). To obtain consistency, expenditures for the Institute for International Politics were removed for the early years. Budgetary expenditures for international technical cooperation and cultural relations with foreign countries (from the budget accounts and from estimations), as well as long term foreign aid were added. Data on the latter, which began only after 1958, were taken from UN worksheets, but differ from the official UN estimates [G21, p. 24] because the latter include short term loans to Indonesia which do not correspond to the definition of foreign aid used in this study. The dollar values of foreign aid were converted to the domestic currency at the official exchange rate. Neither the foreign aid expenditures nor the expenditures for cultural relations with foreign countries are included under 'administration' in the FIS data. One further problem arose in the estimates for 1956 and 1957 in which diplomatic expenditures took a dip and then had a very steep rise in 1958. Although the expenditures of the Foreign Ministry were not available in detail, this dip appears to be an accounting, rather than economic, phenomenon; therefore, for 1957 and 1958 expenditures of the Foreign Ministry were estimated by interpolation.

6. Internal security expenditures were estimated in three steps. First, federal expenditures for courts, public prosecution, etc, and the Ministry of Interior (which includes the secret police, UDBA)

were taken from the budgetary accounts [G159], [G166], and [B167] (whenever possible, the final accounts were used). Second, similar expenditures on the republic level were taken from the budgetary accounts for each republic. Since only 38 out of the necessary 66 budgets (6 republics, 11 years) could be located, a number of interpolations and extrapolations had to be made. (Rather than detailing each of the individual sources, it is simpler to note that most were found in the Government Papers library in the British Museum; locating such budget materials in Yugoslavia proved almost impossible because of the paranoic attitudes of librarians there). Third, local expenditures for internal security were made in three different ways:

(a) It was assumed that the fall in internal security expenditures on the republic level between 1952 and 1954 represented a decentralization of expenditures. Further, it was assumed that total republic and local internal security expenditure remained a constant portion of republic and local administration expenditures during these two years and, thereafter, the ratio of republic to local internal security expenditures remained the same. To the extent that some internal security expenditures were made on the local level in 1952 or that further decentralization occurred after 1954, such estimates are lower than actual expenditures.

(b) Instead of the last assumption above, it was assumed that from 1955 on, internal security expenditures remained a constant ratio of republic and local expenditures, an hypothesis suggested by the relatively constant ratio of federal internal security to administration expenditures and the relatively constant ratio of republic internal security to administration expenditures after 1954. (A constant ratio of republic and local internal security expenditures to administration expenditures for 11 years was not assumed because of a seeming discontinuity in the administration expenditures between 1954 and 1955.) Again, the estimates have a possible downward bias.

(c) *Per capita* internal security expenditures on the republic level were highest in Montenegro, the poorest and least populated republic, and lowest in Serbia, the most populated republic. It was assumed that because of its small size, all internal security expenditures in Montenegro were made on the republic level, and furthermore, that *per capita* republic and local internal security expenditures in the other republics were the same as in Montenegro. To the extent that internal security expenditures were partly made on the local level in Montenegro or that *per capita* internal security expenditures in the other republics were higher, these estimates also have a downward bias.

The first method yielded the highest results but, in the 1960s they were only 3 per cent to 5 per cent higher than the results by the third method. The second method gave results about 15 per cent to 20 per cent lower than the first method. The relative closeness of the results of all three methods offers some confirmation about their reliability. Since all three methods have a downward bias and since only data for scattered years were available for Montenegro, the first method was selected.

7. Data on expenditures for schools and universities were obtained for 1953 through 1962 from [G163, various issues]. (It must be noted that some budgetary expenditures for such purposes are said to be deliberately doubly accounted in [G165, pp. 267–8, 273–4]; nevertheless, the data in [G165, pp. 273–4] are the same as the net figures from [G163]). To this series was added an estimate of expenditures for the administration of the educational system, derived from a datum for such expenditures in 1960 [G35] and the assumption that administration represented the same portion of school expenditures for all years. The datum for education expenditures for 1952 was estimated by extrapolation, using information about the number of teachers and the average change in their salaries.

8. Health expenditures were estimated from data on budgetary accounts ([G164, p. 75] and [G165, pp. 267–8]), accounts of the social insurance fund for health [G164, pp. 79–80], budgetary grants to the independent health organizations [G165, pp. 273–4], and some unpublished data about the small social funds for health in the early 1960s. The data for the social insurance fund for health were adjusted by removing expenditures for inventories and investments as well as for certain services which are classified under welfare for the other countries in this study. Certain minor extrapolations for some of the above accounts had to be made for 1952. A possible source of downward bias in the estimates is discussed in the next note.

9. Welfare expenditures were estimated from data on budgetary accounts ([G164, p. 75] and [G165, pp. 267–8]), and accounts of the social insurance fund for welfare in the early 1960s. The data for the social insurance fund for welfare were adjusted by removing expenditures for inventories and investments and adding certain expenditures from the social insurance fund for health. Certain minor extrapolations for some of the above accounts had to be

made for 1952. To the extent that administration costs of the Federal social insurance institute (which has acted to coordinate the republic and local social insurance funds) are not included in the budgetary accounts, the welfare expenditures are slightly understated. The extent of such bias should be no more than 3 per cent–4 per cent of total welfare expenditures and, for health, even less.

10. The basic data on research and development expenditures for 1956 through 1964 came from the above-cited article by Konvalinka [G160, 11–12/1965] and from unpublished data supplied by him. The fixed-price series for salaries and for materials were reflated with price series similar to those used by the author for deflating the current price series serving as his original source. Finally, the salary data were adjusted upward to include the social insurance and income tax payments which had been netted out. Expenditures for 1952 through 1955 were estimated by extrapolating the ratio of the R and D data for the later years to the national income. It must be noted that these data include expenditures financed by sales to the public and, therefore, overstate public consumption expenditures on R and D. Further, the adjusted Konvalinka datum for 1962 is about 15 per cent higher than the estimate of the Federal Institute of Statistics [G162, No. 374, December, 1965, p. 8].

11. Data come from [G165, p. 85].

Appendix B

NATIONAL INCOME DATA

1. TIME SERIES: CURRENT PRICES

The GNP data of the various market economies except for Italy were calculated according to the OECD standard definitions and were taken from OECD sources ([G17], [G11, various issues], and [G12, various issues]). For West Germany the GNP of West Berlin (from [G157, various issues]) was added for the years it was excluded and the estimated GNP of the Saar was removed from the years it was included. The GNP estimates for Italy are the revised accounts which were published in [G85, 3/1966, supplement].

The GNP estimates for the Soviet Union were taken from the Bergson-RAND Corporation calculations ([B31, [B35], and [B240]). For the other centralized economies, the following three step estimation procedure was employed. First, a series for distributed national income was taken or was estimated from the statistics of the respective nations. Second, a rough adjustment was made for the contribution of the service sector by multiplying the national income estimates by the ratio of the economically active population to economically active in the 'material sectors', those sectors included in the national income. (The labour force data came from Appendix D–2). Third, a final adjustment was made by calculating the ratio of my estimates to some detailed Western estimate of the GNP of the various countries and multiplying my entire national income series by this ratio. These final adjustments were usually quite small. For the individual centrally planned nations the following sources and detailed methods were used:

Bulgaria: the national income series was calculated from data in [B54, p. 154], [G51], scattered sources, and, for the years 1950–52, from a rough estimate. The very detailed estimate of the Bulgarian GNP according to Western definitions for 1956 from [B8] were used for the final adjustment.

Czechoslovakia: the national income series came from [G56, 1965]; the final adjustments were made from detailed estimates of the Czechoslovak GNP according to Western definitions for 1955 and 1956 in [B9].

East Germany: the national income series was estimated from data on the percentage of retail trade in the distributed national income and from data on retail trade, both from [G61, various issues]. The East Germans revised this series in 1964 and the old series was adjusted to the new series for the years in which new-series data were not given. The final adjustments were made from my own estimates of the East German GNP for 1956 (55·23 billion DM) according to Western definitions, which was computed in the following way: Since the East German national income aggregates contain a number of imputations which are usually made in the West but which are not contained in the national income accounts of the other centralized economies (see especially the comments by Kaser and Stolper in [B68] or the remarks of the ECE in [G29, XI, 3/1959, pp. 131–77]), adjustments had only to be made for depreciation and for the value of production of the omitted services. Depreciation was estimated from data in [G61, 1958 and 1962]; the wage bill for the services except those in the 'security sector' (army, police, etc.) came from data on workers in the service, industries and the average wages received [G61, various issues]; the wage bill for the services in the security sector was calculated from data from the sources, and materials used in compiling the public consumption estimates for these services (see Appendix A–5). These GNP calculations differ from my rough estimate which were published in [P74, 3–4/1965] and are, I believe, much improved.

Hungary: the national income data for 1955 through 1965 were taken from [G70] with adjustments made for a change in definition. For 1950 through 1956 data were obtained from the Hungarian Statistical Office. The final adjustments were made from the detailed estimates by [B10] of the Hungarian GNP in 1955 according to Western definitions.

Poland: the national income data for 1955 through 1962 were taken from [G90] and [G91]. For 1950 through 1954, estimates were made from 1950 data on consumption and accumulation (the series of national income in 1950 prices came from [G89]), data on accumulation and consumption in fixed prices [G91], and retail and industrial price indices [G91]. The very detailed estimations of the Polish GNP according to Western definitions for 1954, 1955, and 1956 from [B11] were used for the final adjustments.

Romania: since Romania does not publish any official national income estimates in current prices, a series had to be estimated. As a basis, I have used the Montias estimates of distributed national income, interpolating for the missing years for consumption with the aid of data on retail sales [G93] and my own estimates of military consumption; and for accumulation, from data on total gross investment. For the detailed adjustments, I use an estimate of the Romanian GNP for 1960 which was calculated in the following way. Starting with an estimate of the Romanian GNP for 1960 by Michael Kaser, [P90, Summer, 1966], I recalculated the results using the Montias estimate for distributed national income, depreciation data from [P73, 6/1960 and 9/1960], my own estimates of product originating in government services, and Kaser's estimate for other services. (Household rents and products consumed by producers are included in the consumption fund and do not need to be separately estimated.) My recalculated GNP (126·8 billion Lei) is almost 13 per cent below Kaser's estimate; however the ratio of my GNP and NMP aggregates seem much more in line with this ratio in other countries (using the data from [B8], [B9], and [B10], [B11]), than the Kaser calculations.

The factor price GNPs of all the centralized economies were calculated by subtracting the turnover tax and adding the budgetary subsidies to the GNP estimates. The turnover tax data were obtained from scattered national sources; some of the subsidies were taken from scattered Western or Eastern sources, some were estimated. Any error introduced by such estimations should be very small, however.

2. TIME SERIES: CONSTANT PRICES

For the market economies constant price data were obtained from the same sources as the current price data. For the Soviet Union a constant price series for 1950 through 1961 was obtained from [B261, Appendix P]; from 1961 to 1962 this series was extended from each sector from data taken from scattered Western sources.

For Bulgaria, Czechoslovakia, Hungary, and Poland, the preliminary estimates of the Columbia University Research Project on National Income in East Central Europe were used. I would especially like to thank the director, Thad P. Alton, for letting me use these calculations. For East Germany the constant price series from 1950 through 1958 of [B315] were extended through 1962 by constant price series from [G61] and, for agriculture, services, and housing, from my own estimates. No Western calculations have been made of the growth of the Romanian GNP, so the data used in this study are my own estimates which were made in the following way.

The growth of each of the material economic sectors was assumed to be accurately represented by the official data [G93]; for the services, production was assumed to grow at the same rate as service employment. These various series were weighted according to a 1960 factor-price sector-of-origin values, which were estimated from a market price calculation of the GNP (see above) and the assumption that five-sixths of the turnover taxes and all of the subsidies were on the industrial sector while one-sixth of the turnover taxes were laid on the agricultural sector.

3. DOLLAR SERIES

The 'dollar value GNPs' represent the gross national products of the various countries if all their produced goods and services were valued at US dollar prices. The basis of the estimates for 1956 and 1962 were calculations made for the year 1955.

TABLE B–1

The Dollar Values of the Per Capita Gross National Products of the Sample Nations in 1956 and 1962 (1956 Datum for USA = 100)

Country	1956	1962	Country	1956	1962
USA	100	107	Czechoslovakia	50	67
West Germany	61	79	East Germany	50	67
Austria	41	53	USSR	38	50
Ireland	36	43	Hungary	35	47
Italy	36	51	Poland	32	40
Greece	21	28	Romania	22	34
Yugoslavia	18	27	Bulgaria	21	33

For Bulgaria, Czechoslovakia, East Germany, Hungary, Poland, Romania, the USSR, and Yugoslavia, the 1955 dollar values of the GNP were taken from an improved version of the Staller–Pryor estimates which were published in [P24, July, 1966]. For Belgium, Denmark, France, West Germany, Italy, Netherlands, Norway, and the United Kingdom, the estimates of [B118] were used. Estimates for the remaining West European countries were made in three steps. First, end-use national income aggregates for each country were converted into dollars using the official exchange rate. Second, these aggregates were then adjusted by the ratio of purchasing power parity rates to official exchange rates which were calculated by [B118] for the countries which had roughly similar price structure. Thus, for Sweden and Finland, Norway was used; for Luxembourg, Belgium was the model; for Austria, Germany; for Greece, Italy; for Ireland, the United Kingdom; for Switzerland, Germany and France. Finally, further adjustments were undertaken, specially for the government sector, whenever it was felt that the first adjustments were out-of-line. Data for these final adjustments came from [G153] and [G6].

For all countries the 1955 dollar value estimates were extended to 1956 and 1962 by adjusting each sector (measured in dollars) with the volume index of growth of that sector (measured in national currencies).

4. NOTES ON THE EXPENDITURES/GNP RATIO

There is a low level controversy in the economic literature about the appropriate concepts to use in calculating public expenditures/GNP ratios. Although such matters can be discussed at considerable length. I do not feel that a resusitation of the various issues would be particularly profitable since, to a large extent, the choice of concepts to be used depends on what one is trying to measure or investigate. Several brief points must be made, however.

In the cross-section analysis a factor price GNP is used because the expenditures data are essentially factor price data, i.e. the portion of public consumption expenditures represented by payment of net indirect taxes is extremely small. Thus the expenditures/GNP ratio has factor price data for both the denominator and the numerator and, therefore, more accurately reflects the portion of real production financed by public consumption expenditures. For the time-series analysis a market price GNP is used because factor price GNPS could not be easily estimated for all years.

Transfer expenditures are included in the public consumption expenditures data for two reasons. First, all public consumption expenditures can be considered as transfers, and the division between transfers in money and kind is quite arbitrary. Second, it proved impossible statistically to separate transfers in money and kind for certain nations.

Appendix C

CALCULATION OF CONSTANT PRICE INDICES

1. GENERAL APPROACH

There are two general methods of constructing constant price indices of government expenditures. One can build up such indices with the use of physical indicators of production or one can deflate current price data by an appropriate price index. The first method requires highly detailed data which were quite unavailable for most of the sample nations; therefore, the second method was chosen.

In using the deflation methods, several procedures are available. One can separate out various components (usually wage payments, expenditures on goods, and transfer payments) and deflate each of these components by the appropriate price index; or one can construct some composite price index and deflate the aggregated expenditures series as a whole. Although the first method is preferable, it is often difficult to separate out the various economic components of the different expenditures.

Three major objections can be raised against such deflation procedures. First, selecting a proper deflator for the various components of government expenditures is quite difficult. Government wages often do not move at the same rate as wages in the rest of the economy. Although using a wholesale price index excluding agricultural goods for the deflator of government purchases of goods does not introduce much error (since wages are the largest component of most government expenditures), such an index is usually not available for the centralized economies and a retail price index of non-food items must be employed.

Second, price indices are usually of the Laspayres type which means that the derived volume index is a Paasche index. Since the GNP volume series is a Laspayres type, the derived elasticities are calculated from mixed indices.

Finally, such a method neglects changes in productivity in the government sector. Although it is generally assumed that such productivity changes are very small, detailed analysis of performance of different US agencies during the 1950s has shown average annual labour productivity changes ranging from $-4\cdot0$ per cent to $+9\cdot8$ per cent. (These data come from [G102] and [P79, XLI, November, 1959, pp. 341–60]. They were calculated from data on output and labour inputs and the effects of changes in the capital input were neglected. Because no adequate data on the capital stock employed in the various functional sectors were available for most of the sample nations, this precedent is followed in this discussion.)

In the calculation of income elasticity of public expenditures, the exact effect of differences in productivity changes in the public and private sectors depends on the ratio of government expenditures to GNP, the 'wage ratio', and the respective productivity changes.

If we assume that the productivities in the two sectors increase at the same rate and that the wages in the two sectors also move parallel to each other, then prices will move at the same rate in both sectors and current price data can be used to calculate income elasticities in fixed prices. If we assume that productivity changes in the non-government sector are greater than in the government sector, then from the income elasticities calculated with both the deflated and with the current price data, we can fortunately bracket the errors introduced by the differential productivity changes. By making certain qualitative judgment about relative productivity changes (e.g. in education, productivity of teachers probably changes very little), then it is possible to narrow the range of variation of the calculated elasticities even more.

The following procedure was therefore adopted for this study. Both current and fixed price elasticities were calculated. Although the current price elasticities are presented in a text, some mention is always made of the constant price elasticity so that the range of variation can be noted.

2. SOURCES OF DATA AND SPECIFIC STATISTICAL PROCEDURES

A. *Sources of Data*

For all expenditures except military, three types of series were collected for use in the deflation of the current price data: wage data, non-agricultural wholesale price indices (for the centralized economies, retail non-agricultural price indices), and cost of living indices. For these three series (the methods used for deflating military expenditures are discussed below), all data came from the respective national statistical yearbooks unless otherwise noted. Minor extrapolations or interpolations are not discussed.

Austria: wholesale price and cost of living data came from the national statistical yearbook and [G8, various issues]. Wage data were average wages of workers and employees in all sectors and came from the national statistical yearbook and [G6, various years].

Bulgaria: an index of retail prices of non-food items was used instead of a wholesale price index. A composite index calculated from overall retail prices and wages was used for the cost of living index. A composite series of wages of workers in administration, education, health, and security was used for a general governmental wage index; for the individual sectors of health and education, wage data of these sectors were employed.

Czechoslovakia: retail prices of industrial goods were used instead of wholesale prices. A regular cost of living index was used, extrapolated in the early years with the aid of information from [B252]. A composite index of wages in administration, education, health, and social work was used for a general government wage index; however, for the individual sectors of health and education, wage data of these sectors were employed.

East Germany: retail prices of industrial goods were used instead of wholesale prices, while a regular cost of living index was used. Average wages of all employees and workers in the socialist sector were used as the government wage index.

West Germany: regular industrial wholesale and cost of living data were used; wage data of public administration employees were used for the government wage index.

Greece: regular wholesale and cost of living indices from [G8, various issues] were used. Since no wage data were available, an index based on total consumption per employed worker was used as a proxy for the wages in government.

Hungary: retail prices of industrial goods were used instead of wholesale while a regular cost of living index was employed. An index of wages of industrial workers and employees was used for government workers' wages.

Ireland: regular wholesale and cost of living indices were used; average wages of all non-agricultural workers from [G6, various issues] were employed.

Italy: industrial wholesale and regular standard of living indices were used; a special series of government workers salaries (Group B) was used for average wages of all government workers.

Poland: retail prices of industrial goods were used instead of wholesale prices, while a regular cost of living index was employed. A composite index of wages in health, education, and government administration was used for the general wage index; however, for the individual sectors of health and education, wage data of these sectors were used.

Romania: non-food retail prices were used instead of wholesale prices. A cost of living index was calculated from a retail price index and a wage index. For government wages an index of average wages for all workers and employees was used, with interpolations made between 1950 and 1955.

USSR: retail non-food prices were used for wholesale prices. A cost of living index was constructed for 1950–55 from data on the movement of total consumption in real and fixed prices [B31, pp. 300–4], and, for 1955–62, from an index of total retail prices and a wage index. For government wages a wage index was estimated from data in [B31, p. 100] and [G129, p. 66].

USA: regular non-agricultural wholesale and cost of living indices were used. The wage index was calculated from data in [G105, Vol. VI, pp. 53–5] and the national statistical yearbook; for education an index of teachers wages was used.

Yugoslavia: an index of industrial prices was calculated for data in [G165, p. 230], while a regular cost of living index was used. A wage index of government workers was taken to be similar to average wages in the non-productive sectors [G165, p. 64].

B. *Adjustments for Individual Sectors*

Administration: a composite index of wages and wholesale prices, at a ratio of 8 to 2, was used to deflate the current expenditure series.

Military: two different methods were employed for these calculations. For the market economies except Yugoslavia, deflators especially for military expenditures are already available in the national accounts data and were taken from data on defence expenditures in current and constant prices which are published in [G12] and [G17] or, for Italy, from [G85, 3/1966]. For Yugoslavia a composite price deflator was calculated by weighting the price index of manufacturing production by 7 and wages by 3. Since information on the components of such expenditures or a better deflator are not available, no better method could be found.

For the centralized economies, constant price estimates were made in three steps. First, a wage bill for military personnel was calculated for each year. For the Soviet Union average military wages and subsistence allowances were assumed to be 95 per cent of average industrial waves, the ratio for 1958 [B240, p. 33]; for Bulgaria, Czechoslovakia, Hungary, and Romania, average military wages and subsistence allowances were assumed to be 53·7 per cent of average industrial wages, the ratio for Hungary in 1955 [B10, p. 148]. Wage estimates for East Germany are described in Appendix A–5. For all countries average wages of security personnel included in the military and civilian personnel attached to the military were assumed equal to the average industrial wage. The total wage bill was then subtracted from total military expenditures to derive non-personnel expenditures. Finally, the non-personnel expenditures were deflated by price indices for industrial production for all countries except the Soviet Union and Romania. For the USSR, a price index of machinery production was used [B226]; for Romania, a retail price index of manufactured goods was used (calculated from [G93], various issues) since no better price indices were available. For Bulgaria, Czechoslovakia, East Germany, Hungary, and Poland, industrial price indices were derived from national current price series of industrial production and the following Western estimates of industrial production in constant prices: [B346], [P3, June, 1962, pp. 385–407], [B315], [B93], and preliminary estimates for Hungary calculated by Laszlo Czirjak. Since some of the military equipment used by these countries was imported from the Soviet Union, such a procedure leaves something to be desired. However, as the imported share of military equipment of these nations is not known and the prices charged by the Soviet Union are also not known, no better alternative method of estimation was open.

Non-military external security: For the market economies, diplomatic expenditures were separated from foreign aid and other expenditures. The diplomatic expenditures were deflated by a composite index of wages and wholesale prices at a ratio of 7 to 3, while the foreign aid and other expenditures were deflated by a wholesale price index. Because of the very rough nature of the non-military external security estimates for the centralized economies and the special way in which foreign aid expenditures were converted into national currency units, no deflation was attempted for these countries.

Internal security, education, health, and research and development: a composite index of wages and wholesale prices, at a ratio of 7 to 3, was employed. For the US health expenditures a special price deflator for this sector (Bureau of Labour Statistics) was used instead of the composite index. Since none of these expenditures contain any monetary transfer expenditures of consequence, no adjustments were needed for this purpose.

Welfare: a composite index of wages and the cost of living, at a ratio of 1 to 9, was used since the overwhelming bulk of these expenditures were monetary transfers.

3. EVALUATION OF RESULTS

For the market economies the results seemed to be reasonable, i.e. the direction of difference between the current and constant price elasticities followed *a priori* expectations. For the centralized economies, however, extremely peculiar results were obtained, which required further investigation into the nature of the price statistics for these nations. As a first step, average rates of change of various price and wage indices were calculated for each country and compared with similar rates of change of market economies.

First, the cost-of-living and the retail price indices rose much slower than one would suspect from the wage indices in some of the centralized economies. It is well known that a number of nations (e.g. Israel and France) have deliberately chosen products for inclusion in the official cost-of-living indices which have had particularly low price increases and the same phenomenon appears to have occurred in several of the Eastern European Nations.

Second, the price deflators of the net material products (NMP) rose at a much higher rate than one would suspect from the retail price indices in the centralized economies. This might also reflect the phenomenon mentioned above.

Finally, there was a considerable difference in the rise of implicit price deflators for the national NMP estimates and the Western estimates of GNP of the centralized economies. This is one facet of the Western contention that East European NMP indices have an upward bias.

One interesting result of these three differences is the following. The average increases in the wholesale price and cost of living indices are much greater among the sample market economies than the sample centralized economies. However, there is no difference in the average growth of the GNP deflators in the two groups of countries when Western estimates are used.

Since data on government wages and on prices of goods bought by governments are not available for most of the centralized economies, calculating appropriate indices for deflating the current price expenditures data would be an impossible task. Therefore, it was decided to calculate only the current price elasticities and to report the average difference between current and fixed price elasticities for the market economies so that a rough idea of magnitudes could be gained.

Appendix D

MISCELLANEOUS STATISTICAL NOTES

APPENDIX D–1: POPULATION DATA

For the market economies the main sources of data were the national statistical yearbooks and the following other sources: [G13, various years], [G109, Series P–25, Nos. 265 (May 1963), 293 (October 1964)], [G151, various issues], [G155, various issues], and [G19, 1959, 1960, 1963]. With the exception of Ireland, for which fairly extensive estimates had to be made, there were few difficulties in preparing the population data.

For the centralized economies the main sources of data were the national statistical yearbooks and the following other sources: [G111], [G132], [G110], [G115], and [G19, various issues]. Although data on the population by age group were available for certain years, the other years had to be estimated by interpolation and extrapolation, using bench mark census years and data on birth and death rates for the intervening years whenever possible.

APPENDIX D–2: LABOUR FORCE DATA

The labour force concept used is 'economically active persons', which includes soldiers as well as unemployed persons looking for work. For the centralized economies it is very difficult to know whether certain countries include these latter categories of workers in the labour force data. For those countries where such details are known, appropriate adjustments were made whenever possible. All such calculations were based on the extensive studies of the labour forces in these economies which are cited below.

For the market economies, data were obtained from the various national statistical yearbooks and the following sources: [B201, p. 64], [G13, various issues], [P78, 1955, No. 32, pp. 99–108], [B90], and [G156, various issues]. Estimates had to be made for missing years for several countries by means of interpolation or extrapolation. Extensive estimates had to be made for Austria and Greece in the following way. For Austria a series had to be built up from data for all years on employed workers from [G50], data on the entire labour force from the 1951 and 1961 censuses (reported in [G50]), data on the self-employed workers (obtained from the various associations of self employed workers), and data on soldiers [G50]. For Greece, the data on the labour force in the 1951 and 1961 censuses are not comparable and so special comparable estimates prepared by Mr Marmatakis for these two years were taken as a base. The labour force for the other years was estimated by interpolation of the participation ratios.

For the centralized economies data were obtained from the various national statistical yearbooks and the following sources: [B26], [B27], [B28], [B348], [B265], [B266], [G111], [G129], [G131], and [G132]. Labour force for the missing years was estimated by interpolation of the participation ratios.

APPENDIX D–3: URBANIZATION DATA

The measure of urbanization is the percentage of the population living in urban 'places' larger than 10,000; this measure was chosen in order to avoid some of the well known incomparabilities which arise when a lower cut-off point is chosen.

The data were obtained primarily from the various national statistical yearbooks, supplemented by [G19, 1955, 1962, and 1963] and [B302]. For Austria, Czechoslovakia, Greece, Hungary, the United States, and Yugoslavia, data for 1956 are not available and the figures presented in the table were estimated by interpolation from census data (with the assumption that the urbanization ratio increased exponentially during the period under examination).

APPENDIX D–4: NUMBER, STATUS, AND AVERAGE POPULATION OF THE LARGEST TERRITORIAL GOVERNMENTAL SUBUNITS

A 'federal' governmental system designates the existence of a constitutional division of powers between central and local governments; nevertheless, many difficulties arise in applying this definition. For instance, the Czechoslovak constitution in force in 1956 designated the country as a unitary state of Czechs and Slovaks, and yet specifically gave local governmental units power over matters of local concern. In the Soviet Union the country is formally 'federal'

TABLE D-1

Number, Status, and Average Population of the Largest Territorial Governmental Subunits

Country	Status	Territorial Units, 1956		Territorial Units, 1962	
	Federal or unitary	Number	Average population (1000s)	Number	Average population (1000s)
USA	F	49	3,447	51	3,659
West Germany	F	10	5,202	10	5,585
Austria	F	9	776	9	792
Ireland	U	4	724	4	706
Italy	U	19	2,552	19	2,679
Greece	U	10	803	10	845
Yugoslavia	F	6	2,948	6	3,140
Czechoslovakia	U	19	697	11	1,260
East Germany	U	15	1,181	15	1,140
USSR	F	16	12,475	15	14,767
Hungary	U	24	413	24	419
Poland	U	22	1,260	22	1,378
Romania	U	17	1,034	18	1,038
Bulgaria	U	13	583	30	267

but the degree to which the country is actually 'federal' is open to some doubt.

Difficulties in compiling this table were also caused by the existence of 'independent' cities. For the USA, Washington, DC, is considered as a state; for West Germany, West Berlin is included as a Land but the Saar was excluded; for East Germany, East Berlin is considered as a Bezirk; for Czechoslovakia, although Slovakia as a whole is an 'independent region', only the Kraje are counted; for Poland each of the independent cities is considered as a Wojewodztwo; for Hungary each of the independent cities is considered to be a Magya; and for Bulgaria, Sofia is considered as an Okrug.

Data on the status of the territorial units come from [B344] and from materials collected by R. J. Rummel, Dimensionality of Nations Project, Yale University. Population data come from Appendix D-1; data on the number of territorial units come from the national statistical yearbooks.

APPENDIX D-5: LONG-TERM TRENDS IN THE CENTRALIZATION OF GOVERNMENT EXPENDITURES

The trends were determined by comparing the ratio of total government expenditures accounted for by the central government and its agencies in the base and final years. All expenditures are measured in current prices but are not necessarily completely comparable. Data for other nations are available but usually only for shorter periods.

For the individual countries, data were obtained from the following sources:

(a) *United Kingdom:* from Jindřich Veverka, 'The Growth of Government Expenditures in the United Kingdom since 1790', in [P84, X, pp. 111–27].

(b) *United States:* [G105, Vol. IV, No. 4].

(c) *Canada:* estimated from data from [B327].

(d) *Australia:* [B268].

(e) *France:* [G168].

(f) *Germany:* Süphan Andic and Jindřich Veverka, 'The Growth of Government Expenditures in Germany since the Unification', in [P30, XXIII, January, 1964, pp. 169–289].

(g) *Norway:* [G169] and [G170].

(h) *Sweden:* [B153].

(i) *Japan:* [B92, p. 97]. The trend in centralization, particularly in the period 1881–1910, depends considerably on how local government expenditures are defined. With a narrower definition, the centralization ratio fell slightly during the period [B92, p. 99].

APPENDIX D–6: THE NUMBER OF MILITARY PERSONNEL

A. *Centralized Economies*

For the USSR, estimates were based on data from J. G. Godaire, 'The Claim of the Soviet Military Establishment', in [G132, p. 43] and from [P58, various issues]. Sources and methods of estimating security troops are given in Appendix A–12.

For East Germany the 'Barracked People's Police', and the National People's Army, the border guards, the alert police and the motorized alert police are designated as military personnel. Sources and methods of estimation are given in Appendix A–5.

For Bulgaria, Czechoslovakia, Hungary, and Romania estimates were made in three steps. For the first three countries the basic data on military and security troops were obtained from calculations made by Thad P. Alton, Director of the Columbia University Eastern European National Income Project, to whom I would like to express my appreciation. Second, data on military personnel were also gathered from the files of the Institute for Strategic Studies in

London and were supplemented by data from the following sources [P8, December 1961], [P13, October 1963], [P17, March 1961], [P82, No. 351, 1963], [B57], [B70], [B91], [B101], [B131], [B141], [P58, various issues], [B316] and [G121]. Finally, the Alton estimates were modified in a number of cases by the data from these other sources.

Since no estimates of the number of civilians attached to the military establishments are available for any of the centralized economies, a very crude technique had to be employed. In the late 1950s, about 12·5 per cent of the total military personnel in the US were officers, while in the Soviet Union this percentage was about 25 per cent. (Malinowski, cited by L. M. Chassin in [P81, February 1961, pp. 171–93]). This suggests that many officers in the Soviet Union are doing work which is carried out by high ranking civilian personnel in the US and that the relative portion of civilian personnel is correspondingly lower. Therefore, for the Soviet Union, I estimated civilian personnel attached to the military to amount to 10 per cent of total military personnel and for the other centralized economies, 5 per cent.

B. *Market Economies*

For the United States, West Germany, and Italy, data on military personnel come from [G13]. For the United States, data on civilians attached to the military come from [G114] and [G116, various issues]; for West Germany, [G154, various issues] and [G155, various issues]. For Italy, such civilians were estimated as 15 per cent of total military personnel. For Austria, data on both military and civilians attached to the military establishment were kindly supplied by the Bundesministerium fuer Landesverteidigung. For Greece, data on military personnel come from [G140] and from materials kindly supplied by the government of Greece; civilian personnel attached to the military establishment were estimated from data in [G68, 1962, pp. 79, 84, 97] and from several assumptions about relative rates of pay of different classifications of personnel. For Ireland, data on military personnel come from [G78, various issues], civilians were estimated as 10 per cent total military personnel. For Yugoslavia, data come from [P56, July 1957] and from files of the Institute for Strategic Studies.

C. *Other Countries*

Data on military personnel come from [G13], [P58], [P92], and from scattered sources. Data on civilian personnel attached to the military establishment come from national statistical yearbooks and, where unavailable, were estimated as 15 per cent of total military personnel in the larger nations and 10 per cent of total military personnel in the smaller nations. Military data for France come from [G13]; this differed considerably from the data in the national statistical yearbook, however.

APPENDIX D-7: DYNAMIC BEHAVIOUR OF MILITARY EXPENDITURES

TABLE D-2

Ratio-Income-Elasticities of Defence Expenditures, 1950 to 1962

Country	Ratio-income-elasticity	Country	Ratio-income-elasticity
USA	+ 0·28	East Germany	− 1·47*
West Germany	− 0·68*	Czechoslovakia	− 0·71*
Austria	+ 2·58	USSR	− 1·09*
Ireland	− 0·57	Hungary	− 3·06*
Italy	− 0·53*	Poland	− 0·12
Greece	− 0·70*	Romania	− 1·54*
Yugoslavia	− 1·30*	Bulgaria	− 1·04*

Yugoslav data cover 1952 through 1962. Occupation expenditures in West Germany, East Germany, and Austria were considered as military expenditures. Asterisks denote whether the derived co-efficient is statistically significant (0·05 level). The data come from Appendix A and B. Constant price ratio-income-elasticities for the market economies average 0·21 below such elasticities in current prices.

TABLE D-3

Trends and Fluctuations of Defence Expenditures in Fixed Prices for West and East Europe, 1950 to 1962

NATO			WARSAW PACT		
Country	Average annual increase	Correlation coefficient	Country	Average annual increase	Correlation coefficient
USA	3·1%	0·44	USSR	1·4%	0·41
UK	− 0·6	0·20	East Germany	− 3·5	0·57*
West Germany	3·0	0·50	Poland	5·8	0·74*
France	2·0	0·62*	Czechoslovakia	3·2	0·66*
Italy	1·0	0·86*	Romania	− 5·3	0·82*
Canada	0·1	0·02	Hungary	− 8·3	0·62*
Netherlands	2·1	0·54	Bulgaria	1·1	0·34
Belgium	0·9	0·18	Non-Pact European Nations		
Turkey	n.a.	n.a.			
Denmark	3·9	0·67*	Sweden	7·4	0·92*
Norway	3·1	0·53	Spain	n.a.	n.a.
Greece	0·9	0·54	Switzerland	6·4	0·79*
Portugal	9·6	0·90*	Yugoslavia	0·6	0·17
Iceland	0·0	1·00*	Austria	3·2	0·43
Luxembourg	− 6·0	0·76*	Finland	n.a.	n.a.
			Ireland	4·1	0·13

In Table D-3 countries are arranged according to the order of the total value of the GNP.

OECD data were used for the NATO countries except Italy and the non-pact nations except Yugoslavia. Estimates discussed in Appendix A were used for Italy, Yugoslavia, and the Warsaw Pact nations. Asterisks denote statistical significance.

Trend values using my definition of military expenditure differ considerably from the OECD definition.

APPENDIX D-8: DATA ON TOTAL US EXPENDITURES FOR HEALTH AND WELFARE

Public consumption expenditures data for both health and welfare come from Appendix A-13.

The data on private health expenditures, including those paid directly by the health service recipients as well as those made by philanthropies, industrial enterprises (inplant medical services) and insurance companies for health insurance benefits, come from Ida Merriman, 'Social Welfare Expenditures 1960-61', [G126, XXV, November 1962]. From private direct payments were subtracted the payments for health benefits financed by tort payments which are reported by Robert L. Bombaugh, 'The Economic Significance of Loss-Shifting in the United States', [P46, XXVIII, December, 1961]. The significance of such tort liability payments is analysed by [B63] in greater detail.

Data on payments against short term income losses incurred during illness by private enterprises and government agencies (such payments are not included in the public consumption expenditures for welfare) are from Alfred M. Skolnik, 'Income Loss Protection Against Short Term Sickness, 1948-59', [G126, XXIV, January 1961]. From the Skolnik data expenditures financed through publicly operated cash sickness funds were removed since they are included as public consumption. From the same source data on uninsured benefits for all wage and salary workers in private industry (supplementary unemployment benefits, pension benefits, etc.) were obtained. Data on insurance, annuity, and pension payments of life insurance companies, fraternal orders, and assessment life insurance and savings bank life insurance companies, were obtained from various issues of [P54] and [G116].

Philanthropic payments for welfare services presented considerable difficulties. Although a number of estimates from different sources are available, [P33, various issues]; Thomas Karter, 'Voluntary Agency Expenditures for Health and Welfare from Philanthropic Contributions, 1930–55', [G126, XXI, February 1958]; [B73, p. 431]; [B78, pp. 17 ff.]; and [B228, p. 259], the range exhibited by such estimates is quite wide. Rather than prepare new estimates, a conservative average of the above cited sources of $1 billion was made.

APPENDIX D–9: TRENDS IN HEALTH INPUTS IN THE UNITED STATES, 1900 THROUGH 1960

TABLE D–4

Trends in Health Inputs in the United States, 1900 through 1960

Year	Health personnel as ratio of population	Physicians as a ratio of total health personnel	Physicians, dentists and nurses as a ratio of total health personnel	Hospital beds per 100 population
1900	0·43%	33%	48%	n.a.
1910	0·51	30	56	4·7
1920	0·57	24	58	7·7
1930	0·70	18	61	7·8
1940	0·76	16	62	9·3
1950	0·91	14	55	9·6
1960	1·09	12	49	9·1

Health occupations include physicians and surgeons, dentists, and professional and student nurses as well as chiropractors, hospital attendants, pharmacists, practical nurses and midwives, physicians' and dentists' office attendants, medical and dental technicians, optometrists, osteopaths, and therapists and healers. In several cases, minor extrapolations were made for the earlier years. It must be noted that the above health personnel constitute 74 per cent and 81 per cent of the respective 1960 and 1950 aggregative personnel in the medical and health services, as defined by the Census Bureau. Unfortunately, the aggregative series does not extend back past 1950. The data in Table D–4 are not quite comparable with the data in Table D–5 because of the definition of nurses.

Hospital beds *per capita* for 1909 are used for 1910; the 1960 datum was adjusted to take into account a discontinuity in the series between 1950 and 1960.

The data come from [G114, Series B196, B210, D1 and D123], [G106] and [G116, various issues].

O

TABLE D–5

Health Inputs and Outputs for the Sample Nations, 1956 and 1962

Country	Health inputs per 1000 population					Health outputs		
	Physi- cians	Dent- ists	Nurses	Hospital beds	Infant mortality	Life expectancy		
						Men	Women	Year
Market economies								
USA								
1956	1·2	·53	3·0	9·6	26·0	66·6	72·8	1956
1962	1·3	·51	4·2	9·1	25·3	66·8	73·4	1962
West Germany								
1956	1·4	·59	2·6	10·8	38·6	n.a.	n.a.	—
1962	1·5	·56	2·7	10·4	29·2	66·9	72·4	1960/62
Austria								
1956	1·6	·55	2·3	10·5	43·3	61·9	67·0	1949/50
1962	1·6	·54	2·6	10·6	32·8	65·0	71·0	1960
Ireland								
1956	n.a.	n.a.	n.a.	16·2	35·6	64·5	67·1	1950/52
1962	1·0	·20	n.a.	21·3	29·1	n.a.	n.a.	—
Italy								
1956	1·3	n.a.	1·5	8·1	48·8	65·8	70·0	1954/57
1962	1·3	n.a.	1·6	9·2	41·8	n.a.	n.a.	—
Greece								
1956	1·0	·30	0·6	5·3	38·7	n.a.	n.a.	—
1962	1·3	·38	0·5	5·8	40·4	67·5	70·7	1960/62
Yugoslavia								
1956	0·6	·09	0·5	4·1	98·3	56·9	59·3	1952/54
1962	0·7	·14	n.a.	5·0	84·2	62·2	65·3	1960/61
Centralized economies								
Czechoslovakia								
1956	1·3	·31	3·6	9·2	31·4	66·6	71·6	1956
1962	1·7	·32	3·9	12·5	22·8	67·2	72·8	1962
East Germany								
1956	0·8	·40	n.a.	11·8	46·5	66·3	70·6	1955/56
1962	0·9	·34	2·4	12·1	31·6	67·3	72·2	1960/61
USSR								
1956	1·6	·19	4·4	6·5	47	63	69	1955/56
1962	1·9	·24	4·8	8·5	32	65	73	1960/61
Hungary								
1956	1·2	·23	1·8	6·9	58·8	65·0	68·9	1955
1962	1·6	n.a.	3·1	7·0	47·9	65·2	69·6	1959/60
Poland								
1956	·7	·28	2·4	6·6	70·7	62·4	67·8	1956
1962	1·1	·34	2·5	7·2	54·8	64·8	70·5	1960/61
Romania								
1956	1·2	n.a.	2·1	6·8	81·5	61·5	65·0	1956
1962	1·3	·13	2·2	7·4	60·3	64·2	67·7	1961
Bulgaria								
1956	1·2	·28	1·6	7·1	72·0	64·2	67·6	1956/57
1962	1·5	·32	2·5	7·7	37·3	n.a.	n.a.	—

A. General

The data on physicians cover active physicians and exclude stomatologists (which are included with dentists) and osteopaths. Nurses cover both licensed and certified nurses and midwives as well as feldschers. Infant mortality rates are infant deaths per 1,000 live births. Life expectancy data are life expectance at birth.

The data come from various issues of [G19], and [G40], supplemented by [G61] and [G93].

B. Country notes

Austria: nurses include only those working in hospitals.

Bulgaria: 1961 health inputs are used instead of 1962.

East Germany: 1955 physician and dentists rates are used for 1956; 1960 nurses rate is used for 1962 and was estimated from data from [G60, Nr. 16, February 8, 1960], and the assumption that nurses equalled two-thirds of total nurses, medical laboratory assistants, diet-cooks, and assistants, masseurs, hygiene inspectors, medical-social workers and 'doctors' helpers'. The data on physicians is considerably higher than Western estimates (e.g. [B138, p. 6]) and may include medical students as well.

West Germany: data for both years excludes West Berlin; 1956 data exclude and 1962 data include the Saar.

Greece: the 1960 nurse rate is used for 1962. The infant mortality rate is higher in 1962 than in 1956 because the infant mortality rate in the latter year was much lower than in the preceding years. The trend over time was downwards, however.

Hungary: 1961 inputs are used for 1962. Feldschers for both years were estimated from data from the intervening years.

Ireland: 1961 rates for physicians, dentists, and nurses are used instead of 1962; 1960 hospital bed rate is used for 1962. The hospital bed rate was double-checked with the yearbook datum and proved to be correct.

Italy: 1961 input data are used for 1962. For 1961 certified nurses were estimated from such data for previous years. Nineteen fifty-six nurses include only those working in hospitals.

United States: the 1955 physician rate is used for 1956; nurses exclude midwives which are numerically very small.

Yugoslavia: the 1960 hospital bed rate is used for 1962.

USSR: 1961 hospital bed rate is used for 1962.

APPENDIX D-11: HEALTH EXPENDITURES IN THE
UNITED STATES BY INDIVIDUAL STATES

For advice and aid in making these estimates I would like to thank Louis R. Reed. However, he is in no way responsible for any errors.

Estimates for health expenditures by state in 1962 were based on a set of estimates of different aggregates of health expenditures for the United States as a whole (Louis S. Reed and Dorothy P. Rice, 'National Health Expenditures: Object of Expenditures and Source of Funds, 1962' [G126, XXVII, August 1964, pp. 11–21] and two different sets of estimated indices for the individual expenditures components by state. The component indices were combined according to the national weights.

The following major elements of total national health expenditures were included; expenditures on hospital care, physicians' service, dentists' service, other professional services, drugs and drug supplies, eyeglasses and appliances, and nursing-home care. Excluded were military hospitals, net cost of insurance, government public health activities, medical activities in federal units other than hospitals, private voluntary health agencies, school health services, industrial inplant health services, medical research and medical-facilities construction. In total, my more restricted measurement of health expenditures amounted to about 82 per cent the total expenditures reported by Reed and Rice.

Estimates A: Primarily from Physical Indicators

The first set of estimates consisted of the following components:

(a) Physicians and osteopaths: Data by state for 1960 were obtained from [G106]. National expenditures for physicians and osteopaths were distributed according to the percentage of such personnel.

(b) Dentists: Data on dentists by state for 1960 were obtained from [G106]. Dentist expenditures by state were estimated in the same way as for physicians.

(c) Hospital care, other professional services, and nursing-home care were estimated in three steps

1. First, data on nurses, student nurses, and midwives; practical nurses; hospital attendants; medical technicians and therapists, healers, and chiropracters; were obtained for all states for 1960 from [G106].

2. These various types of health personnel were weighted by the median salary of the respective groups for the nation

as a whole and were combined. An index of relative health personnel *per capita* by state was calculated.

3. The number of sickdays in all non-federal hospitals for 1960 was obtained from [B269], and an index of sick days *per capita* by state was calculated.

4. An index of hospital care, other professional services, and nursing home care was constructed, weighting the index of health personnel *per capita* by 4 and the index of sickdays by 1.

(d) Drugs and drug sundries and eyeglasses and appliances expenditures were estimated in three steps

1. Data on optometrists and lens-grinders by state were obtained for 1960 from [G106]. An index by state was constructed by weighting optometrists by 2 and lens-grinders by 1, and this index was used as a proxy for expenditures on eyeglasses and appliances.

2. Data on pharmacists by state for 1960 were obtained from [G106] and data on drug-store sales by state for 1963 were obtained from [G103]. Each of these series was divided by the state population and a *per capita* index was constructed for each. These two indices were then combined, weighting each component by unity.

3. The index for drug and drug sundries and the index for eyeglasses and appliances were combined by weighting each according to the total national expenditures.

(e) Military hospitals: Data on gross expenditures of individual military hospitals were obtained from [P39, 1963]. Missing data were estimated from average bed/expenditure ratios. A *per capita* index by state was calculated. These were removed from the total of *a* through *d*.

Estimates B: Primarily from Expenditures Data

(a) Private expenditures on physicians. Data on *per capita* expenditures for services of physicians by state were obtained from income tax data of physicians, reported in [B269]. Missing data were estimated from data on the number of physicians in each state (see above).

(b) Private expenditures on dentists. Data on *per capita* expenditures for dentists by state were obtained from income tax data of dentists, reported in [B269]. Missing data were estimated from data on the number of dentists in each state (see above).

(c) Private expenditures on hospitals, nursing care, and other professional services. Data on private expenditures for hos-

TABLE D–6

Public and Private Health Expenditures in the USA by States in 1962 (Mil. Dollars)

State	Total health expenditures	Government health expenditures
Alabama	330·4	52·4
Alaska	36·8	14·1
Arizona	191·8	33·5
Arkansas	193·5	42·2
California	2,686·5	515·2
Colorado	325·0	57·3
Connecticut	449·2	68·0
Delaware	96·0	9·9
Florida	658·1	108·1
Georgia	412·6	67·1
Hawaii	99·8	17·8
Idaho	95·4	11·4
Illinois	1,538·9	283·6
Indiana	586·2	75·3
Iowa	375·6	57·1
Kansas	337·4	56·3
Kentucky	320·3	46·7
Louisiana	366·4	103·4
Maine	134·3	23·3
Maryland	439·0	93·7
Massachusetts	979·0	190·4
Michigan	1,125·6	179·2
Minnesota	561·4	121·4
Mississippi	189·3	30·8
Missouri	603·9	98·6
Montana	114·2	12·6
Nebraska	220·6	32·9
Nevada	71·2	8·6
New Hampshire	107·7	13·2
New Jersey	876·0	145·9
New Mexico	114·3	27·5
New York	3,040·5	683·7
North Carolina	429·2	65·4
North Dakota	108·3	14·2
Ohio	1,340·2	201·7
Oklahoma	318·5	70·0
Oregon	292·5	54·2
Pennsylvania	1,516·7	217·7
Rhode Island	163·8	22·2
South Carolina	209·8	28·4
South Dakota	105·8	17·5
Tennessee	425·2	65·1
Texas	1,094·2	183·2
Utah	146·4	20·8
Vermont	87·7	10·8
Virginia	441·1	64·0
Washington	464·2	109·4
West Virginia	219·5	36·4
Wisconsin	567·6	122·9
Wyoming	72·3	10·0
Washington DC	202·8	70·1

pital services by state were obtained for each state from [B269].

(d) Public expenditures on physicians, dentists, hospital care, nursing homes, and other professional services. Indices derived for the various components discussed below were weighted by the national totals reported by Reed and Rice, *op. cit.*

1. State and local health expenditures for 1961–62 were obtained from [G105].
2. Workmen's compensation expenditures for medical care by state were obtained for 1962 from [G116, 1962]. Workmen's compensation for Federal employees was estimated from the total amount and the number of Federal employees reported in [G105].
3. State and local vendor payments for medical care by state come from [G126, *Annual Statistical Supplement*, 1962].
4. Veterans Administration and other federal hospital expenditures by state were obtained from [P39, 1963].
5. Other federal health expenditures were assumed to be distributed in the same proportion as state and local expenditures.

(e) Drugs and drug sundries and eyeglasses and appliances. Same as in Estimates A above.

Estimates A and B were quite similar. After removing California, the standard deviation of the two sets of estimates from the mean of the two estimates for each state was somewhat more than 10 per cent. Since both sets of estimates have defects, the mean of the two estimates for each state was used.

Data on health insurance of Blue Cross, Blue Shield, and other hospital medical plans came from [P88, 1964]. Data on health insurance from life insurance companies for 1962 came from [P54, 1964].

APPENDIX D–12: DATA ON PHYSICIAN/POPULATION RATIOS IN THE USA AND USSR

For the United States, data on population and physicians by state come from [G116, 1959, pp. 10, 69]. For the Soviet Union, such data come from [G100, pp. 20 ff., 81 ff.].

In the United States there were 12 civilian physicians per 10,000 people; in the Soviet Union, 18. Comparing the standard deviation of the physician/population ratio in the two countries presented a minor methodological difficulty since there were 51 administrative units in the former country and over 150 in the latter country. Therefore, it was necessary to combine the various administrative units (Krai, Oblast') into 51 units for the Soviet Union so that the chosen measurement of dispersion would be unaffected by the number of units. The rule for combining the administrative units in the Soviet Union was based on the principle of contiguity of units; groups of 2 to 6 units bordering each other were randomly combined to form 51 larger units.

The ratio of the standard deviation to the average doctor/population ratio was $0 \cdot 28$ in the USA and $0 \cdot 51$ in the Soviet Union. Although different combinations of the Soviet administrative units would have yielded different results, it is extremely unlikely that the gap between the two nations would have been substantially reduced.

APPENDIX D–13: DATA ON SALARIES OF MEDICAL PERSONNEL

The relative salaries of physicians seem to vary greatly among nations. The United States and East Germany are 'high physician salary countries' since such salaries are over three and a half times the average industrial wages (data from [P57, October 24, 1960] and [B45, pp. 116–17]). On the other hand West Germany and the Soviet Union seem to be 'low physician salary countries' since such salaries are less than two and a half times the average industrial wages (data from [B45, pp. 116–17] and [B98, p. 104]. (Data for other countries can be found in [B74, pp. 339, 359]).

In interpreting such data, account must be taken of the relations of earnings differentials between professionals and non-professionals in the course of economic development (see esp. Tibor Scitovsky [P3, March 1966, pp. 24–43]) and, indeed, some economists (e.g. [B74]) suggest that most cross-section differentials attributed in physicians' salaries can be to this one factor. Other economists (e.g. W. Lee Hansen, [B55]) present evidence that private costs of medical education are the most important factor in salary differentials between physicians and industrial workers.

Nurses wages show some variation *vis-à-vis* average industrial wages in different countries but this variation seems much smaller than for physicians (data on nurses wages from [G4]). Salaries of most other types of health personnel seem even more closely related to the general wage level of the economy.

Since physicians and nurses are only part of total health personnel, we must be wary about generalizing from their salaries to the entire wage component of health expenditures.

APPENDIX D–14: RENT SUBSIDIES IN CENTRALIZED ECONOMIES

The full magnitudes of rent subsidies are extremely difficult to estimate. Although certain data on the matter have been collected by international organizations [e.g. Economic Commission of Europe, *Financing of Housing in Europe* (Geneva, 1958, Chpt. IV)] the quality of such data is not known. This appendix gives alternative sources of data.

Soviet Union: Soviet rent subsidies can be estimated in several ways. Source [B59, p. 140, ftn. 39] cites a 1959 Soviet source which states that government subsidies on housing exceeded rents by 2 to 3 (old) rubles per square metre per month. Furthermore, we know that the maximum rent in the postwar years was $1 \cdot 32$ (old) rubles per square metres per month. Finally, [B5, pp. 305–308] gives a numerical example of an oblast' housing administrations's budget in 1960 in which a housing subsidy of $3 \cdot 26$ (old) rubles per square metre per month and a rent of $1 \cdot 15$ (old) rubles per square metres per month can be calculated. Therefore, the magnitudes of the housing subsidies can be bracketed.

Since rents, with certain exceptions, have not appreciably changed in the postwar years [B172, pp. 253–4] and since we can assume that the major portion of housing subsidies went to maintenance and repair personnel, a series can be estimated from the above data on subsidies per square metre, data on the number of square metres of socialized housing [G99] and a wage index [G129].

Bulgaria, Czechoslovakia, Hungary, Poland: Rent subsidies are discussed in the national income estimates by Thad Alton [[B8], [B9], [B10] and [B11].

East Germany and Romania: Aside from the information given in Appendices A–5 and A–11, no materials about such rent subsidies could be located.

APPENDIX D–15: DATA ON STUDENTS AND TEACHERS IN PRIMARY AND SECONDARY SCHOOLS

For the classification of different types of schools, the UNESCO definitions were followed. Data on primary and secondary schools

O*

presented in Chapter V exclude data on vocational, technical and special schools. Only full-time students were counted, but both part-time and full-time teachers were included.

The basic sources of information were the following UNESCO sources: [G33], [G34], and [G36, 1963]. The UNESCO data are, unfortunately, often inconsistent and were therefore supplemented, whenever possible, with data from the various national statistical yearbooks and for the US, from [G122, various issues]. A number of estimates had to be made, especially to add part-time teachers; in most cases such estimates were made from ratios of part- to full-time teachers obtained for 1954 and 1957. Adjustments for the specific countries are listed below:

Austria: Certain estimates for students in private schools were made from the 1954 and 1957 ratios of children in public and private schools. Teachers in private secondary schools were estimated by assuming that the teacher/pupil ratio was the same as in public schools.

Bulgaria: Data were taken only from the national statistical yearbook as UNESCO data include part-time and night students. Minor adjustments were made to remove teachers in night schools.

Czechoslovakia: No estimations had to be made.

East Germany: Part-time teachers were estimated from ratios of part-time to full-time teachers in 1954.

Greece: Data from UNESCO and from official government sources were inconsistent so that only data from the national statistical yearbook were used. These were supplemented by information supplied by the Ministry of Education and Religion in Greece.

Hungary: Estimates for students and teachers in secondary schools were made for 1950–52 by extrapolation.

Ireland: There are a number of perplexing inconsistencies between the UNESCO data and the data in the national statistical yearbook, so the latter were used exclusively. Infants in national schools were removed and teachers of infant classes were estimated by assuming that the teacher/pupil ratio was the same as for the national schools as a whole. Teachers both with and without certification were included. Both students and teachers from non-recognized primary schools are not included.

Italy: The UNESCO classification of Italian schools was changed with the merger of the prevocational schools with the regular secondary schools. For comparability, therefore, the prevocational schools were counted as a regular secondary school for all years.

Poland: Part-time teachers were estimated from data on full- and part-time teachers given in UNESCO sources.

Romania: Evening and part-time students in secondary schools for later years were estimated for different categories of students for the early years and were removed. Secondary teachers of part-time and night students were estimated by assuming that the teacher/pupil ratio was half that of the day students and were also excluded.

USA: Pupils in kindergartens were removed and teachers of kindergartens were estimated by assuming that the teacher/pupil ratio was the same as for all primary grades. To the data on regular public primary and secondary schools were added data on Indian schools, schools on federal installations, primary and secondary schools operated by universities, and private schools. For all these added schools, a number of interpolations and extrapolations had to be made, although any introduced error should be very small.

USSR: Teacher data from UNESCO sources exclude teachers of music, handicrafts, etc. Teacher data from Soviet sources include these as well as headmasters and principals. An estimate of teachers of music, handicrafts, etc., was made, but headmasters and principals were excluded, so that my definition is different from either UNESCO or official Soviet sources.

West Germany: Data include West Germany and West Berlin. Part-time teachers were estimated from data for 1954 and 1957.

Yugoslavia: UNESCO data for teachers apparently include both full- and part-time teachers and, therefore, were used instead of data from the national statistical yearbook.

APPENDIX D–16: TEACHERS' SALARIES AND AVERAGE BLUE CROSS INDUSTRIAL WAGES

I would especially like to thank Mr Hercik of UNESCO in Paris for helping me to locate source materials.

Data on average teachers' salaries are extremely difficult to obtain. Basic wage scale information (available in [B160] or [B161] is not very helpful because of the importance of wage supplements, bonuses, and special allowances. Furthermore, different national sources give data which are sometimes quite divergent. Finally, when data are available, teachers' salaries are sometimes combined with wage data of other professional groups.

In order to escape these problems, letters of enquiry about average teachers' wages were sent to the Ministers of Education of 10 of the sample countries; of these replies were received from Austria, Czechoslovakia, Greece, Hungary, Ireland, and Yugoslavia, but useful data were sent only by three of the six respondents. Only for Czechoslovakia do we have data available from the Ministry which can be checked against other information. According to [G56] the average salary of workers in education and culture in 1963 was

TABLE D-7

Ratio of Teachers' Wages to Average Blue Collar Industrial Wages in 1958

Country	Ratios	Country	Ratios
USA	105%	Czechoslovakia	86%
West Germany	188	East Germany	192
Austria	185	USSR	91
Ireland	193	Hungary	99
Italy	164	Poland	81
Greece	n.a.	Romania	n.a.
Yugoslavia	n.a.	Bulgaria	89

15,072 Kcs; according to the Ministry in 1963 or 1965 (the year is not specified) the average annual salary for a fully qualified teacher with 5 to 10 years experience and with a family of two children was 17,760 (1st–5th grades), 21,288 (6th–9th grades) and 23,376 (secondary school). Thus the average data on wages in education and culture seem to have a downward bias in Czechoslovakia and the ratio of teachers wages to average blue collar wages may have been slightly over 100 per cent. The biases in the other data in the above table are unknown; sources and methods of obtaining the data for the above table are outlined below.

Austria: There is a considerably greater range of salaries for teachers in Austria than for any other sample nation and, therefore, estimating an average salary is very hazardous. Minimum and maximum salaries (including supplements) are given in [G5, p. 19]; it was assumed that the relation between the range and the average salary was the same as in West Germany. Average teachers wages were assumed to change at the same rate as average wages in all sectors. Average industrial blue collar wages come from [G6, 1963].

Bulgaria: Data on average wages in the field on education, culture, and art for most years come from [G51, various issues] and were estimated for the remaining years by interpolation or extrapolation, using changes in wages of other sectors as guideposts. Average blue collar industrial wages come from the same source.

Czechoslovakia: Data on average wages for most years in the fields of education and culture come from [G56, various years], and were estimated for the remaining years by extrapolation, using changes in wages of other sectors as guideposts. Average industrial wages come from the same source.

East Germany: Data on teachers' wages for 1956 come from [B45, p. 77]; for other years it was assumed that teachers' salaries changed at the same rate as salaries of all full-time workers and employees. Blue collar industrial wages are not available; average wages of full-time workers and employees come from [G61, 1965].

Greece: Data on minimum and maximum salaries for teachers come from [G5, p. 19] and were adjusted in the same way as the data for Austria. For other years teachers' salaries were assumed to move at the same rate as consumption per member of the labour force. Average blue collar industrial wage data are not available.

Hungary: Data on teachers' salaries in 1963 come from the Ministry of Culture of Hungary, to whom I would like to express my appreciation. For other years teachers' salaries were assumed to change at the same rate as average wages. Average industrial blue collar wages come from [G70].

Ireland: Data on teachers' salaries in 1964 come from the Department of Education of Ireland, to whom I would like to express my gratitude. For other years teachers' salaries were assumed to change at the same rate as average wages. Data on average blue collar industrial wages come from [G6].

Italy: Data on minimum and maximum salaries for teachers come from [G5] and were adjusted in the same way as the Austrian data. For other years teachers' salaries were assumed to move at the same rate as average salaries in government. Average blue collar industrial wages come from [G82].

Poland: Data on average salaries for workers in education, culture, and science come from [G91, various issues] for most years and were estimated for the remaining years. Average blue collar industrial wages come from [G91].

Romania: No data on teachers' salaries could be located.

USSR: Data on teachers' salaries may be found in a number of sources including [B77, pp. 810–13], [G124, p. 16], [G98, August 1964], and an article by Bereday and Schlesinger surveying the results of these and many other sources [P11, VI, February 1963, pp. 200–8]. The datum in the table is an 'average' figure and is very close to the datum cited by [G124]. For other years it was assumed that teachers' salaries changed at the same rate as average wages and salaries. Data on average blue collar industrial wages come from [G129, p. 66].

USA: Data on average teachers' salaries are from [G116, 1964, p. 127] supplemented with data from [G114, p. 97]. Average blue collar industrial wages come from [G116, 1964].

West Germany: Data on teachers' wages for 1956 come from [B45, p. 77]; for other years it was assumed that teachers' salaries changed at the same rate as average salaries and wages in the economy. Average industrial blue collar wages come from [G6, 1963].

Yugoslavia: No data on teachers' salaries could be located.

APPENDIX D-17: MISCELLANEOUS DATA ON EDUCATION

TABLE D-8

Primary and Secondary School Education Indicators for the Sample Nations in 1962

Country	Percentage of Population in School Ages	Percentage of School-age Population in School (Enrolment rates)	Pupils Per Teacher
Market Economies			
USA	20%	114%	27
West Germany	14	87	26
Austria	14	80	20
Ireland	20	76	27
Italy	16	74	17
Greece	17	84	34
Yugoslavia	21	77	32
Centralized Economies			
Czechoslovakia	19%	91%	24
East Germany	14	90	20
USSR	20	86	22
Hungary	18	90	24
Poland	22	80	31
Romania	19	84	25
Bulgaria	17	19	23

The data for the above table come from Appendices D-15 and D-1.

TABLE D-9

Ratios of Primary and Secondary School Teachers to the Total Labour Force

Country	1956	1962	Country	1956	1962
USA	1·8%	2·2%	Czechoslovakia	1·9%	1·4%
West Germany	1·0	1·0	East Germany	0·9	1·3
Austria	1·2	1·2	USSR	1·5	1·7
Ireland	1·3	1·5	Hungary	1·2	1·3
Italy	1·6	1·8	Poland	0·9	1·2
Greece	0·8	1·0	Romania	0·8	1·1
Yugoslavia	0·9	1·2	Bulgaria	1·1	1·2

The data for the above table come from Appendices D-15 and D-2.

TABLE D–10

Degrees from Institutions of Higher Learning in the Sample Nations in 1956 and 1962 per ten thousand in the population.

Country	1956	1962
Market Economies		
USA	22·6	27·7
West Germany	7·4	10·4
Austria	4·4	5·9
Ireland	6·2	8·3
Italy	4·3	4·6
Greece	5·8	6·5
Yugoslavia	4·6	12·2
Centralized Economies		
Czechoslovakia	7·1	10·2
East Germany	5·8	10·2
USSR	13·4	14·7
Poland	7·9	7·2
Hungary	7·6	6·8
Romania	6·8	6·1
Bulgaria	7·8	8·5

The sources for this table are
given in the footnotes in
Table 5–2.

APPENDIX D–18: COSTS AND FINANCING OF EDUCATION IN THE USA AND THE USSR

TABLE D–11

Costs and Financing of Education in the USA and the USSR

	USA[4] 1957–58 million $	USSR[5] 1957 million new R
Costs		
Resource-use-costs (current costs)[1]		
Government budgetary expenditures	9,970	4,115
Other	3,212	184
Resource-loss-costs (opportunity costs)[2]	14,972	2,036
Total	28,154	6,335
Financing[3]		
Monetary transfer expenditures	950	686
Gifts	576	0
Endowment	145	0
Government	9,970	4,115
Others	16,513	1,534
Total	28,154	6,335

1. In order to achieve comparability, only direct current monetary costs were included. Depreciation and imputed costs of books and supplies of students which are not included in the government budgetary expenditure are excluded.

2. In order to achieve comparability, only income foregone by students in the eighth and higher grades are included. Interest and

rent foregone, imputed values of tax exemption, and other opportunity costs are excluded.

3. Gifts and endowment income for current expenditures are assumed to cover only the resource-use-costs covered above. No allowances have been made for financing of costs excluded in the calculations.

4. The government budgetary expenditures reported in Appendix A–13 cover expenditures of all public schools and institutions of higher learning (which were not financed by fees or sales), government grants to private schools and institutions of higher learning and transfer payments to veterans and other students. Data for 1957 and 1958 were averaged to obtain such expenditures for the 1957–58 school year. Transfer payments were estimated on the basis of unpublished data supplied by the Census Bureau and were removed.

Other resource-use-costs cover: expenditures of public schools and institutions of higher learning financed by student fees [G122, 1957–58, Chapter 1]; current expenditures of private schools and institutions of higher learning (estimated from data from [G122, 1957–58, Chapters 1 and 4]); and current expenditures of private commercial vocational schools not included elsewhere (from Rudoph Blitz, 'The Nations' Educational Outlay', in [B233]). Current expenditures of private primary and secondary schools were estimated from data on total current expenditures and an adjustment to remove expenditures for kindergartens. Current expenditures of private institutions of higher learning were estimated from total current expenditures after the removal of funds received from various public agencies and an estimate of research expenditures financed by non-governmental sources. Transfer payments of all private institutions of learning were not included in the current expenditures data so that no adjustments were necessary.

Data on income forgone by students at various levels in 1956 come from Theodore W. Schultz, 'Capital Formation by Education' [P49, LXVIII, December 1960, p. 575]. These were adjusted to 1957–58 by assuming that such income forgone increased at the same rate as average industrial wages. Total income forgone was estimated from these data and from data on full-time students above the seventh grade [G122, 1957–58, Chapter 1].

Monetary transfer expenditures cover transfers from public schools and institutions of higher learning (noted above) and private institutions of higher learning [G122, 1957–58, Chapter 4]. In addition direct transfers to students by enterprises and private institutions [B137, p. 246] were included. Monetary transfers by private primary and secondary schools were assumed to be negligible.

Data on gifts and grants used for current educational purposes come from [G122, 1957–58, Chapters 1 and 4]. Gifts and grants for current purposes in private primary and secondary schools were estimated by assuming that the ratio of such gifts to total revenue 'from all other sources' was the same as in private institutions of higher learning.

Estimates of endowment earnings used for current purposes were made on the basis of data from [G122, 1957–58, Chapters 1 and 4]. It was assumed that endowment earnings were split between current and capital costs at the same ratio as total expenditures. It proved impossible to estimate endowment earnings of private primary and secondary schools.

5. The datum for state budgetary expenditures in Appendix A–12 is adjusted to be similar in content to the US datum. It must be noted that this datum is larger than the figure which is often cited in the West (e.g. [B77, p. 68]) because I have attributed all the relevant residuals in the budget on education and cultural services to education. From the budgetary datum, transfer payments [G99] are removed.

Other resource-use expenditures cover those education expenditures financed by student fees, enterprise expenditures, etc., and are included in 'extra-budgetary' expenditures of educational institutions. It is difficult to separate these expenditures into current and capital components and even more difficult to separate current expenditures into expenditures of auxiliary enterprises (e.g. dormitories, student cafeterias) and other expenditures. On the basis of scattered data in [G99, 1958, 1959] a figure for current extra-budgetary expenditures in education was derived. It was then arbitrarily assumed that one-third of these expenditures were not expenditures of auxiliary enterprises.

Income foregone by students above the seventh grade has been estimated for 1955 [B76, p. 91]. By assuming that the income foregone per pupil increased at the same rate as the wage rate between 1955 and 1957, total income foregone by pupils and students was estimated from data on full-time students at various levels [B77, Appendices].

Monetary transfers to students from the budget on education were discussed above. It was assumed that monetary transfers to students and pupils from other parts of the budget or from outside agencies (e.g. enterprises) were negligible.

It was assumed that gifts to schools and institutions of higher learning were negligible. These institutions do not have endowment funds.

APPENDIX D-19: SOURCES OF DATA FOR TOTAL CURRENT SCIENCE EXPENDITURES

(a) *United States:* [G116, 1966, p. 543].

(b) *West Germany:* Public expenditures come from Appendix A-14; private expenditures from [G145, p. 16].

(c) *Italy:* Public expenditures come from Appendix A-9; private expenditures were estimated from data for 1963 'Indigine sulla spesa per la ricerca scientifica in Italia', [G86, II, June, 1966].

(d) *Greece:* [B167].

(e) *Czechoslovakia:* [G53].

(f) *USSR:* [G99, 1962, p. 637].

APPENDIX D-20: FOREIGN AID BY THE CENTRALIZED ECONOMIES

I would especially like to thank Stanisław Braun for the use of the UN worksheets and Milton Kovner for his advice in making these estimates.

Since data on foreign aid payments of the centralized economies are not published by these countries, estimates must be made. Two basic approaches are open.

A small number of recipients of foreign aid from the centralized economies publish the annual amounts of such aid which they receive ([G7] and various national sources). Since such data are not closely broken down by donating country, they can be used only as supplementary evidence and not as the basis of complete estimates.

Considerable amount of information is available about foreign aid promises of the various centralized economies. With certain assumptions about the rate of disbursement of such payments, the estimates can be made. Unfortunately, many problems arise in carrying out such a task.

Although a number of lists of such foreign aid commitments have been published (the most complete lists are [G29, 1/1959], [P71, 6/1958], [G26], [G30, 1957], [B37], [B79], [B85], [B166], [B215], [B285], [B300], [B303], [B306]), interpretation of such information must be made cautiously. Sometimes a single aid commitment is announced several times and in different amounts as negotiations proceed. Sometimes the original offer is not accepted, or, if accepted, is not used. A detailed knowledge of each offer is necessary to judge such a matter, a task which involves an enormous amount of research.

One option is to base estimates on detailed previous studies of the balance of payments of the various nations. Unfortunately, such studies are available only for East Germany [B176] and the Soviet Union (Marcello Caiola, 'The Balance of Payments of the USSR, 1955-58' [P91, March, 1962] and Marcello Caiola, 'The Balance of Payments of the USSR, 1959-60' [G132, pp. 145-63]). In addition, there are a set of estimates of foreign aid disbursements of the centralized economies published annually by the US Department of State, but only numerical data of such disbursements for the bloc as a whole are presented with no explanation on how such estimates are made. Finally, there is a running list of foreign aid commitments made by the various centralized economies which is carefully maintained by the United Nations and presented in various UN publications (e.g. [G20], [G23]).

The first step of the estimates was making a list of loans and grants promised by the centralized economies. For such foreign aid to the underdeveloped countries, the basis of my estimates was the UN list, occasionally supplemented by the sources cited above when it appeared that the UN list was incomplete. For the loans between centralized economies, information was taken from most of the above cited sources. Since much military aid by the centralized economies is not recorded, a downward bias in the results is introduced.

The second step was estimating the drawings upon the foreign aid promises of the centralized economies. Here it was assumed that all promised aid was actually given, except in those cases where data by the receiving countries were available. Following a procedure described by [B37], the foreign aid disbursements were distributed over an estimated period. The assumption of complete disbursement introduces an obvious upward bias in the results. It was hoped that this bias would cancel out the bias introduced in the first step.

The final step was converting the aid deliveries in dollars into national currencies. Here a purchasing-power-parity exchange rate for all industry was used, calculated from data on the net industrial production in domestic currency and the Pryor–Staller estimates of the dollar value of industrial production [P24, July, 1966].

Footnotes to Table on facing page

1 In this table only the financing of consumption, rather than investment, is considered. Moreover, ownership is interpreted in a strict legal sense, rather than in its broader connotation of 'control'.

2 In the Soviet Union, unlike most other socialist nations, *all* land belongs to the state and the collective farms legally lease it.

Appendix E

RESEARCH NOTES

APPENDIX E–1: A THREEFOLD CLASSIFICATION OF MODES OF COLLECTIVIZATION

TABLE E–1

Combinations of Forms of Ownership, Financing, And Administration[1]

Financing of expenditures	Ownership of productive facilities	Management of productive facilities	Examples
Public	Public	Public	Production of public education in the USA and the USSR.
Public	Public	Private	General Electric Co. administrating Oak Ridge Facilities for US government; Soviet government purchases of paintings from artists in state ateliers.
Public	Private	Public	Government leasing of private land for recreational facilities in USA; government trusteeship of private factories selling to the government in East Germany.
Public	Private	Private	Government purchases of handicraft articles in USA and USSR.
Private	Public	Public	Electricity sold to private individuals by publicly owned and operated electricity plants in the USA and USSR.
Private	Public	Private	Private leasing and operating of government owned hotels in Canada; private agricultural production for market by peasants on a co-operative farm in the USSR.[2]
Private	Private	Public	Federal Reserve Bank in USA; government trusteeship of private factories selling to public in East Germany.
Private	Private	Private	Production of small handicraft goods or services sold to private individuals in USA and USSR.

APPENDIX E-2: THE PROPRIETY OF ISOLATING PUBLIC
CONSUMPTION EXPENDITURES

Implicit in almost every study of public expenditures is the assumption that public expenditures can be isolated and studied in relation to a few selected explanatory variables. The reasonableness of this assumption is questioned by Peacock and Wiseman's [B249] hypothesis relating the 'stickiness' of taxes and postwar public expenditures as well as by Harley Hindrich's [B145] discovery that the structure of taxes, especially the relative importance of levies of foreign trade, is an extremely important variable in understanding variations of public expenditures between economically underdeveloped nations. On a less aggregative level Henry Aaron [B86] demonstrates that the extent of social insurance payments in different nations partly depends on whether the system is financed by earmarked taxes or by the general budget revenues. Furthermore, studies of US local governments have also suggested several significant relations between expenditures and certain types of taxes (especially [P61, XIX, September, 1966, pp. 259–75]).

Once the problem about the propriety of separating taxes and expenditures is raised, a number of other questions about isolating public expenditures can also be asked. For instance, are we justified in isolating different types of public expenditures from each other? Or is it meaningful to discuss public expenditures apart from private expenditures for the same service? Some quantitative data are available for empirically examining these matters.

Taxes can influence expenditures through the effects of the tax structure or through constraints placed on expenditures due to the total receipt available. Each of these influences is examined in turn.

The structure of taxes can affect expenditures in two specific ways. First, the existence of a highly centralized tax system may allow a greater amount of taxes to be raised than if taxing powers are decentralized among a number of smaller subunits, and the greater overall taxing ability may lead to higher expenditures. Second, the existence of a particular tax source or the use of a particular type of tax may permit governments to raise more revenue to finance more expenditures. Both of these hypotheses can be tested much more easily with cross-section than time-series data, because changes in the tax structure occur very slowly over time and, therefore, extremely sensitive statistical tests are necessary to detect any structural constraints.

For a sample of 18 economically developed economies in Europe and America and for a much larger sample of 50 US states, regressions of the following type were calculated:[1]

For international tests:

$$E/Y = a + b\,(Y/P) + c\,[R_c/(R_c + R_1)]$$

For intranational tests:

$$F/P = a + b\,(Z/P) + c\,(U) + d\,[R_s/(R_s + R_r)]$$

where

E/Y = current public expenditures as a ratio of the factor price
        GNP
Y/P = GNP *per capita* (in dollars)
R_c = current revenues of the central government
R_1 = current revenues of the local governments
F/P = public expenditures (separately, total public expenditures
        and current public expenditures) *per capita*
Z/P = personal income *per capita*
U = urbanization
R_s = total state revenues
R_r = total revenues of local governments
a, b, c, d = calculated regression coefficient.

Both linear and logarithmic forms of the regressions were calculated, but in no case was the calculated coefficient for the tax variable (in the first equation 'c'; in the second, 'd') significantly larger than zero. At least this type of structural effect seemed to be absent.

In examining the other mechanism by which the tax structure directly influences expenditures, account must be taken of two phenomena; there are administrative and political limits on revenues which can be raised from particular tax sources; furthermore, some tax sources are not open to governments in certain situations. It seems likely that the relative limits on different tax sources are lower in under-developed than in mature economies and, in addition, that the non-availability of tax sources should occur more often in the former group of countries. Following such expectations, Hindrich's empirical studies [B145] show that foreign trade taxes play a determining role in public expenditures, but only for the economically underdeveloped nations.

For testing such effects of tax structure on expenditures, use of

[1] For the international tests, the data on income *per capita* in dollars come from Appendix B and the other data come from [G25, 1965]. For the intranational tests the data come from [G105], [G116], and [G120].

cross-section data for nations presents statistical problems. The relative importance of certain types of taxes appears significantly related to income *per capita* so that it is difficult to separate out the two effects in a completely satisfactory manner. Nevertheless, regressions of the following type were calculated:

For international tests:

$$E/Y = a + b\,(Y/P) + c(T_x/R_t)$$

For intranational tests:

$$F/P = a + b\,(Z/P) + c(U) + d(T_z/P)$$
$$F/P = a + b\,(Z/P) + c(U) + d(T_z/T_t)$$

where

T_x = tax under examination (total indirect taxes; total direct taxes)

R_t = total current revenues

T_z = tax under examination (property taxes; sales taxes; income taxes)

T_t = total taxes

(all other variables have the same meaning as above).

Both linear and logarithmic forms of the regressions were calculated for total indirect and for total direct taxes, but in no case was the calculated coefficient for the tax variable significantly larger than zero. However, for the international tests total direct personal taxes were also used as a tax variable and a significant relationship with expenditures was found. This seems to reflect the discovery of Aaron [B86] that social insurance expenditures are related to tied taxes. Unfortunately, the data were not sufficiently detailed or comparable enough for further experiments. With the intra-national data other experiments, were also attempted, but with similar negative results. My conclusions for the United States contradict the opinions of H. Kenneth Allen and Richard F. Fryman, [P61, XVII, December, 1964, pp. 357–65]; however their analysis is marred by the fact that the differences which they discover are very small and would not be statistically significant if confidence limits had been calculated.

The influence of tax receipts in determining the total volume of expenditures is a much more difficult matter to test since the lines of causality are hard to distinguish. In analysing such problems, three issues must be separated. First, in the short run to what extent are public expenditures limited by the government's inability to borrow in order to cover a deficit? Second, to what extent are public expenditures constrained by the fact that taxation is reaching a level at which adverse effects in the rest of the economy are bound to occur?[1] And finally, to what extent are long run increases in public expenditures limited by the abilities or desires of governments to raise taxes?

To investigate this matter regressions of the following type were calculated:

For international tests:

$$E/Y = a + b\,(Y/P) + c\,(S/Y)$$

For intranational tests:

$$F/P = a + b\,(Z/P) + c\,(U) + d\,(Q/Y)$$
$$F/P = a + b\,(Z/P) + c\,(U) + d\,(Q/P)$$

where

S = difference between current state revenues and expenditures
Q = difference between total state and local revenues and expenditures

(all other variables have the same meaning as above).

In the international tests the calculated coefficient 'c' was not statistically significant and thus borrowing did not appear as a significant restraint on expenditures.[2] On the other hand US state and local expenditures seemed to be significantly affected by difficulties in borrowing. Such different results merely reflect the well-known fact that central governments can borrow (or print money) considerably easier than local units. Since this study focuses primarily on expenditures of all levels of governments and since a large part of such expenditures are financed on the central government level (see Chapter II), this borrowing constraint should not greatly affect the results.

In examining the constraint on public expenditures which arise from some limit placed on the level of taxation, a relatively simple test can be devised. If a nation were approaching this limit, then one would expect a special kind of substitution to occur between

[1] The thesis about the limits of taxation has been most vigorously propounded by Colin Clark [P22, December, 1945, pp. 371–89]. The literature on this question is summarized by Amotz Morag [B227].

[2] Legitimate objections can be raised against the international tests because the differences between current (rather than total) receipts and expenditures are used. Unfortunately, comparable and adequate data for total receipts and expenditures could not be located for such an experiment to be made.

expenditures. That is, in comparing two similar political units, if expenditures *per capita* on *A* in the first unit is higher, its *per capita* expenditures on *B* should be lower.

For nations both time-series and cross-section tests using military and civilian public expenditures are conducted in Chapter III. In general, such substitution does not seem to occur although certain specific cases are noted where such an effect is statistically significant. For the United States state and local governments, regressions of the following type were calculated:

$$J/P = a + b\,(Z/P) + c\,(M) + d(K/P)$$

where

> *J, K* = expenditures under examination [education, health and hospitals, welfare, highways, internal security (fire, police, correction), administration, and natural resources]
>
> *M* = other relevant independent variables

(other variables have the same meaning as above).

In no case was coefficient '*d*' negative and statistically significant (although, it must be added, several positive and statistically significant coefficients appeared). The results were not completely conclusive, primarily because there was relatively little variation of expenditures between states once the effect of *per capita* income, urbanization, and several other independent variables had been removed.

Devising suitable statistical tests for examining the long run implications of the size of tax revenues on the volume of public expenditures proved infeasible because of lack of sufficient comparable data. Nevertheless, few economists have been bold enough to predict that long term state debts have had a very great dampening effect on public expenditures, especially in the post-World War II era when such debts have not been considered as evidence of financial sin or fiscal irresponsibility on the part of governments.

Four errors in interpreting these statistical experiments should be avoided. First, the results do not mean that at some levels of government, there are no such relationships. Second, they do not mean that if expenditures and taxes were more disaggregated, such relationships would not appear. Certainly expenditures which are legislatively tied to certain taxes (e.g. highways financed by user-fees through petrol taxes; the question of whether such fees are 'really' taxes is avoided here) violate such a generalization. Third, the results do not mean that significant relationships between tax structure and public expenditures do not appear over time. Unfortunately, sufficient data for state and local governments were not available for an adequate time-series analysis to be carried out. Finally, the results do not mean that there are no statistically significant relations between taxes (rather than tax structure) and expenditures.

Although many of my experiments for this purpose are quite crude, the results of such tests give confidence to the general impression that for developed economies in the period under examination, taxes and the tax structure seemed to respond to changes in aggregate public expenditures, rather than the reverse.[1] This impression further suggests that analysis of the major components of public expenditures will not greatly suffer when tax considerations are omitted from discussion; and it is on this assumption that this study is based. It must be added that such an assumption implicitly underlies almost all of the empirical studies on the behaviour of public expenditures which have been made by other economists, a phenomenon which does not make the assumption correct but which indicates the general consensus of opinion in the profession.

APPENDIX E-3: AN ANALYSIS OF THE DISPLACEMENT EFFECT OF MESSRS PEACOCK AND WISEMAN[2]

According to the 'displacement effect' hypothesis, the basic constraint on the increase of government expenditures is the difficulty of increasing the tax rates to finance such expenditures. Citizens supposedly have strong notions about the 'tolerable burden of taxation' which remain fairly stable in peacetime but which are subject to change in periods of national crises such as the outbreak of war. After wars are over, it is unlikely that taxes and government expenditures return to their previous level but, instead, probably remain at a somewhat higher level so that the pattern of public expenditures over time looks like a series of steps. Peacock and

---

[1] This does not mean that taxes do not influence expenditures; obviously, tax revenues are (or should be) very much in the mind of planners and legislators dealing with expenditures. Nevertheless, this assumption means that inclusion of a tax variable would not aid in the analysis of expenditures which is carried out in the following pages.

[2] Alan T. Peacock and Jack Wiseman, *The Growth of Public Expenditures in the United Kingdom* (Princeton: Princeton U. Press for NBER, 1961). Extensive comments on the displacement effect are also made by Musgrave [B230] and Gupta [B129].

Wiseman point to the United Kingdom as an excellent example of the operation of such a mechanism.

Three major objections can be raised against this theory:

In the first place, if the tax rates are progressive, if all tax revenues are expended, and if GNP *per capita* is increasing, then government expenditures as a ratio of GNP will rise and a 'displacement effect' is not needed to explain the rise in relative expenditures.[1] Furthermore, if the government is permitted to borrow in order to finance its expenditures, then difficulties in changing the tax rate are no longer such an important restraint.[2]

Second, the 'displacement effect' due to war does not seem useful in explaining the pattern of public expenditures in certain postwar cases, e.g. Japan.[3] Furthermore, displacements have occurred in various nations in cases other than war, e.g. in the great depression in the United States.[4] If 'social upheavals' causing 'displacements' are used to explain changes in the pattern of public expenditures *a posteriori*, then the theory cannot be refuted and loses its character as a scientific statement.

Finally, there is some doubt about the magnitude of the 'displacement effect' in the United Kingdom. Peacock and Wiseman use graphical evidence to support their hypothesis and do not attempt to test the statistical significance of their displacement. Nevertheless, this can be easily performed by estimating regression equations using dummy variables to designate periods before and after different wars.[5] To this end least squares regressions were calculated according to the following formula with data from the UK:

$$\ln G = v + xT + yA + zB$$
$$\ln C = v + xT + yA + zB$$
$$\ln G = v + w \ln Y + yA + zB$$
$$\ln C = v + w \ln Y + yA + zB$$

[1] Peacock and Wiseman recognize this as a possibility but dismiss its applicability to the UK.

[2] This point is emphasized by Tait and O'Donoghue in their forthcoming study of Ireland.

[3] Peacock and Wiseman assert that the displacement can be downward as well as upward (p. 28); nevertheless, if the theory can justify any occurrence, then it is not refutable by empirical evidence and is not a scientific theory.

[4] This is emphasized and analysed by Gupta [B129] in an interesting manner.

[5] Gupta [B129], has an alternative approach in which he fits regression lines to segments of the function relating government expenditures and GNP. This has the advantage of showing not only shifts but changes in the slope of the function that are caused by the displacement. My formulation is simple but can be used to illuminate several facets of the matter which he does not discuss.

Symbols:

T = time

G = total government expenditures *per capita* (in tenths of £'s, in the prices of 1900)

C = government expenditures minus expenditures of defence and war related purposes (in tenths of £'s, in the prices of 1900)

Y = national income *per capita* (in tenths of £'s, in prices of 1900)

A = 0, 1890–1913; = 1, 1923–37; 1950–61

B = 0, 1890–1913, 1923–37; = 1, 1950–61

v, w, x, y, z = calculated regression coefficients.

The results of these experiments are given in the table below.

TABLE E–2

Regression Experiments to Test the 'Displacement Effect'[1]

Dependent variable	Independent variables				Number of observations	Correlation coefficient
	w	x	y	z		
G	—	0·019* (0·003)	0·352* (0·085)	0·242* (0·074)	28	0·992*
C	—	0·031* (0·002)	0·023 (0·063)	− 0·001 (0·055)	28	0·997*
G	1·173* (0·244)	—	0·744* (0·054)	0·401* (0·075)	28	0·988*
C	1·710* (0·325)	—	0·685* (0·072)	0·306* (0·100)	28	0·980*

Taking time as one of the explanatory variables the 'displacement effect' for total government expenditures *per capita* is, indeed, important; it is equal in its effect to about eighteen years for the interwar period and about thirteen years in the post-World War II period. Nevertheless, if we look at *per capita* government civilian expenditures, it is noteworthy that the displacement is not statistically significant in either period. This means that the displacement which occurred was entirely due to increases for defence and war-related purposes. Although Peacock and Wiseman follow Wagner in formulating their hypothesis with time as an independent variable,

[1] Coefficients marked with an asterisk are significant to the 0·05 level; standard errors of estimates are placed in parentheses below the coefficients.

The data are from [B249, pp. 153, 154, and 173]. An estimate for 1961 was made on the basis of data presented by [P84, X, 1/1963, pp. 111–27]. In order to avoid distortions caused by war, the year preceding and the five years following each major war were omitted.

this type of analysis is somewhat unsatisfactory since the relation between government expenditures and time is not entirely clear.

If we reformulate the displacement hypothesis with *per capita* national income as an explanatory variable instead of time, the displacement is statistically significant both for total and for civilian *per capita* expenditures, but the magnitudes are less impressive. After World War I the displacement in 1923 was equal to about six years for total government expenditures *per capita* and to about three years for civilian expenditures *per capita*, if we use as the reference point the average annual growth rate of GNP *per capita* during the entire interwar period. After World War II the displacement in 1950 was equal to about three years for total government expenditures *per capita* and about one year for civilian government expenditures *per capita*, if we use as the reference point the average annual growth rate of GNP *per capita* for the 1950–61 period.

Although the 'displacement effect' does not seem very great, we are left with one important insight. In certain periods the tax system might act as a restraint to government expenditures. This system might act as a constaint to government expenditures. This phenomenon is investigated in Appendix E–2.

APPENDIX E–4: RECENT EMPIRICAL STUDIES OF PUBLIC EXPENDITURES

A. *Long-Time-Series Studies of Nations*

1. *Argentina:* Ernest F. Patterson, 'The Extent and Pattern of the Expenditures of the Argentine National Government', *Public Finance/Finances publiques*, XI, 1/1956, pp. 36–55. Federico Julio Herschel and Samuel Itzcovich, 'Fiscal Policy in Argentina', *Public Finance/Finances publiques*, XII, 2/1957, pp. 97–117; and 3/1957, pp. 208–32.

2. *Australia:* B. U. Ratchford. *Public Expenditures in Australia.* Durham, NC; Duke University Press, 1959.

3. *El Salvador:* Henry C. Wallich and John H. Adler, *et al. Public Finance in a Developing Country: El Salvador—A Case Study.* Cambridge, Mass., Harvard Univ. Press, 1951.

4. *Germany:* Suphan Andic and Jiřndich Veverka, 'The Growth of Government Expenditures in Germany since the Unification', *Finanzarchiv*, NF Band 23, Heft 2, January, 1964, pp. 169–278. Horst C. Recktenwalt, 'Die Entwicklung der oeffentlichen Ausgaben in der Bundesrepublik' in Heinz Koenig, ed., *Wandlungen der*

Wirtschaftstruktur in der Bundesrepublik Deutschland. Berlin, Duncker and Humblot, 1962, pp. 199–249.

5. *Ireland:* Alan Tait and Martin O'Donoghue, 'Public Expenditures in Ireland'. In J. Bristol and A. Tait, eds., *Economic Policy in Ireland.* Dublin, Institute of Public Administration, 1968.

6. *Italy:* Francesco A. Repaci. *La finanza pubblica italiana nel secolo 1861–1960.* Bologna, Zanichelli editore, 1962.

7. *Japan:* Koichi Emi. *Government Fiscal Activity and Economic Growth in Japan. 1868–1960.* Tokyo, Kinokuniya Bookstore Co. Ltd., 1963.

8. *Portugal:* V. K. Pintado. *Public Expenditures and Economic Growth, with Special Reference to Portugal.* Ph.D. dissertation, University of Edinburgh, October, 1960.

9. *Sierra Leone:* N. A. Cox-George. *Finance and Development in West Africa: The Sierra Leone Experience.* London, 1961.

10. *South Africa:* T. van Waasdijk. *Public Expenditures in South Africa.* Johannesburg, Witwatersrand Univ. Press, 1964.

11. *Sweden:* Erik Höök. *Den offentliga sektorns expension: En studie av de offentliga civila utgifternas utveckling åren 1913–1958.* Stockholm, Almqvist and Wiksell, 1962.

12. *United Kingdom:* Alan T. Peacock and Jack Wiseman. *The Growth of Public Expenditure in the United Kingdom.* Princeton Univ. Press for NBER, 1961. Jindřich Veverka, 'The Growth of Government Expenditure in the United Kingdom since 1790', *Scottish Journal of Political Economy,* X, 1/1963.

13. *USA:* A number of studies have been made; the most important are: M. Slade Kendrick. *A Century and a Half of Federal Expenditures.* Bureau of Economic Research Occasional Paper 48. New York, 1955. R. A. Musgrave and J. M. Culberton, 'The Growth of Public Expenditures in the United States, 1890–1948', *National Tax Journal,* VI, 2/1953, pp. 97–115. Solomon Fabricant. *The Trend of Government Activity in the United States since 1900.* New York National Bureau of Economic Research, 1952.

14. *Yugoslavia:* Jindřich Veverka and Dubrovko Matko. 'Public Expenditures in Yugoslavia' (forthcoming).

Long Time-Series data can also be found for:

15. *Canada:* M. C. Urquhart and K. A. H. Buckley, eds. *Historical Statistics of Canada.* Toronto, Macmillan, 1965.

16. *France:* Institut national de la statistique et des études économiques. *Annuaire statistiques de la France: Retrospectif.* Paris, 1961.

17. *Norway:* Statistisk sentralbyrå. *Statistiske oversikter 1948.* Oslo, 1949; and *Statistiske oversikter 1958.* Oslo, 1959.

B. *Recent Econometric Studies of State and Local Government Expenditures in the USA*

1. Robert Frank Adams. *Determinants of Local Government Expenditures.* Ph.D. dissertation, University of Michigan, 1963. Ann Arbor, Michigan, University Microfilms.

2. Robert F. Adams, 'The Fiscal Response to Intergovernmental Transfers in Less Developed Areas of the United States', *Review of Economics and Statistics* (forthcoming).

3. Robert F. Adams. 'On the Variation in the Consumption of Public Services', *Review of Economics and Statistics,* XLVII, November 1965, pp. 400–5.

4. Albert Ando, E. Cary Brown, and Earl W. Adams, 'Government Revenues and Expenditures', in J. S. Duesenberry, *et al.* eds. *The Brookings Quarterly Econometric Model of the United States.* Chicago, Rand McNally, 1965, pp. 533–85.

5. R. W. Bahl and R. J. Saunders, 'Determinants of Changes in State and Local Government Expenditures', *National Tax Journal,* XVIII, March 1965, pp. 50–8.

6. Roy W. Bahl, Jr, and Robert J. Saunders, 'Factors Associated with Variations in State and Local Government Spending', *Journal of Finance,* XXI, September 1966, pp. 523–35.

7. George A. Bishop, 'Stimulative versus Substitutive Effects of State School Aid in New England', *National Tax Journal,* XVIII, June 1964.

8. John C. Bollens, *et al. Exploring the Metropolitan Community.* Berkeley, Univ. of California Press, 1957.

9. Bernard H. Booms, 'City Governmental Form and Public Expenditures Levels', *National Tax Journal,* XIX, June 1966, pp. 187–200.

10. Harvey E. Brazer. *City Expenditures in the United States.* New York, National Bureau of Economic Research, 1959.

11. Murray Brown and Paul Taubman, 'A Forecasting Model of Federal Purchases of Goods and Services', *Journal of the American Statistical Association,* LVII, September 1962, pp. 633–47.

12. Lora Collins, 'Determinants of Public Assistance Expenditures', in Otto Eckstein, ed. *Economics of Income Maintenance.* Washington, DC, The Brookings Institution, 1966.

13. Otto A. Davis, 'Empirical Evidence of Political Influences upon the Expenditure Policies of Public Schools', in Julius Margolis,

ed., *The Public Economy of Urban Communities*, Washington, DC, Resources for the Future, 1965, pp. 92–111.

14. Otto Davis and George H. Haines, 'A Political Approach to a Theory of Public Expenditures', *National Tax Journal*, XIX, September 1966, pp. 259–75.

15. Richard E. Dawson and James A. Robinson, 'Interparty Competition, Economic Variables, and Welfare Policies in American States', *Journal of Politics*, XXV, 2/1963, pp. 265–89.

16. Thomas R. Dye. *Politics, Economics and the Public: Policy Outcomes in the American States*. New York, Rand McNally, 1967.

17. Solomon Fabricant. *The Trend of Government Activity in the United States since 1900*. New York, National Bureau of Economic Research, 1952.

18. Glenn W. Fischer, 'Determinants of State and Local Government Expenditures: A Preliminary Analysis', *National Tax Journal*, XIV, 4/1961, pp. 349–55.

19. Glenn W. Fischer, 'Interstate Variation in State and Local Government Expenditures', *National Tax Journal*, XVII, March 1964, pp. 57–74.

20. Glenn W. Fischer, 'Public Assistance Expenditures', in *Report of the Commission on Revenue of the State of Illinois*. Springfield, Ill., 1963.

21. Bruce L. Gensemer. *Determinants of the Fiscal Policy Decisions of Local Governments in Urban Areas: Public Safety and Public Education*. Ph.D. dissertation, University of Michigan, 1966.

22. Karl D. Gregory. *Variations in State and Local Appropriations for Publicly Supported Institutions of Higher Education, by State*. Ph.D. dissertation, University of Michigan, 1961. Ann Arbor, University Microfilms.

23. Amos H. Hawley, 'Metropolitan Population and Municipal Government Expenditures in Central Cities', in Paul K. Hatt and Albert J. Reiss, Jr, eds. *Cities and Societies*. Glencoe, Free Press, 1957.

24. Niles M. Hansen, 'The Structure and Determinants of Local Public Investment Expenditures', *Review of Economics and Statistics*, XLVII, February 1965, pp. 150–62.

25. Nels W. Hanson, 'Economy of Scale as a Cost Factor in Financing Public Schools', *National Tax Journal*, XVI, March 1964, pp. 92–96.

26. Robert L. Harlow. *Factors Affecting American State Expenditures*. Ph.D. dissertation, Yale University, 1966.

27. Walter Hettich. *Equalization Grants, Minimum Standards and*

P

Unit Cost Differences in Education. Ph.D. dissertation, Yale University, 1967.

28. Werner Z. Hirsch. *Analysis of the Rising Costs of Public Education.* Study Paper 4 for the Joint Economic Committee of the US Congress. Washington, DC: GPO, 1959.

29. Werner Z. Hirsch, 'Cost Function of an Urban Government: Refuse Collection', *Review of Economics and Statistics,* XLVII, February 1965, pp. 87–92.

30. Werner Z. Hirsch, 'Determinants of Public Education Expenditures', *National Tax Journal,* XIII, March 1960, pp. 29–40.

31. Werner Z. Hirsch, 'Expenditure Implications of Metropolitan Growth and Consolidation', *Review of Economics and Statistics,* XLI, August 1959, pp. 232–41.

32. Henry Thomas James, *et al. Wealth, Expenditure and Decision Making in Education,* Stanford, Stanford University. Mimeo, 1963.

33. Woo Sik Kee, 'Central City Expenditures and Metropolitan Areas', *National Tax Journal,* XVIII, December 1965, pp. 337–53.

34. Richard F. Kosobud. *An Econometric Approach to Forecasting Selected Government Expenditures and Revenues.* Ph.D. thesis, Univ. of Pennsylvania, Philadelphia, 1964.

35. Ernest Kurnow, 'Determinants of State and Local Expenditures Re-examined', *National Tax Journal,* XVI, September 1963, pp. 252–5.

36. Jerry Miner, *Social and Economic Factors in Spending for Public Education.* Syracuse, Syracuse University Press, 1963.

37. Elliott R. Morss, J. Eric Fredland, and Saul H. Hymans, 'Fluctuations in State Expenditures: An Econometric Analysis', *Southern Economic Journal* (forthcoming).

38. George Pidot, Jr. *The Public Finances of Local Government in the Metropolitan United States.* Ph.D. dissertation, Harvard University, 1965.

39. E. F. Renshaw, 'A Note on Expenditure Effect of State Aid to Education', *Journal of Political Economy,* LXVIII, April 1960, pp. 170–4.

40. Seymour Sacks, 'Spatial and Locational Aspects of Local Government Expenditures', in Howard G. Schaller, ed., *Public Expenditures Decisions in the Urban Community.* Baltimore: Johns Hopkins Press, 1963.

41. Seymour Sacks and Robert Harris, 'The Determinants of State and Local Government Expenditures and Intergovernmental Flow of Funds', *National Tax Journal,* XVII, March 1964, pp. 75–85.

42. Seymour Sacks and William F. Hellmuth, Jr. *Financing*

Government in a Metropolitan Area. New York: Free Press of Glencoe, 1960.

43. Henry J. Schmandt and C. Ross Stevens, 'Local Government Expenditure Patterns in the United States', *Land Economics,* XXXIX, November 1963, pp. 397–406.

44. Henry J. Schmandt and C. Ross Stevens, 'Measuring Municipal Output', *National Tax Journal,* XIII, 4/1960, pp. 369–75.

45. Stanley Scott and Edward L. Feder. *Factors Associated with Variation in Municipal Expenditure Levels.* Berkeley: Bureau of Public Administration, University of California, 1957.

46. Harvey Shapiro, 'Economies of Scale and Local Government Finance', *Land Economics,* XXXIX, May 1963, pp. 175–86.

47. Harvey Shapiro, 'Measuring Local Government Output: A Comment', *National Tax Journal,* XIV, 4/1961, pp. 394–7.

48. Sherman Shapiro, 'Some Socio-economic Determinants of Expenditures for Education', *Comparative Education Review,* VI, 2/1962, pp. 160–6.

49. John A. Vieg, *et al. California Local Finance.* Stanford: Stanford University Press, 1960.

50. Robert E. Will, 'Scaler Economies and Urban Service Requirements', *Yale Economic Essays,* V, 1/1965, pp. 3–61.

51. Oliver P. Williams. *Suburban Differences and Metropolitan Policies.* Philadelphia: University of Pennsylvania Press, 1965.

52. Robert C. Wood. *1400 Governments.* Cambridge: Harvard Univ. Press, 1961.

APPENDIX E–5: A BRIEF HISTORY OF DOCTRINE ON THE RELATIONSHIPS OF INCOME AND PUBLIC CONSUMPTION EXPENDITURES

As noted in the text a number of early economists discussed relationships between the level of development and public consumption expenditures. However, Adolph Wagner was the first to buttress such remarks with an extensive theoretical foundation.

In brief, Wagner [B333, B334] asserted that in growing economies the share of public consumption expenditures in the national income increases. In order to justify this generalization in a theoretical fashion Wagner divided public expenditures into two categories: expenditures for internal and external security; and expenditures for 'culture and welfare' which include education, health, culture, and welfare, as well as expenditures for different types of 'economic' functions such as transportation, communication, banking, insurance, etc. He argued that expenditures for external security would increase in a growing economy as the nature of the use of force by the state changes from simple aggression to prevention of attack by others and as armies increasingly use more capital equipment. For internal security he foresaw greater expenditures because of increasing 'friction' between economic units and between people as urbanization and industrialization progressed. Expenditures for 'culture and welfare' would increase as the public sector gradually began to encroach upon the private sector, since the former could more effectively and efficiently produce certain goods and services.[1] Moreover, as basic needs for food, shelter, and clothing become increasingly satisfied, people begin to demand more services, especially those provided by the public sector (or, in modern language, the income elasticity for government services is greater than unity). Although Wagner certainly did not prove, either analytically or empirically, that any type of public expenditure would become an increasing ratio of national income, he did present convincing arguments that the absolute level of public expenditures of a growing nation would increase with time.

Wagner has been attacked by Arnold Brecht [B49], who argues that the key factors are really urbanization and its accompanying phenomena (e.g. break up of the extended family, increasing interdependence of economic activities, etc.) which lie behind the rising demand for public expenditures accompanying an increase in the GNP *per capita*. Karl Deutsch [P5, LX, September 1961, pp. 493–515] has taken this argument one step further by noting that economic development is associated with a greater mobilization of public opinion which allows greater pressures to be placed for increased government expenditures. S. P. Gupta [B129] presents another facet of such political considerations: voters desire increased public expenditures as long as the brunt of taxation can be placed on richer minorities. At some point, however, the tax base is such that such expenditures can only be financed by additional taxes on the majority of voters; after this critical point has been reached, politicians gradually realize the inexpediency of such action and the share of public expenditures to the GNP stops rising.

Other types of more economic considerations are also brought to bear on this problem. Oshima [P3, XLVII, June 1957, pp. 381–90]

---

[1] He based this on three reasons: the public sector can produce goods and services of much higher quality that the private sector; the public sector can raise more capital and administer much larger economic units; and public sector production can avoid many of the market crises which beset private firms.

argues that as the level of economic development rises, governments have a much larger tax base after basic human consumption needs have been met and, therefore, that needed public expenditures can then be financed.[1] Peacock and Wiseman [B249] focus their attention on a particular kind of ratchet effect whereby tax rates never decline to their previous levels after certain types of social upheavals such as wars when taxes have been 'temporarily' raised. (This hypothesis is analysed in detail in Appendix E-3.) Martin and Lewis [P55, XXVI, September 1956, pp. 203–44] advance the hypothesis that the rising share of government expenditures in the GNP is due to the rapid expansion of 'non-basic' government expenditures (which they designate as administration, health, and education). On this line Richard Thorn [P69, forthcoming] argues that the relative increase of social expenditures (those for education, health, and welfare) provides the major thrust in growth of government expenditures. More elaborate considerations about the behaviour of individual portions of public expenditures are offered by others (e.g. Musgrave [B230]).

The theme of the secular increase in the public expenditures/GNP ratio is attacked in a different way by J. G. Williamson [P55, XXIX, 1/1961, pp. 43–57], who suggests that as the level of economic development rises, the tendencies toward secular stagnation and permanent unemployment also increase unless the government increases its expenditures to maintain aggregate demand at the full employment level.[2] Ideological factors are also brought into the analysis, especially in the examination of time series where it is asserted that a dramatic shift in world opinion toward such public expenditures has also taken place.[3]

---

[1] Marxists such as Paul Baran [B23] who lay great stress on the 'economic surplus' of a nation have a similar approach to this matter. For a recent restatement of such beliefs, see [B24, p. 147].

[2] Williamson also notes that nations with higher *per capita* incomes have less need for publicly financed social overhead or welfare expenditures so that there are certain countervailing pressures.

[3] This change is illustrated dramatically in the following two statements by US Presidents (cited by Arnold M. Soloway [G133, pp. 19–60]:

'. . . I do not believe that the power and duty of the General Government ought to be extended to the relief of individual suffering which is in no manner properly related to the public service or benefit. A prevalent tendency to disregard the limited mission of this power and duty should, I think, be steadfastly resisted, to the end that the lesson should be constantly enforced that though the people support the Government, the Government should not support the people.' (Grover Cleveland, February 16, 1887.)

'. . . The human problems of individual citizens are a proper and important con-

Finally, some economists (e.g. Andic and Veverka [P30, January 1964, pp. 169–278]) have pointed out that because productivity rises more slowly in those services financed by government revenues than for the aggregate of other goods and services, the relative costs of such 'government services' rises *vis-à-vis* the other costs. Thus the share of public expenditures in the GNP in current prices could rise with economic development, even though this share remains the same in constant price calculations. This change in relative prices bedevils both time-series and cross-section empirical analyses and is discussed in the text.

In addition to such general political and economic factors, a number of special factors are adduced to explain the behaviour of public expenditures in specific countries, e.g. class structure, centralization of tax system, ideology, and so forth. Such reasons are too numerous to outline systematically and, because many are advanced for particular cases, have little general value.[1]

APPENDIX E–6: SOCIO-POLITICAL APPROACHES TO THE STUDY OF PUBLIC EXPENDITURES

The socio-political approach is the attempt to explain public expenditures by reference to sociological or political factors which underlie the decision-making process for public expenditures. By bringing in such broader considerations, the practitioners of this approach hope to avoid the parochialism which characterizes much of the strictly economic analyses on the subject. A number of different lines of attack have been made with this approach and are briefly discussed below.

One line of attack is the construction of abstract models of government behaviour; recent studies in this area include monographs by Anthony Downs [B82], James M. Buchanan and Gordon Tullock [B52], and James M. Buchanan [B50a]. Downs views democratic governments in terms of a vote maximization procedure by politicians and derives such propositions as: democratic governments tend to redistribute income from the rich to the poor, or

cern of our Government. . . . To reduce both the fear and the incidence of destitution to the minimum, to promote the confidence of every individual in the future —these are proper aims of all levels of government, including the Federal Government.' (Dwight D. Eisenhower, January 14, 1954.)

1 For time-series changes in the rate of increase in public expenditures have been explained by changes in government (e.g. the Meiji restoration in Japan, the assumption of power by Salazar in Portugal or by Hitler in Germany), by political crises (the Great Depression in the United States), particular political

democratic governments tend to favour producers more than consumers in their actions. The Buchanan–Tullock approach focuses more on implications of voting systems and the mechanisms for political action. The Buchanan study analyses the effects of fiscal institutions on political behaviour of individuals as they participate in decision-making processes of democracies. Buchanan also summarizes a good deal of the Italian literature on these matters. A number of provocative hypotheses are advanced, but fairly detailed data are necessary for testing them.

From such basic models several economists have tried to derive and test specific macro-economic hypotheses about public expenditures. For instance, Suphan Andic and Jindřich Veverka [P30, Band 23, Heft 2, January 1964, pp. 169–278] argue that public consumption expenditures for welfare purposes will exceed the growth of public consumption expenditures for 'input services' (e.g. education, transportation) because voters are much more conscious of the benefits of the former. Or Burton A. Weisbrod [B337] argues that the greater the mobility of the population in and out of a state, the lower the education expenditures because the voters are reluctant to pay for such expenditures of which the benefits may eventually accrue to other states. As noted in the text S. P. Gupta [B129] puts forward a voting mechanism explanation of the growth of public expenditures as well.

A more traditional use of the socio-economic approach is the inclusion of political variables in the multi-variate analysis of specific types of expenditures. Such variables include the degree of party competition in the political units, the control of the legislature and the governmentship by different political parties, and so forth. Such attempts are still quite primitive (e.g. [B84], and [P48, XXV, 2/1963, pp. 265–89]) and an attempt to carry out such an analysis in this study for US state and local public expenditures for health ended in failure. Another line of enquiry along such lines lies in the response of government units to transfer payments from other levels of government. Some theoretical studies in 'fiscal federalism' include:

reforms (e.g. the Gladstone reforms in England including the extension of the suffrage) and by transfers in financing certain services from the private to the public sector (e.g. in Sweden in the field of education). In cross-section studies, for instance, Martin and Lewis argue that the public expenditures/GNP ratio is low in India and Nigeria because the class structures of these countries are rigid and the political elites are cut off from the needs of the masses. Oshima, on the other hand, explains the Indian case as due to the fact that local, rather than federal governments, have the exclusive right to tax agricultural land, income, and product and, therefore, the central government is handicapped by lack of funds.

[B235, pp. 97–134], [B139] and [P9, XXXI, 2/1965]; in addition, a number of empirical studies have also been carried out.

A different kind of approach is that of 'fiscal psychology'—the attempt to explain the type and amount of public consumption expenditures by analysis of public opinion concerning such expenditures, the attitudes of governmental legislative and administrative bodies, and general sociological phenomena surrounding the expenditure process.

Methods used for such studies include linguistic analysis [B296], public opinion polls ([B292] and [P77, LXXVII, May 1963, pp. 210–35]) and depth interviews with important figures in the political decision making bodies [B293]. Since this is a relatively new field of research (overall views may be found in [B291] and [B192]) few generalizations have been derived which are of use in this study.[1]

APPENDIX E–7: POSSIBLE CAUSES OF DIFFERENCES BETWEEN CROSS-SECTION AND TIME-SERIES ELASTICITIES FOR PUBLIC CONSUMPTION EXPENDITURES

A. Technology

The effect of technological changes, both on the demand and supply side, seem more apparent over time than at a single point in time. Over time on the demand side, for instance, more education per student is required as the level of technology increases, while at a single point in time this differential requirement for education should not be so apparent. Over time on the supply side, the relative prices of goods and labour change considerably, while at a single point in time, such relative prices may be quite similar in different geographical areas.

[1] It seems curious that the fiscal psychologists have not turned to the field of *belles lettres* in their research. For instance, it is of fiscal-psychological interest that in literature public officials engaged in making government expenditures are usually directing such expenditures toward such negative purposes as repression (war, police, or prisons) or the personal needs of the ruler and his entourage, rather than for such positive goals as health, welfare, or roads. Furthermore, in such cases of 'good' expenditures the officials are usually portrayed extremely unfavourably (e.g. the supercilious wastrels in Gogol's works or the villains in Dickens' novels), rather than sympathetically. Indeed, there seem only two notable exceptions to this rule in world literature: the first exponent of counter-cyclical public finance (Joseph in the Bible); and the aged Faust directing public works projects (Part II, Act V). The authors in the socialist-realism school are trying to change the literary image of officials making public expenditures, although their efforts have not yet had notable success.

B. *Population*

Over time the age-distribution of the population has shifted considerably so that, for instance, there is a much higher proportion of people over 65. Over space, on the other hand, such different age-distributions may not be so apparent in various geographical areas. Other aspects of the population structure such as urban-rural ratios, labour force participation rates, etc., may also be related to different factors over time and space.

C. *Differential change in ideology*

Over time, ideological changes can occur which are not associated with changes in *per capita* income on a cross-section basis.

D. *Resistance to change (consumption lags) and anticipation effects (consumption leads)*

Time-series data are supposed to reflect the relative strengths of two phenomena: the time which it takes consumers to adjust their consumption patterns to different incomes or prices; and the change in buying patterns, in anticipation of changed income and prices. Generally, the former effect is assumed to be stronger and, since neither effect is supposed to be reflected in cross-section elasticities, time-series elasticities are expected to be *lower* than the cross-section elasticities. The analogy with government expenditures has a certain relevance and, although such aspects of public expenditures are not examined in this study, considerable empirical research can and should be carried out on this topic.

E. *Effects of stocks and hoarding*

Time-series data are also supposed to reflect the relative importance of the existence of stocks and the desire for more hoarding for consumer expenditures. If the 'stock effect' is more important, the consumer demand for durables would show greater fluctuations over the business cycle than demand for non-durables; similarly, the reverse would be true if consumer desire to hoard were stronger. Since cross-section data are not supposed to reflect such phenomena, cross-section and time-series will again be different. Analysing government expenditures with such concepts is difficult. Although some governmental services can be classified in this way (police services are a 'non-durable'; road construction is a 'durable') other services such as education show characteristics of both, depending on whether they are viewed as consumption or investment.

P*

F. *Interdependence of preferences and desire for uniqueness*

Among similar units of government there is some pressure for uniformity of expenditures. (A cursory reading of the legislative digests of the various US states shows that there is considerable awareness about the expenditures of other states.) Furthermore, in order to reduce certain tensions, central governments often provide certain equalizing grants for local public expenditures. On the other hand, decision makers of a unit may feel that their policy problems are unique and may deliberately avoid expenditure patterns similar to other such units. The relative strength of these two effects is reflected differently in cross-section and time-series data. An empirical investigation of such differences may be found in Chapter III, when the inter-relations between Soviet and US military expenditures are examined.

G. *Other changes*

The inequality of income can be associated with changes in *per capita* income in a different way over time than over space. Over time lengthy political or economic events (wars, depressions) can take place which would affect time-series data for the period without making much impact on the cross-section data. On the other hand, certain regional variables might play an important cross-sectional role which would not affect time-series, e.g. in the USA, cross-section regressions of government expenditures are strongly affected by the fact that the preferences of citizens in the southern states for some expenditures seem different from those in other states and, moreover, that regional variables are highly correlated with important economic variables (e.g. income); time-series data should not be affected by such regionalism, however, unless the relative influence of the region were changing.

H. *Statistical effects*

In time-series data, most of the economic variables are more correlated with each other than in cross-section data. This greater multicollinearity in time-series means that the coefficients are much more sensitive to the specific variables which are included in the analysis. In addition, divergences in the calculated coefficients of cross-section and time-series analyses would also be brought about by different identification problems, auto-correlation in time-series, and other such statistical nightmares.

APPENDIX E–8: THE CENTRALIZATION OF US STATE AND LOCAL PUBLIC EXPENDITURES

Centralization of government expenditures in this appendix refers to the degree to which state and local public expenditures are made at the state government level.[1] The purpose of this note is to explore certain of the hypotheses discussed in Chapter VII in greater detail.

A. *The Behaviour of Aggregate State and Local Expenditures*

As we might expect, the degree of centralization of state and local public expenditures rose over the last half century; from 1913 to 1962 the centralization ratio increased from 14 per cent to 38 per cent. If the proportion of expenditures is held constant so that the effects of a change in the structure of expenditures can be eliminated, quite similar results are obtained: the rise being from 14 per cent to 33 per cent (1913 structure) and from 16 per cent to 38 per cent (1962 structure). In other words, contrary to the case of centralization of total government expenditures (federal expenditures as a ratio of total government expenditures), the rise in centralization of state and local expenditures cannot be attributed to a structural shift in relative importance of the major expenditure categories. This does not mean, of course, that a shift in relative importance of different types of expenditures *within* the major categories did not underlie the rising centralization ratio.

On a cross-section basis the importance of income *per capita* and population, which are discussed in the text, can be easily examined by calculating the following regressions for the 50 states in 1962:

$$\ln C_1 = 2 \cdot 33 - 0 \cdot 20^* \ln (Y/P) - 0 \cdot 25 \ln P \quad R^2 = 0 \cdot 53^*$$
$$(0 \cdot 03) \qquad\qquad (0 \cdot 14)$$
$$\ln C_2 = 4 \cdot 11 - 0 \cdot 18^* \ln (Y/P) - 0 \cdot 48^* \ln P \quad R^2 = 0 \cdot 59^*$$
$$(0 \cdot 02) \qquad\qquad (0 \cdot 13)$$

where

C_1 = centralization ratio for current state and local expenditures
C_2 = centralization ratio for total state and local expenditures
Y = personal income
P = population.

The regressions show that the centralization ratio decreased as income *per capita* and population increased, a result which seems contrary to the time-series data (where centralization increased as

[1] All data for government expenditures come from [G105]; personal income and population data come from [G116] and [G120].

per capita income and population increased). A resolution of this apparent difference requires examination of the centralization ratio of individual types of expenditures, a problem which is attacked below in two different ways.

B. *The Relative Degree of Centralization of Different Types of State and Local Public Expenditures*

By means of a rank order analysis, exclusive attention can be focused on the following question: does the relative degree of centralization of different types of state and local public expenditure follow some pattern or does it merely reflect random factors? The 1962 data for the 50 states were treated in the following way: First, the seven most important public expenditures were chosen; second, centralization ratios were calculated,[1] third, the ratios were ranked for each state.

One measure of the degree to which the rank orders are similar is the 'coefficient of concordance', a statistic which is equal to $1 \cdot 00$ when the rank orders of centralization ratio are the same in each state and which is equal to $0 \cdot 00$ when the rank orders follow a random pattern. [This statistic is analysed by Maurice G. Kendall, *Rank Correlation Methods*, 2nd ed. (New York: Hafner Publ., 1955)]. For the data under consideration, its value is $0 \cdot 59$, which is statistically significant ($0 \cdot 05$ level). That is, a statistically significant rank order pattern appears and, moreover, the particular order which is revealed is the following (arranged according to degree of declining centralization ratios): natural resources, health services (health and hospitals), welfare, highway, police (police and correction), administration (financial administration, general control, and general public building) and education.

Although it seems quite reasonable that natural resource expenditures, for which certain public good properties and externalities are readily apparent, should be centralized; but the order of centralization ratios for the other expenditures seems quite peculiar. Certainly on an *a priori* basis it would have been difficult to predict that expenditures for health services or welfare could be more centralized than expenditures for highways or education. More insights into the rank order can be gained by listing the number of occurrences in which the centralization ratio of one expenditure was higher than that of another (see Table E–3).

The table shows that the centralization ratios of expenditures for natural resources were higher in a majority of cases for other

[1] Both current and capital expenditures were included.

individual expenditures, while the centralization ratios of education expenditures were lower. The centralization ratio for welfare expenditures show the most peculiar pattern since in some states they were relatively high (in twenty-four cases out of fifty it was higher than the ratio for natural resources) while in other states they were relatively low (in thirteen cases out of fifty they were lower than the ratios for education). All other ratios showed a much more regular pattern.

TABLE E–3

Comparison of Individual Pairs of Centralized Ratios for US State and Local Public Expenditures in 1962.

Number of times centralization ratios of expenditure listed in columns were higher than centralization ratios of expenditure listed in rows.

	Natural resources	Health services	Welfare	Highways	Police	Administration	Education
Natural resources	—	26	26	40	48	50	50
Health services	24	—	20	40	48	50	49
Welfare	24	30	—	32	35	36	37
Highways	10	10	18	—	48	50	49
Police	2	2	15	2	—	26	48
Administration	0	0	14	0	24	—	44
Education	0	1	13	1	2	6	—

Interpreting these results is difficult. Although a pattern appears, we are at a loss to explain it. Two important factors must be noted, however. First, the pattern is quite different from the pattern which was found and discussed in the text concerning the centralization ratios of total government expenditures in the EEC nations (e.g. in these nations health expenditures were the most decentralized and education expenditures were more centralized). Second, there are no grounds to conclude that the order is due to any particular economic factor; indeed, the data in the table could well reflect historical or institutional forces as well. In order to examine the effects of such forces, it is useful to examine the causal factors behind the absolute value of the centralization ratios of particular expenditures.

C. *The Centralization Ratios of Individual Expenditures*

In the economic literature there are few hypotheses about the causal determinants of variation of the degree of centralization for a single expenditure.[1] A start can be made by considering the effect of *per capita* income and population, the variables which have been discussed above. The results of regression calculations using these variables in the cross-section analysis are noteworthy particularly when compared to a 50-year time trend.[2]

TABLE E–4

Cross-Section and Time-Series Analyses of Centralization of State and Local Expenditures[3]

Expenditures	Cross-section analysis: 1962 Elasticity coefficients		Centralization trend, 1902–1962 Average annual rate of increase
	Y/P	P	
Education	− 0·49*	− 0·21*	+ 1·6*
	(0·20)	(0·04)	(0·1)
Public welfare	− 2·10*	− 0·46*	+ 1·4*
	(0·80)	(0·15)	(0·2)
Police	− 0·02	− 0·23*	+ 4·2*
	(0·17)	(0·15)	(0·3)
Highways	− 0·13	− 0·08*	+ 4·3*
	(0·12)	(0·02)	(0·5)
Administration	+ 0·04	− 0·15*	+ 1·3*
	(0·02)	(0·04)	(0·2)
Health services	− 0·14	− 0·07	+ 0·1
	(0·23)	(0·04)	(0·1)
Natural resources	0·05	− 0·03	—
	(0·14)	(0·03)	

[1] One hypothesis has been suggested by Burton Weisbrod [B337] and concerns the effect of outward migration on centralization for those expenditures with external benefits. Unfortunately, adequate data on outward migration are not available and it was not felt that this hypothesis could be adequately tested.

[2] Strictly speaking one cannot compare the cross-section and time-series results because they are at different levels of aggregation. That is, the time series might be affected by an increase in relative expenditures of those states which have a higher or lower relative degree of centralization for the expenditure being analysed. Such composition effects, however, did not seem very important in the cases under examination.

[3] For the cross-section analysis the regression coefficients were calculated according to the following formula: $\ln C = a + b_1 \ln (Y/P) + b_2 \ln P$, where Y is personal income. For the time-series analysis the regression coefficients were calculated according to the following formula: $\ln C = a + b T$, where T is time.

Since local government expenditures for natural resources did not begin on any scale until three decades after 1902, no time trend was calculated.

Although time-series calculations were also made according to the same formula used for the cross-section analysis, multicollinearity between the two independent variables prevented a meaningful separation of the two causal factors. Therefore, only the trend was calculated.

In the cross-section analysis, centralization ratios of all expenditures except health and natural resources are significantly (0·05 level) and negatively related to population; in education and public welfare, centralization is also significantly and negatively related to *per capita* income. For all the expenditures except those for health services, however, centralization increased over time when both the population and the *per capita* income were increasing. Fortunately, we are in a position to probe into the reasons for this discrepancy between the cross-section and time-series results. The causes seem most clear-cut for education.

If we split education expenditures into two parts, those for local schools and those for other educational purposes (universities, special schools, etc.) and recalculate the regressions, some startling differences appear.

TABLE E–5

Centralization of State and Local Expenditures for Education

Expenditures	Cross-section analysis: 1962		Centralization trend, 1902–1962
	Elasticity coefficients		Average annual rate of increase
	Y/P	P	
Local schools	− 6·89*	− 0·08*	+ 4·2*
	(2·87)	(0·55)	(1·0)
Other education	− 0·06	− 0·09*	− 0·16*
	(0·05)	(0·01)	(0·04)
Total education	− 0·49*	− 0·21*	+ 1·6*
	(0·20)	(0·04)	(0·1)
	Distribution of expenditures		Centralization ratios
	1902	1962	1902	1962
Local schools	93%	80%	0%	1%
Other education	7	20	100	91
Total education	100	100	7	18

In the cross-section regressions centralization is significantly and negatively related to both income *per capita* and population for both components of education. However, over time the centralization ratio of expenditures increased for local schools and decreased for other education. Since the centralization ratio for local schools was so low, its increase over time could have been easily offset by the decrease in the centralization ratio for other education. It was the shift in relative expenditures toward 'other education', which has the highest centralization ratio, that was responsible for the rising trend of centralization for education as a whole.

If the same experiment is repeated for welfare (which can be divided into cash and other welfare expenditures) and health services (which can be divided into hospital and public health expenditures) it becomes clear that the shift in composition of expenditures is the primary factor behind the rising time trend of centralization. On the other hand, the cross-section regressions for the different components give roughly the same results as the regression for total expenditures.

All this suggests that the major factor behind the contradictory cross-section and time-series results are structural shifts in the relative importance of different categories of expenditures which accompany a rising income *per capita* and population over time, but not at a single point in time. In other words, cross-section and time-series determinants for the relative volume of expenditures are different, a subject which is discussed in the text.

Two major approaches toward analysing these differences in determinants of expenditures and their influence on the centralization ratios can be taken. One line of attack is pursued in the text—close attention is paid to different supply and demand factors operating across space and over time. For instance, there has been a rising technological complexity in the world over the last half century so that the calculated income elasticity of demand for higher education is quite different when viewed at a single point in time or over a time period. For other types of expenditures, similar conclusions can be drawn.

A second approach in explaining the differences between the time-series and cross-section analyses of the centralization ratio is more speculative. If we consider government expenditures for some new purposes as an expenditure 'innovation', then evidence from other studies suggests that the major factor behind the rapid increase in government expenditure over time has occurred in those areas where expenditure innovations are made (see [B94]). Furthermore, most such expenditure innovations seem to be made at the higher levels of government and only slowly are decentralized. Thus the state governments financed the first institutions of higher learning and only later did communities begin to establish and finance their own colleges and universities. Although the expenditure innovations may be finally made at the local level, particularly in states with relatively large populations or *per capita* incomes (this is reflected in the cross-section analysis), there is a considerable lag which, in turn, leads to the rising centralization ratio for expenditure aggregatives over time. At one point in time, however, the effects of this lag are not apparent and only population or *per capita* income act as determinants for the level of centralization.

Of course, this second explanation for the contradictory results of the cross-section and time-series studies of centralization of US state and local government expenditures needs considerably more empirical research before it can be confirmed. If the evidence is positive, then the problem of decentralization of public expenditures becomes one of devising new institutional mechanisms by which funds from higher instances can be transferred to local governmental organs, rather than the problem of circumventing inexorable economic forces. In view of the importance of centralization as a political issue, it is surprising that economists have not yet begun to examine more deeply the relevant determinants of the current centralization of public expenditures.

APPENDIX E-9: AGE DISTRIBUTION OF WELFARE RECIPIENTS IN SIX NATIONS

Some idea of the overall age distribution of welfare recipients can be gained by classifying each of the different welfare programmes according to the broad age group to which the programme was intended. For instance, out-of-school athletic expenditures go to youth; unemployment benefits and income supports for illness go to people in the working ages; and pensions go to the old age. General assistance measures, etc., are classified as 'not specified' unless qualitative evidence is available which gives some guidepost for distributing them among the different age groups. Although such a statistical exercise involves many problems,[1] and although the resulting data can only be considered to be indicative of general magnitudes, certain broad conclusions can be drawn (see Table E-6 on the next page).

First, it appears that the centralized economies give relatively larger shares of their welfare expenditures to infants and youth. A closer examination shows that a large portion of such expenditures in all three centralized economies went for infant care, nurseries, etc., which allow women to continue as active members of the labour force. The relatively higher percentage of expenditures going to infants and youth in Austria, *vis-à-vis* the other market economies

---

[1] The results are particularly sensitive to the assumptions made in spreading the expenditures of vaguely specified programmes to specific age groups. Additional qualitative evidence leading to different assumptions in spreading certain expenditures yield somewhat different results for East Germany than in a previous estimate of mine. [P74, 3–4/1965)].

and in Poland, *vis-à-vis* the other centralized economies, seems to reflect the general tendency of countries which are predominently Roman Catholic to have higher children's allowances [B122].

Second, the market economies seem to give a higher percentage of their welfare expenditures to members of the population who are of working age. This includes not only unemployment compensation, but, in the case of Austria, fairly high sick-pay as well.

TABLE E–6

Welfare Expenditures According to Age Categories of Recipients in 1958

Age groups	USA	West Germany	Austria	East Germany	USSR	Poland
			(in percentages)			
Infants and youth	5	4	11	10	18	44
Working age	25	27	11	12	15	11
Old age	62	56	63	65	64	34
Not specified	8	12	15	12	3	11

General sources for the estimates are given for the respective countries in Appendix A. Data may not add to 100 per cent because of rounding. Detailed data for such similar calculations for other sample nations are not available. The major assumptions used in making the estimates in the table were as follows:

(*a*) *United States:* 'Veterans expenditures not elsewhere classified' were assumed to be given half to working aged, half to old aged.

(*b*) *West Germany:* Expenditures for war victims and for social expenditures of the LAG were assumed to be given half to the working aged, half to the old aged. Fiscal 1958 was used.

(*c*) *Austria:* One half of the local expenditures for youth and other social purposes was assumed to go to youth; and one half to 'not specified'.

(*d*) *East Germany:* One half of the expenditures for social facilities was assumed to go to the working aged; one half, to the old aged. General welfare expenditures were placed under 'not specified'. (Both of these assumptions are different in a previous calculation which I published).

(*e*) *Soviet Union:* No major assumptions needed to be made.

(*f*) *Poland:* No major assumptions needed to be made.

APPENDIX E–10: SOCIAL INSURANCE PROGRAMMES IN THE SAMPLE NATIONS[1]

Following a standard classification in the various social insurance programmes can be divided into five categories:

A. *Payments for old age, invalidism, and death*

In the 1950–62 period all of the sample nations had nationwide programmes for such purposes and in almost all of these countries, such programmes constituted the largest portion of welfare expenditures. The initiation of such programmes started in the Germanies in 1889 and, by 1930 included all the sample nations except the United States, Greece, and Yugoslavia (all of which began such programmes by 1937). With the exception of Czechoslovakia, which had a social service pension arrangement, all of these programmes in the 1950s were administered by social insurance systems.

In the market economies by 1962 all major groups in the labour force were covered, although inclusion of agricultural workers or self employed farmers was not complete in many of these countries. In the centralized economies at this time the only major groups which were not covered were co-operative and private farmers in Romania and the Soviet Union and private farmers in Poland.[2]

With the exception of Ireland, where a flat pension was given, all of the other sample nations linked benefits to previous contributions; and in none of these nations did the social insurance system take into account greater objective needs of one or more population groups for such old age pensions. Although the financing of such social insurance payments differed among nations, consideration of this factor is beyond the scope of this chapter.[3]

---

[1] Most of the information for this appendix comes from [G127].

[2] Since 1962 state pension systems for cooperative farmers have been introduced in both Romania and the Soviet Union. Although private farmers are not covered in most of the centralized economies, by 1962 they were numerically unimportant in all these countries except Poland.

[3] Although considerable attention is given to the relative shares of employer and employee contributions to the social insurance payments, the practical difference seems to be very small. Both payments act as a wedge between take-home wages and labour costs and changing the distribution between the two types of contributions affects primarily the base on which gross wages are calculated. On the other hand, the relative contribution of government to the social insurance system is important and raises a number of questions about the incidence of taxation which are discussed in Chapter VII.

B. *Income supports for lost time caused by work injuries*

All of the sample nations had nationwide insurance programmes for such purposes, although such insurance was carried by private companies in the United States and Ireland. Such programmes were usually the oldest social insurance arrangements, dating back before World War I in most countries. The volume of such expenditures was relatively very small, however.

C. *Income supports during sickness or maternity*

Of the sample nations only the United States did not have such a specific nationwide system of public expenditures for such purposes. In all other countries the system was organized on a social insurance basis and, in most cases, dated back before the 1920s. Major excluded groups among the market economies included certain self-employed groups; among the centralized economies, collective farm workers in the Soviet Union and private farm workers in most of the other countries.

D. *Unemployment payments*

All of the market economies had nationwide public unemployment insurance systems; of the centralized economies, however, only East Germany and Hungary had such systems. The adoption date of such programmes varied from 1911 to 1957 for the sample nations with such expenditures. Although such unemployment payments existed at one time in the Soviet Union, they were abolished at the time of the first five year plan; however, there has been certain agitation for their re-introduction.[1]

With the exception of Yugoslavia and Hungary, unemployment benefit systems were organized on an insurance basis. Coverage of such benefits did not extend in most countries to all workers; the most important excluded groups were agricultural workers in the USA, West Germany, Yugoslavia, and Greece.

E. *Family allowances*

These are the newest type of social insurance expenditures and, of the sample nations, the United States was the only country without a nationwide public programme for such purposes (although specific assistance programmes were especially designated for families with children). In all the other countries except Ireland, East Germany,

[1] E.g. see Ye. Manevich, 'Vseobshchnost' truda i problemi ratsional'nogo ispol'zovaniya rabochey sily v sssr' [P97, 6/1965, pp. 23–31].

and the Soviet Union, such supports were given through employment related systems. In the latter three countries, such payments were made through social service payments. The size of families qualifying for such supports varied from one to four children.[1]

APPENDIX E–11: SOME REMARKS ON THE EFFECTS OF FINANCING MEDICAL CARE EXPENDITURES IN DIFFERENT WAYS

In this Appendix I briefly outline some of the major pros and cons for financing medical expenditures through fee-for-service, insurance, and public service methods.

The major advantage of the direct fee-for-service method of financing medical care expenditures is that the physician has a financial stake in giving the customer high quality medical care. Thus in certain countries such as Poland and the Soviet Union, where medical expenditures are provided free as a public service, citizens often pay for private medical care if they want particularly high quality treatment or special attention.[2] On the other hand, three disadvantages are readily apparent. Because of financial limitations of certain low income groups, medical care is not necessarily distributed in the most equitable or, from the viewpoint of the economy, in the most productive way. This seems especially true in regard to maternity care and is discussed in the text. Furthermore, the physician has a certain financial advantage in keeping the patient longer under medical care, especially if the patient has little technical understanding of his condition. For instance, in the United States there are frequent complaints about the large number of unnecessary operations.[3] Finally, the fee-for-service introduces a certain measure

[1] In order to discourage large families, family allowances are being withheld after the family has had three or four children in Mainland China [P66, April 27, 1966]. On the other hand, Poland, which has the greatest over-population problem in East Europe, has also the highest relative amount of children's allowances.

[2] For the Soviet Union, see Luk and Tardov [P54a, December 8, 1966, p. 2]. For Poland I have relied on interviews with several Polish economists. In certain centrally planned economies such as Czechoslovakia, physicians are highly restricted in taking private patients or charging special fees for service. Czechoslovak citizens have told me that it is quite common, however, to 'tip' physicians with money or presents.

[3] The statistics on this matter are discussed by [B326, pp. 45 ff.]. George Bernard Shaw [B301, Vol. I, p. 1] once wrote:
'That any sane nation, having observed that you could provide for the supply of bread by giving bakers a pecuniary interest in baking for you, should go on to

of uncertainty into a person's financial future which many people do not like to bear.[1]

Financing medical expenditures through some type of insurance arrangement, either public or private, can be carried out in a number of ways. Either the physician can charge only a certain fee for each type of treatment, which is then paid to him by the insurance company, or he can charge any fee and the patient is reimbursed a certain set amount for each treatment; or the physician belongs to a group which accepts all patients at a certain prepaid fee.

The primary advantage of financing medical expenditures through any type of insurance arrangement is that the major risks stemming from high or unexpected medical expenditures can be alleviated while the patient is allowed the freedom of selecting his own doctor.[2] On the other hand, there are also certain disadvantages of an insurance scheme. First of all, many insurance systems do not cover all types of medical treatment and, as a result, certain distortions are introduced. Thus, because hospital insurance is much easier to obtain than insurance for doctors' fees in the United States, increasingly more routine medical tests are being performed in hospitals, rather than in physicians' offices. Second, 'experience-rating' type health insurance acts to drive out other types of health insurance and leaves certain high risk groups of the population without health insurance except at extremely high costs.[3] Third, health insurance can lead to 'health malingering' and subsequential crowding of medical facilities so that the quality of medical care

give a surgeon a pecuniary interest in cutting off your leg, is enough to make one despair of political humanity. But that is precisely what we have done. And the more appalling the mutilation, the more the mutilator is paid.'
Consistency was not one of Shaw's virtues, for it must be noted, 12 pages later he was complaining about the poverty among the doctors.

[1] In interviews with Soviet refugees, Field [B98 Chapter 12] found that a majority of the refugees in West Germany preferred the German over the Soviet system of medicine while in the United States, a majority favoured the Soviet over the US system. These data, that are the only large scale opinion data I could find of polled groups which have lived under a number of types of medical systems, give an interesting insight about general attitudes toward personal risk bearing in the medical area.

[2] There is considerable controversy about the advantages and disadvantages of different types of insurance arrangements which I am omitting. This controversy is summarized by [B309, Part V] and [B174].

[3] Seymour Harris [B136, Chpt. XX] particularly emphasizes this point when writing 'bad insurance drives out the good'. Such 'risk skimming' is defended on economic grounds by Duncan M. MacIntyre [B55, pp. 148–73].

deteriorates.[1] Furthermore, some insurance schemes limit the choice of doctors by patients which often leads to a lowering of the quality of medical care as well. Finally, administration costs of insurance can add considerably to the cost of medical care and, indeed, can lead to the exclusion of certain population groups from medical insurance because of the high costs of sales and servicing.[2]

The major advantages of financing medical expenditures as a public service (medical care is financed by a central agency and is available to all eligible citizens) are that emphasis can be placed on preventive medicine and that large population groups are not excluded from receiving such care. Preventive medicine can lead to long run lessening of the burden on medical facilities and the non-exclusiveness of benefits can lead to the breaking of vicious circles of poverty and disease which characterize certain groups in several of the sample nations. Physicians can be paid either salaries, fees per patient, or fees for service. Two major disadvantages are apparent. First, administration costs of such a system can be paralysing. For instance, recent reports indicate that about 50 per cent of the time of physicians in the Soviet Union and Czechoslovakia is spent filling out various governmental forms.[3] Second, if patients cannot easily change doctors, or if doctors are salaried, they may have very little economic incentive for providing high quality medical care.[4] Third, such a system economizes 'medical malingering' and wastage.[5]

The balancing of the pros and cons of each method of financing medical expenditures is an intricate matter in which the special

[1] This point is examined for a number of countries in [B294]. However the general conclusions of this study are hotly disputed in the case of the United States by [B15], and [B309]. The debate is summarized by [B174, esp. pp. 31 ff.].

[2] This issue is debated by Arrow [P3, LVIII, December, 1963, pp. 941–73] and Lees and Rice [P3, LX, March 1965, pp. 140–54]. Data on the high cost of administration, especially for specialized policies, are presented in [B309, Chpt. 14]. The adequacy of health insurance coverage, especially in the low income groups, is analysed by [B15]. One interesting theoretical point about insurance which is not mentioned by the protagonists in the debate is that there are increasing returns in risk bearing, a proposition which is discussed mathematically in [B246, Chpt. VII and Appendix by Aryeh Dvoretzky].

[3] For the Soviet Union, see Boris Petrovsky [P76, March 3, 1966]; for Czechoslovakia, Jan Vrtis [P75, July 21, 1964].

[4] [B294] discusses this situation in a number of countries. Field [B98] has certain contrary conclusions from interview materials of Soviet refugees.

[5] The whole question of 'wastage' due to providing free medical care is extremely difficult to analyse. For instance, in Poland there have been reports (e.g. [P36, October 6, 1964]) that eyeglasses are extremely difficult to obtain and that patients must wait years for them. But such a situation may reflect less on the system *per se* than on the incompetency of the responsible officials.

conditions of the country and the period must be taken closely into account. There has been considerable variation of the role of the public sector in the area of health over the centuries[1] and many types of public devices for the distribution of medical care which are often considered 'socialistic', such as the free polyclinic, have been developed by 'capitalist' nations.[2] Indeed, of the sample nations, all of the countries except the United States, Greece, and Yugoslavia had introduced extensive publicly financed medical care programmes before 1925 and most of these systems had been established before 1900. Within the sample nations, there is considerable diversity in the role played by the public sector.

Among the sample centralized economies during the 1950–62 period, medical care was provided as a public service in Czechoslovakia, the Soviet Union, Romania, and Bulgaria, and on an insurance basis in the remaining countries.[3] Coverage ranged from 57 per cent of the population in Poland (1960) to almost 100 per cent in Hungary, Czechoslovakia, and the Soviet Union.[4] In the latter country, publicly financed expenditures covered in the late 1950s about 90 per cent of total expenditures for medical care, a percentage which has been achieved in some market economies such as the United Kingdom, as well.[5]

Among the sample market economies, in this period, medical care was provided as a public service only in Ireland. In four of the countries, West Germany, Austria, Italy, and Yugoslavia, public insurance programmes covered sizeable portions of the population, ranging from 49 per cent in Yugoslavia (1960) to 80 per cent in West Germany (1960).[6] In 1960 the public medical insurance programme in Greece covered about 18 per cent of the population and in the United States, about 2 per cent. Indeed, the latter country and South Africa were the only two economically developed nations

[1] See [B280] or, for a briefer treatment of such matters, George Rosen in [B106, pp. 17–69].

[2] See especially [B239]. For example, free polyclinics were operative in inter-war Hungary [B239, Vol. II, Chpt. V].

[3] The public provisions for medical care are briefly summarized for every country in the world in [G127]. For the centralized economies the Akademie fuer Staatsmedizin in Hamburg has published more than 25 volumes in its series: *Zur Entwicklung und Organization des Gesundheitswesens in Sovjetrussland, in osteuropaeischen Volksdemokratien und in Mitteldeutschland.*

[4] [G6, 1961]. These data are not completely comparable and the ILO has ceased publication of such information.

[5] The datum for the Soviet Union was estimated by [B240, pp. 62–3]; the datum for the UK, [B136, p. 279].

[6] [G6, 1961].

without such extensive programmes and the United States with the introduction in 1966 of public medical insurance for the aged, is slowly moving out of this category. It must also be added that in cases where government medical insurance does not cover large segments of the population, private medical insurance often fulfils the same role. For instance, in the United States over 70 per cent of the population was covered by private medical insurance of one kind or another and, in addition, such private medical insurance was expanding in coverage of both individuals and of different types of expenditures.[1]

APPENDIX E-12: CAUSAL FACTORS BEHIND THE ESTABLISHMENTS OF SOCIAL INSURANCE SYSTEMS

I tried to isolate the causal factors behind the establishment of social insurance systems (either pension or national health insurance) by looking at the differential characteristics of nations at the eve of World War I which had, or did not have, such systems. For examining single characteristics, chi-square tests using the following arrangement of data were used.

	Nations with social insurance systems in 1913	Nations without social insurance systems in 1913
Nations with less than A of characteristic X in 1913		
Nations with more than A of characteristic X in 1913		

For testing the influence of several factors at the same time, regressions of the following type were calculated: $S = a + b X + c Y$; where S is a dummy variable designating whether the nation had a social insurance system in 1913, Y and Z are the independent variables which were tested, and a, b, and c are the calculated regression coefficients.

In the sample of nations I tried to include all independent European nations plus the developed nations of North America and the British Commonwealth. If a larger sample of nations had been used, the causal factors behind the establishment of social insurance systems would have been the level of economic development (meas-

---

[1] For data on individuals covered, see [G116, various issues]. For detailed data on type of coverage, amount of coverage, and relation of insurance to various socio-economic characteristics of family, see [B15] and [B14].

ured by GNP *per capita*) or industrialization (measured by portion of the labour force in industry or outside of agriculture), since none of the less developed, non-industrialized nations had social insurance systems. However, most of these nations were colonies (in Africa and Asia, but not Latin America), which raises a problem of multi-collinearity, and in all of these nations, statistics were of very poor quality. By excluding these poorer nations, attention is focused on more immediate causal factors, rather than the most basic causal factor of the level of economic development.

Information about the founding date of the social insurance systems come from [G127]; *per capita* GNP data, from [B60a]; labour force and population data, from [G9, 1926]; unionization data, from [B335a, p. 602]; and other data, from [G9] and scattered sources.

With the 25 or so nations in the sample there was no statistically significant relation between the existence of a social insurance system and the level of economic development (measured by GNP *per capita*). Zoellner's [B350] hypothesis concerning the influence of industrialization (measured both in terms of percentage of the labour force in industry, mining, and manufacturing and percentage of the labour force outside of agriculture) and the establishment of a social insurance system also did not show statistically significant results.

A number of variants of an hypothesis proposed by Henry Aaron (in [B86]) that the age distribution played an important role in the establishment of social insurance systems were tested, but no statistically significant relation was found. A multivariate analysis using income *per capita* as the second variable was also attempted, but in vain.

Other types of economic hypotheses culled from the literature were tested, but no statistically significant associations could be unearthed.[1] I also examined a number of more political variables (for which data are considerably more scarce) such as the proposition advanced by the French historian Elie Halévy that colonial empires and social insurance systems were related (for Great Britain, he claimed that both were manifestations of the desire for 'security'). But negative results were also obtained in these experiments.

Finally one factor was found—the relative importance of union-ization (measured in terms both of the proportion of labour union members in the labour force and the proportion of union members

[1] Most of this work was carried out by Mr Philip Shea and I would like to express my appreciation to him.

among the non-agricultural labour force)—that was significantly associated with the existence of a social insurance system in a 19 nation sample for which data are available. Indeed, among all the experiments that were performed, this was the only one for which such a positive relationship was revealed.

We must be cautious in interpreting this relation between unionization and social insurance systems. Although it suggests that labour unions acted as a political force for the establishment of such systems, it could also be interpreted to mean that both are related to some common cause. For instance, it is well known that Bismarck instituted the social insurance system in Germany in order to forestall increases in power of the Social Democratic Party. That is, the percentage of unionization may be merely a measure of the political interest or mobilization of the workers.

APPENDIX E–13: PRODUCTION OF PRIVATE EDUCATION

There is considerable information in regard to the degree of private schooling on various levels of education. For the United States the ratio of pupils or students in private schools rises steadily from primary school, through secondary schools, to undergraduate colleges and universities, and to graduate schools.[1] For all of the other sample market economies for which data are available, the relative importance of private schools is higher in secondary education than in primary education[2]; however, the relative importance of private colleges and universities is very small for all of these nations. Such a phenomenon can be found in most of the other industrialized nations of the world as well.[3]

The question of the relationship between private schooling and a rising *per capita* income can be examined with both time-series and cross-section data. In the United States and Sweden, two countries for which data on public and private primary and secondary schooling for a fifty-year period are readily available, the relative import-

[1] [G122, 1957-58, Chapters 1 and 4].

[2] [G34]. Although the ratio of pupils in private vocational schools to total pupils in vocational schools was higher than a similar ratio for general secondary schools in the four sample market economies for which good data were available, the situation was different in many other market economies for which information could be obtained.

[3] For Sweden the quantitative importance of public and private schools is discussed by [B153].

ance of private school children has increased in the former country and decreased in the latter. The situation is complicated in the United States because the relative importance of private school children has increased in the primary schools, but decreased in the secondary schools.[1] In the short run period under consideration in this study (1950–62), the relative importance of private primary and secondary pupils increased very slightly in the United States and Italy and at a slow but steady rate in Greece. (The latter is probably one of the few countries in the world where the relative number of pupils in private primary and secondary schools is planned to increase.[2]) Because of the importance of historical, religious and political factors outside the purview of this study, it does not seem meaningful to make cross-country comparisons at a single point in time.[3]

APPENDIX E–14: DISCRIMINATION IN HIGHER EDUCATION

Operationally, we can define 'discrimination' in education as the differences to which education is denied to pupils and students from different social groups on bases other than intellectual merit.

If we assume that intellectual merit is distributed evenly between men and women, then determination of the sex composition of students in institutions of higher learning should be the first step in an analysis of discrimination (see Table E–7 on the next page).

Although the proportion of women among students in institutions of higher learning did not seem related to *per capita* income of the nation, a result also noted by others,[4] the proportion was significantly greater (0·05 degree of confidence) in the centralized economies than

---

[1] [G122, Chapter 1].

[2] [G18, pp. 162 ff]. The primary reasons for the relative increase in private schools is that private schools are relatively more important in urban than in rural areas and there has been an increase in urbanization. Since the rate of increase of private and public schools in urban areas is expected to be about the same, the relative importance of private schools in the country as a whole is expected to increase.

[3] It should be noted that religious factors seem to operate in a peculiar fashion. Countries with considerable religious heterogeniety, such as the United States or Holland, often seem to have a relatively important private school sector. Countries with religious homogeniety, such as Ireland, Sweden, or Italy, may have a relatively high or low ratio of private school students, depending on a number of historical factors too complicated to set forth in this economic study.

[4] C. Arnold Anderson, 'The Social Status of Students in Relation to Type of Economy: An International Comparison', in [B133].

The Proportion of Women Among Students in All Institutions of Higher Learning in 1960[1]

Country	Ratio of women	Country	Ratio of women
USA	37%	East Germany	32%
West Germany	23	Czechoslovakia	34
Austria	23	USSR	43
Ireland	30	Poland	41
Italy	28	Hungary	33
Yugoslavia	29	Romania	33
Greece	26	Bulgaria	40

in the market economies. Since women account for about 50 per cent of the relevant age bracket in all countries, this suggests that discrimination against women is greater in the market economies. However, one additional factor must also be taken into consideration before this conclusion can be made with confidence.

Aspiration levels for a college education may be different among sexes. For instance, in both the United States and the Soviet Union, aspirations for higher education appear to be lower for women than for men;[2] and this is undoubtedly true in all the other sample nations as well.

Once an aspiration factor is introduced into the analysis, difficulties arise. For instance, although no one has ever claimed that discrimination against women in higher education is increasing in the United States, it is a fact that women as a percentage of students receiving college degrees declined between 1930 and 1960.[3] The cause of this decline seems due more to a change in *relative* aspirations for a college education, linked with a change in the self image of American girls, than to economic discrimination.[4] Thus for the data in Table E-7 to be employed in analysis of discrimination, data about

[1] Data from [G36, 1963, pp. 219–40]. The datum for West Germany excludes West Berlin; the datum for Ireland excludes the National College for Arts; the datum for Czechoslovakia and Bulgaria cover both day and evening students; the datum for Hungary includes correspondence courses.

[2] For the United States, recent evidence is available in [B189, Chap. VI], and [B228, Chap. 26 ff.]. For the Soviet Union, evidence is available in [B25, Chapter VI].

[3] Data from [G116, 1962, p. 131] and [G114, p. 211].

[4] This phenomenon has been analysed in social-psychological terms in a number of popular books such as Betty Friedan, *The Feminine Mystique* (New York: Norton, 1963).

relative aspiration levels for higher education also need to be known. Since certain survey results suggest that education aspiration levels may be relatively higher for women in socialist countries than elsewhere,[1] there may not be any real difference between the two systems in discrimination against women. Considerably more evidence is needed, however, before definite conclusions can be drawn.

Another important type of discrimination in higher education is against certain social classes in the population. This may be due to the fact that only certain classes in the society can afford higher education, or it may be due to deliberate policy by the government. In either case selection of students for higher education is not based on the intellectual merit of the student. Such discrimination is particularly important when viewing social mobility since managerial, technical, and intellectual elites in all countries have increasingly come to be composed of individuals with higher education. Thus education has become increasingly necessary, though not sufficient, for high status positions.[2] Of course, since education is often not the most important qualification for such jobs, other channels for social mobility also remain.

It is well known that in different periods, the governments of all of the East European nations have promulgated measures acting to favour the admission of sons and daughters of workers and peasants over children of parents from other social classes.[3] In certain cases the quantitative effect of this can be easily seen, e.g. in 1964 in East Germany the children of members of the intelligencia composed only $18 \cdot 5$ per cent of those attending college and universities during the day, but $58 \cdot 9$ per cent of those attending institutions of higher learning in the evening; the corresponding percentages for children of workers was $42 \cdot 2$ per cent and $17 \cdot 7$ per cent.[4] Among the market economies such type of government directed class discrimination seems unknown.

The social class discrimination in the market economies seems due almost entirely to the fact that students in institutions of higher learning in these nations receive relatively low transfer payments,

[1] Survey of attitudes toward education and work of women in the Soviet Union are briefly discussed bv [B25, Chaps. VI and VIII]. For the USA [B189] and [B228], have analyses of these factors.

[2] The importance of education as the most important factor of social mobility has been recently questioned by C. Arnold Anderson, 'A Skeptical Note on the Relation of Vertical Mobility to Education', [P4, LXVI, May, 1961, pp. 560–70].

[3] Accessible information on this may be found in [B53], [B77, pp. 246 ff.] and [B181, pp. 170 ff.].

[4] Data from [G61, 1965, p. 465].

so that only children from families with considerable income can afford to attend college or university. Some idea about the quantitative effects of class discrimination in both centralized and market economies may be gained from data about the social composition of college and university students.

In the centralized economies there are considerable differences in the proportion of students in institutions of higher learning whose parents were workers and peasants, ranging in the late 1950s from about 35 per cent in the Soviet Union and about 38 per cent in East Germany to about 54 per cent in Hungary and 63 per cent in Bulgaria.[1] In the market economies the proportion of students whose parents were workers or farmers ranged from about 8 per cent in Austria and 16 per cent in West Germany to about 40 per cent in the USA and 48 per cent in Greece.[2] Unfortunately, these data are not completely comparable not only because of differences in definition of social class but because of the different class composition of the labour force in these countries.

If we calculate 'representation indices' by computing the ratio of the proportion of students from a particular social background to the proportion of the entire population in this social group and then index such ratios so that the average representation ratio for the entire nation is 100, we have a good measure of the relative degree of inequality in representation of different social groups in higher education. In a three category comparison between the United States and the Soviet Union (parental status recorded as non-manual, manual, and farmer), the Soviet Union and the United States were quite similar for non-manual and farmer, but the relative representation index for manual workers was somewhat higher in the USSR.[3] In a different three category comparison between East and West

[1] The Soviet datum comes from a speech by Khrushchev, cited by [B77, p. 247]. Abundant data for the other centralized economies except Romania can be found in the various national statistical year books, although the definitions employed in determining the different social statuses are not clear and comparability is doubtful.

[2] The USA datum was estimated from 1947 data cited by Anderson, 'The Social Status of University Students in Relation to Type of Economy', [B133] and data for 1948 and 1960, given by Robert J. Havinghurst, 'Social Class Influences in American Education', in [B142]; the West German datum was estimated from data from [B313, pp. 43–4], the datum for Austria, from [G45, p. 44]; the datum for Greece, from [G18, p. 67].

[3] Robert A. Feldmesser. 'Social Status and Access to Higher Education: A Comparison of the United States and the Soviet Union', [P38, XXVII, Spring 1957, pp. 92–106]. [B25, Chap. VI] also has some interesting remarks on the subject.

Germany (fathers' status recorded as worker or employee; independent farmer or member of collective farm; and independent) the results were remarkably similar although lumping workers and employees together masked the fact that the relative representation index for workers alone appeared much higher in East Germany.[1]

There are a morass of problems concerning comparability and aggregation of the data which cannot be discussed here. Nevertheless, from the above evidence and from information from other sources, three tentative generalizations seem possible. First, in cross-sectional comparisons of market economies the relationship between *per capita* income and relative representation indices of different classes are not significant.[2] On the other hand, with a rising *per capita* income, the proportion of students from working class backgrounds, and relative differences in representation indices seem to narrow over time.[3] Second, in centralized economies, there does not also seem to be a significant relationship in the cross-section data between *per capita* income and the proportion of students from working class backgrounds or relative representation indices of different classes. Nevertheless, over time the proportion of students from worker and peasant backgrounds seem to decline[4] and it does not seem accidental that in the Soviet Union, the country which has had a centralized economy the longest, the proportion of worker and peasant students is the lowest. Such evidence suggests that relative differences in the representation indices may be slightly rising. Third, the proportion of students from worker and peasant backgrounds is greater on the average in the centralized than in the market economies. In the future, however, these differences will probably decline.

Before any of these data can be interpreted as indicating discrimination, attention must again be paid to aspiration levels. Since

[1] The distribution of males by social category in the labour force for West Germany were estimated from data from the 1961 Census of Occupations, presented in [G154, 1964, pp. 147–8]. The distribution of males by social category in East Germany was estimated from data from [G61, 1965, pp. 54–60]. The number of male production workers had to be roughly estimated for both countries from scattered data in the above cited sources.

[2] Data from Anderson, 'The Social Status of University Students', [B133] show a very weak positive relationship between income *per capita* and percentage of students from working class backgrounds.

[3] Time series evidence for the USA over a long period is presented by Havinghurst, *op. cit.* For a short interval data are available for West Germany [B313] and Austria [G45].

[4] Data from the various national statistical yearbooks. For several of the countries this trend is not very strong, and East Germany appears an exception.

aspirations for higher education are strongly correlated with social class in both the Soviet Union and the United States,[1] and since the same appears true in the other sample nations as well, data on the class structure of college students do not *directly* indicate discrimination. Furthermore, a number of other factors also enter into the determination of the class structure of students in institutions of higher learning. For instance, in the United States it was found that the class background of students in community and junior colleges very much paralleled the class division of the community while the class background of students in large colleges and universities was very much different.[2] This means that the geographical dispersion of institutions of higher education is important for the class composition of students. Finally, scattered evidence suggests that children from rural areas in all countries suffer disadvantages in entering colleges because of the lower quality of their secondary schooling than in urban areas. Certainly, in almost all countries the children of farmers and peasants are a lower percentage of college students *vis-à-vis* the percentage of the labour force represented by their parents (i.e. their representation index is lower) than any other major occupational groups.[3] Similar to the discussion about discrimination against women in higher educational institutions, no definite conclusions about class discriminations can be drawn from the existing data. Nevertheless, although workers and peasants make up the majority of the labour force in all countries, the relative under-representation of students from such backgrounds in all the sample countries suggests that parental status, rather than the methods by which education is financed, is the single most important factor for determining the class composition of students in institutions of higher learning.

APPENDIX E-15: SCHOOL CURRICULA DIFFERENCES AMONG THE SAMPLE NATIONS

For primary and secondary schools considerable comparable quantitative data on hours devoted to various subjects in different types of schools are available;[4] and, as far as I know, have been

---

[1] For the Soviet Union, survey data are available in [B25, Chap. V]; for the USA [B228, Part VI].

[2] See [B60, pp. 54 ff.]

[3] Anderson, 'The Social Status of University Students', [B133].

[4] E.g. [G33], [G34], [B158], and [B159].

Q

relatively unexploited by comparative educationists. However, among the sample nations there seemed surprisingly few differences in the subject distribution of the curricula at a single point in time and an analysis in depth of these differences would be extremely arduous. Although time series data for the sample nations could not be found, studies of other nations have shown a considerable shift in the amount of time devoted to different subjects over the century.[1] Most of this shift seems related to the increasing technological and sociological complexity of society, rather than to a rising *per capita* income or the type of economic system.

TABLE E–8:

Distribution of Degrees Granted by Institutions of Higher Learning in 1960 According t Field of Specialization[2]
(in percentages)

Country	Human- ities	Fine arts	Law	Social science	Natural science	Engin- eering	Agricul- ture	Medi- cine	Not spec.
Market Economies									
USA	13	7	3	38	16	12	2	7	2
West Germany	6	3	12	10	7	43	3	16	0
Austria	9	10	22	23	3	18	5	9	0
Ireland	50	1	2	12	10	7	6	12	0
Italy	17	2	24	13	13	11	3	17	0
Yugoslavia	16	5	10	23	7	13	9	16	0
Greece	18	2	15	30	8	7	2	14	3
Centralized Economies									
Czechoslovakia	3	4	3	10	4	45	16	15	0
East Germany	4	3	2	8	13	34	11	25	0
USSR	—5—		3	12	5	49	15	11	1
Poland	5	5	3	8	6	40	11	21	0
Hungary	2	5	6	6	2	30	21	28	0
Romania	11	4	9	10	9	27	13	18	0
Bulgaria	7	4	2	18	4	29	19	16	0

[1] [B287] has data for Japan, Sweden and the United States for number of school hours devoted to different subjects over a long time period and draws a number of provocative conclusions. These conclusions do not seem as valid for cross-section analysis, however.

[2] Data cover all types of institutions of higher education but omit degrees in education, as such degrees are reported in a non-comparable manner in the various countries.

For Bulgaria and the Soviet Union, data cover 1959 and 1957 respectively. For East Germany and the Soviet Union, the distribution of students, rather than granted degrees, is presented. For Bulgaria, only first degrees are included. For West Germany (including West Berlin) degrees in fine arts were estimated from the number of students in this area. For the United States, the data are reported according to a slightly different classification than the rest.

Data come from [G36, 1963, Tables 16 and 20]; and, for the Soviet Union, from [G34].

Qualitative differences in primary and secondary school curricula between the sample nations are much more difficult to analyse. Although considerable literature is available about the formal guidelines to teachers in various nations, the extent to which such guidelines are actually followed is unknown.[1] Moreover, until unified achievement tests can be given to children in different countries and until there is considerably more direct visiting of classes in many nations by trained observers, such qualitative analyses must remain on a fairly primitive level.

For higher education, some ideas about differences in curricula can be gained from examination of the distribution of granted degrees.

No generalizations can be made about the effect of *per capita* income on the distribution of degrees; however, the effect of economic system seems quite evident. On the average, market economies grant a higher percentage of degrees in humanities, law, and the social and natural sciences; while centralized economies grant a higher number of degrees in engineering, agriculture, and medicine, fields which are most directly related to material production. Other measures of the structure of higher education output show the same results, although the quantitative amounts are somewhat different.[2]

APPENDIX E–16: ECONOMETRIC EXPERIMENTS WITH EDUCATION EXPENDITURES OF US STATE AND LOCAL GOVERNMENTS

For the determinants of education expenditures of US state and local governments I carried out a number of econometric experiments in order to see the stability of the coefficients for various years. Many economists have hypothesized that *per capita* government expenditures for education are directly related to *per capita* income (a factor

---

[1] For the centralized economies, such information is available for the school syllabi. For instance. in the 1952 syllabus to math teachers in the Soviet Union it was stated: '. . . while teaching mathematics, the teacher should realize the general goals of a communist upbringing—the formation of a Marxist-Leninist outlook, inculcation of Soviet patriotism and Soviet national pride, and the development of willpower and character', [B181, p. 70]. But this still does not tell us whether the teacher *actually* spent his time inculcating a Marxist-Leninist world outlook or teaching mathematics or both.

[2] Data on the distribution of students are also available in [G36, 1963] but are less comparable because of the different handling of part time, night, and non-degree students as well as the inclusion or exclusion of higher educational institutions which are not equivalent to the colleges and universities.

affecting both supply and demand) and the ratio of school-age children to the general population (a demand factor) and are inversely related to the population density (a supply factor which is supposed to be important because of economies of scale in the production of education). Therefore these three factors are used in the experiments. The calculated income elasticities are different from the ratio-income-elasticities used in the text but are monotonically related such that if the computed coefficients are greater than, equal to, or less than unity, their respective ratio-income-elasticities are greater than, equal to, or less than zero.

For the calculations the following regression forms are used:

$$\ln E_s = w + x (\ln I_s) + y(\ln D_s) + z(\ln C_s) \quad \text{(cross-section analysis)}$$
$$\ln E_n = w + z (\ln I_n) + y(\ln D_n) + z(\ln C_n) \quad \text{(time-series analysis)}$$

where

E = education expenditures *per capita*,

I = personal income *per capita*,

D = population density,

C = ratio of school-age children to the total population,

s = state level (for expenditures, expenditures of state and local governments),

n = national level (for expenditures, expenditures of combined state and local governments), and

w, x, y, z = calculated regression coefficients.

The results for the important regression coefficients are presented in Table E–9 below.

In the analyses at a single point in time (the first five regressions), it should be noted that the size of the calculated coefficients depends very much on the year chosen for analysis, although 1957 and 1962 are quite similar in two out of three coefficients; 1932 and 1942 were, of course, quite unusual years, but had to be chosen because of availability of data. It is also noteworthy that one variable, the ratio of school-age children to the total population, is statistically significant for only one of the four years in which the model was tested. Since this phenomenon may reflect either a statistical quirk or something important, further research on this point is necessary. Finally, in all of the cross-section regressions there is an identification problem of the following type; although education expenditures may be, in a sense, determined by *per capita* income, *per capita* income is a function of previous education expenditures so that the lines of causation are not entirely clear in the statistical model as presented. It does not seem very likely, however, that this identification problem would greatly affect the results of the cross national comparisons, although this is an assumption of the study and not the result of an empirical investigation.

TABLE E-9

Econometric Experiments with US State and Local Governmental Education Expenditures[1]

Year or period	x	y	z	Number of observations	Correlation coefficient
1932	0·29	− 0·08*	− 0·74	21	0·79*
	(0·22)	(0·03)	(0·67)		
1942	0·59	− 0·09*	− 0·68	48	0·68*
	(0·31)	(0·03)	(0·74)		
1957	0·80*	− 0·07*	− 0·55*	48	0·86*
	(0·09)	(0·01)	(0·24)		
1962	0·78*	− 0·06*	0·18	48	0·82*
	(0·08)	(0·01)	(0·15)		
1962	0·66*	—	—	48	0·71*
	(0·10)				
1930–1962	0·09	0·40	1·20*	22	0·92*
	(0·12)	(0·24)	(0·23)		
1948–1962	0·70	4·14*	− 3·11*	13	0·99*
	(0·34)	(0·67)	(0·54)		
1948–1962	1·85*	—	—	13	0·96*
	(0·16)				

[1] Standard errors of estimates are placed in parentheses; coefficients marked with an asterisk are statistically significant at the 0·05 level.

Government expenditures data for cross-section studies come from [G104], [G105, Vol. VI, No. 4] and [G112]. The 1932 and 1942 data are gross current expenditures for 'schools' and probably contain expenditures for colleges and universities. Data for 1957 and 1962 are gross current expenditures for local schools. Time-series data are gross current expenditures for local schools. The basic series was taken from [B146, p. 33] and was extended from data on current education expenditures [G105, Vol. VI, No. 4] and from price indices derived from [G114, p. 97] and [G116, 1965, p. 126]. In all cases expenditures of Alaska and Hawaii are excluded.

The population data come from [G106, Vol. I, Table 15], [G109, Nos. 139, 168, 265, 273, and 293], and [G114, p. 7]. Ratios of children in school ages to total populations by state were estimated by interpolation from the census years. Area data come from [G116, 1962, p. 170] personal income data come from [G119] and [G120, 4/1965, pp. 18 ff]; these current price data were deflated in the time-series analysis by an index of prices for consumer expenditures.

The time-series regressions (the last three regressions) were calculated in constant prices and show enormous variability. Noteworthy is the fact that contrary to the cross-section results, the sizes of the coefficients are extremely dependent on the variables included in the analysis, a feature arising from the lack of statistical independence between the various 'independent' variables.[1] Thus, the coefficient relating income *per capita* and education expenditures *per capita* for the period 1948–62 increases by 164 per cent when the two other independent variables are dropped, while in the cross-section analysis for 1962, the change is only 15 per cent. Another interesting feature is that the coefficients z for the school-age children's ratio are statistically significant in the two regressions, but have the opposite signs. Although a number of explanations can be given for this phenomenon, the choice of the right reason requires more research. Another statistical pitfall is demonstrated by the lack of statistical significance of income *per capita* in the regressions with three independent variables. Although income *per capita* may be the key variable, both education expenditures *per capita* and population density show less variability around their respective long run trends in the postwar years than income *per capita*, and thus they appear highly correlated although no causal interaction may be involved.

The results of the time-series and the cross-section analyses are very different in a number of respects. Part of this is due to the fact that individual states are being compared at a single point in time, while the aggregate of states is being compared over time, so that an aggregation problem arises. Part of the difference between the cross-section and time-series results may be due to the situation where variables reflect different phenomena in the two types of analyses. Thus the measure for density (persons per square mile) probably reflects this phenomenon in the cross-section analyses but in the time-series studies it really reflects the growth of population since the area under consideration did not change. Finally, results from the two analyses may also differ because different causal forces are operating over time and across space. The fact that the technological level is positively related to the *per capita* income in the time-series but not the cross-section data seems the most important such difference.

[1] A rough indication of the multicollinearity between the variables is the fact that the sum of the coefficients for all three regressions is approximately equal, i.e. 1·69, 1·73, and 1·85.

APPENDIX E–17: THE SPATIAL REDISTRIBUTION OF
INCOME THROUGH THE GOVERNMENT BUDGET IN THE
USA, THE USSR, AND EAST AND WEST GERMANY

This appendix describes in detail the experiment reported in Chapter VII and the asumptions underlying the interpretation of the results.

A. *Sources of Data*

USA: State and local public consumption expenditures for the fiscal year 1957 were calculated from data on gross expenditures and receipts from sales to the public from [G104]. Tax data were obtained from the same source; the tax concept covers both property, sales, income, and miscellaneous taxes, but omits charges and other types of non-tax revenues. Population data came from [G116].

USSR: Republic and local public consumption expenditures for 1956 were calculated by combining data on such expenditures for the local and republic levels from [G95] and [G96]. Social expenditures excluded expenditures from the social insurance system. Data on taxes were obtained from the same source; the tax concept covered all taxes collected on the local level plus the following taxes collected at the republic level: turnover taxes, MTS taxes, income taxes collected from republic and local enterprises, and other taxes collected at the local level (categories I, II, IV, and V). Taxes split with the federal government, taxes on enterprises selling at a national level, and other such taxes were excluded. Such decisions were based on some hypothetical propositions concerning the local and national incidence of various taxes. Population data came from [G99, 1956].

The Soviet data contain one difficulty. The Russian republic includes more than one half of the total population and the Ukrainian republic includes more than one half of the remaining population. Since weighted averages were used, it was considered best to exclude these two republics. In the case of the distribution of average public consumption expenditures, such an exclusion made little difference; but for the analysis of expenditures and taxes, the exclusion was of considerable importance. In a footnote in the text, all results are reported.

West Germany: Gross expenditures data of the Laender and local governments for the fiscal year 1956 were obtained from [G155, no. 227]; taxes were obtained from the same source and covered 'general taxes'. From experiments with data from the USA, it was discovered that use of gross expenditures data instead of public consumption data affects the results very little. Populations data came from [G154].

East Germany: Gross expenditures data for the Bezirke for 1958 were obtained from [G61, 1958]; local government expenditures were not available but are believed to be very small. Since tax data are not available, total tax receipts of Bezirke governments (from the same source) were used as a substitute. For these reasons the results are not completely comparable with those from the other three countries. Population data also came from [G61, 1958]. East Berlin expenditures and taxes were excluded from the calculations because certain expenditures made on the federal level in the other Bezirke were made on the local level for this city and the data were therefore not comparable.

B. *Aggregation*

To avoid problems arising from a different number of political units for each country, these units were combined in each country so that ten regions were created. Two rules were followed for such aggregation: only spatially adjoining units could be joined; and only the smallest units (in terms of population) were joined. For the United States the nine areas designated in statistical reports of the Census Bureau were used, with the South Atlantic group (which had the most states) split. For the USSR different combinations of republics were combined to form 10 regions excluding the RSFSR and the Ukraine, excluding the RSFSR but including the Ukraine, and including both. A similar procedure was followed for East Germany in regard to East Berlin. Only for West Germany, which had 10 Laender (West Berlin included; the Saar excluded) were no aggregations made.

In the calculations the regions are weighted by their population in order to eliminate effects arising from differences in the size distribution of regions between the four nations.

C. *Analysis*

This analysis is based on the assumption that the more wealthy regions have higher *per capita* expenditures and taxes than the poorer regions, an assumption which in most cases is quite reasonable. Regressions of the following type were calculated for each country:

$\ln (E/P) = a + b \ln (T/P)$, where E = local public expenditures for health, education, and welfare of the region; P = population; T = local taxes collected in the region; and 'a' and 'b' are the calculated regression coefficients.

If funds are transferred from the wealthy to the poorer regions, then the wealthy regions should spend less than their taxes and the poorer regions should spend more than their taxes. Therefore, the 'b' coefficient would be less than unity. If each region spent the same as it received in taxes so that there would be no redistribution, then the 'b' coefficient should be unity.

Complications enter into this interpretation when a region is subsidized from national funds. Still other difficulties arise when one region 'dominates' the regression because of its size. Thus in the Soviet Union, the Russian and Ukrainian republics include 75 per cent of the Soviet population and their inclusion in the regressions dominate the results. Their inclusion or exclusion in the regression greatly changes the 'b' coefficient because the regressions are weighted. If they are removed, however, the removal of any other republic does not change the results very much. Similarly, inclusion of East Berlin dis-stabilizes the regression results for the 'b' coefficient, while no other Bezirke affects the regressions in this way. Therefore, removing these cases seems the preferable procedure although other results are reported in a footnote below.

TABLE E–10

Net Spatial Redistribution of Public Expenditures and Revenues[1]

USA	1·02	(·09)
West Germany	·50	(·06)
East Germany (excl. East Berlin)	·93	(·22)
USSR (excl. RSFSR and the Ukraine)	1·12	(·22)

West Germany is the only country out of the four which appears to have a statistically significant progressive net spatial redistribution of budgetary funds. The United States and the Soviet Union (both including and excluding the Russian and Ukrainian Republics) do not have a redistribution coefficient significantly different from unity. This means that we cannot attribute any net spatial redistribution to them. If East Berlin is excluded from the calculation, East Germany does not also have any net spatial redistribution of budgetary funds; if East Berlin is included, it does.

[1] Standard errors are given in parentheses. If East Berlin is included in East Germany, the 'b' coefficient drops to ·36 (·14); if the Ukrainian republic is ncluded in the USSR, the 'b' coefficient increases to 1·33 (·35); if both the Russian and the Ukrainian republics are included, the coefficient is ·65 (·21). The effect of such changes illustrate the difficulties introduced by the 'aggregation problem' in making international comparisons.

Q*

Appendix F

GLOSSARY

The following non-technical definitions give only the meanings of the terms as they are used in this study. For more complete and precise definitions, particularly for the statistical terms, the reader must turn to the technical literature. All terms defined in this glossary are italicized.

Administration/budget ratio: the ratio of *public consumption expenditures* for administration to total *adjusted expenditures*. The *ratio-budget-elasticity* is the percentage increase in the *administration/budget ratio* that accompanies a one per cent increase in *per capita* income.

Adjusted expenditures: these are *public consumption expenditures* for administration, internal and external security, education, health, welfare, and research and development which have been adjusted to fit the statistical definitions set forth in Appendix A–1.

Capitalism: an economy in which most of the productive capital is privately owned.

Centralization ratio: in the context of expenditures of all levels of government, the ratio of direct central government expenditures to total government expenditures. In the context of state and local public expenditures, the ratio of direct state expenditures to total state and local public expenditures.

Coefficient of multiple determination: in a *multiple regression* this is a measure of the percentage of the variation in the *dependent variable* (the variable to be explained) that is explained by changes of other variables (the *independent* or *explanatory variables*), combined in some predetermined function, e.g. $X = a + bW + cZ$ (X is the *dependent variable*; W and Z are the *independent variables* and a, b, and c, are the calculated coefficients). If the dependent variable is completely determined by the independent variables, the *coefficient of multiple determination* is equal to unity; if the dependent variable has no relation to the independent variables in the predetermined function, the *coefficient of multiple determination* is equal to zero. The *coefficient of determination* is similar to the *coefficient of multiple determination* but applies only to *simple regressions* (a regression with one independent variable). The square roots of the *coefficient of multiple determination* and the *coefficient of determination* are, respectively, the coefficient of multiple correlation and the correlation coefficient.

Coefficient of variation: the ratio of the *standard deviation* to the arithmetic mean.

Collinearity: see *multicollinearity*.

Complementarity: in the context of this study, two public expenditures are complementary if they both increase or decrease at the same time when major determinants of both expenditures (such as income and economic system) are held constant.

Centrally planned (or *centralized*) *economy:* an economy in which the allocation of productive resources is primarily guided by commands emanating from a central planning body. A *centrally planned economy* need not be *socialist*.

Consumption unit: the decision making unit that direct decisions about the amount and type of personal consumption of individuals is made. This can be the individual himself, his family, or, for *public consumption expenditures*, the government.

Covariance analysis: a statistical technique used in this study to determine whether two samples come from the same universe.

Cross-section analysis: the analysis of a set of variables in different geographic areas at a single point in time, rather than over a time span.

Dependent variable: see *coefficient of multiple determination*.

Degree of freedom: a certain minimum number of observations are necessary to define any statistic (e.g. an arithmetic mean or a standard deviation). For instance, two points are necessary to define *regression line*. The degrees of freedom designate the number of observations above this crucial number. Other things being equal, the more degrees of freedom, the more faith one can place in the estimated statistic.

Dollar value GNP: see *gross national product*.

Dummy variable: in a *regression*, a variable which takes on a small number of values designating some qualitative property of the observations. For instance, a dummy variable D could equal zero if the observed nation were capitalist; and one, if the observed nation were socialist.

Economies of scale: if the prices of *factors of production* (land, raw materials, labour and capital) remain the same but if the amount of each factor is increased by the same percentage, economies of scale designate the fall in average unit costs of production.

Economic system: in this study economic system is defined in terms of a *market economy* and a *centrally planned economy*. In certain cases economic system is defined in terms of *socialism* and *capitalism* instead.

Exclusivity (exclusion principle): if a person buying a certain good or service cannot prevent others from consuming or utilizing it without paying, there is lack of *'exclusivity'*. A person who drains a malaria swamp cannot prevent other people living in the area from benefiting.

Externality: on the production side this is a cost or benefit which accrues to a producer that he does not contract or pay for. For instance, smoke pollution from a steel factory might increase the costs of a laundry (a cost); similarly, this laundry might act to further pollute the air without paying others for the damage caused (which would save the laundry the costs of a filter). On the consumption side an externality is a benefit or 'unbenefit' which a person receives that he does not contract or pay for. For instance, a person can enjoy a fireworks demonstration of his neighbour without paying for it; similarly, a non-smoker is bothered when smokers pollute the air around him. An *externality* embraces a broader class of phenomena than those exhibiting a lack of *exclusivity*.

Factor costs: see *gross national product*.

Factor income effect: the centrally planned nations did not include a charge for capital (interest) or land (rent) in their calculations of costs. Therefore, the value ratios of expenditures for services (primarily labour costs) to the GNP are higher than if these interest and rent charges had been included in calculating the value of the denominator of the fraction.

Factors of production: see *economies of scale*.

Gini coefficient: a measure of the inequality of income measured from a Lorenz curve construction.

Gross expenditures: in this study gross expenditures are the public expenditures as defined and presented by the statistical services of the individual nations. Such data are rarely comparable because of the different definitions and practices that are used by each national statistical service.

Gross national product (GNP): the money value of the total production of goods and services in a country during a year before subtracting allowances for depreciation. The GNP can be valued in terms of *market prices*, i.e. the prices at which such goods and services are sold to the ultimate consumers, or *factor prices*, the wages, rents, or profits which the *factors of production* receive. The difference between gross national product in market and factor prices is accounted for by *net indirect taxes*, i.e. the indirect taxes (e.g. sales taxes) minus government subsidies to producers. The *dollar value gross national product* is the value of the GNP when all goods and services are valued at market prices which such goods and services receive in the United States.

GPO: Government Printing Office.

Income elasticity: the percentage by which a particular public expenditure changes when the GNP changes one per cent.

Income effect: if income rises and if relative prices of all goods remain the same, usually more of all goods are sold. See also *substitution effect.*

Independent variable: see *coefficient of multiple determination.*

Index number problems: such problems arise from trying to compare two sets of quantities of production (e.g. apples and oranges) at two different points in time (e.g. production of apples and oranges in 1955 and 1956) or points in space (e.g. production of apples and oranges in the USA and Canada), by evaluating them in some common monetary denominator. For comparisons in time a *Laspeyres index* is when production is valued in the prices of some base year in the past; while a *Paasche index* is when production is valued at current prices. In most circumstances the two indices give quite different results. Similarly for comparisons across space, the results depend upon the currency used for evaluating the products and calculating the index.

Keynesian type unemployment: when labour unemployment is brought about by an insufficiency of aggregate demand. In such cases unemployment of labour is accompanied by unemployment of capital as well.

Laspeyres index: see *index number problem.*

Least squares: see *regression.*

Level of development: in this study the *per capita gross national product* is used as a measure.

ln: natural logarithm.

Market economy: an economy in which the allocation of productive resources and consumer goods is primarily regulated by a market mechanism. A *market economy* need not be *capitalist.*

Material product: a concept of aggregate production which excludes services. The *gross material product* is roughly the *gross national product* without most services (e.g. government, finance, real estate, bootblacks, etc.). The *net material product* is the *gross material product* excluding depreciation. The *global material product* is the gross material product plus the value of all intermediate goods, a statistical concept which is falling in gradual disuse in those countries using a material produce concept for defining aggregate production.

Multicollinearity: when the explanatory variables in a regression are correlated with each other.

Multivariate regression analysis or multiple regression: see *regression analysis.*

Modified ratio-income-elasticity: see *ratio-income-elasticity.*

n.a.: not available.

NATO: North Atlantic Treaty Organization.

Normative theory: a theory dealing with the desired behaviour of variables, rather than their actual behaviour. Attention is focused on the 'ought', rather than the 'is'.

Paasche index: see *index number problems.*

Positive theory: a theory dealing with actual behaviour of variables, rather than the desired behaviour. Attention is focused on the 'is', rather than the 'ought'.

Public consumption expenditures: current expenditures and transfer payments of governments which are financed by taxes or government borrowing. The individuals or groups which utilize or receive such goods, services, or transfer payments, make no direct payment for them. The exact concept used in this study is defined at length in Appendix A–1.

Public expenditures: expenditures of governments which include public consumption expenditures but which may also include expenditures financed by user-fees or sales to the public. Capital expenditures, and subsidies may also be included.

Public goods: goods or services that have two properties: *non-exclusiveness* and small increases in costs when an additional person enjoys such goods and services. Thus no one in a country can be excluded from enjoying the benefits of a retaliatory missile force and, furthermore, an immigrant to that country enjoys this service at no additional cost to anyone.

Price elasticity: the percentage change in the quantity sold of a good or service when its price is changed by one per cent.

Public service: a service is provided as a public service when it can be received free by any citizen who goes to the place where it is dispensed.

R^2: coefficient of multiple determination or coefficient of determination.

Ratio-income-elasticity: the percentage change in the public expenditures/GNP ratio (both defined in current prices) when *per capita* income (defined in constant prices) changes by one per cent.

A mathematical definition is given in Chapter II. The *modified-ratio-income-elasticity* used in Chapter V is the ratio-income-elasticity with the ratio of education expenditures per child to the GNP substituted for the public expenditures/GNP ratio.

Regression: the calculation of the relationship between variables when the functional form is specified. *A simple linear regression* (see diagram) is the calculation of the relationship between two variables which are linked in a simple linear form ($Y = a + b X$, where Y is the *dependent variable*, X is the *independent variable*, and a and b are the *calculated regression coefficients*). In the diagram the *regression line* is estimated by the *method of least squares*, i.e. coefficients 'a' and 'b' are calculated so as to minimize the square of the distance from the actual observations to the calculated line. A *multiple or multivariate regression* is when more than one *independent variable* is used.

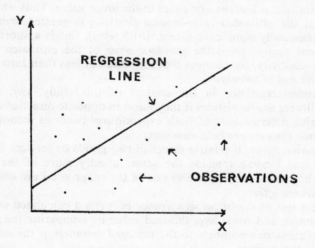

Risk skimming: the process occurring with 'experience rating' in insurance where low risk individuals receive insurance at very low rates and high risk individuals, at very high rates.

Socialism: an economy in which most of the productive capital is publicly owned.

Standard deviation: a measure of the dispersion of observations around the arithmetic mean of these observations. It is calculated by taking the square root of the sum of the squares of the distance of the various observations from the arithmetic mean divided by the number of observations. An *adjusted standard deviation* is when the sum of squares of the distance of the various observations from the arithmetic mean is divided by the number of observations minus the *degrees of freedom*.

Standard error: this is the *standard deviation* of an estimated *regression* coefficient. The *standard error of estimate* is the *standard deviation* of the difference between the predicted and observed dependent variable and represents the unexplained residual in the regression.

Statistical significance: In testing the significance of an estimated statistic (e.g. an arithmetic mean, a ratio-income-elasticity, etc.), we are asking about the probability that it is different from some given value, e.g. zero. The range of significance is determined by the *standard deviation* or *standard error* of the statistic and a probability statement of the following kind: the chances are less than one out of twenty (or one out of a hundred) that the estimated value of the statistic is less than or equal to the given value. Thus when we say that the estimated ratio-income-elasticity is greater than zero to a statistically significant extent (0·05 level), this is a short-hand statement that if given the *standard error* of the estimated ratio-income-elasticity, the chances that it is equal or less than zero is less than one out of twenty.

Substitution relations: in the context of this study, two public expenditures are substitutes if they move in opposite directions when the major determinants of both expenditures (such as income and economic system) are held constant.

Substitution effect: if relative prices of two goods or services change but if real income remains the same, usually more of the good which has become cheaper and less of the other good are sold. See also *income effect*.

T-test: a test of *statistical significance* between a calculated statistic of a sample and some hypothesized value by comparing the difference of these two numbers to the *standard deviation* or the *standard error* of the statistic.

Urbanization: the ratio of population living in urban places over 10,000 to the total population.

Variance: the square of the *standard deviation*.

WTO: Warsaw Treaty Organization.

Wagner's Law: an economic 'law' stating that as income *per capita* increases, the share of public expenditures in the GNP also increases.

Bibliography

PERIODICALS[1]

P1. *Administration*. Dublin: Institute of Public Administration, quarterly.

P2. *The American Behavioral Scientist*. Princeton: Metron Inc., monthly.

P3. *American Economic Review*. Menasha, Wisconsin: American Economic Association, five times yearly.

P4. *American Journal of Sociology*. Chicago: University of Chicago Press, six times yearly.

P5. *American Political Science Review*. Menasha, Wisconsin: American Political Science Association, quarterly.

P6. *American Sociological Review*. Albany, NY: American Sociological Association, six times per year.

P7. *Applied Statistics*. Edinburgh: Oliver and Boyd for Royal Statistical Society, three times per year.

P8. *Aussenpolitik*. Stuttgart: Deutsche Verlags-Anstalt, monthly.

P9. *Canadian Journal of Economics and Political Science*. Toronto: Political Science Association, quarterly.

P10. *Chemical and Engineering News*. Washington, DC: American Chemical Society, weekly.

P11. *Comparative Education Review*. New York: Comparative Education Society, three times yearly.

P12. *Current Digest of the Soviet Press*. New York: Joint Committee on Slavic Studies, weekly.

P13. *Current History*. Philadelphia: Current History Inc., monthly.

P14. *Den'gi i kredit*. Moscow: Gosudarstuennyy bank SSSR, monthly.

P15. *Deutsche Finanzwirtschaft*. East Berlin: Verlag Die Wirtschaft, twice monthly.

P16. *Der Donauraum*. Graz: Bolhaus Verlag, quarterly.

P17. *East Europe*. New York: Free Europe Committee, monthly.

P18. *Eastern Underwriter*. New York: Eastern Underwriter Co., weekly.

P19. *Economica*. Hereford: Hereford Times Ltd. for London School of Economics, quarterly.

P20. *Econometrica*. New Haven: Econometric Society, quarterly.

---

[1] Periodicals include non-official governmental publications; official governmental periodicals are listed in the third section of the bibliography.

P21. *Economic Development and Cultural Change.* Chicago: University of Chicago Press, quarterly.
P22. *Economic Journal.* London: Royal Economic Society, quarterly.
P23. *Economic Record.* Melbourne: Melbourne University Press, quarterly.
P24. *Economics of Planning.* Oslo: A. W. Brøggers, three times yearly.
P25. *Ekonomicheskaya gazeta.* Moscow: Tsentral'nyy komitet K.P.S.S., weekly.
P26. *Finance a úvěr.* Prague: Ministerstvo financí, monthly.
P27. *Finanse.* Warsaw: Polskie Wydawnictwa Gospodarcze, six times yearly.
P28. *Finansi i kredit.* Sofia: monthly.
P29. *Finante si credit.* Bucharest: monthly.
P30. *Finanzarchiv.* Tuebingen: J. C. B. Mohr, quarterly.
P31. *Foreign Affairs.* New York: Council on Foreign Relations, quarterly.
P32. *Freie Rundschau.* Munich: Zentralverband politischer Emigranten aus der UdSSR, six times yearly.
P33. *Giving, U.S.A.* New York: American Association of Fund-Raising Council, annual.
P34. *G.D.R. Review.* Dresden: Verlag Zeit im Bild for German Democratic Republic League for Friendship among the Peoples, irregular.
P35. *General Systems Yearbook.* Ann Arbor: Society for General Systems Research, annual.
P36. *Głos Pracy.* Warsaw: daily newspaper.
P37. *Gospodarka Planowa.* Warsaw: Polskie Wydawnictwa Gospodarcze, monthly.
P38. *Harvard Educational Review.* Cambridge, Massachusetts: Harvard University.
P39. *Hospitals, Guide Issue.* Chicago: American Hospital Association, annual.
P40. *Ikonomicheska misŭl.* Sofia: 4 to 10 times a year.
P41. *Indian Economic Review.* Bombay: Asia Publishing House, twice yearly.
P42. *International Economic Review.* Osaka: Kansai Economic Federation, three times a year.
P43. *Journal of the American Statistical Association.* Menasha, Wisc.: American Statistical Association, quarterly.
P44. *Journal of the Irish Statistical and Social Inquiry Society.* Dublin: yearly.

P45. *Journal of Finance.* Worcester, Massachusetts: American Finance Association, quarterly.

P46. *Journal of Insurance.* Bloomington: American Risk and Insurance Association, quarterly.

P47. *Journal of Peace Research.* Ann Arbor: Center for Research on Conflict Resolution, quarterly.

P48. *Journal of Politics.* Jacksonville, Florida: Southern Political Science Association, quarterly.

P49. *Journal of Political Economy.* Chicago: University of Chicago Press, six times yearly.

P50. *Komsomol'skaya pravda.* Moscow: daily newspaper.

P51. *Közgazdasági szemle.* Budapest: Magyar Tudományos Akadémia, monthly.

P52. *Kyklos.* Basel: List Gesellschaft, quarterly.

P53. *Land Economics.* Madison: University of Wisconsin Press, quarterly.

P54. *Life Insurance Fact Book.* New York: Institute of Life Insurance, annual.

P54a. *Literaturnaya Gazeta.* Moscow: 3 times a week.

P55. *Manchester School.* Manchester: Norbary Lockwood & Co. for University of Manchester, three times a year.

P56. *Marine Corps Gazette.* Quantico, Virginia: Marine Corps Association, monthly.

P57. *Medical Economics.* Oradell, New Jersey: Medical Economics, Inc., fortnightly.

P58. *The Military Balance.* London: Institute for Strategic Studies, annual.

P59. *Minerva.* London: Committee on Science and Freedom, quarterly.

P60. *National Institute Economic Review.* London: National Institute of Economic and Social Research, quarterly.

P61. *National Tax Journal.* Lancaster, Pennsylvania: National Tax Association, quarterly.

P62. *Natural Law Forum.* Notre Dame, Ind.: Notre Dame Law School, irregular.

P63. *Neues Deutschland.* East Berlin: Sozialistische Einheitspartei Deutschlands, daily newspaper.

P64. *Népszabadság.* Budapest: daily newspaper.

P65. *New Scientist.* London: Cromwell House, weekly.

P66. *New York Times.* New York: daily newspaper.

P67. *Orbis.* Philadelphia: Foreign Policy Research Institute, quarterly.

P68. *Ost-West Kurier.* Frankfurt a.M.: Heimat Verlag, weekly.

P69. *Oxford Economic Papers.* London: Oxford University, three times yearly.

P70. *Plánované hospodářství.* Prague: Státní plánovací komise, monthly.

P71. *Planovo stopanstvo.* Sofia: Družhavna planova komisiya, six times yearly.

P72. *Die Presse der Sowjetunion.* East Berlin: Verlag Volk und Welt, irregular.

P73. *Probleme economice.* Bucharest: Akademia R.P.R., Institutul de Cercetări Economice, monthly.

P74. *Public Finance/Finances Publiques.* The Hague: quarterly.

P75. *Pravda.* Bratislava: daily newspaper.

P76. *Pravda.* Moscow: daily newspaper.

P77. *Quarterly Journal of Economics.* Cambridge, Massachusetts: Harvard University Press, quarterly.

P78. *Quarterly Review.* Rome: Banco Nazionale del Lavoro, quarterly.

P79. *Review of Economics and Statistics.* Cambridge, Massachusetts: Harvard University Press, six times yearly.

P80. *Revue de science et de législation financière.* (now *Revue de science financière*). Paris: Librairie générale de droit et de jurisprudence, quarterly.

P81. *Revue militaire générale.* Paris: Berger-Levrault for Institut des études stratégiques, monthly.

P82. *Revue militaire d'information.* Paris: Ministère des armées, monthly.

P83. *Rudé právo.* Prague: daily newspaper.

P84. *Scottish Journal of Political Economy.* Edinburgh: Oliver & Boyd for Scottish Economic Society, three times yearly.

P85. *Scientific American.* New York: monthly.

P86. *Slavic Review.* Urbana, Ill: American Association for the Advancement of Slavic Studies, quarterly.

P87. *Soldat und Technik.* Frankfurt a.M.: Umschau Verlag, monthly.

P88. *Source Book of Health Insurance Data.* New York: Health Insurance Institute, annual.

P89. *South African Journal of Economics.* Johannesburg: Economic Society of South Africa, quarterly.

P90. *Soviet Studies.* Oxford: Blackwell, quarterly.

P91. *Staff Papers.* Washington, D.C.: International Monetary Fund, quarterly.

P92. *Statesman's Yearbook.* London: Macmillan, annual.

P93. *Statisztikai szemle.* Budapest: Központi Statisztikai Hivatal, monthly.

P94. *Tagesspiegel.* West Berlin: daily newspaper.

P95. *Transactions of the Society of Actuaries.* Chicago: quarterly.

P96. *Trybuna Ludu.* Warsaw: daily newspaper.

P97. *Voprosy ekonomiki.* Moscow: Akademiya nauk S.S.S.R., monthly.

P98. *Die Wirtschaft.* East Berlin: Verlag Die Wirtschaft, weekly.

P99. *Die wirtschaftliche und soziale Entwicklung in Ost Berlin und der sowjetischen Besatzungszone.* West Berlin: Karl C. Thalheim, mimeo., irregular.

P100. *Wochenbericht.* West Berlin: Deutsches Institut fuer Wirtschaftsforschung, weekly.

P101. *World Politics.* Princeton: Princeton University Press, quarterly.

P102. *Yale Economic Essays.* New Haven: Yale University Economics Department, three times yearly.

P103. *Zeitschrift fuer die gesamte Staatswissenschaft.* Tuebingen: J.C.B. Mohr, quarterly.

BOOKS AND PAMPHLETS[1]

B1. Abel-Smith, Brian. *Paying for Health Services: A Study of Costs and Sources of Finance in Six Countries.* Geneva: W.H.O., 1963.

B2. Adams, Henry Carter. *The Science of Finance.* New York: Henry Holt, 1899.

B3. Adams, Robert Frank. *Determinants of Local Government Expenditures.* Ph. D. dissertation, University of Michigan, 1963. Ann Arbor, Michigan: University Microfilms.

B4. Akademie fuer Staatsmedizin. *Zur Entwicklung und Organization des Gesundheitswesens in Sowjet Russland, in osteuropaeischen Volksdemokratien und in Mitteldeutschland.* Hamburg: various years.

B5. Alexandrov, A. M. (ed.). *Gosudarstvennyy byudzhet S.S.S.R.* Moscow: Gosfinizdat, 1961.

B6. Allakhverdian, D. A., *et al. Finansy S.S.S.R.* Moscow: Gosfinizdat, 1962.

B7. Allen, Julius W. *Subsidy and Subsidylike Programs of the U.S. Government.* Materials prepared for the Joint Economic Committee, Congress of the US, Washington, DC: GPO., 1960.

[1] Official publications of governments and intergovernmental organizations are in the next section of the bibliography.

B8. Alton, Thad P., *et al.*, *Bulgarian National Income and Product, 1956.* New York: Columbia University Press, forthcoming.

B9. Alton, Thad P., *et al.*, *Czechoslovak National Income and Product, 1947–1948 and 1955–1956.* New York: Columbia University Press, 1962.

B10. Alton, Thad P., *et al. Hungarian National Income and Product in 1955.* New York: Columbia University Press, 1963.

B11. Alton, Thad P., *et al. Polish National Income and Product in 1954, 1955 and 1956.* New York: Columbia University Press, 1963.

B12. Ames, Edward. *Soviet Economic Processes.* Homewood, Ill: Irwin, 1965.

B13. Anatol, A., and V. Martin. *Statistica Financiară.* Bucharest: Editura Ştiinţifică, 1956.

B14. Anderson, Odin W., *et al. Changes in Family Medical Care Expenditures and Voluntary Health Insurance: A Five Year Resurvey.* Cambridge, Mass.: Harvard University Press, 1963.

B15. Anderson, Odin W., and Jacob J. Feldman. *Family Medical Costs and Voluntary Health Insurance: A Nationwide Survey.* New York: McGraw-Hill, 1956.

B16. Andrzejewski, Stanisław. *Military Organization and Society.* London: Routledge & Kegan Paul, 1954.

B17. Andreski, Stanislav. *Elements of Comparative Sociology.* London: Weidenfeld and Nicolson, 1964.

B18. Angelov, A. S. *Finansovo pravo na Narodna republika Bŭlgariya.* Sofia: 1960.

B19. Arndt, Klaus Dieter. *Wohnverhaeltnisse und Wohungsbedarf in der sowjetischen Besatzungszone.* Deutsches Institut fuer Wirtschaftsforschung, Sonderheft 50, Reihe A. West Berlin: Duncker & Humblot, 1960.

B20. Bader, Heinrich, *et al. Das Finanzsystem der D.D.R.* East Berlin: Verlag Die Wirtschaft, 1962.

B21. Baer, Werner and Isaac Kerstenetzky, (eds.). *Inflation and Growth in Latin America.* Homewood, Illinois: Irwin, 1964.

B22. Bakule, Josef, Vladimir Kyzlink, Frantisek Picmaus, and Miroslav Tuček. *Finance a úvěr v Č.S.R.* Prague: S.N.P.L., 1959.

B23. Baran, Paul. *The Political Economy of Growth.* New York: Monthly Review Press, 1957.

B24. Baran, Paul and Paul Sweezy. *Monopoly Capitalism.* New York: Monthly Review Press, 1966.

B25. Bauer, Raymond A. and Alex Inkeles. *The Soviet Citizen.* Cambridge, Mass.: Harvard University Press, 1959.

B26. Baum, Samuel. *The Labor Force of Hungary*. US Bureau of the Census. International Population Statistics Reports. Series P-90, No. 18. Washington, DC: GPO, 1961.

B27. Baum, Samuel. *The Labor Force of Rumania*. US Bureau of the Census. International Population Statistics Reports. Series P-90. No. 14. Washington, DC: 1961.

B28. Baum, Samuel and Jerry W. Combs, Jr. *The Labor Force of the Soviet Zone of Germany and the Soviet Sector of Berlin*. US Bureau of the Census, International Population Statistics Reports. Series P-90. No. 11, Washington, DC: GPO, 1959.

B29. Becker, Abraham S. *Prices of Producers' Durables in the United States and the U.S.S.R. in 1955*. RAND Corporation Memorandum RM-2432. Santa Monica: 1959.

B30. Becker, Abraham S. *Soviet Military Outlays Since 1955*. RAND Corporation Memorandum RM-3886-PR. Santa Monica: July 1964.

B31. Becker, Abraham S. *Soviet National Income and Product, 1958–1962*. RAND Corporation Memorandum RM-4394-PR. Santa Monica: June 1965.

B32. Becker, Gary S. *Human Capital: A Theoretical and Empirical Analysis with Specific Reference to Education*. New York: National Bureau of Economic Research, 1964.

B33. Benoit, Emile (ed.). *Disarmament and World Economic Inter-dependence*. Oslo: Universitetsforlaget, 1966.

B34. Benoit, Emile & Kenneth E. Boulding (eds.). *Disarmament and the Economy*. New York: Harper & Row, 1963.

B35. Bergson, Abram. *The Real National Income of Soviet Russia since 1928*. Cambridge, Massachusets: Harvard University Press, 1961.

B36. Berliner, Joseph S. *Factory and Manager in the U.S.S.R.* Cambridge, Mass.: Harvard University Press, 1957.

B37. Berliner, Joseph S. *Soviet Economic Aid*. New York: Praeger, 1958.

B38. Billerbeck, Klaus. *Soviet Bloc Foreign Aid to the Under-developed Countries: An Analysis and Prognosis*. Hamburg: Hamburg Archives of World Economy, 1960.

B39. Blank, David M. and George J. Stigler. *The Demand and Supply of Scientific Personnel*. New York: National Bureau of Economic Research, 1957.

B40. Bodenman, Paul S. *Education in the Soviet Zone of Germany*. US Department of Health, Education, and Welfare. Bulletin 26/1959. Washington DC: GPO, 1959.

B41. Bodnar, Artur. *Gospodarka europejskich krajów socjalistycznych*. Warsaw: Książka i Wiedza, 1962.

B42. Bohn, Helmut. *Die Aufruestung in der sowjetischen Besatzungszone Deutschlands*. Bonn: Bundesministerium fuer gesamtdeutsche Fragen, 1958.

B43. Boldyrow, B. G. *Die Finanzen der europaeischen Laender der Volksdemokratie*. East Berlin: Verlag Die Wirtschaft, 1953.

B44. Bollens, John C., *et al. Exploring the Metropolitan Community*. Berkeley: University of California, 1961.

B45. Bosch, Werner. *Die Sozialstruktur in West- und Mitteldeutschland*. Bonn: Bundesministerium fuer gesamtdeutsche Fragen, 1958.

B46. Boulding, Kenneth E. *Conflict, and Defense: A General Theory*. New York: Harper and Row, 1962.

B47. Boulding, Kenneth E. *The Organizational Revolution*. New York: Harper, 1953.

B48. Brazer, Harvey E. *City Expenditures in the United States*. New York: National Bureau of Economic Research, 1959.

B49. Brecht, Arnold. *Internationaler Vergleich der oeffentlichen Ausgaben*. Vol. 2. Series *Grundfragen der internationalen Politik*. Leipzig & Berlin: B. G. Teubner, 1932.

B49a. Bristol, J. and Alan Tait, (Eds.). *Economic Policy in Ireland*. Dublin: Institute of Public Administration, 1968.

B50. Brzezinski, Zbigniew K. *The Soviet Bloc: Unity and Conflict*. Cambridge, Massachusetts: Harvard Univeristy Press, 1960.

B50a. Buchanan, James M. *Public Finance in Democratic Process*. Chapel Hill: U. of North Carolina Press, 1967.

B51. Buchanan, James M. *The Public Finances*. 2nd Edition. Homewood, Ill.: Irwin, 1965.

B52. Buchanan, James M. and Gordon Tullock. *The Calculus of Consent: Logical Foundations of Constitutional Democracy*. Ann Arbor: University of Michigan Press, 1962.

B53. Buhler, Neal and Stanley Zukowski. *Discrimination in Education in the People's Democracies*. Mid-European Studies Center Publication 24. New York: Free Europe Committee, 1955.

B54. Bŭlgarska akademiya na naukite. *Ekonomichesko i sotsialno razvitie na N.R.B.* Sofia: 1964.

B55. Bureau of Public Health Economics and Department of Economics. *The Economics of Health and Medical Care*. Ann Arbor: University of Michigan Press, 1964.

B56. Burns, Eveline M. *Social Security and Public Policy*. New York: McGraw-Hill, 1956.

B57. Busek, Vratislav and Nicholas Spulber (eds.). *Czechoslovakia*.

Mid-European Studies Center of the Free Europe Committee. New York: Praeger, 1956.

B58. Butakov, D., V. Bochkova, and I. Shevel': *Finansy stran narodnoy demokratii.* Moscow: Gosfinizdat, 1959.

B59. Chapman, Janet G. *Real Wages in Soviet Russia since 1928.* Cambridge, Mass.: Harvard University Press, 1963.

B60. Clark, Burton, R. *The Open Door College: A Case Study.* New York: McGraw-Hill, 1960.

B60a. Clark, Colin. *The Conditions of Economic Progress.* 3rd ed. London: Macmillan, 1957.

B61. Clark, Colin and Geer Struvel (eds.). *Income and Wealth, Series X, Income Redistribution and the Statistical Foundation of Economic Policy.* New Haven: International Association for Income and Wealth, 1964.

B62. Colm, Gerhard and Peter Wagner. *Federal Budget Projections.* Washington, D.C.: Brookings Institution, 1966.

B63. Conard, Alfred, *et al. The Economics of Injury Reparation.* Forthcoming.

B64. Coppock, Joseph D. *International Economic Instability.* New York: McGraw-Hill, 1962.

B65. Cornelisse, Peter A., *et al. The Educational Structure of the Labour Force: A Statistical Analysis.* Rotterdam: Netherlands Economic Institute, March 1966.

B66. Correa, Hector. *The Economics of Human Resources.* Amsterdam: North-Holland Publishing Co., 1963.

B67. Cox-George, N. A. *Finance and Development in West Africa: The Sierra Leone Experience.* London: D. Dobson, 1961.

B68. Deane, Phyllis (ed.). *Income and Wealth, Series IX: Studies in Social and Financial Accounting.* Chicago: Quadrangle Books, 1961.

B69. Delarue, Jacques. *The Gestapo: A History of Horror.* New York: William Morrow, 1964.

B70. Dellin, L. A. D. (ed.). *Bulgaria.* Mid-European Studies Center of the Free Europe Committee. New York: Praeger, 1956.

B71. Denison, Edward F. *The Sources of Economic Growth in the United States and the Alternatives before us.* Washington, DC: Committee for Economic Development, 1962.

B72. Derkach, N. *The Differences in Soviet Portrayal of their Aid to Underdeveloped Countries in English and Russian.* RAND Paper P-2853. Santa Monica: January, 1964.

B73. Dewhurst, J. Frederic, *et al. America's Needs and Resources: A New Survey.* New York: 20th Century Fund, 1955.

B74. Dewhurst, J. Frederic, *et al. Europe's Needs and Resources*. New York: 20th Century Fund, 1961.

B75. Degras, Jane (ed.). *Soviet Planning: Essays in Honour of Naum Jasny*. Oxford: Blackwell, 1964.

B76. DeWitt, Nicholas. *Costs and Returns in Education in the U.S.S.R.* Ph.D. dissertation, Harvard University, 1962.

B77. DeWitt, Nicholas. *Education and Professional Employment in the U.S.S.R.* National Science Foundation 61-40. Washington, DC GPO, 1961.

B78. Dickinson, Frank R. (ed.). *Philanthropy and Public Policy*. New York: National Bureau of Economic Research, 1962.

B79. Domdey, Karl Heinz. *Neokolonialismus oder Unabhaengigkeit und sozialistische Wirtschaftshilfe*. East Berlin: Werlag Die Wirtschaft, 1962.

B80. Dorfman, Robert (ed.). *Measuring Benefits of Government Investments*. Washington, DC: Brookings Institution, 1963.

B81. Dormont, Alexis. *La nouvelle armée allemande est là*. Paris: Amiot-Dumont, 1957.

B82. Downs, Anthony. *An Economic Theory of Democracy*. New York: Harper, 1957.

B83. Duesenberry, J. S., *et al. The Brookings Quarterly Econometric Model of the United States*. Chicago: Rand McNally, 1965.

B84. Dye, Thomas R. *Politics, Economics, and the Public: Policy Outcomes in the American States*. New York: Rand McNally, 1967.

B85. Eckstein, Alexander. *Communist China's Economic Growth and Foreign Trade*. New York: McGraw-Hill, 1966.

B86. Eckstein, Otto (ed.). *Economics of Income Maintenance*. Washington, DC: Brookings Institution, 1966.

B87. Edwards, Alberta *et al. Report of the American Marketing Delegation to the Soviet Union 1960*. Cambridge, Massachusetts: Harvard Business School, mimeo., n.d.

B88. *Economia Romîniei între anii 1944–1959*. Bucharest: Editura Académiei Republicii Populare Romîne, 1959.

B89. Edding, Friedrich. *Internationale Tendenzen in der Entwicklung der Ausgaben fuer Schulen und Hochschulen*. Kieler Studien 47. Kiel: 1958.

B90. Elias, Andrew. *The Labor Force of Yugoslavia*. US Bureau of the Census. International Population Statistics Reports. Series P-90, No. 22. Washington, DC: GPO, 1965.

B91. Ely, Louis B. *The Red Army Today*. Harrisburg, Penn.: Military Service Publishing Co., 1953.

B92. Emi, Koichi. *Government Fiscal Activity and Economic Growth in Japan, 1868–1960.* Tokyo: Kinokuniya Bookstore Co. Ltd., 1963.

B93. Ernst, Maurice C. *Polish Industrial Production, 1937–1960.* Occasional Paper of the Research Project on National Income in East Central Europe. New York: 1966.

B94. Fabricant, Solomon. *The Trend of Government Activity in the United States since 1900.* New York: National Bureau of Economic Research, 1952.

B95. Fein, Rashi. *Economics of Mental Illness.* New York: Basic Books, 1958.

B96. Feiwel, George R. *The Economics of a Socialist Enterprise: A Case Study of the Polish Firm.* New York: Preager, 1965.

B97. Fenichel, Otto. *The Psychoanalytic Theory of Neurosis.* New York: Norton, 1945.

B98. Field, Mark G. *Doctor and Patient in Soviet Russia.* Cambridge, Mass.: Harvard University Press, 1957.

B99. *Finanse polski ludowej w latach 1944–1960.* Warsaw: Pánstwowe Wydawnictwo Ekónomiczne, 1964.

B100. *Finansite i sotsialisticheskoto stroitelstvo v Narodna Republika Bŭlgariya, sbornik 1949–1959.* Sofia: Nauka i izkustvo, 1959.

B101. Fischer-Galati, Stephen (ed.). *Romania.* Mid-European Studies Center of the Free Europe Committee. New York: Praeger, 1956.

B102. Foot, M. R. D. *Men in Uniform.* New York: Praeger, 1961.

B103. Forster, Thomas M. *NVA, Die Armee der Sowjetzone.* Cologne: Markus Verlag, 1964.

B103a. Form, William H., and Delbert C. Miller. *Industry, Labor, and Community.* New York: Harper and Bros., 1960.

B104. Freeman, Christopher. *Science, Economic Growth, and Government Policy.* Paris: O.E.C.D., 1963.

B105. Freeman, Christopher, A. Young, *et al. The Research and Development Effort in Western Europe, North America, and the Soviet Union.* Paris: OECD, 1965.

B106. Freeman, Howard E., *et al. Handbook of Medical Sociology.* Englewood Cliffs, New Jersey: Prentice Hall, 1963.

B107. Frei, Rudolf (ed.). *Economic Systems of the West.* Tuebingen: J. C. B. Mohr for the List Gesellschaft, 1957.

B108. Friedman, Milton. *Capitalism and Freedom.* Chicago: University of Chicago Press, 1962.

B109. Friedman, Milton. *Essays in Positive Economics.* Chicago: University of Chicago Press, 1953.

B110. Fuchs, Victor R. *Productivity Trends in the Goods and Services Sectors 1929–1961.* National Bureau of Economic Research

Occasional Paper 89. New York: Columbia University Press, 1964.

B111. Galbraith, John Kenneth. *The Affluent Society*. Boston: Houghton Mifflin Co., 1958.

B112. Galbraith, John Kenneth. *American Capitalism*. Boston: Houghton Mifflin Co., 1952.

B113. Galenson, Walter and Graham Pyatt. *The Quality of Labour and Economic Development in Certain Countries*. Geneva: International Labour Office, 1964.

B114. Gallik, Daniel. *The Classification of Revenues and Expenditures in the Soviet Budget*. Foreign Demographic Analysis Division, US Bureau of the Census. Washington, DC: mimeo., March, 1964.

B115. Gensemer, Bruce L. *Determinants of the Fiscal Policy Decisions of Local Governments in Urban Areas: Public Safety and Public Education*. Ph.D. dissertation, University of Michigan, 1966. Ann Arbor: University Microfilms.

B116. Gerloff, Wilhelm. *Die oeffentliche Finanzwirtschaft*. Frankfurt a.M.: Klostermann, 1948.

B117. Gerloff, Wilhelm and Fritz Neumark (eds.). *Handbuch der Finanzwissenschaft, IV*. Tuebingen: J. C. B. Mohr, 1965.

B118. Gilbert, Milton, *et al. Comparative National Products and Price Levels*. Paris: OEEC, 1958.

B119. Goldman, Marshall I. *Soviet Aid and Trade with Less Developed Countries*. New York: Praeger, 1966.

B120. Goldsmith, Raymond and Christopher Saunders, (eds.). *Income and Wealth*. Series VIII. *The Measurement of National Wealth*. London: Bowes & Bowes, 1959.

B121. Goloshchapov, V. A. (ed.). *Byudzhetnyy uchet*. Moscow: Gosfinizdat, 1962.

B122. Gordon, Margaret S. *The Economics of Welfare Policies*. New York: Columbia University Press, 1963.

B123. Gort, Michael. *Diversification and Integration in American Industry*. Princeton: Princeton University Press for NBER, 1962.

B124. de Gramont, Sanche. *The Secret War*. New York: Putnam, 1962.

B125. Granick, David. *The European Executive*. Garden City, New York: Doubleday, 1962.

B126. Gregory, Karl D. *Variations in State and Local Appropriations for Publicly Supported Institutions of Higher Education, by State*. Ph.D. dissertation, University of Michigan, 1961. Ann Arbor: University Microfilms.

B127. Griffith, William. *The New Course and Thaw*. New Haven: Yale University Press, forthcoming.

B128. Grzybowski, Kazimierz. *The Socialist Commonwealth of*

Nations: Organizations and Institutions. New Haven: Yale University Press, 1964.

B129. Gupta, Shibshankar Prasad. *The Size and Growth of Government Expenditures: A Time-Series and Cross-Section Analysis.* Ph.D. dissertation, University of York (England), 1966.

B130. Haire, Mason (ed.). *Modern Organization Theory.* New York: Wiley, 1959.

B131. Halecki, Oscar (ed.). *Poland.* Mid-European Studies Center of the Free Europe Committee. New York: Praeger, 1956.

B132. Haley, Bernard F. (ed.). *A Survey of Contemporary Economics.* Homewood, Ill.: Irwin, 1952.

B133. Halsey, A. H., *et al.* (eds.). *Education, Economy and Society.* New York: Free Press of Glencoe, 1961.

B134. Harbison, Frederick and Charles A. Myers. *Education, Manpower and Economic Growth.* New York: McGraw-Hill, 1964.

B135. Harlow, Robert L. *Factors Affecting American State Expenditures.* Ph.D. dissertation, Yale University, 1966.

B136. Harris, Seymour E. *The Economics of American Medicine.* New York: Macmillan, 1964.

B137. Harris, Seymour. *Higher Education, Resources and Finances.* New York: McGraw-Hill, 1962.

B138. Harsen, Hans. *Der Perspektivplan zur Entwicklung der medizinischen Wissenschaft und des Gesundheitswesens in Mitteldeutschland und Ost Berlin: 1959/60.* Hamburg: Akademie fuer Staatsmedizin in Hamburg, 1962.

B139. Haskell, Mark A. *The Influence of Federal Grants on State and Local Expenditures.* Ph.D. dissertation, Rutgers University, 1962. Ann Arbor: University Microfilms.

B140. Hatt, Paul K., and Albert J. Reiss, Jr. (eds.). *Cities and Societies.* Glencoe, Free Press, 1957.

B141. Helmreich, Ernst C. (ed.). *Hungary.* Mid-European Studies Center of the Free Europe Committee. New York: Praeger, 1956.

B142. Henry, Nelson B. (ed.). *Social Forces Influencing American Education, Part II.* Chicago: University of Chicago Press, 1961.

B143. Herscher, Karl. *Der Zahlungsverkehr der D.D.R. mit dem Ausland.* East Berlin: Verlag Die Wirtschaft, 1958.

B144. Hettich, Walter. *Equalization Grants, Minimum Standards, and Unit Cost Differences in Education.* Ph.D. dissertation, Yale University, 1966.

B145. Hindrichs, Harley H. *A General Theory of Tax Structure Change during Economic Development.* Cambridge, Massachusetts: Law School of Harvard University, 1966.

B146. Hirsch, Werner Z. *Analysis of the Rising Costs of Public Education*. Study Paper 4. Joint Economic Committee of the US Congress, Washington, DC: GPO, 1959.

B147. Hirst, F. W. *The Political Economy of War*. London: J. M. Dent, 1915.

B148. Hitch, Charles J. *The Character of Research and Development in a Competitive Economy*. RAND Corporation Paper P-1297. Santa Monica: 1958.

B149. Hoeffding, Oleg and Nancy Nimitz. *Soviet National Income and Product, 1949–1955*. RAND Corporation Memorandum RM 2101. Santa Monica: April, 1959.

B150. Hoffman, George W. and Fred W. Neal. *Yugoslavia and the New Communism*. New York: 20th Century Fund, 1962.

B151. Holzman, Franklyn D. *Soviet Taxation*. Cambridge, Massachusetts: Harvard University Press, 1955.

B152. Horelick, Arnold L. and Myron Rush. *Strategic Power and Soviet Foreign Policy*. Chicago: University of Chicago Press, 1966.

B153. Höök, Erik. *Den offentliga sektorns expansion: En studie av de offentliga civila utgifternas utveckling åren, 1913–1958*. Stockholm: Almqvist and Wiksell, 1962.

B154. Huntington, Samuel P. *The Common Defense: Strategic Problems in National Politics*. New York: Columbia University Press, 1961.

B155. Institut international de finances publiques. *Les effets économiques des dépenses publiques*. Paris: Editions de l'épargne, 1957.

B156. Institut international de finances publiques. *L'importance et la structure des recettes et des dépenses publiques*. Brussels: Emile Bruylant, 1960.

B157. International Bureau of Education. *Financing of Education*. Publ. No. 163. Geneva: 1955.

B158. International Bureau of Education. *Preparation of General Secondary School Curricula*. Publ. No. 216. Geneva: 1960.

B159. International Bureau of Education. *Preparation and Issuing of the Primary School Curricula*. Publ. No. 194. Geneva: 1958.

B160. International Bureau of Education. *Primary Teachers' Salaries*. Publ. No. 147. Geneva: 1952.

B161. International Bureau of Education. *Secondary Teachers' Salaries*. Publ. No. 157. Geneva: 1954.

B162. Isaev, Boris L. *Denezhno-kreditnaya sistema Narodnoy respubliki Bolgarii*. Moscow: Gosfinizdat, 1956.

B163. James, Henry Thomas, *et al*. *Wealth, Expenditures and*

Decision Making in Education. Stanford: School of Education, Stanford University, nimeo, 1963.

B164. Janowitz, Morris. *The Professional Soldier.* Glencoe, Ill.: The Free Press, 1960.

B165. Jaworski, Władysław. *Systemy Kredytowe Europejskich krajów socjalistycznych.* Warsaw: Pánstwowe Wydawnictwo Ekonomiczne, 1962.

B166. Kakkarov, A. K. and G. M. Prokhorov. *Druzheskaya pomoshch ivzaimovygodnoye sotrudnichestvo.* Moscow: Izd. vost. lit., 1959.

B167. Kalogeris, Angelos. *I organosis tis epistimonikis ke technikis erenis en Helladi.* Athens: Ekdosis Illinikou Kendrou Paragogikotitos, 1963.

B168. Kapp, K. William. *Social Costs of Business Enterprise.* London: Asia Publishing House, 1963.

B169. Keenan, Stella and Pauline Atherton. *The Journal Literature of Physics.* New York: American Institute of Physics, 1964.

B170. Keith, E. Gordon (ed.). *Foreign Tax Policies and Economic Growth.* New York: Columbia University Press for NBER, 1966.

B171. Kendrick, M. Slade. *A Century and a Half of Federal Expenditures.* National Bureau of Economic Research Occasional Paper 48. New York: 1955.

B172. Kirillov, L. A. *Finansy otrasley narodnogo khozyaystva.* Moscow: Gosfinizdat, 1958.

B173. Kirschen, E. S., *et al. Economic Policy in Our Time.* Amsterdam: North-Holland, 1964.

B174. Klarman, Herbert E. *The Economics of Health.* New York: Columbia University Press, 1965.

B175. Kleinsorge, Paul K. (ed.). *Public Finance and Welfare: Essays in Honour of C. Ward Macy.* Eugene: University of Oregon Press, 1966.

B176. Koehler, Heinz. *Economic Integration in the Soviet Bloc with an East German Case Study.* New York: Praeger, 1966.

B177. Koenig, Heinz (ed.). *Wandlungen der Wirtschaftsstruktur in der Bundesrepublik Deutschland.* Berlin: Duncker & Humblot, 1962.

B178. Komissarov, V. *Finansovo- kreditnaya sistema Chekhoslovatskoy respubliki.* Moscow: Gosfinizdat, 1956.

B179. Komissarov, V. P. and Popov, A. N. *Den'gi, kredit, i finansy evropeyskich stran narodnoy demokratii.* Moscow: Izd. sotsial'noekonomicheskoy literatury, 1960.

B180. Koopmans, Tjallings C. *Three Essays on the State of Economic Science.* New York: McGraw-Hill, 1957.

B181. Korol, Alexander. *Soviet Education for Science and Technology.* Cambridge, Massachusetts: Technology Press of MIT, 1957.

B182. Korol, Alexander. *Soviet Research and Development: Its Organization, Personnel and Funds.* Cambridge, Massachusetts: MIT Press, 1965.

B183. Kosobud, Richard F. *An Econometric Approach to Forecasting Selected Government Expenditures and Revenues.* Ph.D. thesis, University of Pennsylvania, 1964.

B184. Kozlov, Yu.M. (ed.). *Sovetskoye administrativnoye pravo: Osobennaya chast'.* Moscow: Izdatel'stvo yuridicheskaya literatura, 1964.

B185. Kramish, Arnold. *Research and Development in the Common Market vis-a-vis the U.K., U.S., and U.S.S.R.* RAND Corporation Paper P-2742, Santa Monica: 1963.

B186. Kurowski, Leon. *Les finances dans les états socialistes.* Paris: Pichon et Durand-Auzais, 1962.

B187. Kuusinen, O. W. (ed.). *Fundamentals of Marxism–Leninism.* Moscow: Foreign Language Publishing House, n.d.

B.188. Lange, Oskar and Fred M. Taylor. *On the Economic Theory of Socialism.* Minneapolis: University of Minnesota Press, 1952.

B188a. Lange, Oskar. *Political Economy,* Vol. I. Oxford: Pergamon Press, 1967.

B189. Lansing, John B., *et al. How People Pay for College.* Ann Arbor, Michigan: Survey Research Center, Institute for Social Research, University of Michigan, September, 1960.

B190. Lasky, Melvin. *The Ugly Russian.* New York: Trident Press, 1965.

B191. Laufenburger, Henry. *Finances comparées: Etats-Unis, France, Angleterre, U.R.S.S.* Paris: Sirey, 1957.

B192. Laufenburger, Henry. *Théorie économique et psychologique des finances publiques.* Paris: 1956.

B193. Lavrov, V., P. Kudryashov, and A. Shuvalov. *Gosudarstvennyy byudzhet.* Moscow: Gosfinizdat, 1961.

B194. Lazarov, Kiril (ed.). *Finansite i sotsialisticheskoto stroitelstvo na Narodna Republika Bŭlgariya,* 1949–1959 godina. Sofia: Nauka i izkustvo, 1959.

B195. Lazarov, Kiril. *Finansovata sistema na Narodna Republika Bŭlgariya.* Sofia: Izdatelstvo na Bŭlgarskata komunisticheska partiya, 1957.

B196. Lazarov, Kiril. *Ikonomichesko razvitie na Narodna Republika Bŭlgariya.* Sofia: 1961.

B197. Lees, D. S. *Health through Choice.* London: Institute of Economic Affairs, 1961.

B198. Lenin, V. I. *Imperialism, the Highest Stage of Capitalism*. New York: International Publishers, 1939.

B199. Little, I. M. D. and J. M. Clifford. *International Aid: A Discussion of the Flow of Public Resources from Rich to Poor Countries*. Chicago: Aldine, 1966.

B200. Lubscher, Gerhard and Guenther Thude. *Sozialversicherung in der D. D. R.* East Berlin: Tribuene Verlag, 1960.

B201. Lutz, Vera. *Italy, A Study in Economic Development*. London: Oxford University Press, 1962.

B202. Macesich, George. *Yugoslavia: The Theory and Practice of Development Planning*. Charlottesville, Virginia: University of Virginia Press, 1964.

B203. Machiavelli, Niccolo. *The Prince*. New York: Appleton-Century-Croft, 1947.

B204. Machlup, Fritz. *The Production and Distribution of Knowledge in the United States*. Princeton, New Jersey: Princeton University Press, 1962.

B205. MacIver, R. M. *Social Causation*. New York: Harper, 1964.

B206. Maddison, Angus. *Economic Growth in the West*. New York: 20th Century Fund, 1964.

B207. Mangus, Philip (ed.). *Edmund Burke, Selected Prose*. London: Falcon Press, 1948.

B208. Maneschi, Andrea. *The Scope of Allocation in the Public Sector*. Yale University, Economic Growth Center Discussion Paper No. 3. New Haven: February, 1966.

B209. Maréchal, A., *et al. Fundamental Research and the Policies of Governments*. Paris: OECD, 1966.

B210. Margolis, Julius (ed.). *The Public Economy of Urban Communities*. Washington, DC: Resources for the Future, 1965.

B211. Markovich, Stefan. *Povishavane rolyata na mestnite byudzheti za uskoryavane razvitieto na narodnoto stopanstvo*. Varna: Dŭrzhavno izdatelstvo, 1961.

B212. Marx, Karl. *Capital*. Vol. I. Moscow: Foreign Languages Publishing House, 1961.

B213. Mastalygina, N. A. *Bukhgalterskiy uchet v byudzhetnykh organizatsiyakh*. Moscow: Gosfinizdat, 1962.

B214. Maxwell, James, *Financing State and Local Government*. Washington, DC: Brookings Institution, 1965.

B215. McAuley, Alastair and Dubravko Matko. *The Real Cost of Soviet Foreign Aid*. Glasgow: University of Glasgow, Department of International Economic Studies, 1966. Mimeo.

R

B216. Meade, J. E. *Efficiency, Equality and the Ownership of Property.* London: George Allen and Unwin Ltd., 1964.

B217. Meier, Helmut. *Die Entwicklung des Haushaltswesens in der sowjetischen Besatzungszone Deutschlands.* Berlin: Duncker & Humblot, 1960.

B218. Melman, Seymour. *Dynamic Factors in Industrial Productivity.* New York: Wiley, 1956.

B219. Menz, Gertraud. *Die Entwicklung der sowjetischen Besteuerung unter besonderer Beruecksichtigung der ordnungspolitischen Funktionen.* Berlin: Duncker & Humblot, 1960.

B220. Mergelov, G. S. *Planirovaniye i finansirovaniye raskhodov na upravleniye.* Moscow: Gosfinizdat, 1962.

B221. Merritt, Richard L. and Stein Rokkan (eds.). *Comparing Nations: The Use of Quantitative Data in Cross National Research.* New Haven: Yale University Press, 1966.

B222. Mesmer, Theodore Charles. *Government Expenditures and Economic Growth: An International Comparative Study.* Ph.D. dissertation, University of Wisconsin, 1962. Ann Arbor, Michigan: University Microfilms.

B223. Miner, Jerry. *Social and Economic Factors in Spending for Public Education.* Syracuse: Syracuse University Press, 1963.

B224. Minkoff, Jack. *The Soviet Social Insurance System Since 1921.* Ph.D. dissertation. Columbia University, 1960. Ann Arbor: University Microfilms.

B225. Mitchell, B. R. and Phyllis Deane. *Abstract of British Historical Statistics.* Cambridge University Press, 1962.

B226. Moorstein, Richard. *Prices and Production of Machinery in the Soviet Union, 1928–1958.* Cambridge, Massachusetts: Harvard University Press, 1960.

B227. Morag, Amotz. *On Taxes and Inflation.* New York: Random House, 1965.

B228. Morgan, James N., *et al. Income and Welfare in the United States.* New York: McGraw-Hill, 1962.

B229. Musgrave, Richard A. (ed.). *Essays in Fiscal Federalism.* Washington, DC: Brookings Institution, 1965.

B230. Musgrave, Richard A. *Fiscal Systems.* New Haven: Yale University Press, 1968.

B231. Musgrave, Richard A. *The Theory of Public Finance.* New York: McGraw-Hill, 1959.

B232. Musgrave, Richard A. and Alan T. Peacock (eds.). *Classics in the Theory of Public Finance.* New York: Macmillan, 1958.

B233. Mushkin, Selma (ed.). *Economics of Higher Education*. Washington, DC: GPO, 1962.

B234. Myrdal, Gunnar. *The Political Element in the Development of Economic Theory*. English edition. Cambridge, Massachusetts: Harvard University Press, 1955.

B235. National Bureau of Economic Research. *Public Finances: Needs, Sources and Utilization*. Princeton: Princeton University Press, 1961.

B236. Nelson, Richard R. (ed.). *The Rate and Direction of Inventive Activity: Economic and Social Factors*. Princeton, NJ: Princeton University Press for NBER, 1962.

B237. Nelson, Richard R., Merton J. Peck and Edward Kalachek. *Technology, Economic Growth and Public Policies*. Washington, DC: Brookings Institution, 1967.

B238. *Népgazdasági tervezés, II kötet*. Budapest: Közgazdasági És Jogi Könyvkiadó, 1964.

B239. Newsholme, Arthur. *International Studies on the Relation between the Private and Official Practice of Medicine with Special Reference to the Prevention of Disease*. London: George Allen and Unwin, 1931.

B240. Nimitz, Nancy. *Soviet National Income and Product, 1956–1958*. RAND Corporation Memorandum RM-3112-PR. Santa Monica: June, 1962.

B241. Novick, David (ed.). *Program Budgeting: Program Analysis and the Federal Budget*. Cambridge, Massachusetts: Harvard University Press, 1965.

B242. Olson, Mancur. *The Logic of Collective Action*. Cambridge, Mass.: Harvard University Press, 1965.

B243. Olson, Mancur and Richard Zeckhauser. *An Economic Theory of Alliances*. RAND Corporation Memorandum RM-4297-ISA, Santa Monica, California: 1965.

B244. Palyi, Melchior. *Compulsory Medical Care and the Welfare State*. Chicago: National Institute of Professional Services, 1949.

B245. Parkinson, C. Northcote. *Parkinson's Law*. Boston: Houghton Mifflin, 1957.

B246. Patinkin, Don. *Money, Interest, and Prices*. Evanston, Ill.: Row, Peterson, and Company, 1956.

B247. Peacock, Alan T. (ed.). *Income Redistribution and Social Policy*. London: Jonathan Cape, 1954.

B248. Peacock, Alan T. and Jack Wiseman. *Education for Democrats: A Study of the Financing of Education in a Free Society*. London: Institute of Economic Affairs, 1964.

B249. Peacock, Alan T. and Jack Wiseman. *The Growth of Public Expenditures in The United Kingdom.* Princeton: Princeton University Press for NBER, 1961.

B250. Pearson, Karl. *The Life, Letters, and Labours of Francis Galton.* Cambridge University Press, 1911–30.

B251. Peck, Merton J. and Frederic M. Scherer. *The Weapons Acquisition Process: An Economic Analysis.* Boston, Mass.: Graduate School of Business Administration, Harvard, 1962.

B252. Pesek, Boris. *Gross National Product of Czechoslovakia in Monetary and Real Terms, 1946–1958.* Chicago: University of Chicago Press, 1965.

B253. Pidot, George. *The Public Finances of Local Government in the Metropolitan United States.* Ph.D. dissertation, Harvard University, 1965.

B254. Pincus, John A. *Economic Aid and International Cost Sharing.* Baltimore: Johns Hopkins Press, 1965.

B255. Pintado, V. Z. *Public Expenditures and Economic Growth, with Special Reference to Portugal.* Ph.D. dissertation, University of Edinburgh, October, 1960.

B256. Plotnikov, K. *Gosudarstvennyy byudzhet S.S.S.R.* Moscow: Gosfinizdat, 1959.

B257. Pokrovsky, G. I. *Science and Technology in Contemporary War.* New York: Praeger, 1959.

B258. *Una politica per la ricerca scientifica.* Rome: Edizione 5 luni, 1962.

B259. Popovivi, Mircea. *Sistemul bugetar al R.P.R.* Bucharest: Editura Ştiinţifică, 1964.

B260. Popper, Karl. *The Open Society and Its Enemies.* Princeton, NJ: Princeton University Press, 1950.

B261. Powell, Raymond P., and Richard Moorstein. *The Soviet Capital Stock, 1928–1961.* Homewood, Ill.: Irwin, 1965.

B262. Prais, S., and H. S. Houthakker. *The Analysis of Family Budgets.* Cambridge, England: University Press, 1955.

B263. Price, Derek J. deSolla. *Little Science, Big Science.* New York: Columbia University Press, 1963.

B264. Price, Derek J. deSolla. *Science Since Babylon.* New Haven: Yale University Press, 1961.

B265. Prochazka, Zora. *The Labor Force of Bulgaria.* U.S. Bureau of the Census. International Population Statistics Reports. Series P-90, No. 16, Washington, DC: GPO, 1962.

B266. Prochazka, Zora, and Jerry W. Combs, Jr. *The Labor Force of Poland.* US Bureau of the Census. International Population

Statistics Reports. Series P-90, No. 20, Washington, DC: GPO, 1964.

B267. Pryor, Frederic L. *The Communist Foreign Trade System.* Cambridge, Mass.: MIT Press, 1963.

B268. Ratchford, B. U. *Public Expenditures in Australia.* Durham, NC: Duke University Press, 1959.

B269. Reed, Louis. *Per Capita Expenditures for Hospital Care and for the Services of Physicians and Dentists, by Region and State.* Research and Statistics Note No. 18/1964. Social Security Administration, US Department of Health, Education and Welfare. Washington, DC: December 18, 1964.

B270. Reifman, Lucille (ed.). *Financing of Education for Economic Growth.* Paris: OECD, n.d.

B271. Repaci, Francesco. *La finanza pubblica italiana nel socolo 1861–1960.* Bologna: Zanichelli Editore, 1962.

B272. Richardson, J. Henry. *Economic and Financial Aspects of Social Security.* Toronto: University of Toronto Press, 1960.

B273. Richardson, Lewis F. *Arms and Insecurity.* Pittsburgh: Boxwood Press, 1960.

B274. Robbins, Lionel. *The Theory of Economic Policy in English Classical Political Economy.* London: Macmillan, 1952.

B275. Roberts, Ffrangcon. *The Cost of Health.* London: Turnstile Press, 1952.

B276. Robinson, E. A. G. (ed.). *Economic Consequences of the Size of Nations.* New York: St Martin's Press, 1960.

B277. Rogers, Daniel. *The Effects of Education on Earnings: A Case Study.* Ph.D. dissertation, Yale University, 1967.

B278. Rohde, Erwin and Heinz Fengler. *Der Staatshaushalt der Deutschen Demokratischen Republik.* East Berlin: Verlag Die Wirtschaft, 1959.

B279. Rosa, Josef and Ján Petrenka. *Štátný rozpočet Československej socialistickej republiky.* Bratislava: SVPL, 1961.

B280. Rosen, George. *A History of Public Health.* New York: MD Publications, 1958.

B281. Roskamp, Karl W. *Capital Formation in West Germany.* Detroit: Wayne State University Press, 1965.

B282. Rovinskiy, N. N. *Gosudarstvennyy byudzhet S.S.S.R.* Moscow: Gosfinizdat, 1949.

B283. Royal Institute of International Affairs. *Documents on International Affairs, 1947–1948.* London: Oxford University Press, 1952.

B284. Russett, Bruce M. *et al. World Handbook of Political and Social Indicators.* New Haven: Yale University Press, 1964.

B285. Rymalov, Victor V. *Economic Cooperation between the U.S.S.R and Underdeveloped Countries.* Moscow: FLPH, 1962.

B286. Sacks, Seymore and William F. Hellmuth, Jr. *Financing Government in a Metropolitan Area.* New York: Free Press of Glencoe, 1960.

B287. Saunders, Donald Perry. *Patterns of Educational Change During Economic Growth.* Ph.D. dissertation, Stanford University, 1962. Ann Arbor: University Microfilms, n.d.

B288. Schaller, Howard G. (ed). *Public Expenditure Decisions in the Urban Community.* Baltimore: Johns Hopkins Press, 1962.

B289. Schilling, Warner R., *et al. Strategy, Politics, and Defense Budgets.* New York: Columbia University Press, 1962.

B290. Schmidt, Ádám. *Az adóztatás igazságossága: Az alapvetó problémát eltakaró részletkérdés.* Budapest: 1962.

B291. Schmoelders, Guenter. *Finanzpolitik.* West Berlin: Springer Verlag, 1955.

B292. Schmoelders, Guenter. *Das Irrationale in der oeffentlichen Finanzwirtschaft.* Hamburg: Rowohlt, 1960.

B293. Schmoelders, Guenter. *Der Politiker und die Waehrung.* Frankfurt a.M.: Knapp Verlag, 1959.

B294. Schoeck, Helmut (ed.). *Financing Medical Care.* Caldwell, Idaho: Caxton Printers, 1962.

B295. Schoeck, Helmut, and James W. Wiggins (eds.). *The New Argument in Economics: The Public versus the Private Sector.* Princeton, NJ: Van Nostrand, 1963.

B296. Scholten, H. *Die Steuermentalitaet der Voelker im Spiegel ihrer Sprache.* Cologne: 1952.

B296a. Schuette, Ehrenfried. *Das Versicherungswesen der Sowjet-Union.* West Berlin: Duncker und Humblot, 1966.

B297. Schraeder, Herbert L. *No Other Way.* New York: McKay, 1964.

B298. Schultz, Theodore M. *The Economic Value of Education.* New York: Columbia University Press, 1963.

B299. Scott, Stanley, and Edward L. Feder. *Factors Associated with Variation in Municipal Expenditure Levels.* Berkeley: Bureau of Public Administration, University of California, 1957.

B300. Sergeyev, S. D. *Ekonomicheskoye sotrudnichestvo i vzaimopomoshch stran sotsialisticheskogo lagerya.* Moscow: Vneshtorgizdat, 1959.

B301. Shaw, George Bernard. *Complete Plays with Prefaces.* Vol. I. New York: Dodd, Mead & Co., 1963.

B302. Siegel, Jacob S. *The Population of Hungary.* US Bureau of the

Census, International Population Statistics Reports. Series P-90 No. 9, Washington, DC: GPO, 1958.

B303. Simon, Maurice David. *Communist System Interaction with the Developing States, 1954–1962: A Preliminary Analysis.* Stanford Studies of the Communist System. Research Paper 10. Stanford: mimeo., 1966.

B304. Slamecka, Vladimir. *Science in Czechoslovakia.* New York: Columbia University Press, 1963.

B305. Slamecka, Vladimir. *Science in East Germany.* New York: Columbia University Press, 1963.

B306. Smirnov, S. M. *Mezhdunarodnye valutnye i kreditnye otnosheniya S.S.S.R.* Moscow: Vneshtorgizdat, 1960.

B307. Smith, Adam. *An Inquiry into the Nature and Causes of the Wealth of Nations.* New York: Modern Library, 1937.

B308. Snyder, Glenn H. *Deterrence and Defense.* Princeton, NJ: Princeton University Press, 1961.

B309. Somers, Herbert Miles and Ann Ramsay Somers. *Doctors, Patients, and Health Insurance.* Washington, DC: Brookings Institution, 1962.

B310. Sorokin, Pitirim. *Social and Cultural Dynamics.* Vol. III, New York: American Book Co., 1937.

B311. Spáčil, Bedřich (ed.). *Československé finanční právo.* Prague: Orbis, 1959.

B312. Spulber, Nicolas. *The Economics of Communist Eastern Europe.* Cambridge, Massachusetts: Technology Press of MIT, 1957.

B313. Stifterverband fuer die deutsche Wissenschaft. *Wissenschaft in Daten.* Essen: 1962.

B314. Stockfisch, Jacob A. (ed.). *Planning and Forecasting in the Defense Industries.* Belmont, California: Wadsworth Publishing Co., 1962.

B315. Stolper, Wolfgang, and Karl Roskamp. *The Structure of the East German Economy.* Cambridge, Massachusetts: Harvard University Press, 1960.

B316. Stowe, Leland. *Conquest by Terror.* New York: Random House, 1951.

B317. Surányi-Unger, Theo. *Studien zum Wirtschaftswachstum Suedosteuropas.* Stuttart: Gustav Fischer Verlag, 1964.

B318. Survey Research Center, University of Michigan. *Life Insurance 1954.* Ann Arbor: n.d.

B319. Svrakov, G., N. Karbashakov, M. Rusenov, and L. Ralchev. *Finansi i kredit na sotsialisticheskata dŭrzhava.* Sofia: Nauka i izkustvo, 1957.

B320. Swianiewicz, S. *Forced Labor and Economic Development: An Enquiry into the Experience of Soviet Industrialization.* London: Oxford University Press, 1965.

B321. Timár, Mátyás. *Költségvetés, pénzügyek, gazdaságirányitás.* Budapest: Közgazdasági És Jogi Könyvkiadó, 1964.

B322. Trevelyan, George Otto. *George the Third and Charles Fox.* Vol. II. New York: Longmans Green and Co., 1914.

B323. Tsankin, N. *Finansy i kredit Germanskoy demokratischeskoy respubliki.* Moscow: Gosfinizdat, 1959.

B324. Tybout, Richard A. (ed.). *Economics of Research and Development.* Columbus, Ohio: Ohio State University Press, 1965.

B325. Tuček, Miroslav, *et al. Socialistické finance.* Prague: NPL, 1965.

B326. Tunley, Roul. *The American Health Scandal.* New York: Harper & Row, 1966.

B327. Urquhart, M. C., and K. A. H. Buckley, (eds.). *Historical Statistics of Canada.* Toronto: Macmillan, 1965.

B328. Veltruský, Ladislav (ed.). *Československé finance.* Prague: SNP, 1956.

B329. Veltruský, Ladislav (ed.). *Československé finance.* Prague: Orbis, 1959.

B330. Vieg, John A. *et al. California Local Finance.* Stanford: Stanford University Press, 1960.

B331. de Viti de Marco, Antonio. *First Principles of Public Finance.* London: Jonathan Cape, 1936.

B332. van Waasdijk, T. *Public Expenditures in South Africa.* Johannesburg: Witwatersrand University Press, 1964.

B333. Wagner, Adolph. *Finanzwissenschaft: Erster Teil,* 3rd ed., Leipzig: Winter Verlag, 1883.

B334. Wagner, Adolph. *Grundlegung der politischen Oekonomie.* 1st part, 3rd. edition, Leipzig: C. F. Winter, 1893.

B335. Wallich, Henry C., John H. Adler, *et al. Public Finance in a Developing Country: El Salvador. A Case Study.* Cambridge, Massachusetts: Harvard University Press, 1951.

B335a. Webb, Augustos D. *The New Dictionary of Statistics,* London: George Routledge, 1911.

B336. Weisbrod, Burton A. *Economics of Public Health.* Philadelphia: University of Pennsylvania Press, 1961.

B337. Weisbrod, Burton A. *External Benefits of Public Education.* Princeton, NJ: Industrial Relations Section. Department of Economics, Princeton University Press, 1964.

B338. Weitzman, Murray S. *Comparison of the U.S. and U.S.S.R.*

Employment in Industry: 1939–1958. Washington, DC: GPO, January, 1963.

B339. West, E. G. *Education and the State: A Study in Political Economy.* London: Institute of Economic Affairs, 1965.

B340. Wiles, Peter. *The Political Economy of Communism.* Cambridge, Mass.: Harvard University Press, 1962.

B341. Williams, Oliver P. *Suburban Differences and Metropolitan Policies.* Philadelphia: University of Pennsylvania Press, 1965.

B342. Wolin, Simon and Robert Slusser, (eds.). *The Soviet Secret Police.* New York: Praeger, 1957.

B343. Wood, Robert C. *1400 Governments.* Cambridge, Massachusetts: Harvard University Press, 1961.

B344. *The Worldmark Encyclopedia of Nations.* New York: Worldmark Press, 1960.

B345. Wright, Quincy. *A Study of War,* 2nd ed. Chicago: University of Chicago Press, 1965.

B346. Wynnyczuk, Alexander. *Growth of Bulgarian Industrial Production, 1939 and 1948–1962.* Occasional Paper of the Research Project on National Income in East Central Europe. New York: 1966.

B347. van Ypersele de Strihou, Jacques M. *Sharing the Defense Burden among Western Allies.* Ph.D. dissertation. Yale University, New Haven, Conn.: 1966.

B348. Ypsilantis, James N. *The Labor Force of Czechoslovakia.* US Bureau of the Census, International Population Statistics Reports. Series P-90, No. 13, Washington, DC: GPO, 1960.

B349. Zaleski, Eugene. *Planification de la croissance et fluctuations économiques en U.R.S.S.* Paris: 1962.

B350. Zoellner, Detler. *Oeffentliche Sozialleistungen und wirtschaftliche Entwicklung: Ein zeitlicher und internationaler Vergleich.* West Berlin: Duncker and Humblot, 1963.

OFFICIAL PUBLICATIONS OF GOVERNMENTAL AND INTER-GOVERNMENTAL ORGANIZATIONS[1]

Inter-governmental Organizations

G1. European Economic Community. *Die Einnahmen und Ausgaben der oeffentlichen Verwaltung in den Laendern der E.W.G.* Study 2, Reihe Wirtschaft und Finanzen. Brussels: 1964.

[1] Non-official publications of governmental and inter-governmental organizations are contained in the previous two sections of the bibliography.

R*

G2. International Labour Office. *The Cost of Medical Care*. Geneva: 1959.

G3. International Labour Office. *The Cost of Social Security*. Geneva: various years.

G4. International Labour Office. *Employment and Conditions of Work of Nurses*. Geneva: 1960.

G5. International Labour Office. Meeting of Experts on Teachers' Problems. *Principles Underlying the Determination of Teachers' Salaries*. Geneva: mimeo, 1958.

G6. International Labour Office. *Yearbook of Labour Statistics*. Geneva: annual.

G7. International Monetary Fund. *Balance of Payments Yearbook*. Washington, DC: annual.

G8. International Monetary Fund. *International Financial Statistics*. Washington, DC: monthly.

G9. League of Nations. *Statistical Yearbook*. Geneva: various years.

G10. OECD *Economic Aspects of Higher Education*. Paris: 1964.

G11. OECD *Economic Survey: Socialist Federal Republic of Yugoslavia*. Paris: annual.

G12. OECD. *General Statistics*. Paris: monthly.

G13. OECD. *Manpower Statistics*. Paris: annual.

G14. OECD. *Policy Conference on Economic Growth and Investment in Education*. Paris: 1962.

G15. OECD. *The Residual Factor and Economic Growth*. Paris: 1964.

G16. OECD. *Review of National Science Policy: Greece*. Paris: 1965.

G17. OECD. *Statistics of National Accounts, 1950–1961*. Paris: 1964.

G18. OECD. Mediterranean Regional Project. *Greece*. Paris: 1965.

G19. United Nations. *Demographic Yearbook*. New York: annual.

G20. United Nations. *International Flow of Long Term Capital*. New York: irregular.

G21. United Nations. *International Flow of Long Term Capital and Official Donations, 1961–1965*. New York: 1966.

G22. United Nations. *Statistical Yearbook*. New York: annual.

G23. United Nations. *World Economic Survey*. New York: annual.

G24. United Nations. *Yearbook*. New York: annual.

G25. United Nations. *Yearbook of National Income Accounts*. New York: annual.

G26. United Nations. Conference on Trade and Development. *Proceedings of the United Nations Conference on Trade and Development, Vol. VI*. Part 1, Geneva: 1964.

G27. United Nations, Department of Economic and Social Affairs. *Economic and Social Consequences of Disarmament*. New York: 1962.

G28. United Nations, Department of Economic and Social Affairs. *A Manual for Economic and Functional Classification of Government Transactions*. New York: 1958.

G29. United Nations. Economic Commission for Europe. *Economic Bulletin of Europe*. Geneva: three times a year.

G30. United Nations. Economic Commission for Europe. *Economic Survey of Europe*. Geneva: annual.

G31. United Nations. Economic Commission for Europe. *Some Factors in Economic Growth in Europe during the 1950s*. Geneva: 1964.

G32. United Nations Educational, Scientific and Cultural Organization. *Manual of Educational Statistics*. Paris: 1961.

G33. United Nations Educational, Scientific and Cultural Organization. *World Survey of Education, II*. Paris: 1958.

G34. United Nations Educational, Scientific, and Cultural Organization. *World Survey of Education, III*. New York: International Documents Service, 1961.

G35. United Nations Educational, Scientific, and Cultural Organization. *World Survey of Education, IV*. New York: UNESCO Publications Centre, 1966.

G36. United Nations, Educational, Scientific and Cultural Organization. *Statistical Yearbook 1963*. Paris: 1964.

G37. United Nations. Research Institute for Social Development. *Aspects of Social and Economic Growth*. Geneva: October, 1965.

G38. World Health Organization. *Annual Epidemiological and Vital Statistics*. Geneva: annual.

G39. World Health Organization. *Epidemiological and Vital Statistics Report*. Geneva: irregular.

G40. World Health Organization. *World Health Statistics Annual*. Geneva: annual.

Austria

G41. Bundesrechnungskammer, *Bundesrechnungsabschluss*. Vienna: Oesterreichische Staatsdruckerei, annual.

G42. City of Vienna. *Rechnungsabschluss der Bundeshauptstadt Wien fuer das Jahr 1958, umgeformt nach den Richtlinien des Erlasses des Bundesministerium fuer Finanzen vom 9. Juli, 1949*. Vienna: mimeo, n. d.

G43. Hauptverband der oesterreichischen Sozialversicherungstraeger. *Jahrbuch der oesterreichischen Sozialversicherung*. Vienna: Verlag Carl Ueberreuter, annual.

G44. Hauptverband der oesterreichischen Sozialversicherungstraeger. *Jahresbericht*. Vienna: annual.

G45. Oesterreichisches Statistisches Zentralamt. 'Oesterreichische Hochschulstatistik, Wintersemester 1959/60'. Heft 60. *Beitraege zur oesterreichischen Statistik*. Vienna: 1961.

G46. Oesterreichisches Statistisches Zentralamt. *Gebaerungsuebersichter fuer die Bundeslaender, Bezirksfuersorgeverbaende, Gemeindeverbaende und Gemeinde*. (title varies). Vienna: annual.

G47. Oesterreichisches Statistisches Zentralamt und Oesterreichisches Institut fuer Wirtschaftsforschung. *Oesterreichs Volkseinkommen im Jahre 1958*, Beilage. *Statistische Nachrichten*, XIV. 11/1959, Vienna: 1959.

G48. Oesterreichisches Statistisches Zentralamt und Oesterreichisches Institut fuer Wirtschaftsforschung. *Oesterreichs Volkseinkommen 1950 bis 1960: Neuberechnung*. Sonderheft. *Statistische Nachrichten*. Vienna: 1963.

G49. Oesterreichisches Statistisches Zentralamt and Oesterreichisches Institut fuer Wirtschaftsforschung. *Oesterreichs Volkseinkommen 1961 und 1962*, Beilage *Statistische Nachrichten*, XIX, 4/1964. Vienna: 1964.

G50. Statistisches Zentralamt. *Statistisches Handbuch*. Vienna: annual.

Bulgaria

G51. Tsentralno statistichesko upravleniye pri Ministerskiya sǔvet. *Statisticheski godishnik na Narodna republika Bǔlgariya*. Sofia: annual.

Czechoslovakia

G51a. Ministry of Finance. *Basic Questions of the Financial Economy* Prague: mimeo, 1965.

G52. Ministry of Finance. *Statement on the State Budget for 1962 Made to the National Assembly of the Czechoslovak Socialist Republic*. Prague: mimeo., n.d.

G53. Ministry of Finance. *Statement on the State Budget for 1963 Made to the National Assembly of the Czechoslovak Socialist Republic*. Prague: mimeo., n.d.

G54. Narodní shromáždění. *Sbírka zákonů a nařízení republiky Československé*. Prague: irregular.

G55. Narodní shromáždění. *Těsnopisecké zprávy o schůzích Narodního shromáždění republiky Československé*. Prague: irregular.

G56. Ústřední komise lidové kontroly a statistiky. *Statistická ročenka Československé socialistické republiky*. Prague: SNTL, annual.

G58. Výzkumný ústav Ministerstva financí. *Úloha financí v soůcasné ekonomice Československa.* Prague: SNPL, 1961.

East Germany

G59. Buero des Praesidiums des Ministerrates der DDR *Gesetzblatt.* East Berlin: irregular.
G60. Presseamt beim Vorsitzenden des Ministerrates der DDR. *Presse Informationen.* East Berlin: irregular.
G61. Staatliche Zentralverwaltung fuer Statistik. *Statistiches Jahrbuch der Deutschen Demokratischen Republik.* East Berlin: annual.

Greece

G62. Hypourgeion Ikonomikon *Genikos proipologismos.* Athens: annual.
G63. Hypourgeion Ikonomikon. *Prosorinos apologismos ton esodon ke exodon tou kratous.* Athens: annual.
G64. Hypourgeion Syntonismou. *Ethniki logariasmi tis Héllados, 1958–1963.* Athens: Ethnikon Typographeion, 1964.
G65. Ministry of Coordination. *National Accounts of Greece, 1948–1959.* Athens: National Printing Office, 1961.
G66. Ministry of Coordination. *National Accounts of Greece, 1960.* Athens: National Printing Office, 1962.
G67. National Statistical Service. *Statistical Yearbook of Greece.* Athens: National Printing Office, annual.
G68. National Statistical Service. *Statistical Yearbook of Public Finance.* Athens: National Printing Office, annual.
G69. Ministry of Finance. *Budget Message for the Fiscal Year.* Athens: mimeo., annual.

Hungary

G70. Központi Statisztikai Hivatal. *Statisztikai évkönyv.* Budapest: annual.
G71. Ministry of Finance. *The State Budget of the Hungarian People's Republic for 1954.* Budapest: Athenaeum Printing Office, 1954.
G72. Magyar Forradalmi Munkás-Paraszt Kormány, Titkárság. *Magyar közlöny: a magyar népköztársaság hivatalos lapja.* Budapest: irregular.
G73. Ministère des Affaires Etrangères. *Faits et chiffres sur la Hongrie: Le budget hongrois pour 1950.* Budapest: mimeo., 1950.
G74. Ministère des Affaires Etrangères. *Faits et chiffres sur la Hongrie: Le budget hongrois pour 1951.* Budapest: mimeo., 1951.

G75. Ministère des Affaires Etrangères. *Faits et chiffres sur la Hongrie: Le budget hongrois pour 1952.* Budapest: mimeo., 1952.

Ireland

G76. Comptroller and Auditor General. *Appropriation Accounts.* Dublin: Stationery Office, annual.

G77. Central Statistics Office. *National Income and Expenditures.* Dublin: Stationery Office, annual.

G78. Central Statistics Office. *Statistical Abstract of Ireland.* Dublin: Stationery Office, annual.

G79. Department of Local Government. *Returns of Local Taxation.* Dublin: Stationery Office, annual.

Italy

G80. Camera dei Deputati (presented by the Ministero del Tesoro and the Ministero del Bilancio). *Relazione generale sulla situazione economica del paese.* Rome: annual.

G81. Camera dei Deputati. *Rendiconto generale del' amministrazione dello stato.* Rome: TCD, annual.

G82. Istituto Centrale di Statistica. *Annuario di statistiche del lavoro e dell' emigrazione.* Rome: annual.

G83. Istituto Centrale di Statistica. *Annuario statistico italiano.* Rome: annual.

G84. Istituto Centrale di Statistica. *Bilanci delle amministrazioni regionale, provinciali e comunale.* Rome: annual.

G85. Istituto Centrale di Statistica. *Bollettino mensile di statistica.* Rome: monthly.

G86. Istituto Centrale di Statistica. *Notiziaro I.S.T.A.T.* Rome: irregular.

G87. Ministero del Tesoro. *Bilancio di previsione dello stato.* Rome: IPS, annual.

G88. Ministero del Tesoro, Ragioneria Generale dello Stato. *Note informative sul bilancio dello stato.* Rome: IPS, irregular.

Poland

G89. Główny Urząd Statystyczny. *Dochód Narodowy Polski 1954–1955.* Warsaw: 1957.

G90. Główny Urząd Statystyczny. *Dochód Narodowy Polski 1955–1960.* Warsaw: 1962.

G91. Główny Urząd Statystyczny. *Rocvnik Statystyczny.* Warsaw: Nakładem Głownego Urządu Statystycznego, annual.

G92. Urząd Rady Ministrow. *Dziennik Ustaw Polskiej Rzeczypos-politej Ludowej*. Warsaw: irregular.

Romania

G93. Direcţia Centrală de Statistică. *Anuarul statistic al* RPR Bucharest: annual.

U.S.S.R.

G94. Ministerstvo finansov SSSR, Byudzhetno upravleniye. *Gosu-darstvennyy byudzhet soyuznykh respublik v pyatoy pyatiletke: Statisticheskiy sbornik*. Moscow: Gosfinizdat, 1957.

G95. Ministerstvo finansov SSSR, Byudzhetno upravleniye. *Gosu-darstvennyy byudzhet S.S.S.R. i byudzhety soyuznykh respublik: Statisticheskiy sbornik*. Moscow: Gosfinizdat, 1962.

G96. Ministerstvo finansov SSSR, Byudzhetno upravleniye. *Mestny-ye byudzhety S.S.S.R.: Statisticheskiy sbornik*. Moscow: Gosfini-zdat, 1960.

G97. Ministerstvo finansov SSSR, Byudzhetno upravleniye. *Rask-hody na sotsial'no kulturnyye meropriyatiya po gosudarstvennomu byudzhetu S.S.S.R.: Statisticheskiy sbornik*. Moscow: Gosfinizdat, 1958.

G98. Ministerstvo prosveshcheniya RSFSR. *Narodnoye obrazovaniye*. Moscow: annual.

G99. Tsentral'noe statisticheskoye upravleniye. *Narodnoye khozy-aystvo*. Moscow: annual.

G100. Tsentral'noe statisticheskoye upravleniye. *Zdravookhraneniye v S.S.S.R.* Moscow: Gosstatizdat, 1960.

U.S.A.

G101. Bureau of the Budget. *The Budget of the United States Govern-ment*. Washington, DC: GPO, annual.

G102. Bureau of the Budget. *Measuring Productivity of Federal Government Organizations*. Washington, DC: GPO, 1964.

G103. Bureau of the Census. *Census of Business: 1963*. Washington, DC: GPO, 1965.

G104. Bureau of the Census. *Census of Governments: 1957*. Washing-ton, DC: GPO, 1959.

G105. Bureau of the Census. *Census of Governments: 1962*. Washing-ton, DC: GPO, 1964.

G106. Bureau of the Census. *1960 Census of Population*. Washington, DC: GPO, 1964.

G107. Bureau of the Census. *Compendium of City Government Finances.* Washington, DC: annual .

G108. Bureau of the Census. *Compendium of State Finances.* Washington, DC: annual.

G109. Bureau of the Census. *Current Population Reports.* Washington, DC: irregular.

C110. Bureau of the Census. *Estimates and Projections of the Population of the U.S.S.R. and of the Communist Countries of Eastern Europe by Age and Sex.* Washington, DC: April, 1964.

G111. Bureau of the Census. *Estimates and Projections of the Population and Labor Force of the European Communist Countries: 1950, and 1955 to 1965.* Washington, DC: mimeo, March, 1965.

G112. Bureau of the Census. *Financial Statistics of State and Local Governments: 1932.* Washington, DC: GPO, 1935.

G113. Bureau of the Census. *Governmental Finances.* Washington, DC: annual.

G114. Bureau of the Census. *Historical Statistics of the United States.* Washington, DC: GPO, 1960.

G115. Bureau of the Census. *International Population Reports: Projections of the Population of Poland, by Age and Sex.* Series P-91, No. 6. Washington, DC: May, 1958.

G116. Bureau of the Census. *Statistical Abstract of the United States.* Washington, DC: GPO, annual.

G117. Bureau of the Census. *Summary of Governmental Finances.* Washington, DC: annual.

G118. Department of Commerce. Office of Business Economics. *Balance of Payments: Statistical Supplement.* (Rev. ed.). Washington, DC: GPO, 1963.

G119. Department of Commerce. Office of Business Economics. *Personal Income by States.* Washington, DC: GPO, 1956.

G120. Department of Commerce. Office of Business Economics. *Survey of Current Business.* Washington, DC: GPO, monthly.

G121. Department of Defense, Army. *Handbook of the Satellite Armies.* Washington, DC: irregular.

G122. Department of Health, Education, and Welfare. *Biennial Survey of Education.* Washington, DC: GPO, biennial.

G123. Department of Health, Education, and Welfare. *Education in the U.S.S.R.* Publ. 14/1957. Washington, DC: GPO, 1957.

G124. Department of Health, Education, and Welfare. *Soviet Commitment to Education.* Washington, DC: GPO, 1959.

G125. Department of Health, Education, and Welfare, Public

Health Service. *Health Statistics from the U.S. National Health Survey*. Washington, D.C.: GPO, March, 1961.

G126. Department of Health, Education, and Welfare. Social Security Administration. *Social Security Bulletin*. Washington, DC: GPO, monthly.

G127. Department of Health, Education, and Welfare. Social Security Administration. *Social Security Programs Throughout the World, 1964*. Washington, DC: GPO, 1964.

G128. Federal Bureau of Investigation. Crime in the United States: *Uniform Crime Reports*. Washington, DC: annual.

G129. Joint Economic Committee. US Congress. *Annual Economic Indicators for the U.S.S.R.* Washington, DC: GPO, 1964.

G130. Joint Economic Committee. US Congress. *Comparisons of the United States and Soviet Economies*. Washington, DC: GPO, 1959.

G131. Joint Economic Committee, US Congress. *Current Economic Indicators for the U.S.S.R.* Washington, DC: GPO, 1965.

G132. Joint Economic Committee, US Congress. *Dimensions of Soviet Economic Power*, Washington, DC: GPO, 1962.

G133. Joint Economic Committee, US Congress. *Federal Expenditure Policy for Economic Growth and Stability*. Washington, DC: GPO, November, 1957.

G134. Joint Economic Committee, US Congress. *New Directions in the Soviet Economy*. Washington, DC: GPO, 1966.

G135. Federal Reserve Bank. *Federal Reserve Bulletin*. Washington, DC: monthly.

G136. National Science Foundation. *Federal Funds for Research, Development and Other Scientific Activities*. Washington, DC: GPO, annual.

G137. National Science Foundation. *Federal Funds for Science*. Washington, DC: GPO, annual.

G138. National Science Foundation. *Industrial R and D Funds in Relation to Other Economic Variables*. Washington, DC: GPO, 1964.

G139. National Science Foundation. *Scientific Activities in Six State Governments*. Washington, DC: GPO, 1958.

G140. Operations Mission to Greece. *Statistical Data Book, 1953/54*. Vol. II. Athens: mimeo., June, 1955.

West Germany

G141. Bundesministerium fuer Arbeit und Sozialordnung. *Arbeit- und Sozialstatistische Mitteilungen*. Bonn: monthly.

G142. Bundesministerium fuer gesamtdeutsche Fragen. *S.B.Z. Archive*. Bonn: twice monthly.

G143. Bundesministerium fuer gesamtdeutsche Fragen. *S.B.Z. von A bis Z.* Bonn: various editions.

G144. Bundesministerium fuer Wirtschaft. *Leistungen der Bundesrepublik Deutschland auf dem Gebiet der Entwicklungshilfe.* Mimeo, Bonn: October 1, 1964.

G145. Bundesminister fuer wissenschaftliche Forschung. *Bericht der Bundesregierung ueber Stand und Zusammenhang aller Massnahmen des Bundes zur Foerderung wissenschaftlicher Forschung,* Drucksache IV/2963. Bad Godesberg: Verlag Dr Heger, January, 1965.

G146. Ministerium der Finanzen. *Finanzbericht.* Bonn:Bundesdruckerei, annual.

G147. Presse- und Informationsamt. *Bulletin der Bundesregierung.* Bonn: irregular.

G148. Presse- und Informationsamt. *Deutsche Politik: Taetigkeit der Bundesregierung.* Bonn: annual.

G149. Presse- und Informationsamt. *Deutschland im Wiederaufbau: Taetigkeit der Bundesregierung.* Bonn: annual.

G150. Presse- und Informationsamt. *Germany Reports.* Bonn: 1961.

G151. Statistisches Bundesamt. *Bevoelkerung und Kultur.* Reihe 1, *Bevoelkerungsstand und -entwicklung.* Stuttgart and Mainz: Kohlhammer Verlag, annual.

G152. Statistisches Bundesamt. *Finanzen und Steuern.* Mainz and Stuttgart: W. Kohlhammer Verlag, irregular.

G153. Statistisches Bundesamt. *Internationaler Vergleich der Preise fuer die Lebenshaltung.* Mainz and Stuttgart: W. Kohlhammer Verlag, irregular.

G154. Statistisches Bundesamt. *Statistiches Jahrbuch fuer die Bundesrepublik Deutschland.* Bonn: annual.

G155. Statistisches Bundesamt. *Statistik der Bundesrepublik Deutschland.* Mainz and Stuttgart: W. Kohlhammer Verlag, irregular.

G156. Statistisches Bundesamt. *Wirtschaft und Statistik.* Mainz and Stuttgart: W. Kohlhammer Verlag, monthly.

G157. Statistisches Landesamt, Berlin. *Berliner Statistik.* West Berlin: irregular.

Yugoslavia

G158. Narodna banka. *Statistički bilten.* Belgrade: monthly.

G159. Savezni državni sekretarijat za poslove financija. *Savezni budžet.* Belgrade: annual.

G160. Savezni zavod za javnu upravu. *Radna idruštvena zajednica.* Belgrade: monthly.

G161. Savezni zavod za statistiku. *Indeks.* Belgrade: monthly.

G162. Savezni zavod za statistiku. *Statistički bilten.* Belgrade: irregular.

G163. Savezni zavod za statistiku. *Statistički godišnjak S.F.R.J.* Belgrade: annual.

G164. Savezni zavod za statistiku. *Studije, analize i prikazi.* Belgrade: irregular.

G165. Savezni zavod za statistiku. *Jugoslavija 1945–1964, Statistički pregled.* Belgrade: November, 1965.

G166. Savezno izvrsno veće (author varies). *Zakon o završnom računu F.N.R.J.* (title varies). Belgrade: annual.

G167. Savezno izvršno veće (author varies). *Predlog zakona o završnom* računu o izvrzenju savešnog budžeta (title varies). Belgrade: annual.

Other Nations

G168. France, Institut national de la statistique et des études économiques. *Annuaire statistique de la France: Rétrospective.* Paris: 1961.

G169. Norway, Statistisk Sentralbyrå. *Statistiske Oversikter 1948.* Oslo: 1949.

G170. Norway, Statistisk Sentralbyrå. *Statistiske Oversikter 1958.* Oslo: 1959.

INDEX